JOHN MCCALLUM has written extensively about Australian theatre and drama since the 1970s. He currently lectures in theatre at the University of New South Wales and is Sydney theatre critic for the *Australian*.

For Ann McCallum, my mother,
and in memory of Doug McCallum, my father

BELONGING
AUSTRALIAN PLAYWRITING IN THE 20TH CENTURY

JOHN McCALLUM

Currency Press, Sydney

First published in 2009 by
Currency Press Pty Ltd
PO Box 2287
Strawberry Hills NSW 2012 Australia
www.currency.com.au
enquiries@currency.com.au

Copyright © John McCallum, 2009

Copying for Educational Purposes:

The *Copyright Act 1968 (Commonwealth)* ('the Act') allows a maximum of one chapter or 10% of this book, whichever is the greater, to be copied by any educational institution for its educational purposes provided that the educational institution (or the body that administers it) has given a remuneration notice to Copyright Agency Limited (CAL) under the Act. For details of the CAL licence for educational institutions please contact CAL, 19/157 Liverpool Street, Sydney, NSW 2000, tel (02) 9394 7600, fax (02) 9394 7601, email: info@copyright.com.au.

Copying for Other Purposes:

Except as permitted under the Act, for example a fair dealing for the purposes of study, research, criticism or review, no part of this book may be reproduced, stored in a retrieval system, or transmitted in any form or by any means without prior written permission. All inquiries should be made to the publisher at the above address.

In accordance with the requirement of the Australian Media and Arts Alliance, Currency Press has made every effort to identify, and gain permission of, the artists who appear in the photographs. Every reasonable effort has been made to identify and gain permission of any material that is copyright. Any enquiries should be addressed to the publisher at the above address.

Indigenous Australians are advised that this publication includes images or names of people now deceased.

National Library of Australia Cataloguing-in-Publication Data:
Author:	McCallum, John, 1952-
Title:	Belonging / John McCallum.
ISBN:	9780868196589 (pbk.)
Notes:	Includes index.
	Bibliography.
Subjects:	Australian drama--History and criticism
	Theater--Australia--History.
	Nationalism--Australia.
	Cosmopolitanism--Australia.
Dewey Number:	822.009

Cover and book design by Laura McLean, Currency Press
Index by Alan Walker
Typeset in Revival 565BT 10.5 / 14.5.

Publication of this title was assisted by the Commonwealth Government through the Australia Council, its arts funding and advisory body.

CONTENTS

Introduction	vii
Chapter One: The turn of the century	1
Chapter Two: Bush and city	23
Chapter Three: Settling the land	51
Chapter Four: Into the city	77
Chapter Five: Patrick White	91
Chapter Six: Playwrights in the 60s	113
Chapter Seven: The New Wave	139
Chapter Eight: David Williamson	167
Chapter Nine: Playwrights in the 70s	187
Chapter Ten: The new internationalism	209
Chapter Eleven: Playwrights in the 80s	239
Chapter Twelve: Identity and Community	265
Chapter Thirteen: Immigrants and exiles	281
Chapter Fourteen: Aboriginal theatre	301
Chapter Fifteen: Playwrights in the 90s	327
Chapter Sixteen: The end of the twentieth century	347
Conclusion	373
Endnotes	381
Play List	399
Works Cited	453
Index	461

Currency Press acknowledges the Traditional Owners of the Country on which we live and work. We pay our respects to all Aboriginal and Torres Strait Islander Elders, past and present.

INTRODUCTION

Australia as a continent is a strangely vacant place, in which many people have struggled to find a sense of belonging—from the original immigrants, who arrived 40,000 or more years ago, to the waves of invaders, settlers and new immigrants who have arrived since 1788. The drama of the twentieth century, the subject of this book, is part of the record of this struggle.

In the popular theatre of the nineteenth century the Dharug, the Gamaraigal, the Dharawul, and further afield the Awabakal, the Darkinung, the Gandangara, the Wadi-Wadi and the Gurangada, and beyond the Sydney basin the rest of the six hundred cultures of pre-1788 Australia became simply 'blacks'. They were represented theatrically in familiar stock characters from European genres that went back to the trickster servants of Greco-Roman comedy. In the minstrel shows, pantomimes and vaudevilles the 'blackfella' took over from the stage Irishman in English melodrama, or became a local version of the comic American plantation slave.[1]

For the first invaders—convicts and their jailers huddled on the coast—there was at first nothing out there. The notorious 'dead heart' of the continent didn't exist until a series of narratives constructed it as a barren and empty landscape waiting to be tamed and settled. As the theatre moved away from the conventions of the nineteenth century

BELONGING

these narratives at first became flatter, more episodic, laconically understated and underplotted. Many of the new Australian plays of the early twentieth century have little incident, few big speeches and hardly any strikingly idiosyncratic characters. They are plays written in a marginal land by and for exiles. The dark plays expressed a kind of gloom and despair and the comic ones, a mischievously ironic rebellion. Early twentieth-century Australian drama is, for the most part, short on heroes and visionaries. The larrikin and the suicide are two of the most important character types. You laugh it off or go mad and kill yourself.

These feelings of alienation were repeated, culturally, many times during the ensuing century, as new immigrant settlers joined the old. Again and again new groups of people, especially from Europe but later from other continents, have washed up on these shores, sometimes literally, and discovered a strangeness. Different waves found different problems and formed their theatres in different ways. This book is partly about the variety of dramatic voices that have flickered into life here. It explores how Australian playwriting in the twentieth century started out as a search for unity and a national identity and eventually came to revel in diversity.

The characters who have peopled the stages are a motley crew: convicts, soldiers and entrepreneurs; Scottish Presbyterians, English Anglicans and Irish Catholics; hard-working ex-prisoners who established pastoral empires and dissolute aristocrats living on remittances from Home; hard-bitten working men with their whores; tough battling women and their weak men addled by the bush struggle, shell-shocked, emasculated or pathologically introverted; loners, bastards, madmen, drifters, larrikins; sentimentalists, socialists, dreamers; immigrants, refugees and aliens. Exiles all, looking to belong.

Following the discovery of gold in the 1850s, the population quickly doubled. Gold also brought the first Chinese to Australia and, for a brief time, traditional Chinese opera flourished on the diggings.[2] In the early 1920s Greek, Italian and Scandinavian immigrants were on the Australian stage—no longer the stock types of melodrama. One of the greatest popular successes of Australian culture, Arthur Hoey Davis's *On Our Selection* stories, resisted for a time the homogenising

INTRODUCTION

effects of the 1890s 'legend', which for at least sixty years tried to construct a single Australian identity. Davis populated the Darling Downs, cow-cocky country in Queensland, with a range of European characters, although the stage and screen versions allowed them to slip away again.[3] Jewish refugees from Europe, before and after World War II, brought with them a sophisticated European culture that eventually supplied the tastes and some of the skills that went into the late twentieth-century opera, ballet and music, although it was to be another thirty-odd years before they began to make their presence felt in the theatre. Since the 1970s there have been waves of Vietnamese, Lebanese and other immigrants whose voices could be heard on the stage in the 1980s and 1990s, as the idea of a homogenous Australian national character retreated.

'Nowt more outcastin'', says Queenie Ayre in Louis Nowra's *The Golden Age* (1985). At the end of the play her daughter Betsheb, having returned to the wilderness whence she came, repeats Ayre's phrase and adds, ''Ome. I come 'ome'.[4] Nowra's play dramatises the extraordinary complexity of what ''ome' might mean in a country full of exiles and the dispossessed.

In recent Aboriginal drama the dancer, the dreamer and the singer/storyteller are powerful figures, ghosts from a much more ancient past. Jack Davis, the great social realist Aboriginal playwright of the 1980s and 1990s, allowed such figures to invade the mission kitchens of his comedy-dramas of Aboriginal life on the marginal lands in the darkness at the edge of white towns. In Robert Merritt's *The Cake Man* (1975) the mystical figure of the Eurie-Woman is an ethereal vision for the leading character as he abandons mission life and heads for the city. She reminds him of his world. 'Not yours', he says to the white audience, 'mine'.

Ghostly figures pervade white Australian drama too. The ghosts of explorers wander through the desert and end up mad or dead. Murdered soldiers return from distant imperial wars to speak to their loved ones from beyond the grave. Refugees from sophisticated European cultures, carrying on their shoulders a thousand years of bloody history, disappear in floods and meet up with ancient spirits cut off from their aboriginal connections with the land.

BELONGING

On a more domestic level, women in drab bush huts eke out a lonely existence without men in an arid sunblasted world. Their men are no help, laconic almost to the point of catatonia, only capable of silent communion around the campfire with recently-encountered strangers whom they like to call their 'mates'.

The men from the bush got lost in the new city world. The inner-city slums are, in many of the plays, just as much a wasteland as the bush. Later, some peace might be found amongst the hydrangeas, with a Holden in the driveway and a lamb roast on the table of a Sunday, but there is a dead heart in the suburbs too.

And always there is that yearning for a home. From Louis Esson to Daniel Keene Australian drama has been about the difficulty of belonging.

This book is a description of the Australian dramatic repertoire of the twentieth century. It is not a history of the theatre. There are many great works for the twentieth-century Australian theatre that are not covered here because the scripts are not readily available. Any book about theatre is about traces and in this one the traces are the scripts. Almost all of the plays discussed here are published or, especially for some of the neglected plays of the 1930s and 1940s, readily available on inter-library loan. In a few cases, where the matter seemed urgent, I have included plays that readers will not easily be able to consult.

Our current understanding of the history of life on this planet is dominated by the fact that, in the ground, bones and teeth last longer than flesh, just as our understanding of the history of human culture is dominated, and just as warped, by the fact that stone survives better than wood or fibre. Playscripts are, perhaps unfortunately, the bones and stones of our theatre. More thorough historians than I are beginning to explore other traces and their work will tell a different story. One of them is Geoffrey Milne, whose comprehensive survey of twentieth-century Australian theatre I recommend.[5] Other resources, by many fine scholars, are given in the endnotes. The plays are listed at the end.

A book such as this delivers, inevitably, something that looks very like a canon of Australian drama. It is not (entirely) my choice but

INTRODUCTION

rather one that has been determined by all the contingencies that have affected the survival of our theatre's traces. But in the end this is clearly my book and the responsibility for its selection and commentary is mine.

I have had a wonderful time revisiting the repertoire and writing about it. I would like to thank Katharine Brisbane, who first suggested the idea; my editor at Currency, Victoria Chance, who has been very patient and helpful as she has waited for the result; and my colleague and friend John Golder.

I'd also like to thank the playwrights whose work is covered here, and also those many fine ones whose work I haven't had space to cover. Sometimes I think that writers have taught me more about life than has life itself.

Above all I would like to thank those frontline artists whose work scarcely gets a mention here. This book is dedicated to all the great actors whose work has given me so much pleasure in more than forty years of theatregoing, and without whom there is nothing in the theatre worth writing about.

1
THE TURN OF THE CENTURY

'Australians are fond of the drama, but have no drama of their own.'

Alfred Johnson Buchanan, 1907[1]

For much of the twentieth century, Australian drama had very little to do with Australian theatre—local plays were not often performed. That basic fact pervades this book. While huge theatres at the end of the nineteenth century were filled with sensations, pageants, choruses, ballets, orchestras, comedy, sex, violence and passion—things we all still want—the first seventy years of this book is mostly a tale of small activities in small rooms.

On the nineteenth-century stage the whole world, and a few other worlds besides, was dragged kicking and screaming into the theatre. Real horses galloped up scenic mountainsides, jumped vast gorges and fell into flooded rivers as their riders leapt to safety. Overblown exotic scenes were transformed into even more extravagant worlds of fairies, wizards and tricksters. Crowds of up to two hundred performers danced, sang or fought battles across great stages. Lovers lost and found each other, villains crowed and underdogs triumphed. When white heroes wilted they were saved, at least in Australia, by women and blackfellas.

BELONGING

This spectacular melodrama was appropriated from England and the United States and localised by the great Australian actor–managers. It outlasted its forbears, surviving in Australia into the twentieth century. In addition to melodrama the theatre boasted grand historical and military dramas that have their equivalents in Hollywood epics and war movies; early stage forms of theatrical farce and domestic comedy whose descendants are sitcoms and soap operas; and pantomime and the music hall, whose traditions have been inherited by Tonight shows and reality television.

One of the last of the great hands-on actor–managers was George Musgrove. He had been part of 'The Firm', as J. C. Williamson's (JCW's), the largest commercial company, was known. When Musgrove retired, businessmen who had never performed in the theatre began to take over and the commercial theatre changed its emphasis. In the 1920s and 1930s, under the management of the Tait brothers, Williamson's began producing imported thrillers and plays of intrigue alongside their trademark musical theatre repertoire.[2] They had long specialised in the musical theatre, doing everything from light musicals to grand opera, and especially Gilbert and Sullivan, to which they had early acquired the Australian rights. The few commercial producers who did Australian work also began to change their repertoire—from sensation melodrama through domestic melodrama to bucolic comedy.

By 1915, some of the old forms, particularly melodrama, had begun to disappear but the commercial theatre flourished until the 'talkies' started up in 1928. A Commonwealth Government Entertainment Tax introduced in 1916 was compounded by an additional state tax from the late 1920s. Because the new cinemas had lower ticket prices and could avoid them, entertainment taxes discriminated against live theatre. The taxes, the talkies and the Depression combined to destroy mass live entertainment as a lucrative business. At the beginning of 1929 Melbourne had ten live theatres. Eighteen months later there were five.[3] Between 1929 and 1939 the number of live theatres in Sydney fell from ten to three.[4]

Some commercial theatre survived partly by moving to the high-cultural or middle-class end of the market. JCW's, overwhelmingly the dominant entrepreneur until the early 1970s, did particularly well

1: THE TURN OF THE CENTURY

touring opera and operetta, training a generation that would later form the core of the national opera company. They also managed the 1932 tour of Lewis Casson and Sybil Thorndike.

On the vaudeville circuits, a golden age of Australian comedy (Roy ('Mo') Rene, George Wallace and Jim Gerald especially) lasted, despite hiccoughs, until just after World War II, when David N. Martin took over the new Tivoli circuit and looked overseas for performers. Australian variety artists who had made a good living at the Tivoli in the 1930s drifted into radio and later television. The rural touring companies, tent-shows doing the rounds of local agricultural shows in country towns, lasted a little longer. George Sorlie, for instance, was known as 'J. C. Williamson of the road'.[5] When he died in 1948 Bobby le Brun and Sorlie's wife, Grace, kept Sorlie's going until 1961. (In 2001, Margery and Michael Forde wrote a tribute to the old tent-shows, *Way Out West*, which toured Queensland for the Centenary of Federation.)

In the same year that Sorlie's folded, Patrick White first gained attention as Australia's greatest modernist playwright when *The Ham Funeral* was produced in Adelaide. Also in the 1960s the Music Hall Theatre Restaurant in Sydney nostalgically, and with proper respect, parodied the traditions of melodrama. Its success sparked the establishment of a series of suburban theatre restaurants with names like 'Dirty Dick's' that burlesqued (another grand nineteenth-century tradition) the old forms and styles. With more earnest aims, and without the commercialism, many nineteenth-century popular theatre conventions were gleefully appropriated and reworked during the neo-nationalist New Wave of the late 1960s and early 1970s. In 1970, for instance, the Australian Performing Group produced *Marvellous Melbourne*, scripted by New Wave writers Jack Hibberd and John Romeril and created by the company. It incorporated scenes from Alfred Dampier's popular 1889 melodrama of the same name and also exploited twentieth-century vaudeville and music-hall performance styles. To top it off, one of its characters was a gloomy Louis Esson, whose work as a polemicist and playwright is discussed in the next chapter.

BELONGING

The transition period

At the beginning of the twentieth century, the starting-point for this book, such an appropriation of old genres was a long way off. Instead writers and campaigners rebelled, in some cases perversely given their populist hopes, against the sensations and passions of the popular theatre of the day. Some sought refuge in the new middle-class genres of European drama. Others looked for models in the nationalist dramas of countries outside the imperial centre—America, Ireland, Russia.

The most extreme turned to a localised drama of exile. Its themes of alienation and a searching for home and identity are common to postcolonial cultures everywhere. Polemicists in the journals and small literary magazines frequently wrote about using art to build a new nation, either by importing European high culture or by starting afresh to define a new Australian identity. For at least fifty years dramatists turned their backs on popular culture, even as they used the rhetoric of 'folk' and 'the people' to explain their work. Some of their projects look quaint now but many have had an extraordinary longevity.

The theatre in the first three decades of the twentieth century may be loosely divided into three categories. In drastically decreasing order of size these are the commercial theatre already described; the repertory theatre movement, which dealt mostly with the 'serious' contemporary repertoire from overseas; and the nationalist theatre, which focused on local drama. In a very small theatre scene, the three were intimately interconnected with writers, actors and producers constantly moving between them. The Adelaide Repertory Theatre, for example, produced two plays by Arthur H. Adams, a writer who had sold his first script, *Tapu*, to JCW's, for whom he later worked on salary. Gregan McMahon had been an actor in the commercial theatre before he started a couple of amateur repertory companies and then sold out (according to many of the amateurs who were suddenly left out in the cold) to Williamson's new managers, J. and N. Tait. The Taits put him on a retainer to run repertory companies in Sydney and Melbourne, funding the productions and taking both the members' subscriptions and the supposed profits. At a crucial point in his battle to establish a nationalist theatre Louis Esson, the patriotic

1: THE TURN OF THE CENTURY

purist, found that his friend and collaborator Vance Palmer had sent one of his (Palmer's) plays to McMahon, who had in turn sent it up the commercial line to actor–entrepreneur Bert Bailey, where it sank without commercial trace.[6]

The year 1922, when Esson's *The Battler* launched the Pioneer Players, may be taken as exemplary in the interplay between commercial and amateur theatre. JCW's imported a company from Dublin's Abbey Theatre, the source of Esson's chief influences, W. B. Yeats and J. M. Synge. The Abbey toured Synge's *The Shadow of the Glen* and other plays from their repertoire. They travelled around the country from early June to late October but the tour was not a box-office success. It took an average of £470 a week at a time when Williamson's New Comic Opera tour was taking in £2,380.[7]

Also in 1922 Arthur Hoey Davis, writing as Steele Rudd, tried to repair his financially ailing fortunes by embarking on a national lecture tour. He took a print of Raymond Longford's silent film version of his *On Our Selection* stories. Bert Bailey had already had a huge commercial success with the stage version, which had opened ten years previously and was still revived, but Davis was making nothing out of it. Some commentators saw Esson's *The Battler* as a response to the commercialism of *On Our Selection*.

These sorts of overlaps and connections lead to one of the vexed questions that faced every producer in the 1920s and that pervaded discussion of Australian drama until at least the late 1970s—that of 'Australianness'. As in many postcolonial cultures, especially settler colonies such as Australia, this starts with an interest in 'local colour' within adopted forms and genres. Then come periods of strident nationalism, interspersed with times of outward-looking internationalism, which, in Australia's case, lasted through the century.[8] During the 1920s local theatre workers and writers began to disentangle themselves from the centralised structures of commerce and empire and look for what they called frontiers. Pretty soon, as the land began to open and fill up, these became border zones and marginal lands.

BELONGING

'Australianness' and Australian playwrights

By the 1920s the bush legend of the 1890s (re-mythologised in the 1950s by writers and historians, and again in the 1970s by filmmakers and advertisers) was well-entrenched. The scenic spectacle of the grand melodrama of the late nineteenth century had already, ironically, become tangled up with new notions of realism. A desire for 'authentic' Australian settings became part of this otherwise highly artificial and conventional form.

In this celebration of 'Australianness' a new interest in local colour was twinned with the spectacle demanded by theatrical tradition. Animals loomed large in this project. In the 1890s, late in his career, the prolific 'Gorgeous' George Darrell (best remembered now for *The Sunny South* (1883)[9]) produced a dramatic version of a racing novel, *The Double Game*, in the 1890s in which he staged the running of the Melbourne Cup with twenty real horses.[10] Bland Holt's 1903 production of Arthur Shirley's *The Breaking of the Drought* was, one critic wrote, full of 'charming fidelity' to bush life, at least partly because it included a 'casual emu wandering about the homestead' and, for the famous drought scene, real crows flying down from the flies and picking at the skeletons of cows dotted picturesquely about the stage.[11] *The Squatter's Daughter* (1907) opened with a flock of sheep, a pack of dogs and, on cue as the stage lights came up, trained kookaburras that started laughing at 'dawn'.[12]

Some of this theatrical splendour continued into the early twentieth century, but its days were nearing an end, and not simply because of commercial pressures. The tone of the reviewers and columnists became increasingly cynical—sarcastic, even—from the late nineteenth century. In 1911 Edmund Duggan's *My Mate: A Bush Love Story* was advertised (not just reviewed) as having a 'saving sense of restraint running through it'.[13] In the commercial theatre the thrills were increasingly based in realistic spectacle: a horse falling into a flooded river for instance.

This emphasis on realism was the crucial link between the old commercial theatre and the new drama. The huge technical resources of the nineteenth century popular theatre were being directed towards a project that the Australian-produced commercial theatre and the

1: THE TURN OF THE CENTURY

nationalist drama came to have in common: representing Australians to themselves. It proved an impossible task. By the time the amateur theatre had grown professional during the 1950s, and the professional theatre had relaxed enough to accept Australian plays during the 1970s, the whole idea of Australia as a homogenous entity had begun to fall apart.

But for about a hundred years from the 1870s distinctively Australian scenic representations were an important aspect of the national drama, wherever it was staged. Other types of plays were unjustly ignored as the great Australian Legend was constructed. In the 1910s and 1920s, the commercial theatre and the embryonic nationalist drama were pursuing essentially the same material, despite their different motivations and a great deal of mutual antagonism. It is one of the ironies of early twentieth-century Australian drama that for nearly thirty years the new nationalist playwrights reviled the commercial theatre, and the commercial theatre scorned the new drama, as both sought to exploit the mythology of a bush legend.

In the 1920s Australian writers who were making lucrative careers from the box office were ignored or condemned by the nationalists. The most successful were Bert Bailey and Kate Howarde. Howarde was the last and longest surviving of the nineteenth-century actor–managers, especially with her great touring tent-show hit, *Possum Paddock* (1919), which did almost as much as the Davis–Rudd–Bailey team to establish bucolic comedy as a popular dramatic form.

But far and away the most popular work of the early twentieth-century Australian theatre was *On Our Selection*, the reach and influence of which is unlikely to be seen again on the stage. Indeed the remarkable longevity of the stories in their different forms is a classic example of how nineteenth-century theatre conventions were taken up by the new media.[14]

On Our Selection

In December 1895, Arthur Hoey Davis, writing as Steele Rudd, published a story in the *Bulletin* entitled 'Starting the Selection' in which Dad Rudd takes up a 'selection', or small farm, at a place called Emu Creek. Davis eventually produced ten books of stories about the adventures of an increasingly complicated family growing up on the farm. *On Our Selection*, published in 1899, was the first.[15] The original stories were character- and incident-based vignettes which combined observations of the struggles of rural life (based, at least initially, on Davis' own experience) with dry rustic humour. Davis came to be caught up in his persona as Steele Rudd much as Samuel Clemens used and became trapped in the persona of Mark Twain.[16] Over the next quarter of a century (the tenth volume was *The Rudd Family* in 1926) the characters changed and the tone became increasingly one of generic bucolic farce, but that was nothing compared to the changes the stories underwent when they were translated to the stage, radio and the screen.

Davis himself wrote six plays based on the stories but, unfortunately for his financial wellbeing in his declining years, not the one that took the Rudd family into the commercial theatre.[17] In their stage version of *On Our Selection*, Edmund Duggan and Bert Bailey reset the characters and incidents in a stock melodramatic plot. More than a million people saw it between 1912 and 1916 and Bailey was still reviving the role on which he built his career—Dad, later Grandad, Rudd—in 1929.[18]

The script of the play strings together incidents from the stories, bits of local colour and comic stage routines, using a stock melodramatic plot involving a mean squatter, a murder and an innocent suspect who is finally vindicated in an unlikely revelation scene. The forced marriage between the folk stories and the generic plotting required by the theatre is most obvious in the characters of the young lovers Kate and Sandy—the juvenile leads—who seem to have wandered in from another world. Nevertheless, the basic family set-up—a tyrannical Dad, a long-suffering Mum and a collection of more or less dissatisfied children—established a pattern that continued in Australian drama until the early 1960s. This tradition is discussed in the next chapter.

Almost immediately a series of imitative backblocks-farce films were produced about Rudd-like families—the 'Hayseeds' and the 'Waybacks'.[19] In directing his silent film version in 1920, Raymond Longford tried to reclaim the spirit of the original stories, and when the Bailey/Duggan stage version finally reached the screen, in 1932, he assumed it would be 'melodramatic tripe':

1: THE TURN OF THE CENTURY

> [W]hen I made my picture, [I] prefer[red] the starkly true Australian characters of the book to the puppets of the play, with all its trappings of mortgages, flinty-hearted moneylenders, black-moustached heavies in polo suits, and various other borrowed stage traditions.[20]

The talkie version of *On Our Selection* that Longford so crabbily anticipated was directed by Ken G. Hall in his first feature-length film. It was full of picturesque nationalistic elements, including lots of patriotic speeches and bush panoramas. It brought Bailey, now 64, out of retirement to play Dad Rudd yet again, after two decades playing the old bugger. Bailey made three spin-off films with Hall in the 1930s, at last looking almost as old as the character.

In the stories Dad Rudd was a battling selector with five kids when he first came to Emu Creek in 1895. Even after he was elected to Parliament at the end of the second book of stories (*Our New Selection*, 1903) he was still a battling selector made good. In the films Dad was put through such a series of transformations that the original bush stories were completely lost. In *Dad and Dave Come to Town* (1938) he inherits a glamorous city department store, full of ladies' fashions. By the time we get to *Dad Rudd, M.P.* (1940) he is a fully-fledged respectable member of a new middle class and the old selection is long forgotten. Instead of droughts, fires and squatters, Dad is now struggling with the recalcitrants who resist Australia's commitment to the new war.

The theatre wheel turned full circle when the original play came back in 1979 in a version adapted by George Whaley as a nostalgic production for middle-class audiences in the new subsidised theatre of the New Wave.

Dad and Dave were also characters in a long-running radio serial, a 1972 television series starring Gordon Chater and Garry McDonald and another movie released in 1995, directed by Whaley, that starred Leo McKern and Joan Sutherland as Dad and Mum. In addition Dad and Dave are the butts of a fifty-year tradition of obscene jokes that still circulate on the internet.

BELONGING

Authenticity, melodrama and realism

The exoticism of the bush legend appealed to commercial theatre audiences and to the new playwrights working on a new self-consciously Australianist drama. In both cases the rhetoric, or at least the publicity, was based on a new discourse of the 'real', as in the much-abused phrase, 'the real Australia'. This emphasis on authenticity, however, was a problem. Margaret Williams has wittily documented the contradiction in the reviews of the late melodrama between the requirements of convention and the value placed on *vraisemblance*— as critics who praised lifelikeness measured the plays up against the stock conventions of the genre:

> The more the Australian melodrama satisfied the critics' and audiences' expectations of lifelikeness in the local characters and familiarity in the settings, the less it could satisfy the expectation of probability [within melodramatic conventions]. [...] The closer to familiar reality the Australian plays came, the less likely seemed the stock situation of the theatre.[21]

Increasingly, the critics complained of the form's incredible features. Black-hatted villains may be at home in London but they didn't look right on outback stations. The call for colonial 'authenticity' and lifelikeness, as much as commercial failure in the face of the growing film industry, led to the decline of melodrama. Critics who now mock Esson and his colleagues for turning their backs on the still busy commercial theatre in their quest for a new 'Australianness' ignore this failure.

The new writers thought they had solved the problem. They embraced a new kind of flat (or under-plotted) realism, which came to be called 'naturalism'. This was a long way from the five-act sensation melodrama, with its dizzying highs and comic intrusions, and also from the more relaxed 'well-made' play, with its neater three-act structure, rising action and climax.

The Touch of Silk

A final example of the interaction between the nineteenth-century conventions and the nationalist realism can be seen in Betty Roland's *The Touch of Silk* (1928), the best-known of the early bush realist plays. It is a transitional play which shows the melodramatic style

1: THE TURN OF THE CENTURY

of early twentieth-century realistic drama, a feature that has often been commented on, usually negatively. Indeed, Roland rewrote *The Touch of Silk* in 1954 to expunge some of its melodrama. But, as Philip Parsons pointed out, the principal dramatic influence on Roland, who had great success in the Little Theatres, was not the new realism and nationalism with which she later became identified, but George Pierce Baker's 1919 *Dramatic Technique*, a playwriting textbook 'grounded squarely in the quality commercial theatre'. Parsons writes:

> The playwright's job, says Baker, is above all to make people feel. To achieve this he must develop a clear, strong narrative which involves his characters in arresting and expressive situations—the confrontations and discoveries of the well-made play formula as propounded originally by Eugene Scribe. Other things are important too, of course: characterisation must be plausibly motivated, and dialogue must be clear and characteristic of the speaker while moving the action along. But essential to all is a story working through a powerful situation.[22]

The book was based on lectures Baker had been giving to playwriting students at Harvard since 1913, and his principles govern much writing for the stage to this day (and much training in traditional American-style drama courses) especially because they have been codified, refined and expanded as the basis of the Hollywood 'three-act structure' for films and much commercial television drama.

As Pamela Heckenberg and Philip Parsons put it, '[T]he power of Betty Roland's play [...] lies precisely in the fact that she does not disdain, as Esson does, the popular tradition of Australian melodrama'.[23] Like many playwrights of her time Roland went on to write, among other things, commercial drama for radio, as a way of earning a living.

Commercial theatres

It is a commonplace in criticism and commentary on twentieth-century Australian theatre that the commercial theatre largely ignored local writers. This idea was introduced by the early nationalists, who rejected the melodrama and other locally-written popular forms, and started a series of what their most prominent historian Leslie Rees dubbed 'rallying calls' for a local drama that was more serious, or more engaged with local culture, or simply had more local colour. The campaign, linked with various pleas for a national theatre, or a series of state theatres, was led in 1907 by the columnist 'Stargazer' writing in the new journal *Lone Hand*. It was carried on, with different proposals written in a range of rhetorical styles, well into the 1950s.[24] At first the campaigners called for commercial entrepreneurs to take on the cause of serious Australian playwrights, but when it became clear that this was not going to happen they fell back on the repertory movement, and later on a scattering of nationalist projects, of which the Pioneer Players is the best known.

It is quite true that, apart from Bailey and Howarde, commercial producers neglected Australian dramatists. A few of the amateur theatres and the new radio producers were the only avenues for Australian writers. JCW's scarcely did Australian drama at all. While Bailey made enough money from his extended career as actor, writer and producer to set himself up in a nice house in Sydney's Potts Point, Williamson's did a string of Gilbert and Sullivan operettas, one of their main money-spinners for many years.

JCW's explained their neglect of Australian plays in terms that were still familiar in the 1970s: none were any good, able to pull a crowd, at all reliable for a producer with an eye on the box-office. Plays from London or New York had been developed and refined through the extensive out-of-town tryout system that feeds solidly researched box-office material into the West End and Broadway; the local press had reported regularly on them; they came to Australia already tried and with good advance publicity. Add to that the actors imported to support this overseas repertoire and the arguments of these sensible men of business seemed incontestable.

The commercial theatre was a little more attentive to the serious modern repertoire that constituted the staple of the repertory theatres, but not much. From the late 1920s until just after World War II the Firm occasionally produced serious drama from overseas, and with stars such as the Oliviers they had some modest financial success. But overall they felt, as Nevin Tait put it, that 'the Australian public is really not so keen on the higher drama'. As another Williamson's man said:

1: THE TURN OF THE CENTURY

> It makes one absolutely frightened of the repertory type of play when the big money seems to come for *Ladies Night in a Turkish Bath*, *See How They Run*, *Worm's Eye View* and farce comedies. Personally I love to see these wonderfully produced ['repertory type'] shows with their superlative casts when I am in London or New York, but we don't seem to make any money with them out here. [...] I am afraid that the I.Q. of our public is not very high, and therefore the audience for the highbrow plays [...] is very limited.[25]

Similar complaints about the vulgar taste of the Australian public abound, but commercial entrepreneurs were not investing the resources that might bring to Australia the new serious English repertoire. Dramatists such Arthur Wing Pinero, Henry Arthur Jones, John Galsworthy, John Masefield, Somerset Maugham, Arnold Bennett and George Bernard Shaw were having commercial success in the English theatre at the beginning of the century but their plays were rarely given commercial production in Australia. A commercial tour of *A Doll's House* in 1889 by Janet Achurch and her actor-husband Charles Charrington had done little to introduce Ibsen to Australia other than allow local journalists and moralists to revive the scandal that the play had already provoked in England.[26]

Many critics blamed the monopoly of the Firm for what they saw as the crude populism of the Australian commercial theatre. The harshest of these was Allan Ashbolt, who, looking back in 1978, wrote of the Tait brothers, who had dominated the commercial performing arts for more than forty years:

> They strangled artistic enterprise, distorted and retarded the growth of indigenous theatrical practice, debased public understanding with creaking revivals of trivial musical comedies, goaded actors into unemployment and exile, charged exorbitant seat prices for productions by mediocre overseas companies, bought, sold, exploited and rented either buildings or performers by the ubiquitous slide-rule of profit. They were commodity dealers, neither evil nor greedy nor ill-intentioned, merely devout cynics, mawkishly susceptible to the dreamworld of make-believe, dressing-up and grease-paint.[27]

Ashbolt argued that the Taits were 'penny wise and pound foolish' for not investing in productions that might have created a demand for a type of quality theatre that could have withstood the challenges of entertainment taxes, the depression, and the rise of the movies.

Lady Viola Tait's defence of JCW's record of producing Australian writing, in her 1971 book *A Family of Brothers*, is revealing because it is so weak. All she could point to was *Pommy* (1954), a comedy drama by W. P. Lipscombe and Victor Weston and 'Ray Lawlor's [sic] world premiere of *The Piccadilly Bushman* in 1959'.[28] The first is now obscure and the second an easy exploitation of the spectacular success of *Summer of the Seventeenth Doll*, a centre of media attention since its triumphant opening a few years earlier. In the New Wave of the late 1960s, she writes, the company rejected the new type of 'violent, colourful, tragicomedy plays'. They knocked back *Who's Afraid of Virginia Woolf*, *The Boys in the Band* and *Hair*—all of which became huge successes for other commercial producers, especially Harry M. Miller.[29]

Tait doesn't mention several other Australian plays that JCW's produced over the years, including Doris Egerton Jones's jobbing detective thriller *The Flaw*, co-written with and for its star, the English actress Emelie Polini in 1923; the successful stage and radio writer Max Afford's comedy thrillers *Lady in Danger* and *Mischief in the Air* in the 1940s and in the late 1950s and early 1960s Barbara Vernon's *The Multi-Coloured Umbrella* and Peggy Caine's *Who'll Come A-Waltzing*.

Repertory theatres

In general, the repertory theatres were not much better. Like their English counterparts they were created to take up the contemporary repertoire that the commercial theatre ignored, which in Australia, as we have seen, was most of it. Many of them produced the farces, thrillers and drawing-room comedies that in a larger theatre scene might have been done commercially. In part this was because they needed to keep an eye on the box office. The more serious-minded companies had an interest in the new 'intellectual drama', based around 'Ibshaw' (Ibsen, Shaw, Pinero and others); in the new avant-garde; or, in a few cases, in Australian writing.

The term 'repertory theatre' was taken from the English model, although the Australian companies did not play true repertory seasons,

1: THE TURN OF THE CENTURY

nor were they professional. In the 1930s the term 'Little Theatres' became fashionable, partly to acknowledge this. Some companies used the term 'art theatre', after the Moscow Art Theatre, to distinguish their work from the bland repertoire of conventional repertory companies, which mostly played to small but respectable subscription audiences. Hugh Hunt, the founding director of the Australian Elizabethan Theatre Trust, described such groups in 1958 as 'the middle-aged, the middle-class and the middle-brow'.[30]

The Little Theatre Movement was an eclectic group of small amateur companies, societies and clubs with mostly low production standards. As Virginia Kirby-Smith points out, in the only serious discussion of this movement, the fact that small companies led by enthusiasts kept the serious repertoire alive from the 1920s to 1950s should not blind us to the fact that it was essentially an amateur movement. This issue was to become controversial during the campaign for a national theatre in the 1940s and 1950s and the competition for public subsidy in the 1970s.[31]

It is easy to mock the efforts of the movement now. Many otherwise supportive commentators hinted at the low standards of these theatres. Allan Ashbolt drew their implied reservations together in 1948, in a damning but convincing account of Gregan McMahon's cheap and slipshod working methods.[32] The professionalism that Harley Granville Barker had worked for at the Royal Court Theatre in London since 1904 was, when transplanted to Australia, always 'tenuously rooted' in the repertory companies, which were characterised by a happily amateur approach and 'an air of social chic'.[33] Paul Hasluck, a drama critic better known as a politician and later as Governor–General, wrote of his involvement with the Perth Repertory Club that, 'amateurs are not only actors on stage but also in the clubroom'.[34]

More generally, though, it was commercial theatre productions that were described by journalists, writers and polemicists alike as 'cheap and slipshod'. The phrase is Alice Grant Rosnan's, writing in *Lone Hand* in 1909 of Treharne's company, and drawing a comparison with the 'eager and ever growing public' for the Adelaide Repertory Theatre that created a need for a larger hall and longer seasons (two nights, that is, rather than one) for the new repertoire.[35] Obviously we are talking about hundreds rather than thousands of people here but there was nevertheless an audience that valued the new drama and rejected the old, and it was an audience that stayed loyal, grew steadily for the rest of the century and formed the basis of the middle-class audience for the professional theatre now. It is possible to exaggerate the significance of the repertory companies as standard bearers of serious drama, and it is certainly an error to suppose that they were pioneers of Australian playwriting, but there can be no doubt that they played a vital role in developing audiences.

Several of the new companies, including Treharne's, did produce Australian plays, particularly in the 1930s and 1940s, once the repertoire had started to grow. The Pioneer Players in Melbourne in the early 1920s, and in Sydney Carrie Tennant's Community Playhouse in the late 1920s and early 1930s and Doris Fitton's Independent Theatre, also in Sydney, from the 1930s to the 1970s, were seriously committed to Australian writing. Tennant's Play Society, set up in 1931, attempted to draw together the disparate activities of the Little Theatres interested in Australian drama by publishing lists of available scripts.

But for the most part the Little Theatres paid only lip-service to the work of local dramatists. McMahon's Repertory Theatre in Melbourne from 1911–1917 staged productions of thirteen Australian plays out of total of sixty-five. His Sydney company, between 1920 and 1927, did four out of seventy.[36] Back in Melbourne, between 1929 and 1941 (when McMahon died), his Gregan McMahon Players produced five in a repertoire of 110.[37] The philosophic base of the repertory movement was a deep respect for serious drama that seems to have precluded an acceptance of what producers and committees saw as weak and undeveloped Australian writing. McMahon himself was not interested in nurturing new local work. His mission was to offer excellence, in the form of the new European repertoire, to Australian audiences, and to offer it also to Australian writers, as a model of what they might one day achieve.[38] None of these producers had any idea about how to develop the work of new writers, other than to present them to audiences at 'Club Night' readings.

A few explored the European avant-garde—such as Duncan McDougall's Playbox Art Theatre in the 1920s, which did productions

1: THE TURN OF THE CENTURY

of plays by Frank Wedekind, Eugene O'Neill and Sean O'Casey in Sydney; and Alan Harkness and Kester Baruch's Ab Intra Theatre in Adelaide, which produced symbolist plays, using heightened design and dance in the 1930s. Most, however, did the standard repertoire of the sophisticated London theatre of the day. The genres and styles of the old commercial, popular theatre pervaded much of their work but the movement that began with what Arthur H. Adams called seasons of 'one consecutive night' culminated when John Sumner's Union Theatre Repertory Company produced *Summer of the Seventeenth Doll*, the greatest popular success of an Australian play since *On Our Selection*. The company became one of the new state flagship companies—non-commercial but professional—in the dawning age of publicly subsidised theatre in the 1970s and was renamed the Melbourne Theatre Company.

One of the very early pioneers of non-commercial Australian writing was journalist, art historian and hopeful playwright William Moore. He never had a company of his own, but he organised a series of annual Australian Drama Nights in Melbourne between 1909 and 1912 and is often credited with launching the new nationalist Australian drama. His own plays were stilted and trivial, although *The Tea-Room Girl* was at least full of Melbourne colour. It was published in 1910 by T. C. Lothian as the first volume of a projected series entitled 'Plays with Local Background'. Set in what we would now call a fashionable restaurant its opening lines, between two patrons who have just been to the theatre, mark another transition from the old to the new:

> ADMIRER: [...] Great spectacular show, wasn't it? Good old melodrama; I haven't seen one for a long time.
> BLOCK GIRL: Weren't the horses lovely? I adore plays with gee-gees in them. (p. 8)

The little play they are in, as opposed to the grand production that they have just seen, was performed at the Turn Verein Hall in 1910, along with one-acters by Katharine Susannah Prichard and Louis Esson. It concerns a Melbourne journalist who, having found fame and wealth in London as a successful commercial playwright, has returned to claim his tea-room girl. It was a dream that many amateur dramatists were to write about for the next fifty years.

BELONGING

The Nationalist Theatre

The same arguments used about the commercial, the repertory and the little art theatres in introducing a serious overseas repertoire to Australian audiences were also employed in relation to the local repertoire—or rather the lack of one. Aside from the campaign launched by *Lone Hand*'s anonymous 'Stargazer' already mentioned, *Triad* editor and playwright L. L. Woolacott started arguing in the 1920s, as did Ashbolt later, that a repertoire of Australian plays might have been the very thing to save the commercial theatre.[39] But the Taits, who controlled distribution, refused to spend money on the product and, like McMahon, had little interest in developing new Australian work.

It took Australian writers a little while to realise that the commercial entrepreneurs were not interested. There were in fact a great many attempts by hopeful dramatists to write plays for the commercial stage between the 1920s and the 1950s—plays that ended up falling in a gap between the commercial and the nationalist theatres and sometimes found a place in the repertory theatres by default. A great deal of very good writing for the stage from this period has been neglected because would-be professional writers wrote plays in conventional genres, hoping they would be picked up by the commercial theatre. They weren't, and since that time these forgotten plays have not been seen as either serious or nationalist enough to be included in the canon of Australian drama.

In a different context but for similar reasons the plays of the socialist playwrights have also been neglected. One of the most prolific and eclectic of all Australian dramatists last century, Mona Brand, was 'alternative' in the sense that she wrote for the socialist New Theatre movement, and also created, in the 1960s, the antecedents of the theatricalist New Wave of vaudeville history plays of the 1970s. Yet her large output has never been admitted to the canon because she wrote mostly in genre. Her work is also discussed in the Chapter Three.

Small though the nationalist drama was at the beginning of the century, it is better remembered now and has come to be seen as a movement that triumphed over both the nineteenth century commercial tradition and the early twentieth century repertory tradition. We

1: THE TURN OF THE CENTURY

might introduce it by discussing a polemical attack launched by one of the first of the new nationalists, Louis Esson, against one of the genre writers, Arthur H. Adams.

Esson and Adams

Adams had been produced on the commercial stage. In 1897 he sold to JCW's a libretto he had written for an operetta, *Tapu* (composed by Alfred Hill) and was employed to work for the next two years as their literary secretary, writing the book and lyrics for pantomimes such as *The Forty Thieves* in 1899.[40] For many years he tried to persuade commercial managements to produce his plays, documenting their failure to do so, and bewailing the fate of the Australian writer, in a series of articles in *Lone Hand* and *The Theatre*. He is best known now (insofar as you can say that about a writer whom most people have never heard of) for a series of plays of urban life, published in 1914 and reviewed in vitriolic terms by Esson.[41] 'These plays were written for the Australian stage', Adams wrote, 'One of the many drawbacks to their production is that there is no Australian stage'.

He was clear about his aims as a writer:

> These plays do not claim to be Repertory plays: they were written for the Australian commercial theatre—though it must be admitted that, so far, the controlling destinies of the Australian commercial stage have not quite grasped my intention.[42]

He advised other writers that they should try to get their plays produced, for the sake of developing their craft, even if it meant turning to bad amateur companies; and that is what he finally did himself, although he denied the companies he used were bad.[43] He had some success in this, with productions in Adelaide by Treharne's company, and in Sydney and London. He managed to sell the rights to his last play *Gallipoli Bill* to Bert Bailey—but no production eventuated.

Adams wrote well-made plays about very modern problems faced by articulate city characters who live in nice houses with Sydney harbour views. He was the first dramatist to use Sydney's 'southerly buster'—a refreshing wind that blows away the heat at the end of a hot summer day—as a dramatic device. But he fell between two stools: for JCW's he was Australian and therefore uncommercial and for Esson he was commercial and therefore unAustralian. Now that the evangelism of the nationalists has faded and genre writing is more accepted, at least ironically, it might be time to revisit his plays.[44] Making allowance for the fact that, because his plays were rarely performed, his dramatic skills remained undeveloped, he looks very much like a precursor to David Williamson.

Adams's plays are formulaic but they have charm and humour. One can understand his chagrin that they were not produced, when equally light plays that had received the imperial imprimatur were. But, of course, it was success at Home that both Australian producers and audiences looked for in their theatre.

The Wasters is a comedy about the marital problems and money scandals of a wealthy business-class family in Sydney's Potts Point. *Mrs Pretty and the Premier* is a political comedy with the sort of implausible plot that outraged the new realists at the time but is standard fare in the commercial cinema and television today. *Galahad Jones* is a pleasantly silly farce about an otherwise dull middle-aged bank clerk who gets drawn into an innocent association with a romantic young woman dying of pernicious anaemia. In the process of resolving the misunderstandings he and his wife rediscover their youthful love for each other. The southerly buster blows away all the farcical complications at the end.

Louis Esson was a particularly outspoken enemy of the commercial theatre, and he came to identify Adams with it, in spite of Adams's lack of commercial success. Esson denied that money had any role whatsoever in the production of art, and claimed that no important writer ever wrote for financial reward. Synge, he commented with apparent approval, had written 'the greatest plays [...] in English since Webster', yet received no payment for them.[45]

Some allowance must be made for the rhetorical exuberance of Esson's critical and polemic writing, and also for the frustration he so obviously felt at the apparent failure of his dream for a National Drama. Certainly he never made any money himself out of writing plays. But one of his most savage attacks was directed at Adams rather than, say, at commercial entrepreneurs such as Bert Bailey and Kate Howarde. He accused Adams of selling his soul, in spite of the fact

1: THE TURN OF THE CENTURY

that since 1899 Adams had made no more money out from his plays than he had himself. In a series of early articles about Australian drama he referred to Adams in fairly neutral tones as a fellow playwright whose plays he had not seen. In 1914 he wrote:

> My complaint against the author is not that he has written a bad play—everybody writes bad plays—but that he has not even faintly realised that it was his duty to do his best for Australian drama. Adams was working for himself, not for the movement: thinking, maybe, of a motor-launch, and forgetting altogether that he was making the road harder for the rest of us.[46]

The reference is to a series of light magazine stories published in book form by Adams the previous year under the title *The Knight of the Motor Launch*.[47] They follow the amorous adventures of a rich young man racing around Sydney Harbour in his boat, and they make pleasant, if quaint, reading today. Esson's tone reveals how deeply committed he had become to the bush legend at the expense of the trivialities of city life. Reviewing Adams's volume of plays he writes:

> In an authentic Australian play there should be a real atmosphere—some space and sunshine, wild nature or primitive character, something with a cow in it would have been much better; closer to the earth and reality.[48]

Only two years earlier, at the Melbourne Repertory Theatre, Gregan McMahon had produced Esson's own society play, the political comedy *The Time Is Not Yet Ripe*—a fecklessly commercial play, according to its 1973 editor, written by a playwright 'as yet unharried by inner contradictions'.[49] It has been compared favourably with Adams's comedies, especially *Mrs Pretty and the Premier*, as pap for the Repertory audiences.[50] But even as he wrote it, Esson was complaining that it was five years old in style and he later came to disown it.[51] His other city plays, discussed in the next chapter, are set in the exotic bohemian inner city rather than high society. By 1914 his 'inner contradictions' were already beginning to trouble him, and that was eight years before he embarked on his major project—the creation of an Australian repertoire for his company, The Pioneer Players. Never again would Esson write for the repertory theatre.

BELONGING

In 1920, after his second meeting with his mentor W. B. Yeats he wrote to Vance Palmer about a debate at Dublin's Abbey theatre that the Australian repertory theatres might have had. The Abbey's patron Mrs Horniman wanted the company to stage European masterpieces alongside the new Irish repertoire. Yeats wavered but Synge protested 'and Irish drama was saved':

> 'A theatre like that', said Synge, 'never creates anything'. Isn't that true? What did McMahon create? What did Hilda's University Society that did Shaw, Galsworthy, etc., create? They should have discovered me for a start, but they didn't! What has Adelaide ever done, with all its list of plays?[52]

McMahon had produced *The Time Is Not Yet Ripe*. Adelaide (by which he meant Treharne's company) had done the two Adams plays. Hilda, his wife, was to become one of his greatest supporters, even after their marriage was effectively over.[53] But Esson was as disenchanted with the repertory theatres as he was with the commercial ones. After the failure of the Pioneer Players his work started to decline. He wrote *Shipwreck* in the late 1920s but it has never been given a full production—too melodramatic for the new realist theatre and too serious for the commercial theatre. It ought to be revived. It is discussed in the next chapter.

2
BUSH AND CITY

'The worst of it is that the plays become out-of-date, without being known'

Vance Palmer, 1939[1]

'I had always imagined Australia as a free and happy land of eternal sunshine. But what impressed me most about your country's plays is their Greek gloom. They are full of the atmosphere of Greek tragedies.'

St John Ervine[2]

The bush legend

The bush legend was always going to be a problem for the new realist theatre because the central protagonist was a land not a person. Instead of individuals, the agents that prompted dramatic events were oppressive heat, huge distances or long droughts suddenly interrupted by devastating floods or fires. The dramatic characters were the least significant things in a landscape that, hostile or seductive, was brought into imagined being over the course of a century. In many of the

BELONGING

most enduring stories the characters were, literally, lost in it. Their identity—and by extension the much discussed Australian Identity, or Australian National Character, or Australian Legend—was constructed by talking and performing about this loss and an associated search for a sense of belonging.

Even vast spaces have to have people in them, at least in plays, so a series of character types that reflected these ideas was born: laconic men with suppressed emotions, battling women who tamed theirs, rebellious young men and women not yet defeated or others who do not appreciate the values of pioneering life. (In the best plays, of course, all these contradictory attitudes are present.) And inevitably, in a theatre based on realistic illusion, a lot the attention was focused on the sets.

Most of the plays written about the harshness of the bush and the struggle of life on the land between the 1890s and the 1950s were staged according to the 'authentic' staging requirements of late melodrama, or with the simple representational realism called for by the new nationalist drama. In both cases the settings were supposed to be mimetic. Today a designer can call up a desert, a fire and a flood, in any of a number of ways. Then, the commercial and the amateur theatre alike used stage conventions that were increasingly challenged by the new photographic conventions of film. In an amateur theatre based on a visual vocabulary of painted backdrops, wings, flats and borders the bush life quickly became a series of set clichés.

The predominant cliché, found in *On Our Selection*, *Possum Paddock* and a whole swathe of plays right up until the 1950s (and even today in some fine retro-realist plays), showed a veranda and a bit of the homestead garden. A gate and the strainer post of the fence were upstage, with old logs, pieces of furniture or other set pieces dotted about. As David Malouf has observed, the veranda is a place where nature and culture intersect.[3] Although part of the homestead intrudes onto the stage—either the veranda itself or, in the more elaborate sets, a glimpse of the interior—essentially the setting is outdoors. A backcloth shows the far hills or the nearer tree line of the river, and restless cattle, or perhaps a corroboree down at the blacks' camp, can be heard in the distance. The action often moves indoors, leaving the

2: BUSH AND CITY

landscape behind as the drama focuses on the characters. In Harry Tighe's *Open Spaces* (1927) the producer is given the choice: while the action suggests it moves indoors in Acts 3 and 4, Tighe, mindful of costs, says in the stage directions that these acts can, if necessary, be played on the outside set.

The alternative standard set, especially in the more grimly realistic plays, is indoors. In play after play the setting is the interior of a simple bush hut, with walls made of hessian, rough timber slabs or flattened kerosene tins and a few pathetic attempts to enliven the room: such as pictures torn from the newspaper colour supplements tacked to the walls, gay print curtains at the windows and a few geraniums outside on which the woman of the house lavishes the last of the water from the dry creek bed. There may be a rough deal table centre stage and other simple items of furniture, made, perhaps, of undressed saplings. There is usually a gun somewhere, to be used on the marauding kangaroos (or escaped convicts in the historical plays), and which an intruder sometimes turns on the inhabitants of the lonely dwelling. The windows (often flanking a central door, like two eyes in a face) look out on the dry harsh land. There might be silhouettes of dead trees on the distant painted hills, or an open sky, expressed in brilliant blue on the cyclorama. Or if it is sunrise or sunset, as it often is, a simple cross-fade of the standard old ground-row lighting suddenly floods the sky with vivid oranges and reds. When the drought breaks at the end of the play, as it tends to do, the rain pounds on the tin roof, and a slow curtain falls on the defeated, but sometimes newly hopeful, characters.

In Betty Roland's *The Touch of Silk*, a play in this vein, an ominous knife, which Jim uses to put dying sheep out of their misery, hangs on a hook next to the door. In Act 2 a blind flapping in the dry north wind brings the outside inside. At the end of the play, Jeanne, the pretty, sophisticated European wife of the shell-shocked digger, collapses as, in line with her prediction, God finally sends down his rain to mock their tragedy. In Katharine Susannah Prichard's *Pioneers* (1937), a door and a window open out on the small patch of land that the pioneers have cleared, with the wilderness beyond. In Millicent Armstrong's *Drought* (1958) the only window has a blanket pinned across it against the

BELONGING

heat and light of the blasted dry country outside. At the final curtain a blinding glare of lighting and an earth-shaking crash of thunder all but drown out the rifle-shot as the depressed farmer shoots himself, and the gush and pour of wild rain drowns out the tears of his grieving wife.

Henrietta Drake-Brockman's three-act *Men Without Wives* (1938) has three sets without any windows, but outside the harsh sun beats through the veiled door and we hear the sound of the river in flood during the climactic scene. In Dymphna Cusack's *Red Sky at Morning* (1942) the figures onstage watch as two desperate characters flee the tight confines of the inn in which they are trapped only to be drowned crossing the rising river. In Mona Brand's *Flood Tide* (1955) the land literally invades the Act 1 set. Two characters are forced to sit upstairs and listen to the crashing of the waters. By Act 3 volunteer helpers have dug six feet of mud out of the house.

The box sets are closed off in direct proportion to the threat of the land. The cheerful plays, about pioneers looking to make a new world, are set on verandas with the domestic interior offstage. The tragedies are set indoors, in a vain attempt to shut out the land.

Realism, and the theatrical conventions of the time, required such sets to represent or evoke the land. As they separated onstage from off and inside from out, the sets mirrored the plays' interest in the interactions between individuals and their environment. Inside, the domestic, was inhabited by the women who put up the pictures and watered the geraniums. Outside, in the other world, were the men who cleared the land, got the supplies, and mustered the cattle. Between the two is continual traffic.[4]

In the plays, the city always looms beyond the bush, promising escape, with its civilisation, attractions, comforts, satisfactions and lures; and obversely its wickedness and corruption. The traffic between the huts and the outside bush is nothing to the traffic between them and the city. Flighty young city women are lured to the bush, where they either pine or grow tough. Sensitive young bushmen with poetic souls are torn between staying on the farm and fleeing to the bright lights and cafés. Battling pioneers, who have spent their energy fighting the land, grow old and need city hospitals; or they are persuaded by their

2: BUSH AND CITY

long-suffering wives to give the land up to their sons. In *Men Without Wives*, Ma Bates, the toughest old chook of all, happily welcomes the flood that cuts her off from the city world, even though it means her death. In Tighe's *Open Spaces* the elemental battle between the two women of the play—a long-suffering bush wife and her husband's new city mistress—becomes a bitter struggle to see who can stay on the longest and so win. In Henrietta Drake-Brockman's *The Man from the Bush* an old bushman with a shearing cheque to spend sits on a city bench and ponders the supposedly civilised city types, before giving his cheque to a poor young urban mother who is suffering in the world they have created.

It is, of course, the city perspective that makes the bush plays possible. They were, after all, written and produced in urban centres, where the bush was a myth, a 'projection onto the outback of values revered by an alienated urban intelligentsia'.[5] It may have only become the legend during the 1950s but it was a potent idea in plays from the 1920s. The civilised theatrical conventions of the bush realist plays call for a city perspective, framing the land as a landscape and its people as characters.

The conventions of realism constrained the characters as much as they did the settings. H. G. Kippax first summed up the problem:

> Realistic drama makes much of scene: but what stage could hold the Australian bush and plains? In the event, playwrights avoided the problem. They mirrored the hardness of the land in the hardness of characters dominated by the land; they peopled their plays with men who were brutes or virtuous boobies and with women who were drab Griseldas or neurotics. They dramatised the violence of the land by substituting human violence: when one thinks of the Australian outback play, one thinks of a set of hard-bitten characters who nag, in a flat monotonous way, about the droughts or the floods or the fires—and then, because something has to happen in a play, begin fighting each other.[6]

Although it was fair comment at the time, it's worth noting that Kippax was writing in 1963 at the height of his enthusiasm for the new plays of Patrick White. White had done a great deal to transcend these limitations by mixing new theatrical styles. Further the bush tradition

BELONGING

Kippax was writing about had culminated in a series of urban realist plays that had brought it to an end—literally so, in the case of *Summer of the Seventeenth Doll*—shouting and fighting its way into the city.

The bush realist plays between the 1920s and the 1950s were often criticised for not being realistic. The characters were stereotyped or two-dimensional; their motivations unmotivated or contrived; their development unconvincing or incomplete. In 1954 Betty Roland took to heart criticisms that her 'realism' was too 'melodramatic' and re-wrote *The Touch of Silk*, one of the most successful plays of the first half of the century. Kippax commented negatively on the play's melodrama in 1963. Indeed Kippax relentlessly asserted that drama was the representation of individuals in conflict. And this assertion from a leading critic over thirty years did a great deal to entrench the idea that plays that attempted other things, such as plot-driven narratives, were failures.

The negative sense of the word 'melodramatic' has a long history. It is still used by people who are otherwise happy to watch commercial TV and go to the movies. If we stop thinking of the bush plays as bad realism and start thinking of them as good melodrama then we might rehabilitate many unfairly neglected works. The best bush plays have an excess rooted in popular culture that is not appropriate in traditional realism, but which justifies attention now that directors, actors and audiences are exploring new forms of presentational theatre that are frank about their theatricality. There is nothing drably representational about early Australian melodramatic realism, but in the quest for Australianness what people noticed was the local colour, not the form.

Louis Esson

Foremost among the writers who were asking for more than the conventions of the theatre at the time could provide was Louis Esson. He ignored all the interiors, the deal tables and the verandas, and set his most famous play, *The Drovers* (1923), on the open plain. This classic early bush play opens with the offstage sound of a gunshot and cattle stampede. Briglow Bill, a drover injured by the stampede, is brought

2: BUSH AND CITY

on stage. He will be left to die, according to the hard law of the stock routes, so that the thirsty cattle can be taken to the next waterhole. Both he and the men accept this with a simple fatalism. His mates even start chatting with him about how they'll divvy up his cheque. But the city-bred Jackeroo, who had caused the stampede by firing at a dingo, is appalled. This bush–city opposition at the core of the play was, as Margaret Williams points out, clearly written from a city point of view.[7] If the audience shared the stoic attitudes of the drovers then the dramatic situation would collapse. The play romanticises the bush legend for urban audiences.

The Boss is a tough, laconic, capable leader, respected by his men:

> MICK: ... D'ya remember when he took those steers from the yellow waterhole at Murrimji, the short cut through the devil-devil country, where the ground broke under your feet, and the ants would eat you alive—only three of us and a myall nigger! We got one drink for the mob in a hundred miles. He's a marvel, the old man is, and delivered only six short of his number. (p. 230)

The 'myall nigger' in this play is Pigeon, a stock stage Aborigine who is given the task of staying with the dying Briglow and mourning over the body. 'You, Briglow, and old man Boss, you savvy bush all-the-same blackfellow', he says (p. 238). Briglow's cheerful acceptance of his fate is a classic statement of the legend:

> It don't matter. It had to come sooner or later. I've lived my life, careless and free, looking after my work when I was at it, and splashing my cheque up like a good one when I struck civilisation. I've lived hard, droving and horse-breaking, station work, and overlanding, the hard life of the bush, but there's nothing better, and death's come quick, before I'm played out—it's the way I wanted. (p. 235)

Dead Timber (1911), set on an isolated selection in Gippsland, is the gloomiest of all Esson's plays—perhaps of the entire bush repertoire—one of those that reminded St John Ervine of Greek tragedies. The setting is a slab hut, with a bench and logs strewn around, and in the distance, silhouetted against the sky, the dead trees that come to represent the broken family who live there. It is winter and a

BELONGING

thunderstorm the night before is taken by the depressed Farmer as a sign of God's judgement on his daughter Mary, who is pregnant to an itinerant horse breaker camped nearby. Joe and Abe, his two sons, tramp reluctantly through the mud to bring in the cattle, while the Wife, 'careworn but resigned', struggles to keep everyone together. When the Farmer discovers Mary's sin he shoots himself. The play is like a particularly sombre episode of On Our Selection, stripped of all humour and pushing the grim struggle of the selectors to its conclusion.

The call of the city is more insistent than in *The Drovers*. Mary has been driven into the arms of her lover by a wretched feeling of weariness at the hard life in the bush—a feeling she continually voices. None of the other characters finds any comfort in their battle against the land, nor any solace in the legend. In these two plays it is as if Esson were laying out the opposing sides in a bush–city debate that became one of the dominant themes in early twentieth-century Australian drama.

Two of Esson's later short bush plays and both his full-length ones are set in the open air. *Vagabond Camp* brings two city crooks on the run from the law to a riverside camp where they team up with Sarah, 'a woman of the roads', to rob a crippled ex-digger who has been living peaceably with Bess for five years. It is a clumsy play, self-consciously colourful, with an old fisherman who keeps wandering in and out, spouting aphorisms of bush philosophy. *Andeganora* is set at the camp of a violent brumby-runner and the blacks he travels with. It is a genuine attempt to tell from the Aboriginal side of their exploitation by the tough men of the outback but the politics of black–white relations since have diminished its relevance.

Mother and Son is one of Esson's more successful plays, and the principal forerunner of a succession of bush realist dramas in the decades after its 1923 premiere. It is centred on the relationship between Mrs Lind, a tough battler who has long struggled to make a living out of the land, and her son, Harry, whose wild streak leads him into poaching, sheep-stealing and the arms of a loose woman at the local shanty. His wildness has a romantic side to it, which he expresses by playing violin. Although uncertain of his talent his artistic side is

2: BUSH AND CITY

clearly very important—a sort of spirituality he finds in the harsh dull rural life.

The others are there mostly to support this central pair but while derived from nineteenth-century drama types they are more than stock characters. Peter, Harry's father, is an old battler now enfeebled. The bush philosopher, Tom Henderson, is a swaggie with an obsession for the *Koran*. He settles with them for a while but heads on the road again and eventually dies under a tree. Peggy, a good woman, does little more than wait for Harry to pull himself together, but the bad woman, Emma, is sympathetically drawn and the rich squatter's son is much more than the traditional melodramatic villain. The third act is rather overcrowded, as the threads of all these lives are drawn together, but the play has a power through its atmospheric evocation of the landscape in which these people are so isolated.

The setting is a lonely bee farm in a forest clearing in the Wimmera district of Victoria. 'Everything is wild and primitive.' The opening set has the usual elements—the yard, the sliprails, the hut with a porch and a bench and logs strewn around. It is autumn and the children are bee-hunting. Harry has had a fling with Emma but she has moved on, and everything seems fine between him and Peggy. He leaves for a duck-shooting tour of the lakes but promises to return.

The second act moves indoors as winter approaches, and Peter dies as a wild storm rages in the night outside. Harry and Emma enter, together again, having been caught in the storm returning from the shanty. At the end of the act a heartbroken Peggy rushes out into the rain. In the third act it is again night outside and after a series of revelations. Harry, drunk again and more restless than ever, goes for a wild horse-ride through the dark trees and is killed.

The melodramatic elements in the story, as in so much Australian realism, are probably not the problem for audiences they once were. The almost gothic use of weather and the intensity of the conflicts make this a play ripe for bold new theatrical treatment.

The final play in this group is *The Battler*. Set in and around an old shanty called 'The Diggers' Rest', it is a cheerful portrait of an old gold-mining community, once lively and prosperous but now declined into very quiet rural isolation. 'Its glory has departed but it just faintly remembers its romantic past.' A legendary miner from the roaring days, George Ogilvie, returns to look for a Lost Reef and revive the town. The gold is found, the town comes briefly to life—The Diggers' Rest is renamed The Commercial Hotel—but then the reef is lost at a fault line. Ogilvie leaves again and the community reverts to its former quiet ways.

The landscape is not the most important part of this play (although at one stage we are told rather more about the geology of gold-mining than we need to know—Esson liked to show that he'd done his homework). It is the sense of community, and a nostalgia for a romantic past, that give this play its charm. The outsider who stirs up a community and leaves it again is a familiar device in Australian drama.[8]

It is also the central device in J. M. Synge's *The Playboy of the Western World*, which leads us back to the Irish influence on Esson. One critic of the Pioneer Players' production of *The Battler* wrote, 'The play strikes the right note but the blow is insufficiently hard'.[9] More than any other Esson play, *The Battler* illustrates his reaction against melodramatic excess, against, even, the Ibsenite drama based on the 'conflict of wills'. He quoted with approval George Moore's phrase to describe Synge's dramaturgy: the 'drama of drift'.[10]

Esson's bush plays, which anticipate so much of the drama that followed, were a direct result of the influence of Yeats and Synge. Yeats told him that in Australia he had the people and the land and that his job was to try to get the right relationship between them. Synge said: 'You ought to have plenty of material for drama in Australia. All those outback stations with shepherds going mad in lonely huts'.[11] It is one of the ironies of the nationalist drama movement that its main inspiration should have come from overseas. Another is that Esson was by inclination a cosmopolitan with an interest in the bohemian life of cities and the advanced art of his time. But under the influence of his Irish mentors he turned his back on that and started to work towards a folk drama modelled on the work of Synge. Each of his two bursts of playwriting activity came after a visit ('pilgrimage' was his word) abroad.

He first travelled in 1904 when he met Synge in London, visited the Abbey, met Yeats and received advice that the young admirer of

2: BUSH AND CITY

Montmartre and Bloomsbury didn't want to hear: 'Keep within your own borders!' and 'If you want to do anything you must regard your own country as the centre of the universe'.[12] Esson had written many polemical articles about the philistinism of his country, and continued to do so for many years. He had come to Europe to be part of an artistic world that he felt did not exist at home. But Yeats urged him to write country comedies, which 'build up a country, where dramas of ideas tend to divide and shatter it'.[13] He returned home and produced *Dead Timber*, two one-act city plays of the under classes (*The Woman Tamer* and *The Sacred Place*) and the very urbane political society comedy *The Time Is Not Yet Ripe*. During his second trip abroad, which lasted from 1916 to 1921, Yeats read a volume of the three one-acters and *The Drovers* and told Esson that on the whole he thought he might do his best things in tragedy.[14] Unphased, and perverse again, Esson came back home and wrote his only country comedy *The Battler*. He also wrote his bush tragedy, *Mother and Son*.

Esson admired and respected Yeats in the same way (to use his own religious imagery) that students of divinity in the Middle Ages admired St Thomas Aquinas.[15] He seems to have been a man in need of heroes and he found them abroad.[16]

He was also a highly impressionable dramatist who tended to write plays in the style of the playwright who had most recently influenced him. *The Battler* has, like *Dead Timber*, been said to be a reworking of *On Our Selection*[17] but it owes more to Synge's *The Playboy of the Western World*. *Vagabond Camp* is a road play very like Synge's *The Tinker's Wedding* and *The Drovers* owes a lot to *Riders to the Sea* (although not as much as does Sydney Tomholt's *The Women Wait*, which is almost a direct adaptation). *Andeganora* was written a few years after Katharine Susannah Prichard won a *Triad* play-competition with *Brumby Innes*, one of the most extraordinary plays of the entire period (Esson had submitted his plodding historical drama *The Southern Cross*). It is much slighter than Prichard's play but obviously heavily indebted to it. Esson was evidently impressed, intimidated and a bit shocked by *Brumby Innes*, with its very frank treatment of interracial sex and violence, and he is slightly coy when he picks up the same themes in *Andeganora*.[18]

BELONGING

The Time Is Not Yet Ripe is written in a genre made familiar by a number of playwrights, especially Oscar Wilde, whose *The Soul of Man Under Socialism* influenced Esson's political thinking.[19] Both *Mother and Son* and *Shipwreck* are clearly influenced by Eugene O'Neill. The episodic structure of *The Quest* owes much to that of the German expressionists, whom Esson had read and praised for breaking away from linear plots.[20] None of this is to say that Esson was a mere imitator. Like many other Australian playwrights, especially those of the late 1960s and 1970s, he was more a bower bird, seizing on techniques and styles that seemed useful to him.

His historical dramas *The Quest* and *The Southern Cross* are his least successful plays (if we discount the brief conversation pieces *Terra Australia* and *Australia Felix*). *The Quest* is a series of scenes from the life of de Quiros, a great Spanish navigator who dreamed of discovering the great south land but never did. Each scene leads to a departure as de Quiros moves further away from his family and homeland and deeper into the uncharted southern ocean, where he eventually perishes. It is an ideal theme for Esson, and the scenic structure has so much potential that it is a pity he does not make more of it.

The Southern Cross might have been more successful if it, too, had employed an episodic structure. It is so concerned with telling the whole story, and getting the detail right, that narration overwhelms it. It has an impossibly large cast: 24 named characters plus 'Diggers, Troopers, Soldiers, Officials, Jurymen, Pikemen, Women and Children, Immigrants of various nationalities'.

The last category of characters is particularly interesting. Here and even more so in his city plays Esson's interest in local colour extends to the variety of national types he finds in Australia, belying the myth that before the community theatre movement of the early 1980s the drama was only interested in Anglo-Australians. Esson's characters are often types, displaying their ethnicity in ways that we now find stereotyped, but they are not the stock types of the nineteenth-century theatre. Rather they are clearly based on his observations during his bohemian days when he frequented Fasoli's café in Melbourne and enjoyed its mix of artists, students, late-night revellers and petty criminals. *Ballades*

2: BUSH AND CITY

of Old Bohemia includes many articles, stories and verses recording his impressions, and he also wrote one full-length and two one-act plays based on this material. *The Sacred Place* is a little scene about a disputed debt in Mohammedan Melbourne, showing the difference between traditional Islamic law and the Australian court system. *The Woman Tamer* is a neat short play about loyalty and manhood in the world of small-time Fitzroy spivs and their women.

Act 1 of *The Bride of Gospel Place* is set in a café very like Fasoli's, and much of it is taken up with the colourful characters who come and go as the night wears on. It is presided over by a Greek named Spiro and there is much comic play with the distinctions to be made between Greeks, Dagos and Chows. The carefully researched language is an elaborately colourful underworld argot. The act ends with one of the most abrupt courtships in a repertoire full of plot-driven abruptness.

The model this time is Puccini's *La Bohème*, but it is a determinedly grim and deromanticised version. The bride of the title is Lily. Her lover is a small-time boxer who dreams of winning an important fight but drifts into crime. When she challenges him he bashes her and leaves, thinking she has betrayed him. Lily's death from TB and the revelation that she has been a loyal crook's girl shakes him out of his decline and he decides to go back to boxing. 'Think of your girl, and be a man, for her sake', says the loyal old fortune teller who has been Lily's friend (p.141).

In his aims, though, Esson was reacting against the conventions of the old theatre and seeking, under Yeats's influence, something more 'real': simple representations of the life of a new country, written with a naturalism (Yeats' word, this time, for the early one-acters) that was authentic and unforced. His wife Hilda, introducing a posthumous tributary collection of his plays, wrote,

Overleaf: Valma Pratt as Lady Pillsbury, Sandy Gore as Miss Perkins, Tony Llewellyn-Jones as Bertie Wainwright and Sydney Conabere as Sir Joseph Quiverton with hecklers in the 1973 Melbourne Theatre Company production of Louis Esson's The Time Is Not Yet Ripe.

BELONGING

> [H]is work gives an authentic and valuable record of [the period he wrote in…]. Its authenticity may even be a reproach. Perhaps he disciplined himself too rigidly, sacrificing everything to fidelity of impression.[21]

At the other end of the scale, one of Esson's most exciting, fully-plotted plays is *Shipwreck* (1984), which has been neglected partly because it hasn't been easily available until recently and partly perhaps because its simple unabashed excess was unappealing to producers and audiences used to contemplative, character-based realism. Hilda Esson rejected it for the tributary volume writing that although it 'undoubtedly has some scenes of macabre and powerful beauty', she felt that its violence was alien to Esson's temperament and therefore not well done.[22] But the theatre could do it well today: it demands a grand treatment and deserves to be revived.

On a wild and isolated cliff top overlooking the Great Southern Ocean, 'Stumpy' Johnson keeps a shanty, runs a team of bullocks and makes a bit on the side scavenging the many shipwrecks on the dangerous rocks below, sometimes dynamiting the remains to remove the evidence. 'He is over sixty, with a wooden leg; but he gives the impression of a man in his prime, for he is powerfully built, and still vigorous and active.'(p.159) He lusts after Madge, a spirited 19-year-old girl of the bush, and buys her from her mercenary mother to be his bride. He keeps her locked up in the shanty where her only visitors are two rough but likeable sailors who periodically deliver the stores.

Stumpy has an estranged son, Tom, a cattle-man who once fancied Madge himself and with whom, after a few complications, she naturally falls in love. When the old man is arrested for his scavenging and sent to prison Madge and Tom set up house in his shanty (rather foolishly, you'd say, if this were a realistic play) and have a baby. Stumpy returns a year later and after a fine scene in which he is quietly sinister for a while he kills the baby and then Tom. In the last act he chains Madge to the wall and sets off with his bullocks through a particularly bad patch of 'debbil-debbil country' where blacks were once massacred, and that is so cursed that the lizards won't crawl and the birds won't fly over it. Of course the bullocks won't cross it either. Stumpy is mortally injured trying to force them, and blinded by the backlash of

2: BUSH AND CITY

the barbed wire he has tied to the end of his whip. He crawls brokenly back to the shanty but Madge refuses to help him, happy to watch him die. The play's only concession to sentimentality is in the final scene when the two sailors turn up to rescue Madge at the last minute and dump Stumpy's body into the sea. The ending would be much more powerful if that scene were cut and the play's last words were Madge's last, crowing to her oppressor, crumpled on the floor with his wooden leg now useless under him:

> MADGE: The light's fadin'. It'll be dark in a minute. [*Pause.*] How are you now, Stumpy? You're boss, are you, and you can do as you like. … You do look funny, lyin' there, crumpled up agen the wall. … You must be done in, Stumpy. … Can't you move? (p. 201)

Neither can she, of course, still chained to the wall.

This script, perhaps overblown and unintentionally comic in places, is a fine example of what Esson might have achieved, had he a real theatre to write for. Its psychology has the grand simplicity of its Greek model. The landscape is powerful, and haunted: Stumpy can exploit the storms of the Southern Ocean but he is defeated by a land cursed by the ghosts of the slaughtered when he turns inland.

Esson's plays, whether by direct influence or not, set the tone and style for much of the drama from the 1930s to the 1950s. Hilda Esson's 1946 anthology, and Vance Palmer's annotated edition of his letters two years later (*Louis Esson and the Australian Theatre*), did a great deal to cement his reputation. He is still the best known and most written about Australian playwright of his time, even if his plays are seldom produced. Both Hilda Esson and Palmer acknowledged that his aspiration far outweighed his achievement. Most subsequent critics have agreed. This is partly because he wasn't a naturally gifted playwright, and never claimed to be. His comments on his own work are usually humble and self-deprecating. He spent most of his playwriting life simply trying to provide repertoire for the national theatre that he believed Australia should have.

BELONGING

Writers without a theatre

The main reason why Louis Esson didn't achieve as much he dreamed was that he never got to work in an active theatre. Ray Lawler, who with *Summer of the Seventeenth Doll* brought the rural tradition back into the city, had been an actor and dramatist for many years before he produced the *Doll*, apparently his fourteenth play.[23] By the late 1960s and the time of the New Wave, it was becoming generally accepted that playwrights were, or ought to be, theatre workers who wrote, rather than writers who did plays. There are playwrights today with less flair than Esson who are doing good work because they have theatres to work with and write for.

Esson did have the Pioneer Players but this was short-lived and, reading between the lines, its production standards appear to have been woeful. Even when things went well and the actors remembered their lines, the venue, the Russell Street Temperance Hall in central Melbourne, had an atmosphere that Palmer described as 'gross with the memory of many dreary Saturday night entertainments'. Fellow dramatist Sydney Tomholt thought that it was 'a place to kill any play—its atmosphere so deadening and dreary'.[24] Nettie Palmer wrote, after the opening night, 'I miss the socialist audience that greeted the repertory movement with a cheer, a dozen years ago'.[25]

In Esson's time, and at least up until the late 1950s, Australian playwrights were mostly writing in a theatrical vacuum. Many were journalists and novelists who loved the theatre or were prompted to write plays for political reasons as members of the international labour movement, or by the proliferation of playwriting competitions.

Vance Palmer, best known as a novelist, was Esson's most loyal supporter in the founding of the Pioneer Players, and contributed to its repertoire. *A Happy Family* (1921) from the opening season is a cheerful play, a sort of bush *Romeo and Juliet* with a happy ending. Two old mates, once good bushmen who have settled on the land, have fallen out and drawn their families into their feud. But their children are in love. Before a tragedy can develop there is a sentimental *scène à faire* in which the long-awaited confrontation between the two enemies dissolves into a pleasant reunion. They smoke and drink rum together as they reminisce about the good old days.

2: BUSH AND CITY

In 1924 Palmer published a volume of three short plays that exemplified the minimalist naturalism that he and Esson sought—no elaborate plotting, understated dialogue, laconic characters. *The Black Horse*, performed in the Pioneer Players' 1923 season, is the best known. It dramatises a confrontation between a wife's city values and her grim husband's bush values, as they wrangle over their son's future. The father's bush toughness kills their troubled son, who is pressured to prove his manliness by riding, unsuccessfully, the wild black horse of the title. *The Prisoner* (1924) is set in a cosy little shanty where a thief and the trooper who has just arrested him gather with other characters around the fire, as flooding rains pour down outside. Trapped together they discover their common humanity and basic decency. In *Travellers* (1924), a group of characters from different classes huddle inside a bush hut as, again, the rain beats down outside. This time the upper-class move on, leaving their victuals and drink to be enjoyed by the shanty-keeper and the coach driver in simple comradeship. Another one-acter, *Ancestors* (1937), is about Peter, an Australian soldier who, with another soldier, is visiting his relatives. Walking across the downs Peter feels the urge to kill a sheep. When they are arrested at the end it is revealed that Peter's grandfather had been transported for life for the same crime eighty years earlier. Taken seriously, it might be about inheriting the notorious convict stain, but it is really just a ghost story.

Palmer kept writing plays after the failure of the Pioneer Players but they are mostly more readable than playable. *Hail Tomorrow*, (1947) about the 1890s shearers' strike, deals with the conflicts and issues of the birth of the Australian labour movement mostly through a series of wordy debates between the leaders. It comes alive dramatically in Act 4, when its two main characters—the earnest political worker Alec Glover and the visionary William Lane finally have the discussion they have been anticipating throughout the previous three acts. It works theatrically because there is something at stake between them—a choice, with consequences for the plot, between Lane's visionary but escapist vision and Glover's determination to keep battling at home.

Palmer was good at plot, in a conventional way, and his characters are always surprising. His other full-length plays include *Christine* (1930), *The Fledgling* and *Meadowsweet* (1945). The most interesting,

BELONGING

and the best candidate for revival, is *Prisoner's Country* (1960), a bush drama of miscegenation set on a lonely cattle station, exploring the mix of colour, race and different memories. It, too, is full of debate, but here it is theatrically vivid in presenting the unstable and difficult relationship between people and the land. 'This is the place of exile', says the disturbed young son, 'the prisoner's country'.

The central relationship is between the ageing Cunningham, who has battled to build his station Karoola into a successful pastoral property, and Duggan, his Aboriginal head stockman whom he thinks of as a mate even though, as he eventually realises, he has been exploiting him for twenty years. After four years as a Japanese prisoner-of-war, his son Floyd has returned to the station. Duggan's daughter Warrie is trapped between her spiritual connection with the blacks camped down by the river and the whitefellas' education she has received growing up as a servant in the homestead. Floyd is killed in a riding accident and, in the final scene, Warrie gives birth to their child. Cunningham and Duggan, who have spent decades trying to come to an understanding of their difference in the face of the memories that bind them, sit together on the veranda and welcome their grandchild. Cunningham's wife Thea has already expressed the feeling of alienation that pervades this play when she says to her son, 'I feel scattered'.

All of these characters are dislocated, ghosts in a landscape. The play's understated naturalistic style, and the sense of community that it tries to establish between the different types of 'prisoners', are Palmer's best legacy to the theatre that Esson strove to create.

The other Pioneer Players writers were Stewart Macky, Gerald Byrne, Frank Brown, Katharine Susannah Prichard, Alan Mulgan, Furnley Maurice and Ernest O'Ferrall. Macky was a doctor who was involved with the venture from the beginning. He wrote an intense little one-acter for the 1923 season, *The Trap*, in which the enlightened Captain McConochie, on Norfolk Island in the 1840s, tries to reform the penal system by showing humanity to the convicts. He attempts to win the trust of 'Swinger Strude', one of the toughest, by leaving him alone with his wife for five minutes. Pretty tough herself, she manages to appeal briefly to Strude's better side.

2: BUSH AND CITY

Brown was Louis Esson's half-brother, an ex-boxer who became a well-known sports journalist. Unlike Esson he had genuine bush experience. Esson's most recent editor, John Senczuk, has attributed to him co-authorship of *The Drovers* and in return attributed to Esson co-authorship of *Mates*, which was produced in the 1923 season under Brown's name.[26] *Mates* has an ironic take on mateship, like a cheerfully cynical version of *Vagabond Camp*. Bill is a simple bushman who has befriended Joe, a larrikin city jockey, on the trail. When Joe becomes bushwhacked, Bill carries him ten miles on his back to Carrie's shanty. Carrie is a delightfully mischievous woman, completely in control as first Bill and then Joe try to chat her up. Her husband Ned turns up at the end. The script is undeveloped but it is very neat.

Another Pioneer Players supporter was Leon Brodzky, an early friend of Esson and as committed to a nationalist theatre. They met up in England after Esson's first visit to Dublin in 1904. Brodzky wrote many polemical articles calling for a national repertoire but he left the country in 1914, finally settling in New York. He wrote a prefatory tribute to Esson in the script of his play, *Rebel Smith*, published under his new name Spencer Brodney in New York in 1925. The play was written for the Pioneer Players but they had folded before it was finished which is perhaps just as well. It is an earnest, plodding attempt to write politics into a realistic drama of character by letting the characters talk a lot about socialism as they fall in love.

The national repertoire that Esson yearned to create with the Pioneer Players, cajoling his friends to write, never eventuated—apart, perhaps, from some of his own plays. The only Pioneer Player to contribute seriously to the repertoire was Katharine Susannah Prichard but not with *The Great Man* or *Pioneers*, her Pioneer plays. The first was an inconsequential three-act comedy, which Prichard herself considered 'a poor thing', about a young couple coping with a new baby; and the second an historical convict drama in which a sensible woman left alone in an isolated bush hut brings some humanity to the harsh male world of the convicts and troopers who invade it from the world outside.[27]

Prichard was an almost inadvertent playwright. Like Palmer she is much better known as a novelist, and she used some of her plays to try out ideas for her novels. Katharine Brisbane, the editor of two of her major plays, wrote that they 'outshine the novels in their directness. We lost a most distinctive dramatist when Katharine Susannah Prichard grew tired of waiting for an Australian theatre to be born'.[28]

Prichard was a founding member of the Communist Party in 1920—unlike many others of her generation, she remained a member until her death in 1969 at the age of 86—and wrote many of her plays in its support. These included *Forward One*, about a shop-floor protest; *The Great Strike*, set in the mining industry and ending with a dying heroine singing the Internationale; and *The Women of Spain*, written as a fundraiser during the Spanish Civil War. *Solidarity* is also about a miners' strike, opening with an accident underground and then pursuing in eleven fluid scenes the miners' struggle for safer and better conditions.

Her 1927 play *Bid Me To Love* is a nicely wry comedy about an experiment in open marriage, anticipating her novel *Intimate Strangers*. It is a marital comedy like many others of its time, but more thoughtful than most. In a gentle way it deals with the ex-bohemian Louise's continued yearnings for independence and some degree of sexual freedom.

But Prichard's greatest play is *Brumby Innes*, written for the 1927 *Triad* playwriting competition. Against the wishes of L. L. Woolacott, the *Triad*'s editor and co-judge with Gregan McMahon, it won. Woolacott preferred E. Coulson Davidson's *The Forerunners*, about the Eureka Stockade.[29] However, he let McMahon have his choice because, as part of the prize, McMahon was to produce the play for JCW's and he thought that *Brumby Innes* might therefore actually get a production. It didn't. *Brumby Innes* wasn't staged until 1972, when an Indigenous company, Nindethana Theatre, produced it in association with the Australian Performing Group. The fact that it wasn't produced when it was written may, as Brisbane suggests, have turned Prichard away from the theatre, but her play needed a collaboration between a white and a black company. It is one of the best plays of its time, it is still controversial, and it has yet to be given the large scale production it deserves.

Alone among the bush plays it opens not in a bush hut or homestead but in the nearby blacks' camp, usually offstage in other plays, with

2: BUSH AND CITY

a corroboree scene. Prichard researched the language and dance for this in north-west Australia. The corroboree's three parts deal with a stranger in a new land, and with the ritual driving away of the narloos (Naalus)—mythic figures who had to be dealt with. According to Carl von Brandenstein the Naalus are human-like creatures who live in the ranges and have giant penises, with a hook in the end, which they can push underground for miles and use to snare and impregnate human women.[30] This is a detail Prichard leaves out. More immediately the scene is a celebration of Indigenous culture, until interrupted by the local station-owner Brumby Innes. Brumby is explicitly a savage white invader who staggers on drunkenly, gun blazing, to drag the pretty young Wylba out of the camp and off to his bed. It is the most theatrically powerful opening of all the bush plays—a rape made emblematic of an invasion.

But Brumby is no simple villain. Like Stumpy in Esson's *Shipwreck* he is 'a powerful man, handsome and attractive in a rough and brutal way' (p. 56). The second act is set in his kitchen, an uncompromisingly male version of the standard bush home. Through the windows is that 'sun-blasted country stretching to a far horizon under the glimmer of dawn'. He deals coolly with the people he has abused: Polly, the gin who has been his servant and mate until the forced arrival of Wylba; the boys from the camp who come to try to rescue Wylba and whom she helps to raid the stores; and John Hallinan, the decent neighbour whose cattle Brumby has been stealing. The act ends with another rape, as Brumby drags Hallinan's nice city-girl niece, May, who has been naïvely flirting with him, 'struggling, but yielding' into his bunk. 'I like 'em thoroughbred and buckin' a bit at first', he says (p. 83).

By the third act May has married him, and the kitchen setting has become a little feminised—more the standard bush hut, with a jar of flowers and some brightly-coloured magazines lying about. May has become the classic bored city-girl in the bush but still somehow in Brumby's thrall, partly because she is pregnant. She is the homestead lady now. The blacks from the camp come to her for supplies and she helps them. When Hallinan visits she begs to be taken away, but Brumby bashes him and he submits. The old retainer Jack assures Hallinan that rough as he is Brumby treats his women well. Brumby reaffirms this

BELONGING

to May when he says, in one of the play's most notorious lines, 'What you've got to understand is, you're one of Brumby's mares. You gallop with the mob' (p. 97).

What follows is one of the frankest exchanges about the sexual economy of life in the bush in the genre and the period. It ends with May gloomily accepting the contract—Brumby provides well for his mares, and expects only offspring in return. The third act ends not with a rape but with something else he has to offer—a bit of fun. May is too abject to accept it so Brumby's final dance is with Wylba, who understands the terms of the contract better than May ever will. The play ends with Brumby and Wylba dancing to the 'harsh music of the gramophone' (p. 99), an ironic reprise of the music of the corroboree that opened the play, and a perfect image of the white invasion.

What made this play shocking and unproduceable at the time was the directness with which it dealt with sex and violence on the border of white invasion, and perhaps the way it reconfigured the great pioneering legend, in terms of invasion and rape. What makes it controversial now is that the invader and rapist, Brumby, is such a vital and attractive figure—a brutal animalistic man of the land and therefore part of the legend.

Brumby Innes is an exceptional work. Prichard knew it would probably 'be considered unproduceable' because of its subject matter.[31] But one of the most remarkable features of the inter-war drama was that it was so dominated by women writers who wrote boldly and passionately about issues of social justice and female sexuality even when they were writing within genre. While their male counterparts such as Max Afford, Alexander Turner, Edmund Barclay, George Farwell and Leslie Haylen were turning out solid workmanlike pieces (for the most part), women like Roland, Prichard and Cusack were writing about politics and sex in plays that are still powerful. Of the men only George Landen Dann dealt as seriously with social issues. And two non-political dramatists whose plays deserve to be remembered are Henrietta Drake-Brockman and Dorothy Blewett.

2: BUSH AND CITY

Bush women

The role of women in the bush legend has been much debated. On the one hand the legend is overwhelmingly male and white. The land, discursively constructed as a landscape loaded with ideological meanings, has been seen as both 'no place for a woman' and also as the place of the Other, represented as feminine. In this view the battling Mums and drovers' wives, such as Ma Bates in Drake-Brockman's *Men Without Wives* (1938), are seen as Lacanian phallic mother-figures who have internalised the maleness of the legend and become its representatives.[32] On the other hand, for the drama at least (and most of the discussion has been about novelists), these characters and their struggles can now be re-read in subversive, oppositional ways.[33] Ma Bates might be a bit of a bloke, with her men's trousers and her bush toughness, but on stage she is also a woman. The mythic figure she represents turns up repeatedly in the bush drama written by women dramatists.

Men Without Wives revolves around the difference between two white women, and their position in the hard life of the North, where the men go 'combo' with the black women if their white women don't stick around. Mrs Bates is a tough old battler who has worn the pants alongside her husband. Mrs Abbott is a pretty young city bride brought to a lonely outback station by its proud owner. At the beginning the two women just miss each other at Kooli Crossing, at a station on the route from the south, before heading off to their isolated homes. They first meet in Act Three, set two years later, by which time they have realised through the hardships they have endured what the hard lonely life on the land means to them. Mrs Bates has a cancer and is being sent south for an operation against her will. Mrs Abbott, weary of the heat, the flies and the loneliness, is fleeing. Before either of them can leave, though, the river rises in flood. They are stuck for at least two months. It is a happy ending for both of them. Mrs Bates can die peacefully in the land she loves. Mrs Abbott, partly inspired by her example, decides to stick it out with her husband. Mrs Bates has two daughters who reflect the same basic division between women in the bush: Lulu, with her dependable

BELONGING

boyfriend Andy, is content to stay on the land; Clara yearns for pretty clothes and fun in the city.

Like *Brumby Innes* the play explores the sexual economy of bush life and in both plays the issues are complicated by black–white relationships, although in very different ways. Brumby's harsh contract with his white bride May is a much better deal than he offers to his black mistress Wylba, but the sexual terms, and more importantly the ethical terms, are similar. In *Men Without Wives* all the characters see the men going 'combo' as an outrageous moral problem. Ma Bates puts the case to Mrs Abbott in terms that Brumby, for all he might have respected her manly bush skills and endurance, would have found disgustingly feminine. Mrs Abbott has had their stockman Jencks fired for sleeping with the black women from the camp:

> MRS BATES: I mean I don't shut me eyes to nothing. All the yeller babies—and never knowing who the fathers are. ... Could be me own grandchildren. I got sons. I wouldn't like to have grandchildren growing up in a nigger camp. ... Now here you are leaving Jack on his own again.
> MRS ABBOTT: [*coldly*] Mrs Bates, your implications. ...
> MRS BATES: Oh, Jack's a white feller, and no mistake. But I've watched just as white as him go black in twenty years.
> (p. 62)

The owner of Kooli Station, Lovatt, has done precisely this, losing his wife and baby when the river was last in flood and now keeping a harem of young black women down at their camp.

Ma Bates clearly sees it as part of her responsibility to stay and keep the men honest—a 'God's police' role familiar in Australian culture and literature.[34] In the process she has become masculinised, from her appearance in men's trousers to her scorn for the make-up and pretty clothes that interest Clara. At the same time she is an Earth-Mother figure who wants to lose herself in the land. In a speech that might be set alongside Briglow Bill's male version in Esson's *The Drovers*, quoted earlier, Mrs Bates describes her own transformation. The abandonment of subjectivity is as strongly expressed here as anywhere in the Australian literature of the bush legend:

2: BUSH AND CITY

> I wouldn't like ter live south now. Once—well, maybe Clara'd not believe it, but I've had me moments. I used ter think it 'ud be fine ter have our own place, I'd imagine meself being one er the nobs. … women are like that, when they're young. Joe, he'd talk of his station, and I'd sit staring at the trees all silhouetted by the campfire … sit dreaming me silly young-woman dreams. … But up here, you live ter learn sense. … Night after night, sleeping out on the earth, looking up through yer mosquito-net at stars a lot brighter and gayer nor all yer diamonds, lying still and listening ter the soft munching of the horses and the rustling er the leaves—and sniffing the sorter smell yer can only catch outside, when yer lying on the earth in the night-time. … (*Wistfully*) You get ter feel small—yer know it don't reely matter a twopenny cuss what yer may want—that yer of no more account nor a blade of grass. … Yet it makes yer feel good, that feeling. Because somehow yer seem ter just be as much part of the earth as that same grass—a little bit er the universe that's movin' and breathing all round you. (p. 48)

That's belonging.

3
SETTLING THE LAND

'There seems to be a natural affinity between pioneering a literature and literature about pioneering a land.'

A. D. Hope[1]

Station and historical dramas

A series of station dramas and historical dramas in the 1930s developed the pioneering plays using many of its themes. These plays explore the painful transition from pioneering days to a new life based in a hard-won tradition of family and settlement. In the sets of these plays the old bush shack has become the living room and veranda of an established homestead with nice furniture and portraits of ancestors on the walls, especially in the family sagas. As in the earlier plays, the home paddock or a horse-yard or cattle-shed is suggested offstage. The constant struggle with the weather, produce prices and the banks makes everything unstable. But while the young folk are still yearning for the city, they are now struggling to escape the oppressiveness of family pastoral traditions, rather than the isolation of the land.

Many station dramas simply used this background to tell genre narratives. The remote homestead, for example, becomes an

BELONGING

Australian version of the lonely manor house of the English detective-thriller tradition, or an exotic hothouse location for romance between characters thrown together by isolation. The well-known prevalence in outback Australia of wandering poets, Irish rebels embracing bush socialism, passionate European immigrants and dispossessed aristocrats provides a ready source of dangerously attractive young men to tempt free-thinking independence-seeking young daughters away from the respectable sons of neighbouring squatters. In vain might their fathers want them to marry and consolidate two properties as a hedge against the next drought. Flooded rivers and washaways on damaged roads cut a place off from civilisation as effectively as any storm on a blasted English moor, especially if the homestead is already several hundred miles from its neighbour.

Such a play is Millicent Armstrong's *Goblin Gold* (1932), about a wealthy woman station owner who clings to her property in the hope that her long-lost son will turn up, and about the mystery when a plausible claimant does. Armstrong wrote many strongly imagined plays, driven by mood and incident. *Fire* (1923) is a grand romantic drama about faith, love and loyalty, set in a homestead with a bushfire raging in the distance and metaphorically threatening the characters. One of her most vivid plays is the one-act *At Dusk* (1937), a highly atmospheric ghost story, full of sinister moonlight and sexual menace. In it a young woman, once threatened by a crazed sadist who loved her, fears that he will return to kill her. Eventually, as a ghost, he does. *As The Moon Sets* (1958) is an extravagant mystery thriller, set on a lonely farm cut off by floods, full of rain and sinister night effects. It concerns a woman with a sexually violent husband and a neurotically devoted station-manager. A Hitchcockian third act and denouement include a body in a car down an abandoned mineshaft. A mad old woman turns out to be the murderer.

Marjorie McLeod's *Horizons* (1952) is a treacly script about young love thwarted, for a while, by an irascible father. The Mum figure gives another version of the standard pioneering speech about the importance of battling on in the face of adversity. The daughter's lover is a European immigrant and war-refugee. The play has the standard station set but the refugee, David, is not referring to that when he

3: SETTLING THE LAND

complains to the station owners: 'We may not venture nearer than the outskirts—the verandas of your lives'. It is a fine image, of a pioneering country that builds homesteads on other people's land, sets down traditions, and then allows more recent immigrants no further than the veranda. McLeod also wrote *Mine a Sad One* (1958), a sad historical romance about a lively young show-girl's thwarted love for the Burke of Burke and Wills; and *Within These Walls*, a family saga discussed below.

Dulcie Dunlop Ladds's *We Have Our Dreams* was written in 1936 but lay in a drawer until its premiere in 1957 when it had a very good run in the repertory theatres here and a professional production in Germany. It was dogged in London, as a commercial Australian play, by the success of *Summer of the Seventeenth Doll*. Ladds was a popular short-story writer for women's magazines and the play is a lively station romance, set on an isolated banana plantation in south-eastern Queensland, with all the elements of the genre: a tyrannical father, long-suffering mother and a rebellious daughter who has a brief affair with her stay-at-home sister's fiancé but, rather than become the ruined woman of the tradition, shrugs off the stain and leaves to find independence in the city.

This genre reached its climax in 1959—in the first season of the Trust Players, the professional repertory company set up by Hugh Hunt at the Australian Elizabethan Theatre Trust—with Anthony Coburn's *The Bastard Country*. Sometimes linked with the new urban realist plays that followed *Summer of the Seventeenth Doll*, the play is in fact a testosterone-driven version of the traditional station drama. Re-titled *Fire on the Wind*, it toured the country in a second season and was produced and published in England as an exotic Australian bush drama. It is like a lurid parody of *Brumby Innes*—an intense bush tragedy, with a grim and violent action, full of negative versions of the standard tropes.

John Willy is the Brumby figure, who rules his mistress/housekeeper Connie, his daughter May and his downtrodden sons Billy and Possum with an iron toughness. A mysterious Greek, Diargos, arrives at their isolated homestead, with a terrible hold over John, based on events that happened in the war. It emerges that John raped and killed Diargos's wife while Diargos was fighting with the partisans in the hills (rather different from the heroic version of Australians in Crete given in Catherine Duncan's *Sons of the Morning*). To put him off, John offers him May in marriage, and he accepts. Although May is frightened and abject, she wants a man and their marriage is represented as a happy one.

The action intensifies as bushfires threaten the property. It turns out that John has also killed his first wife and he grows increasingly mad, bashing his son and then May. After several violent confrontations and altercations Diargos brings this strongly-written melodramatic play to an end by killing him, just as the drought breaks, as it did with similar timing in *The Touch of Silk*.

Family sagas

The best station dramas were those that grew into family sagas. There are many minor examples and many one-act plays that explore generations of settlers, but the main plays, which found success in the repertory theatres, include Marjorie McLeod's *Within These Walls* (1936), Lynn Foster's *There Is No Armour* (1939) and, most successful of all, Dorothy Blewett's *The First Joanna* (1948). Another less successful play was George Landen Dann's *How Far Returning*.

In these plays the battling mum of the early bush dramas has become a matriarch, struggling to make good the sacrifice of her femininity to the pioneering life, as she dominates succeeding generations. Her fierce commitment to the station is reflected in her resistance to backsliding sons who want to wander the world as poets or minstrels and daughters in search of independence as New Women in the wicked city. There are no Brumbys in these plays. The founding fathers are simple, hard-working men who leave the vision to their wives, a vision that keeps the unstable tradition alive.

In each case the action spans many years, from the family's pioneering days to modern times, when the new generation is resisting the established tradition. The span of *Within These Walls* is 1855–1912, *There Is No Armour* 1858–1938, *How Far Returning* 1914–1932 and *The First Joanna* 1837–1945.

3: SETTLING THE LAND

McLeod's *Within These Walls* is a drama of matriarchal imperialism centred on Janet Cameron—at the beginning of the play a gaily chattering young bride and at the end a sick old woman desperately clinging to her vision of Blair Gowrie, the colonial homestead she has presided over for nearly sixty years. The house becomes her obsession, representing civilisation and the sanctity of the family, until a series of last-act revelations undermines her dream. She is consumed in a bushfire that finally destroys her hard-fought world.

A similar character is Elizabeth Barry in Foster's *There Is No Armour*, who lasts eighty years, the performer being required to play her, in successive scenes, aged 17, 40, 71, 75 and 98. Her matriarchal fortress is Minnabooka, the pastoral property that she refers to as the Barry family's 'destiny.' In each generation, as the narrative marches on, most of her descendants try to give it up, but by sheer strength of will, she manages to persuade one of them to keep battling. When she finally dies, her restless great-grandson Jimmie, who has been yearning to get away to the city, realises his destiny is to keep the property going. The play has two framing scenes in which a supernatural connection is established between Jimmie and his great-grandfather James, Elizabeth's husband. It is a link that binds the generations together as pioneers who have tamed the land, established a tradition and survived long enough to have ghosts.

Dorothy Blewett's *The First Joanna*, the finest example of the genre, found itself a place in the Little Theatre repertoire.[2] It is a grandly romantic pioneering story framed within a contemporary (in 1948) story of a sophisticated young European woman, Joanna. Like Jeanne in *The Touch of Silk* but more rebelliously, Joanna is horrified to find herself trapped in the Australian bush with a husband, Stephen, whom she met and married in Europe. The play has the standard veranda setting on the homestead of a vineyard planted in South Australia by the first Stephen, a century earlier, using cuttings brought out from Germany. Joanna is scornful of her Stephen's obsession with this family tradition, comparing it with her family's eight-century heritage.

But, just as she is about to leave her embarrassingly colonial husband to go on a jolly jaunt with her frivolous aristocratic friends, she

BELONGING

discovers the first Joanna's diaries and sits down to read them. What she reads is acted out in the middle section of the play. She discovers that the revered matriarch whose reputation haunts her was originally a convict transported at 13 for trying to shoot the 'benefactor' who had raped her; that at 17, with the help of the first Stephen, she had absconded from the house in which she was an abused servant; and that when, twenty-five years later, one of her abusers turned up and tried to destroy the decent life she had since built with Stephen, she killed him. Reading all this, the second Joanna is attracted by the first's passion and commitment in the face of much hardship. In an outburst in the final scene she speaks of it to her new family, who have been anxious to hide all this away:

> You should rattle your manacles—you should take your skeletons out of their cupboards—you should clothe them with your own romance, and then turn them into history.
> (p. 49)

This, of course, is precisely what the play does.

Betty Roland's *Granite Peak* (1952) picks up on many station drama themes. A pioneering family, the old Carmichaels of Granite Peak station, have put down roots in the land and face the familiar crisis when their grandson Roger wants to leave. (The middle generation have already disappeared, the son dead and his wife left for Europe.) Charlie, their part-Aboriginal adopted grandson, has become a doctor to prove his worth, yet he still works on the station. Their granddaughter Kate loves him but the social obstacles are too great to allow them to inherit the tradition together. There is a happy ending, of sorts, when Roger's apparently doomed romance with a 'ruined' young woman in the nearby town turns out well and he accepts her coming baby as his own. It is a romantic and sentimental play.

Roland's *Morning* (1937), written twenty years earlier, is a bleak and still quite shocking little one-acter. An absconded ticket-of-leave convict and his wife, living in poverty in a lonely bush hut, are threatened by a particularly nasty prospector who stumbles on their seclusion. They are decent battlers but, faced with a dilemma like that faced by the first Joanna in Blewett's play, they kill the intruder and use his gold to set themselves up in a respectable life. Roland apparently

3: SETTLING THE LAND

intended this as the beginning of a full-length play.[3] It reads like Act 1 of a pioneering family saga.

These sagas are still appearing. Dorothy Hewett, Alex Buzo, Louis Nowra, Stephen Sewell and John Romeril have all contributed to the genre over the years. In 2003 Hannie Rayson and Katherine Thomson both produced contemporary versions (*Inheritance* and *Wonderlands*, respectively) that were welcomed by critics and audiences who had little idea of the long tradition behind them.

Country practices

Between the bush and the city was the country town which produced another group of plays that have enough in common—in settings, issues, mood and characters—to be discussed together. Like the bush dramas country-town comedies and dramas concern the yearning to belong, to put down roots, a common theme in early twentieth-century drama. The prototype is Louis Esson's *The Battler*, and like that play they celebrate (or critique) an idea of community that it is still strong in the discourses surrounding Australian rural life.

These communities, like those in the early bush dramas, are defined and challenged by outsider figures (often from the city or from Europe) and the harsh landscape, in addition to more complicated outside pressures. The growing country towns must also cope with an urbanised nation growing big and powerful over the horizon, sending out railway lines, city politicians and creeping suburbs as the new city wealthy buy up the old cockies' farms. As with the family sagas such plays are still being written, because the issues are still current.

After *The Battler* the first and still the most influential country-town drama is a play that links the old formulaic playwriting traditions with the new nationalist interest in the realistic representation of Australian life—Betty Roland's *The Touch of Silk*, already referred to. In this play Jeanne, a Parisian woman with refined tastes and a passion for the beautiful things in life, has been brought out to a small, drought-stricken farm by her husband Jim, a shell-shocked Australian soldier whom she met and fell in love with in France during the First World War. Their sexual passion for each other, her sophistication and his

BELONGING

unsettled state of mind all threaten the solid, conservative, dull rural values of the nearby town, represented by Jim's mother, Mrs Davidson, who struggles to bring Jim back to his roots in the Australian soil. The play becomes a battle between Jeanne's city cosmopolitan values and Mrs Davidson's rural colonial ones, fought far from Paris and Flanders' fields. Jim and Jeanne are oppressed by drought, haunted by dying sheep and threatened by the bank manager Ritchie who holds Jim's financial fate in his hands, and, in a different way, by the charming Clifford Osborne, an Australian-born wanderer who has returned to his home town to work as a travelling salesman for the local store. He sells Jeanne the expensive and frivolous silk underwear that gives the play its title, and so provokes the crisis, when Jim needs to meet the mortgage repayment that will stave off the ruin he faces in the drought.

Jeanne, unforgivably from a bush point of view, is so excited by her touch of silk that she forgets to pass on a message about a damaged fence, and many sheep die. Jim is so excited by his touch of silk, Jeanne, that when she goes off to a dance with Osborne and returns late, he bashes Osborne, who is fatally injured when he falls to the ground and strikes his head on a stone. The only way Jeanne can save the situation, as Jim faces a murder charge, is to pretend that she was having an affair with Osborne, so that Jim's violence will be justified, at least in the eyes of the town and the courts.

The play first appeared in 1928 and, as already noted, Roland rewrote it in 1955 to soften its melodramatic plot. She wrote much more openly about women's independence and sexuality in her autobiographies than she ever did in her plays.[4] Jeanne's denial of her desire, in her sad and vain attempt to conform to country town morality, is what has really dated. In the twenty-seven years between the two versions it wasn't just the form of Australian drama that had changed. In the later plays the Jeanne figures had bold flirtatious affairs with their Osbornes, and often abandoned their needy, clinging Jims.

As we have seen, such independent New Woman characters emerged first in the city genre plays, but by the 1950s they had moved into the country towns, just as the men, such as Roo and Barney in *Summer of the Seventeenth Doll*, were moving into the cities. A little fancifully,

3: SETTLING THE LAND

Barney's sexual failure—his particular contribution to the overall sense of disillusionment that pervades the *Doll*—might be attributed to the influx of new women into the country towns in which he has left his string of abandoned lovers, mothers and children.

One of the women who might have contributed to Barney's emasculation is Jenny Milford, the heroine of the play that shared the 1955 Playwrights Advisory Board prize with the *Doll* but not its theatrical success—Oriel Gray's *The Torrents*. It is a fine, spirited comedy about a lively, independent New Woman who arrives to take up a position on the town's local paper, when they were expecting a man. Jenny sweeps into Koolgalla determined to make a life for herself.

She soon becomes embroiled in all sorts of local problems—personal and public. Rufus Torrent, her editor, doesn't approve of a woman journalist, but her competence and strength—and a spark of the battler in her that he shares, because of his poor Irish background—wins him over. His feckless son Ben, a decent man weakened by his fear of his father, falls in love with her.

The public, social part of the story is the vision of a young man named Kingsley, who is in love with Ben's fiancée Gwynne. Koolgalla is a prosperous but declining gold-town and Kingsley has a scheme for arresting its decline by using irrigation to turn it into an agricultural centre. Partly due to a device of Jenny's, on which the plot turns, all the other characters are in different ways drawn into this scheme. The implications—of ruthless exploitation versus sustainable development—are broad and, though it is an historical play (set in the 1890s) it is more topical today than the *Doll*.

There is no easy resolution—the play ends with the real battles, personal and public, only just beginning, but the characters have a clearer view of themselves and what they must do. At the end Jenny rejects Ben and determines to marry his father Rufus and work with him on the grand fight. We can feel another family saga coming on.

Other, earlier, country-town community comedies include George Beeby's *The Banner* (1923) (like *The Torrents* about an independent woman journalist, who in this case actually runs the newspaper because the editor, her father, is a cheerfully incompetent drunk); Vance

BELONGING

Palmer's *A Happy Family* (1915) and *Christine* (1930); and Gwen Meredith's *Wives Have Their Uses* (1944). A group of good hospital dramas, impossible to revive now because the form has become such a television staple, includes Dorothy Blewett's well-written *Quiet Night* (1941), with interesting characters whose lives and problems we care about; and Meredith's *Ask No Questions* (1940), in which a handsome doctor's jealous wife checks into his hospital as a patient to spy on him. Eunice Hanger's *2D* is a more meditative portrait of daily life in a public hospital's accident ward, using lots of direct audience-address to explore a closed, tightly knit community of nurses and patients united against their respective enemies, the doctors and the visitors. Hanger's *Flood* (1955) is a country-town drama, in free, theatrically–speakable verse, that combines a celebration of community with an ironic treatment of the old bush legend. When flood waters overrun a small town it forces all the characters to congregate in a house on the hill, where their prejudices and personal differences are played out. Here the outsider figure is Robert, a 'new Australian' migrant who, like Kingsley in *The Torrents*, has a vision for transforming the land. He is subjected to a great deal of racial vilification before he can prove himself a contributor to the rebuilding of the town after the waters have subsided.

All these plays revolve around a personal or family situation but they also celebrate the positive aspects of small communities, often in opposition to the values of the city or the cosmopolitan centres. This was and still is one of the great obsessions of dozens of Australian radio and television serials, such as Meredith's *The Lawsons* and, especially, *Blue Hills*, which ran on radio for over thirty years. Oriel Gray worked on the writing team of the television serial *Bellbird* for a decade from the late 1960s. There have been many others. In the 1980s and 1990s a new generation of women dramatists such as Katherine Thomson and Debra Oswald wrote plays for the stage about people in communities and also contributed some of the best episodes to long-running television series such as *Police Rescue* and *GP*. Another inheritor of the tradition of *The Lawsons* was the series *SeaChange*. Centred on a corporate lawyer who forsakes the city to start afresh in a backwater community, it was a huge success for the Australian Broadcasting Corporation in the late 1990s.

3: SETTLING THE LAND

There was a darker side to country-town life, of course, and many plays explored it. One of the best is Oriel Gray's *Burst of Summer* (1960)—a powerful drama of racial prejudice in a town in the far north of NSW. The local council decides to build low-cost housing and so bring into town the Aboriginal population, who currently live in 'the Flats', a camp near the river. The action is based mainly around the milk bar run by the Italian Joe, who finds himself caught up in a feud between a group of white racists, led by the disturbed Mav, and the young Aboriginal men, including Eddy, a cheerfully indolent youth who works for Joe. In the violent climax, a brawl offstage in the street outside, Mav smashes a broken bottle into Eddy's face, blinding him.

Adding new levels to this conflict, the play shows the ways in which the barriers between races and classes are constructed, and varying personal responses to displacement. As it opens a film star Mayrah Dinjarra, known to the town as Peggy, the black girl who used to do the dishes at Joe's, is returning for the premiere of her film amid a blaze of publicity. Once the film opens, she is quickly forgotten, of course, and the play charts her attempt to find a place for herself, caught as she is between two societies. She becomes engaged for a while to a man who appears to have done this—an earnest and sensitive black activist Don Reynolds who devotes his life to helping his people while also trying, through friendship, to open the eyes of white racists. Peggy eventually decides that he is too good for her to endure: she wants to keep feeling her anger. She leaves with Don's white friend, an irresponsible but charming journalist Clinton Hunter, who can help her establish a new life for herself in the city.

The work of many fine writers for the amateur theatres was swept aside when the non-commercial theatre went professional. Like Gray, many of these writers wrote professionally for radio and television.[5] But there was no professional stage. Oriel Gray would have been regarded today as a major dramatist, had she a theatre to write for. The same is true of three other important playwrights of the period—Dymphna Cusack, George Landen Dann and Mona Brand.

BELONGING

Dymphna Cusack

Dymphna Cusack was a socially committed materialist feminist, with a strong streak of almost girl-like romanticism who wrote within established genres. Perhaps this explains the neglect her plays have suffered.[6] Like Roland she was an enthusiastically heterosexual woman who wrote radically about gender politics and patriarchy in the context of middle-class suburban morality.[7] In many of her plays she brought her romantic sensibilities to bear on her political work, producing works that might be seen as sentimental but, equally, they could be produced, with a touch of irony, as highly emotional works of deep political conviction. Roland and Prichard wrote political agitprop pieces, while Cusack exploited the emotionality of popular film genres in the same radical cause.

In the most clichéd dramatic situations (and she wrote many of these) her dialogue is always witty and full of surprises. Her settings, the closed rooms of the realist tradition, are so vividly described in her stage directions, and are used to such strong effect in the action, that they become conceptual, not just decorative, challenges to new designers. Her best plays are the corniest, the most contrived, the ones that outrage every standard of well-made realism. She avoids the understated naturalism of Esson and Palmer and goes for broke, like Roland but more often. She had an ability to take what Leslie Rees called a 'type-idea' for a play and turn it naïvely and passionately into something fresh.[8]

Red Sky at Morning (1942) is a colonial melodrama, set in a lonely inn in the bush wilderness of Parramatta in 1812. The characters include a genial landlord, a nagging landlady and a drab daughter who lusts after their assigned convict servant, a charismatic Irishman named Michael. The play opens at sunset with, offstage, a red sky, a wild storm and a mysterious woman knocking at the door. She is Alicia, fleeing from the torture of being the kept woman of an unnamed military officer who soon turns up in pursuit and is utterly villainous. In the next few hours, with the storm raging outside and the river rising, Michael and Alicia fall in love and make an apparently suicidal pact to flee across the raging torrent. Against all odds they get away.

3: SETTLING THE LAND

The play is like a riposte to the sentimentality of T. Stuart Gurr and Varney Monk's musical *Collits' Inn*, which had opened three years earlier with a similar situation and plot, except that the innkeeper's daughter is the heroine, and she falls in love with the officer, not the convict. For all its 'type-ideas' *Red Sky at Morning* reveals the difference between the new literary theatre and the commercial theatre, which, even under the relatively adventurous entrepreneur Frank W. Thring, who produced *Collits' Inn*, remained highly conventional.

Like most of her generation, Cusack produced a series of one-act plays, for which there was then a great demand by the repertory theatres for their 'club nights', and which now read like tryouts for more sustained work. *Anniversary* (1935) is an Anzac ghost play, one of many written after the First World War, in which an old digger discovers one Anzac Day that he has more in common with his dead mates from the war than with the new world to which he has returned.[9] *Second Rhapsody* and *Shallow Cups*, also written in the 1930s, explore issues of family and sexual politics that loom large in the sudden burst of dramatic activity that Cusack had during World War II. In the early 1940s she conducted a series of dramaturgical laboratory experiments in her full-length plays, bringing together disparate groups of characters in artificially confined situations where they discover their personal and political differences.

Only one of these plays remains in the repertoire and, ironically, given the non-realistic theatrical vocabulary that the Australian theatre has developed since the 1970s, it is the most constrained and the least adventurous. *Morning Sacrifice* (1942), revived by Sydney's Griffin Theatre Company in 1986, by the State Theatre Company of South Australia in 1994 and by the Sydney Theatre Company in 2000, is set in the staff room of a girls' school and deals with the personal interactions between the teachers as they cope with various crises. It is a passionate celebration of liberal values in education and also in social attitudes to girls' and women's sexuality. Its oblique treatment of lesbian issues has caused comment because, in the political interests of asserting women's rights to both marry and work, it appears to demonise its lesbian characters as repressive and socially conservative.[10] Its most attractive characters are lively young women with romantic attachments to exciting but decent young men whom we never meet. Spinsters are mocked. The behaviour of the villainess, Portia Kingsbury, who uses the rhetoric of respectability to destroy the life of a pretty young protégée who has moved away from her, suggests a suppressed homoeroticism.

In *Comets Soon Pass* (1943) a group of characters are marooned by a flood, like the characters in Eunice Hanger's *Flood*. They are in the house of a successful city doctor, John Smith, who has had a Damascene conversion and gone bush to pursue a less glamorous but more satisfying life in a small community. An unlikely but nevertheless interesting and volatile collection of people are trapped together for several days as they wait to be rescued. The dramatic laboratory is interesting because the characters are so disparate: a right-wing local businessman, Talbot, and his enemy the local communist agitator, Jack Smith; a philandering society artist from the city and his unhappy wife (who turns out also to be John's estranged wife); a staid local clinging to old traditions of Anglo decency; as well as two young women—John's adopted daughter and an errant servant, Trallie. The latter has been abused and betrayed by Talbot's fascist son, recently killed in a riot which involved Jack Smith.

The play deals vividly and stirringly with the conflict between responsibilities to self and responsibilities to others, especially for independent women who would like to have men in their lives but not live in an oppressively patriarchal society. It offers an alternative to bourgeois marriage (like *Summer of the Seventeenth Doll* and many New Wave plays) with Jack Smith and Trallie entering into a socialist marriage contract at the end.

Shoulder the Sky (1945) is even more sentimental at the narrative level, but looser dramaturgically and therefore, perhaps, more interesting now. The laboratory here is the Australia League Canteen, run mostly by volunteer women as a haven for a wild mix of military servicemen and women on short term leave during World War II. It includes the interwoven (but mostly distinct) stories of a collection of drunken soldiers, tired nurses, good-time girls and injured war heroes as they gather in the Canteen's dance hall and try to find partners. It has several burgeoning romances, a lot of comic scenes verging on

3: SETTLING THE LAND

farce and a few serious scenes of anti-war polemic. Its heart is the volunteer women, all with exhausting daytime war-service jobs, who turn up each night to do their bit not for the war but for the men who have to go off to fight it, or have returned from it with damaged minds and bodies. Their struggles, weaknesses and desires are infused with courage, explored comically in a way that could be done now with a light irony without losing the spirit of the original. Its nearest relation in recent theatre is Wesley Enoch's 2000 musical, *The Sunshine Club*.

Cusack wrote two later plays worth mentioning: *Pacific Paradise* and *The Golden Girls*, both written in 1955. *Pacific Paradise* is a passionately polemical piece about the threat of nuclear testing on a small Pacific island community, which successfully resists the power of the military–industrial complex that wants to blow up their happy island as collateral damage in the Cold War. It is naïve and sentimental for contemporary tastes, but it has considerable polemical and emotional power. It is an early theatrical celebration of the political power of ordinary people when the islanders discover radio and manage to talk about their crisis by intervening in regular news bulletins. This brings huge protesting crowds to throng the streets of cities around the world. It was a fanciful idea at the time but it is standard practice now among a new internet generation of anti-globalisation protestors.

The Golden Girls is a splendidly gothic family drama about the power of the patriarchy, and how its influence can continue long after the actual patriarch is dead. Major Prendergast, an awful old paterfamilias with rigid Victorian moral and social codes, moulds his four daughters to serve his own vanity by trying to marry them off to a succession of society figures and English aristocrats, the last of whom is revealed, just in time, to be a dissolute bigamist. We discover the *nouveau riche* Major has used his dead wife's money to set himself up in the gold mines and is determined to achieve English respectability.

Only one daughter, Rosalind, escapes, by eloping with a romantic young artist. The others linger on in the house for fifty years, accumulating money they never spend. The terrible Angelica has internalised her father's values so completely that she eventually outdoes him in vileness. The younger twins are under her control. As the room decays like Miss Haversham's, and piles of cash gather dust in every nook and cranny, the sisters slowly starve. Two neat framing scenes set in the present (1948) introduce a young doctor Rosalind Hall who in the prologue comes to examine a corpse. In the epilogue she turns out to be the original Rosalind's daughter and the corpse turns out to be Angelica's. In the last of many surprises the twins are discovered locked in a room upstairs alive, but utterly demented. They have fled there after vengefully allowing Angelica to die when she was too feeble to feed herself. The whole play has a splendid excess about it which, if revived, would offer great acting and design opportunities.

Cusack is better known today as a novelist. In 1997 Jonathon Hardy wrote a fine stage adaptation of her first novel *Jungfrau*, which, given that the theatre she wrote for never gave her the attention she deserved, stands as one of her greatest theatrical legacies. The play reveals her very modern feminism, presenting three remarkable professional women, and telling the tragedy of one of them, through their interactions both with each other and with a series of mostly disappointing but occasionally exciting men.

George Landen Dann

The one male playwright of the 1930s who dealt successfully with issues of gender and race was the reclusive Queenslander George Landen Dann. He produced a series of mostly neglected plays that deserve to be part of the repertoire—including one fine play, *How Far Returning*, that has somehow escaped mention in the standard sources. His *Fountains Beyond* (1942) was revived in 2000 by the Queensland Theatre Company in an adaptation by Wesley Enoch, and QTC have a playwriting award named in his honour. His only other published play is the unremarkable *Caroline Chisholm* (1939), but others deserve to be known.

He was controversial from the beginning. *In Beauty It Is Finished* won a competition and subsequent production from the Brisbane Repertory Theatre in 1931. Before it opened news leaked out that it was, as *Smith's Weekly* put it, a 'sordid drama of miscegenation' about 'the dubious romance of a self-confessed woman of the streets and a half-caste'.[11] The harlot and the half-caste, as Marian and Tom call themselves in the script, were seen as thoroughly unwholesome

3: SETTLING THE LAND

characters treated with too much sympathy. The controversy, typically, made little of the play's complexity, but it's fair to say it would probably still be controversial, albeit for different reasons. Today Marian and Tom appear as marginalised people who have internalised their oppression. Dann represents the pair as full of self-loathing and guilt, yet the secrets that make them outcast—Marian's promiscuous sexuality and Tom's hidden Aboriginality—might now be sources of pride. In the play Marian aspires to a respectability, and Tom to a whiteness, that they cannot achieve; today they would not be expected to yearn for it. Finally they run away together defeated; today that ending might be represented as a triumph.

The play is not simply moralistic, however, and it contains many ideas and images that Dann was to explore again in later plays. His sympathy for Aboriginal people was genuine and based in first-hand experience. Many of the issues he dramatises are still current.

Fountains Beyond, his best-known play on the politics of Aboriginality, has a situation similar to that in Oriel Gray's *Burst of Summer*. The respectable white middle class in a small country town want to shift the black fringe dwellers so they can develop the site as a white children's playground. A visiting English journalist, Miss Harnett, takes up the black cause, and forms a political alliance with the central character, Vic Filmer, a local Aboriginal leader not prepared to sell out to the whites. But events turn out badly. Vic's wife Peggy, a straightforward mission black who just wants to live quietly, resists her husband's activism because it will lead to trouble. Like Tom in *In Beauty It Is Finished*, she has internalised her oppression and blames herself for her abjection. When she is accidentally killed in an argument with Vic, he is forced to quit the struggle and flee. At the end of the play Vic, with the help of an elder, takes Peggy's body back to sacred land where the whites cannot reach them. But in doing so he is forced to give up white politics. In terms of contemporary politics it is a profoundly ambivalent conclusion: Vic rediscovers his roots but loses an important battle in the process. Today, perhaps, he would not be asked to choose.

How to deal with plays written about black issues by sympathetic white writers is an issue that will come up again in Chapter 14. In the 1930s, like Vance Palmer and Katharine Susannah Prichard, but perhaps more so, Dann wrote from experience. He had a sensitive interest in the individual and social implications of the politics of black–white relations. But those politics have changed so much since his time that much of his sympathy now seems condescending, more like pastoral care. In contemporary terms, Dann's plays are post-assimilation in their politics, but they were written, radically, when assimilation was the standard assumption. Although, at least implicitly, they celebrated and valorised Aboriginal people, in the contemporary politics of difference they probably have no place. The rise of Indigenous drama and theatre since the late 1970s, and the issues of authenticity of voice that arose with them, have left the plays of these early white writers behind.

A more recent play in this vein is Louis Nowra's stage adaptation of Xavier Herbert's 1938 novel *Capricornia*. Herbert was another sympathetic writer who knew something of the Indigenous culture he was writing about. The play was produced during the 1988 Bicentennial and revived, again in a production by Wesley Enoch, by Sydney's Company B in 2006.

In other plays Dann wrote about women's experience. In *How Far Returning* and *No Incense Rising* he showed women trapped in the social constructions of family. In both plays the main character has spent years suppressing her desires in order to be a dutiful daughter, and in both cases she is in some way complicit in her own oppression. The two plays are respectively the happy and the sad versions of the clash between social conformity and unacted desire.

How Far Returning tells the story of Jessie, trapped as much by her own timidity as by her family and her responsibilities. The play is a family saga, told in flashback, and framed by two scenes set in the present during the Depression (1932). Her father's business, which she has been running effectively for eighteen years, is bankrupt and the family faces an uncertain future. Jim, a married man for whom she has been yearning for years, asks her to run away with him. She promises to answer him that day. Then she lapses into a reverie during which the key events in her life of self-sacrifice are played out before her. For most of the play she sits and watches from her chair as her

3: SETTLING THE LAND

memories, like ghosts, come alive. She conducts a running dialogue with her younger self, played by another performer, about the meaning of her life and its missed opportunities. She has knocked Jim back on at least two occasions because she wanted to do the right thing. She has still not made up her mind when the action returns to the present for the final scene. Her family have no notion of what she has done for them and are smug and patronising about her future. Unaware that Jessie was the person who has secretly provided for his future, her father dismisses her, suggesting that she go to live with her aged aunt. At this point she decides. 'I don't want you to think for me. I'm quite capable of doing that for myself', she says (p. 59). The play closes with her suddenly exultant as she rings Jim to say yes.

No Incense Rising (1937) is the tragic version of the same story. It is a grand drama of desire and abjection, like Cusack's *The Golden Girls*, set in a small, isolated fishing community accessible only by boat. Another dutiful daughter, Ada, is trapped minding her mother, Mrs Bergman, after the loss of her father and brother at sea some years earlier and the recent wedding of her sister Ellen. The drab little room in which Ada and her mother do battle; the constant sound of the sea outside; and the eerie green phosphorescent glow of the seaweed beds on the far headland where their men died and the ghosts still live for Mrs Bergman—all contribute to the theatrical mood. Ada has an enthusiastic fiancé, Carl, but her mother has asked her never to marry so she makes him wait until she becomes so trapped that she can never escape. At the end of Act 2 she commits herself to Carl, when her mother says that she has been invited to stay with Ellen. But then her mother commits suicide in what looks like a last desperate attempt to bind Ada to her forever. It works. At the end of the play Ada, apparently mad and unable to leave the house, hides from Carl as he pounds on her door wanting to be let in.

A bush–city play in theme, although the bush is here a lonely island, *No Incense Rising* has the familiar character of a pretty young restless woman. In this case it is Mary, who escapes to the city and while there is a hint that she will go wild and become a harlot like Marian in *In Beauty It Is Finished*, there is no suggestion that this will do her anything but good. It will certainly allow her to escape Ada's fate.

BELONGING

Within the standards of his time Dann was a radical writer, even though he was writing to formula. His 1958 play, *Ring Out Wild Bells!*, is a very slight small-town comedy, but at his best his eye and ear were good, his dramaturgy sound and his material lively and interesting. Always on the side of the marginalised, he tries to give a voice to people who didn't have one when he was writing. According to Katharine Brisbane he was a solitary man, who had wanted in his youth to become a minister to isolated Aboriginal communities but lacked the necessary education and the resources. He spent a great deal of his life travelling around the outback and the coastal fringes, however, and wrote about this in his plays.[12] The classic example of the talented playwright who did not have an active theatre to write for, his best plays are extraordinarily vivid.

Mona Brand

The best of the political genre writers was Mona Brand, who worked for the New Theatre movement and was one of the most successful and unfairly neglected of all twentieth-century Australian playwrights. Her early plays, during the Cold War, were often dismissed as propaganda, although they now read like plays that simply have something to say. She wrote in 1948 about racial issues in rural Australia; in 1952 about British imperialism in Malaya; in 1953 about the social injustice caused by politically motivated 'tough-on-crime' campaigns; and in 1958 about the American CIA intervention in South–East Asia. Nothing she portrays comes across today as particularly radical or controversial. Although her plays now have a period feel about them—which is not the same thing as saying they are dated—the political and social issues she wrote about are still potent. Most of her supposed propaganda is now well-known fact.

During the 1950s and 1960s she also wrote a large number of satirical sketches for the famous New Theatre political revues, which had started in 1941 with *I'd Rather Be Left* and which had one of their great successes in 1968 with *On Stage Vietnam*, a collaborative show, of which Brand was the principal writer. The fashionable middle-class Phillip Street revues in Sydney were the antecedents to television's

3: SETTLING THE LAND

The Mavis Bramston Show in the late 1960s and to much of the intellectual left-wing political satire since, including the television work of satirists and performers like Patrick Cook and Max Gillies, and later John Clarke and the Sydney Theatre Company's Wharf Revue team. The more radical New Theatre revues, on the other hand, were the antecedents of the larrikin playwrights of the early 1970s New Wave, a movement which, convinced it was pioneering something new, forgot some of its own history and failed to acknowledge them.[13]

Mona Brand's plays have also been the most internationally successful Australian plays ever written, but only in the former Soviet bloc and in China, and so they have not been respected in her own country. Three of her best plays are only available now because they were published in Moscow.

Even those 1950s critics who thought her social-issue plays to be mere propaganda grudgingly respected her skill.[14] Along with repertory writers such as Gwen Meredith, Brand knew her people, and wrote in a popular genre with great ability. Between the 1940s and the 1960s she turned out a type of socialist realism—a form which was rooted in the structure of the 'well-made play', which constituted the basis of the society comedies and dramas of the repertory movement—with a sense of humour and a freedom from dogmatism that many other examples in the genre lacked. She wrote strong, lively, well-differentiated characters and effective 'curtains' (sudden revelations at the end of each act or scene). Her plots were well done: she was good at controlling the rate of release of dramatic information. Her endings were usually happy, or at least uplifting.

Her first full-length play was *Here Under Heaven* (1948), a station drama like so many before it, that introduced issues of racism. Like Vance Palmer's *Prisoner's Country*, it used the genre in new ways. Set during World War II, it concerns Mrs Hamilton, the matriarch of an old pioneering family, and her three sons. Two of them have gone off to fight and the third, crippled by childhood polio, has stayed behind to manage the property. But the central character is Lola, a civilised, sophisticated woman whom the eldest son, John, has married in Singapore, just before it fell to the Japanese and he disappeared. At Mrs Hamilton's special request Lola has come to Australia as a refugee.

BELONGING

To Mrs Hamilton's great distress Lola turns out to be Chinese. In a series of splendidly written revelations we watch as Lola deals with Mrs Hamilton's racism, discovers the blacks' camp on the property and decides to care for a sick child there. This child turns out to be the half-caste daughter of one of Mrs Hamilton's heroic warrior sons. The curtain to the first scene of the final act sums up the spirit of the play. Simply because she cares, Lola has brought the dying child up to the homestead to be nursed. Mrs Hamilton refuses to have an Aboriginal in her house:

> MRS HAMILTON: I'll have no half caste children here—will you please remember what I say?
> LOLA: Yes, I will. September will come soon, and my own child will be born—and I will remember what you say.
> (pp. 175–6)

Having announced that she is about to produce another 'half-caste' Hamilton, Lola reveals that her husband John, in theory the inheritor of a patriarchal tradition but, as we discover, actually his family's liberator from entrenched squattocratic attitudes, is dead. No one has thought to ask her if she knew of his fate, so obsessed were they with her ethnicity. The closing moments of the play hint that she may be reconciled with her mother-in-law, in a tentative way that may or may not offer the hope of a new beginning.

Strangers in the Land, a political drama about British imperialism in Malaya during the communist insurgency, was banned in the United Kingdom when it was first produced in 1952 by the Unity Theatre in London's East End. Christine, another strong young woman, has come to Malaya to marry an English planter. He turns out to be a viciously unscrupulous fighter against the native resistance. The play ends when, horrified by what she learns about the local situation and the terrorist tactics of the British, Christine flees before the marriage can take place. *No Strings Attached* (1958) is also about Western imperialism in South–East Asia, specifically American interference in the democratic process of an imaginary country called Taikong. A businessman travelling with his innocent wife and daughter is, in reality, a CIA agent. He engages in various corrupt and increasingly violent practices to ensure the re-election of a right-wing government

3: SETTLING THE LAND

that will allow an American air base to be built. His unknowing wife inadvertently subverts his plans and at the end his daughter elopes with a member of the local royal family.

In the shadow of 'The Doll'

Alongside the genre writers before the professionalisation of the non-commercial theatre in the 1950s, there were a few playwrights who wrote in lyrical non-naturalist styles, and one who wrote in verse.

Ray Mathew's *We Find the Bunyip* (1955) is the first great existentialist comedy written in Australia. First produced at Sydney's Independent Theatre in 1955, on the eve of the success of the *Doll*, it would have received a lot more attention had its title not made it look like a play for children. It draws on a long tradition of plays set in small country towns a long way from the civilised world of the cities. As in Esson's *The Battler*, which pioneered the genre, it has very little story. Its people do nothing much, except struggle on together with noisy but relaxed desperation. It is both a celebration and a critique of that fractured and alienated groping for a sense of community that is at the heart of the way the bush legend is represented in Australian drama.

The mood is like an ironic, bittersweet revision of Gorky's *The Lower Depths* or O'Neill's *The Iceman Cometh*. The characters, a loose collection of comic grotesques, barely make contact with each other. Their dialogue is a rhythmic pattern of disconnected phrases, representing yearnings that were once real, but which have become by the end a litany of comfortable sayings drained of meaning. A dispossessed desperate lot thrown together—old drunken men, battling bush mums, disillusioned trapped young lovers, outsider figures of all kinds—they sit around in the kitchen of a bush pub drinking, squabbling and dreaming of a better life.

One of them is Tony the Talker, a romantic young schoolteacher with an Italian background. He flirts with the old women but he is obsessed by Denise, a stern young woman who spends the entire night rejecting his love. At the end of Act 1, Tony inspires them to go off into the night to find the bunyip. A local legend based on noises heard after dark, the bunyip comes to represent all their desires and fears. They don't find it, but in the process of their search they start connecting with one another.

Mathew also wrote *A Spring Song* (1957), a lyrical country town comedy about love and the difficulty of belonging in the bush. It has most of the elements of the bush, station and rural community plays—the land with a farm imposed on it, the old parents, the lure of the city for the young and the romantic outsider figure from the city—but its heightened poetic style takes it far beyond the simple representation of rural life. It is a play about the desire to belong in a place and the difficulty of finding a home. Similarly, his city play, *The Life of the Party* (1960), is about a group of bohemians living in Sydney's Kings Cross, looking vainly for a purpose in life. Its central character is a histrionic but closeted gay man whose succession of female lovers keep trying to pin him down. Mathew's one-acter, *The Bones of My Toe* (1964), is an absurdist family comedy about a boy who believes, with some justification, that he lives in a madhouse. All Mathew's plays show a feeling for pattern and rhythm in the dialogue that is poetic without being verse.

Sumner Locke Elliott's *Rusty Bugles* (1948) is similar in mood to *We Find the Bunyip*, but even less happens. While World War II is going on somewhere over the horizon, a group of disaffected, alienated soldiers are trapped in an isolated ordnance depot in the Northern Territory, far from both home and the war. The main character Rod, who represents the author's experience, is an educated man who is at first rather shocked to find himself in this rough company. Gradually, though, he comes to respect and admire the others, adopting their crude language and their desperate joking style of behaviour as they suffer small tragedies. The play created a controversy when it was first produced at Sydney's Independent Theatre because of its frank language.[15]

When he arrives at the camp, Rod's new mates are a classic bunch of ocker Australian men, dealing with their problems through chiacking humour. The 'Gig Ape' is a big boofhead who practises bad hygiene as he desperately tries to get dermatitis in order to be invalided back home. Ot is a little battler, obsessed with his fiancée back home, who loses all his larrikin panache when she gives up waiting for him and

3: SETTLING THE LAND

marries someone else. There is a tragically neurotic character whom everyone calls 'Dean Maitland', a reference to Ken G. Hall's 1934 film *The Silence of Dean Maitland*. He never speaks and no-one ever speaks to him.

Every time the whistle blows on the ordnance train in the distance there are cries all around the camp: 'Here come the replacements!'. All of them are obsessed with getting home, except for Vic Richards, who wants to get to the war and fight. In the most poignant scene several of them are queuing to place brief phone calls to their loved ones down south. They shout their intimacies into the handpiece, with their mates hearing every word, but the connection is bad and nothing of their longing is communicated down the line.

The play is about dreams of escape, not from war but from the dull oppression of bureaucracy. It is a triumph of the quiet documentary naturalism that Esson looked for, that also comes across as an absurdist comedy about the futility of life.

Douglas Stewart was a major poet who also had a huge influence as editor of the *Bulletin*'s Red Page from 1940 to 1961 and was a literary editor for the publisher Angus & Robertson for the ten years following. He is Australia's only major verse dramatist and although his plays have had more impact on the page (and in classrooms) than on the stage, they deserve to be remembered.

The Golden Lover (1943 radio, 1953 stage), a love-triangle story based on a Maori legend, and *Fire on the Snow* (1941 radio), a self-consciously heroic retelling of the tragic journey to the South Pole of Scott of the Antarctic (as he was known to a generation of Australian and New Zealand schoolchildren), were both written for radio. The latter, though, has also had many stage productions including one in 1968 when it was paired, unsuccessfully, with Alexander Buzo's *Norm and Ahmed* at the Australian Play Season of Sydney's Old Tote Theatre. The play uses an all-knowing Narrator, and its effects are more poetic than dramatic, but it anticipates Stewart's interest in Australian legend-building, and the need, as he saw it, to create the myths for a new nation to live by.

Shipwreck (1949) is a poetic drama based on the 1629 wreck of the Dutch ship *Batavia* on an island off the coast of Western Australia, and

BELONGING

the subsequent mutiny, with its murders, rapes and savage struggles for survival. In a morally and lyrically complex drama, Stewart takes pains to give the violent mutineers a voice, while noting the victory of the supposedly humble butler Heynorick, a classic low-lying, smooth-talking bureaucratic figure of the type who always triumph over the heroes. The play also focuses on the way in which the women characters accommodate themselves in individual ways to the new savagery. In 2001 Richard Mills turned the story into an award-winning opera, *Batavia*, for Opera Australia.

Ned Kelly (1942) remains Stewart's best play. Written in 1940 and staged during the 1956 Melbourne Olympics as a feature production starring expatriate Leo McKern, it was controversial because it was a heroic drama about a wicked bushranger. Kelly is presented as a troubled, violently rebellious hero, a simple representative of brute rebellion, dimly aware of his oppression, with a lingering grievance against the injustice he and his family have suffered. He is supported by a much more contemplative gang member in Joe Byrne, a philosophical Irish dreamer who likes to love and be wept for, with some great speeches about what it means to be an outcast in the Australian bush. The poetry of the play gives a beautifully detailed evocation of the romance of the bush legend, and it includes some fine argument between Ned and the bureaucratic town-dwellers, middle-class descendants of Heynorick, whom he keeps bailing up. The play is the nearest thing, in mid-twentieth-century Australian drama, to a romantic historical tragedy. Byrne dies heroically at the end in the gunfight after the siege of Glenrowan but Stewart doesn't deal with the fact that Ned survives to be captured and hanged by the representatives of the bourgeois town-dwellers. Instead, in the real tragedy for the legend that Stewart is drawing on, Ned, clad in his iconic sheet-tin armour, is pathetically shot.

The genre plays discussed in this chapter are now neglected partly, as we shall see, because waves of nationalist rhetoric in the 1950s and 1970s valued originality and newness. When the bush moved into the city, with the sudden success of Ray Lawler's *Summer of the Seventeenth Doll*, a new urban genre emerged.

4
INTO THE CITY

'If you find that for some reason or other you do have an interesting character, have him shot about halfway down page one by a boring character. Make it obvious that the boring character didn't actually decide to shoot the interesting character, he was forced to do it by the crushing heartlessness of the postwar fusion of urban and rural society.'

Fred Dagg (John Clarke)[1]

The end of an era: the *Doll* School

In 1955 *We Find The Bunyip* was produced, Betty Roland rewrote *The Touch of Silk*, and both Alan Seymour's *Swamp Creatures* and Eunice Hanger's *Flood* appeared. In the same year Ray Lawler's *Summer of the Seventeenth Doll* was joint-winner of the Playwrights Advisory Board play competition, with Oriel Gray's *The Torrents*. Dymphna Cusack's *Pacific Paradise* was runner-up. According to one of the judges, Leslie Rees, the panel thought *The Torrents* the 'more complete' play but they were so impressed by the subject-matter of the other play that they decided it should share the prize.[2] The subsequent history of the *Doll*, which went on to become the most famous Australian play ever written or produced, with the possible exception of *On Our Selection*, is a perfect illustration of a theme that campaigners for a national drama had been emphasising for fifty years: playwrights need a professional theatre to write for. None of the playwrights so far discussed had that, and many prize-winning plays had sunk without a production.[3] It is still happening.

But in 1955 the newly-created Australian Elizabethan Theatre Trust was named for the new young queen of England who had recently toured the country. The AETT, inspired by its declared mission to make theatre as vital to Australian life as it was to England in the first Elizabeth's reign when Shakespeare was working, was looking for an Australian play to help start the process.[4] In a pattern reproduced many times with the rise of the subsidised state companies, they were also keen to bring out contemporary overseas successes and the classics. With characteristic timidity, the AETT initially provided limited financial support for a production of the *Doll* by Melbourne's Union Theatre Repertory Company.

Between sharing the prize and being taken up by the AETT, the *Doll* was given a lot of development work, so much, indeed, that one of the competition judges barely recognised the revised script when he saw it produced.[5] The media interest it attracted set it on the way to becoming the first Great Australian Play and the huge critical and popular success it has received is well-deserved. But, out of respect for the earlier lost dramatists, it must also be said that the *Doll* was the first professionally-produced Australian play outside the commercial theatre to receive any serious professional support and backing. Much of the *Doll*'s success was in the timing.

Its action, plot and characterisation brought the bush legend kicking and screaming into the city, almost literally. Its structure is firmly based in the well-made-play tradition that was never again to have the same authority—the tradition that Esson, Palmer, Locke Elliott (in *Rusty Bugles*) and Mathew (in *We Find the Bunyip*) had resisted in their attempts to create their new, flatter, more naturalistic dramaturgy.

The *Doll* is so well-known, and has been written about so widely, that it is difficult to discuss it without cliché or, more importantly, without implicitly supporting one or other of the standard critical perspectives.[6]

4: INTO THE CITY

Is it a socio-cultural document of its time or an individual drama of personal interactions? Is it a story of the failure of childish illusions or a proud assertion of a new vision? Is it a hard-nosed study of a new urban Australia or a sentimental elegy for a lost past? No-one gets killed in it but there are a few stoushes: were they forced to do this, as Fred Dagg puts it in his epigraph to this chapter, 'by the crushing heartlessness of the postwar fusion of urban and rural society'?

The story itself is straightforward. For sixteen years Olive has been working as a barmaid in Melbourne, living with her mother Emma and waiting for the annual migration south of her lover Roo, a manly and exciting canecutter from Queensland, and his mate Barney. Roo and Barney have a five-month summer lay-off in Melbourne spending their cheques and living it up with Olive and her best friend, the wildly playful Nancy. This summer is different. Nancy, who never appears, has suddenly married. Olive has persuaded Pearl, another barmaid who likes to think of herself as a respectable widow, to step into Nancy's place to keep the tradition going.

When the men arrive it is immediately obvious that Nancy's defection is not the only problem. Roo is broke, because after being challenged by a younger man, Dowd, he left his gang and spent two months alone in Brisbane spending his cheque and getting drunk. Barney, it later emerges, stayed with the gang, an act that both he and Roo see as a betrayal of their longstanding mateship. Roo is too proud to let either Olive or Barney support him through the lay-off and takes a job in an inner-city paint factory, a degrading thing for a bushman to do.

As the play unfolds it becomes clear that the excitement has gone and all their old pleasures have turned sour. Pearl is a witness to their misery, as her early suspicions are confirmed; and the young woman next door, Bubba, who has grown up with the dream and still believes in it, is another. Barney tries to salvage the situation by various schemes but they have all suddenly grown old. Roo is no longer top dog on the canefields, and Barney is no longer the successful womaniser. After a series of increasingly violent confrontations they come to realise what they have lost. Only Bubba, who wants to team up with Dowd, still has the dream.

BELONGING

The crisis comes when Roo, his role as a tough bushman shattered, asks Olive to marry him and settle down. She is horrified. 'You think I'll let it all end up in marriage—every day—a paint factory—you think I'll marry you?' She is clinging to what they used to have. She breaks down, and then picks herself up again and leaves for her shift at the pub, where she is covering for Pearl, who has already fled. Roo is devastated. All he can do is pick up the tinselly kewpie doll of the title and smash it to pieces. Barney leads him out, dumb and hurt.

The initial response was to the play's local colour. It was Australian in a way that seemed to vindicate fifty years of dramatic realism. Its subject was so recognisable that the conventions of its highly contrived form—well-made, in three acts with effective curtains and a crisis scene—became invisible to some critics:

> [A]s the curtain went up a miracle happened. The theatre disappeared, there was no acting on the stage, there was no play to act in. We were in Melbourne, on a hot summer afternoon, in a stuffy terrace house, living the lives of some strangers who were us.[7]

In fact, of course, these canecutters and barmaids were as exotic for Australian middle-class theatregoers and journalists as were the characters in the plays of J. M. Synge and Tennessee Williams, the overseas comparisons that were instantly made.[8] As the play made its way to London and New York public discussion turned to its 'universal values' rather than its local colour. It was a play about the disillusionment that age imposes on youthful dreams. Olive came to be seen as a little girl who never grew up—cuddling her kewpie doll as a baby substitute, and rejecting Roo's proposal of marriage because she is incapable of relinquishing her childish dream of the lay-off. Then, as the play itself settled into legend, a new cultural reading began to take over. It became a metaphor for the development and maturation of the country itself. As the critic H. G. Kippax put it in 1963, the play 'brought the outback into the city and confronted the "Australianist" legend with the realities of modern, urbanised, industrialised Australia'.[9]

It is not hard to see how this progression in the play's reputation—from local colour, to universalism, to cultural document—came about. Everything that Olive says about the men and her dream can be read at

4: INTO THE CITY

all three levels. She is a colourful and lively character who speaks with personal passion but her words can easily be interpreted in a wider sense. Roo and Barney, she says to Pearl, are like 'a coupla kings' when they walk into the bar of an afternoon and the soft city blokes stand aside for them. They are like 'eagles flying down out of the sun' for the mating season—an image that comes to us in the play via Pearl's cynical retelling of Olive's original enthusiasm. At the personal level Olive is a passionate lover when she says these things, but she also went on to become a representative of both female dreaming foolishness and the romantic side of the old bush legend.[10]

In terms of the bush legend Roo and Barney are defeated by their encounter with the city, but at the end of the play they walk off romantically into the sunset—still mates. The supposedly victorious city has no alternative to offer. The bush legend is celebrated nostalgically. The only alternative future offered is Bubba's, and her hopes of a new life with Dowd, a new version of Olive's dream.

Lawler himself said that his play was simply a study of an 'alternative to marriage'.[11] If so then Olive becomes a more complicated character after the second wave of feminism. In 1975 Anne Summers pointed out how abject Olive was, and yet how triumphant in the way that she clings to her dream despite what amounts to a psychological assault first as Roo meets his 'existential crisis' and then when Roo and Barney reassert their mateship: 'Lawler does not dare even suggest what will happen to Olive, left to sink hopelessly among the smithereens of the seventeenth doll'.[12] What we see her do, of course, in spite of everything, is summon up the strength to go to work.[13]

Wherever such cultural and gender readings might have led, the *Doll* collapsed happily back into a comedy–drama of individual life in the mid-1970s when Lawler wrote two new plays to make a trilogy. He had always claimed, in response to the academic enthusiasm for the *Doll* as a cultural document, that what he was really interested in was creating a night's entertainment in the theatre.[14] The new plays refocused interest on the characters, as if they were real people. The sexual politics of the original play might have been bold for the 1950s but by 1975 Lawler was able to expand on that aspect and turn the play back into something approaching high-class theatrical soap opera.

BELONGING

Kid Stakes, set in the first summer, is a charming play, full of detail about the characters' youthful sex life, self-consciously dramatising the back story to the 17-year-old fantasy. The central conflict is between Olive and her mother Emma, who wants to run a respectable boarding house and set her daughter up in a good career in millinery. Olive's innocent flirtation with Roo becomes a rite-of-passage story as she lets him into her life and then, after much agonising, into her bed. She has a suitor, Dickie Pouncett from the millinery shop, who represents the nice, middle-class values that she rejects when she falls for Roo, quits her job, and becomes a barmaid so that Roo and Barney can visit her during her working day. Nancy and Barney are much more sophisticated: they agree to go along for the ride until whenever it ends. Olive and Roo feel obliged, before they have sex for the first time, to make the extra-marital commitment that sets up the dream of the next sixteen summers. Olive accepts the kewpie doll that Roo has bought her as a substitute for a wedding ring, and for children.

Other Times is set in the winter of the ninth year of their agreement, 1945. It is the only play of the trilogy that could not easily stand alone—a grim middle act sandwiched between the optimism of *Kid Stakes* and the tragic conclusion of the *Doll*. It is full of incident and an almost overwhelming wartime bitterness. Dickie Pouncett has died at sea; Emma has become involved in a black market racket in which she loses most of her life savings; Nancy, practically alcoholic, has had an abortion; and a new character Josef Hultz, a refugee Austrian Jew, is introduced briefly and then dismissed by Olive. Roo reveals his propensity for existential crisis when he breaks down, after being demobbed from the army, and comes close to destroying the house as he burns his army gear in a bonfire in the backyard. He is full of anguish because he has spent the war as a private—for the sake of his no-hoper mate Barney—watching good men die. He knows that if he had been their ganger they would have lived. Olive goes along with this macho fantasy, and our respect for her diminishes. There is a scene, extraordinary now, in which Nancy tells the story of her abortion. Barney cries, because it was his child, and Nancy comforts him instead of belting him.

4: INTO THE CITY

When the trilogy was first performed as a whole in 1978 part of the interest for audiences who knew the *Doll* was to meet Nancy at last and to watch as all the familiar incidents and revelations in the earlier play were anticipated. Most surprisingly the whole romantic dream of the layoffs is undermined. The first summer was happy enough but in the ninth winter we learn that five summers have been missed while the men were away at war and things are already looking rather bleak. After seeing Nancy's drunken disillusionment in *Other Times*, the great surprise is that she hangs on for another seven years until the penultimate summer.

The trilogy depends to a large extent on our belief in Roo and Barney as genuine bush heroes—however battered and finally defeated. Roo's dumb pride and Barney's sneaky scheming drive most of the action and cause most of the damage in all three plays. Without a basic respect and admiration for them, therefore, the whole thing becomes infuriating. Just as Esson's *The Drovers* depended for its effect on our acceptance of the city values of the Jackeroo, so this final confrontation between the bush and the city depends on our acceptance of the bush legend. If the audience shared the values of 'soft city blokes' such as Dickie Pouncett then the whole drama would collapse. In clinging to the dream Olive would only be desperate and foolish, and Roo's rejection of her years of self-sacrifice, when he proposes marriage at the end of the third play, unfeeling and mean.

When the *Doll* first appeared it was heralded as launching a new 'school' of Australian playwriting called, by Hugh Hunt, 'backyard realism'.[15] It was characterised by an interest in the urban poor, explored in a well-made three-act dramatic structure, often involving a climax in which the tensions of inarticulate characters burst out in violence. Eunice Hanger called it a 'recipe':

> the slum or mean or sordid setting, the doll or baby or other child symbol, the violence of the climax at the end of the second act, the conflict of sex or family or race, resolved unhappily or only partly resolved by compromise or by death.[16]

It was not, Hanger pointed out, Lawler's recipe, although it was believed to be. His next play, *The Piccadilly Bushman* (1959), was in part a satire on the new artistically-inclined middle class that

BELONGING

had patronised the *Doll* and its successors. In the play an expatriate Australian actor, Alec Ritchie, who has had success in England, returns, against his wishes it turns out, to star in a commercial film adaptation of a successful Australian novel. Staying in the luxury harbourside house of a *nouveau riche* business couple he resists their colonial cringe mentality. He tries to mediate between the English producer and screenwriter and the larrikin Australian novelist, and later confronts his own feelings about his international identity. He is briefly provoked to assert his Australianness by his alcoholic wife, Grace, who wants to return to the country town where she grew up. At the end, after a revealing speech in which Alec expresses the anguish he feels about his expatriate rootlessness, he returns to England.

The play was produced by Williamson's in 1959. Leslie Norman's film version of the *Doll* was released in New York in 1962 under the title *Season of Passion*, with Hollywood stars Ernest Borgnine (Roo), John Mills (Barney), Ann Baxter (Olive) and Angela Lansbury (Pearl). The film has an early scene in which Roo and Barney, fresh from the canefields, are met at Circular Quay in Sydney by their girls and whisked off on a ferry that chugs out of the Quay and turns left under the Sydney Harbour Bridge, which lurks in every scene, heading for Bondi Beach (actually in the other direction), where they all have a beer. Barney woos Pearl in the beauty parlour where Pearl works, while he is getting his nails done. For the New Year's Eve scene they all go off to Luna Park, where Roo fights a sideshow tent-boxer and, after a few setbacks, defeats him. It ends with Bubba going to join Dowd on the canefields, and Roo walking back into Olive's bar, presumably to marry her. It is a ludicrous travesty of the original, of the sort that Alec Ritchie briefly resists but then settles for in *The Piccadilly Bushman*.

The *Doll* 'school' was rather small. Were it not for the air of excitement about the sudden professionalisation of the non-commercial theatre, it would not have been critically constructed at all. Several of the plays from this 'school' are not set in either the slums or a backyard. Anthony Coburn's *The Bastard Country* (1959), a bush melodrama, was included because of its timing. Barbara Vernon's *The Multi-Coloured Umbrella* (1957), JCW's attempt to cash in on the new interest in Australian plays, is interesting chiefly for bringing a new

4: INTO THE CITY

class of Australians onto the stage, a sordid but by no means poor family of successful bookmakers living in a tasteless but expensive beachside house. In a contrived way the play dramatises various financial and sexual conflicts among them. Ru Pullan's *Curly on the Rack*, Robert Wales's *The Grotto* and John Hepworth's gritty urban dramas *The Beast in View* and *The End of the Rainbow* are other examples.[17]

Peter Kenna's *The Slaughter of St Teresa's Day* (1959), his first successful play, is a special case. It is set in the slums of Sydney's Paddington in the 1950s, in a colourful criminal underworld of the sort that Esson had flirted with in *The Bride of Gospel Place*, reinvigorated by the influence of subsequent Hollywood gangster movies. The play is written in the rambling storytelling style that Esson used, with sudden eruptions of violent incident, a style that emerged again in the in-yer-face urban plays of the late 1990s and early 2000s by playwrights such as Raimondo Cortese.

In Kenna's play Oola McGuire is an aging queen of the underworld whose annual St Teresa's day party is interrupted first by her daughter Thelma, unexpectedly arriving home from her convent school, and then, as the party hots up, by a gun battle among the guests, who include a lot of lively Irish Catholic Australians who sit around yarning in Act 2 before they start shooting each other. In the aftermath Oola is forced to take stock of her life and her neglect of her relationship with her daughter.

Aside from these there are really only two other plays in the supposed 'school' started by *Summer of the Seventeenth Doll*: Richard Beynon's *The Shifting Heart* and Alan Seymour's *The One Day of the Year*. What unites these three highly-influential plays was not just the recipe described by Hanger but the fact that they were concerned with what P. H. Davison, in an influential article, called 'national myths under criticism'.[18] The *Doll* examined the bush legend, *The Shifting Heart* (1957) did tolerance and *The One Day of the Year* (1960) took on the Anzac tradition.

Richard Beynon's later plays include *Summer Shadows* and *Simpson J. 202*. In *Summer Shadows* (1986) he tells the story of his grandparents and their struggles in working-class Melbourne in the early 1920s, with poverty, conflict within the family, a beautiful daughter dying of tuberculosis, a son moving towards a life of crime and above all their 15-year-old independent daughter Ali, who falls in love with a shell-shocked ex-soldier, Davie. Ali and Davie's young determination to be together and to find stability is the core of the play. They are all struggling, and recovering from the war. None of them knows, of course, that the Depression is only a few years away, but we do. It is a very poignant family drama.

But Beynon is best known for *The Shifting Heart*, a play that won a 1956 competition (Vernon's was the runner-up) and came second in an international competition run by the London *Observer*. It is the only 'backyard realist' play actually set in a backyard—that of the Bianchis, a family of Italian immigrants. The son Gino wants to be accepted as an Australian and the pregnant daughter Maria has married an Anglo-Australian, Clarrie, who runs a trucking business. Clarrie employs Gino but is reluctant to take him on as a partner. Momma and Poppa Bianchi are colourful 'new Australians' engaged in a continual feud with a neighbour who keeps flinging her rubbish over their fence. On the other side of their yard there is a more sympathetic woman, with an ocker husband who gets violently drunk every Christmas, when the play is set. (Another feature of Eunice Hanger's recipe is the setting of the plays on national holidays, when the characters can justifiably get drunk and release their suppressed tensions. A crucial scene in the *Doll* is set on New Year's Eve, and the *Day* is set around Anzac Day.)

The action of the *Heart* revolves around Gino's attempts to be accepted at the local dance hall and Clarrie's inability to embrace the fact that he has married into a 'wog' family. At the climax Gino is fatally wounded in a knife fight at the dance hall and, when Maria's baby is born, Clarrie finally accepts his new world and decides to name the boy Gino. There is a great deal of backyard colour in the first half, before the sudden rush of incident in the second.

The Shifting Heart was the first Australian play about immigrant experience to attract much attention, and its success—again partly a result of timing—has obscured some bold earlier plays with similar themes. Sydney Tomholt's *Anoli the Blind*, published in 1936, is a tight, fierce little melodrama, set in a lonely bush hut and full of evocative stage effects and outbursts of European passion, about a

4: INTO THE CITY

vendetta imported to the Australian bush from Velletri in Italy. The vivid contrast between Anoli's passion and the aridity of his new environment is evoked with a theatrical excess that lifts it to an almost mythic level.

Jean Devanny's *Paradise Flow*, also written in the 1930s, is more ambitious. It is set in the Queensland canefields, and gives a very different view from that of the bronzed white heroes implied in the *Doll*. Devanny's canefields, swarming with people of different nationalities, are a place where the great political struggles between communism and fascism are played out under the same sun that beat down on Roo and Barney. It is a very raw script but its mingling of personal and political issues, its interest in multiculturalism and its sexual frankness anticipated a great deal of later drama. Esson's *The Sacred Place*, Marjorie McLeod's *Horizons*, Oriel Gray's *Sky Without Birds* and Eunice Hanger's *Flood* have already been mentioned.

The national myth under criticism in the third major play of the tiny *Doll* school, *The One Day of the Year*, proved to be the most controversial. So much so that for a time the basic family drama of the play, a classic father–son conflict, was ignored. The Drama Advisory Committee of the first Adelaide Festival in 1960 selected the play but the Festival Board of Governors rejected it, apparently because they thought it might offend the Returned Services League. It was the first play to explore the relations between the pre-War generation of ockers and mums and their postwar children, who were being educated beyond the expectations, and often beyond the understanding, of their parents.

In 1960 the new generation was represented by Hughie Cook, a university student in conflict with his lift-driver father Alf, a bigoted old digger. Alf celebrates his Australianness by railing against the Poms and the I-ties (the upper-class English and the Italian New Australians) and by commemorating Anzac Day each year with a drunken mixture of patriotic rhetoric and maudlin sentimentality. Hughie has an upper middle-class girlfriend, Jan, from Sydney's wealthy North Shore, whom he met at university. Together they plan a student newspaper exposé of the hypocrisy and drunken excess of Anzac Day as they see it. Alf has a mate Wacka, an old digger who fought at Gallipoli, a simple decent man with none of Alf's strident nationalism. The clash between these two pairs is presided over by Dot, a classic figure of the long-suffering mum struggling to persuade her men to talk to each other. The situation has a long tradition in bush drama.

The second-act crisis comes after Hughie refuses to join his father in the customary Anzac Day march and goes off instead with Jan to take photographs of drunken diggers. Alf sees their article in the student paper and, uncharacteristically, bashes Hughie, provoking a confrontation. Hughie realises that his political objection to Anzac Day is in fact a personal reaction to the oppressive influence of his father and his class. He breaks up with Jan and ends up staying on in the fractured family home, hoping to work his way through his personal crisis before attempting to deal with the wider issues. This rather weak ending dates the play now, and belies its iconoclastic reputation. In a 1985 revision Jan is given a similar conflict in her own family and finally leaves. At the end she leaves asking Hughie to wish her luck in her struggle with her father. In neither version is there any doubt that the main task is some sort of reconciliation, or at least weary accommodation, with the demands of the father.

Each of these plays ends up reaffirming the values of the national myths they supposedly criticise: they have none of the passionate polemic and social critique that writers such as Prichard, Gray, Dann and Brand extracted from the generic forms they exploited. In the New Wave the often violent reaction against naturalism (a term by then used more broadly to include the well-made realism of the *Doll* group of plays) was motivated by a frustration with all varieties of realistic form as tools for dealing with anything outside the daily lives of specific individuals.

This frustration had begun at the same time as the new urban realist plays were hitting the boards. In 1963 H. G. Kippax lamented that Australian nationalist writers had ignored 'the discoveries of the anti-naturalists like the later O'Neill' and 'the much more relevant use of the chronicle play by Brecht to project an epic drama'. He agreed with Hugh Hunt that naturalistic dialogue could never rise to great dramatic heights in the mouths of inarticulate characters.[19]

4: INTO THE CITY

There would be later urban realist plays just as there are good plays being written today that have their roots in the bush realist tradition. Dorothy Hewett's first play, *This Old Man Comes Rolling Home* (1967) is firmly based on Hanger's recipe but it adds an expressionist chorus and a non-realistic heightened language that foreshadowed the important role she was to play in the new drama of the 1970s. Peter Kenna's *A Hard God* revisited the territory in a new way in 1974. John O'Donoghue's colourful *A Happy and Holy Occasion* in 1976 used some non-realistic narrative devices but it, too, dealt with the struggles of an Irish Catholic working-class family, in this case in Newcastle, NSW. But overall one of the remarkable things about the longevity of the *Doll* group of plays is that, while they were being written about by academic critics, set for study in schools and universities, and sometimes revived in the new professional theatres of the last quarter of the century, they had virtually no impact on the playwrights of the 1960s, nor those of the New Wave in the early 1970s, and they have not had much substantial influence since. In terms of both theme and dramaturgy, they brought an end to the whole bush–city era for a time—until writers such as Katherine Thomson, Debra Oswald and Hannie Rayson later revived some of its concerns.

After the early 1960s bush realism, country-town comedy-drama, slum realism and most of their related genres moved off, mostly, into film and television, just as the nineteenth-century melodrama had done fifty years before. The old amateur and the new professional theatres passed each other by like ships in the night, except for the brief moment of contact in the 1950s that has since become such a legend.

Kippax concluded the introduction to his influential 1963 collection *Three Australian Plays* by introducing Patrick White as an exciting new playwright. Like *The One Day of the Year*, White's *The Ham Funeral* was first produced in Adelaide by an amateur company. The Board of Governors had rejected *The One Day of the Year* for its inaugural 1960 Festival and now for the second Festival in 1962 they duly and dully rejected *The Ham Funeral*. In both cases an amateur company stepped in, picked up the rejected play and carried it on to success. If this were a history of the theatre then White's early plays might conclude this

BELONGING

chapter as the last gasp of the amateur theatre. But it is a history of the drama so his plays launch the next chapter. As Kippax wrote, by 1963 Australian drama had 'reached the end of its beginnings'.

5
PATRICK WHITE

The prevailing model of the history of Australian drama since the mid-twentieth century is of two separate surges of activity. The first in the 1950s, the *Doll* school, petered out. The second, the New Wave, started in the late 1960s and endured. The notion was parodied by Barry Humphries in the late 1970s when Edna Everage claimed that one of the good things about being Australian was 'all those wonderful cultural renaissances we're always having'. Alex Buzo wrote that 'one of the characteristics of Australian cultural life is that every few years it starts all over again'. This, he said, was because the top jobs always went to Poms who had never been here and who therefore had to spend a few years getting to know everyone.[1]

This model, however, ignores a number of writers and, most importantly, it overlooks the fact that in the transition from the 1950s upsurge to the New Wave came the first four plays of one of the most influential writers for the Australian stage, Patrick White.

White, Australia's only literary Nobel Prize winner, wrote his first surviving play, *The Ham Funeral*, in 1947 and his last, *Shepherd on the Rocks*, forty years later. His influence looms over the drama of the second half of the century—a challenge to the genre and realist playwrights, an inspiration to others and, though much appreciated, never broadly popular. For the most part his plays were successful at the box office and favoured by the critics, because they gave them so much to write about. They were always controversial. In academia he is one of the most discussed Australian dramatists, and for more than a decade of theatrical neglect academics kept his reputation as a playwright alive, partly as an offshoot of his reputation as an internationally renowned novelist.[2]

His often cantankerous relationship with the theatre profession is legendary. He formed close artistic links with a few favoured directors, and in the case of the first, John Tasker, had a dramatic falling out.[3] In White's first flurry of theatrical success in the early 1960s, Tasker directed three plays in just over three years for the Adelaide University Theatre Guild, and John Sumner directed *A Cheery Soul* for the Union Theatre Repertory Company in Melbourne. After that, partly as a result of a controversial relationship with the Adelaide Festival Board of Governors, and partly as a result of the hostility of the popular press (at the opening of *The Season at Sarsaparilla* a banner headline in the Sydney *Daily Mirror* read 'New Play Stinks'[4]) White lapsed into theatrical silence for thirteen years. In 1976, prompted by the success of director Jim Sharman's revival of *The Season at Sarsaparilla*, White started writing plays again.

His second phase as a dramatist, in the 1970s and 1980s, is associated both with Sharman and also Neil Armfield, the director who has done more than any other since Tasker to bring White's plays into the theatrical repertoire and to establish him as one of the most important Australian stage writers of the twentieth century. Armfield directed three very different productions of *Signal Driver*, demonstrating how a sympathetic and creative director can explore a play by returning to it in new ways, treatment that few Australian playwrights have experienced. He also directed the premiere of *Shepherd on the Rocks* and major revivals of *Night on Bald Mountain* and *A Cheery Soul*. In 2000 a new generation director, Michael Kantor, did *The Ham Funeral* at Sydney's Belvoir St Theatre in a style of Meyerholdian grotesque. In 2007 Benedict Andrews directed a highly imaginative production of *The Season at Sarsaparilla*, set in a revolving Californian bungalow fitted with fly-on-the-wall cameras, for the Sydney Theatre Company. White is one of the few Australian

5: PATRICK WHITE

playwrights to attract new generations of theatre artists eager to test themselves on his work.

White was the first successful modernist dramatist in the special Australian sense of the word, meaning 'non-naturalistic'. He was the last playwright of the golden age of the amateur theatre and more successfully than his predecessors he took on board the full range of European dramatists of the post-realist avant-garde. He has dramaturgical links with the surrealists, Strindberg, the German expressionists and the post–Second World War absurdists. He also drew on the popular theatrical traditions of vaudeville.

He was not afraid to mix this up, bringing together literary, popular and experimental styles. In this he anticipated the theatrical adventurism of the New Wave, although at the time he faced considerable negative criticism. As late as 1985 critics with theatrical understanding, such as Katharine Brisbane, were lamenting that everyone read him but no-one produced him.[5] Yet the weaknesses that even his most avid supporters saw when his plays first appeared have since proven to be strengths. The excess of his plays and their stylistic promiscuity, a problem when the realistic representation of Australian life dominated the theatres, now offer exciting theatrical opportunities to adventurous actors, designers and directors.

The early plays were an exultant rebellion against realism. In form, style and subject White re-worked the details of everyday life and invested them with a new spirituality. This was based in a troubled, ambivalent but sincere reverence for the immediacy of sensual experience and a respect for the basic facts of life—birth, sex, death—and the hope for some sort of cyclical continuity between them. Two of his plays from the 1960s, *The Season at Sarsaparilla* and *A Cheery Soul*, anticipated the New Wave's satirical interest in suburban middle-class Australia, with a lyrically heightened style, in language and in theatrical effect. New Wave writers and directors, busy reinventing the wheel, took a long time to discover this. It has taken the Australian theatre nearly forty years to catch up with White's early plays.

The second group of plays seems like a riposte to the New Wave, mocking its achievements by embracing, half in parody, the old drama. *Big Toys* is a version of a traditional drawing-room comedy such as

BELONGING

Arthur Adams or Gwen Meredith might have written, reconfigured in White's distinctive way. *Signal Driver* is a bleak, Beckettian version of the classic family saga and *Netherwood* a burlesque of a closed-house family drama. There is a neat parallel between White's two most excessive plays: *Night on Bald Mountain*, which ended his first period and *Shepherd on the Rocks*, which ended his second period, a play with a grandly melodramatic conclusion and every bit as misunderstood, with its exaggerated style, as *Night on Bald Mountain*.

The Ham Funeral

White's first plays, *Bread and Butter Women* and *School for Friends*, were produced at Bryant's Playhouse in Sydney in 1935 and 1937 respectively. *Return to Abyssinia* was scheduled for a production in London in 1939 but the war intervened and it was not produced until 1947. None of these survive.[6] In 1947, just before he returned to Australia, he wrote *The Ham Funeral*, inspired, apparently, by 'The Dead Landlord', which William Dobell had painted from his experience living in a London boarding-house before the war. For thirteen years White's play floated around, attracting some interest from Keith Michell and George Devine in London and Hugh Hunt and Doris Fitton in Sydney. But it was not until 1961, when Geoffrey Dutton was looking for an Australian play for the second Adelaide Festival, that White's first tumultuous period in the theatre began in earnest. The Board of Governors of the Festival rejected the play—largely, it seems, because of a scene in which two vaudevillian bag-ladies discover an aborted foetus in a rubbish bin. However, like Alan Seymour's *The One Day of the Year*, it was picked up elsewhere, this time by the amateur Adelaide University Theatre Guild and directed in a fringe production by John Tasker, who had been hand-picked for the job by White himself. It was a success, especially with H. G. Kippax, who became one of White's most influential supporters and who publicly welcomed a new Australian play that transcended the bounds of well-made urban realism. White's position as the first great non-naturalistic dramatist of the Australian theatre was assured.[7]

5: PATRICK WHITE

The Ham Funeral deals with the inability of a sensitive and self-conscious Young Man with aspirations as a poet to engage meaningfully with life. He spends much of his time at his lodgings lying on his bed thinking and dreaming, which is expressed on stage by his communing with his anima, the Girl in the room across the landing. Downstairs in the basement his restlessly sensual Landlady, Alma Lusty, prowls around the kitchen while her solid husband, Will, sits at their deal table in massive silence. Alma persuades the Young Man to come down for tea and so launches the first of his journeys towards the understanding he craves. The Landlord, after a brief transcendently articulate moment, suddenly dies. Alma lets down her hair and sends her young lodger off to fetch the relatives for a funeral feast at which she decides, luxuriously, to serve ham.

As in all of White's plays the theatrical geography is important. He conceived and described the sets for his first four plays realistically, but they also have a highly symbolic significance. In *The Ham Funeral* the entire house is represented. In the Landlady's basement earthy life goes on; upstairs the Young Man lies on his bed listening to the sounds below. The stairs and the hall in between are spaces where the body and the mind intersect. Both the Landlady and the Young Man pause there, on their way up or down, and consider the direction they are taking. Aside from a brief scene in which the lodger who actually occupies the Girl's room returns from work, neither the Landlord nor the Girl leaves their respective area. At the end, when the Young Man escapes out into life, the stage direction calls for the whole back wall to dissolve so that he can be seen walking off into the distance. In Neil Armfield's 1989 revival at the Sydney Theatre Company he simply ran out through the auditorium into the world from which the audience had come.

A revelation by the Landlord in Act 1, Scene 4 prompts the Young Man to embark on the next phase of his quest. He has already articulated his restlessness and his desire to be an artist but it is clear that a life spent lolling around on his bed until the late afternoon has not much in it to express. Will Lusty speaks suddenly, just before he dies, of his centredness in a world of physical things: 'I sit 'ere. I am content. Life, at last, is wherever a man 'appens to be. This 'ouse is life. I watch it

BELONGING

fill with light, an' darken. These are my days and nights'. When Alma objects that it is natural, also, to love he replies, 'This table is love ... if you can get to know it'. (p. 27) The couple have grown wearily and bitterly old, revealing glimpses of a long past life together: their first sex, Will's boxing, their struggle to make a living in a sweet-shop, Alma's adultery, their dead child. These far-off, filtered memories are more real than the Young Man's tortuous introspection.

There are moments of grotesque comedy after the Landlord's death. Alma and the Young Man struggle to get his fat corpse up onto the bed, to lay him out. The Young Man, on his journey to fetch the relatives, meets the two old bag ladies, who flee on discovering the foetus. He is left to his philosophising and has one of many moments of self-discovery as he stares at the foetus: 'So much for visions! Who'll ever tell where the flesh begins ... or ends? The landlord and the dead child are one'. (p. 43) The relatives are an expressionist chorus who when they arrive drink the stout and eat the ham and like harpies taunt Alma for her dumb but deeply felt grief and for the sensuality of her memories.

Finally the Young Man throws them out and returns to confront Alma, who, befuddled by booze and loss, starts to embrace him as her lover and her lost son, and at last awakens some fire in him. But, appalled by her desperate sensual need, he flees upstairs yet again. The Girl, by now clearly revealed as himself in a less self-protective mode, prompts his final self-revelation. He says of Alma, 'Lunging and plunging, she raped life, and won ... [...] whereas *my* attempts have amounted to little more than acts of self-abuse in an empty room' (pp. 70–71). After a final farewell he rushes out into the world.

The biggest problem with the play is the Young Man's earnestly self-absorbed introspection and priggishness but the actor Tyler Coppin, in Armfield's revival, showed that the character can work if played with enough insouciant charm and flair. Alma Lusty is the first of many of White's complex women—loose-hipped but childless or barren—who embody spiritual yearnings in the flesh and its failings. *The Ham Funeral* is a coming-of-age story for the Young Man and a coming-to-terms story for Alma.

5: PATRICK WHITE

The Season at Sarsaparilla

White's next play, *The Season at Sarsaparilla*, subtitled 'A Charade of Suburbia', was written in a heat of rage at the shallow, philistinism of Australia after the controversy over *The Ham Funeral*. A new young man, Roy Child, whose anguish is like that of the Young Man in *The Ham Funeral* is, if anything, even more detached and cruel. Nola Boyle, a passionate older woman, is more comfortable with her sensuality than Alma.

The play is set in Mildred Street, Sarsaparilla, the fictitious Australian outer suburb of White's novel *Riders in the Chariot* and many of the stories in *The Burnt Ones*. In the theatre we are looking from the back lane onto the rear of three nearly identical houses, the homes of the Pogsons (Clive is a minor business executive), the Knotts (Harry is a men's wear salesman) and the Boyles (Ernie is a sanitary man, who empties the dunny cans). The season of the title is that of a bitch in heat, roaming the streets pursued by a pack of lustful dogs—a source of disquiet for the respectable Mrs Girlie Pogson and of fascination for Pippy, her young daughter. The barking of the dogs punctuates the monotony of the suburb and reflects the desires that suburban respectability masks—the births, sexual encounters and deaths that drive the inhabitants' lives. The action moves between the three houses, satirically pointing out the routine mundanity but also catching the characters in moments of fear, passion or simple tenderness—what Judy Pogson, the other daughter of that household, calls 'loving-kindness' (p. 162).

The shifting moods of *The Season at Sarsaparilla* are presided over by Roy, Mavis Knott's schoolteacher brother, a chronic observer who detaches himself from the action to tell us what he sees but cannot live. He introduces the 'razzle-dazzle', a lighting effect for mechanical human activity. He is an outsider, half drawn into the action via his relationships with the sweet Judy Pogson and her fast friend, the model Julia, but who, like the Young Man, leaves at the end. In a sign of the play's ambivalence about suburbia, however, he acknowledges that he will return. 'You can't shed your skin ... even if it itches like hell!'. (p. 177)

Girlie Pogson is an extravagantly respectable 1950s Australian suburban housewife, a character that has few real antecedents in the earlier drama but is clearly related to Barry Humphries's Edna Everage and has a long line of descendants in the new middle-class drama of the late 1960s and 1970s. Her relentless fussy niceness conceals a dissatisfaction with her uncommunicative husband and her uneventful life, expressed in a ritualised nostalgia for Rosedale, the rural property where she grew up. Her cleanliness is now the only control she can exert over the world.

The elder Pogsons are the principal objects of White's satire, while their children, and the Knotts and the Boyles, get on with life. One of the play's extraordinary features is the way the satire keeps being taken over by the sufferings and triumphs of the characters. It is as if White found his distaste for them melting away as he dug deeper into the 'charade'.[8] Judy rejects Roy and settles for the duller but more dependable postal clerk who dotes on her. Mavis Knott, suffering through her pregnancy, manages to unite the street when the baby arrives. Nola has a one-night-stand with 'Digger' Masson, Ernie's old mate from the war, but her remorse and her genuine passion for Ernie force a quick reconciliation between them. With the possible exception of the Pogsons, a mutual tenderness keeps each couple together.

The weary aspect of all this suburban mundanity is underscored by the rebellious child Pippy and by the awful casualness used in telling the story of Judy's friend Julia. In a series of abrupt little scenes we learn that Julia is a successful model; that she is having an affair with a local councillor; that she has fallen pregnant and would like Roy, who has always expressed a passion for her, to help her; and that, when he refuses, she kills herself and her unborn child by driving into a tree. It is like a little soap opera from the Mildred Street wireless sets. (In Andrews's 2007 production the whole play was played out in the reality TV style of 'Big Brother', with surveillance cameras relentlessly recording everything the characters did.) It provokes questions about the relationship between individuality and social conformity and between creativity and submission—issues most clearly explored in the monstrous, tragic Miss Docker, the awesome figure who dominates White's next Sarsaparillan play.

5: PATRICK WHITE

A Cheery Soul

A Cheery Soul has a mixture of styles that divided critics from the beginning.[9] White physicalises Miss Docker's great journey from irritating neighbourhood busybody to nightmarish paragon of 'goodness' and finally tragic heroine judged by God as the play journeys from straightforward realism through increasing expressionism to a final moment in which the existentialist void appears to sweep away Sarsaparilla and its poor struggling individuals altogether.

Each act is self-contained. Act 1 is a mini suburban drama in which Mrs Custance, motivated by a sense of her inadequacy as a good Christian soul, persuades her dour but decent husband to take in the recently evicted Miss Docker as a non-paying boarder. Miss Docker arrives in an explosion of aggressive cheerfulness and threatens to disrupt the Custances's tenderly affectionate but quiet domesticity so they find her a place in a nursing home and ask her to leave. At the end of the act, they settle back into their dull but warm regard for each other. This is Miss Docker's first knock-back. We do not meet the Custances again.

Act 2 is set in Sarsaparilla's Sundown Home for Old People. Miss Docker rules the roost until a chorus of grotesque old women who at first idolise her start to turn against her. The act is dominated by a flashback story about her brutal intervention in the life of one of the residents, Mrs Lillie, when she commandeered Tom Lillie in his last weeks. Her relentless do-goodery is revealed as a desperate and pathetic grasp for attention. Mrs Lillie, once beautiful and rich, is now poor and suffering from palsy. Her memories of the sensuality of her youth, filtered like Alma's and Nola's, are expressed in one of the most beautiful and evocative scenes in Australian drama. We watch images of the Lillies as a young romantic couple, dancing in the background, as Mrs Lillie, old and crippled, sits on stage remembering what she once had but has now lost:

> Even in our beginning I was haunted by our end. What would come to our rescue if the flesh lost its divinity? We travelled, of course ... Europe ... the Nile. ... As the dahabiah carried us deeper into Egypt, I looked for answers in the stone hieroglyphs. It puzzled Tom. It was too

BELONGING

> perverse ... irrational. ... So I joined my mouth to his. His kisses smelt of claret. I grew gratefully drunk on them. But, as the boat rocked us into deeper moonlight, sometimes the dust would reach out from the eroded shore ... and I would taste ... the desert ... on my lips ... (p. 218)

After this interlude Miss Docker suffers her second rejection in the play. In a scene narrated in Brechtian style, she is abandoned by the suddenly rebellious members of Tom's funeral procession on the way to the crematorium. She is left to walk the dusty road back to Sarsaparilla.

In Act 3 Miss Docker's goodness and cheerfulness have become hubristic. By now militantly virtuous, she intervenes with fatal results in the life, career and hopes of the local clergyman, Mr Wakeman, a man of strong faith but weak ability. In the interest of doing good she invades the rectory, challenges the Wakeman household and disrupts Wakeman's sermon, causing his death. She is left abandoned at the end of the play, wandering the streets of Sarsaparilla like a bag-lady, mocked by passing children and talking to a stray dog that ends up pissing on her leg. A passing swagman interprets this as a judgement from God but in the ambivalent spirit of all White's plays she rejects this, with comic defiance: 'If Gawd was goin' to judge yer, 'E wouldn't use a blooming dawg'. (p. 263) But He has. Miss Docker wanders off, supposedly back to Sundown nursing home, but really into the emptiness.

While the three acts of this play are self-contained, they also cohere as one. The early critical qualms that it lacked a unity of style were swept aside in the theatre by both Jim Sharman's 1979 and Neil Armfield's 2001 revivals. The freeing of stage design from the constraints of realism since 1963 has been particularly important in allowing the symbolic significance of White's sets to be explored much more imaginatively than his old-fashioned stage directions suggested. Brian Thomson's design for the 1979 production progressively stripped the stage, so that by the end Miss Docker was left alone in a vast empty theatrical space from which all vestiges of Sarsaparilla as an actual place had vanished. Dale Ferguson's design for the 2001 production had a similar impact. In both productions Miss Docker was played by Robyn Nevin, who gave performances of such power that the jarring shifts in style became part of her journey.

5: PATRICK WHITE

Night on Bald Mountain

The last play of this first period is *Night on Bald Mountain*, a gothic melodrama with roots in the nineteenth-century theatre of effect, characters drawn from Freudian and Jungian psychology and a grand theme—the destructive power of reason when it fails to love enough or to understand the forces of nature. It opens on an outcrop of Bald Mountain, hard but desolately beautiful land, with one of White's wildest women, Miss Quodling, a tough old battler descended from Ma Bates in Drake-Brockman's *Men Without Wives*. She lives in contented solitude tending her goats, away from the city lights that she can see, like inverted stars, shining far below her craggy retreat. To her comes the sweetly confident and capable young nurse Stella Summerhayes, who has been engaged to look after Miriam Sword, the alcoholic wife of Hugo Sword, a desiccated professor of literature and failed writer who has retreated to the old house at the top of the mountain. Miss Quodling takes one look at Stella and predicts that she will turn out to be not as tough as she thinks she is.

Stella is attracted to Professor Sword, in a respectful way, because he reminds her of the beloved father with whom she has lived alone since she was a child. One of Sword's acolytes, another academic and failed writer, Denis Craig, is attracted to her; but after a motoring trip during which Miriam breaks out in an alcoholic binge everything starts to unravel. In the recriminations that follow, Sword's self-crippling intellectual detachment from life, and the cruelly destructive effects of this on Miriam, are revealed. Sword sees in Stella some life-force that will reconnect him with the world, and he clumsily attempts to seduce her. Fearing that her attraction to him is, as he suggests, a reflection of an incestuous sexual feeling for her father, she flees into the mountain night and dies falling off a cliff into the valley below. Hugo and Miriam have a weary reconciliation and return to the mansion on the hill. Miss Quodling is left with her goats. The play ends with her apocalyptic vision of a world in which everything has been ground into dust, perhaps—in the great cyclical vision of death and rebirth that is a theme in all White's plays—to be reborn into a place fit for life again.

This play, not well received critically at its first production in 1964 by the still faithful Adelaide University Theatre Guild, was not revived

BELONGING

until 1996 when Neil Armfield directed it in Adelaide and Sydney. Armfield's production again revealed how long it had taken for the Australian theatre to catch up with White. If taken literally, the script's scenic demands are enormous. It moves from Miss Quodling's goat farm with its view of the city, via a lonely mountain path beneath a craggy rock, to the two-storey, six-room Sword house where interconnected scenes are played in each of the rooms simultaneously, emphasising the loneliness of the characters. Then the action moves back to the goat farm via the path. Anna Borghesi's design showed how this sort of symbolic staging can work: one theatrical space, full of mystery and ambiguity, can suggest many places—especially in an expressionist play that partly takes place in the mind.

More important is the problem of Stella's sudden death and, if we take it to be suicide, her improbable motivation. Critics at the time assumed that she was horrified by her sudden discovery, provoked by Sword's advances, of her lust for her father. But, as Essie Davis played it in Armfield's revival, the crucial scene (pp. 342–3) can also be read as a revelation of sexual abuse.

These four plays were produced within four years, and three of them were written in that time. They have had an enormous, if mostly unacknowledged, influence on subsequent writers. White was the first Australian playwright to write ironically about the new postwar middle-class suburbia and the first to use a wide range of theatrical styles. He asked big questions and mixed them up in a complex web of issues: the interaction between the private and the public, between intellect and passion, between sex and sensibility. In his second group of plays he added a political dimension.

Big Toys

White started to write *Big Toys* immediately after the success of Sharman's 1976 revival of *The Season at Sarsaparilla*, partly for the actors Kate Fitzpatrick and Max Cullen, who had played Nola and Ernie Boyle in that production. Cullen played the unionist Terry Legge and Fitzpatrick was Mag Bosanquet, a society wife flirting with activism. It opened at Sydney's Parade Theatre in 1977, less than nine months after the opening night of *The Season at Sarsaparilla*.

5: PATRICK WHITE

It is a play of its time, motivated by White's involvement in the Green Bans and the anti-uranium-mining movements in the mid-1970s. It is also his least adventurous play stylistically—a glamorous bedroom comedy set in the Sydney harbourside high-rise apartment of QC Ritchie Bosanquet and his beautiful toy wife Mag, a woman who has clawed her way into society from the wrong side of the tracks. Terry Legge is an honest old-style trade-union leader—modelled on Jack Mundey who invented the Green Bans—who is a witness for the prosecution in a corruption case that Ritchie is defending. Mag seduces him, and Ritchie half tries to as well. They offer him the 'big toys' of high society and at the end, after Terry has given his evidence—not lying but not telling the whole story—Ritchie, who has won, gives him the keys to a Ferrari parked out in the street. Terry takes it for a spin but then returns, handing back the keys and walking out with his integrity more or less intact.

As a political protest play it has a light touch and some of White's trademarks. Mag is a complex character whose radical-chic society activism is paper thin but who has dragged herself out of degradation, battled hard and humiliated herself to get where she is. A doll-wife at the beginning she is revealed by the end to be deeply troubled by her hedonistic love of the big toys, and by Terry's integrity when she finally fails to tempt him with them. She is terrified to the core by the black north-westerly winds that blow in on her glittering eyrie. Brian Thomson's design for Sharman's production was one of the most exciting things about it—an apparently realistic panorama of the Sydney Harbour skyline, which, during Mag's most fearful moments, suddenly opened to reveal a black void.

Big Toys was White's only contribution to the New Wave. Perhaps he felt he'd already done it. He was theatrically silent until another burst of activity in the 1980s, when Sharman moved to Adelaide to transform the State Theatre Company of South Australia into the Lighthouse Company, an ensemble that brought together, briefly, a group of collaborators—Neil Armfield, Louis Nowra, Alan John, Geoffrey Rush, John Wood, Kerry Walker and Gillian Jones—who were to become leading theatre artists in the late 1980s. White wrote *Signal Driver* for Lighthouse in 1982, *Netherwood* in 1983 and then, after a short gap, his maddest and most extravagant play, *Shepherd on the Rocks*, in 1987.

BELONGING

Signal Driver

Signal Driver is one of White's best plays, a perfect marriage of wildness and classicism. Like *A Cheery Soul* it has a tripartite structure but in this case it is contained and neat, its wildness supplied by two old existentialist derelicts, the two Beings, avatars of God. In a mischievously vaudevillian style they provide the social, spiritual and cosmic context of the small human comedy-drama of the play. Its three acts are three slices of experience from a long marriage, set against a backdrop, literally, of the city's growth and the threat of the destruction of their world. Ivy and Theo Vokes stay together because neither has the courage to leave. By the end of the play this weakness has become a strength, a tribute to their endurance.

The theatrical set-up is simple. Each act is set in a public transport shelter on the outskirts of town as either Theo or Ivy attempts to escape. This crisis moment is introduced and framed by the two Beings. The Vokes are in their 20s, their late 50s and then suddenly their 80s and still yearning. The tram or bus that might carry them away to another life keeps thundering up to their shelter but they fail to signal the driver—so it never stops.

In Act 1 the escapee is Theo, fleeing the suffocation of a wife who needs and desires him more than he wants or can comprehend. He has a vision of living in solitude in a bare room by the sea, working in wood to make spiritually meaningful furniture, like the Landlord's table in *The Ham Funeral*. In Act 2 Ivy is fleeing Theo's need, trying to get away from him to meet her rich lover but drawn back to the domestic centre of her life to make sure that Theo knows his tea is on the stove. In Act 3 both of them have forgotten, at last, what they are fleeing from. They sit together in the shelter shed and watch the lights of the Aurora Australis rise and bloom in the sky above them. After fifty years of mutual disappointment, following a brief romantic young love, they have somehow grown together again.

Meanwhile, over the same period, the city grows huge around them. White's script specifies a road separating the audience from the shelter and a hillside in the background. At first this is an outer suburban thoroughfare with horse carts and a tramline and the hillside is bare; in Act 2 it has become a busy highway with cars and buses while the

5: PATRICK WHITE

hillside is dotted with the lights of houses; finally the constant traffic presents an almost impassable barrier and the hillside is covered with tower blocks. At the beginning of each act Ivy and Theo emerge from the audience and cross the road to the shelter where they are watched over by the Beings. In Act 3 Ivy finds it almost impossible to cross, but the traffic parts like the Red Sea, when Theo crosses to join her.

Neil Armfield's three productions tested the symbolism of this simple, suggestive setting by progressively theatricalising it. In 1982 in Adelaide, designer Stephen Curtis followed White's directions: the invisible trams in Act 1 thundered past in front of the stage with a cascade of sparks from the electric cable above and the hillside behind blossomed with the lights of houses in Act 2, just as White described. In Act 3 two giant billboards advertising cars appeared on either side of the shelter and obliterated the growing suburb. At the end the Aurora Australis invaded the theatre literally: a huge billowing cloth swept out over the auditorium to envelop the audience.

In Brisbane in 1983, designer Mike Bridges turned the transport shelter into a stagehouse, a little theatre within the theatre, as in classical Japanese Noh drama. This formally framed Ivy and Theo's story in order to focus and magnify it. Two years later in Sydney, Stephen Curtis reduced the staging to its bare essentials. The Beings prowled the open, empty Belvoir St space, cued the music, orchestrated the entrances of the Vokes, and created the road at the beginning of each act, painting the road markings—a dotted line, then an unbroken line, then a double yellow line—on the floor with a colourless stuff that gradually brightened and glowed as each act got underway.

These three productions of the one text reflect the shift from representational realism in Australian theatre as it developed an extended theatrical vocabulary. Even more than through its direct influence on other playwrights, in the work of directors such as Sharman and Armfield and their designers, White's adventurous dramaturgy helped provoke a new theatrical articulacy that, in turn,

Overleaf: John Wood as Theo Vokes and Melissa Jaffer as Ivy Vokes in the 1982 Lighthouse Company production of Signal Driver. *(Photographer: David Wilson.)*

JOY OF SL/X

BELONGING

has made new demands on writers. The playwrights of the age of the amateur realist theatre would have squirmed with frustration. Had a Neil Armfield directed *Shipwreck* for Louis Esson, the history of Australian playwriting might have been very different.

Netherwood

In his last two plays, White took to the new theatre like a kid let loose in a lolly shop. *Netherwood* and *Shepherd on the Rocks* are wildly theatrical and mysterious pieces, so full of excess that the effect is sometimes inadvertently comic. They mix grotesque humour with extravagantly visionary and apocalyptic speeches and images; and switch abruptly from the savage to the tender and back again. Both plays are determinedly theatrical, with their shifting and unstable representations of the world continually subverted as they slide from realism into a series of memories, fantasies and expressionist manifestations of both interior states and public (social and political) scenarios.

Netherwood is an allegory of the world reproduced in microcosm in a house, like Shaw's *Heartbreak House*—wilder and crazier but with similarly layered personal, social and political resonances. Like the 'great, damp crumbling house in which people are living' in *The Ham Funeral* (p. 15), or the Swords's mansion on the hill in *Night On Bald Mountain*, the set has huge symbolic significance, most importantly in the way in which it cuts off the outside world but also allows it to invade at the end.[10] Netherwood is 'a large, dilapidated Australian country house' (p. 99), straight out of the pastoral tradition of the station dramas and family sagas. It is presided over by Alice and Royce Best who claim to have permission from the local mental hospital to gather together and nurture some of the inmates in the hope that they can be healed through love. As the play progresses it becomes clear that Alice and Royce are themselves disturbed and on probation. The experiment is supervised by the director of the hospital, Miss Jelbart, who keeps the house under constant surveillance with the help of the sinister Dr Eberhard, and the unwanted assistance of Netherwood's self-interested interfering neighbours, Fred and Flo Stubbs.

The residents are a collection of characters who might very well be crazy but who are so disturbed by their memories and fantasies, so

5: PATRICK WHITE

unsure of their identities and so close to desperation that it is difficult not to see them as ordinary people bruised by experience and rejected by society. By the end Dora Pillbeam, who thinks she is there in her professional capacity as a music therapist, unravels completely. Mog, a lumpish, apparently retarded, woman with a knack of suddenly striking to the truth, still grieves for her baby whom she killed long ago when the priest who fathered it in the orphanage wouldn't help. There is Harry, a broken-down alcoholic ex-boxer, vicious and violent, who kept two women in separate households and abused them both. He didn't want children with either of them, but now he cherishes a sentimental father–son relationship with Royce.

All these characters have sexually transgressive relationships in almost every possible coupling. Dr Eberhard once treated both Alice and Royce and there was a sexual element in his interactions with each. Harry hates Mog, and all women, with a lustful passion. Alice and Royce are a long-married couple for whom sex has ceased to be an issue, although in one of the tender moments it surfaces again.

The core relationships are between Royce and Harry and between Mog and Alice. From the beginning it is difficult to say who looks after and supports whom. Each pair is given a fantasy scene in which they interact and play out roles from the past for each other, and in each relationship there is a homoerotic attraction.

In the apocalyptic ending the outsiders, as if in dumb outrage, drag in the police to the closed world of Netherwood and many of the characters are killed in an onstage shoot-out. Jelbart and Eberhard and Royce and Alice survive but the final line is left to the Sarge suddenly hesitant about what the operation has achieved: 'Comical bastards, us humans. Seems like we sorter *choose* ter shoot it out … to find out who's the bigger dill'. It is an image of modern warfare, like that which pervaded *Heartbreak House*.

Shepherd on the Rocks

White's last play, *Shepherd on the Rocks*, is based on the true story of a vicar in the northern English town of Stiffkey, who was thrown out of the Church for the carnal zeal with which he extended his missionary work among the whores of London. He goes on the stage,

BELONGING

finally meeting up with a circus where he is eaten by a lion. In White's extraordinary hands this bizarre tale becomes a grotesque tragedy of spirituality, the search for faith and the enduring power of love.

Stiffkey becomes Budgiwank, a seaside version of Sarsaparilla with its chorus of respectable lower-middle-class citizens, this time the congregation of Daniel Shepherd's church. Danny is an ex-vaudeville entertainer who has found God. He has a mission to spread his message of love and so travels regularly to Kings Cross to minister to prostitutes. There is something of King O'Malley in his peculiar combination of carnality and faith which is reflected in the play's mixture of vaudeville vulgarity and visionary spiritualism.[11] His great Experiment is to bring the girls and their hangers-on to Budgiwank to mingle with his congregation in the hope that each group will learn from the other.

The media catch on and the Church establishment wants to get rid of him. The Church's representative, Archbishop Bigge, a sort of alter-ego to Danny, proves to be far more corrupt than the flawed but well-meaning Danny. Bigge employs a private investigator to follow him, attempts to bribe one of the prostitutes and offers to supply her with heroin. There is also a hint that he is engaged in shady land deals. Like Danny he can explain everything he does to his own satisfaction in terms of his faith and his work. The moral implications are obvious, if a little forced: it is one thing to enjoy sex and to use it in love to further God's work ('Carnal love is not a sin if he wills us to experience it', 178) but the corrupt use of institutional and economic power to destroy a man is quite another.

Destroy him they do, however, and Danny, after a humiliating attempt to raise money for his great Experiment by embarking on a travelling roadshow, flees with his devoted, long-suffering wife Elizabeth on a long pilgrimage up the coast. They arrive eventually in Tiddler's Bay, famous in the media but for saving whales rather than souls, and then journey on to the Bay's market town, Jerusalem. The circus is in town and they meet up with several of their flock from the Experiment. Daniel enters the lion's cage and is killed.

The idiosyncratic meandering of the plot is apparently because White followed the original story quite closely.[12] Some commentators

5: PATRICK WHITE

have made grand claims for the visionary power of religious faith that lies behind Danny's hypocritical and absurd behaviour.[13] These claims are supported by several typical White touches that go some way towards turning a tale of sexual conquest and betrayal into a spiritual quest. The two prostitutes, Queenie and Bell, not only genuinely love Danny but, as well as enjoying the sexual side, find nourishment in the spiritual side of his love and his promise of God's love (pp. 182–5). Elizabeth, resigned and devoted, follows him to Jerusalem, seeing her love for both his vision and his weaknesses as part of what her Christian faith demands of her (p. 210).

Most importantly, Danny is given three key speeches in which he struggles to explain his vision: an interior monologue as he travels on the train to Kings Cross to meet his fallen women (p. 178); a sermon to the mixed congregation of the Experiment (p. 195–6); and a final speech to his circus audience, another sermon really, just before his death (p. 229). Each of these is full of the ambivalence and complexity that White had been exploring since 1947, when the Young Man in *The Ham Funeral* tried to reconcile the challenges of the flesh in the basement with the glimpses of the spirit in his room upstairs. Danny might be that same Young Man forty years later: still childish and self-obsessed but with a more developed vision of the healing power of loving-kindness, a vision based in both faith and experience; still a bit of a prick perhaps but at least he has battled to understand himself and tried to understand and to help others; still an egomaniac but one who has turned out towards the greater social world from which he would like to, but cannot, hide.

The Ham Funeral and *The Season at Sarsaparilla* end more or less optimistically with their young men going out into life like Stephen Dedalus at the end of Joyce's *Portrait of the Artist as a Young Man*. White's subsequent plays explore what they find there and end in the creative individual's defeat, at the hands of either the drably conformist or the venally materialist social and political world. In the final moments, though, there tends to be a flicker of spiritual optimism. Miss Docker is pissed on by an avatar of God but she struggles back to the Sundown Home to pray again. Stella Summerhayes falls—or jumps, or is pushed—off her cliff but Miss Quodling is left behind

BELONGING

to dream of a post-apocalyptic world in which 'the silence will breed again' (p. 356). The Vokes survive fifty years of living with their demons and each other. As the material city rises around them, they are left emotionally destitute, but at the end the Aurora swells above them to invade the theatre 'like a visible projection of love'.[14]

In the last two plays the endings turn darker and more grotesque, but there is still a hint of old man White's enduring hope. The comic carnage at the end of *Netherwood* concludes with the Sarge's sudden doubt. After Danny's death at the end of *Shepherd on the Rocks* his three women gather together round his body like the three Marys. Tilda Scutt, an old woman of Tiddlers Bay who likes to feed people, expresses a faint hope that Danny might rise again.

Danny's final sermon to the circus crowd has often been quoted. Both White's biographer David Marr, and his most sympathetic critic May-Brit Akerholt use its opening line as a type of obituary: 'Are you for magic? I am'. If any other playwright had written it, the ensuing speech would be called a theatrically incoherent shambles, but it represents well White's great achievement in the Australian theatre—to fracture the artificiality of its old genres and forms and open them up to fresh ideas, innovative styles and a new concern with the transcendent.

6
PLAYWRIGHTS IN THE 60S

Dorothy Hewett

More than any other playwright, Dorothy Hewett picked up White's style, passion and interests. Her first play appeared three years after *Night on Bald Mountain* and she was still writing up until her death in 2002. Hewett was a poet and had written a novel when her first plays appeared.[1] Politically she was in the tradition of the red witches (a term she coined) such as Katharine Susannah Prichard. But she was always an original—an unconventional communist until she teamed up with Les Flood and lived with him for nine years in the slums of Redfern, Sydney, doing Party work and having babies. Flood thought that her writing was a bourgeois indulgence and burned much of it except for *Bobbin' Up*, a factory novel based on her experiences in Redfern, which appeared in 1959 and was a success. But she had much more in store for her theatre audiences, who for most of her writing career were divided in their responses between enthusiasm and revulsion.

She shares with White a passionate conviction that the impulses of the flesh are more important to an understanding of life than the tortuous workings of the rational mind; and an urgent interest in the creative individual's search for an identity—both in a visionary

BELONGING

struggle against the forces and effects of social and political authority and, in her case, the simpler but more immediate forces of male and female passions and drives. Her playwriting, like White's, is vividly theatrical, drawing on a broad and eclectic range of styles and forms, from vaudeville through Brechtian expressionism to realism. Her plays are full of poetry, songs, dances, fights and moments when the immediacy of raw experience suddenly brings her flights of passion back to earth with a thud—sex, birth, death; a menopausal flooding, a botched abortion, a suicide's bathtub full of blood. Her language is always heightened and poetic, and much more seductive than White's—drenched in sensuality, sometimes violent, often tender, always lyrical, and continually invaded by visions, memories and a passionate resistance to growing old.

Like White she was way ahead of her time, and perhaps still is, at least in the mainstream theatre. 'It's not so much that we're repelled by the thought of having menstrual blood flowing onstage', said one observer. 'It's her language. It is literary rather than dramatic. She relies on inner action and to get this across to audiences, you need actors with incredible energy.'[2] We have seen such actors in the recent productions of White's plays, as well as directors and designers with the theatrical language to do such bold plays. If you can do White, you can certainly do Hewett.

Her first play, *This Old Man Comes Rolling Home*, was inspired, ironically, by her experience of seeing performances of *Summer of the Seventeenth Doll* and *The Shifting Heart*, 'the only bourgeois thing I [did] in those nine years of living with [Flood]'. She started it in 1957, though it only appeared ten years later. A belated member of the *Doll* school of slum realism, set in the poor inner-city Sydney suburb of Redfern, it chronicles the struggles of the Dockerty family to survive poverty and a string of its attendant disasters and to realise some of their visions for a better life. The mother Laurie dreams of the days when she was the privileged Belle of Bundaberg but is sunk for most of the play in alcoholic oblivion. Her husband Tom dreams of a communist revolution and drags his 13-year-old daughter Joycee around the streets at night to paint revolutionary slogans on the walls. He settles in the end for simply getting his job back. Their tough but

6: PLAYWRIGHTS IN THE 60S

sensitive daughter Julie dreams of a good man who will value her abilities but the only one she loves is a drifter who leaves her. Edie, an outsider from the nearby suburb of Surry Hills, marries the Dockerty's son Lan and dreams of a house in the suburbs, but settles finally for life in Redfern supporting the family she has married into. There are many other characters—a mixture of small-time criminals, losers and no-hopers—whose stories are sketched in this rich play. One of the saddest is the English immigrant Fay, who has fled the slums of East London. Julie meets her while fruit-picking in Tasmania and brings her back to stay. In Redfern she meets the spiviest of boys, gets pregnant, is abandoned by him, and flees to die in a pool of blood in a cheap hotel after attempting a self-abortion.

On its initial appearance in Sydney one critic called it 'old, old-fashioned', just ten years after its subject had been hailed as the new way forward for Australian drama. But the play is not a piece of well-made slum realism: the dialogue is richly poetic, full of songs and poems that heighten its realism, it has a trio of old Redfern women who have nothing to do with the plot but who function like a lyrical chorus, and it has a mysteriously wise old derro who sleeps under newspapers on a bench outside the Dockerty house—'Old Father Time, perhaps' (p. 3). It shows a playwright trying to work within a genre but with a talent too large for it.

Angry at the dull response to her first play, Hewett reacted shortly afterwards with a new play intended to shock. *Mrs Porter and the Angel* was first produced in Sydney in 1969 but not published until 1992, in the first volume of her *Collected Plays*. It is a wildly extravagant and formally eclectic play but its dominant style is expressionism. The story deals with the intertwined lives of a small, mostly academic community of lonely people living in Circe Circle, a suburban cul-de-sac of houses with dark secrets behind their facades. Mrs Porter is an alcoholic drama lecturer who teaches Chekhov's *The Cherry Orchard* and wanders the street with her imaginary friend, a dog called Angel who has been killed on the road but whom she still cherishes. Her husband Edgar, twenty years her junior, is, like Professor Sword in White's *Night on Bald Mountain*, a distant intellectual figure who rejects her sensuality. In one of the most

BELONGING

confronting scenes in the play, he humiliates her for wanting him. An aging gay couple, Burke and Will, have a secret represented by the mysterious Tatty Hollow, who they keep locked in their broom cupboard. Tatty is a surreal figure, a universal whore on a pedestal, whom all the characters have desired. Hewett later devotes an entire play to her. There's Wendy and Peter—a woman with deep longings and a husband who won't satisfy them. And looming unseen in the background is the sinister Professor Shaddow—to whose house the action leads in a final comic-horror *Walpurgisnacht* in which deep passions come to the surface.

But this is to extract plot details from what is really a theatrical extravaganza—a glorious celebration of the libido and other bodily urges and failures, with lots of obscenity, grotesquely comic violence and blood. Will's mother arrives, like an untrammelled Miss Docker, to torture him with her violent nurturing; Wendy roasts her baby and serves it up to her husband for dinner; Mrs Porter, after her humiliation by Edgar, finally confronts her father, the Vice-Chancellor of the university. He had been sexually abusing her for twenty years before she encountered Edgar and, wanting him, got him a job. Two characters, Girlsie and Boysee, who represent students, function as a chorus linking the scenes. Girlsie says at the first segue: 'I like *The Cherry Orchard* better ... it's well-written'. (p. 95)

It would all be like a particularly lurid daytime soap opera if it weren't for the wonderfully poetic transformation of everyday language; the highly theatrical staging—with songs, music, dance, and carnivalesque scenes of transgression; and above all the grand mocking array of different theatrical styles—from slapstick vaudeville to expressionist nightmare.

One continuing theme is the destructive but needy emotional distance of the men, and the sometimes abject yet still passionate engagement, and occasionally glorious defiance, of the women— especially Mrs Porter and her alter ego Tatty. This became a theme in Hewett's first, intensely personal period as a dramatist in the plays *The Chapel Perilous, Bon-Bons and Roses for Dolly, Catspaw, The Tatty Hollow Story, Joan, The Beautiful Mrs Portland* and *The Golden Oldies*. These plays represent an extraordinary range of forms—from

6: PLAYWRIGHTS IN THE 60S

the epic musical *Joan* to the well-made realistic melodrama of *The Beautiful Mrs Portland*—but all of them contain a romantic quest, a modern female version of the wandering medieval knight. The most famous (and notorious) is Sally Banner from her best-known, most often revived (at least in amateur and university productions) and most successful play, *The Chapel Perilous*. Sally is the most complete evocation of the wildly romantic, sexual, visionary, feminine, rebellious and subversive character that many early critics and audiences took, with some justification, to be Hewett's representation of herself. Dolly, Tatty, Joan, and the offstage figure of Becca in *The Golden Oldies*, one of her best plays of this early period, can all be seen as versions of Sally. In the 1970s, Hewett was criticised by male and female critics alike for this apparently autobiographical element in her work while equally autobiographical male writers such as David Williamson were not.[3]

The Chapel Perilous is a remarkable play. In 1971, on the crest of the male New Wave, it was the first Australian play to exploit the new theatricality without losing richly poetic language; and the first to create characters who were placed in their time and social milieu but were also mythic and unconstrained by the everyday realism of the tradition. Its nearest contemporary male equivalent is Jack Hibberd's 1972 one-man play *A Stretch of the Imagination*. By contrast, *The Chapel Perilous* has eleven named characters and a huge collection of chorus and crowd figures. Its roots are in English Elizabethan drama and it was written for Marshall Clifton's New Fortune theatre on the campus of the University of Western Australia, a theatre modelled on the dimensions of Edward Alleyn's 1600 Fortune Theatre in London. It is full of poems, songs, theatrical show-pieces and lyrical heightened speech. It stands now like a bridge over the New Wave, linking the vision of Patrick White to the post-naturalistic, epic work of 1980s writers such as Louis Nowra and Stephen Sewell.

An iconic image from the play is of Sally Banner, wearing her long golden hair like armour as she approaches the chapel perilous and confronts the world. Early on, as a rebellious schoolgirl, she confronts masked figures of institutional authority with a defiant assertion of

BELONGING

her individuality which later leads her into a great deal of trouble. It also reveals her vulnerability, resilience and strength—her ability to 'walk naked through the world'. The play is partly the story of one woman's journey through the mid twentieth century, from the outbreak of World War II (with flashbacks to the older world of her stitched-up parents) to the rebellions of the late 1960s, when the relations between the personal and the political became public rhetoric. But for Sally these relations are always a private quest. The defiant girl who refuses to bow at the altar at the beginning, becomes a communist agitator, and then a member of the Light That Failed generation. Stalin's betrayal of communism leaves her bereft—for Sally losing communism is like losing a lover. A wild scene of political carnival at the beginning of Act 2 turns, after various revelations and developments in her personal life, into an expressionist courtroom scene in which her political activism is put on trial and tied in with her personal rebellion.

The main movement of the play follows Sally's personal rebellion—especially her hungry, half-abject and half-defiant response to, and treatment of, the succession of her lovers whose stories drive the plot: Judith, her first love, the cool, life-denying girl at school who eventually becomes one of the Authority figures; Michael, the rough man who never offers her warmth but to whom she keeps returning for his brutal honesty and sexual energy; the nice but dry boy David; the husband Thomas, devoted but dull; and the inspiring party-political agitator Saul. She lies down with them all, and then gets up and leaves them, one by one, or is left by them, to pursue her own sense of truth—her faith in, and hope for, herself.

Sally, and the visionary, sexually rapacious women of Hewett's later plays, attracted criticism from some second-wave feminists in the 1970s, for their dependence on men and their consciousness of their abjection. But they have survived in the post-second-wave feminist world as women with a defiantly politicised sexuality. Every boy wants Sally, and she wants them. She seeks a new type of independence that will allow her to escape the old power dependencies without having to give up sex with the thrilling enemy.

The Chapel Perilous has inspired generations of young women who

6: PLAYWRIGHTS IN THE 60S

have identified with Sally and written to Hewett telling her so.[4] Sally's glorious embodiment of divine whore, bitch goddess, political agitator and romantic dreamer has endured through the transformations of feminism since the early 1970s. Walking naked, crying to herself, bruised, resilient, visionary and proud, Sally Banner is one of the great survivors.

The musical play *Joan* (1984) also portrays the romantic feminine quest. It is a contemporised, musical version of the Joan of Arc story that divides its multi-faceted heroine into four separate characters—Peasant Joan, Soldier Joan, Witch Joan and Saint Joan. They run the quest like a relay race. Each Joan likes what she's achieved but is forced to hand on the baton to the next one, as the quest continues in the face of changing authoritarian pressures and personal traumas. The composite Joan is by turns a struggler, a fighter, a whore and, finally, a complete rebel, perhaps even a saint. Near the end the Witch Joan tells one of her inquisitors, 'I'm a threat to your rules, the security of your lives. I try to bring about justice and love on earth and it's dangerous, because it's different'. (p. 66)

Bon-Bons and Roses For Dolly (1972) and *The Tatty Hollow Story* (1974) are two grandly theatrical and lyrical plays that celebrate the dreams of passionately rebellious women such as Sally Banner and Joan. *Bon-Bons and Roses for Dolly* is a bitter-sweet musical extravaganza full of wonderfully detailed nostalgia for the lives, dreams and failures of three generations of women and their men in provincial Western Australia. Their lives are recalled and romanticised in memory, filtered through old movies, washed in the glow of movie lights, and accompanied by the tunes of an old cinema organ that rises from the pit like a ghost from the past. The play's structure charts the rise and fall of the Crystal Palace movie parlour—a place of dreams and disillusionment which still survives in Perth. Like all Hewett's plays it is about starting young, growing old and then being young again. It shifts constantly between the glitteringly theatrical and the darkly disillusioned. Along the way there is an earthiness—a romantic elegy for the dreams and beauties of youth combined with a vivid enthusiasm for the basics of life, and a sadness at their loss, however sordid and desperate they might have been.

BELONGING

The Tatty Hollow Story is a darker play, taking the Tatty of *Mrs Porter and the Angel* and turning her into a mythic, mysteriously absent figure. For most of the play she is represented on stage by a glamorous but frozen mannequin in a telephone booth. A collection of ex-lovers gather to come to terms with what Tatty might have meant to them. She appears to be haunting them all, as her name starts to appear in mysterious graffiti throughout the city. As they try to recall her none of their memories agree, especially with regard to a strange figure named P. Laureate. Several men claim him as their son, and say Tatty has since taken him as a lover. At last, as the play ends, we meet what may now be the 'real' Tatty, an old bag lady who, like Sydney's notorious Bea Miles, sells Shakespeare recitations on the streets, and who, yes, paints her name up on the walls of the city. Perhaps she has finally found her voice.

Pandora's Cross (1978) is a theatrically extravagant play, in the style of *Bon-Bons and Roses for Dolly* and *The Tatty Hollow Story*, about bohemian life in Sydney's Kings Cross. *The Golden Oldies* (1977) is an achingly beautiful, classically simple play written for two women performers and two male mannequins, who sit immobile in a stylised suburban living room behind a scrim. They are like frozen reminders of the sets of the urban and suburban realist dramas that White and Hewett were leaving behind. The play explores the lives of three generations of women, as in their different ways they mourn and celebrate the passing of the previous. In each case a grotesque nurse-figure, like Miss Docker in White's *A Cheery Soul*, aggressively presides over the passing. The women are also haunted by a wild, Sally-like character, Becca, who never appears but who dominates the play, defiantly committing suicide at the end and dying in a bathtub full of blood.

The radio play, *Susannah's Dreaming* (1980), is a highly lyrical evocation of the lonely life of a yearning young girl who lives by the sea with her mother and who falls in love with a romantic abalone diver. It has the fable-like resonances of an ancient Greek myth. Hewett's two poetic plays for children, *Golden Valley* (1981) and *Song of the Seals* (1983) also draw on myths, the latter transposing a darker version of mermaid stories, the half-human and half-seal Celtic Selchie, to an Australian seaside setting.

6: PLAYWRIGHTS IN THE 60S

In nationally publicised libel suits *The Chapel Perilous* and one of Hewett's poems 'Uninvited Guest' were the subject of a legal storm in the 1970s and their sale was prohibited in Western Australia.[5] So it was amidst much controversy that Hewett was commissioned by Perth's National Theatre to write a play for the West Australian sesquicentennial celebrations of 1979. The result, *The Man From Mukinupin*, was a gloriously bipolar celebration of life in an emblematic wheat-belt town east of the rabbit-proof fence during and just after the First World War. The theatrical and musical style of the play draws not only on the rural comedy-dramas of the early twentieth century, but also on nineteenth-century theatre, when travelling players were left to fend for themselves after the collapse of the old touring circuits. It tells, in a fine pastiche, the story of a romantic young couple, Jack Tuesday and Polly Perkins, and their battles with their respectable small town parents, a story straight out of the ancient Greek New Comedy via Shakespeare. Alongside this couple, and played by the same actors, are their doppelgangers from the dark side of town, Jack's brother Harry Tuesday and Polly's half sister, Lily Perkins. Lily is Polly's father's bastard child by a black woman from the camps, just as in the old dramas of the 1930s and 1940s. The town calls her Touch-of-the-Tar. The interplay between the two stories brings to light a vengeful and savage massacre of the blacks that still haunts the town.

The play combines these two worlds in a harvest festival fantasia, presided over by Clarry and Clemmy Hummer, a chorus of two old show-business crones who unite the light and the dark. On the day side there is a splendidly comic collection of earnest country types: Polly's father the storekeeper Eek Perkins and his wife Edie; and Cecil, a clumsy travelling salesman whose toupee keeps falling off and who loves Polly but hasn't got a chance. On the other side is a group of characters who only come out at night: Jack and Harry's weird mother, the Widow Tuesday; Eek's crazed brother Zeek; and the Flasher, a cheerfully sinister character who prowls the town doing what flashers do and briefly scaring pretty Polly. Jack and Harry both enlist to fight in the War. On their return, Jack is welcomed by the community, while Harry, the dark troubled hero, comes back shell-shocked and takes to the bush.

BELONGING

In some splendidly comic scenes the travelling players Max and Mercy Montebello give a performance of their show, 'The Strangling of Desdemona'. After a brief entanglement with them, Jack and Polly go off to become stars with JCW's, while Harry and Lily leave for the back country together. Cecil gives up on Polly and marries Mercy and they open up a fish-and-chip shop in Mukinupin. It is, finally, a happy play in which Hewett sets aside the personal quest of her earlier work and creates a joyous celebration of rural Australian life, in which the dark side still lurks.

Hewett found her voice as a theatrical poet in the 1970s but with *Man from Mukinupin*, she embarked on a new phase as a writer of celebratory community plays. *The Fields of Heaven*, another rural play, explored the decline through bad management and greed of a long-established pastoral property. In 2002, as a vehicle for his graduating students, National Institute of Dramatic Art director John Clark produced a condensed version of *Jarrabin*, an unproduced epic trilogy that Hewett had written in the late 1990s about life in another imaginary WA wheat-belt town. Her last play, commissioned by Aubrey Mellor for Melbourne's Playbox Theatre in the year before she died, was *Nowhere* (2001), another visionary fable of Australian life. In this play three social outcasts—Josh, an old communist derelict; Blue, a disturbed Vietnam veteran and Vonnie, a young Aboriginal reformed heroin addict fleeing her pimp and dealer—meet and find some comfort living together in the decayed old showground of a small town. At the end an apocalyptic flood threatens the fragile and embattled community that they have managed to create for themselves. Blue and Vonnie flee deeper into the outback to search for a place named 'Nowhere' (a name that Hewett once saw on a road sign in the Nullarbor Desert) where they might find peace. Josh cannot leave his hard-won 'home' and is swept away in the flood. It is, by Hewett's standards, a simple, small-scale drama, but like her larger scale works it manages to draw on decades of Australian social and political history and focus them in an intensely personal story told with poetic vision.

6: PLAYWRIGHTS IN THE 60S

Peter Kenna

Peter Kenna was part of, but not central to, the waves of both the 1950s and the 1970s. His *The Slaughter of St Teresa's Day* has already been discussed in relation to the *Doll* School. His most successful play, *A Hard God*, was one of Nimrod Theatre's greatest productions at the height of the New Wave. But Kenna's 'quiet, self-effacing talent', as one critic described it, did not sit easily with the exuberant self-confidence of the younger writers.[6] His plays are concerned with the personal isolation of his characters, none of whom manage to connect in a satisfying way with the people they live with, nor with those with whom they fall in love. Any brief fleeting moments of intimacy serve to underline their loneliness. Families are battlefields of conflicting loyalties, intimacies fail, the God that they feel obliged to love is no real help and sexual closeness is a constant source of anxiety and guilt. These were not New Wave issues or values.

Talk to the Moon (1963) is a grim drama about a family that is tearing itself apart in a quiet, steady, everyday kind of a way. Individual pairs have close ties that keep breaking. As a group they are incapable of offering lasting companionship to one another but they somehow manage to battle on as a family. In *Trespassers Will Be Prosecuted* a fight between lonely individuals becomes a theatrical metaphor for intimacy. A closed-off culvert under a railway line gives the drama a vividly symbolic setting. In this secret hideaway, a disturbed young rich boy keeps insects, birds and animals in jars and cages and sadistically feeds them to each other. When an old derelict alcoholic falls into the culvert, the boy keeps him too and tortures him, psychologically. Finally, however, they have a brief moment of closeness during which they acknowledge each other's vulnerability.

Listen Closely (1972) is a cheerful country-town comedy, rich in the comedy of recognition of its time. Local lore requires every father to buy his son his first beer on his eighteenth birthday and see he lays the barmaid Flora who cheerfully raffles herself every Friday night to raise money for the local hospital. But Henry, returned from university with girlfriend Lesley in tow has other values. In a farcical battle of the sexes, Flora, Lesley and Henry's termagant mother Lily, wreak havoc

BELONGING

on the men while the pub starts to collapse, literally, around them.

Mates (1975), a play more in the spirit of the 1970s, explores the connections between four disparate characters—an old shearer, a former prostitute and now cleaner, a drag queen and her secret boyfriend, a macho football star. The shearer uses his old-fashioned vision of bush mateship to try to come to terms with the relationship between the two gay men. When the latter go off to patch up their troubled relationship he and the cleaner wearily shake their heads at the mystery of youthful sexual passion.

Kenna's most important work is *The Cassidy Album*, a trilogy of plays built around *A Hard God* (1973), one of the great comic realist dramas in the repertoire, much loved by audiences, studied in schools and often revived, most recently by the Sydney Theatre Company in 2006. The role of Aggie in the original Nimrod production was played by Gloria Dawn, a variety and musical comedy star, born into a circus family that went back six generations on both sides, who first appeared on stage when she was three. (Her first dramatic role was Oola Maguire which Kenna had asked her to take on in a revival of *The Slaughter of St Teresa's Day* the previous year.) Her performance as Aggie, one of the greatest battling Mum figures of the realist dramatic tradition, played for Nimrod, one of the most successful larrikin theatres of the early 1970s, underlined the eclecticism of the New Wave.

A Hard God is set in the western suburbs of Sydney in 1946 in the home of a struggling Irish-Australian working-class couple. Aggie and Dan Cassidy have survived the Depression and a great deal of hardship. They are sustained by their love for each other, despite a lot of family disruption. Dan and his brothers Martin and Paddy are dispossessed bushies, who were driven by a long drought off the land that their father had worked. They have spent years wandering and learning the legend of the bush before meeting up again in the city. Martin is a dreamer and Paddy a loser. They both need Dan, who is desperately ill but always ready, with Aggie's help, to pick up the pieces of their troubled lives.

The play has two lines of action: the story of Aggie and Dan and their eccentric relatives; and the story of their son Joe, a lonely 16-year-old struggling to come to terms with his budding homosexuality,

6: PLAYWRIGHTS IN THE 60S

in an anguished relationship with his friend Jack Shannon. Jack, after what for him is obviously just an adolescent fling, finally dumps Joe, leaving him numb with grief.

The story of the older generation sets the tragi-comic adventures of Dan's brothers against the quiet domestic tragedy of Dan's illness and Aggie's loving stoicism. Martin, who has fled from his obsessive-neurotic wife Monica, to become a labourer and anti-communist union organiser, is found dead. After his death Monica, a religious fanatic, goes quietly, comically mad. Paddy's wild wife, Sophie, gets drunk, goes on an insane gambling spree and chases Paddy through the streets of Sydney threatening to slice him up with a razor. In the midst of all this chaos Aggie finally learns, from a doctor in the hospital corridor, that Dan has a fatal cancer. She flees. When Joe later suggests that she should have listened to the details she finally rebels:

> AGGIE: I don't believe it! I don't believe any of it! How *could* I believe such a thing? Why, I might just as well believe the ground was going to open up and swallow me.
> JOE: You might have to believe it.
> AGGIE: I won't! I won't! At least ... not yet. (p. 88)

Aggie is the stronger character but Joe Cassidy became the central character of the trilogy. In *Furtive Love* he is 24, and an actor, working with a small travelling theatre company. He is still a virgin and agonising about whether or not to accept his sexuality and succumb to the advances of his best friend's lover. In *An Eager Hope* he is 35, seriously ill with a kidney disease, battling to become a successful playwright, but abject in his love for a man whose sexual interests obviously lie elsewhere. Aggie reappears as an old woman, but still tough and sympathetic. The play also introduces Francis, Joe's rascally brother, whose lying Irish charm is like a throwback to Martin and Paddy, his uncles. At the end of the play Francis has a spectacularly unjust gambling success, winning an unlikely fortune on a horse race using stolen money. Meanwhile Joe is sacked from his theatre company and admitted to hospital. The impact is of a monstrous practical joke played on Joe by the God with whom he has been so obsessed for so long.

BELONGING

Hal Porter

A final playwright of the 1960s is another gay writer, Hal Porter, who wrote two genre plays with their roots in the old commercial theatre. Porter's plays had some impact because he was a well-known prose writer. *The Tower* had some influence when it was published in H. G. Kippax's successful and often reprinted 1963 anthology *Three Australian Plays*, which also included Alan Seymour's *The One Day of the Year* and Douglas Stewart's *Ned Kelly*. It is a grand historical drama, full of narrative excess, set in convict Hobart in the 1850s, with an extravagant plot underpinned by a lurking sexuality. *The Professor* is queerer—an old-fashioned strong drama with an exotic setting and a hidden sexual–political agenda. Today it reads like a closeted gay play, but even if outed it would still be controversial, with its highly exploitative triangular relationship between Gilbert, a cruel Anglo-Australian professor living in Japan; Toda Inagaki, a pretty boy who is his pupil and acolyte; and Fusehime, a young woman who adores Toda and prostitutes herself to a series of Western visitors in order to supply him with cash to buy expensive presents for Gilbert. It comes across now as a highly misogynistic play.

We have seen how, in his satires of suburbia in *The Season at Sarsaparilla* and *A Cheery Soul*, Patrick White anticipated the spirit of the New Wave. Mona Brand and the satirical political revues produced by Sydney's New Theatre from the 1940s also helped to lay down the basics of the rough-theatre style of the early 1970s. So, too, did the Philip Street revues in Sydney in the 1950s, which developed into the successful 1960s television series *The Mavis Bramston Show*. But the most important influence in the 1960s on what was to become the new nationalist larrikin drama of the 1970s was the meteoric rise of a character who outlived them all. After the New Wave, she went on to become a media superstar, but her origins were in rural Victoria where she was created in 1955 in the back of a bus.

6: PLAYWRIGHTS IN THE 60S

Barry Humphries

The bus belonged to the touring Union Theatre Repertory Company and on it, touring *Twelfth Night*, in which he played Orsino—very badly by all accounts including his own—was the young Barry Humphries. In between stops he entertained his fellow actors with an impersonation of the lady mayoresses who in each town greeted them with tea, tiny cakes and speeches. Humphries wanted company members Zoë Caldwell or June Jago to play the character on stage in *Return Fare*, a UTRC end-of-year revue, but they urged him to do it himself. And so, as they say, a legend was born—Edna Everage.

The following year, Humphries released Edna's first record, *Wild Life in Suburbia*. On the B side he introduced his other great character, Sandy Stone, who represented the poignant dimension of the satire. Several years later when he was living in London, he wrote a comic strip with cartoonist Nicholas Garland for *Private Eye* magazine about the adventures of an Australian innocent abroad in the wilds of 1960s London and Barry ('Bazza') McKenzie entered the scene.

Edna, Sandy and Bazza established the peculiar mixture of celebration and self-mockery that marked the nationalism of the New Wave. Humphries's delight in reproducing and, more usually, inventing a colourful idiomatic language for his characters, introduced a vernacular style that Jack Hibberd, Alex Buzo and David Williamson later exploited for a range of dramatic purposes. His characters' speech entered the language, in that odd combination of aspiration and linguistic incompetence at the heart of catchphrases such as Edna's 'Excuse I!' and 'I mean that in a nice way!' (after a particularly offensive remark); or Sandy's 'I had a bit of trouble parking the vehicle' and 'It was a very nice night's entertainment', which he applies to a series of utterly banal activities in his first monologue, *Days of the Week*. 'A nice night's entertainment' became a slogan and it was the title of Humphries's first solo show in 1962 and also his first volume of collected scripts, published in 1981 by Currency Press as a sort of classic plays anthology, with historical notes by Humphries himself.

Humphries' exultant invention of a whole new language, alternately cringing and strutting, found its New Wave expression in Alex Buzo's

BELONGING

Norm and Ahmed. Norm's confused feelings of inadequacy and aggression are so challenged by his late-night confrontation with the educated, well-spoken Pakistani student Ahmed that before bashing him he feels obliged to explain himself. He's a foreman in a factory (but 'I wear a white collar under me dustcoat') who spends a lot of time in the office 'rectifying a few anomalies'.

Barry McKenzie was based on a character created in 1960, Buster Thompson, and also on two monologues about young men drunkenly vomiting, with accompanying songs, from the 1964 show *Excuse I*. Bazza became a star when some of his adventures were recorded in two tribute movies made at the height of the New Wave. In the second of these, *Barry McKenzie Holds His Own* in 1974, Edna was made a Dame by Prime Minister Gough Whitlam, a surprise that she seized on with malicious glee and turned into a new international career gimmick.

For the original character of Bazza McKenzie, Humphries invented a whole new surreally ocker language that was so convincing and comically attractive that a generation grew up thinking of it as its own. When Bazza went to the toilet he 'pointed Percy at the porcelain' and so, therefore, did many hip young Australian men in the late 1960s. His obsession with sinking a few Fosters and having a quick chunder before scoring a root (he usually only succeeded in the first two) became part of a new mythology, a Bahktinian carnival of excess for a generation of educated sons of ocker who wanted to enjoy, and at the same time challenge, their heritage. Humphries's characters and their language introduced a new irony to Australian popular culture—the irony of aggressively asserting what you lack—although Humphries added an element of supercilious disdain. They have their descendants in the Melbourne comedy boom of the late 1970s and 1980s and postmodern ironic comedians such as Roy Slaven and H. G. Nelson (performed by John Doyle and Greig Pickhaver) in the 1990s. But Bazza's spirit first animated vernacular plays such as Hibberd's *White With Wire Wheels* and Williamson's *The Coming of Stork*—two of the great subversions of the old high culture from the late 1960s.

Earlier that decade Humphries had introduced a range of characters who set the model for many New Wave stereotypes, but who were

6: PLAYWRIGHTS IN THE 60S

created with decidedly more comic malice. Humphries emigrated to England in 1959, returning only to tour shows or promote his career, yet he continued to draw on Australia for his material, relying increasingly on locally-based research assistants to supply the vocabulary and the detail.[7]

Debbie Thwaite, created in 1960, is a female Bazza, an Australian girl in London so obsessed with the details of flat-sharing in Earl's Court, then an Australian ghetto, and with gossip about her visiting Australian friends, that she is scarcely aware that she is no longer in Melbourne. Morrie Tate, in 1962, is a pretentious beatnik, and an antecedent of other characters through which Humphries satirised 1960s rebels. One of these was Big Sonia, in 1968, a stupid but passionately committed protest singer who wants to go to Vietnam and sing for the Aussie troops but only if Viet Cong troops can be in the audience as well. She oozes unctuous care and commitment. ('I sing a song of suffering/ Of agony and pain/ And if you haven't suffered/ I'll sing my song again.') Neil Singleton, who first appeared in 1965, and returned in 1974, is a narcissistic, hypocritical left-wing academic anxious to be fashionably rebellious long before the invention of the term 'radical chic'. Martin Agrippa is an equally pretentious and self-obsessed alternative filmmaker. A 1968 sketch included the screening of a parody of an 'underground' short film, directed by a young Bruce Beresford, which Humphries claims was taken for real and acclaimed as a masterpiece at several international film festivals.[8]

In the early 1960s Humphries also began what was to become a series of 'fat cat' characters satirising the beneficiaries of the burgeoning cultural nationalism that had begun in the mid-1950s and reached a pinnacle in the Whitlam years of the early 1970s. These characters were still spending taxpayers' money on world trips, luxury hotels and nubile young 'escorts' and 'research assistants' well into the 1990s.

Their forerunner, in 1962, was a sinister unnamed Orwellian character who claimed to be the Minister for National Identity, announcing a program to 'scientifically and, if necessary, surgically' implant every expatriate Australian with the new 'official Oz–Image' (p. 63). Rex Lear, created in 1968, is a nouveau-riche businessman, drunkenly outrageous at his daughter's wedding, dimly aware that she loathes his vulgarity but is quite prepared to spend his money.

Lance Boyle is the corrupt and venal general secretary of a powerful trade union, with the acronym ACUNT, who is capable of bringing the nation to its knees whenever he wants to prevent his wife from getting home in time to catch him with his secretary. Morrie O'Connor is a media-savvy car salesman who has turned his attention to the art world, with his Magic Mile of Masterpieces.

Humphries's most popularly successful character in this vein, Sir Les Patterson, first appeared in 1974 but came into his own in the 1980s and 1990s as a monstrous Aristophanic clown, with a huge phallus that he kept fondling, a gargantuan appetite for drink and sex, and a comical line of patter about Australian cultural achievements. He claims to have been, back in the 1960s, the Federal Minister for Shark Conservation. He served in the Whitlam government in the early 1970s and learned to love what he calls 'the Yartz'. Fat (or 'ventripotent', as Humphries likes to put it) and drunkenly complacent, he also once sat on the Cheese Board. In the fiction of the Les Patterson routines Prime Minister Gough Whitlam finally appoints him, in the twilight of a venal political career, Cultural Attaché to the Court of St James. The Queen of Australia, 'Betty Windsor', knights him. When she touches him on the shoulder with her royal sword he bids his past farewell with 'Stuff Socialism! Are you with me?' (p. 181).

In all these characters Humphries exults in his love of banal detail. Many of his sketches are a litany of names of products, brands, streets, suburbs and other obscure minutiae of Australian suburban life. He does lists like a comically deranged folklorist. The shock of recognition element in his humour seems sometimes to be the act of an anthropologist of suburbia gone feral.

This obsession began with his greatest character, Sandy Stone, a dry wisp of a suburban man, with a thin, high-pitched sibilant voice—the result of ill-fitting dentures—and a slow, quiet way of reporting on the everyday details of his quiet life. Humphries has said that Sandy is the *adagio* movement in his otherwise hyped-up, physically and musically energetic solo performances. He originally created the character as a Dadaist exercise 'to see how unutterably boring one could be, and

6: PLAYWRIGHTS IN THE 60S

for how long, before an audience would rise in revolt', in an attempt to provoke his audience 'into some kind of confrontation with their lives'.[9]

Sandy simply sits there on stage—in pyjamas and dressing-gown in his old Genoa velvet armchair clutching his hot-water bottle, always about to go to bed with a mug of hot Milo—and talks on and on about the very ordinary events of his humdrum existence. The comic point is that he has no idea of how profoundly dull he is. To him life is a constant buzz of frenetic activity. He whizzes, in his own mind, from one 'nice night's entertainment' to the next. His supposedly devoted wife Beryl has clearly lost interest in him years ago. She eventually goes off on a *Women's Weekly* World Discovery Cruise, during which he dies, although in no way does this put an end to his relentless capacity for reflection.

Created in 1958, Sandy continues still to haunt Humphries's shows, appearing as recently as 2007 in *Back with a Vengeance*. For half a century he has sailed on, through the chaos of an unexamined life, oblivious of Beryl's passions and regrets. He is the ultimate dull dumb nice guy, undisturbed even by his own demise. He has one of the great lines in Australian drama, at the beginning of 'Sandy Soldiers On', in 1978: 'I am deceased. With the resultant consequence that there has been a considerable change in my lifestyle…'[10]

Sandy is a Beckettian figure, comic but ineffably sad, created with a compassion that the usually malicious Humphries exhibits in no other character. As Clive James wrote, Sandy seems to be the one character on whom Humphries does not want to take revenge. 'To Sandy, and to Sandy alone, he is fair.'[11]

Such is Humphries's comic genius as a performer, that the inspired tedium of Sandy's monologues illustrates the old saw that some performers can get laughs reading from the telephone directory. But it was Edna Everage who scaled the heights. The humour of the early Edna sketches again lay in the catalogue of suburban values and commonplaces that she represented. Some of her monologues and songs from the 1950s and early 1960s were so mundane that they read like Sunday newspaper advertising supplements. In those days she had simply to mention gladioli—the tawdry flowers that in later

BELONGING

years became the great phallic symbol of her aggression—to get an easy laugh of recognition.

Edna became very famous and, being the sort of character she was, it went to her head. She started out a simple suburban mum and went on to become a 'housewife superstar' and later a self-styled 'megastar'. She loved every minute of it and as her fame grew her supposed suburban ordinariness assumed extravagantly surreal proportions. As Edna Humphries took on the popular media, just as with the early Sandy he had taken on the advanced modernist drama of his time—Beckett, Pinter and the Absurdists. While the more narrowly nationalist writers of the 1950s were using the conventions of well-made realism to represent Australian life, Humphries was appropriating, for the same purpose, the avant-garde of European culture, not its traditions.

By the 1980s Humphries was using Edna to take on one of the great forms of contemporary media culture—the glamorous celebrity chat show. Edna's television productions of that time, *An Audience with Dame Edna* and *The Dame Edna Experience*, had different versions in England, Australia and the United States, each country providing its own 'international' stars. She mocked the whole notion that any star could be as internationally successful as she, while never letting go of her essentially provincial personality. In 2005, fifty years after his original invention of the Edna character, and after playing *Back with a Vengeance* 163 times on Broadway, Humphries won a Tony Award.

In all this Humphries set the agenda, with his character types and his material, and established the tone, through his satire, for a great deal of the New Wave. His comedy was so exuberant that audiences embraced the types with an enthusiasm that helped pave the way for their commercial exploitation in the 1980s by the advertising industry, and for the success of affectionate versions of them, such as Paul Hogan's character Crocodile Dundee and later, in the 1990s and early 2000s, the commercial phenomenon of the 'Crocodile Hunter' Steve Irwin.

6: PLAYWRIGHTS IN THE 60S

Other precursors of the New Wave

Another writer who anticipated the New Wave, especially its larrikin interest in vernacular idiom and its celebration of popular theatrical and cultural traditions, was Alan Hopgood, who was promoted by John Sumner's Union Theatre Repertory Company, which in 1968 became the Melbourne Theatre Company. Sumner was part of the 1950s 'Anglo' generation who believed strongly that the key to the creation of a vibrant Australian theatre was the establishment and maintenance of professional 'standards'. But he was also instrumental in the early success of the *Doll* and continued to take an interest in local playwrights.[12] It was Sumner who established the formula that became the standard for the repertoire of the new state theatre companies after the 1960s: a third classics, a third contemporary overseas plays and a third Australian works. In his view the UTRC's productions in the early 1960s of *Sweeney Todd*, *The Mystery of the Hansom Cab* and Reg Livermore's *The Good Ship Walter Raleigh* anticipated the rough, open theatricalist style of the New Wave.[13]

For Sumner Hopgood produced a series of exaggerated farcical comedies, starting with one of the most popularly successful plays of the 1960s, *And The Big Men Fly* (1963), an amiable bush–city tall tale. It concerns a hayseed named Achilles Brown who can drop kick bags of wheat in his bare feet and who is signed up by an unscrupulous football club manager to win his ailing team their first premiership in forty years. Acky, as he is known to his friend Lil, wins the Brownlow Medal for the fairest and best player of the year, but he is not interested in fame, fortune or football. When he realises that he is being manipulated he throws the Grand Final in protest and it ends up a draw. Acky retires leaving his supposedly revitalised team to battle the replay by themselves. David Williamson's 1977 play *The Club* returned to the theme, without the bucolic touch and with a tougher satirical edge but with a similar sentimentality about the gap between the corrupt managers and the decent players.

Hopgood's *The Golden Legion of Cleaning Women* (1967) is a similar tall tale about corrupt business practices and a triumphant revolt by ordinary people. In it a group of cheerful cleaners suddenly

BELONGING

realise that knowledge is power when they start exploiting the contents of the waste-paper bins they clear every morning. *And Here Comes Bucknuckle* (1980) is a sequel to *And The Big Men Fly*. Acky has acquired a horse, equal to his own prodigious talent and just as stupid, who is signed by the same unscrupulous manager to win the Melbourne Cup. Bucknuckle falls in love with another horse, and Acky finally kisses Lil, but only to get her to stop hitting him.

Private Yuk Objects (1966) starts out like another country comedy but very soon becomes a play of ideas about the war in Vietnam, which in 1966, when the play was written, had not yet divided Australia as it was about to do. It is a reasoned series of arguments about the rights and wrongs of conscription, conscientious objection and the morality of the war—introducing two sympathetic Viet Cong characters who argue their case. With hindsight, it comes across as too even-handed—the protestors all end up going off to fight—but it is interesting as an early document of its time.

Jane Street

A month after *Private Yuk Objects* opened in Melbourne the new professional theatrical establishment in Sydney, represented by NIDA, the Old Tote Theatre Company, the University of New South Wales Drama Foundation and the new School of Drama—all under the direction or influence of Robert Quentin (Tom Brown was the director of NIDA at the time)—launched an initiative that anticipated the rumblings of the New Wave. The Jane Street Theatre, a small converted church in suburban Randwick, was established partly as a venue, some said a ghetto, for new Australian plays. It had its most important influence after 1969, when it was taken over by NIDA under its new director John Clark, but between 1966 and 1969 it produced a number of new Australian plays.

The first program, in 1966, included two one-act plays that reflected in negative terms on some upcoming issues, the new radicalism and the new sexual openness, without actually capturing the spirit of the post-1968 cultural change. These were Tony Morphett's absurdist black comedy, *I've Come About the Assassination*, which mocked

6: PLAYWRIGHTS IN THE 60S

the banality of violence and the brutality of revolutionary fervour, and Michael Thomas's *The Pier*, a wordy play about a sexually sadomasochistic relationship between two decrepit old men (rather more shocking, you'd think, than the plays such as Buzo's *Norm and Ahmed* that were at the forefront of the battle against censorship a few years later.)

Other new plays were James Searle's *The Lucky Streak*, a Pinteresque drama about the interplay between two young men in a boarding house, their prurient landlady, her halfwit son and a bold, tough young woman from next door; and Rodney Milgate's *A Refined Look at Existence*, an elaborately contrived Australianised version of Euripides' *The Bacchae* set in the outback. Milgate's play is full of arch comedy, non sequiturs, poetry, songs and dances, and satirical recognition humour about consumerist and media culture. The final play of the season was novelist Thomas Keneally's first play, *Halloran's Little Boat*, a convict romance that looks back to the historical dramas of the 1940s and 1950s. The season also included a revival of the convict Edward Geoghegan's 1844 play *The Currency Lass*.

Whether or not the institution-based work at Jane Street truly reflected the radical tone of the New Wave has been much debated.[14] The following year's work seemed to prove that it did: Jim Sharman's production, *Terror Australis*, was in the spirit of the old New Theatre revues and anticipated the loose theatricalist style of the early 1970s. It included a playful subversion of the traditional actor–audience relationship of the kind that La Mama and the Australian Performing Group were later to make their own. The audience were led into the tiny theatre via a railed race of the kind that is used on outback stations for dipping sheep. No script has been published of this remarkable production, but it romped gleefully through 180 years of Australian history with great larrikin disrespect.

In 1968 the Jane Street 'ghetto' was opened up, when a season of new Australian plays was mounted at the Old Tote Theatre on the UNSW campus, a small tin-shed theatre but the home of the main company's early professional work. The Australian play season included Keneally's *Childermas*, a revival of Rodney Milgate's *A Refined Look*

BELONGING

at Existence, a production of Dorothy Hewett's *This Old Man Comes Rolling Home*, and a new Milgate play, *At Least You Get Something Out of That*.

Keneally's *Childermas* is more interesting than his convict drama *Halloran's Little Boat* and, as another play written in response to the war in Vietnam, is more complex than Hopgood's *Private Yuk Objects*. Set in the 97th summer of a mythic war, it is a Brechtian–Bondian allegory, about the journey of three knights in search of a new holy child whom they hope to protect from the clutches of the militarists. They are captured and tortured by a Herod figure who brainwashes them in the art of terror. They lead him, with the help of his spy, to the holy child, whom he kills in a terrible barrage of firepower that also wipes out a mysterious chorus of singing children who have been following the young lama figure in a sort of crusade. After this apocalypse a single, hopeful, child's voice is heard singing faintly in the distance. It is still a shocking play.

The most influential play of the 1968 season was Alex Buzo's *Norm and Ahmed*, which helped spark the anti-censorship campaign, portrayed a cultural clash that was unique in the early New Wave, and introduced a new young writer whose dialogue exploited the vernacular of Humphries and Hopgood for new purposes. It was presented with a revival of Douglas Stewart's radio classic *Fire on the Snow*, and blew Stewart's play out of the water.

Jane Street included Buzo's *Rooted* in 1969, but his work was brought to national attention when his third play *The Front Room Boys*, was included in the La Mama Company's first professional season at the 1970 Perth Festival. This is discussed in Chapter 9. Also in the 1969 Jane Street season was Tony Morphett's *The Rise and Fall of Boronia Avenue*.

The Jane Street seasons, which lasted until 1977, generated a great deal of critical disagreement about their importance in the new Australian writing of the 1970s. Their greatest success was with Michael Boddy and Robert (now Bob) Ellis's *The Legend of King O'Malley* in 1970. John Clark's 1972 production of David Williamson's *Don's Party*, in a revised version, firmly established Williamson's reputation.

After 1972 Jane Street never repeated the critical and popular

6: PLAYWRIGHTS IN THE 60S

success of these two seasons and it was often criticised in the press. But the 1973 season included productions of Alma De Groen's *The After-Life of Arthur Cravan* and Dorothy Hewett's *Bon-Bons and Roses for Dolly*—the two major women writers of the ensuing years. In 1971, 1973 and 1975 Jane Street did productions of plays—*Childhead's Doll, Cooper and Borges* and *Interplay*—written by Willy Young, now better known as the photographer and performance artist William Yang.

Several members of the 1970 *The Legend of King O'Malley* company went on to join Rex Cramphorn's innovative group, the Performance Syndicate, which, along with the APG's Stasis Group, introduced to Australia the body-as-text performance techniques and theories of Antonin Artaud and Jerzy Grotowski. A group of performers called the Human Body, performing at Sydney's PACT, had begun to explore this sort of work in the late 1960s.

After the collapse of the Performance Syndicate, Cramphorn directed productions for the Jane Street seasons from 1974 to 1976. The success of the new playwrights of the 1970s has eclipsed a lot of the experimental non-script-based theatrical work of that time, including the Human Body, the Performance Syndicate and the work of Syd Clayton, who did happenings, and Doug Anders's improvisational group Tribe, both at La Mama. This work has been forgotten to such an extent that it had to be reinvented by contemporary performance artists of the late 1980s and 1990s, such as the Sydney Front.

In the 1960s though, all this activity laid down the groundwork for the most important and influential period of the twentieth-century theatre—the New Wave.

7

THE NEW WAVE

'The New Wave' is a misleading term when applied to playwrights because it implies that the writers who helped shape the sudden explosion of theatre in Australia from the late 1960s shared a common set of goals and interests. They didn't, although they appeared to. They were a group of mostly young, educated, middle-class men—rebellious larrikins swept up in the new nationalistic fervour and the social and political upheaval of the period. They wanted to get the individual and social issues of the world they were experiencing onto the stage—including the polarisation created by the Vietnam War, the sexual revolution and the emergence of a globalised media culture. They wanted to appropriate and rework Australian history, reclaiming popular theatrical traditions that their immediate theatrical forebears had dismissed as vulgar and commercial. Many of them were left-wing, but aside from a brief surge of agitprop to protest the Vietnam War, and the work of John Romeril, they tended not to engage seriously with politics. For the most part they seemed untroubled by too much understanding of the identity politics that became driving forces in the late 1970s and 1980s.

The New Wave blokes, especially David Williamson, Jack Hibberd and Alex Buzo, belonged to the generation of the new professional middle class that Williamson would later chronicle in his plays.

BELONGING

Hibberd's young men in *White With Wire Wheels*, like Buzo's in *The Front Room Boys* and *Rooted*, and Williamson's in his first play, *The Coming of Stork*, were what Max Harris called the 'sons of Ocker'—a postwar baby-boomer generation which, according to your view, were either educated beyond their capacity to take part in civilised society, or triumphantly disrespectful of it.[1] Some of the self-interested entrepreneurs of the 1980s, whose exploits were explored in the theatre by, among others, Stephen Sewell and Louis Nowra, emerged from this generation.

With hindsight, however, the similarities between these writers seem less important than their differences. The central four—Hibberd, Romeril, Buzo and Williamson—now look like as disparate a bunch of writers as you might find. Hibberd became for a time one of Australia's most interesting dramatic experimenters, working in and against the traditions of the European avant-garde and appropriating them for subtly subversive ends. Before Stephen Sewell, Romeril was the most important political playwright—a 'public servant of the pen', he once called himself—bringing to the community theatre movement of the early 1980s a depth of political knowledge, craft experience and skills without which it could scarcely have got off the ground.[2] Buzo was a sophisticated stylist, who wrote a series of elegant, humanist comedies of manners with characters trapped in their roles, wanting to be let out. Williamson went on to become a comic chronicler of his times, for forty years his every play eagerly awaited by audiences and producers, his every utterance recorded by an avid press. He is the only New Wave playwright whose name is known among the general middle-class public.

Hard as it is to imagine this varied group as part of a single 'New Wave', that is how they were seen at the time. Between 1968 and 1975, the dates used here for the New Wave, something came alive in Australian theatre. It was both the last gasp of modernism, in its revolutionary fervour, and the first breath of postmodernism, in its use of irony, its breaking-up of traditional forms, and its stylistic eclecticism. It celebrated a new nationalism and proclaimed a supposedly unifying rhetoric of Australianness. At the same time it exposed 'new voices', thus laying down paths for the new theatres of identity politics of the 1980s. For young theatregoers brought up in the 1960s, as I was, this

7: THE NEW WAVE

tension between tradition and iconoclasm made the early 1970s a very heady time.

The term 'New Wave' also describes a group of practices and ideas accompanied by radical changes in the conditions and processes by which the theatre was produced and consumed. There was a new audience and a new generation of practitioners who were suddenly talking to one another in ways that seemed revolutionary. There are many theatre practitioners and critics today who still see the early 1970s as a golden age in which the theatre suddenly mattered, culturally and socially, in ways that it didn't before and hasn't since.

The only sustained analysis of the New Wave in these terms is *See How It Runs*, by Julian Meyrick, who defines it in generational terms, as a reaction against the Anglophile directors and actors of the 1950s and 1960s (who in turn had defined their own practice in opposition to that of the commercial theatre, as Esson and the first wave of nationalists had done in the 1920s).[3] He finds three new cultural perspectives in his discussion of Nimrod's history, and asks what happened to them and how they might be understood: a new understanding of 'professionalism' based on new ideas of expressiveness, relevance and spontaneity instead of traditions and standards; a response to the old National Theatre debate (which goes back to the beginning of last century); and a positioning of the New Wave as in itself Australian, even when it wasn't doing Australian plays. He puts these together into what he calls 'the New Wave syllogism'.[4]

This syllogism starts out as 'Theatre→Politics→The World'.[5] The middle term changes as Nimrod's work changes, but Meyrick's point remains that for Nimrod, like the APG in Melbourne, the theatre was connected with the social, cultural and political world in a new sense. As a creative activity it didn't just describe or represent the world, it replicated it. There was a new vocabulary for this idea of theatre, introduced by one of the theatrical gurus of the late 1960s, the director Peter Brook, whose highly influential book, *The Empty Space*, threw aside old terms such as 'good' and 'bad' and suggested a new taxonomy—'holy', 'rough' and 'deadly'.[6]

In the rhetoric of the New Wave, the deadly theatre was that of the old Anglo directors, especially John Sumner's Melbourne Theatre

BELONGING

Company, and in Sydney Robert Quentin's Old Tote Theatre Company, which by the early 1970s had become a suitably traditional institution for Nimrod to oppose. The exuberant larrikin work of the APG and the early Nimrod exemplified what Brook called 'rough theatre', and 'holy theatre' described the more inward-looking work of their offshoots, such as the APG's Stasis Group and Nightshift in Melbourne and Rex Cramphorn's Performance Syndicate in Sydney.

La Mama, the APG, Nimrod

In 1967, when Sharman's *Terror Australis* was produced in Sydney, Betty Burstall opened Café La Mama in Melbourne as a venue for new and experimental work. It was modelled on the Off-Off-Broadway theatres she had recently visited in New York, including La MaMa there—just as the Pioneer Players had been modelled on the Abbey Theatre after Esson visited Dublin. Melbourne's La Mama, a tiny venue in an old shirt-and-underwear factory in Carlton, was still operating at the time of writing. It is a curated venue rather than a theatre company and it has also nurtured poets and musicians. But its greatest success has been as a space for new writers and new performance artists and companies.

The early work at La Mama included Happenings and improvisational work; political street and guerrilla theatre projects; and a series of workshops based on the new American and European radical political theatre of the 1960s.[7]

The venue opened, with an evening that included Jack Hibberd's *Three Old Friends*, on 30 July 1967. In the next two years it presented more new Australian works than all the established companies put together—including plays by Hibberd, Romeril, Kris Hemensley and Frank Bren. A series of mock-absurdist 'micro-plays', written by Hibberd the previous year, became part of a program called *Brainrot* ('An Evening of Pathology and Violence and Love and Friendship') at Melbourne University in April 1968.[8] The *Brainrot* team went on to become the La Mama Company, which began life three months later with a production of Hibberd's *One of Nature's Gentlemen*. After a tour to the Perth Festival in 1970—with Hibberd's *Who?* and *White*

7: THE NEW WAVE

With Wire Wheels, Romeril's *Chicago, Chicago* and Buzo's *The Front Room Boys*—the La Mama Company became the Australian Performing Group (APG), opening in December with a production of Hibberd and Romeril's *Marvellous Melbourne*. The Perth Festival plays became the key texts of the early New Wave when they were published by Penguin with an introduction by Graeme Blundell. *Marvellous Melbourne*, along with Michael Boddy and Bob Ellis's *The Legend of King O'Malley*, also became key texts—ushering in the vaudeville history plays that represented the rough side of the new theatre.

The APG and the Nimrod were the two dominant companies of the New Wave. Both started up in 1970, imbued with the spirit of the times, but their different styles, working methods and agendas soon saw them drift apart.

The APG was a fiercely collective company with political and artistic visions that led ultimately to internal arguments over process, and industrial and workplace management issues. It nurtured or generated an extraordinary number of spin-off groups, including Stasis, the Women's Theatre Group and Circus Oz. Its venue was the legendary Pram Factory, a dilapidated building, also in Carlton, with a Front Theatre, a smaller Back Theatre and a Tower in which some of the company members played out interpersonally the hippie lifestyle that was a key feature of the New Age dream of a theatre contiguous with life. The Pram Factory was sold in 1980 for a supermarket development. The APG limped on into 1981, but the collective disbanded after appointing, with little regard for continuity and no plan at all for the future, a new young group to carry on the flag. It collapsed after one season.

The Nimrod, a looser collection of individual talents united by an ability to work together and an enthusiastically opportunistic openness to new projects, achieved more mainstream success. It started out in a tiny old wedge-shaped building in Nimrod Street in Sydney's Kings Cross (now the SBW Stables Theatre), then moved in 1974 to a converted factory in Surry Hills. When Nimrod moved out in the mid-1980s, this became Belvoir St Theatre, currently the home of director Neil Armfield's Company B and the last surviving high-profile theatre company in which the spirit of the New Wave survives.

BELONGING

With a rhetoric of revolutionary solidarity, the APG was driven by a visionary collective committed to collaborative processes of theatre production, but still rife with individual passions. The group was also divided into ideological factions that kept threatening to tear it apart.[9] Hibberd and Romeril figured prominently, partly because they were prolific, and also because they stayed, Hibberd until 1977 and Romeril until 1980. While Nimrod paid more lip-service to writers, there was still a great deal of cross-over of roles there. Both companies placed a strong emphasis on new theatre work.

Like La Mama, both companies produced a considerable number of Australian plays written by a wide range of new playwrights.[10] Meyrick gives rough comparative statistics from which it is difficult to draw conclusions, but they suggest that a few house writers wrote a large proportion of the local repertoire. Between 1970 and 1981, Hibberd and Romeril wrote 31 per cent of the APG's locally-written productions (86.8 per cent of the overall repertoire), and Romeril wrote two thirds of that.[11] Between 1970 and 1985, Alex Buzo, Ron Blair and David Williamson dominated the Australian part of Nimrod's repertoire (62 per cent), with eighteen productions between them, compared to twenty written by Nimrod's other top three writers, William Shakespeare, Tom Stoppard and Anton Chekhov.

Such figures are merely indicative, for they don't compare like with like and the samples vary wildly: the APG staged 74 plays in eleven years, compared to Nimrod's 171 in fifteen years. Like all methods of quantitative arts accounting, the raw statistics are overwhelmed by more interesting factors. At Nimrod a series of artistic directors had a great influence. There was John Bell's special interest in Shakespeare, which provoked an influential new style and found further expression later in his highly successful Bell Shakespeare Company.[12] There was Ken Horler's interest in Stoppard, shared by Nimrod audiences at the time, Aubrey Mellor's interest in Chekhov, realised in a series of successful and critically acclaimed productions, and Richard Wherrett's interest in the new Australian repertoire.

Such was the turmoil of the New Wave, as it moved into the mainstream, that its original directors travelled around the new companies like hippies in a Kombi van. Horler was ousted from Nimrod

7: THE NEW WAVE

in a palace coup in 1980 and didn't direct again. Mellor, who had been Artistic Director of the Jane Street seasons in 1978–79, at Nimrod from 1981 to 1983, and at the Queensland Theatre Company from 1988 to 1993, became Artistic Director of Melbourne's Playbox Theatre in 1993. Playbox had been founded in 1976 as Hoopla Productions by former APG stalwarts Graeme Blundell and Garrie Hutchinson, together with Carrillo Gantner. Rex Cramphorn, whose Performance Syndicate had been established in 1969, was a resident director there from 1981 to 1985. He died in 1991.

Outside Melbourne and Sydney, other companies followed the model of the APG and Nimrod. Originally founded in 1965, Perth's Hole-in-the-Wall Theatre was remodelled along Nimrod lines for a short period in the mid-1970s by its artistic director John Milson. Troupe, formed as a collective in Adelaide in 1976, hosted visiting La Mama and APG productions and produced new work by David Allen, one of its founders, and Doreen Clarke. Based in Brisbane, the Popular Theatre Troupe was a political theatre company, like the agitprop arm of the APG, that used popular musical and comic styles and toured shows to non-theatre venues, with a great deal of political controversy, until its demise in 1982.[13] The playwrights, unlike the performers, directors and designers, will not loom as large as they do today, when theatre historians come to write about the New Wave theatre.[14]

Oakley, Blair, Reed

At first glance Barry Oakley was an unlikely member of the New Wave. Wry, urbane and literary, he was ten years older than most, an ex-teacher, advertising copywriter and public servant. In a neat blue suit at his first opening night, in 1967, he was, like many of his characters, a solitary figure in the company of bohemian actors and audience members wearing baggy jumpers and jeans.[15] His short satirical-absurd comedy about office life, *Eugene Flockhart's Desk*, was one of the last plays to be produced, in a rehearsed reading, at Wal Cherry's Emerald Hill Theatre in Melbourne in 1967. A similar play, *Witzenhausen, Where Are You?* was produced by the Leeton Dramatic Society in the same year and was one of the early productions at La Mama. *A Lesson*

BELONGING

in English (1969), also produced at La Mama, is a short, wild classroom comedy that anticipates Ron Blair's *The Christian Brothers*. It is the first of several comedies in which Oakley explores the loneliness of a small-time character performing on a big stage, whose performance is haunted by a sense of his own failure. *The Great God Mogadon* carries this to an extreme when a humble clerk, called on to impersonate the Prime Minister for a day, is harassed by an obscure group of right-wing establishment terrorists who end up trying to assassinate him. The best play in this vein is *Scanlan*, a short monodrama in which an anxious and confused man breaks down while giving a public academic lecture, and allows his personal life to become comically, embarrassingly public. *Bedfellows* (1975) develops the theme domestically in a sad comedy about marital disillusion and infidelity. *Marsupials* (1979) explores it further, showing a comically bitter and drunken middle-aged publisher's editor who prefers to retreat into himself rather than take the necessary steps to save his marriage and his life. In the early 1970s Oakley was one of the staple writers for the APG, where he produced a series of satirical history plays, discussed below, that married his wit to the APG's larrikin house style.

Ron Blair, in Sydney, was one of the diverse talents that founded the Nimrod Theatre and in 1970, with Michael Boddy and Marcus Cooney, was co-writer of the new company's first show, *Biggles*, a mock-imperialist romp in the style established by *The Legend of King O'Malley*. He wrote another vaudeville history play during Nimrod's first year, *Flash Jim Vaux*, and the pantomime *Hamlet on Ice*.

Blair's first straight play for Nimrod was *President Wilson in Paris* (1973), a psychological thriller with political implications. In it a megalomaniac who is rich enough to act out his fantasies, like the central character in Pirandello's *Henry IV*, plays out a pathological fantasy role that is alarmingly close to the supposedly normal public roles played by world leaders. In 1976, *Mad, Bad and Dangerous to Know*, a monodrama about Byron, was a vehicle for a tour de force performance by John Bell. *Marx* (1978) is an ironic drama about Karl Marx the Man, living in poverty in London, neglecting his wife, getting his maid pregnant and pawning his possessions, while Karl Marx the Intellectual struggles to understand the material causes of

7: THE NEW WAVE

the capitalist oppression of the working class. The roots of *Last Day in Woolloomooloo* (1979) lie in the slum realism of the 1950s, yet its bizarrely surreal quality anticipates the critique of materialist urban alienation in some 1980s and 1990s drama, such as the later plays of Stephen Sewell and Louis Nowra, and those of Andrew Bovell, Daniel Keene and Raimondo Cortese.

Blair's most enduring play is *The Christian Brothers*, a monodrama first produced at the Nimrod Theatre in 1975. It was revived by the original director Richard Wherrett, designer Larry Eastwood and actor Peter Carroll in 2001, by which time Carroll, as he said in the press, had reached the right age for the part. The play takes the form of a lesson conducted by an aging Brother whose commitment to his pupils far outweighs his teaching ability. In what becomes a grand confessional monologue, he tries to beat, cajole and intimidate his boys into knowledge and, more importantly for him, into understanding the personal basis of his vocation: a vision he once had, of the Virgin Mary, to which he now clings like a man drowning. The play was a huge success—partly as a recognition comedy for a generation of Catholics educated in systemic Catholic schools and partly as a portrait of a flawed but well-meaning man who is incapable of separating his personal faith and passion from his pedagogic duty.

In the 1970s, working-class Irish-Catholic Australia was still, in the drama at least, a world outside the middle-class ocker construction of the new Australianness. Ron Blair and Peter Kenna's Catholic plays were forerunners of the challenges to that old nationalism that were to multiply and flourish in the late 1970s and for the remainder of the century, especially in the work of Nick Enright—whose plays are discussed in Chapter 11.

Bill Reed came out of left field in the late 1960s and produced several non-realistic plays, influential at the time but now largely forgotten. A stylised historical drama about the disastrous Burke and Wills expedition, *Burke's Company* (1968) incorporates songs and a heightened introspective language into dream and flashback scenes. Intended for an open stage, which represents the vast desert landscape over which Burke and Wills and Brahe crawl, it was the first play to use Brecht as a dramaturgical model for staging Australian pioneering experience.

BELONGING

Reed's later plays became increasingly obscure. *Truganinni* (1970), about the English massacre of the first-contact Indigenous people in Tasmania, is a trio of one-act plays in different styles that now come across as well-intentioned rather than relevant. *Mr Siggie Morrison with his Comb and Paper* (1972), like Peter Kenna's 1965 play *Trespassers Will Be Prosecuted*, is about an old man trapped in a culvert tormented by cruel children, but the script has so much elaborate wordplay and metatheatrical trickery that it is almost impenetrable.[16] *Cass Butcher Bunting* (1976) is his best play—an intense, highly theatrical drama about three very different men trapped underground after a mine explosion. They review the country-town memories and tensions of their lives together, while all the time the hope of rescue keeps tapping (literally) on the outside walls of the cave in which they are imprisoned. It offers terrific opportunities for set and sound designers and a director to revisit the text in a contemporary theatricalist style.

Jack Hibberd

Jack Hibberd was there at the beginning of most of the important early stages of the New Wave—the first night at La Mama, the first plays by the La Mama Company (which became the APG), and, with John Romeril, the first play at the Pram Factory. By 1972 he had written *Dimboola*, one of Australia's biggest commercial successes since *On Our Selection*, and also *A Stretch of the Imagination*, its greatest critical success, which historian Margaret Williams hailed as 'the first unmistakable Australian theatrical classic'.[17] For many years he was one of the country's most interesting, eclectic and often idiosyncratic playwrights. As a polemicist he was a constant irritant, like a tick in the scalp of the hairy new theatrical establishment of the 1970s. His longstanding role as the Australian theatre's resident ratbag, and his almost single-handed introduction of many of the new forms and theatrical styles that the New Wave explored in its politicised battle against naturalism, were almost as important as the remarkable and varied series of plays that he kept producing.[18]

The eclecticism of this early writing has continued throughout his career. He has written some of the most obscure and verbally

7: THE NEW WAVE

sophisticated plays in the repertoire, and also some of the most raucously vulgar. He was the supreme larrikin of his time, like the mad rooter with a classical education that was Monk O'Neill in *A Stretch of the Imagination*. He has translated Baudelaire, adapted Aristophanes, Arrabal, Gogol and de Maupassant and has also been responsible for some of the most groan-inducing puns, crudest slapstick and coarsest sexual comedy in Australian drama. More than any other New Wave writer he rebelled against the civilised theatrical 'standards' represented by the old Anglo generation, but he knew and exploited the culture he was battling. His work is the first great carnivalesque subversion of European high culture in the Australian theatre—confidently disrespectful, playfully ironic, gleeful in its appropriation and pastiche collection of colourful scraps of the Great Tradition.[19]

Early plays such as *Three Old Friends* and the *Brainrot* series—*Just Before the Honeymoon, O, This Great Gap of Time, No Time Like the Present, Who?* and *One of Nature's Gentlemen*—which appeared in 1967 are a collection of mysterious encounters between characters who have their dramatic origins in Pinter-style absurdism, but find their roots, in both senses, in the everyday life of Australian inner-city urban culture in the 1960s. Steve, Ron and Herb in *Three Old Friends* go through the rituals of mateship, but their rituals don't work when the easy camaraderie that Steve expects slips away, as Ron and Herb refuse to know him and finally kill him, in a logical development of the hollowness of their friendship. *O* is a brutal story of the casual murder of a woman by a man she has just taken to bed, made creepy by the circular plotting, in which we see the murder before we see the preceding intimacy. In *Who?* and *One of Nature's Gentlemen*, the social rituals of mateship and male competition and aggression are exaggerated into absurdist comic violence—like works of theatrical anthropology exploring the strange customs and mating habits of the Australian Male. Hibberd once referred to himself as an 'anthropologist of rituals' and, although the label by no means sums up all his work, it is a consistent part of his writing.[20] Later plays in the 1980s extended the style to include female rituals. *Mothballs* (1980) is a monologue for a widow sitting in vigil by her husband's coffin, trying to find the emotion, or simply the pose, appropriate for a grief

BELONGING

that she has difficulty feeling. In *Glycerine Tears* (1982), two society women sit at a table drinking tea and champagne and eating pikelets and sponge cake, as one disingenuously expresses support for the other in her recent bereavement. They end up talking about their current men, in each case one of the other's former lovers/partners, before anticipating lunch—a piece of succulent, pink lamb that the widow has prepared for her comforter. As in the earlier plays about men, we are left at the end with a hollowness, a disturbing feeling that these people are alienated from life by their customary behaviour, and that they deserve to be.

Hibberd's first full-length play, *White With Wire Wheels* (1967), one of the most influential plays of the early New Wave, is still one of the best. It is classically formal in its construction—a series of neat scenes in which three blokes, flatmates obsessed with cars and women (and scarcely able to distinguish between the two), behave like animals, treat their girlfriends like dirt, try to crack onto the new woman upstairs and then finally get their come-uppance.

Mal, Simon and Rod spend most of their time recovering from last night's binge or anticipating tonight's. In a series of matched scenes, each separates from his current girlfriend and prepares to chat up Helen, the mysteriously emasculating woman who has moved into the flat upstairs. The girlfriends and Helen are all played by one actress. After the boys have finally met Helen, there is an expressionist scene in which each comes to her late at night with his inner fears. She sets them up by agreeing to a date—all on the same night. When she turns up at their flat, she takes them outside, one by one, to tell them something that we never hear. Whatever it is, they are cowed, and retreat into their ritualised mateship. They decide to drive to a pub in the hills and get trashed, but at the end, like Gogo and Didi in *Waiting for Godot*, they do not move. The play is one of the first great studies of the new Australian male, part satirical, part celebratory but finally very bleak.

Peggy Sue, in some ways a companion piece to *White With Wire Wheels* but appearing seven years later, is much tougher. It follows the lives of three young women from the mid-1950s to the mid-1960s as they are abused and abandoned by their men, forced into prostitution

7: THE NEW WAVE

to support their babies, and eventually sent to jail. This time all the male characters are played by one actor, and one of them, Aussie, is the philandering husband of all three women. The savagery of the play, and its obscenity, indicate how much Australian theatre had changed in the seven short years between 1967 and 1974.

Dimboola (1969) is the first of three defiantly populist celebration plays, each based on a simple idea that must have had other writers and producers kicking themselves for not thinking of it.[21] In *Dimboola*, the audience are the dinner guests at a cheerfully awful wedding reception, a night of drunkenness and predatory sexuality. At the official table the families of the bride and groom battle out their differences, interrupted by two larrikin interlopers, a drunken uncle who sings most of the songs and a primly Methodist maiden aunt who ends up under the table before leaving with the sozzled Catholic priest. The audience are invited to sing and dance along. The batty bride and gormless groom, Maureen and Morrie, sit at the official table and watch as their evening collapses into chaos. Each has a tag-line: 'Ain't it awful?' says Maureen; 'No worries', says Morrie. The play is a triumph of New Wave irreverence.

It opened at La Mama in 1969, and was then revived by the APG at the Pram Factory in 1973 in a production by David Williamson, before being taken up by commercial theatre-restaurant managements. Hibberd was particularly satisfied by the play's popularity among amateur groups, who staged up to thirty productions of it a year during the 1970s and early 1980s in community halls and clubs.[22] A film version was directed by John Duigan in 1978 and the same year Tim Robertson published a novelisation. The success of the play has done a great deal to blur the boundaries between populist commercial and popular amateur theatre, partly as a result of Hibberd's mischievous and exultant rejection of the old standards of theatrical decorum and good taste.

Hibberd's second celebration play was *Goodbye Ted* (1975), co-authored by John Timlin. The gimmick this time is a testimonial dinner for an aging Aussie Rules football star, but it relies less than *Dimboola* did on audience involvement. The script here is a scaffold for gags, slapstick, dirty jokes and yarns, especially by the eponymous Ted. In true theatre-restaurant style, there are lots of randy blokes groping large-breasted sheilas, although there is also a political angle: club chairman Sir Cyclops Garnish rips off money from the decent ordinary battlers who have supported the club all their lives. Like Hopgood's *And the Big Men Fly*, the play is an attempt to capitalise on Melbourne's football mania. In one scene the new recruit smokes dope and shares his joint with Sir Cyclops's unsuspecting wife. David Williamson did this gag much better two years later in *The Club*, a play that treads the fine line between satire and celebration—something Hibberd called for, and which Williamson mastered.[23] Hibberd's third celebration play was *Liquid Amber* (1982), in which the audience are again involved, but this time without much to do, as guests at a chaotic golden wedding anniversary party. Here *Dimboola*'s cheerful awfulness is more strained.

A Stretch of the Imagination opened at the Pram Factory in 1972, with Peter Cummins in a role that has attracted many fine actors, each of whom has brought to it something different.[24] As Hibberd has been keen to point out, it is not a monologue, but a one-actor drama in which the recluse Monk O'Neill struggles through 'yet another penultimate day' as he journeys towards death.[25] In the process he replays some of the great encounters in his life—sexual, social, cultural and mythic.

Monk lives in a corrugated iron hut, straight out the bush tradition of the 1920s and 1930s, at a place called One Tree Hill. There is no tree, because Monk cut it down when he first arrived, so as not to draw attention to himself. Every day he fertilises a replacement sapling, planted out of guilt, with his own nitrogenous wastes drawn from the 44-gallon drum he pisses into. On the penultimate day in question he wakes to the ringing clock, checks the thermometer, raises his shade umbrella, performs his ablutions, tends his tomato crop, eats three meals and then retires again, crawling on all fours, to his shelter.

This simple day, which starts out blisteringly hot and turns savagely and absurdly cold, is studded with re-enacted memories: of his only visitor at One Tree Hill, a bushwhacked bikie named Mort Lazarus who died of Monk's hospitality in a snap frost in the night and is buried under the spot where he now places his alarm clock; of the time Dorabella seduced him in a beer garden and her husband, his mate Merv, beat the shit out of him; of dining in a Paris café, when he berated the waiter

7: THE NEW WAVE

and met up with Proust; of saving his dying brother from a deathbed conversion at the hands of the Catholics by driving the priest out of the room at gunpoint; of his chats about philosophy and politics with the legendary boxer Les Darcy and his impromptu bout with him on the top of Mt Kosciusko. In 1972, Cummins played these scenes as reminiscences. In 1976, for Max Gillies, they became flashbacks, disrupting the activity of the day. Nine years later, Bruce Spence played the whole thing—the present and the memories—as a highly theatrical performance of stereotypes of individual and cultural identity.

At the end of the play Monk returns to the present. He remembers how his beloved horse Cromwell was killed by the falling tree he had chopped down; he scratches his tinea with his old rosary beads ('drops of blood from the Blessed Oliver Plunkett's decapitated neck') and he takes a pencil and alters his will—leaving all his lands and property to 'the Aboriginal peoples of Australia', or, if they turn out to be extinct by the time he dies, to the 'populous Oriental nations of the north':

> On no account must my domain fall into the clutches of the predatory and upstart albino. I believe that the tides of history will swamp and wash aside this small pink tribe of mistletoe men, like insects. *(With pencil)* Change insects to dead leaves. (pp. 43–4)

Monk's last reminiscence is having sex with his best friend's widow, on the friend's grave after the funeral. Then he tells us about the grave that he has dug for himself and into which he has put a silk mattress. In his last moments he will fall onto this and, as he finally expires and the walls of clay cave in on him, he will lie looking up at the Southern Cross. He has a last celebratory meal—a meat pie and a bottle of beer—and crawls back into his hut.

In their imaginative range and density both the interpolated scenes and Monk's present ramblings come to represent the memory of a nation and a civilisation. He is the last decrepit relic, living out his final days in isolation in a stolen land now dry and barren. Monk is a true blue ocker—a drinker, a womaniser and a sportsman.[26] But, as he ironically exploits his classical education, he is also an inheritor of European high culture. He could be the last person left alive on the planet. As Margaret Williams says, *A Stretch of the Imagination* evokes the death

BELONGING

> not just of the Australian legend but a whole civilisation with its roots in the classical world, and beyond that, the death of the world itself through some destroyed relation between man and his environment [...] or ultimately through some second engulfing Ice Age.[27]

In later plays Hibberd showed that he wasn't trying to kill off European civilisation, he just wanted to appropriate it for trickster Australian ends. After 1976 he turned away from the self-conscious Australianness of the New Wave and embraced the European influences that had always informed his plays. His adaptation of Gogol's *The Overcoat* (1976) is a sophisticated expressionist staging of the story, using music and (in the published script) Meyerholdian stylised design suggestions, but it is still full of scatological humour. *Odyssey of a Prostitute*, a companion musical piece written eight years later, is based on a story by Guy de Maupassant, but reconfigured theatrically with lots of excess and a mischievous, postcolonial ironic 'distance', such as Brecht might have appreciated. In 1984 Hibberd published *Squibs*, an anthology of what he called 'microplays', including some from the *Brainrot* series and several previously unproduced ones from that period. One of his most extraordinary pieces of writing, published at this time in the journal *Scripsi*, is *Death Warmed Up*: spotlit and speaking directly to us, like figures in Beckett's late work, Thea Limbo delivers a number of brief fragments of texts controlled by a series of playing-style stage directions. She seems to be searching for a way of uttering, of being, of understanding her past, her present and her approaching death; trying to understand how her words are related to the supposed 'real' of her remembered experience and how her speaking of them is related to the here-and-now of her performance.

Hibberd has written many other short works, and in 2001 he returned to Melbourne's Playbox Theatre with another short play, *The Prodigal Son*. He might have been a major writer for contemporary performance companies in the 1990s if he hadn't turned his back on it all, and if he hadn't been tainted, for the new generation of performance makers, by his youthful macho association with the early New Wave. *Death Warmed Up* reads like a farewell to the theatre.

7: THE NEW WAVE

John Romeril

John Romeril was the most prolific of the New Wave writers, and is also the most critically neglected.[28] As noted above, he wrote roughly twenty per cent of the APG's repertoire, and since that company's collapse he has continued to write at an extraordinary rate. In 1987 he told a member of a federal parliamentary Waste Watch Committee, who had asked what he did, that he had written 50, 'maybe 60' plays.[29] That was before many of his major works of the late 1980s and 1990s, including *Lost Weekend*, *Top End*, *Black Cargo*, *Love Suicides*, and, in 2001, *Miss Tanaka*.

More than any other New Wave writer, Romeril kept faith with the radical political and industrial spirit of the theatre in those times. In a time of collective creation he saw himself as a jobbing writer whose responsibility was 'to record what is and what is said, to get it down, fabricate images out of it'.[30] In 1978, after the popular, critical and commercial success of the new generation of Australian playwrights, he said:

> I guess writers have won a demarcation dispute they should never have fought. The real author of a play is the company, when it gives birth to a production. [...] A text can enslave or liberate the performer. To see performers on a stage, performers whose self-image is that of the simple-minded executor of either the director's or writer's higher dramatic will—that is to witness the work of slaves.[31]

This sort of self-effacing commitment to collective creation is rare among writers. Graham Pitts, who in 1979 with Don Mamouney founded the Sidetrack Theatre Company, and Scott Rankin, who in 1992 with John Bakes established Big hART, one of the foremost community cultural development companies in Australia, are among the few who still subscribe to it, although in the 1980s it was an important part of the working practices of the community theatre movement (see Chapter 12).

Both David Williamson and Barry Oakley have written of their disillusionment with the APG collective approach, because it downplayed the authority of the playwright, but for a long time Romeril seemed happy to be one of the 'literary bureaucrats' who were 'public servants of the pen' working with and in communities.[32] In an interview sixteen years later he looked back on a career based in community theatre and theatre-in-education and seemed to want, belatedly, to assert his independence as a writer. 'Unless you're careful', he said, 'you become a kind of bureaucratised pen'.[33]

Many of Romeril's early plays were occasional pieces, written for a particular protest event. One of his most notorious short scripts, for example, was *Whatever Happened to Realism*, written in response to the censorship furore over Buzo's *Norm and Ahmed*. It provoked a key event in the anti-censorship campaign of the late 1960s, when the audience followed the arrested actors all the way to the police station chanting obscenities.[34] For the activist wing of the APG, performing in workplaces and at demonstrations, he also wrote *Mr Big the Big Big Pig*, *The American Independence Hour*, *Dr Karl's Cure* and *Brudder Humphrey*.

The plays that have entered the canon are, typically, the ones that have been published, including *Chicago, Chicago* and *The Floating World*. *I Don't Know Who To Feel Sorry For* exemplifies the distinctive 'super-naturalist' style of La Mama and the APG—intensely grim, and sometimes blackly comic, plays in which the audience, in the small confines of the performance space, were pressed hard up against actors performing a new reconstruction of Australianness in urban life. Another example is *Kitchen Table* (1971), in which a burglar discovers to his horror that the nice suburban couple he is robbing are far more violently criminal than he has ever been. It has a touch of Pinteresque absurdism and menace similar to some of Hibberd's early plays. *Bastardy* (1972) is a play about alienated urban fringe-dwellers, set in a derelict building inhabited by a decrepit couple, an old prostitute and her companion, and visited by a younger Aboriginal man whose dispossession is ironically allegorised in the setting, when the old building turns out to be a warehouse full of stolen luxury goods.

I Don't Know Who To Feel Sorry For (1969) is one of the most revivable of the early plays. In a style Romeril described as 'a kind of naturalism that talks back to its audiences', and with an added touch of farce,[35] it seems at first like a classic New Wave larrikin comedy, if rather bleaker than most, about the emptiness of sexual relationships.

7: THE NEW WAVE

But after a bitter scene between Lenny and Celia, the central couple, and a party scene in which the women flee their crass men, it spins first into expressionism with a bizarre scene in a hamburger shop, before spiralling down into a climactic moment of surrealism when Celia's mother betrays her daughter. A mixture of naturalism and comedy, the play is a grim study of people trapped in poor mean lives and not coping very well. The weary resignation of the title says it all.

Chicago, Chicago is a revised version of *The Man From Chicago*, which was first produced at La Mama in 1969 and which, under its new title, was part of the 1970 Perth Festival season that established the APG. It was a play ahead of its time. Its fragmented action shows a series of expressionist scenes in which The Man—perhaps a delegate at the notorious 1968 Democratic Convention in Chicago, or perhaps a lonely individual with paranoid fantasies—is presented as an apparatchik and a fractured subject at the same time. Around him swirl disjointed scenes in which the public and private worlds are confused. Demonstrators chant outside his hotel room, then, in an alcoholic ward, a prostitute supplied by the party turns into a nurse who listens to his stories. Personal experiences keep being blown up into media bubbles that suddenly pop out of existence. A middle-American suburban couple, George and Lillian, represented on stage by cardboard cut-outs, watch and discuss the action as if it were a piece of 1960s New York avant-garde performance art. Three psychiatrists who are apparently looking after The Man become gangster figures, and later the President enters and launches into a series of increasingly deranged speeches, until the psychiatrists lead him away. The overall effect is of a political world gone mad, and of a private world of confusion and paranoia struggling to maintain an impossible coherence in the face of it. It anticipates the best of Stephen Sewell's early work—very funny, rather frightening and certainly worth reviving.

The Floating World (1974) is one of the great plays of the repertoire. Like *Chicago, Chicago*, it places its main character, Les Harding, in

Overleaf: Kerry Dwyer as Celia and Peter Cummins as Charlie in the 1969 La Mama production of I Don't Know Who to Feel Sorry For.

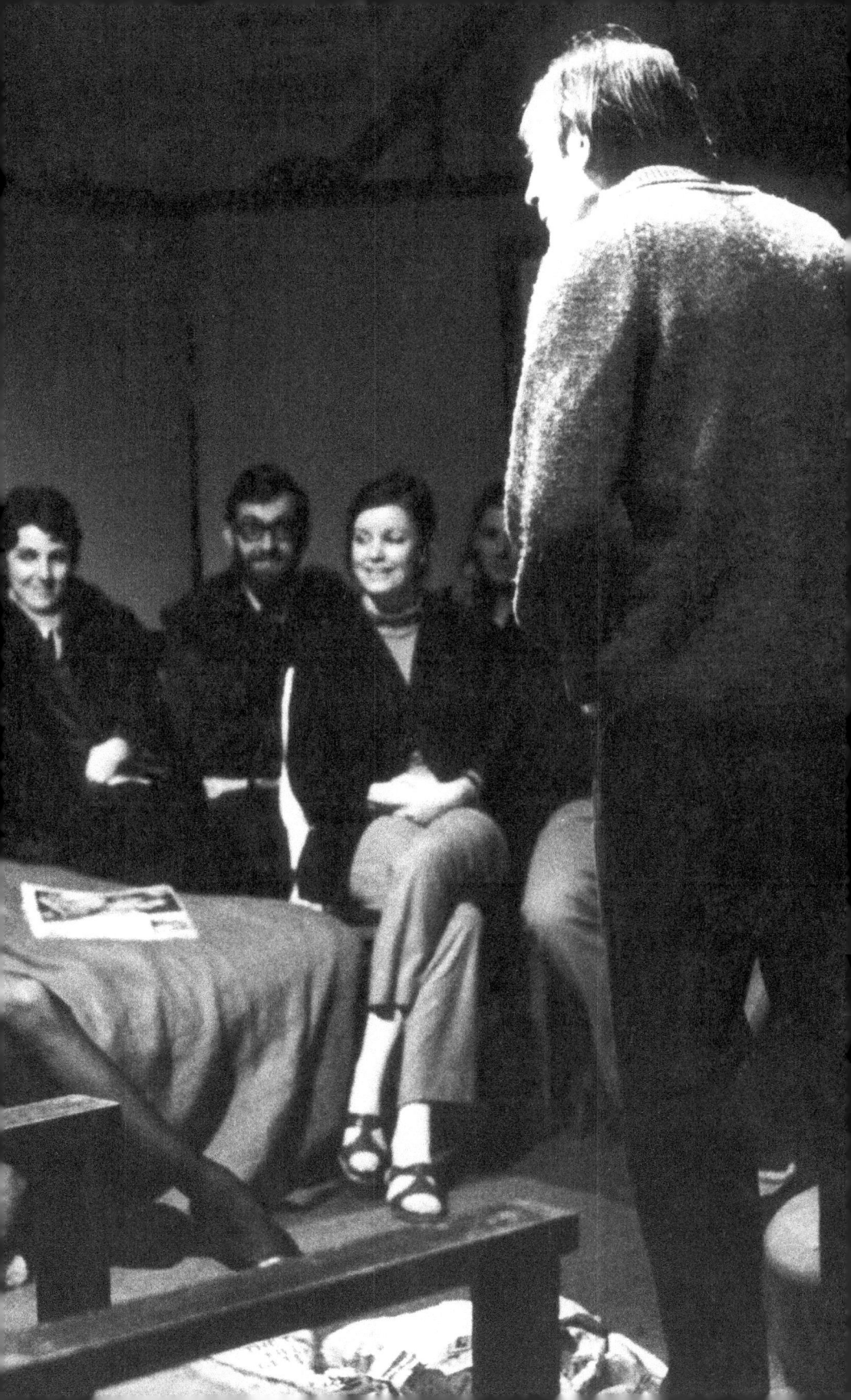

BELONGING

a web of social, cultural and political contexts and anticipates the complexity of the plays written from the late 1970s on by Nowra, Sewell and Michael Gurr among others—about socially constructed individuals caught up in national and international events.

The premise is simple. It is 1974 and Harding and his wife Irene, a classic suburban couple straight out of the early Patrick White or Barry Humphries, are going to Japan on a *Women's Weekly* Cherry Blossom Cruise. Much of the action—a sequence of send-ups of suburbia, crude clubland acts and grotesquely rendered scenes of shipboard life—is larrikin satirical comedy. But, as the play progresses, a deeper and bleaker vision of Australianness emerges. Les appears to have inherited all the racist attitudes of the White Australian tradition, but as a prisoner of war he also survived the forced labour gangs that built the Burma–Thailand Railway in 1942–43. The conditions were appalling: 'Three hundred and four corpses for every mile of track' (p. 92). As the cruise ship approaches Japan, Les begins to fall apart and the play records this in a succession of highly theatrical scenes of increasing paranoia. He sees an innocuous fellow traveller as the ghost of a fellow prisoner whose death he witnessed. A Malay waiter becomes a feared Japanese guard whose casual cruelty he remembers. At the end of the cruise he tries to kill some innocent Japanese, believing them to be his old enemies. The play concludes with a magnificent long speech in which, finally articulate, he recounts his experiences, reveals his survivor guilt and goes quietly mad. In the final powerful moment, strapped into a straitjacket, he tell us the story of his triumph in camp, when he was dying of beri-beri and he stole a Japanese officer's precious Vitamin-B tablets. He kept them from his mates and saved himself. The present Les is about to be carted off to an institution. In his memory of that victory he is finally, as he says, 'well again'.

Theatrically and dramaturgically, *The Floating World* is a complex play, forcing a new engagement with the old masculine discourses of Australianness and the challenges that subsequent counter-discourses had made. Les is an old ocker, stereotyped and satirised, who is offered to the audience as a sympathetic figure, when his experience is suddenly made personal. The Japanese are represented expressionistically, as old oppressors during the war, but also as new economic colonisers in

7: THE NEW WAVE

the opening scene, called Drum Poem One. Their influence in 1970s Australia is represented by the inane toy Dippy Birds that are set up on stage to bob mindlessly up and down throughout the action. The play is dialectical in the Brechtian sense, offering no fixed reference point from which its audience might stand and observe. Its mixture of theatricalism, satire, sympathetic realism and polemic makes for a profoundly unsettling experience that problematises Australian–Asian relationships on both political and individual levels.

Romeril's work with various community companies after the demise of the APG resulted in many occasional pieces, but he has also written several major plays that have not had the impact they deserve. *Top End* (1989), is set in Darwin on the eve of the 1975 Federal election, just after the Indonesian invasion of East Timor. It tells a powerful story of individuals caught up in broad public events. A young, passionately committed journalist, Jill, meets up with an old communist wharfie, Dollie, preparing to impose a union black ban on Indonesian ships in protest against the invasion. With Jill is Rosa, who has been fighting the good fight for many years, nursing in some of the world's worst trouble spots. The two women learn that one of their Fretilin friends has been killed and mutilated by Indonesian forces. Their political and the personal worlds fuse as they try to reconcile their personal desires with their public lives.

Lost Weekend is a city–bush play with an ironic edge. Eric is an old leftie union worker on a farm-stay holiday with his new lover Zelda, the physiotherapist who has helped him recover from a stroke. Over the weekend they do battle with the simple landowners Marg and Charles, who represent the old squattocracy. Eric turns out to have fled a much harder life on the land than Marg or Charles ever had. The play is like a modern, ironic station drama that reframes the bush legend in terms of the politics of class.

In the 1990s Romeril, who had become interested in Australia's position in Asia following *The Floating World*, focused again on Japan. In *Love Suicides* and *Miss Tanaka* the Japanese finally get to have their say.

Love Suicides is based in a respect for the work of Chikamatsu, the late seventeenth- and early eighteenth-century Japanese Bunraku

BELONGING

(puppet theatre) playwright, whom Romeril has called the Japanese Shakespeare and 'the first great playwright of our region'.[36] It is a contemporary Japanese-Australian version of the love-suicide plays that Chikamatsu wrote, of which the best known is *Sonezaki Shinju* (The Love Suicides at Sonezaki)(1703). In Romeril's tribute to the genre, a failed Western Australian tycoon facing jail and a disaffected Japanese woman in revolt against her wealthy family meet in a luxury hotel in Perth, fall in love and embark on a complicated journey that ends with their double suicide. The play takes Chikamatsu's interest in the conflict between social duty and human love and relocates it in the world of late twentieth-century cowboy capitalism. The narrative is complex and morally multivalent, and theatrically the play exploits a sophisticated integration of puppets and live performers playing characters that are realistically conceived.

Miss Tanaka, based on a short story by Xavier Herbert, is another highly theatrical script, telling another complex story of mixed, hybrid and border cultural experiences. Set in 1939 in Broome, Australia's great outpost meeting-point of Indigenous, Asian and European cultures, it uses puppetry, direct Brechtian narration and song and, although it is not as overtly theatricalist as *Love Suicides*, there is still that mix of passionately political and personal material and a theatricality that discourages comfortable subjective identification.

Kazuhiko is an Aboriginal-Japanese man whose father Tanaka, a broken down old pearl diver, yearns to go home to die in Japan. Mott is a sort of new-chum figure, from a tradition that goes back to the nineteenth century, in this case the newly arrived English head of a pearl-trading company. Tanaka drunkenly gets himself into a crippling gambling debt to two tough pearl divers and to save him Kazuhiko dresses up as Miss Kitso, the Miss Tanaka of the title, and fools them into competing for her as a bride. It is subversive and highly comic. Mott wants her, too. All three end up offering a dowry of pearls. During a wild storm, Kazuhiko, a classic postcolonial trickster-figure, ends up taking all their pearls and fleeing with his/her father to the Philippines. Like *Love Suicides*, the play mixes Japanese and European theatrical conventions to tell a story in which the cultures that produced those conventions have themselves become mixed, and transformed. The

7: THE NEW WAVE

other great Broome play, which first explored some of this territory, is Jimmy Chi's exuberantly cross-cultural 1990 musical, *Bran Nue Dae*.

Hibberd, Romeril and other New Wave writers also became identified in the early 1970s with another group of plays, which dealt with popular reclamations of Australian history. These became such an important genre of the New Wave that they deserve a section of their own.

Vaudeville history

Marvellous Melbourne, by Hibberd and Romeril, and *The Legend of King O'Malley*, by Boddy and Ellis, were highly influential early productions of the self-consciously populist side of the New Wave. These two productions pioneered a mini-wave that has been variously referred to as the cartoon or the vaudeville history plays—theatricalised historical stories that celebrated Australian traditions, using a range of popular styles drawn from vaudeville and melodrama and the new rebellious larrikinism. They carnivalised the same past used in the earnestly historical plays of the mid-century with a glibly theatrical style that was easy to write and fun to produce and perform.[37]

Marvellous Melbourne (1970) took its title from a well-known phrase describing that city in its glory years in the second half of the nineteenth century, and in particular from a popular melodrama produced by Alfred Dampier in 1889.[38] Hibberd and Romeril's script is a gleefully irreverent celebration of Melbourne's wild past, with plenty of mocking legend-building; it is also, in the context of the late 1960s, a radical romp about corrupt politicians who witness poverty only incidentally, on their way to visit their whores. With its gallery of villainous rich bastards and lively colourful larrikins, it celebrates the theatre as much as the history it supposedly charts. Several members of the Dampier theatrical family and the dour early modernist playwright Louis Esson appear as characters. One scene, set in an opium den, comes from Alfred Dampier's original play and another, splendidly new and grotesque, is set in a brothel patronised by the rich and powerful.

The Legend of King O'Malley (1970) had a longer life in the theatre and is the best known of the vaudeville history plays. In a happy

BELONGING

variety of theatrical styles, it recounts the saga of King O'Malley, an American revivalist preacher and conman who travelled to Australia after the failure of his church. He became a federal politician, claiming credit for the establishment of the Commonwealth Bank and the city of Canberra before he failed to win a fight with Prime Minister Billy Hughes over conscription in 1917. When the play first appeared, in 1970, conscription for the war in Vietnam was a major issue, but the play's greatest impact derived from its use of popular theatre traditions—including revivalist church singing and music-hall comedy routines—to debunk the pomposity of traditional 'great man' approaches to history.

Other examples of this form included *Biggles*, which inaugurated Sydney's Nimrod Theatre in 1970, a ratbag appropriation by Boddy, Marcus Cooney and Ron Blair of the fictional English hero on whose adventures many Australian boys had been brought up in the 1950s and 1960s; *The Duke of Edinburgh Assassinated*, a play about Henry Parkes by Ellis and Dick Hall, and staged at the Nimrod in 1971; and Blair's *Flash Jim Vaux* (1971), a ballad-opera about the colony's first great recidivist, James Hardy Vaux, a convict who was transported for life three times because he kept getting away and returning to England.

Nimrod's 1971 Christmas show was supposed to be a political revue but, with the 'who cares?' attitude that characterised the early Nimrod, ended up being a mock pantomime called *Hamlet on Ice*, written by Blair, Boddy and Cooney. Kate Fitzpatrick played a buxom Hamlet who, having fallen in love with a hunky Horatio, has had a sex-change operation. The lyrics and music for the show were by Grahame Bond and Rory O'Donoghue, who went on to create *The Aunty Jack Show* (1971–72) and *Wollongong the Brave* (1974) on ABC television. In an attempt to recreate some of the spirit of *Hamlet on Ice*, Bond returned to this pantomime style in 1979, with *Boy's Own McBeth: a really rotten tragedy*, which he co-wrote with Jim Burnett.

In Melbourne, Barry Oakley's plays included *The Feet of Daniel Mannix* (1971), a romp through the career of its eponymous and highly colourful anti-villain Archbishop Mannix and his role, with Bob Santamaria, in the Labor Party split during the 1950s. *Beware*

7: THE NEW WAVE

of Imitations (1973) is a splendidly grotesque portrait of Sir Robert Menzies, presented as an old clown named Wilfred McLuckie, shambling around the stage, drunkenly dictating and re-enacting his memoirs to his faithful manservant Alf, as he struggles to remember and to relive his glory years. *The Ship's Whistle* (1978) is a comic biography of Richard Hengis ('Orion') Horne, a self-promoting English immigrant who worked in various jobs suitable for a gentleman adrift in the colonies, distinguished mainly by his pomposity and his bad poetry.

Oakley wrote these plays for Max Gillies, who played Santamaria, Menzies and Horne and went on to become one of the great Australian comic actors and mimics. In a series of stage and television shows in the 1980s and 1990s he created grotesque caricatures of public figures in Australian politics and culture. With writer Guy Rundle, Gillies returned to this form of topical political satire in *Your Dreaming* in 2001 and *The Big Con* in 2004.[39]

Another show drawing irreverently on popular traditions, again from the APG, was Tim Robertson and John Romeril's *Waltzing Matilda* (1973), a mad version of a nineteenth-century pantomime in which the Demon King becomes a wicked capitalist pie maker, who, in comic defiance of all the laws of the marketplace, is determined to feed the entire population of Australia into his pie-making machine in order to sell more pies to the entire population of Australia. Robertson also wrote *Mary Shelley and the Monsters* (1975) and *Tristram Shandy— Gent* (1982), ocker appropriations of transgressive European texts.

Hibberd picked up again on the populist New Wave style in the early to mid-1970s and produced a number of what he called 'Popular Plays'—larrikin theatrical treatments of figures such as Les Darcy and Nellie Melba.[40] He carnivalised the form even further in *Captain Midnight VC* (1973), a musical romp that creates an imaginary history for its eponymous black trickster hero as he takes on the empire and ends up governor of Tasmania, which has been renamed Truganiniland.

A triumph of this style, because it actively involved its audience, was the Adelaide Troupe Theatre's production of *The Kelly Dance* (1984). Written by Romeril, the show told the Ned Kelly story in a directly experiential way as the audience took part in bush dances in

BELONGING

which they took on group roles in the narrative. The styles of their dances with the performers reflected the politics of the story.

In 1975 the APG had popular touring success with *The Hills Family Show*. A half-mocking and half-reverential comic tribute to the old touring family vaudeville troupes, the show was set up as a comically amateurish revival tour by an old theatrical family on its last legs.[41] The Hills Family—Fanny, Clifton, Sandringham, Adelaide, Antigone, Winston and Fitzroy, together with Granny and their depressed stage manager from Sydney, Mona Vale (names that play on Australian geography)—were a glorious collection of egocentric misfits, supposedly united as a family but in fact in constant conflict, performing sad old acts that were once much loved. The Hills were simply no longer up to it. The show, created out of madcap improvisations by several of the APG's finest performers (including Gillies, Sue Ingleton, Evelyn Krape and Tony Taylor) was full of comic business in the 'ain't it awful' tradition of *Dimboola*. It also had a lingering nostalgic sadness, lamenting the loss of the popular theatrical traditions that had done so much to invigorate the New Wave.

Richard Fotheringham and Albert Hunt's *The White Man's Mission* (1975), the first success for the Brisbane-based Popular Theatre Troupe, draws on the same theatricalist techniques.[42] Like the first half of *The Legend of King O'Malley*, it is presented as a mock religious revivalist meeting, but it is much tougher. It covers the white invasion of Australia, the frontier massacres, the 'Tasmanian solution' and then, in the second half, the importation of Kanaka slaves into Queensland. Like the vaudeville history plays, it is full of gags and songs and is written in a loose agitprop style that uses the company to play the various authority figures and bad men of the story. In a running gag, the audience is invited to play 'True or False', a game of testimony that mocks Australian memory loss and, incidentally, the idea of 'propaganda' in polemical political theatre. The Popular Theatre Troupe helped spawn a political community theatre in Queensland that is discussed in Chapter 12.

8
DAVID WILLIAMSON

Of all the bright young playwrights of the early New Wave the most successful, and later the most controversial, has been David Williamson.[1] He turned up at La Mama late, after the first burst of activity centred on Jack Hibberd, and the influx of radical artists from Monash University centred on John Romeril. He wrote three now forgotten one-acters that were produced at La Mama as well as the pioneering *The Coming of Stork* in 1970 and the now legendary *The Removalists* in 1971. *Don's Party* was produced by the APG at the Pram Factory, also in 1971, with some reluctance by the collective, who did not see its portrayal of the new middle class as sufficiently political. Both it and *The Removalists* came to national and eventually international attention through productions at Jane Street and Nimrod Theatres respectively in 1972, the same year Williamson resigned his teaching position to write full time. He has never looked back, except in his plays. By 2004 he was averaging two plays a year and was by far Australia's most popular playwright at the box-office. In 2005 David Marr observed that of the twenty-five biggest-grossing shows in the history of the Sydney Theatre Company, Williamson had written twelve.[2]

In the early 1970s, Williamson quickly established himself as a writer so in touch with the new audience that he seemed to anticipate, rather

BELONGING

than merely reflect, their concerns. In 1972 he described himself, in a phrase that has since become a mantra, as 'storyteller to the tribe', his tribe being the new urban professionals who made up his public. The theatregoers of the 1950s may have welcomed the *Doll* as being 'about us', in a vague spirit of nationalism, but Williamson was the first popularly successful playwright in Australia to write directly about the lives and worries of the people who were actually sitting in the theatre. For forty years they have loved him for it. As Katharine Brisbane has written he is, like Anton Chekhov, the playwright he most admires, a 'profoundly provincial' writer, sensitive to the emotional climate of his times and interested in the details of its individual obsessions, social organisation and political concerns.[3] This was a huge part of his early success and it still drives his astonishing succession of stage hits.

Three accusations have dogged Williamson throughout his career, all of them related to his ongoing popularity with mainstream audiences. He has been accused of being interested only in the concerns of a privileged social group; of confirming the conservative, or at best soft liberal, opinions and values of this group; and, especially in the first decade of his career, of writing naturalism, a highly-loaded term in New Wave politics and still used derogatorily, rather as the term 'easy listening' is used in relation to music.

Some of these accusations have foundation. Williamson has always admitted, both in the press and via characters who seem to speak for him—Andrew in *What If You Died Tomorrow*, for example, or Colin in *Emerald City*—that he is mostly interested in middle-class Australian society. At the same time, from *The Removalists* in 1971 to *The Jack Manning Trilogy* at the turn of the century, he has occasionally branched out from mining middle-class mores.

The two other criticisms are interconnected and neither is broadly true. The campaign against 'naturalism' was initially based on a serious critique that argued that a naturalistic representation of individuals in conflict normalises and neutralises important divisions. In other words, if you can convincingly explain why everyone did what they did, then you make the state of things appear inevitable and irremediable. In this sense the accusation that Williamson catered to the prejudices of his audiences is intimately linked to his supposed naturalism.

8: DAVID WILLIAMSON

However, Williamson has never written pure naturalism of the kind that requires his characters' behaviour to be psychologically or socially determined. True, he has often flirted with such explanations by allowing his characters to try them out on each other, just as he has argued that aggressive, competitive urges, as well as compassionate, altruistic ones, are intrinsic aspects of human nature. But he also exaggerates the foibles of his characters for comic effect in the style of the comedy of humours, derived from the old Roman comedy and the *commedia dell'arte*; and he has always been good at gags and one-liners.

In the 1990s, perhaps weary of critical attacks on the deterministic view of human nature implied by his supposed naturalism, Williamson addressed the issue head-on in two controversial plays, *Dead White Males* and *Heretic*. The first attacked the argument that the accepted 'truths' of the dominant culture are hegemonically constructed; and the second took issue with the idea that all human behaviour is determined by culture. If representation inevitably has a hidden ideological agenda, then at least he was laying his cards on the table.

What is often not acknowledged is that Williamson is essentially a genre-writer who generally works somewhere between recognition comedy and satire. As a supposedly 'objective' dramatic reporter on the mores and issues of his times, he has had a tendency to editorialise. All satirists do. But by using monstrously outrageous characters and a range of different theatrical styles—in particular, a social comedy that alternates between satire and comedy of manners—he keeps shifting the goalposts of identification. It makes his plays work like a gauge of his audiences' prejudices and opinions. Since *The Coming of Stork*, in which the title character's behaviour and language keep moving between the endearing and the appalling, Williamson has persistently teased his audiences by upsetting the expected balance between sympathy and revulsion. You can tell a lot about someone by asking them which Williamson characters they dislike.

He remains interested in his characters' humanness, but, instead of making them 'fully-rounded' or 'three-dimensional' in the tradition of naturalism, he makes their behaviour and emotions personally and socially recognisable to his audience. He gives actors a lot to do because his characters, for all their humour, emotion and conviction, are like empty vessels waiting to be filled. He also gives audiences a lot to do as he works the changes, so that we identify and are repelled at the same time.

Working the changes is, of course, his craft. Williamson was one of the first generation of Australian dramatists able to collaborate with experienced professional theatre-workers, in pre-production meetings with the central creative team and on the floor in rehearsals. During his career he has developed considerable craft skills in construction, plotting, rhythms and tonal variations.

Before he became a full-time writer he was a lecturer at the Swinburne Institute of Technology in Melbourne in thermodynamics and psychology—a combination so perfect that it would be nice to think it informed his playwriting. (It certainly supplied him with material: *The Department* is set at a staff meeting in the thermodynamics lab of such a college.) At a writers' forum at the Australian National Playwrights' Conference in the late 1970s, he said that one of the skills needed for writing plays can be described in terms of thermodynamics: controlling and manipulating the rate of flow of the release of information; something he has learnt to do superbly. In his continuous-action plays, from *Don's Party* and *The Department* to *Face to Face*, and in the more loosely narrated extended stories that use direct audience address, such as *The Perfectionist*, *Emerald City* and *Money and Friends*, he steers the audience through a sequence of expectations, revelations and reversals with great skill. Robyn Nevin believes that an essential task facing actors and directors of Williamson's plays is getting the rhythms right.[4]

His early work at La Mama and the APG ended with a rift, but it gave him down-to-earth theatre practice. He acted in the La Mama production of *The Removalists* (as the removalist, not a demanding role) and directed the second production of Jack Hibberd's *Dimboola*. Bruce Spence and Graeme Blundell directed his early plays in Melbourne. Once his career took off he worked closely with a number of directors who influenced his dramaturgy. His collaboration with John Clark on the Jane Street revision of *Don's Party* set the pattern for later relationships with Rodney Fisher, Aubrey Mellor, Wayne Harrison, Robyn Nevin, Sandra Bates and Gale Edwards.

8: DAVID WILLIAMSON

Williamson is the first Australian playwright to have written directly for and about his audience, and he has done so continuously for four decades. As most of the other New Wave writers slowed down, Williamson speeded up. By the late 1990s and early 2000s he was producing new plays and having old plays revived at a rate that became hard to track. He was also diversifying—producing satirical comedies such as *Up For Grabs* while exploring a new form, for him, with his community-conferencing plays, *Face To Face*, *A Conversation* and *Charitable Intent*. He has written more than thirty-five plays, as well as screenplays for film and television, including *Gallipoli*, *Phar Lap*, *The Year of Living Dangerously*, *The Last Bastion*, *The Dismissal*, and adaptations of his own plays for the screen.

Williamson's first three full-length plays ranged widely in the social worlds they reported but they all celebrated what their author identified as the 'awful Australian uniqueness'.

The Coming of Stork (1970) is set in a classic shared house, full of young men with bad habits and comfortable incomes to support them, like the young men in Hibberd's *White With Wire Wheels*. Stork, a trickster figure, is a hypochondriac graduate maths student who has dropped out and become a landscape gardener. He spends his time drinking, worrying about his imagined heart problem and trying, with little success, to get a root. His disruption of the household is gleefully irreverent and the conclusion, when he and another loser, West, barricade themselves in the flat and flush their pompous flatmate Clyde's wedding ring down the toilet, is an awful but splendid moment of comic larrikin protest. The play includes the first of many women characters for whom Williamson was criticised. Anna, who has slept happily with most of the boys in the play, settles finally for what they see as the dull respectability of marriage.

The Removalists (1971) is a much darker play, in which a simple set-up is pushed to an extreme conclusion by the power struggles that engage and entrap the characters. In the opening scene, Sergeant Simmonds and Constable Ross are involved in a struggle for power that Simmonds clearly wins. Then two young women, Kate and Fiona, turn up at their small police station to complain of the violent behaviour of Kate's yobbo husband, Kenny. A series of events is unleashed, driven by interpersonal

BELONGING

conflicts, alliances and betrayals, which result in Ross fatally bashing Kenny. In a final 'exorcism of violence', Simmonds and Ross conclude their earlier verbal battle in a stylised scene of brutal violence.

In all the early Williamson plays, there is a tension between satire and celebration. Like Stork, Kenny is one of his many loveable rogues—a character who is, by the social standards of his time, appalling, but who is portrayed with an affection that makes him oddly endearing. Like the devil, he has all the best lines. It is not until his pact with Simmonds at the end, when his corruption seems to betray his earlier jocular resistance, that we finally lose sympathy for him. Soon after that he dies of a massive cerebral haemorrhage caused when the much-provoked Ross beats him. It is a savage ending to a play that until that moment had expressed its conflicts comedically, albeit with a creeping menace.

A minor but key character is the unnamed removalist whom Simmonds and Ross have employed to take away Kenny and Fiona's furniture. Although a comic figure who just goes about his job, his total lack of interest in the way Simmonds tortures Kenny is a satirical comment on the attitude of the apathetic Australian public.

The Removalists was controversial at the time partly because it was seen as an attack on the police, a charge Williamson denied. It is understandable, though, that a play in which two policemen intervene in a minor domestic violence case in the hope of having sex with the victims, and end up killing the perpetrator, might be so taken, especially in the highly-charged atmosphere of the early 1970s. Another controversy surrounded the fact that the women are much thinner characters than the men. Four years after its stage premiere, a film version, directed by Tom Jeffrey, was released and the play remains a staple of the repertoire.

Don's Party, which opened two weeks after *The Removalists* in 1971, set the bittersweet tone and established the middle-class agenda for Williamson's work. The play is set on election night 1969, when, after twenty years in opposition, the Labor Party almost wins power under the new leadership of Gough Whitlam. It explores the disappointments faced by a collection of disillusioned sons of ocker, as they find that their professional careers don't measure up to the bold aspirations of their youth. In a wonderfully orchestrated

8: DAVID WILLIAMSON

single scene Don's election-night party degenerates over two hours into recriminations and pathetic attempts at seduction. The eleven increasingly desperate characters, capable of extraordinary individual vulgarity and insensitivity, collapse drunkenly into a stupor. Their very funny, and eventually sad, personal disillusionment with each other and themselves is punctuated by the live telecast during the evening. Whitlam's party, like Don's, starts out with high expectations but ends in failure, yet again, when voting preferences are distributed. The play closes with a trademark Williamson image that encapsulates the overall mood. Don drunkenly starts to light a cigarette but a moment of rueful reflection distracts him and the match burns his fingers. The last line is, 'Shit!'.

Don's Party also has Williamson's trademark dialogue. All night the boorish Mal tries to crack onto the sexy young Susan. When she chooses Don instead, Mal asks her, drunkenly, 'What's he got that I haven't got?'. 'The nod', she replies.

Williamson too got the nod. *The Removalists* and *Don's Party* were the hot plays in Melbourne and Sydney in 1971 and 1972, and their influence quickly spread around the country. Whether you preferred one or the other divided people, just as the question of whether you were a Stones or a Beatles fan had done in the 1960s: like the Stones, *The Removalists* was hard and serious; like the Beatles, *Don's Party* was soft and sentimental.

The distinction is less obvious now. In any case, during the 1970s and 1980s Williamson himself resolved the dispute by writing new plays that left Kenny, Ross and Simmonds behind as he followed the characters in *Don's Party* on their paths towards middle-class respectability.

Jugglers Three (1972) is Williamson's Vietnam play, but it focuses more on conflicts between individuals than on the war. Graham has just returned from active service in Vietnam to find that his wife Keren has left him to live with a timid university teacher, Neville, who has in turn left his pregnant wife. In a very funny encounter, Graham and Neville thrash out issues of Australian masculinity and their personal antagonisms. A farcical element is introduced when Dennis, Graham's army buddy, turns up. Having also found his wife

BELONGING

with another man, Dennis has stolen their baby and robbed a service station. Pursuing him is a comic policeman who goes away after being bribed. The play successfully mixes different comic styles. The final image is a frenetic game of table tennis as Graham and Keren battle into the darkness, their marital warfare unresolved. *Jugglers Three* was revised in 1997 as *Third World Blues* when some of the farcical elements were dropped and Graham was given more of a chance to speak of his war experience.

What If You Died Tomorrow was written for the Sydney Opera House's opening season of plays, 1973–74. It concerns Andrew Collins, a successful novelist and current darling of the women's magazines, comically struggling to deal with the complications of a new life not unlike Williamson's own at the time—a new wife; professional success that has taken him by surprise (but which he rather enjoys); and complicating intrusions by his agent and rival publishers. The farcical element, this time with a bitter twist, is introduced by Andrew's retired parents, who return from a world cruise with a miserable Norwegian tourist they have picked up as you would a stray dog.

The Department (1974) harks back to Williamson's time as a college lecturer. The setting is a staff meeting in a small, troubled engineering department, and the action is continuous as the play explores institutional politics and the interpersonal issues that underpin them. Next came *A Handful of Friends*, which is discussed below. The popularly successful *The Club* (1977), set in the world of Australian Rules football delves into the same issues. In this case, the characters—the Board member, an ex-player and hypocritical old bastard who dominates the Board; the decent former coach who is in his sights; the smooth-talking new corporate manager; and two players, one traditional but past it, the other new and flashy—become entangled in a web of intrigue and plotting prior to a crucial meeting. The play contains one of Williamson's funniest scenes, in which the new star player gets the old Board member stoned and regales him with the lurid, obviously fabricated, story of his tragic sex life with his legless sister and his mother. Both plays explore the ways in which institutional structures become infected by the personal agendas of the people who control them.

8: DAVID WILLIAMSON

Travelling North (1979) is the culmination and finest play of Williamson's early period. This beautiful study of a turning-point between generations is set during the years of transition between the election that Whitlam lost, in 1969, and the one that he won, in 1972. It reads now like a farewell to the larrikinism of the New Wave, a conciliatory lament for what it left behind, concluding with a determination to go on. It is, as Philip Parsons wrote, an almost religious play.[5]

It is a late-life love story. Frank, in his 70s, is an energetic old communist agitator and Frances, in her 50s, a gentle, warm woman with a quiet religious faith. They seem mismatched but they have a love affair and go north together from cold old Melbourne. They leave behind their children, who are embroiled in the storms and stresses of early adult life—parenting and marital troubles, the troubled world of *Don's Party* and *What If You Died Tomorrow*. Frances's children, particularly her desperately unhappy and needy daughter Helen, pull at her to come back, wanting a babysitter and the maternal support missing when they were children.

Frank and Frances get stuck in Tweed Heads, just south of golden Queensland where they were heading. Frank wants to settle down, but Frances is still restless. Their new neighbours are two old widowers, Freddy, and Frank's doctor, Saul, splendidly comic characters who both fancy Frances and are nervously respectful of Frank.

The couple briefly have romantic happiness, but the idyll sours when Frank gets sick and becomes increasingly demanding and cantankerous. Frances rebels and returns to Melbourne. But she decides that her children have to look after themselves now and, in a belated attempt at commitment, she returns to stay with Frank until the end. They marry just before he dies. During a wicked honeymoon they crash a Brett Whiteley opening, where Frank claims to be the artist's father. After Frank's death Frances looks around her life—her children in Melbourne and the two sad old men they have befriended in Tweed Heads—and decides to continue travelling north. It is one of Williamson's warmest plays.

The Perfectionist (1982) is another study of generations, like *What If You Died Tomorrow*, *Travelling North* and, later, *After the Ball*.

BELONGING

Ostensibly it is about an experiment in open marriage, the power balance shifting back and forth in a fluid sequence of short scenes that comically chart a marital crisis and its uneasy resolution. Stuart, the perfectionist, is an academic economist who for ten years has believed that he is on the verge of a major research breakthrough. He has delayed submitting his PhD thesis until he gets it right, relying for support on his long-suffering wife Barbara. During a teaching posting at a Danish university Barbara starts to rebel and has a fling with Erik, a socially idealistic young dreamer whom they employ to mind their children.

They return to Sydney, where the troubled relationship between Stuart and his highly successful QC father and alcoholic ex-actress mother comes to the fore. Stuart's research collapses and, pricked by Barbara's dissatisfaction and desire to have her own life, he transfers his obsessiveness from his work to his family life. Barbara has a longer affair with Erik when he comes to visit, but that too collapses. Finally, not without some weariness and reluctance, she returns to Stuart. It was Williamson's first serious attempt to deal with the experience of women in the new professional lives he was now documenting. Barbara is the narrator, but Stuart's crises are the main subject.

By the mid-1980s Williamson had established himself as the foremost dramatic chronicler of his times. During the rapaciousness of the late 1980s and early 1990, he started to explore themes of disappointment and disaffection: *Sons of Cain*, *Emerald City*, *Top Silk* and *Money and Friends* are comic studies of public greed, shallowness and corruption.

Sons of Cain (1985) was his first overtly topical political play, in that it tackled directly the subject of institutionalised corruption in government and the police force and let the family and interpersonal issues move into the background. Kevin is an embittered but valiant investigative journalist, who edits a hard-hitting weekly newspaper with a mission to expose the truth. He does this so well that he is muzzled by the proprietor and his political mates. Nothing that Kevin uncovers—a nexus of corruption between politicians, senior police and drug dealers—was particularly surprising at the time, but Williamson's outrage and depression at the impossibility of cleaning up the system is evident. The play appeared in the same year as Stephen Sewell's *The*

8: DAVID WILLIAMSON

Blind Giant is Dancing—a grand and savage political epic on the same subject that makes *Sons of Cain* look rather tame.

Emerald City (1987) returns to a more enclosed, but no less venal, world. Colin, a successful screenwriter, has recently moved to sinful Sydney from earnest Melbourne. He finds himself immersed in, and briefly seduced by, the shallow, bitchy world of the Sydney film industry, obsessed by talk of American studios and lucrative markets into betraying good old Australian storytelling. The parallels with Williamson's own career were obvious and Colin's manifesto might well be his own:

> I know the middle-class shouldn't have emotional problems—they're infinitely better off in a material sense than your average third world villager—but for some perverse reason they successfully screw up their lives with great flair, and I find that interesting, and I'm going to keep charting their perturbations and try and make some sense of it all, and those Chardonnay socialists of Melbourne aren't going to stop me! (p. 4)

Colin is simultaneously satirised and defended. There is a great deal of ironic mockery in his excessive, if brief, enthusiasm for the crass new world—'I don't want to make art films or films with a message, I want to make a product that entertains and I want it to make me awesomely powerful and fabulously rich!'(p. 40). But at the end he goes back to what he does best, leaving another of Williamson's comic monsters, Mike, a brash and blatantly self-seeking commercial filmmaker, to keep trying to woo the Americans. As he did in *The Perfectionist*, and would later do in *Siren*, *Up for Grabs* and *Operator*, Williamson uses direct audience address to steer the narrative and provide a series of comic revelations. Some of the best moments in this very funny play are provided by Colin's wife Kate, a book editor with the serious aim of producing good, not simply commercial, work. Also compromised by her brush with the industry, Kate nevertheless manages to maintain a frank dignity that Colin often loses.

Williamson's final play for the 1980s, *Top Silk*, returns to the issue of corruption. Its tough, clever plot explores the intersection between private and public morality. A brilliant QC, Trevor, who has taken on morally dubious cases in the past, is offered a high profile brief by a ruthless media mogul. His expectation is that, as a reward, the mogul will support his move into politics, which will almost certainly lead to his becoming Premier. His wife Jane, a legal aid solicitor, is a compassionate fighter for the underprivileged. She is assigned the case of an old school friend, Eddie, a heroin user who has been set up for a charge of dealing and who faces a long prison sentence that will leave his wife and children destitute. Eddie is a flawed but decent man and Jane tries to help him by offering the police a bribe. When Tony, Trevor's political enemy discovers this, he threatens exposure unless Trevor backs out of politics. However because Tony happens to have had an affair with Jane that led to an abortion, Jane is able to avert the threat. A subplot concerns the rebellion of Trevor and Jane's son, who has been oppressed by his father.

The play is written in a kind of breathlessly soap-opera style that was later seen in Hannie Rayson's *Two Brothers* and Louis Nowra's *The Boyce Trilogy*. *Top Silk*'s strength is to ask its middle-class audience whether they support Jane's or Trevor's type of corruption, and why.

Siren (1990) appears at first to be another play about public corruption, as a group of detectives holed up in a motel attempt to entrap a mayor who has been taking bribes to push through development applications. The detectives' plan is to exploit the appeal of Liz, the siren of the title, but they become embroiled in several complicated sexual encounters and conflicts. The play turns into a classic bedroom farce, which exacerbated Williamson's by-then troubled relationship with his critics, who thought that he shouldn't be writing that sort of thing.[6]

Williamson's long-standing interest in the intersection between public actions and the individual motives that drive them reached a climax in his best play of the early 1990s. In *Money and Friends* (1991) his satire of the shallow people who win the prizes in the materialist jungle of late capitalism comes up hard against his affectionate treatment of the decent people who don't. Williamson had always written warm characters who represented decent liberal bourgeois human values, and then set them up against monstrously libidinous, self-centred and ego-driven ones. But in *Money and Friends* the decent characters get a serious look-in and, for the first time, a real chance

8: DAVID WILLIAMSON

at some sort of personal success. It was the first hint of Williamson's optimism in the late 1990s.

The distinction between the good guys and the bad guys is sharper in *Money and Friends* than it has ever been. Margaret is a glorious creation, a tough, vitriolic university history lecturer who talks directly to the audience and leads them through a story in which a small pocket of human decency survives, just barely, the general selfishness surrounding it. Her best friend Peter is a professor of pure mathematics. He is also confessor to a group of people who are friends only because they own neighbouring weekenders at a wealthy holiday settlement called Crystal Inlet. Peter faces a financial crisis because, unworldly mathematician that he is, he has gone guarantor for the loans of his brother, whose business has failed in the recession. He needs $40,000 to complete the legal proceedings that will almost certainly see him through. Margaret decides to ask four other couples for the money. As the publicity blurb for the play put it, 'Would *you* lend a friend $10,000?'

On this hook Williamson hangs a loose narrative about a group of terrible people who use Peter's good natured, friendly support to help them through their own emotional problems, but offer nothing in return. The play is the first of Williamson's pure comedies, full of pleasant malice for the frailties and sins of the selfish, but with an underlying warmth that leads to a more or less happy comic ending. It set the tone for *The Great Man*, *Up For Grabs* and *Soulmates*, in which Williamson found a new balance between satire and sympathy.

Before he went there, however, he produced a series of plays of enquiry and debate that again landed him in trouble, although not with his loyal audience. This was partly because he wasn't frightened of dealing with topical issues in politically controversial plays which, although they made a show of being even-handed, were highly tendentious.

Brilliant Lies (1993) is a play about sexual harassment in the workplace, centring on a young woman who seems at first to be manipulating recent anti-discrimination legislation for her own selfish purposes. Although she is clearly vindicated, the means she uses— telling brilliant lies to an official mediator—was seen at the time as a political attack on the new laws. It was the first of Williamson's plays of social conflict in which the processes of formal mediation were offered as a hopeful way through thickets of lies and hypocrisy. *Sanctuary* (1994), is almost as formal, although its action is private. An idealistic young man who is revolted by the media's manipulation of public opinion in the interests of the rich and powerful secretly confronts one of the richest and most powerful commentator in the land. But the young man turns out to be just as sociopathic as—and, if anything, more deranged than—his enemy. In this play the political argument is subsumed in a brutally violent conflict that becomes utterly personal.

Dead White Males (1995) satirises academia and poststructuralism, linking them with what the play portrays as an unfair devaluation of the institution of the family. Its most colourful character is Grant Swain, another comic monster and satirical object. He is a hypocritical university lecturer who teaches poststructural theory and uses his proclaimed subject position of 'non-essentialist feminism and multiculturalism' (p. 7) to seduce his students. The central character is an enquiring young student named Angela, and the older, feminist women in her family are also satirised. *Heretic* (1996) is a vivid dramatic biography of the anthropologist Derek Freeman, acknowledging his personal failings but narrating in heroic terms his life-long academic battle against Margaret Mead. The comic monster figure that began with Stork and was given its most sensitive treatment in Frank, in *Travelling North*, finally gets a play to himself. But while Frank came to some sort of resolution with his women, Derek's dealings with his wife, Monica, consist mainly of repeated and belated apologies for being such a bastard.

Following *Heretic*, Williamson turned away from his brief engagement with intellectual debates and focussed again on personal issues, producing one of his most tenderly autobiographical and earnestly self-exploratory plays, *After the Ball* (1997). The play was written after the death of his mother and he has said that he was partly trying to 'make sense of the family I grew up in and the impact that family has had on me'.[7]

In the play a distinguished émigré film director, Stephen MacCrae, returns to Australia to attend his mother's deathbed alongside his sister Judy, who has stayed in Australia to pursue a more modest career as a teacher with a social conscience. As they sit with her each day,

8: DAVID WILLIAMSON

and retreat each night to her house in the retirement village, the play tells the story of their family, particularly the poisonously bitter and combative relationship between their parents, Kate and Ron, and the effects that this had on each of them as children and young adults. The comic, sad portrayal of the parents' relationship and the sibling rivalry and adult resentments of Stephen and Judy are a culmination of the cross-generational studies of family life that Williamson had been writing for a long time—especially in *What If You Died Tomorrow*, *Travelling North* and *The Perfectionist*. There is something similar in the family scenes in *Dead White Males* and in the relationship between Derek and Monica in *Heretic*.

But *After the Ball* is a much quieter, more elegiac play than any of its predecessors (except, perhaps, *Travelling North*), charged with emotion as Stephen comes down from the hype of his cosmopolitan life in Europe to listen more quietly to his past. He discovers that, until his death, his father Ron carried in his wallet a photo of his first girlfriend, from whom Kate had stolen him. He also reaches a reconciliation of sorts with his sister. Released from his inhibitions because he believes her to be unconscious, he sits and talks frankly to his mother for the first time, and is relieved afterwards when the nurse tells him that often hearing is the last faculty to go. It is an extraordinarily sentimental ending for Williamson. If the play is autobiographical, then perhaps it brings closure to the more cynical and troubled representations of family life in the earlier plays.

Autobiography, or what Williamson calls 'life borrowing'—using the personalities and traumas of his friends as dramatic and comic material—had always been an issue in his writing, or at least a subject of gossip (although he never seemed to suffer critically for it in the way that Dorothy Hewett did). It was said, perhaps apocryphally, that Melbourne in 1972 was full of vain men who claimed to be the model for Cooley in *Don's Party*. In *A Handful of Friends* (1976), Williamson addressed the issue directly via the character of Mark, a filmmaker who has put his friend on screen in an unflattering light. He gives a stumbling, embarrassed self-justification about the re-patterning of life that is required in art (p. 108). That play prompted a notorious article by Bob Ellis and a subsequent public correspondence between him,

BELONGING

Williamson, Kristin Green (now Williamson) and Ellis's wife Anne Brooksbank that aired some dirty linen concerning how they had all been portrayed, and raised again the issue of writers' appropriation of their friends' lives.[8]

In plays of the 1980s and 1990s, Williamson was asking a basic question: how is it possible for a decent small-l liberal to behave well in a world gone mad with greed and corruption? Unlike his successors Louis Nowra and Stephen Sewell, he has never written epic historical or political plays about colonialism or the military-industrial complex or, as their successors Daniel Keene and Andrew Bovell have, explored the world of the alienated underclass of late twentieth-century capitalism. But he nevertheless asks the question, on behalf of his comfortable upper-middle-class audiences.

Since *After the Ball* Williamson has returned in different ways to rework some of the concerns of his early plays. He revisited the politics of the 1970s in *The Great Man*, one of several Australian plays in which a group of women—former wives and lovers—gather at the death of an old patriarch to reflect on his life. Hannie Rayson's *Life After George* and Alma De Groen's *Wicked Sisters* are others. He has revived some of the larrikin spirit of his early years in topical social comedies such as *Up For Grabs* and *Soulmates* (2002). And he has returned to his interest in the complexities of human interaction in formal institutional settings in *The Jack Manning Trilogy*.

The Great Man (2000) revisits the issues of political commitment and personal compromise first raised in *Don's Party*, and asks what happened to the idealism of that generation. If Don and his mates were disillusioned in 1969, then what hope thirty years later, when the dreams of the 1960s socialists had been so comprehensively betrayed by the party they once fought for? When a legend of the Whitlam government, Jack ('The Duke') Barclay, dies, the women who knew him gather, ostensibly to work out his funeral, but in fact to work through their own conflicts as they fight over how the old bugger should be remembered.

The mourners include Eileen, the Duke's bitter but comically cheerful first wife; Fleur, his idealistic companion in his old age; and Tegan, a journalist who interviewed him just before his death and who

8: DAVID WILLIAMSON

has dug up more detail about his life than the other two want to know. He turns out, for all the legend, to have been corrupt. A seedy lawyer enters, with details of shady offshore bank accounts that reveal that Jack has left them a fortune. Only Fleur rejects the money on moral grounds. The play is a sentimental comedy—suggesting that, even if ideals are abandoned in the public world, it is still possible to live by personal ideals.

Corporate Vibes (1999) is another in the new line of optimistic plays. Like *Brilliant Lies* and *The Jack Manning Trilogy*, it is a play about a process of negotiation and reconciliation, and, rather shockingly, the process works. The satire has all but disappeared, replaced by a warmth that is startling. Much is made of the 'inner 6-year-old' who drives a lot of adult behaviour. Williamson's inner 6-year-old seems to be a very nice, polite little boy.

An earlier Williamson, or a tougher playwright, might have satirised a great deal of the material in this play. Deborah Fielding is an inexperienced new human resources officer employed by a housing developer to help arrest the company's declining fortunes which, everyone understands, means to sack people. The real problem, she discovers, is that no-one wants to live in the company's appalling new building, developed under the dictatorial control of the play's comic monster, the bigoted, sexist, aggressive owner Sam Siddons. Deborah asks the key employees—head salesman Brian, architect Angela and marketing manager Megan—to listen to their 'inner song', work together and devise their ideal development. Brian's inner song is to be an interior designer, so he does that; Angela's is to make a radical use of space, to create community areas for the building's inhabitants to get to know each other; Megan's is to be a marketing manager, but she is more successful now that she has something good to market. Because Deborah is Aboriginal, it would be a public relations disaster if Sam sacked her, so he gives the project the go-ahead. It wins architectural awards, it sells and the company is saved. So complete is Sam's conversion by the end that he throws a party, unsuccessfully propositions Deborah and ends up contemplating marriage with Megan. The comedy has little to do with the realities of property development, but its wit, humour and charm are successful, in a cute way.

BELONGING

Face to Face (1999), which opened two months later, is the first of the tightly written, single-action plays in *The Jack Manning Trilogy*, in which disputing parties are brought together to talk through their problems and, if possible, come to a resolution that will keep them out of the courts. Although there is still a lot of humour in these plays, Williamson avoids satire and rebuts the criticism that he only writes about the comfortable middle-class.

The format of each play is the same: a group of characters enter and sit in a semi-circle of chairs. Jack Manning, a facilitator, leads them through the events of the dispute and prompts them to say what they feel about it and what they want from the conference. In each play Williamson has distilled into 90 minutes a process that normally takes three or four hours, and he allows Manning to intervene and express opinions more than a professional facilitator might, but the spirit is reproduced. More than any of his others, these plays bring together Williamson's original twin interests in psychology and thermodynamics—community conferencing, say the professionals, is about the 'mechanics of emotion'.[9]

In *Face to Face* the dispute concerns a simple young man who has deliberately crashed into his boss's car after being dismissed for a violent outburst at work. He has a traumatic past, with a bad father, and this job is the first satisfaction he has ever found. As the details of the troubled workplace environment are exposed, it becomes clear that he is the only worker who actually likes his job, but his naïvety makes him vulnerable to taunting by his workmates and his short temper creates problems. A tentative resolution keeps him out of jail.

A Conversation (2001) raises the stakes. The crime this time is a sadistic rape and murder, so the victim is dead and the perpetrator in a maximum security prison. The conference is for the benefit of the families who have suffered from this terrible experience. A large part of their grief and rage is focussed on that familiar Williamson issue: whether nature or nurture is to blame. A resolution at the end hints at the possibility that the families can now remake their lives.

In *Charitable Intent* (2001) the central conflict is provoked by the efforts of an aggressive new chief executive officer determined to

8: DAVID WILLIAMSON

reform what she views as outdated work practices in a large charitable organisation. In this case it is clear that the new CEO and her supporters are to blame. For the first time in the trilogy the conference collapses but the resolution is simple, and the revelation of incompetent management is a moral vindication of the old ways.

In *Up For Grabs* and *Soulmates* Williamson's satirical malice returns. Again he shows his ability to encapsulate a closely-knit social world, with its peculiar manners and attitudes, and to present it to a general audience with a mixture of horror and amusement. *Up For Grabs* (2001) is set at the fashionable big-money end of the Sydney art scene. It is narrated by Simone, an art dealer who is prepared to sell her soul and body in pursuit of wealth and glamour. With a Brett Whiteley to sell for two million dollars, she embarks on several riotous encounters—first by mobile phone and then, to great comic effect, in the flesh—with a trio of bizarre art collectors. Eventually Simone sells the picture and avoids financial ruin. A substantially trimmed and rewritten version of the play was produced in London in 2002, with Madonna as Simone, the painting a Jackson Pollack and the target price twenty million dollars.[10]

Like *What If You Died Tomorrow*, *A Handful of Friends* and *Emerald City*, *Soulmates* (2002) is a play about writers, focussing on two successful novelists—a popular airport novelist and a serious literary lion—and Danny, a frightfully earnest critic who takes pompous pride in setting literary standards. Danny delights in trashing the work of the popular writer and praising that of the other. His wife Heather, an innocent financial investment advisor adrift in the brutal, no-prisoners-taken world of literature, travels to New York, where she meets both writers and starts an affair with the serious one—who turns out to be a charming hypocritical cad. The climax of the comedy is a Melbourne Writers' Festival forum, chaired by Danny and featuring both novelists, which degenerates into an argument, like those in *Emerald City*, about whether the suffering of the comfortable Western middle classes is as important a subject as the suffering of third world villagers. The play ends as the popular writer starts making notes for a new book about everything we have just seen. Her husband is worried that in doing so she might be betraying her friends:

BELONGING

> GORDON: I'd just hate to think that the woman I loved did anything that wasn't worthy of her.
>
> KATE: Well she's going to. Because she's a writer, and that's what writers do.

In the early 2000s, Williamson extended his prodigious output of social issue comedies narrated in personal terms. In *Birthrights* (2003) a woman agrees to be a surrogate mother for her infertile sister. But when she later wants a baby of her own, she has become infertile. She starts to dote on the first child, competing with her sister for the child's love. *Amigos* (2004) brings together three old friends, members of a once successful Olympic rowing team, who meet up and compare achievements. *Influence* (2005) is a play full of humanist outrage, centred on a right-wing radio shock-jock who has an Islamic cleaner. Even when his family and staff abandon him, his talkback career continues. *Operator* (2005) is a savage comedy about a psychopathic Machiavellian manipulator who joins a small company, destroys the careers of most of his colleagues for the sake of his own advancement, and then leaves, to become, we assume, one of the great business leaders of his time. In all these plays alongside the satire, Williamson is sentimental in his celebration of underdog characters.

Williamson continues to produce new works well after his short-lived retirement (for health reasons) in 2005. *Lotte's Gift* was written as a vehicle for classical guitarist Karin Schaupp in 2007, and the light romantic comedy *Scarlett O'Hara at the Crimson Parrott* for actor/singer/dancer Caroline O'Connor in 2008. Williamson's contribution to the Australian repertoire over forty years has been enormous, and in the process of supplying box-office successes for the mainstream theatres, he has supported a great deal of the more adventurous work that many of those companies have produced. The theatres needed him, other playwrights, although sometimes in his shadow, were supported by him and audiences have continued to love him.

9
PLAYWRIGHTS IN THE 70S

Many of the playwrights of the New Wave rose, shone briefly, and then sank without a trace, in a theatre culture that briefly supported them and then moved on.[1] Some others have been covered in Chapter 7. But Alexander Buzo and Alma De Groen, and to a lesser extent Jim McNeil, were major dramatists whose plays have never become a regular part of the repertoire in the way that the plays of White and Williamson have. This chapter also covers the remarkable work of Reg Livermore, a performer, who wrote his own material in the 1970s for a series of highly original shows.

Alexander Buzo

Alexander Buzo had been the first success of the early New Wave. His 1968 *Norm and Ahmed* was a leading play in the anti-censorship battle of the late 1960s and it provoked John Romeril's *Whatever Happened to Realism*. Still often revived, it is, along with Esson's *The Drovers*, the best-known Australian one-act play. Buzo was also the first New Wave playwright to be produced overseas, when his absurdist comic nightmare *Rooted* had a modest critical success in Hartford, Connecticut and was favourably reviewed by *Time* magazine in 1972, an achievement that at the time counted for a lot. *The Front Room Boys*, first produced in

BELONGING

Sydney in 1969, was part of the pioneering season of Australian plays that the nascent APG took to the 1970 Perth Festival and was published in the influential 1970 volume of plays of that season.² In 1972–73 he was writer-in-residence at the Melbourne Theatre Company, where he wrote *Tom* and, earlier, *Macquarie*, the first play published by Currency Press, in 1971. Until David Williamson's triumph in 1972, Buzo was the best-known New Wave playwright.

Buzo used Australian vernacular language in a new way that was both instantly recognisable yet stylised. Because the New Wave was concerned with a nationalist revival of that old dog, 'Australianness', it was assumed by critics and commentators at the time that his plays were simply satires of Australian characters and behaviour. Norm in *Norm and Ahmed* is like Humphries's Sandy Stone, although much more aggressive. At first glance, the young men in *Rooted* and *The Front Room Boys* seem to be typical sons-of-ocker stereotypes, like those in Hibberd's *White With Wire Wheels* and Williamson's *The Coming of Stork*. Buzo's wit, and his cool detachment, made his early plays seem like comic representations of what Williamson, when he had his first overseas success in London, called the 'awful Australian uniqueness'.

But Buzo was not interested in Australianness for its own sake and, frustrated by critical misunderstanding and a run of bad productions of his plays, he said so.³ He was interested in the ways in which individuals become trapped in discourses that they do not understand (or, in his later plays, which they understand only too well but reject) and in the roles that they consequently, and blindly, play, roles that become fixed as masks.⁴ In his best plays of the 1970s he explored the shy sensitivities of a series of alienated professional protagonists, who find these social constrictions too much to bear and retreat into a kind of neurotic individualism. Coralie in *Coralie Lansdowne Says No*, Edward in *Martello Towers*, Weeks in *Makassar Reef*, Adela in *Big River* and Toby in *The Marginal Farm* have all done well in the public world, then retreated from it. Towards the end of the 1970s, Buzo retreated too, from the sweaty socio-political world of the New Wave. In the 1980s he produced social comedies such as *Stingray* and *Shellcove Road*, and then came back in 1995 with *Pacific Union*, a sophisticated, if dramaturgically old-fashioned, history play about

9: PLAYWRIGHTS IN THE 70S

the role of Doc H. V. Evatt, troubled Labor legend who, as Australia's Foreign Minister, championed the rights of small nations at the 1945 conference in San Francisco that set up the United Nations.

Buzo seems to have been press-ganged into the New Wave. But as its larrikin agenda—based in the rhetoric of newness, spontaneity, rough theatre and Australianness—began to enter the mainstream, his stylish dry wit and middle-class individualism became unfashionable. His plays dropped out of the repertoire and his dramatic output slowed. In spite of his early celebration of the vernacular, his respect for language, craft and standards seemed to link him with the old Anglo generation. Like the generation of genre writers of the 1930s and 1940s, he was outside his time. Had it not been for the rebellious nationalist agenda of the New Wave that first nurtured him, he might be known now for what he was: Australia's first great humanist writer of the comedy of social manners.

He first attracted attention with his play *Norm and Ahmed*, particularly for its last line, 'Fuckin' boong'. In 1968 this fuelled an anti-censorship campaign and sparked police interest and legal action in three states.[5] The play presents a late-night encounter between a blue-collar worker and a Pakistani student who is studying Arts at university under the Colombo scheme. Much of the comedy is based in the incongruity between Ahmed's formally correct English and Norm's equally formal but theatrically more extravagant ocker vernacular. For most of the play the audience is led to believe that Norm and Ahmed are moving tentatively towards a mutual understanding, but at the end Norm suddenly bashes Ahmed viciously, perhaps killing him—a shocking climax that still works. In 2002 Buzo revised the play, in *Normie and Tuan*, substituting a Vietnamese antagonist for his Pakistani original.

Buzo's first full-length play, *Rooted* (1969), is another study of people trapped in language, which the audience but not the characters understand is a form of social and cultural imprisonment. Bentley has two public modes of speaking—one for his mates and one for his bosses—and a private world that he is unable, except in brief moments, to articulate. He lives an absurdist nightmare, hounded out of his home, his marriage and his job by Simmo, whom the audience never see.

BELONGING

The power of this offstage figure—the first truly scary representation of hegemonic corporate power in Australian drama—derives from his refusal to engage in the daily chatter of the people he oppresses and dispossesses. Bentley is an oppressed innocent, a holy fool. Apart from one great scene of self-expression, he is only theatrically eloquent in the concluding scene, when he is silent.

The Front Room Boys (1969) is another formally constructed absurdist comedy, about office workers and the institutional oppression of their individuality. In this case everyone is complicit in their oppression except Jacko, the outsider. The back room boys who oppress them are, like Simmo, mostly offstage figures of power, represented by the laconic Hendo, who silently comes onstage from time to time to note down their transgressions, and by his front room stooge, Robbo. Jacko, the rebel, ends up, in the excess of the final scene, sacked, wrapped in office paper and cast out of the tribe of happy, smiling, unwittingly abject workers.

The first Buzo play staged at Nimrod—a satire about the rising cult of personality on television sport shows, *The Roy Murphy Show* (1971)—reads today like a text-book example of the failure of satire to keep up with the world. Roy, an extreme character at the time, has since been overtaken by real-life television personalities of the type thoroughly parodied by Roy Slaven and H. G. Nelson.

Tom is a surreal comedy about big business and globalisation, written in 1972, partly to satirise the hype surrounding the commercial boom in natural resources stocks that stirred the market at the time. It parodies then-popular television soap operas about high-flying corporate life. The sinister offstage bad guys, sons of Simmo, are represented by Stephen, a very real onstage presence described by Susan, the only character in the play with any real humanity, as an 'unctuous cunt'. Susan is a precursor of the ambivalent tender-tough women in Buzo's plays of the late 1970s.

The first of these is the eponymous heroine of the ironically titled *Coralie Lansdowne Says No* (1974), who has retreated from the awful social world of Simmo, Hendo, Robbo and Stephen, and lives alone, perched in her eyrie on the cliffs above Sydney's Palm Beach. She is surrounded by rich freaks and besieged by old lovers and new suitors,

9: PLAYWRIGHTS IN THE 70S

including the persistent Stuart, a weed of a man to whom she finally says yes. Coralie is brash, witty, bitchy and destructive, but underneath she has a tenderness that she discovers only towards the end of the play. In a mysterious coughing fit in the final scene, she literally chokes on her decision, as she unwraps wedding presents with Stuart. Yet there is a weary acceptance in her final line to Stuart, who is not very interesting but who will support her through everything. 'You'll do', she says.

The play reads now like a riposte to early second-wave feminism in its celebration of a big sassy woman who has seen and done it all, and settles for the comforting support of a quiet unexciting man who says he loves her.

Edward Martello, in *Martello Towers* (1976), is a similar character, a clever wise-cracker with a hidden pain. His retreat is his family's flash holiday house on an island in Pittwater, to the north of Sydney, on which he, his estranged wife Jennifer and his sister Vivien all turn up accidentally on the same weekend with their new lovers. On the surface the play is a clever comedy, with an opening, in which the various couples come and go and keep missing each other, that is pure farce. But it soon becomes much more serious, as the emptiness and longing that Edward, Jennifer and Vivien feel in the face of the 'empty pseuds' who surround them becomes clear. Edward, a second-generation Italian-Australian, is haunted by his family's expectation that he will do well in business and, above all, breed. Jennifer, who has wearied of his supercilious detachment and gone off to look for a new life among the pseuds, finds that she still wants his inner sincerity and is prepared to accept his relentless surface cynicism in order to have it. Vivien is left alone at the end, with the dreaded Martello family tradition closing in around her, in a way that may or may not be comforting for her.

This play and Buzo's next, *Makassar Reef* (1978), are so witty and brittle on the surface that many commentators at the time failed to notice anything else, which led Buzo into a vitriolic public dispute with his critics.[6] The play's original director in 1976, Richard Wherrett, wrote that it took him a while to discover the play's deeper levels, which perhaps were 'buried too deeply in the text'.[7]

BELONGING

Makassar Reef is his darkest play, an apparently genre-based romantic comedy-drama with a bleak undercurrent. Weeks Brown is a high-flying economist on an alcoholic holiday binge with his long-term partner Beth, whom he is about to marry and who, for all he knows in his present drunken stupor, may be pregnant. The play is about their last flicker out of bounds. Weeks falls hopelessly, sincerely and destructively in love with Wendy, a passing tourist and returning expatriate with a young daughter named Camilla. Beth has a brief passionate fling with Perry, a passing yachtsman and smuggler. It is as if the characters were all fleeing from the world of 1970s Australia, as Buzo might have been fleeing, from the New Wave, into a genre movie. There is a great deal of casual adventure and intrigue, involving a comic drug smuggler, a corrupt official and an earnest young Indonesian radical journalist, but in the end, like *Coralie Lansdowne Says No* and *Martello Towers*, the play is about settling down, with a mood of mixed regret and contentment as the characters make compromises with the world.

In the next plays the compromises have been made long before the action opens. The leading characters have retreated into a past, in an attempt to conserve something of value. Adela in *Big River* and Toby in *The Marginal Farm* are both in full flight from the world.

Big River (1980) is set on a country estate outside Albury on the Victoria–NSW border on the eve of Federation and the new century. The play has much in common with the station dramas and family sagas of the 1940s, including the set, which represents the ante-room and veranda of the Hindmarsh family home, threatened now by real-estate development and the passing of the old life. Old Captain Hindmarsh has just died and his lively daughter Adela, a social butterfly and party-girl who works in the city, has returned home. After many complications it becomes clear to the matriarch, Ivy, that of all her children Adela, the rebel, is the one to carry on the family tradition. At the end of the play Adela, though mistress of the estate and pregnant, is left with a perverse sense of personal failure and unease about what the new century and her pregnancy might bring.

In *The Marginal Farm* (1983) Toby, another city-based modern woman fleeing something, arrives in 1950s Fiji, a colony dominated

9: PLAYWRIGHTS IN THE 70S

by imperial commercial interests, to be a governess to the disaffected children of Marshal, the Field Officer for the Colonial Sugar Refining Company. She is full of spirit and determined to have fun. Pursued by a string of men—James, a romantic English pilot, and her pupil Philip, who has an adolescent crush on her—she finally settles for Illy, a Fijian Indian who is a go-getter commercially and sexually. She announces at the beginning that she does not want to become a batty old white woman adrift in the tropics, but by the end that is exactly what she has become. She visits Illy for weekend trysts for which he sends away Taka, his housekeeper and weekday mistress. The once high-flying Illy is a CSR Field Officer, a position Marshal offered him to curb his rebellious independence. As Illy says 'It's an arrangement that's not perfect. But it will do' (p. 150). This echo of Coralie's last line to Stuart neatly sums up the mood of Buzo's best plays, but there is a hint of a new generation when Toby's other pupil, Ellen, returning for a visit, flees in horror when she sees how Toby has turned out.

The creeping mood of weary resignation in this sequence of plays—as Buzo's funniest, liveliest and most rebellious characters started to shrug their shoulders and settle for less—disappointed directors, critics and audiences who had come to love his wit and the sharpness of his characters. As Coralie's pride became Toby's bathos, and Edward Martello's defiance became James the pilot's flippant evasiveness, Buzo's later plays had a feeling of retreat. People who live in the busy world, they seemed to be saying, are disappointing.

Alma De Groen

Alma De Groen was drafted into the New Wave in the early 1970s by commentators and educators as a writer of domestic comedies and marital relationships written from a woman's perspective. But, like Alex Buzo, she was misread. Her early plays, *Going Home* and *Vocations* are fine examples of the new style of middle-class comedy and both were successful. But De Groen is a playwright of ideas who has always been interested in a wide range of forms. In her later work—such as *The Rivers of China*, *The Woman in the Window* and *Wicked Sisters*—she has produced rich, complex plays in which individual characters struggle to discover and position themselves existentially in worlds of thought, created in dystopian visions of society. She has never received the serious critical attention she deserves except from Elizabeth Perkins.[8] In 1998, she became the first playwright to be given the Patrick White Award, which rewards neglected major writers. In 2004, she returned to the country of her birth, New Zealand, after what she called her 'four-decade working holiday in Australia'.[9]

Her early full-length plays from the New Wave period include *The Sweatproof Boy* (1972), an absurdist domestic nightmare in which an alienated and depressed housewife, Olivia, attempts to act out her hidden desires with the help of a mysterious young lodger, Sam. Sam also attracts the intense interest, which may or may not be sexual, of Olivia's otherwise emotionally distant husband, Charles. The play includes an effect that was to become a major feature of her later work—playing on the dramatic ambiguity of the theatrical present—when Olivia manages to destroy Charles, a radio announcer doing his stuff on another part of the stage, by smashing the radio on which she has been listening to him. Later she apparently replaces him with a perhaps fantasised, but theatrically very real, sexual manifestation of Sam. The play was later reworked into the neat little one-acter, *Perfectly All Right* (1973).

Another one-acter, *The Joss Adams Show* (1972), is a bleak absurdist drama in which an alienated mother carries her new baby around in a bag, and later a carry-basket. In a chilling succession of scenes, she encounters the people who ought to be caring for and attending to her. At the end it is revealed that the baby is dead.

The After-Life of Arthur Cravan (1973) is the first of two plays about great eccentrics, in this case the eponymous nephew of Oscar Wilde—a boxer, a poet *manqué*, a scurrilous, vicious critic and generally a cad in Paris and Spain during World War I. Cravan is presented as an inventor of his own life—lazy, self-indulgent and cowardly as he flees the war and every other difficult situation in which he finds himself. But he is oddly attractive in the personal courage he demonstrates in his relentless ability to antagonise everyone he meets and repeatedly get beaten up for it.

9: PLAYWRIGHTS IN THE 70S

The second play dealing with a remarkable eccentric is *Chidley* (1976), about the early twentieth-century Sydney sex-reformer, William Chidley, who believed that all human violence could be traced to the erect penis and preached, among other health messages, the gospel of 'natural coition', whereby the flaccid penis would be gently drawn into the vagina by suction and achieve ejaculation, and thus procreation, without resort to force. Chidley was hounded by the police and eventually committed to Sydney's Callan Park asylum, where he burnt himself to death. A ballad-opera version of this story, *No Room For Dreamers* by George Hutchinson, is a more self-conscious piece of New Wave legend-building. De Groen's more thoughtful version tells the story largely from the point of view of Ada, Chidley's long-suffering neglected wife, and introduces her ex-husband Walt, a nasty piece of work from whom any woman might well want to flee into the arms of a man who didn't want to penetrate her.

Going Home (1976) is De Groen's first major play. Set in a nice middle-class house in Canada, cut off from the outside world by blizzards, it is a closed-house domestic comedy drama. Zoë, an expatriate Australian, has been struggling for a long time to find a life for herself, while Jim, her painter husband, tries to come to terms with the fact that his career has stalled and it is time to go home. They are visited by a number of friends old and new, including the glib Mike Dabro, another expatriate Australian artist, who has schmoozed his way into the New York art scene and who turns up with Molly, the estranged wife of Jim's boss and landlord.

Although this sounds like classic Williamson material, there is an edge to the play, especially in the hard-nosed way in which the comic foibles of the women—Zoë's shopping addiction and Molly's comfort-eating—are presented as signs of their oppression, not of their neurosis.

Vocations (1982) is another domestic play exploring the identity complications in the 1970s, when strong professional women started to assert themselves in relationships that they wanted to make equal and fair. An actress, Vicki, and a writer, Joy, struggle comically with men who just don't get the whole women's career thing. Then, after his infidelity is discovered, Joy's drily academic husband Godfrey

BELONGING

suddenly writes a 'feminist' novel that is a success. Equally suddenly, when Vicki has a baby, Ross, her zoologist partner, who tortures rats in the interests of his scientific research, discovers the joys of fatherhood and becomes, rather oppressively, a reconstructed new-age man. The women look on bemused as their men respond to feminism by taking it over.

The Rivers of China and *The Woman in the Window* are De Groen's most dramaturgically complex works—two intellectually provocative and theatrically powerful plays that explore complex issues of personal and social identity. The past and the future are intimately interconnected in both plays, and each of them intercuts independent stories in a theatrical present tense that permits De Groen to exploit their ambiguities. These are the first great works of serious philosophical science fiction written for the theatre in Australia.

In *The Rivers of China* (1987) the writer Katherine Mansfield travels to Fontainebleau in the 1920s, hoping that the mystic healer and teacher Georgei Gurdjieff might cure her before she dies of tuberculosis. This is juxtaposed with imagined scenes in an alternative present-day Sydney, in which women have seized power over men by using the 'Medusa look'—a female equivalent of male physical violence, used vengefully in a new gynocratic society to oppress men and make them quiescent. The technique was hit upon by a woman who was the victim in a snuff movie—a scene that is re-enacted in propaganda films made by the new regime. All male literature has been suppressed. A young man, left injured and dying after a suicide attempt, has his body and his identity reconstructed by a sympathetic female Dr Rahel. He wakes up as Katherine Mansfield, whose identity and creativity, systematically weakened by Gurdjieff's stern regime of 'therapy', has been channelled into him.

As the action progresses, Katherine's tormented sense of self, oppressed by the male culture in which she has struggled to write, is paralleled in the contemporary story with that of Wayne, a sensitive young nurse who yearns for a poetry that will express his experience. He comes to love Katherine's independent spirit in the body of the injured man he is nursing. The apparently simple gender reversal of the narrative becomes complex when Dr Rahel's experiment goes badly

9: PLAYWRIGHTS IN THE 70S

wrong and the man in the hospital bed inherits not only Mansfield's spiritual identity, but also, mysteriously, her tuberculosis.

The Woman in the Window (1998) is De Groen's masterpiece, carrying the split narrative exploration of identity and interconnectivity further than in *The Rivers of China* and closely linking personal identity politics to two nightmarish visions of social and political oppression. In this case the creative figure is the Soviet-era poet Anna Akhmatova, kept under surveillance since the 1930s. The play is set in the early 1950s when Anna is forced to appear regularly at her window so that KGB agents can see that she hasn't fled. Her life is circumscribed by the universal surveillance of Stalinism, but she retains her independent spirit—not writing down poems, but dictating them to her friend and carer Lilli Kalinovskaya, in order to preserve them. When Lilli is arrested, tortured and murdered, another recorder takes her place: Akhmatova's enduring spirit remains powerful.

This story is intercut with a dystopian vision of a future in which all material needs are supplied by a supreme corporation/state that keeps its subjects satisfied by allowing them to live in a games- and soap-opera-driven virtual reality. It is a disturbing capitalist parallel to the dumb herd-like notion of the masses constructed by Stalinist ideology. Rachel Serekov, one of the few with an actual job, is a 'conference stress consultant', a euphemism for 'hostess' or 'call-girl'. She forms an attachment with one of her clients, Sandor, a 'poet' who also has a job, trawling the massive digital databases in which all past information and culture is recorded, in search of poems about the moon, his area of specialisation. Sandor teaches Rachel to value poetry and the past. Together they exploit his special privilege and raid the databases to retrieve as much poetry as they can before, in the interests of efficiency, all the records are deleted. Sandor then encodes the poetry in a virus in the new multi-net, so that it will forever infect and subvert the smooth new bureaucratic data-driven world.

Overleaf: Frank Gallacher as Matthew and Lynne Williams as The Girl in the 1988 Melbourne Theatre Company production of The Rivers of China. *(Photographer: Jeff Busby.)*

BELONGING

This vision of the internet taken over by corporate capitalism and turned into a new form of Stalinism is very powerful. At the end, Akhmatova and Rachel are connected, as the sophisticated poet watches the naïve call-girl surfing the net and trying, after the arrest and torture of Sandor, to keep the spirit alive in an oppressive totalitarian world. The play ends on a note of hope, as Rachel, watched warmly by Akhmatova from the dim past, starts tentatively to make subversive use of the net.

Between *The Rivers of China* and *The Woman in the Window* came *The Girl Who Saw Everything* (1991), another play of ideas, but also a return in some ways to De Groen's domestic plays about individual politics. A controversial feminist historian, Liz Ransom, has retreated to the Blue Mountains west of Sydney to escape the fuss surrounding her latest book. Gareth, her well-meaning but ineffectual husband, keeps visiting her, asking that she come back home with him to Sydney. On one drive up to the mountains Gareth stops to help a terrified young woman hiding in the bush. She has been brutally raped. Fleeing his offer of help, she runs into the path of an oncoming car and is killed. The image haunts both Gareth and Carol, the other driver, a needy woman, like Molly in *Going Home*. As Liz maintains her distance, Gareth forms a relationship with Carol. After a number of changes in the lives of all the characters (including a painter friend and his new young girlfriend, Edwina) Liz and Gareth are tentatively reconciled. Yet the savage vision of the brutalised girl's arbitrary death, and what it might represent as Liz and Gareth worry about their little lives, overshadows the play.

De Groen's last play before she left Australia was *Wicked Sisters* (2002), a classically constructed real-time confrontational comedy-drama, in which four middle-aged women come together to battle with and console one another after the death of the great man in their lives. Again, but subtly, a scientific metaphor helps the audience to understand what the characters are going through and to explore wider issues of the ways in which interpersonal relationships coalesce to make up general social behaviours and customs.

The dead man, Alec, was a scientific genius who modelled the evolution of artificial life-forms on his computer in an attempt to explore human behaviour and society in brutal Darwinian terms. As

9: PLAYWRIGHTS IN THE 70S

the women's revelations pile up, it seems that he has modelled his own life and relationships in the same way. The play asks whether humans are able to transcend the supposed laws of the jungle.

In his last years, as he sank into Alzheimer's disease, Alec needed constant nursing—as a dying animal or species is nursed—by his wife Meridee. Towards the end of the play Meridee admits that when he started to think that she was his long-term mistress, a woman she had never known existed, she killed him. After a cliff-hanger ending to the first half, the mistress turns out to be her good friend Judith—who is there in the room. In the confusion the other friend in the room, Lydia, also confesses to having had an affair with him.

The outsider figure is Hester, a former student of Alec who now devotes herself to helping others and is fighting to save the planet. The competitive sparring of Meridee, Judith and Lydia seems to emulate Alec's virtual 'critters' warring on the computer (this virtual war ends abruptly in an 'extinction event' as the critters blow themselves up with full audio effects programmed by Alec). But Hester emerges victorious. Alec has stolen her ideas and, in restitution, she demands his lucrative intellectual property rights. These will enable her to look after a dying friend and work on a more human model of evolution. The resolution suggests that real humans, with real feelings and a desire for peace—factors unquantified in Alec's equations—might make a better fist of society than Alec's critters.

Jim McNeil and other prison playwrights

In the early 1970s, with the support of New Wave artists and social activists, a remarkable playwright emerged from the NSW prison system and, to use one of his own most powerful images, briefly flowered. Jim McNeil was serving a 17-year sentence for armed robbery and shooting a policeman when he joined a prison debating group and started to write plays. He represented prisoners as ordinary people with the same needs as outsiders—a new idea at the time, at least in the theatre—and, more importantly, created human dramas in which the cell and the exercise yard became a theatrical microcosm of the world outside the walls.

BELONGING

His first plays, *The Chocolate Frog* (1971) and *The Old Familiar Juice*, were one-acters. In the first Shirker and Tosser, two old lags with a strict prison code of honour, share a cell. Kevin, an educated young Christian with a conventional moral code from outside is put into their cell. He expects a six-month sentence for a fight and robbery in which he claims he had no part, but, because he's on appeal, he hopes his family will be able to bail him out. The play is a debate between them, with two good turning points that raise the stakes: the first when Shirker reveals that he used to dream of outside, until he realised that that world would never have a place for him; and the second when, partly as a result of Kevin's earnest questioning of their code, the two insiders start hurling accusations at each other, and their much vaunted prison camaraderie unravels. They realise that Kevin's presence has provoked this but, just as the confrontation is about to come to a crisis, Kevin is released on bail. After he has gone Shirker and Tosser discover that he has stolen back the cigarettes that Shirker earlier took from him. The plays ends as they settle comfortably back into their culture, philosophically reflecting that you should 'never educate a mug'.

The hints at the sexual codes and mores of prison life in *The Chocolate Frog* are made explicit in *The Old Familiar Juice* (1972), in which McNeil explores what might have happened if Kevin hadn't been suddenly bailed. Bulla is a tough guy who has been in for three years. He has a streak of apparently genuine tenderness for Stanley, a younger, pretty inmate who has only been in for three weeks. The third cellmate is Dadda, an old alcoholic, a vagrant outside, who cares for Stanley in a fatherly way and doesn't want Bulla to get his hands on him. With yeast Bulla has acquired from the prison bakery they make a brew, and as they get drunk, the struggle between Bulla and Dadda over Stanley intensifies. At the end Dadda has lost—too drunk and too weak. Stanley is also drunk and more or less submits when Bulla starts affectionately stroking his hair. In a chilling but oddly tender final moment Dadda sees Bulla with Stanley and rouses himself long enough to ask Bulla what he's doing. Bulla replies, 'Who? Me? I'm doin' fifteen years' (p. 92).

The sexual interplay, and the gentleness with which McNeil represents prison life in these plays, are developed further in *How*

9: PLAYWRIGHTS IN THE 70S

Does Your Garden Grow (1974), his first full-length play, and the last he completed while still in jail. It comes across now as a very light, oddly sentimental drama that only has impact because of the brutal circumstances in which its action takes place.

Again there are three prisoners in a cell, although for the first time other characters, including some from the world outside, are introduced. Mick and George (or 'Brenda', as he is known) are two male prisoners in a domestic relationship: Brenda is a devoted and supportive 'wife', loving but strict, who nags about language and manners and Mick the devoted suburban husband accepting his wife's attentions and appreciating her femininity. They are a delicately mocking, or perhaps yearning, parody of the bourgeois life and marriage outside prison. But Mick is due for parole and his best mate Sam hopes to inherit Brenda. They sit around making inconsequential chat—between Mick and Brenda and Mick and Sam—especially in a long scene set in the exercise yard, as if it were a suburban swimming pool or a nice beach somewhere. When Mick finally comes up for parole, we meet his wife, who is, or has become while he's been inside, an assertive, strong woman who won't put up with any bullshit. After a moment of tenderness between them, we realise that the pretended domesticity offered by Brenda has vanished at the touch of a real woman, even a newly-liberated one, although he returns to the cell and pretends to Sam that he's still the macho boss. In the final scene Sam moves in on Brenda, and there is almost a formal handover ceremony. Brenda makes tea for them and dresses up in feminine finery, using burnt cork for eye makeup, for the new husband Sam.

How Does Your Garden Grow is remarkably gentle. *Jack* (1977), a full-length play completed after his release, opens tenderly, but quickly becomes a powerful work of unleashed fury. It is as if McNeil, finally freed from the observation of prison officers, found his more savage voice. Set in a solitary confinement cell in a notorious prison, the play charts a descent into hell.

From the beginning Jack, half way through a five-year sentence in Parramatta Gaol for car theft, is bitter and angry. He yearns for tenderness and affection, and tells his feelings to his cell mate, Tom. He makes himself a surrogate companion—a plastic bag full of warm water that he snuggles up to each night. He calls it 'Midnight', after his wife, who long ago stopped visiting. Worried that his mate has gone mad, Tom dobs him in to the prison psychiatrist. Jack talks his way out, but at the first-half curtain Tom 'kills' Jack's woman by slashing the bag. When Jack threatens to kill him in return, Tom calls the guards and Jack is transferred to the notorious OBS section of Long Bay Jail.

There, in the second half, Jack encounters a sadistic guard who beats him regularly. He is determined to switch off, so as to remain himself, even without the soft companion that he believes (as he earlier said to Tom) he needs to be complete. He insults the guard, but later expresses contrition. He wants to go back to Parramatta and apologise to Tom. Though the doctor releases him from OBS, it is too late. He is put into maximum security at Grafton—the prison for intractables—where he is savagely beaten as a routine part of the reception process. After a final monologue, he prepares to kill himself.

The play, finished when McNeil was outside and in the process of drinking himself to death, has a wonderfully naked rage and energy. At the time it was considered too melodramatic, but it could be successfully revived if played with intensity. McNeil, who died in 1982, was a powerful force in the New Wave, a gentle voice from a savage world.

Another playwright who began writing while he was in prison is Ray Mooney, for a long time associated with the Melbourne Writers' Theatre. *A Blue Freckle* (1975) is set in a police station and courtroom, and deals with the police habit of 'verballing' prisoners—attributing false confessions to them. The title was chosen because the play was first performed in prison and Mooney didn't want to draw the authorities' attention to its subject. *Everynight, Everynight* (1978) is a tough play about the conduct of the notorious H-division in Victoria's Pentridge Prison, and the prisoners' rebellion. The play paints a graphic picture of the violence, the daily bashings and the ritual humiliation that provoked the prisoners' revolt. Dale, a young prisoner, submits at first to the soul-destroying regime. But he 'resigns' and organises a unified resistance to the old prison culture, rejecting the principle that you never dob anyone in, not even the screws. In a subsequent inquiry the judge refuses to believe the combined voices of the prisoners. Mooney

9: PLAYWRIGHTS IN THE 70S

(who was there) said that no-one believed the play until 1971, when the Jenkinson Inquiry revealed the truth.[10]

Mooney later wrote *Black Rabbit* (1988), a brutal play set in the early 1800s in what was then considered *terra nullius*, a land without inhabitants, about a pair of white men hunting and a black couple living traditional lives. Archie, the experienced old bushman, is mad, full of tough bush philosophy about survival and treating the blacks as animals. Stanley, his young educated offsider, is scared of him and, though repelled by his casual brutality, drawn into the hunt. Djala, a young Aboriginal woman, sings the old stories and tries to maintain the traditions. Her warrior husband, Jala Jala, tries to protect her, but Archie shoots him, captures Djala and rapes her in a sacred cave. Jala Jala crawls off, but returns in revenge, and is finally trapped, killed and beheaded, his head to be sent to London for sale. The play is one of the most savage dramatic accounts of the white invasion of the Australian continent ever written, anticipating Andrew Bovell's *Holy Day*.

The only women's equivalent to McNeil and Mooney's very male prison plays are Therese Collie's *Out of the Blue*, and Somebody's Daughter Theatre's *Tell Her That I Love Her*. Produced by Street Arts in Brisbane in 1991, *Out of the Blue* tells the story of a group of women dealing with the boredom of prison life, and with the remaining shreds of their lives outside. They battle with one another, and with the warders, and hang out for medication time. The women in 'Up Top', the minimum security section of the prison, include Toey, a depressed and angry street kid, who has a fight with one of the screws and ends up in solitary confinement; Delma and Rachael, two Murri Aboriginal women; and Nancy, an old prisoner who is shocked at first by the young women's language and talk, but who ends up bonding with them. All the 'Up Top' women are scared when Kris arrives from 'Max', the maximum security section, but she turns out to be supportive and useful. They organise a fancy dress party which is cancelled by the screws when Toey and Rachael get high and crazy on the prison roof. There is a subplot between an old guard Shepherd and a 'new breed' guard, Jemmy, who is trying to be supportive of the prisoners. At the end, with Kris depressed, Toey and Rachael still defiant, and Nancy released, they gather their strengths together and battle on.

BELONGING

Somebody's Daughter Theatre grew from a drama group at Fairlea Women's Prison in the 1980s that made shows within the prison, directed by Maud Clark. Their first production performed outside was *Tell Her That I Love Her* (1993), a powerful account of women released from prison and coping with heroin addiction. Jess, just released, meets up with Cara, Kate and Caz, who have made it, but her lover Tuesday can't stop using and threatens to drag her down. The other three try to help but Jess's journey is her own. They meet by the beach, a healing and confessional place for them, and each tells her story—abused by fathers, neglected by mothers, beaten up by boyfriends and dealers. Their love for one another binds them and the play together. At the end Tuesday tells Jess to leave, in spite of their intense love for each other, because she knows Jess won't stay clean while she's trying to be strong for Tuesday. Tuesday (who is 18) dies. In a ritual funeral scene just before the end all the dead that they have known in their lives are named. Jess blames herself, but is reassured by the others who stand by her. There is a suggestion at the end that Jess might make it. It's a very strong piece, based on the participant actors' own stories.

Reg Livermore

One of the greatest New Wave transgressive subverters of social stereotypes was Reg Livermore. In a string of shows beginning with *Betty Blokk Buster Follies* in 1975, he introduced a range of grotesque characters grounded in the old myths of Australianness, his performance style drawing on vaudeville traditions in new ways.[11] He often performed in a kind of half-naked drag in which the 'reveal', conventionally the moment when the performer is revealed as a man at the end of an act, was aggressively asserted from the outset. Dressed in a frilly white apron that only served to accentuate Livermore's hairy male muscularity, Betty was a flirtatious Nazi good-time girl, straight out of the cabaret tradition of the Weimar Republic. When she waggled what she thought of as her 'cute little arse', it was a bit like a drunken football player chucking a browneye out of the window of his mate's car. Another character, Vaseline Amalnitrate, was a traditional ocker sportsman, dressed in an extravagant camp headdress and fluffy tutu,

9: PLAYWRIGHTS IN THE 70S

who danced the dying swan from *Swan Lake* on point—because real blokes ought to be able to do such tough physical stuff. In a later show, *Wonderwoman*, Beryl-at-the-sink was a desperate domesticated woman whose anger about her life was deflected onto the crockery that she ritually smashed while washing up. All Livermore's characters were provocatively ambiguous, caught between different social constructions of identity. He took familiar icons of Australian identity—the old digger, the suburban housewife and the virile sportsman—and queered them.

The early shows—*Betty Blokk Buster*, *Wonderwoman* (1976), *Sacred Cow* (1979), *Son of Betty* (1980) and *Firing Squad* (1983)—were lavishly produced, full of songs performed seriously, but always in subversive character. A descendant perhaps is Paul Capsis, an extraordinary cabaret performer of the 1990s and since, who has 'channelled' great singers in a subversive way in a number of shows culminating in *Boulevard Delirium* (2004), directed by Barrie Kosky. Capsis also channelled the ancient Greek gods in *The Lost Echo* (2006), Kosky's and Tom Wright's great version of Ovid's *Metamorphoses*.

Livermore's later shows, after he moved to the Blue Mountains west of Sydney, were intimate small-room cabaret performances, more literary and thoughtful, performed in a local venue, the Clarendon Hotel. After *Wish You Were Here* (Melbourne Festival of the Arts, 1989), these included *Santa on the Planet of the Apes* (1992), *Mother Goose* (1993), *Red Riding Hood, the Speed Hump and the Wolf* (1994) and *Home Sweet Home (Leonard's Last Hurrah)* (1998).

Leonard, who featured in all these shows, was Livermore's most enduring creation—a grotesque old digger in a slouch hat and white-face clown make-up. He first appeared in 1975 as a whining downbeat tribute to the great Australian clown, Mo (Roy Rene), and had his last hurrah in 1998, by which time he had been consigned to an old people's home. In the original production this was represented in cartoon style as a gothic horror-movie mansion, similar to that in *The Rocky Horror Show*, in which Livermore had earlier starred as Frank'n'Furter. (He had also played Berger in *Hair* and Herod in *Jesus Christ Superstar*. More recently, he played Max Bialystock in the musical version of Mel Brooks's *The Producers*.)

BELONGING

By the time of Leonard's impending demise he had become an exotic figure in a wig and an elaborate period frock-coat that still managed to hint, in an extravagant way, at the pyjamas and dressing-gown look of Barry Humphries's Sandy Stone. At heart Leonard was still a sad and lonely, alienated Anglo-Australian old man, blissfully ignorant of his own failure in life and forever complaining selfishly about how he had been mistreated. Like Sandy, he had a long-suffering wife but, unlike Sandy's Beryl, Leonard's Gloria had abandoned him as a hopeless case well before his first appearance on stage. Also unlike the poignantly childless Sandy, Leonard had a hostile daughter Nola who, after Gloria, for all his sickening and hypocritically sentimental effusions of love for her, is the monster in his monologues. Like Sandy, Leonard has always been too self-absorbed to notice other people, especially his supposed loved ones, but, unlike Sandy, he is incapable of taking comfort in the illusion that they still love him.

Livermore's scripts for all his characters, including Leonard, became increasingly elaborate in their use of a language part music-hall (with topical allusions) and part poetic, full of conceits, malapropisms and the sudden comic reawakening of linguistically dead metaphors. In performance he is a master of what Nadia Fletcher calls the 'ambush effect', in which the audience is trapped into laughing at a stereotyped character whose vulnerable humanity is suddenly revealed.[12]

10
THE NEW INTERNATIONALISM

By 1978 the visionary enthusiasm and sense of common purpose that had characterised the New Wave were wearing off. The definitive larrikin New Wave playwright Jack Hibberd was one of the first to write about an 'ennui' and 'weird strain of uncertainty' that he detected in the theatre by the late 1970s.[1] For a while New Wave theatre workers seemed like a gang of partygoers suffering a collective hangover. They had made their mark. In most cases they had not sold out to the mainstream either—the cardinal sin in alternative theatre politics at the time. And if this was sometimes because they didn't have the opportunity, often it was a choice and many sank into obscurity as a result. At the same time a key group disrupted the Anglo mainstream and built a new culture. In their strident attack on naturalism and the old idea of 'drama', this group moved Australian theatre from early realism to a new, sometimes chaotic, eclecticism.

The point at which the New Wave succeeded in doing this, however, was also the point at which it began to feel it had failed. Perhaps New Wavers didn't really want to fragment the monolithic Australianness that they had spent so much energy trying to reinvent. For all its rebellion, the New Wave was just as nationalist and as totalising as anything that had gone before. In the late 1970s many writers, performers, directors and commentators were still seeking a

BELONGING

unitary movement, looking for the next wave. And so came the last of Australia's 'wonderful cultural renaissances', as Edna Everage called them—the 'new cosmopolitanism' of the late 1970s, which, in spite of many attempts to drag other writers into it, really meant Louis Nowra and Stephen Sewell.[2]

From the first, Sewell and Nowra were markedly different from their New Wave predecessors. Their work was less focused on Australianness, more political in its concerns and more cinematic in its dramaturgy—or 'operatic', to use Nowra's term—but certainly not naturalistic or simply representational.[3]

For a start, their plays were set in other countries: Russia and Germany for Sewell; Russia and Paraguay, for Nowra. As late as 1983, Bob Ellis got a good laugh at the Australian National Playwrights' Conference by referring to the absurdity of any Australian playwright setting a play overseas. It was a very late New-Wave moment.

Both writers were quite conscious of what they were doing. They were not interested in what made Australian culture distinctive or 'unique', but in the connections between Australian life and a wider world outside. In 1980, Sewell was already drawing a distinction between what he called 'nationalist' and 'internationalist' schools of Australian playwriting, and identifying himself with the latter:

> [D]rama surely has to have a historical base, otherwise plays are just a lot of snapshots suspended in the air. That's why I don't write about Australia: fine, if you're Williamson to write those accurate, cutting little slices of modern Aussie life, but if they're not integrated into any broader notion of history, and unless you understand that broader notion, why, for instance, the communist ideal collapsed after 1917, then we might just as well go on taking snapshots of each other and sticking them up on stages for ever.[4]

That the plays were set in exotic locations was significant, but it did not simply reflect, as some commentators thought, a desire to get away from Australia, as if it were the artistic equivalent of emigration. Even when Nowra and Sewell turned to write plays set in Australia, it was clear that they didn't share the same interests. Instead of looking at what was distinctively Australian, they examined in broader detail the influences and conditions which affected life in Australia.

10: THE NEW INTERNATIONALISM

Stephen Sewell

Sewell produced a series of large scale works between 1978 and 1986 that established him as Australia's first great political playwright after Romeril. With the contraction of Australian theatre in the late 1980s, he wrote more intimate plays until 1999.[5] During this time, he maintained his large-scale dramatic ambition in *The Golgrutha Trilogy*. In 2003, Sewell returned to his old passionate epic dramaturgy with *Myth, Propaganda and Disaster in Nazi Germany and Contemporary America*. Since then he has remade himself as a writer for the theatre with works in a new Meyerholdian style, *The Secret Death of Salvador Dali* and *Three Furies*; and in his absurdist political farces about the post–9/11 world, *The United States of Nothing, It Just Stopped* and *The Gates of Egypt*.

From the beginning Sewell wrote passionately intense dialogue in epic works constructed with extraordinary dramaturgical complexity. Part of his subject is always the difficulty of knowing, and much of the action in his plays remains ambiguous and unresolved. His characters embrace a series of strongly held beliefs and planned courses of personal or political action, yet they often find themselves betrayed by these beliefs, or else betraying them. Like his great antecedent Bertolt Brecht he is a highly serious playwright with a great sense of fun. His strong interest in politics turns into a concern with the ethics of personal and public human behaviour. At its base is an urgent desire to change the world, and an acknowledgement that art alone cannot do it.

In the late 1970s and 1980s Sewell fell victim to politically motivated criticism of his writing and the objection that he was somehow too earnest. He explored the great issues of his time in a way that has provoked sometimes naïve political responses from his supporters and detractors alike, but his plays are never doctrinaire. He may not be an even-handed writer, but he has always given the devil his due. Like Brecht, he is incapable of not seeing the other side of every question he raises.

Long before other playwrights Sewell was articulating a dramatic response to globalisation and the collapse of nationalism. In 1983 he said:

> [T]he notion of national culture is as outdated as the notion of national economy. Because of the progress of capitalism, it can

> be argued, for example, that institutional changes within the CIA are as significant political developments for the Australian people as they are for the Americans—or anyone else. And my choice of different places and periods is, I suppose, some recognition of this internationalism.[6]

He is probably the first Australian playwright since John Romeril, and before him Katharine Susannah Prichard and Mona Brand, to see his plays as interventionist contributions to public political debate, like newspapers or union meetings. In the context of the 1970s disputes about naturalism, he complained that reviewers were too preoccupied with theatrical values and reluctant to comment on what the playwright was actually trying to say.[7] As Brecht said, when defining realism as 'laying bare society's causal network', realism is not a question of form. It should be judged by criteria of reality, not by criteria of other realist works.[8]

Sewell's plays show people as isolated individuals in a complex and difficult world, a world that reflects individual dreams and worries. Often his characters are obsessed with their own private problems and yet they are driven out into the world, where they confront the social, political and economic conditions of their lives. Sometimes they take their personal dreams and neurotic obsessions into public life, helping to create and mould political or economic systems and imbuing them with their individual irrationality. In this way hope, fear, love and despair are built into the structure of social, economic and political systems and the actual world takes on the qualities of an expressionist nightmare. In turn, the individual characters come to be completely dominated—and sometimes overwhelmed and destroyed—by the conditions of the world which they have helped to create.

Sewell's early plays draw on the conventions of the realistic thriller and *film noir*, and occasionally use expressionist devices to illustrate how the pressures of the world affect the minds and visions of his characters. By means of complex multiple plots and theatrical devices, they also seek to provide a detailed map of the determining conditions from the outside world within which the characters struggle to find personal happiness and love or, as a social expression of love, justice. Sewell's epic dramaturgy always emphasises the historicity of characters and story: the characters are rooted in their time, with

10: THE NEW INTERNATIONALISM

interactions between the story of individual people and the history which conditions it. The epic nature of the early plays derives from this desire to present a complete account of the relationships between his characters and their world, rather than a concentrated, distilled dramatisation. Sewell's insistence on including everything relevant to an understanding of human society sometimes results in a bewildering complexity of action and a great profusion of scenes and atmospheric effects. In the early 1980s he said:

> What I'd like to do finally is produce something where through every character and every scene you can see not only the rest of the play but the rest of the world. [...] I find the world—what exists—really exciting; and my main criticism that I have of my own work is that it has never been complicated enough.[9]

Sewell's first play, *The Father We Loved on a Beach by the Sea*, produced at Brisbane's La Boite Theatre in 1978, is a dense and passionate drama about the phenomenon of working-class reactionary conservatism. It intersperses historical scenes set in the 1950s with scenes from a dystopian future, when Australia has become a fascist state. The beloved father of the title claims to cherish Australia, but has failed to fight for it, and his son, a hunted revolutionary, must flee or be killed by oppressive totalitarian forces. The play is deeply fascinated by the processes of politics and the place of the individual in them, but it is not written from a particular political perspective. Although Mona Brand and George Landen Dann had attempted something similar in the 1940s and 1950s, nothing like this had ever been written on this scale in Australia.

Sewell was one of the last of the enduring writers to be produced by the Australian Performing Group, when in 1979 they commissioned him to write *Traitors*, still one of his best plays. Set in Russia, it is firmly and frankly historical, with framing scenes that take it from just before the 1917 Revolution to the darkest period of World War II. It tells the story of several revolutionaries whose decent Bolshevik aspirations are betrayed by Stalin. They end up either dead or desperately alone and adrift in the chaos of war.

In terms of story and character *Traitors* is the most straightforward of Sewell's plays, but it asks large questions of personal and political

BELONGING

morality. What are we to believe in and fight for? How are we to reconcile individual needs of the self with the self-transcending need to work for a better world? How do we achieve both our personal and public goals? It uses one of the major crises of the twentieth century—the collapse of the communist ideal in Stalinist Russia—to examine the interaction between individuals and history and how they shape each other.

Next Sewell produced the three great works that established his reputation: *Welcome the Bright World*, *The Blind Giant is Dancing* and *Dreams in an Empty City*. There has been no serious large-scale Australian drama since that does not owe something to these extraordinary plays. They are not easy works and mainstream theatre companies have mostly shied away from them, but they tackle big issues, and cry out with a screaming passion that is individual, spiritual and political. Of the three, only *The Blind Giant is Dancing* has been revived. But there is no doubt that they are the most important plays of their time.

Welcome the Bright World (1982) is a family drama and a political thriller rolled into one, with terrorists and secret police and intelligence networks, and 'little people' caught in the midst. It deals with the role and responsibility of those people, in the world and to each other.

The action takes place in Germany between 1974 and 1981. The three principal characters are Max Lewin, a physicist; his colleague in particle physics research, Sebastian Ayalti, a mathematician; and Max's daughter Rebekah, a school student when she is introduced. Max's wife Anat and Sebastian's wife Fay are innocent bystanders in the play's thriller plot. On the human side of the narrative, however, they have major issues with which Max and Sebastian are unwilling or unable to deal.

The play has two central images: the Nazi violence of Crystal Night in 1938 when, as Anat says, the broken glass on the pavement reflected the fragmenting of the world (p. 69); and the bubble chamber experiments that Max and Sebastian are undertaking, smashing bits of atoms together as they investigate the fundamental particles of mid-twentieth-century physics. These images reflect the shattered lives of the characters struggling to find their way through a disintegrating world, but failing to find coherence and purpose in the disorder of experience.

10: THE NEW INTERNATIONALISM

In the thriller plot a powerful neo-fascist network, with close links to the state police, is planning a coup. They are using a new computer police file of all citizens, which, when they succeed, will also be an instrument of state control. The existing Social-Democratic government, represented by a high-ranking Party bureaucrat named Frankl, has initiated work on the computer network as a weapon against a left-wing terrorist movement. A sinister police official named Dr Mencken, ostensibly the link between the Party and the computer network, is in fact a member of the shadowy group planning the coup.

Max, contracted as a consultant to iron out bugs in the computer surveillance network, is a classic twentieth-century 'bomb scientist', politically naïve but in love with the science and thrill of discovery. Sebastian is a soft left-wing political activist, an easy target for both sides in the political struggle. Rebekah, who is introduced to left-wing politics by Sebastian at university, becomes deeply involved with the terrorists, and is targeted by the new anti-terrorist operation. With the aim of setting her up with guns and capturing her, Rebekah is tricked by a police collaborator masking as a terrorist into assassinating a senior political figure.

The assassination, Mencken's brainchild, is supposed to be a bogus scheme. But unbeknownst to Frankl, who considers even that beyond the reasonable bounds of democratic state control, the scheme is not only very real, but the first move of a right-wing coup in which he himself is the target.

Max, working on the computer network, discovers all this. Estranged from Rebekah since she took up with the terrorists, he contacts Sebastian and together they set off to find her in the Berlin slums. In the chaotic final scenes there is a major street demonstration in Berlin, at which Frankl is assassinated—but by the coup leaders, not Rebekah. Max finds Rebekah, who violently rejects him. Sebastian is captured and shot, and Rebekah appears to escape. Max is taken, but not arrested, because, having collaborated with Mencken, he is trusted. When Mencken enters the room where he is being interviewed, however, Max draws a gun, points it at Mencken, and screams 'For my children!'.

A 'psychic side-kick', as a stage direction describes it, initiates a final powerful sequence: all the story-lines and scene-series are integrated

BELONGING

into one long expressionist nightmare, which evokes Max's final terror and despair, as he suddenly realises what his collaboration with the neo-fascist coup-leaders has meant. Today *Welcome the Bright World* remains terribly topical. It is the last Sewell play in which revolutionary violence, however qualified, is presented as a serious option for idealists who want to change the world, and it leads naturally to *The Blind Giant is Dancing* (1983), the only play in which, however wearily, the independent spirit of revolution struggles on—at least until *Myth, Propaganda and Disaster* in 2003.

In *The Blind Giant is Dancing* Sewell draws on his skills in complex structure and multiple narratives to deal with the intersections between the political, corporate and criminal worlds of 1980s Australia, in a way that makes the relaxed larrikin protests of the New Wave seem naïve. Here the analysis of even the most intimate of interpersonal relationships is uncompromisingly political. It looks at power in every arena and in all its forms, from the discursively constructed to the nakedly violent. This is Sewell's wildest, most extravagantly neurotic play, full of individual guilt, public paranoia and fear.

Allen Fitzgerald is a member of the left-wing faction of the governing Social Democratic Party. In his struggle for influence, his initial dilemma is the temptation to enter into an agreement with a criminal businessman in order to defeat Michael Wells, his party enemy and leader of the right-wing faction. The action charts Allen's idealistic rejection of compromise, his subsequent pragmatic acceptance of it, and his eventual slide into a desperate grab for power.

This political action is paralleled with Allen's personal struggle against the emotionally crippling influence of his father, and the guilt which he brings to his relationships with his wife and his lover as a consequence. His marriage is tortured by a confused mixture of jealousy and guilt, and his final ruthless pursuit of public power stems from his most intimate private anxieties.

A crucial influence in this is his relationship with the Mephistophelian Rose Draper, who becomes his mistress and ends up betraying him. Rose is a mysterious journalist who provides him with the material he needs to defeat Wells. Their scenes together are intense and highly concentrated. In the thriller plot it turns out that

10: THE NEW INTERNATIONALISM

she is working for shadowy American, presumably CIA, interests, and has planted false material on him, in order to control him. But her role in the play's moral universe is more significant. As a journalist in the Middle East, she had once betrayed a lover for the sake of a good story and, in spite of her cool self-control, she despairs of ever being able to change the world. Although privately she hopes that she will find consolation in Allen's apparent sincerity, when, in the political thread of the action, she succeeds in setting him up, her personal despair swamps her. 'I hoped you'd win', she mourns, before she kills herself (pp. 131–2).

Dreams in an Empty City (1986) is the culmination of these plays. Its structure is complex, its story dense and tightly narrated and its heightened tone verges on the edge of hysteria. It is full of personal, moral and political passion and anxiety. In the face of the evils and the horrors of the world, its central character cries out, we must affirm the glory of living, even as we fail in our own lives. The last remaining sin in a corrupt world is despair.

It is a great thriller, with an intriguing story of corporate criminality set in the shady world of high finance and commerce. Two mighty egos—Simon Wilson and Derek Wiesland—fight each other like ancient savage kings, and Chris O'Brian, a simple ex-priest, is caught between them. The action leads up to Easter when on Good Friday Chris, like his namesake, is killed. Wilson defeats Wiesland, but in the process, in one of the most extravagant narrative climaxes in Australian drama, the entire globalised economy comes crashing down.

Also involved in the action are Nat Boas and David Kroner, two business high-flyers trying to look after themselves; and Harry Kaufmann and his wife Trish, honest decent capitalists, who become involved in the corruption and implicated in the global economic crisis. Chris's girlfriend Karen and his brother John, pawns and victims of the big players, are the focus of the play's human story.

The relationship between Wilson and Chris forms a father/son subplot that is both human and biblical. When Chris was a priest he left their father's business in the hands of his brother John, who subsequently lost it to Wiesland. Chris went to Thailand as a missionary where he lost his faith watching a child die. He started living with a

BELONGING

young Thai woman and came into contact with the world of the drug overlords. In a fit of savage revenge that now haunts him, he killed a sleazy local policeman after the rape and murder of his girlfriend. He has been left with a despairing obsession about the evil of the world that infects his relationship with Karen.

Wilson is a wealthy, civilised and urbane banker, with a different darkness in his soul. His marriage is empty and loveless, and he is haunted by the death of his son Craig, in whom he seems to have invested the little genuine love of which he is capable.

We watch the developing relationship between Chris and Wilson, knowing that Wilson is planning Chris's murder in order to defeat Wiesland. For his part Wiesland has destroyed John financially and ordered his savage murder. Wilson, now dying of cancer, offers Chris his corrupt world, inviting him to feel and enjoy naked power over the empty city. Chris refuses him. At the end Wilson, riddled with disease and guilt, desperately calls out for Chris to love him.

By this stage the plotlines have come together in a final conflagration which, although divided on the page into some fifteen short scenes, is really one long scene of chaos punctuated by Chris's final messianic message to the world:

> Our lives, our efforts, our civilisation, the works of our hearts and brains mark forever the triumph of human life and the value of the world. We live; our life is glorious; our sin is to deny it and despair. [...] This is the only life we have! [...] Live! (pp. 86–8)

This is the conclusion of a long speech. While Chris is delivering it, the material world is crashing down and millions of people face poverty and starvation. Harry dies of a heart attack as he struggles to hold it together; Wilson finally breaks, accepts Chris and begs for forgiveness. Chris himself is being savagely beaten, almost literally crucified, and as he cries 'Live!' he is shot through the head. But his message is clear enough. It is only the thriller story that ends in gloomy apocalypse. The empty city crashes down, but the dreams continue in a savage world that has no place for them except in the crying heart. *Myth* has a similar ending, with Talbot asserting the triumph of his vision at the moment he is killed.

10: THE NEW INTERNATIONALISM

Sewell's contribution to the 1988 Bicentennial celebrations was *Hate*, the first of several smaller-scale plays. In this closed-house drama the divided members of a high-flying corporate and political family meet and thrash out their individual, ethical and business conflicts. Like *Dreams in an Empty City*, it is based on the story of the passion of Christ and refers to corporate and political corruption on a grand scale.

John Gleason, a businessman and right-wing politician, has called together his fractured family for an Easter retreat at his remote country estate, which is cut off by a sudden flood. A respectable patriarch, with an austere and distant manner, John turns out to be quite unhinged. His wife Eloise seems supportive of him, but is painfully distanced from him by experiences that the plot only gradually reveals. His elder son Raymond is a comic schemer who has embraced his father's corrupt world and is battling to defeat him. His younger son Michael is disturbed and rebellious, driven by Oedipal resentment.

The central character is Celia, John and Eloise's daughter, who has a social conscience and has fled her family and her rich inheritance to become a geriatric nurse. She is drawn back, first for the sake of the family weekend, but later into John's entire corrupt world. Surprisingly, he anoints her as his successor, a role she accepts in spite of herself, in a sudden rush of love based in her abject acceptance of his past sexual abuse of her.

At the climax of the play, out of love for Celia and in an attempt to avenge her, Michael murders his father with an axe. The play ends with his funeral, when all the family secrets have been covered up. Michael is shut away in an asylum, the smilingly manipulative Raymond delivers the eulogy, Celia and Eloise sitting beside him in silent acquiescence. The grim family history has been deftly retold as an heroic saga of corporate success. Like other Bicentennial plays, such as Michael Gow's *1841* and Louis Nowra's *Capricornia*, *Hate* is a tough revisioning of traditional narratives of Australianness. In the late 1990s and early 2000s several playwrights returned to this form of patriarchal drama—including Louis Nowra in his recent *Boyce Trilogy*—but none has repeated the success of Sewell's play.

Sewell's *Sisters* (1991) was another intimate drama, still full of personal anguish and focused on the question 'How are we to live?',

BELONGING

but without the detailed social and political context of the earlier plays. Here his characters simply want to come to terms with their past, deal with their pain, find out what their lives might mean and get on with living. This is not, of course, a simple matter.

After many years apart, Sylvie and Gillian, sisters in their mid-30s, have come to spend a weekend together in the old family beach house. Sylvie has been the independent wild one and Gillian family-oriented and conventional. Over two long days of recriminations and confessions they come to realise that each has longed for the other's life and spent too much time with guilt and envy. In spite of her apparent solidity and sureness, Gillian feels an emptiness inside her that has led her into deep despair. And beneath her apparent hedonism and love of freedom Sylvie yearns for comfort. By the end of their wearying confrontation they discover, tentatively, that they can live in each other's love. It won't be much, when they return to complicated lives in the outside world, but it is something to be going on with.

After many anguished conflicts and revelations the play winds calmly down, its central puzzle, however, still unresolved:

> GILLIAN: [...] Why? Why do you live? You know why you use a car, why you've got to make that ten o'clock appointment; but why do you live? Who knows? (p. 64)

They agree that neither of them does. Gillian offers the despairing Sylvie one reason—'I love you, that's why you should live'—and Sylvie tells a story of their mother's, about a shipwrecked sailor who tried and tried to get back out to sea and who finally turned round and realised that the hinterland behind the shore was his own homeland. They plan to start renovating together. As Gillian comforts Sylvie in her arms, Sylvie reminds us that they both still have a journey ahead.

The Sick Room (1999) is a closed-house family drama, like *Hate*, in which corrupt financial machinations infect personal relationships within a successful corporate and political family. Paul Alexander is a stockbroker who has borrowed massively in order to finance an ambitious deal that blows up in his face. He has drawn into the deal David, his retired senior public-servant father-in-law, who in turn has invested the superannuation savings of his staff—his housekeeper Cecilia and

10: THE NEW INTERNATIONALISM

his groundsman Mr Hilbert. By the end of the play everything has been gambled and lost.

The family is gathered together at David's rural property, where Paul's 17-year-old daughter Kate, terminally ill with cancer, has been brought to die. Her sick room is like a still centre of pain—and, in some scenes, tentative love—compared with the chaotic world outside. She is a redemptive figure and by the end of the play everyone has been touched by her suffering. Kate herself reaches some kind of peace and acceptance although, as always in Sewell's plays, redemption finally proves impossible because it cannot be achieved through suffering alone.

In *The Sick Room* Sewell focuses more clearly than ever on the intersection between the personal and political. Kate's suffering is intimate and her cancer is an individual tragedy. Paul's failure in the public world wreaks widespread economic and social havoc. The failure of their relationship ruptures the world.

King Golgrutha, the first play in a Golgrutha trilogy, was produced by the State Theatre Company of South Australia in 1991. The second, *Dust*, and the third, *The Garden of Earthly Delights*, were also produced in Adelaide with student casts, in 1994. Each has a huge cast.

King Golgrutha is a wild, grotesque play about Gutso, another Père Ubu, who is the ultimate Sewell father-figure—scary and bad, yet somehow beloved. Golgrutha is a mysterious figure, a mythic witness to all life's horrors, who is intimately linked with Gutso and haunts him. The underlying story is similar to that of Sewell's earlier epics, about business families tearing themselves apart, wreaking havoc in a restless search for money and power, and tormented by interpersonal conflicts. Like *Dreams in an Empty City*, the play ends with a massive world-wide financial collapse. The story and the family feud lurk deep beneath a savage carnival of excess.

In *Dust*, the only published play of the trilogy, the savage world outside the lives of the individual characters is hived off into a gothic play-within-a-play, performed in intercut scenes by two of the central characters. These are Doug and Margaret, actors who play Avenal and Dis in violent and rhetorically heightened scenes of war, intrigue and brutality that reflect their 'real life' personal experience. Their

BELONGING

daughter Julie is a schizophrenic dreamer and much of the play seems to be taking place in her head.

In *The Garden of Earthly Delights*, set in a world consumed by war, with resonances of the Bosnian/Serbian/Croatian wars and much else besides, the previous two plays collide in apocalyptic fashion. Gutso and Golgrutha finally discover that they are divided parts of the one self and approach God together. The trilogy is a piece of grand myth-making.

In 2003, Sewell returned to his old epic themes (and his old epic titles) with *Myth, Propaganda and Disaster in Nazi Germany and Contemporary America*, an extraordinary political thriller written in response to the United States' reaction to the attack on the World Trade Centre on 11 September 2001. In common with the early plays it has a claustrophobic narrative in which individual guilt and fear are juxtaposed with social and political oppression and corruption. But here the central couple, Talbot and Eve, are not torn apart by their personal neuroses. Talbot is an Australian with a good job at an American university and Eve is a successful TV and film writer, until the oppressive world of American public paranoia manages to destroy them both. Yet, unlike Max and Anat in *Welcome the Bright World*, or Allen and Louise in *The Blind Giant is Dancing*, Talbot and Eve's love and faith, although severely tested, remain intact until their deaths. Considering that they are both murdered by sinister agents of the American military-industrial complex, the play's ending is remarkably optimistic.

The title of the play is the title of a book written by Talbot in which he argues, from a timidly academic, non-activist perspective, that the security apparatus being put into place as part of the US 'War on Terror' bears comparison with that of Nazi Germany. He then finds himself the victim of a sinister agent, simply called The Man, who keeps turning up mysteriously and threatening to kill him. The Man, who knows everything about him, engages him in a series of Orwellian discussions punctuated by outbursts of brutal violence. This culminates in a long torture scene in which The Man argues that Talbot is the last intellectual who believes in Reason—the last, because The Man's thuggish offsiders are about to kill him. The tone of these scenes recalls the 1930s Stalinist show-trials. As Talbot puts it to Max, another Australian academic, 'This is the end of the American

10: THE NEW INTERNATIONALISM

Republic and the beginning of the American Empire'. Max, who is cheerfully amoral, cynical and self-interested, ends up taking Talbot's job by writing a populist book supporting neo-con America (p. 87). Just before his death, in a speech that rings with passionate defiance, Talbot reaffirms the eventual triumph of Reason.

Following *Myth* Sewell underwent a resurgence and, between 2004 and 2006, produced two extravagantly theatrical, dark carnivalesque plays about painters, *The Secret Death of Salvador Dali* and *Three Furies*, about Francis Bacon. In addition he wrote two political comedy dramas about the United States, *The United States of Nothing*, set in New Orleans in the aftermath of Hurricane Katrina; and *It Just Stopped*, a savage comedy of manners in which an urbane professional couple wake up one morning to find that the world as they know it has suddenly ended. In *The Gates of Egypt*, written in 2007, a recently widowed Australian mum, against her children's wishes, travels to Egypt, where she encounters the Islamic Other in a confrontation of great power. The urgency in Sewell's writing—the desire to get it out quickly—is exhilarating.

Louis Nowra

Louis Nowra is possibly the most prolific playwright of the last thirty years, after Williamson and Romeril. Since the late 1970s he has produced an astonishing succession of plays exploring issues of post-nationalism in Australia, drawing on a wide range of sources and bringing together the personal and the political in provocative new ways.

Nowra was paired with Sewell as part of the new internationalism, but his interest in the links between knowledge and power turned out to be more idiosyncratic than Sewell's. His great academic interpreter, Veronica Kelly, has placed him partly within the critical discourses of post-colonialism, but Nowra has always been a slippery playwright who exploits a range of genres. He is skilful in his craft, strong in his effects, bold in his themes and ideas, but never politically passionate in the way of Sewell.[10] He has been extraordinarily eclectic, from early political allegory plays, through plays about aboriginal issues and others about growing up working class, to his comedy-dramas about politicians, businessmen and the corrupt and degraded world of late twentieth-century capitalism, which he partly celebrates. Nowra has always drawn on the styles and themes of his time. What makes him such an exciting playwright is the vividness with which he takes up different forms and pours new ideas and stories into them.

His early plays look at how people exercise power over others at an individual level by controlling the way in which they see the world. In the one-act *Albert Names Edward* (1975) a man brings home an amnesiac he has found wandering the streets. Tentatively at first, but with increasing confidence, Albert teaches his pupil to live in his own imagined world, modelled on that of the Mickey Spillane novels to which he is devoted. By the end he has named him Edward, 'discovered' him to be his long-lost brother, and started to educate him about his own 'life'—a pastiche of clichéd gumshoe sex and violence. In *The Song Room* (1980) a group of hospital patients with various neurological disorders that affect their speech are introduced to music therapy by Mary, an idealistic young therapist. One of them, Pat, brain-damaged in war and unable to speak of the trauma that he has suffered, responds particularly well. For the first time he finds himself able to speak, or rather sing, of his terrible experiences. Yet, when he tries to tell his daughter at his granddaughter's birthday party and the children banging in rhythm enable him to tell his story, his daughter does not hear it, but instead is fearful and sends the children away. Again, when he takes over a therapy session, he becomes too passionate and is withdrawn from the program. At the end of the play Pat's outburst is forgotten and the rest of the group dully sing 'Row, row, row your boat'.

Both plays were originally written for radio but are perfectly playable on the stage. They show Nowra's ability to reveal the ways in which language, especially inarticulate or damaged language, determines experience and constructs identity.

The first of Nowra's plays to attract wide attention was *Inner Voices* (1977), in a Nimrod Theatre production by John Bell. The play was ostensibly set in Tsarist Russia at the end of the reign of Catherine the Great although, as Nowra writes in his introduction to the published text, it was not a history play, but one set 'in the country of the mind'.[11]

10: THE NEW INTERNATIONALISM

It opens with a chilling scene in which a naked young man who only knows his name—Ivan—is silently washed by prison guards who are forbidden to speak to him.

Ivan is a wild-boy figure who is heir to the throne. He has been imprisoned since babyhood by Catherine the Great, allowed to grow up without language or any significant human contact. When Catherine dies suddenly, he is set free by a soldier, the grotesque opportunist Mirovich, and installed as a puppet-tsar. Mirovich teaches Ivan how to perform the role, using a mix of Enlightenment clichés and sensual pleasures. Ivan learns from Mirovich how to be violent, but not how to rule. In Bell's production, in the black box of the former Nimrod downstairs space (now Belvoir Downstairs), Ivan cowered on stage as his 'lessons' were delivered by disembodied voices from a tangle of pipes looming above him.

Having grown grotesquely fat on the perks of his position, Mirovich eventually dies. Brutality is all that Ivan has learnt and, as he comes into his inheritance as an independent Tsar, he kicks the corpse. He then cuts out the tongues of all his teachers and ends up grimly triumphant, perversely aware of his new power. As the forces of a revolutionary army press around his retreat, Ivan taunts the others—once his mentors, then his followers, now his victims—about the dumbness he has inflicted on them. He starts listening to mysterious voices of his own that we cannot hear. The effect is of him suddenly returning to the silent world of his upbringing, having been taught nothing but violence, and a kind of savagely childlike exultance in the exercise of naked power.

Inner Voices is one of the great plays of the 1970s, and it is astonishing that there has been no mainstage revival since. It is the first of many Nowra works about the effects of dreams, teachings and impositions of power on blank, but always alarmingly receptive, minds. His later plays are increasingly powerful and complex dramas that elaborate on these ideas, but the classical simplicity of *Inner Voices* remains remarkable.

In a dazzling series of plays about the public exercise of power and its intersections with private visions and nightmares, Nowra established his reputation as an extraordinarily imaginative playwright. Violent social and political events are represented as the outpourings

BELONGING

of diseased individual minds, minds that are, in turn, moulded by the large-scale social and political events that they have created. *Visions, Inside the Island, The Precious Woman, Spellbound, Sunrise, The Golden Age* and *The Watchtower* tell a diverse range of stories but in each one Nowra focuses on the interaction between private visions and public events. Images of civilisation and barbarism clash in the context of European imperialism and colonial oppression, so that it is impossible to say which characters are civilised and which barbaric. They are figures with contending visions who dream, or in some cases hallucinate, differently savage worlds.

Visions (1978) is set in nineteenth-century Paraguay during its futile war against the Triple Alliance of Argentina, Uruguay and Brazil. Like *Inner Voices*, it opens with a starkly theatrical scene in which a young man calls out a name, Juana. He finds and leads away a woman in a white dress lying in the mud, perhaps raped, certainly abject. The main action of the play documents President Lopez's assumption of power in his native country and his pointless, egomaniacal propagation of the war. He has returned from Europe with a supposedly sophisticated French wife, Madame Lynch, a courtesan. At first comically, then brutally, her airs and aspirations are subverted as the war escalates, the court flees the city, and her pretty costumes and finery are mired in the swamp. Juana becomes a mute visionary whose magical hallucinations of Paraguay inspire both Lopez and Lynch. At the end, after the tyrants have been shot like animals in the jungle, Juana becomes suddenly articulate in a European way, as if Lopez and Lynch have managed to colonise her after their deaths.

While *Inner Voices* had an Australian resonance, *Inside the Island* (1980) was the first of Nowra's plays to have an unambiguous Australian setting. In it, the colonising power is England and the occupied territory rural Australia during the early years of the last century. It invokes World War I, a European war that still haunts public discourses of Australianness. *Inside the Island* is Nowra's Gallipoli play.

Lillian Dawson is the matriarch of a wealthy pastoral property, like those described in previous chapters, but she is tougher and more brutal. Her husband George is a particularly weak version of the quiescent father figure of the bush and station-dramas.

10: THE NEW INTERNATIONALISM

A troop of soldiers is billeted on Lillian's land. When their commander asks for flour for a picnic cricket match she, knowingly, offers them bad wheat that she's been unable to sell. It turns out to be ergot-contaminated and the soldiers who have eaten it go mad. They rampage through the district, raping and pillaging, killing themselves, each other and most of Lillian's small family in a way that is now familiar, but which seemed at the time to be a shocking extension of the war into a quiet backwater. That all this was happening in Australia in 1912 brought the savagery of the subsequent world war suddenly home. The impact of *Inside the Island* is similar to that of *Blasted*, Sarah Kane's 1995 drama, which relocated the savagery of the Bosnian war to a nice hotel room in Leeds.

The Precious Woman (1980) is Nowra's most straightforwardly Brechtian play, an epic set in warlord China during the early 1920s in which personal choices of moral and political action are set against a background of large-scale historical events. Su-Ling is the sheltered wife of warlord Teng. When he dies, their son Bao pursues his father's ruthless policy of oppressing dissent to terrible extremes; and he exiles his own mother. After a period of grief and introspection, she joins and soon leads the rebels, inventing a successful form of guerrilla warfare called 'nightfighting'. At the end Bao is defeated and his bloody body is brought before the blind and bitter Su-Ling. She kicks the corpse before cradling it in her arms. For the first time in Nowra's plays there is love, albeit thwarted and desperate, in the conclusion.[12]

Sunrise (1983) is a weekend family drama, anticipating Sewell's *Hate* and *The Sick Room*. It resonates both politically and allegorically as a representation of post-colonial Australia and of the tensions between an oppressive European tradition and white Australia's fragile grip on an ancient continent. Its conflicts take place over an Easter long weekend. Clarrie Shelton, a distinguished scientist, is celebrating his 60th birthday at his country property Honey Ant Dreaming, an elegant home built on ancient Aboriginal land. His children and grandchildren have gathered and during the weekend a number of deeply personal traumas are played out, or rather, remembered and dreamed by characters who float around the estate in isolation from each other. The sense of dislocation in the play is very strong.

BELONGING

Clarrie has a particular bond with his 14-year-old granddaughter Venice, a troubled child who grew up in Africa and is haunted by her experiences, feeling separated from the Western world to which she has been returned. There are several non-family characters who are equally adrift: Vince, Clarrie's former colleague, has had a stroke and only Clarrie can understand him; Ly, the gardener, a Vietnamese refugee, cringes in fear whenever a helicopter flies over; and local townspeople, Peggy and her husband Albert, are traditional 'Aussie battlers' but awkward outsiders in this mad company.

A bushfire is raging up the slopes, threatening the property. By the end of the play there are helicopters overhead, smoke and ashes in the air, and gunfire offstage as injured sheep are shot. The effect of war is more apocalyptic than the battlefield-like scenes of *Inside the Island*. Clarrie has been implicated in the nuclear testing at Maralinga. At the end Venice picks up a gun and shoots him dead, to release, she claims, 'the tiger within him'. The play's powerful hallucinatory quality suggests that the violence of the world is a reflection of individual madness which, in turn and in an endless cycle, is itself produced by that violence.

However bizarre it might be in the context of a family weekend, there is much love in Venice's shooting of Clarrie. Like Su-Ling with Bao in *The Precious Woman*, she cradles his body at the end as she watches the sun rise. This culmination of Nowra's first period of playwriting is a play in which love becomes the guiding force of the action, with a resolution that is at once brutal and oddly romantic.

The Golden Age, *The Watchtower* and *Crow* are all set during World War II. Each takes a different point of view but, together with *Inside the Island* and *Sunrise*, they dramatise key stages in the long search for a sense of belonging in white Australia, as groups of troubled misfits cling precariously to an idea and a land that is ambivalently caught between European 'civilisation' and an ancient Indigenous culture. European wars rumble like thunder in the distance and Indigenous ghosts haunt the landscape.

The Golden Age (1985) is the most complex of Nowra's postcolonial allegories. It moves between the worlds of Georgian England; the pristine wilderness of Tasmania to which it cruelly consigned its convicts; the Anglophile society of Hobart in the mid-twentieth

10: THE NEW INTERNATIONALISM

century; and a ravaged Berlin in the final months of World War II.

In 1939, two young men, one from high society and his friend from the wrong side of the tracks, go walking in the Tasmanian wilderness and discover a lost tribe. Descendants of escaped convicts, this tight-knit family group have survived for over a century and created a mini-culture of their own, based on half-remembered snatches of Shakespeare, an argot from the convict hulks and a carefully nurtured love of each other. The boys bring the group back to Hobart on the eve of the war, where they are interned in a mental asylum, hidden away lest their supposedly degenerate condition fuel Nazi race propaganda. In these conditions they die quickly, one by one. By the end of the war, only Betsheb is left, a strong and passionate young woman sustained by the remnants of her culture, especially the matriarch Ayre, and by her love for Francis, the working-class boy who found her and listened to her. Francis is away at war, but when he returns he takes Betsheb back to the Tasmanian wilderness so they can live together in her country. Realistically there is not much hope for the future but spiritually and emotionally we feel this as a victory.

Crow (1994) is set in 1942 in Darwin, depicted here as a crazy provincial outpost, occupied by a colourful collection of Anglo-Australian misfits, corrupt army incompetents and mixed-race battlers. Its early scenes are haunted by the threat of invasion by the half-feared, half-scorned Japanese military forces island-hopping their way south.

At the centre of the play is Crow herself, a glorious Mother Courage figure. An Aboriginal woman, Crow lived for many years with an Irishman named Patrick and together they built a tin mine. Since Patrick's death five years earlier she has been fighting in the white courts for its ownership as she desperately tries to save, support and provide for her two sons. When, in the play's tumultuous finale, the Japanese start bombing Darwin and its tidy white society collapses, she grabs her chance to rewrite history, and takes her daughter back to the world she came from. Patrick keeps appearing as a ghost, full of love and tenderness.

Crow is one of several plays that Nowra wrote about black–white relations, beginning with his adaptation in 1988 of Xavier Herbert's novel *Capricornia*, and continuing with *Byzantine Flowers* (1989)

BELONGING

and *Radiance*. In earlier plays the presence of Aboriginal Australians is suggested obliquely or allegorically. Peter's camp in *Inside the Island*, the lost tribe in *The Golden Age* and the ghosts of Honey Ant Dreaming and Clarrie's memories of the Maralinga tests in *Sunrise* all evoke images of original inhabitants—people who once belonged, but who are now dispossessed fringe-dwellers. Indeed, all Nowra's plays, from *Inner Voices* on, may be read in terms of the dispossession of Indigenous people. But in *Capricornia*, *Byzantine Flowers*, *Radiance* and *Crow* he addresses these issues head-on.

Capricornia was one of a series of Bicentennial plays that made a radical re-examination, not only of the heroic legends of the great Australian tradition, but also of the white histories that were being celebrated in the public hype that year. Several plays were funded by the Bicentennial Authority, including the third and angriest of Jack Davis's *Dreamers* trilogy, *Barungin (Smell the Wind)*, with its litany of the names of Aboriginal men who had died in jail (the Wootten Royal Commission into Aboriginal Deaths in Custody had been set up in October 1987); novelist Frank Hardy's play about Henry Lawson, *Faces in the Street*; the larrikin musical adaptation of Manning Clark's six-volume *History of Australia* by John Romeril, Tim Robertson and Don Watson; Ray Mooney's *Black Rabbit*, a brutal play about the myth of *terra nullius*; Michael Gow's bitter drama, *1841*, about the betrayal of the young colony by violently prosecuted dreams of avarice; and Stephen Sewell's grim dissection of the grand pioneering old-money family dynasties, *Hate*.[13]

Nowra's version of *Capricornia*, revived by Sydney's Company B Belvoir in 2006 in a production by Wesley Enoch, in some ways continues in the tradition of Katharine Susannah Prichard and George Landen Dann and plays such as David Ireland's *Image in the Clay*, Bill Reed's *Truganinni* trilogy, Thomas Keneally's *Bullie's House* and David Malouf's *Blood Relations*. Others, also about black–white relations, such as Ned Manning's *Close to the Bone* and *Luck of the Draw* and Nicholas Parsons's *Dead Heart*, followed later. Although not written from a black perspective, they all treat their Aboriginal characters and their stories with considerable sympathy.

Herbert's novel *Capricornia* appeared in 1938, when it won the Commonwealth Sesquicentenary literary competition. Originally

10: THE NEW INTERNATIONALISM

a short piece entitled 'Black Velvet' (a white man's term for black women they have sex with), the novel grew into an enormous, rambling manuscript, edited, controversially, by P. R. Stephenson down to half its original length. Nowra's brilliantly economical dramatic version, written in haste to meet an emergency deadline, focuses the yarn even further and is undoubtedly the best telling of the story.[14]

For all its economy the play is a grand saga of frontier life in the Northern Territory, which Herbert had called 'Capricornia'. It concentrates on the central character, Norman Shillingsworth, a half-caste who has been educated in Melbourne and returns to Port Zodiac (Darwin) believing that he is the son of a heroic Australian soldier and a Javanese princess. In the first half he meets a number of characters who know more about him than he does himself, and is shocked to learn the truth about his parentage. His white education has taught him to think of this as a sordid heritage and, repulsed, he flees into the bush at the end of Act One. Here he is trapped in the Wet—the annual monsoon season that shuts down much of the Territory—and begins to learn about his Aboriginality. He forms a relationship with Tocky O'Cannon, a feisty half-caste escapee from a mission island (a character much expanded from the novel), and starts out again to run Red Ochre, his white and black family territory, as a black-run station. Norman and Tocky become a new version of the Nowra romantic couple, their love bridging a gulf while events and cultural differences conspire against them. Norman is tried for murder and acquitted, but he suddenly realises it must have been Tocky, in her abject flight from the mission, who was forced to commit the murder. He returns to Red Ochre for the last, tragically ironic scene. To protect her from white men, he has told her to hide in the water-tank whenever she sees them coming. When he returns, she mistakes him for yet another white oppressor, and hides in the water-tank—where months later her sodden body, and that of her baby, are found.

The success of this play is as much in its bizarre collection of peripheral characters—whites gone troppo and dispossessed blacks full of trickster energy—as it is in the tragedy of Norman and Tocky. The hybrid world of Xavier Herbert's *Capricornia* was perfectly suited to Nowra's storytelling skills.

BELONGING

For all its passion and theatricality, *Radiance* (1993) is Nowra's most classically simple play. It brings together three half-sisters who have gathered in a coastal house on the outskirts of the remote North Queensland town of their childhood for the funeral of their mother, who spent her life as an outcast there. Nona is the wild one, with no home base, a sexy dress style and a string of faithless men behind her; Mae is the drab stay-at-home who nursed their mother in her final illness; and Cressy is the glamorous success, a famous opera singer who spends most of her life in lonely hotel rooms. The three estranged women circle each other in their opening negotiations, then gradually come together, and reveal some extraordinary secrets: revelations about their mother—a passionate, loving woman who was exploited by one brutal white man after another and in her abjection loved them all—and about each other.

After a series of comic conflicts they walk drunkenly together across the tidal sand-flats to scatter their mother's ashes on the island from which their people came. It is now a resort for Japanese tourists, to which they are not admitted. They stop half way. Nona wants to go on, but Mae is haunted by memories of her mother's degeneration into the town witch and her oppression as the victim of a string of white lovers—and wants to burn the house down. She does. In a final scene, as the shack burns behind them, Cressy tells Nona that they are mother and daughter. When her had mother discovered that Cressy had been brutally raped under the floorboards by one of her boyfriends, she decided to raise Nona as her own. Horrified by this, Nona runs away across the sand, leaving the self-protective Cressy on the flats, cradling Mae as the incoming tide starts to lap at their feet. The play celebrates the bitter stories of individuals oppressed by past secrets and lies. In 1998, Nowra wrote the screenplay for a film version directed by Rachel Perkins.

Nowra had an extraordinarily prolific period in the early 1990s, producing an opera (*Love Burns* with music by Graeme Koehne) and eight plays in a little over three years: *The Temple, Radiance, Crow, The Incorruptible, Miss Bosnia* and *The Jungle* as well as his two great popular stage successes: *Summer of the Aliens* and *Cosi*. The latter was filmed in 1995, directed by Mark Joffe, and is one of Nowra's best-known works.

10: THE NEW INTERNATIONALISM

Summer of the Aliens and *Cosi* are both centred on a character named Lewis and based in Nowra's own experience. *Summer of the Aliens* (1992), a moving coming-of-age story, is set in 1962, the year of the Cuban Missile Crisis. A Narrator in rattleskin boots introduces us to the bleak outer-suburban Housing Commission wasteland where Nowra grew up—a world of no trees, no bush, no flowers, with backyards of baked dirt and the latest movies a long walk away, across a dry paddock, past the rifle range and the migrant Compound. He introduces us to himself—Lewis aged 14—not yet interested enough in sex as far as his best friend Dulcie is concerned, dreaming of seeing a flying saucer and meeting an alien, and only thinking of the future to the extent of yearning for a pair of rattleskin boots.

Eventually he realises that the aliens are here and they are us, or at least the parents and other grown-ups who stuff us up. They have taken over the minds of his mother, grandmother, sister and absent adventurer father; they have driven the postman mad; they have perverted his best friend Brian, so that he is only interested in sex; they are manifest in the odd Dutch immigrant girl from the Compound with only one arm; and in Lewis's weird show-business uncle and his exotic Japanese girlfriend. With an ingenuous, almost transcendent, naïvety, the young Lewis struggles to take all this on board. Dulcie, sexually abused by her drunken stepfather, is wise beyond her years, but is finally cast out of her family and society. Just before she is taken away Lewis is persuaded by his older self to make contact with her, and they share a tender scene of early teenage love and desperation. But then, like all these figures summoned up from the past, she disappears and he never sees her again. The play is a sentimental lament, a remembrance of things past that pays attention to the present by the simple fact of having being written. In the original production Nowra himself played the Narrator.

Cosi, which appeared a month after *Summer of the Aliens*, is set nine years later against the background of the anti-Vietnam protests. Lewis is now 21, has recently left university and is looking for something to do.[15] He takes a job directing a drama night with inmates of a psychiatric institution. In his discovery of their exhilarating humanity he drifts away from the student friends of his university years. Nothing sets Nowra apart from the spirit of the New Wave dramatists so much

BELONGING

as this nostalgic portrait of himself as a young man, during their golden years, turning his back on Brecht and the protest movement of the time and working with a collection of mad characters on a production of Mozart's *Cosi Fan Tutte*.

The early version of the script (1992) included scenes in Lewis's student household and the break-up of his relationship with his political activist girlfriend who takes up with Nick, his erstwhile friend and mentor. A politics-crazed apparatchik, Nick is a satirical portrait of a typical APG radical theatre-worker. While these characters still remain, the later version of the script focuses on Lewis's adventures with his happy band of patients.

Cosi contains one of Nowra's most successful comic characters in Roy (created on both stage and screen by Barry Otto) a long-institutionalised megalomaniac. Roy's passion for Mozart drives this group of misfits to mount the opera—with a drug-addled accordion player as the orchestra, and a cast of characters whose mental problems almost exactly mismatch the roles they play, speaking them, as they must, since none of them can sing. The women compete for Lewis's sexual attention and the rehearsals are continually interrupted by the pyromaniac Doug, who keeps trying to burn the theatre down. (In the film version he succeeds.)

This funny–sad play combines the elements of Nowra's earlier, more serious work—the interest in knowledge and power; the tensions that result from the meeting of diverse cultures; the carnivalesque excess even in the most domestic scenes—all reworked in a light accessible style.

This new comic exuberance also pervades two political farces from the same period, *The Temple*, a satire on 1980s corporate greed; and *The Incorruptible*, which starts out as a satire on political corruption, but ends up being rather more serious. In *The Jungle*, paying tribute to the then fashionably dark urban comedy of filmmaker Quentin Tarantino, Nowra translated this style of satire into a form of cinematic urban baroque.

The Temple (1993) is a relatively straightforward black comedy that takes an entrepreneurial villain—like Derek Wiesland from Sewell's *Dreams in an Empty City*—and turns him into an outrageous figure of fun. Laurie Blake has enough of the devil in him to be exhilarating,

10: THE NEW INTERNATIONALISM

but not so much as to be frightening. A former abattoir worker, he becomes a major corporate criminal, a vile, evil, obscene character who keeps winning, and winning gloriously. He schmoozes his way through billion-dollar deals that enrich him, impoverish his victims and defeat his corporate enemies. At the end, bankrupt and in exile, he moves into business in post-Soviet Russia, where he will presumably hobnob with a new breed of the corrupt rich.

The Incorruptible (1995) starts out as a similar political satire, when Ion Stafford, a religious bush fundamentalist, is picked up by a corrupt political wheeler-dealer to be set up as a puppet premier. Ion turns out to be an ideologue, incorruptible and incapable of compromise, with the consequence that the entire corrupt world of the state he is running is driven underground and flourishes. Finally, on the night of his triumphant election as Prime Minister, he is shot dead by his publicist, a young woman who has been one of his most devoted supporters. She says she believes he has gone power-mad, but she has her own inner turmoil and might simply be killing a father-figure for fear he will abandon her. This ending, like an echo of Venice's murder of Clarrie at the end of *Sunrise*, is abrupt and contrived, a *deus ex machina* conclusion to a satirical plot that Nowra has cheerfully allowed to go too far.

Two weeks after *The Incorruptible* opened at Melbourne's Playbox Theatre in 1995, *Miss Bosnia* opened in Brisbane, and three months later *The Jungle* opened in Sydney. *Miss Bosnia* is a comedy based on a premise that is bizarre, even for Nowra. A group of desperate women and one man in drag have scurried through the rubble-strewn streets of war-torn Sarajevo to take part in a beauty pageant in which the first prize is a ticket on the last truck out of the besieged city. It is like a carnivalesque inversion of Susan Sontag's well-reported 1993 production of *Waiting for Godot* in that devastated city. The idea is not fully developed in the script, but its elements—the endless comedy of human hopes and sufferings, and the crushing effect of the outside world—are classic Nowra. The characters have to perform idealised media images of womanhood in order to survive in a destroyed city and keep alive their dreams of escaping from it.

The Jungle (1995) is a brilliant sequence of apparently isolated scenes—most of which could be played as short one-acters—which come together as a down-these-mean-streets portrait of 24 hours in the life of a bad wild Sydney.[16] The action opens at dawn with the escape of a teenager, Olive, who like Ivan in *Inner Voices* has been locked away in solitude all her life, drinking vinegar, and beaten and oppressed by a Woman who is perhaps her mother. It closes at the next dawn, when Olive, who has finally found refuge, discovers the sun for the first time in her life and, according to the stage directions, is literally carried away by it.

While Olive is searching for the sun, we travel round the city, peeking into apartments, hospital wards, suburban gardens, hotel rooms, flash restaurants, night clubs, brothels and bars, finding a human story in every place. Some of them are wildly comic, others desperately sad. It gradually becomes clear that all are linked because the city, from its seediest low-life dives to the most glittering meeting places of its cultured elite, is an intricate interconnected web. The play is a wonderful puzzle and great pleasure is to be derived from pursuing the links between these characters, as they manipulate, cajole, betray, kill, torture, rape, trust, love and dream of each other. We follow it all partly with the help of the play's only through-line, the passing of a distinctive blue jacket from scene to scene. The climax takes place in a well-known late-night Sydney venue, the Judgement Bar at Taylor Square. Here a dreamily romantic young drug addict and pimp, who has been murdered earlier in the play but who was astral travelling at the time and so is not yet dead, has finally ended up, in his night-long determination to kill the man who killed him. His soul pops back into his body just a moment too soon, so he dies and is snatched away before he can achieve his death-long ambition.

The aging international rock legend, who has died of a drug overdose at least once during the night but been revived yet again, miraculously survives her concert to deliver the play's final message. In the chaotic desperation of this world, she says, all we can do is comfort one another. Then Olive wakes up, thinking at first that she is back in her cell, before realising that she has found the sun. The play is an exhilarating ride, with a neat conclusion.

In *The Language of the Gods* (1999) Nowra returns to issues he explored in his early epic family dramas. These are set at significant

10: THE NEW INTERNATIONALISM

turning-points in the lives of his characters, whose worlds are about to change forever. Here the key moment occurs when the Dutch return briefly to Indonesia after the defeat of the Japanese in World War II. They attempt to save their colony in the face of the guerrilla wars being fought by the Indonesian republicans.

Peter Braak is the Governor of the Celebes, a decent man who loves his adopted country and understands its ancient culture, but who clings to old imperialist models and realises before anyone else does that the white man's time has passed. He has a difficult family—a surly rebellious son, a teenage daughter who wants to marry a Eurasian, and a new young Australian wife whose affairs become the scandal of the region. As the empire collapses, and the republican guerrillas advance on his home, his happy family starts to fall apart in a mixture of naïvety and selfishness. Still he clings to his love of ancient culture—especially in his relationship with his friend Dely, who is a Bissu, or traditional transvestite priest, with magic powers, including the ability to cut himself without bleeding. Dely's presence repels and fascinates the Dutch characters in differing degrees: in their eyes he is an exotic oriental and sexual other, who likes to dress up in Western frocks and be photographed as Lana Turner. At the end he reveals that he is Braak's Eurasian son by a housemaid. For all his supposed love of the people, Braak had sent the mother back to the *kampong* when she became pregnant. Dely kills Braak in a ritualistic sword dance as the victorious guerrillas encircle the Governor's grand house. In an epilogue set 25 years later we see Dely performing his sacred dances for tourists in an Indonesia that has passed him by. The play gives a powerful account of a time when European imperialism was ending, but also shows that for post-colonial societies the process of 'decolonisation' conceals profound and long-term effects.

The Language of the Gods followed a three-year gap in Nowra's writing for the theatre, if not for other media. He has written radio plays, novels, television dramas and screenplays. Early in his career he published an extraordinary collection of brief, bizarre stories culled from his newspaper scrapbooks, *The Cheated*; he called it his coffee-table book for manic depressives. His novels include *The Misery of Beauty, Palu, Red Nights, Abaza: A Modern Encyclopedia* and, in 2008, *Ice*. His

BELONGING

television dramas include *Displaced Persons*, *Hunger* and *The Lizard King* and with Tim Gooding he wrote a drama series for the ABC, *The Last Resort*. His screenplays include *Map of the Human Heart*, *Heaven's Burning*, *K-19*, *Black and White* and the screen versions of *Radiance* and *Cosi*. He wrote the libretto for the Brian Howard opera, *Whitsunday*. In 2000, he published *The Twelfth of Never*, a memoir about his youth and his troubled family, and in 2004, another, entitled *Shooting the Moon*, about his adult life. He returned to the stage, to Sydney's Griffin Theatre, in 2004 with *The Woman with Dog's Eyes*, a weekend family-reunion confrontation with a rich patriarch in the tradition of *Sunrise* and Sewell's *Hate*. It is the first play in *The Boyce Trilogy*, and was followed, in consecutive years and at the same theatre, by *The Marvellous Boy* and *The Emperor of Sydney*.

Taken together Nowra's plays provide an extraordinary record of the various crises and transitions of twentieth century, especially as they have affected Australians. Beside his, other constructions of Australia seem to have been at best sleeping and dreaming and at worst dangerously stupid about the gathering storms in the world outside their island. In his plays people, societies and cultures internalise their oppression and externalise their visions in ways that are dangerous at all levels. Nowra has demonstrated a remarkable ability to pick up a series of startling stories in which these levels intersect.

Sewell and Nowra reset the agenda of the Australian theatre. The ambitious scope of their early plays, their often brutal interrogation of Australian nationalism and parochialism, their interest in the crushing weight of history on the minds of ordinary people, their big-picture cinematic narrative techniques and the sheer theatrical scale of their early work—with large casts and vast ranges of different settings and scenes, made possible by the new non-naturalistic, non-representational theatrical styles of the 1970s—have seldom been repeated. They were the last of the New Wave, before the 1990s economically-driven contraction of the mainstream theatre and the consequent rediscovery of old genres.[17] Although both kept writing on a smaller scale, from a theatregoer's point of view something was lost when the theatre could no longer keep up with the vision of its best writers.

11
PLAYWRIGHTS IN THE 80S

While Sewell and Nowra were the most influential writers who emerged in the late 1970s, a number of others also produced good work including Steve J. Spears, Barry Dickins, Clem Gorman and Ron Elisha. We turn now to look at their work and that of two others from the late New Wave who went on to become major playwrights: Nick Enright and Michael Gow.

Steve J. Spears was one of the most publicly successful. His one-man play *The Elocution of Benjamin Franklin* (1976) became a national and international success in a production directed by Richard Wherrett and starring Gordon Chater, a well-known revue and television performer.

It tells the story of Robert O'Brien, a once-married cross-dresser who has sexual fantasies about Mick Jagger and may or may not lust after his favourite elocution pupil, an alarmingly sophisticated 12-year-old boy named Benjamin Franklin. Certainly, O'Brien is seduced by something in Ben's preening style. At home in the first act, and in a mental institution in the second, he acts out many of the people in his life with great theatrical flair and bravado. O'Brien is an old actor fallen on hard times and given to the bottle. Fat, fruity and fifty, he likes to go out in public in drag with his happily-married cross-dressing friend Bruce. He has a passionate belief in teaching and in passing

BELONGING

on his love for the pre–New Wave theatrical values of good diction and a reverence for Shakespeare. But his love of grand gestures is his downfall at the end of Act 1 when, besieged by the media, the police and an outraged rock-throwing Toorak public, he takes up a shotgun and shoots his cuckoo clock.

The first edition of the play carries a splendid photo of Chater in a white satin dress and blonde wig with a fat cigar in his mouth, cradling a gun—an image that sums up the peculiarly retro rebellious style of both O'Brien and Spears.[1] O'Brien is an innocent, destroyed by a hypocritical society whose outrage is directed at private fantasies that have never hurt anyone. The play had a new relevance when it was revived in 2002, in the wake of paedophile scandals and a new round of media frenzy.

Five months after *The Elocution of Benjamin Franklin* Nimrod produced Spears's play about the legendary vaudeville and radio star Roy Rene, whose character Mo had been the most famous figure in Australian show business alongside Dad Rudd. Like the APG's *Marvellous Melbourne* and the commercial hit *The Legend of King O'Malley*, the play was an exercise in the larrikin celebration of Australian legends. The full title of Spears's play was *The Resuscitation of the Little Prince Who Couldn't Laugh as Performed by Young Mo at the Height of the Great Depression of 1929*. You needed to know some theatrical history to get the joke of the title, but it was quickly abbreviated to *Young Mo* and the production was a success for Nimrod.[2] Garry McDonald, a fine actor then best known for his own comic creation Norman Gunston, played Mo, and Martin Sharp's stylised image of Mo's comic face, designed for a scenic effect in the show and used in the publicity, became Nimrod's logo.[3]

Young Mo deals reverentially with Mo's early rise to fame as a partner of Nat Phillips and as a co-performer with Queenie Paul, but stops short as he is poised to become a major radio star. With its own theatricality and jokes it contrasts Mo's innocence with Rene's egocentricity backstage and before the press. Mo keeps noticing with surprise the stage devices, as if confused that his life is not being performed realistically. It ends with a surprisingly successful debate between various theatrical stereotypes about the nature and causes of fame.

11: PLAYWRIGHTS IN THE 80S

On the basis of these two vehicles for star actors Spears became for a short time that rare thing in Australia, a star playwright. In the following year Outback Press published a volume of his plays entitled *Early Works*, which included three plays that have not had much impact: *Africa: A Musical*, *People Keep Giving Me Things* and *Mad Jean: They Say She's Crazy Like a Snake*, a hippie musical about a silent woman who challenges a vaguely fascist state and its rabid population by being sweet and nice. These are typical New Wave plays—rebellious and full of bright ideas, but without much structure or sense of purpose. His 1983 play *When They Send Me Three and Fourpence* is a flashback to an earlier time in Robert (then Bob) O'Brien's life. It is set in 1963, when Bob, a fading actor in his forties, is running a very small business teaching dancing to a few lonely pupils. He remembers his glory years, when he returned from overseas with his wife Jeanette who has since left him, hoping to set the rundown beach suburb of St Kilda on fire with his dance classes and his amateur theatre company. He is now alcoholic, but with enough charisma to have attracted both Marion, the niece of the local bishop, and Betty, a young woman who wants to be a real dancer, not just one of his little family of losers. While Betty has a torrid affair with him, Marion wins and in the end reforms him. The play is a rather maudlin celebration of the romantic drunk with a vision, but it also commemorates, with sentimental regret and a lot of music, the death of the old music at the hands of early rock'n'roll, and, in dance, the triumph of the twist over the tango and the stomp over the foxtrot.

King Richard, produced in 1978, is a creaky thriller about political corruption which came across as naïve and unbelievable at the time and still does.

Although he came to the scene rather late and rather young, Spears was in many ways a classic New Wave writer. His best plays, especially *The Elocution of Benjamin Franklin*, *Young Mo* and *When They Send Me Three and Fourpence*, are romantically nostalgic stories about the passing of traditions he was too young to know.

A wilder, darker, less sentimental, but still nostalgic, writer from the late New Wave is Barry Dickins, a vernacular poet of the underclass. He tells colourful stories of self-destructive battlers and desperados who,

BELONGING

by their energy and humour, manage to keep raging against the dying of the light, even as the world crushes them. Like Michael Gurr after him, Dickins is an example of a very good playwright who has been almost completely ignored by theatre companies outside his home city. Geoffrey Milne has suggested that this is because his subject matter is local, but there has to be more to it than that.[4]

Dickins has an exuberant love of the theatrical, in both his settings and the expressionist or vaudevillian action of his plays. A love of theatre itself is the subject or back-story for extravagantly eccentric characters, especially in *The Fool's Shoe Hotel, Lennie Lower, The Golden Goldenbergs* and *A Dickins' Christmas* (1992). The last, a reworking of Charles Dickens's *A Christmas Carol*, is an irreverent celebration of Melbourne theatre in the 1950s, when the dead hand of English directors intent on raising colonial standards was finally challenged and a bloke could finally say 'By Crikey!' on the Australian stage. The Scrooge figure, Fred Gruel, is the snobbish, tight-arsed director of the Maudlin Theatre Company who, with the help of the three ghosts of Christmases past, finally discovers the new Australian drama. You wouldn't want to read too much into this spoof, but the ghosts of the UTRC, John Sumner, Ray Lawler and some of their actors are not hard to detect.

Dickins's characters love to perform. Even the most desperate, lonely and secretive of them do so in the privacy of their retreats, after drinking a slab of beer or a bottle of whisky, for the benefit of parents, siblings, lovers or friends, often long lost or dead. The structure is not sophisticated and many of his plays have a what-shall-I-write-next style that gives the impression of larrikin formlessness. He exults in wordplay—especially puns and non-sequiturs, and has a rich repertoire of often-recycled vernacular phrases and jokes, including one about an elephant and a mouse that he has used in at least three plays.[5]

Dickins also has an original writing style that evokes both Dorothy Hewett and Jack Hibberd and celebrates, with a mixture of brutality and romance, the tragedy and comic resilience of an extraordinary collection of seedy, decrepit, decaying, alcoholic and visionary losers. His language is extravagant and lyrical, his imagination quirky and inventive. His characters, especially in his monodramas, keep moving

11: PLAYWRIGHTS IN THE 80S

from romantic storytelling to comic outbursts of rebellious energy, interspersed with moments of stillness. At the centre of his *One Woman Shoe* (1981), for example, is a short monodrama called 'The Cure', about a woman whose 100th birthday is ruined when she has a stroke. She is imprisoned in a hospital room from which the staff have mysteriously fled. Everyone she knows has long since died, so no-one turns up to celebrate. She jokes, smokes, drinks, swears and remembers her life with a death-defying defiance. Perhaps she is already dead; she certainly refuses to lie down.

In *The Bridal Suite* (1979), one of the best of his early monodramas, a decrepit old woman dressed, like Dickens's Miss Haversham, in a crumbling bridal gown, lives by herself in a derelict shack from the great bush tradition, drinks alone and remembers Jack, her wild, drunken, violent man whom she dearly loved and who died in a truck crash. The play is rich in humour and a poetic vernacular and it has lots of mood swings and different characterisations. Like all Dickins's writing, it exalts in remembered place names, brand names, common phrases and other traces of everyday life.

The Death of Minnie (1980) is another lyrical celebration of life by someone about to leave it. Minnie lives in a single room in a boarding house. On her 40th birthday she is alone, drinking, making raisin toast, telling stories and talking to her Poppa and Mamma in heaven. She remembers her life and what it was like to grow up Jewish, poor and alone in inner Melbourne. The play is her lively and enthusiastic journey towards death. At the end she scatters on the table all her little coloured tablets. 'Which one is cyanide?' She picks one at random. It works. 'That's right, they're all cyanide'. After her death the electric power that has been flickering all night in her squalid room comes back on and all her appliances start to work again, in celebration of her life.

The most passionate and romantic of all the one-actor plays is *Lennie Lower* (1982), about the great and popular humorist who worked for Frank Packer for 20-odd years, churning out daily comic newspaper columns that made Lower loved and Packer rich. During that time, according to Dickins, Lower became increasingly lonely. The play commemorates a remarkable artist who suffered from a charisma leak: he kept giving away bits of himself to his public and never got anything

BELONGING

back for himself, except a kind of hollow fame and a lot of money most of which he pissed up against the wall. Like many of Dickins's characters, Lower was an enthusiastic and riotous alcoholic. There is a story, too good to be true, that he had a row of three terrace houses and kept a typewriter in each of them, so that when he got home pissed he had a reasonable chance of finding a place to write tomorrow's column. The play takes place on the supposed night he waited drunkenly for a throat cancer operation which, apparently bungled by the surgeon (although this is not made clear in the play), killed him at the age of 43.

Dickins's early multi-character dramas are less successful. In *Mag and Bag* (1978) two grotesque old women ritually abuse each other, before dressing up as budgies and flying over the audience. As always in Dickins, its odd mixture of sentiment and grossness has a sort of wild charm. *The Banana Bender* (1980) is an unruly play in which a crazy lonely young agricultural worker and religious maniac who lives with his mother attempts briefly to escape his cramped life by picking up a tart in town and bringing her home. She turns out to be a good woman who offers him escape, but he lacks the courage to go through with it and settles back into his desperately sad life.

In the 1980s and early 1990s Dickins became increasingly nostalgic about the lost world of the working-class 1950s, which he clearly cherishes, at least for its honest ratbaggery. *Beautland* (1985) is an expressionist extravaganza in which a couple who have foolishly and selfishly become part of the 1980s me-generation of cynics and sneerers are taken back on a magical mystery tour of their youth. By meeting up in a series of dreams with their old toys and the ghosts of the family they have left behind, they end up rediscovering their love for each other. *Royboys* (1987), written with a mixture of nostalgia and despair, is about the commercialisation and commodification of sport and the way in which entrepreneurs (represented by Rupert Myxomatosis, the wealthiest and most evil man in the carnival world of this play) have stolen the simple dreams of ordinary working, smoking and drinking people and turned them into commodities.

One of Dickins's toughest plays, *Remember Ronald Ryan* (1994) commemorates the life of the last man to be legally executed in Australia, and represents him as a flawed romantic hero—a larrikin

11: PLAYWRIGHTS IN THE 80S

charmer, loving dad, stupid criminal and, in the end, sad victim of a political and media network obsessed with the idea of law and order. After a thrilling prison-escape opening, the entire first act is taken up by a madcap chase, complete with tense police radio reports, scenes with Ryan and his fellow escapee driving crazily around Melbourne looking for shelter, and flashbacks of Ryan's earlier life, with hints of how things might have turned out differently.

In the second half Ryan has been recaptured and is facing his hanging. There are no trial scenes, and little tension. The mood is contemplative, as Ryan sits waiting in his cell. The play again goes back to his earlier life, showing how he bungled his marriage and most of his crimes. It then lingers over his last days as, one by one, people from his past visit him. Thanks to a friendly guard and an enlightened prison governor, he finds some peace before he is executed. The play is a powerful document against capital punishment, rather than an exciting drama.

Another late New Wave writer who has continued to write is Clem Gorman, whose first play, *A Manual of Trench Warfare* (1974), deals with the homoerotic interplay between two trench-bound soldiers at Gallipoli. A naïve young private, Barry Moon, is drawn to his much older mate, Brendan Barra, who couches his sexual advances in a wild Irish-warrior romanticism. Barra's real enemy is not the Turks, but the homophobic Corporal Byron, who is out to get him. His conflict with Byron reaches a violent climax and he is finally killed. Moon decides to move on, apparently repelled by the whole experience.[6]

Gorman's other plays include *A Night in the Arms of Raeleen* (1981), in which a group of aging bodgies meet to remember the good old days when Raeleen was passed around the gang. Now married to one of them, during the course of their drunken reunion she takes a belated revenge. *The Last Night Club* (1985) is a sentimental eulogy for the days of the old underworld of Sydney's Kings Cross, when crime was cheerfully bohemian, before the American gangs moved in. *The Harding Women* (1981) deals with a battle between a dying woman and her carer, who used to be her husband's lover. Gorman also wrote a stage adaptation of A. B. Facey's well-known and much-loved autobiography of a battler, *A Fortunate Life* (1984).

BELONGING

For more than twenty years Ron Elisha has been one of Australia's most cerebral playwrights, interested in big ideas and constructing highly complex dramatic frameworks for them, using multiple and nested narratives that play clever games with time and subjectivity. *Einstein* (1981), for example, explores its protagonist's recognition, in the last hours of his life, of the contrast between his professional success and his personal and ethical failures. To do this the play uses three Einsteins, played by three actors, who first come together in 1919, the crucial year when the General Theory of Relativity was empirically confirmed and Einstein instantly became a world-famous genius. From that point each Einstein embarks on a separate trajectory. We watch as 'Albert', the young Einstein, moves back in narrative time to 1905, when he first thought of the idea of the mass-energy equation. 'Einstein', the successful physicist, moves forward to 1945, when the bomb was dropped on Hiroshima. And 'The Professor', over two hours in 1955, just before his death, ponders all this, interrogates the others and tries to come to terms with the contradictions.

Elisha also explores in his plays the ambiguity of the represented 'presence' of the character in the theatre, without going so far as to exploit the actual presence of the performer who is doing the representing. *Safe House* (1989) depends for its effect on the device of not having its central character on stage, although he is assumed by the other characters to be present, during scenes in which the story of his life is told in flashback. *Esterhaz*, a play of politics and intrigue, is set in 1772 in the summer palace of Austro-Hungarian Crown Prince Nicholas Esterhazy, with composer Joseph Haydn as a character.

There is a playful inventiveness with genre in Elisha's writing. This is perhaps best seen in one of his most comically dark plays, *The Levine Comedy* (1986), about a Jewish family, whose central character, Asher Levine, jokes and wisecracks his way through an increasingly disastrous sequence of family events; and again *In Duty Bound* (1979), a savage comic critique of Jewish family life with memories of the Holocaust. *Choice* (1994) is an apparently light comedy that turns very dark towards the end. *Pax Americana* is a long philosophical drama about the assassination of President Kennedy.

11: PLAYWRIGHTS IN THE 80S

Two (1983), one of his earliest and still one of his best plays, is a very strong piece, set in 1948 in the months leading up to the end of the British Protectorate in Palestine. A two-hander, it brings an old rabbi, Chaim, face to face with a young gentile woman, Anna, who comes to him to learn Hebrew so that she can go to Palestine to take part in the foundation of the new Jewish state. He discovers that she knew Auschwitz and she eventually confesses that she was not an inmate, but a member of the SS. In the intense conflict that ensues she reveals that she is in fact half-Jewish and that her gentile father so abused and humiliated her Jewish mother during the rise of the Nazis that Anna joined the SS out of self-loathing and a desire to destroy her Jewishness. At the end the authorities come to arrest her for war crimes and Chaim, whose encounter with her has shocked him out of his despair and reclusiveness, packs to go to Israel, writing to her that their meeting had taught him something and that he was grateful to her.

The Holocaust looms over many of Elisha's plays and, although the tone varies, they all explore its great moral questions. Asher Levine, the bitter clown in *The Levine Comedy*, is a playwright who jokes about the fact that he is always harping on the theme. Elisha is Australia's only Jewish playwright to have produced a substantial body of work, and to have probed issues of Holocaust survivors and the second generation that inherited their pain, their feelings of guilt and their grim sense of humour.

Nick Enright

Until his early death in 2003 at the age of 52, Nick Enright was one of the most prolific and wide-ranging playwrights of the previous twenty years, turning out, in addition to comedies and dramas, an extraordinary succession of musicals (*The Venetian Twins*, *Variations*, *Summer Rain*, *Miracle City*, *Mary Bryant* and, most successfully, *The Boy From Oz*), youth and community plays (*A Property of the Clan*, *Spurboard*) and large works, written for drama schools, that enabled him to tell grander and more elaborate stories, particularly after the contraction of the subsidised professional theatres in the 1980s.[7]

BELONGING

One of the most successful of these large-scale works was *Country Music*, produced in 2002 as a NIDA graduation show to open their new lyric theatre on Anzac Parade in Sydney. This country-town comedy-drama, which takes up many of the traditions discussed in earlier chapters, tells a story spanning many generations that is haunted by the ghosts of the dispossessed. Literally lying about the stage are the bones of children lost in the bush, dug up by a dog who is also the play's narrator. It celebrates country-town life, with the kids of the town, the local cop, the respectable shopkeepers, the pastoralists in the big house, and the drifters, immigrants and fringe-dwellers who walk the streets, all made subjects of a case-study for the idea of a wider Australian or global community.

But it is also a twenty-first-century work. There is a refugee detention centre just outside the town; and the characters include an escaped detainee who is outraged by behaviour at an ocker barbecue; a teacher who discovers his aboriginality; and a young woman who suddenly discovers her lesbian sexuality and flees to the city. Left unrevised when Enright died, this magnificently sprawling work has a broad scope, an interest in community and topical social issues, a simple humanity and wry humour that make it a remarkably appropriate culmination of his career.

During the 1980s Enright seemed to be an excellent genre writer with a great deal to express, but without a personal point of view. *On the Wallaby* (1980) is a cheerful ballad-opera about the struggles of the O'Brien family, wharfies in Port Adelaide during the Depression. Like many plays of the New Wave, it uses the past, in this case in music, but it is more nostalgic. *Daylight Saving* (1989), a romantic comedy about life in urbane Sydney in the 1980s, was an early success. Enright was also one of Australia's first major translators of the classic repertoire, including a successful version of Molière's *Don Juan* in 1984.

He collaborated with Terence Clarke, and later with David King and Max Lambert, on a series of musicals that culminated in the hit *The Boy from Oz* in 1998, about the life and music of the singer Peter Allen. With Clarke he wrote *The Venetian Twins* (1979), based on Goldoni's eighteenth-century comedy; and *Summer Rain* (1983),

11: PLAYWRIGHTS IN THE 80S

a musical tribute to the old travelling tent shows. *Summer Rain* focuses on a troupe on its last legs, stranded in the dry western plains of eastern Australia. Its dreaming owner Harold Slocum pushes his sorry little company further west, insisting they play a last show in the tiny outback town of Turnaround Creek. Here various romances and resolutions force many of the characters to come to terms with their past. It is about the need for healing, about new beginnings and the difficulty of saying goodbye.

With King he wrote *Mary Bryant* (1996), about the First Fleet convict who escaped the colony and, after a desperate ocean journey, was betrayed by her man and ended up in England, where she was defended in court by Samuel Johnson's biographer James Boswell. A myth-making colonial story, it should have become a major commercial success but, like so many of Enright's musicals, it didn't. Andrew Lloyd Webber blockbusters were dominating the commercial stage at the time and freezing out local works, just as Gilbert and Sullivan had done earlier in the century.

With Lambert he wrote *Miracle City* (1996), an exuberant musical, with a nicely ironic tone, about small-town American religion. An opportunistic preacher meets his love in a pick-up truck and with her creates an evangelical television empire. They dream of a mighty Christian commercial theme park which gives the show its title.

Enright was a natural collaborator, both as a teacher and a writer. His Oscar-nominated screenplay for the film *Lorenzo's Oil* is co-credited with the film's director George Miller. His adaptation for television of Dymphna Cusack's novel *Come in Spinner* was co-written with Lissa Benyon. With Justin Monjo he adapted Tim Winton's popular novel *Cloudstreet* for the stage.

But in the early 1990s Enright started to produce a series of extraordinary plays in which for the first time he seemed to be writing out of personal experience, while also telling stories plucked from the community. The first was *Mongrels* (1991), based on the interaction between the playwrights Peter Kenna and Jim McNeil. The play is better than most written by either of his subjects—a tender emotional and passionate search for the reason why people love, are loyal and then betray each other.

BELONGING

Edmund Burke, the McNeil character, is a tough prison playwright suddenly let loose in the world of Sydney theatre in the 1970s. He is aggressive, rude and charismatic, a romantic liar who started writing to get out of jail and is bemused by his success with comfortable middle-class theatregoers who are titillated by his underworld background. Vincent O'Hara, the Kenna character, is a sensitive, much more careful writer, whose writing will never be as powerful as Burke's. Although more sophisticated, he tells stories of his own pain too softly, using a series of self-pitying victims. He is a superb play-doctor, however, and against his own interests he nurtures Burke's post-prison career.

For each of these fictional playwrights the suffering is real, but their expression of it somehow false. They hate each other because they understand each other and because they both care. As they flail about they also hurt everyone who flutters around them like moths around a flame. They achieve some sort of grim reconciliation at the end, by which time Burke is dying an alcoholic's death in hospital and O'Hara, barely surviving, finds himself suddenly alone, as the new theatre and the new world sweep past him.

Like many of Enright's plays of the 1990s, *St James Infirmary* (1992) tells a coming-of-age story. Dominic Connolly is a gifted, troubled student at St James, a private Catholic school 'on an island in a river at some distance from a large Australian city', clearly based on St Ignatius' College, Riverview, where Enright went to school. The play is set in 1967 and Dominic is angry and radical about the Vietnam War. It emerges that he also has his own demons, concerning his parents' death when he was four. He has recently discovered that this was a murder–suicide committed by his father, an ex-POW from the Burma railroad. He has an enthusiastic patron in Father D'Arcy, the elderly art teacher who sees his genius and wants a great future for him as an artist.

Dominic paints a savage anti-war mural on the wall of the drill hall just before the Regimental Dinner. He falls while painting it and comes to the infirmary, over which the new Matron Walsh (Jenny) presides. Jenny has fled to this job following the death of her husband Luke, an army surgeon in Vietnam. The other major characters include Bowker, a conventionally high-achieving boy bound for the military academy at Duntroon. Dominic and Bowker have become enemies, although there

11: PLAYWRIGHTS IN THE 80S

is a strong feeling of brotherly affection, at least on Bowker's part. There is also Tim Donohue, a sensitive boy who wants to be an actor, and who is clearly in love with Dominic.

These characters pull Dominic this way and that as he lies in bed, slowly recovering, volatile and full of unresolved anger. As he faces his confusions, he draws pictures—nudes of Jenny, and a double nude of Norma, the cheerful cook, and her husband Kev, the school's groundsman and handyman. Father D'Arcy wants Dominic to conform to the school's stern rules in order to win a scholarship and go to Europe to be a great artist. There is a flickering of feeling between Dominic and Jenny, firmly squashed by her for propriety's sake, but she listens to him as he encourages her to let go of her grief.

In the end Dominic takes his little forbidden dinghy and rows across the river to the real world outside the protective and oppressive school, literally burning his boat behind him. He has given Jenny a sketch of the scene beforehand, a Viking funeral, and she understands its significance for her. He strikes out into the dark on his own having rejected Tim, who wants to come with him; and also Bowker.

Good Works (1994) is a dark epic family saga, in which acts of betrayal and loving friendship are gradually revealed in a complex discontinuous narrative that covers more than sixty years. At its heart are two betrayals, involving two pairs of friends: two mothers and their sons. In each case one is timid and the other wild, and in each case it is the timid one who succeeds, and who carries feelings of guilt through a long life.

Of the mothers it is the decently proper Mary Margaret, an orphan brought up by nuns, who does well. Her passionate school friend Rita Kennedy attracts the boys, one of whom writes her erotic letters that prove to be innocent fantasies but nonetheless destroy her reputation. We first meet their sons—the timid Tim and the wild Shane—in a gay bar many years after they have lost contact with each other. Shane pretends that he is someone else—rough sex trade, dangerous. For Tim he remains a ghostly memory of a genuinely tender youthful relationship.

The key past event that haunts them all is the central revelation of the play. A sadistic Brother at the school was savagely beating Tim when Shane stumbled on the scene, fatally stabbed the Brother in defence of his friend, and was convicted and sent to jail. Their lives,

BELONGING

and old relationships, were irrevocably altered. A souvenir snowdome belonging to Tim becomes the play's central metaphor. Trapped in its glass—as in Citizen Kane's—are memories, which are stirred in the swirling white flakes when you shake them up, but then settle when you let it rest. At the end of the premiere production at the Q Theatre in NSW, directed by Adam Cook, miraculous snow suddenly started falling all over the stage, like memories. It is a mystery why this great play has never been revived.

In 1992, Enright was commissioned by Newcastle's theatre-in-education company, Freewheels Theatre, to write a play about the impact on the local community of the rape and murder of a teenager, Leigh Leigh, at a beach party at Stockton, a battling-class suburb just north of the city. The result was *A Property of the Clan*, the first of several highly influential works in which Enright explored the crises faced by boys at around 16 to 18 years of age, when confronted by peer-group and social pressures. 'There is a window of opportunity which boys have at that age', he once said. 'If they can go through it, then they can go on to become young adult men. If not, they are lost.'[8]

In *A Property of the Clan* the boy Jared just makes it through the window. He is a product of Blackrock, a working-class suburb of an industrial city. He is caught in a web of three influences—his battling single mum Diane and naïve young sister Jade; his middle-class girlfriend Rachel, who lives across the river in the nice part of town; and his old mate Ricko, a surfie friend who has left school to go hooning up the coast. Ricko comes back and throws a keg-party on the beach, during which Jade's extrovert friend Tracy is pack-raped and murdered. The rest of the play chronicles the response of the community and Jared's journey to maturity.

Rachel is shocked, and tries to find out why this crime could have happened. Jade, in a series of scenes by Tracy's grave, simply wants communion with her lost friend. The boys in the community want to forget about it, except for the gentle, nascently gay Glen, who works with Rachel on her inquiry.

Jared's torment represents the pressures in the aftermath of the murder, which tears the community apart. The three boys who raped Tracy are arrested, but no-one knows who killed her. It emerges that it

11: PLAYWRIGHTS IN THE 80S

was Ricko, who found her after she had been left staggering along the beach. Denied his piece of the action, he killed her in a rage. Because she had acted like a slut, he says—she was lively, fun and flirtatious—he thought she was one. He discovers that until that terrible night she had been a virgin. 'People have to act the way they are', he says, in dumb confusion (p. 46).

Meanwhile Jared is drifting away. Diane tries to talk to him. Rachel brings him a pottery mug she has made, but he smashes it angrily and tells her what he told Ricko—that he saw the rape and did nothing. He is obviously consumed with confused guilt. Rachel leaves him, horrified.

In the final scene Rachel and Jade are by the grave—still wondering. 'What was the last thing she saw?' ... 'Hatred. Just hatred. Blind hate.' Then in the distance Jared appears, carrying a small bunch of flowers.

In 1995 Enright rewrote the play for mainstream adult audiences as *Blackrock*, and this version became a successful 1997 film. *Blackrock* is more fully developed than *A Property of the Clan*, especially in the way it brings in the parents as a context for the young people's attitudes and behaviour.

Jade has been replaced by Cherie, Jared's cousin, and her mother Glenys. Glenys expresses an adult equivalent of the boys' view, that, by being lively, dressing sexy and flirting with boys, Tracy was a slut who was asking for trouble. The party is hosted by Rachel's brother, Toby, who turns out to be one of the rapists. Her father, Stewart, makes ads using images of sexy women. The story of Jared's mother Diane is considerably expanded. She has to go into hospital for a mastectomy while struggling to deal with her estranged son. The party scene in *A Property of the Clan* is interspersed in *Blackrock* with scenes from the adult world, and the adults play a more significant role in the aftermath. At one point Diane and Glenys, sisters and mothers, brood together.

> GLENYS: You've done a good job so far. The boy's nearly there.
> DIANE: Where?

Overleaf: Kristina Bidenko as Tiffany, Joel Edgerton as Toby and Simon Lyndon as Jared in the 1995 Sydney Theatre Company production of Blackrock. *(Photographer: Tracey Schramm.)*

BELONGING

Michael Gow

Gow's first successful play was *The Kid* (1983), a tough passionate comic drama that presents in Wagnerian terms the journey of a small band of battling underclass heroes cruising down the highway to their Götterdämmerung—Sydney. Here they hope to get compensation for the sick and mentally disturbed Aspro, whom they claim has been hit by a bus. They are all kids (17–19), but they act as a family. Dean is a charismatic tough guy, lazy and opportunistic, but with hidden qualities that emerge when the chips are down. Snake is a resilient girl who keeps the family together as she half mothers the others and half fights with them like a kid sister. The only adults are a collection of weird, dysfunctional types they meet in their travels. From the beginning it is clearly a hopeless cause, but they are driven by a great passion and a loyalty towards one another.

In Sydney they rent a flat, using money supplied by Donald, a gay boy they have picked up on the road who is excited to escape his country town. Snake takes Aspro to the 'welfare department', where he fails to get his compensation ('a loophole', says Snake vaguely). Dean discovers Desiree, a thin smelly girl who lives upstairs. He wants to rescue her from her psychopath father, who distributes pamphlets about the coming of the end of the world, and who beats her and locks her in a cupboard tied up to a shotgun. As one increasingly desperate scene follows another, the family is torn apart. Dean rescues Desiree and kills her father but, unable to get through to her, leaves her out in the open, perhaps free at last. The city is ringed by fires and in the distance sirens wail constantly. Aspro dies, Snake and Donald leave after Snake challenges Dean to respond to it all: 'Yell. Go on. Yell. Cry out. Go on'. Way cool to the end, he won't, but left alone in the flat he starts taking pills. It is an apocalyptic study of desperate kids living with a wild kind of heroism that is at last defeated. The play's most recent revival was in a 2008 production by Tom Healey at Sydney's Griffin Theatre.

The Kid has resonances of Wagner, but *Away* is romantically Shakespearean, at once a summer comedy and a winter elegy, bittersweet, tragic and uplifting. Gow may have come to resent the

11: PLAYWRIGHTS IN THE 80S

way its enormous popular success has overshadowed his later work, but it remains one of the best-loved plays of the post-New Wave.

The action takes place during the summer of 1967–68, when the war in Vietnam was a worry for many Australians, but not yet as nationally divisive as it was to become a year later, after the Tet Offensive. Partly about the theatre, *Away* opens with a school performance of *A Midsummer Night's Dream*, in which the central character Tom is playing Puck. Three families, of different social classes but all living in the suburbs, are brought together in that night, the last of the school year, before going on holidays.

Their destinations, up and down the east coast, become places of crisis and renewal, like the woods outside Athens in the *Dream*. Gwen, the mother of his friend Meg, is on the verge of a nervous breakdown. The headmaster's wife Coral is grieving desperately for her son who has been killed in Vietnam. Tom is dying of leukaemia. In their different holiday spots each family confronts the issues that they have kept hidden, although we hear nothing of what they talk about. A sudden storm, initiated and performed by the fairies from the *Dream*, brings them all together at the very ordinary campsite where Tom and his working-class parents are staying. On its long lonely beach they start to connect with one another.

At the happy campers' amateur night Tom, who knows that he is dying even though his parents have never told him, performs with Coral a strange little mermaid play he has written about healing. It is a great success and they all troop happily down to the beach for a bonfire. At the end of the holiday each family is renewed. In a coda scene, set at the beginning of the next school year, the drama teacher who had produced the *Dream* takes her new class into the open to work on *King Lear*. This is their rite of passage into adulthood, dealing with death in a new way. In the original production the dying Tom is asked to read Lear's opening lines

> Know that we have divided
> In three our kingdom; and 'tis our fast intent
> To shake all cares and business from our age,
> Conferring them on younger strengths, while we
> Unburden'd crawl toward death. (p. 57)

BELONGING

In the STC production directed by Gow in 1992, Tom had died before this last scene and Lear's lines were read by Meg. Meg read again in the 2006 QTC/Griffin production, but the ghost of Tom was onstage watching.

Away captures the beginnings of a major turning point in the lives, social rituals and institutions of suburban Australians, a moment when a new generation is poised to take over from the old. Although set just before the major upheavals of the late 1960s and early 1970s, it was written and first produced nearly twenty years later, in a tone of haunted nostalgia, half cynical and half tender. *On Top of the World*, which appeared six months after *Away*, was written earlier.[9] Its ending is similarly redemptive, but for most of the play the tone is harsher and the conflicts between the generations, the same generations as in *Away* but fifteen to twenty years older, are much sharper.

Stephanie and Marcus are siblings, established in careers that are so appropriate to their personalities that the effect is satirical, almost Jonsonian: she is an academic semiotician, he a depressed real-estate agent. Their mother has recently died and their relationship with both parents is a mixture of resented emotional attachment and a hidden longing for release. This emerges in a series of savage confrontations that are resolved at the end. Stephanie has sold their old suburban home, and forced their dying father Clive to leave behind all his belongings. She sets him up on top of the world in a high-rise apartment on Queensland's Gold Coast. From this eyrie he could, like Buzo's Coralie Lansdowne, look out at the sea, the stars and the moon—except that he doesn't want to.

Clive is crabby and resentful. Stephanie feels guilty and Marcus, when he arrives, is withdrawn and unhappy. The family who gather to celebrate Clive's 73rd birthday are bitter and fractured. The redemptive figure is Baby, an elderly neighbour whom Marcus has dragged along like a stray cat. In a long monologue, a comic tour de force, Baby describes a life of caring for others which stops short the family squabbles and brings them to an uneasy resolution.

Again like Buzo's *Coralie Lansdowne Says No*, the play is an odd mixture of realism and stylised formalism. Though the style is

11: PLAYWRIGHTS IN THE 80S

Australian suburban, the advances in the story are told mainly through long set speeches, in the manner of Spanish Renaissance tragedy.

Gow's respect for the traditions of the European dramatic canon, and his extraordinarily ability to use them to tell vernacular stories of middle-class Australian life, became an important feature of his work when he was STC Associate Director between 1991 and 1993, running its research and development arm. Previously this had been devoted to new Australian plays but Gow renamed it New Stages and dedicated it to an experimental program of innovative productions of the classics—including Euripides' *Women of Troy* and Shakespeare's *Titus Andronicus*—intended to reawaken new Australian playwrights to old forms that had been ignored in the nationalist larrikin revival of the New Wave. One of his great successes as a director at that time was an austerely passionate production of Racine's *Phèdre*, a play from the seventeenth century of Louis XIV, a period that had never before influenced Australian playwriting, but which was subsequently to leave its mark on his own writing, especially *Sweet Phoebe* in 1994.

Gow had earlier dramatised his interest in the interplay between Australia and its imperial centre in his two-hander, *Europe*, first produced in 1987, six months after the premiere of *Away*. In it a young Australian actor travels to Europe to stalk a distinguished European actress with whom he has had a brief affair. Haunted by his love for her, his abject and unreciprocated passion becomes inextricably bound up with issues of colony and empire and his cringing nationalism.

For the 1988 Bicentennial celebrations Gow wrote *1841*, a passionate reworking of Australian colonial history, critically panned at the time, for what look like political reasons, and unfairly neglected since. Once again, Gow was ahead of his time. The play gives a bleak and savage account of the brutality of frontier life, more historically detailed than Ray Mooney's *Black Rabbit* of the same year. For a play produced in association with the official Australian Bicentennial Authority, it is extraordinarily rebellious and angry, anticipating Andrew Bovell's *Holy Day*, which appeared in 2001 after a new round of debates between historians and revisionists about the extent of white massacres of the Indigenous population. Both plays rework the pioneering legends of the frontier plays from 1930s to 1950s in much darker terms.

BELONGING

The play's title refers to the last year a convict transport ship landed on the east coast. On board the ship and evoking, at the end of the first act, Delacroix's celebrated 1830 painting, *Liberty Leading the People*, is Aurora, fleeing after the final collapse of the ideals of the French and American Revolutions and hoping to reawaken them in the southern reaches of the New World. Instead she discovers a world that fails to care about even the most basic human rights and which, far from pursuing the revolutionary dreams of a better society, seems intent on becoming mired in a series of ever more nightmarish horrors of greed and violence.

After encounters with brutal soldiers and convicts, a hypocritically genteel ruling class and ineffectual artists, Aurora allows herself to be drawn into a journey to the heart of darkness, the bush, where proto-capitalists are tearing the guts out of the new land and selling it off for profit. She is led by a charismatic, idealistic but increasingly despairing drunk named Sullivan, and his naïve supporter Lynch. Lynch is a tough, hard-working convict with a head of steel that helps him to cope with beatings, and a child-like innocence that finally fails to help him cope with the world. Deep in the bush everyone gives up their humanity. Aurora's friend Mercy, a serving woman who wants to make a decent new life for herself, goes off with a group of white settlers who have casually massacred a tribe of blacks as if it were an innocent land-clearing exercise. Sullivan is murdered in his tent with an axe by one of his former protégés, now in power. Lynch is framed for the murder and in his simplicity refuses to respond to his accusers or, when she confronts him at the end, to Aurora's revolutionary fervour. In the last scene he is hanged. All Aurora's revolutionary dreams of a better world are destroyed. It was not a message that Australians wanted to hear.

Furious (1990) is full of a more intimately emotional brutality and a kind of wild anger. Its central character is Roland Henning, a successful playwright who has had a great popular hit much loved for its sunniness and its magical sense of renewal, a success that dogs him as a string of mindless foyer 'friends', journalists, critics, students, academics and aspiring playwrights pursue him in a sort of feeding frenzy, soaking up his supposed sunniness and leaving him feeling constantly cold.

11: PLAYWRIGHTS IN THE 80S

In a savage opening scene he visits a bleak Old People's Home, where he takes possession of a box of papers that has been left him by Bonnie, a mad old woman who has recently died, and whom he didn't know. The box is filled with newspaper clippings about him. It emerges that Bonnie was his father's first wife, abandoned with a young baby and subsequently erased from the family's history. She brought up the baby girl by herself in poverty. The girl eventually had a baby of her own that she gave up for adoption. She left her mother to run off with her bloke. Abandoned again, Bonnie stopped speaking and was sent to the Home where, after living in silence for sixteen years, she died.

Roland is shocked, appalled and fascinated by these revelations and, as he moves through his glittering theatre world, he is haunted by them. He starts to write a new play, which pours out of him uncontrolled. Frightened by this, he lashes out at his agent, disrupts an award ceremony, seduces a schoolboy who is writing an essay about him, and is brutal with the boy's mother when she confronts him about it.

Scenes from Bonnie's life and that of her lost daughter begin to appear mysteriously in the play. They start to repeat details of the opening scene in the Home, and depict events that we know could not have occurred, such as Roland taking Bonnie to confront her lost daughter—his sister. Slowly we realise that we are watching the play Roland has been writing, using it to reconstruct the recently discovered family. The implication of this complex and powerfully reflexive work is that Gow is doing the same thing.

Like *The Kid*, *Sweet Phoebe* (1994) charts a journey through the heart of the modern city, but this time the travellers are from the right side of the tracks. Frazer and Helen, a childless professional couple absorbed in their careers, reluctantly agree to mind a dog named Phoebe for their friends, who want to go away for a week-long Intensive Couples Workshop. As they become smitten with the dog, their professional lives begin to unravel, and when Phoebe goes missing they become obsessed, searching for her as if she were a child lost in the bush. In the process, as they visit the people who answer their lost-dog ads, they separately encounter and confront an otherworld that disturbs them profoundly. They keep bringing back to each other stories of their encounters with a collection of lonely individuals and

BELONGING

cheerful outsider families whose values challenge their own. Frazer has an affair with one of the respondents. Stumbling across them in her own search for the dog, Helen disappears to lick her wounds and to find peace with a crazy underclass family with whom she spends a weekend. She's overdue and might be pregnant. At the end Frazer finds the dog, happy with a new master. He leaves her there and goes back to Helen. Perhaps their relationship is renewed.

The play is written with a classically simple theatrical lyricism, a return, after the savagery of *1841* and *Furious*, to the formally spare understated romanticism of *Away*. *Away* had dramatised the cusp between the generation of the 1950s and that of their children, to whom they were reluctant to give way. *On Top of the World* is about the same transition told from the point of view of the younger generation, now grown-up and looking back on their aging parents as a burden not yet lifted. In *Sweet Phoebe* a new generation, brought up during the greed-is-good 1980s, suddenly faces a similar crisis of succession. But their successors are now represented by a lost dog and Helen's missed period.

In 1999 Gow became Artistic Director of the Queensland Theatre Company and his next play, a stage adaptation of Henry Handel Richardson's *The Fortunes of Richard Mahony*, appeared there three years later. It is a skilful theatrical condensation of an epic three-volume novel that originally appeared between 1917 and 1929, about a protagonist whose career starts on the Victorian goldfields in the early 1850s and ends many decades later in a lunatic asylum. Although scenes with the mad old Mahony effectively bookend the dramatisation, the intervening scenes are a less successful attempt to force the novel's sprawling narrative into a more condensed dramatic shape.

In 2007 Gow came up with another play about Roland Henning, the playwright in *Furious*. In *Toy Symphony* Roland is troubled by a controversy surrounding a play he once wrote. It seems to be very like Gow's *Sweet Phoebe*. Roland has not written a new play for many years; neither had Gow in 2007. Again Roland travels back to his earlier life—this time to terrible events from his childhood that he feels led him to betray a dying friend for whom he wrote a school play, titled *Toy Symphony*. He is deeply troubled by the connections between his life

11: PLAYWRIGHTS IN THE 80S

and his art, and perhaps redeems himself by writing the extraordinarily moving and powerful play we are watching, which, for all its apparent interest in art, is really, very definitely, about life.

Sewell, Nowra, Enright, Gow and the other writers who started out in the late 1970s were in no way a movement or a group of playwrights with a common cause. The 'new internationalist' label that was applied to Sewell and Nowra now seems contrived. But these were the first playwrights to move away from the New Wave and they were still writing in the early twenty-first century. In the 1990s a new collection of writers started exploring the collapse of the ideals of the New Wave in the bleak streets of the postmodern city. Before this happened, however, there emerged a range of theatre workers who brought identity politics into the theatre in the 1980s. In their various celebrations of difference and otherness they did become, ironically, a new movement.

12
IDENTITY AND COMMUNITY

After the New Wave few people other than politicians and advertisers ever spoke again with confidence about the Australian National Character. In the theatre, as elsewhere in the 1980s, the idea that such a complex notion as 'Australianness' could ever be summed up in a simple drama of representation came to be seen as absurd. Difference was celebrated. The politics of personal and social identity became key determinants in the way in which new plays were produced and read by their audiences.

A new theatre of identity politics had been emerging for some time. It had its roots in the ocker rhetoric of New Wave blokes reacting against the conventional, tradition-based theatre they had grown up with. Many identity politics groups picked up the New Wave trickster model of resistance and transgression, even as they contested its narrow politics. The larrikin forms of the New Wave also provided theatrical and dramaturgical techniques, including direct audience involvement, songs, physical comedy and mime, and non-realistic theatricalist modes of address. Even so, as new, often separatist, movements sought a voice for their communities many of the old realistic modes of representation survived dramaturgically, embedded in the new styles. As David Watt has pointed out, many of the new theatrical forms, at least on the overtly political side of the community theatre movement, were based

BELONGING

on the work and performance styles of radical theatre groups of the 1960s—El Teatro Campesino, the Bread and Puppet Theatre and the San Francisco Mime Troupe in the USA and Welfare State, Red Ladder and John McGrath's 7:84 company in the UK—theatres that had influenced the New Wave but had somehow been forgotten.[1] In the 1980s the influence of Brecht was claimed more than it had ever been before.[2]

The new stories focused on communities and individuals who had previously been the Other in Australian drama—represented by 'stereotypes' in a drama that valued 'characters'. While it can be difficult to pin down what critics, theatre workers and people in foyers actually meant by these loaded terms, stereotypes—or, as Watt calls them, 'typifications'—were reappropriated by the new writers as the idea of the realistically 'fully-rounded' character retreated. Groups without a voice in the mainstream sought new ways and places in which to speak and perform. They challenged ideas about identity and culture and the relationship between the mainstream centre and the margins. In doing so they opened up new conceptions of border and liminal spaces in 1980s debates about multiculturalism.

The early work of these new practitioners was based on ideas of 'culture' and 'community' that were strongly contested from the outset.[3] As each new cultural or community group was labelled, deeper fractal levels of difference kept emerging. The old mainstream words—such as 'ethnic' and 'homosexual'—were rejected because they objectified individual felt-experience and ended up occluding, rather than celebrating, difference. There was a proliferation of new terms—'homosexual' became 'gay', for example, then 'gay and lesbian', and then, via a series of increasingly refined groupings, each of which created a new taxonomy, eventually the acronym, GLBTQ, meaning the Gay, Lesbian, Bisexual, Transgender and Queer community. 'Community' here is obviously a strategic construction. The abbreviation is unlikely to catch on, but it may turn out to be an important rhetorical step. In the 1970s, for instance, the alternative spelling 'wimmin' was immediately mocked by the patriarchy and has not survived, but at the time it was important in deconstructing the hidden ideology of language.

For a time in the 1980s adding 'women', 'multicultural' and

12. IDENTITY AND COMMUNITY

'gay', to 'theatre' created a politically useful, strategically essentialist celebration of community. No one now believes that these labels ever identified a unified group of people who shared a single culture and common set of personal and social values but for a brief period a broadly inclusive sense of the Other became the defining characteristic of a lot of theatre. ('Aboriginal theatre', a term which also dates from this time, is discussed in Chapter 14.) Even the vocabulary was revised and many of the old abusive words—'girl', 'wog', 'queen', 'dyke'—were reappropriated as badges of new pride.

Whether they were positive or negative, however, the generalised counter-hegemonic 'identity' labels of the 1980s masked a wide range of intracultural difference within the groups they were labelling. Women's theatre, workers' theatre, Aboriginal theatre, multicultural theatre, gay theatre—buzz categories, all still used—were just as totalising as older strategic terms, including that earlier all pervasive term: 'Australian drama'.

Feminist Theatre

The pioneers of identity-based theatre were the feminist groups of the early- to mid-1970s who reacted against the white male-dominated New Wave. Groups led by white, middle-class women were at the forefront in exploring artistic practices whereby political, economic, social and hegemonic power might be resisted.

It started when a group of disillusioned and dissident women in the APG produced *Betty Can Jump* (1972). Although the APG was run collectively, its often rowdy meetings tended to be dominated by the men with the loudest voices.[4] *Betty Can Jump* was the precursor to the Melbourne Women's Theatre Group (1974–77), a collective of women whose work was directed at audiences 'composed largely of inner-city feminists'. From the beginning it provoked debates about separatism and target audiences, and there were divisions within the group about whether to introduce 'women only nights'.[5]

As second-wave feminism flourished in the 1970s, in both the theatre and educational institutions, the mainstream writers Dorothy Hewett and Alma De Groen were strategically co-opted into what was

BELONGING

then called 'the women's movement'. (In a similar way playwrights discussed in the next chapter were drafted, sometimes against their wills, into the project of multiculturalism.) It was always an uneasy relationship, and particularly in the case of Hewett it led to strong disagreements, but it succeeded in making the work of women playwrights more visible and influential. During this period, too, the 'red witches' of the 1930s and 1940s, discussed in Chapter Three, were rediscovered.

An early work at Sydney's Nimrod was Jennifer Compton's *Crossfire* (1975, titled *No Man's Land* when it was first produced[6]), which intercut stories from the first and second waves of feminism, one set in 1910 and the other in 1975. It looked at the difficulties experienced by women from both generations in negotiating the conflicts between the desire to do paid work and the desire to be mothers. In the 1910 story, Jane Onslow, the wife of a tea merchant Samuel, is writing a book arguing that women should be allowed to work. She cannot have children (or perhaps it is Samuel), but her maid Rose is pregnant, after what we would now call a date-rape. Jane helps Rose find a husband, Tom, by bribing him to accept Rose's baby as his own.

In the 1975 story, Cilla, also childless and not in paid work, is a new generation feminist whose patient and long-suffering husband Sam is a stockbroker. They take in and support an unmarried mother, Mim, who is homely but bright and alert. She and Sam hit it off, but do not have the affair both would like. Cilla picks up a rough sexist man, Lam, and wants to have an affair with him, but he flees from the complications when he learns about Sam and Mim. Mim, the supposedly abject single mother, comes off best—a sensible woman who, unlike the feminists and the male chauvinists on either side of her, seems to know her own mind free of ideology. Controversial at the time because it revealed the simplicities of the gender wars in the 1970s, it is nonetheless a thoughtful play.

Compton later wrote *Barefoot* (1994), a short farce produced as part of Griffin's *Passion* season. In it an ironically grieving mother and her two passionate daughters yearn mockingly for a passion that no actual man can offer. One of the daughters is engaged in an absurd IVF project. The other is fleeing a violent but pathetic husband whom

12. IDENTITY AND COMMUNITY

she is trying to evict, and starts a relationship with the policeman who arrives to protect her. The four male characters, played by a single actor named in the cast list as 'All-Purpose Man', keep appearing comically at the door and being turned away. It is lively and pleasantly man-hating.

In 1999 Compton returned to Griffin with *The Big Picture*, a tribute to the lives of a group of rural underclass women trapped by poverty; and by the desperate desire for fun in their lives, which they equate with having a man. Three single mothers on pensions with few opportunities for escape cling to the one loser man who turns up. He is Guy, a desperado no-hoper petty criminal and drug-dealer who leaves behind him a trail of physical and emotional damage. Eventually, to save them all, Guy's sister Joy dobs him in to the police. There is a suggestion that she, at least, has begun to haul herself out of her situation. In a final scene, Joy talks to Guy in prison, on the phone he had reconnected with the aid of his drug money. It is a strong play about people who are inadvertently complicit in their own victimization, because they neither can nor ever will understand and take control of the instruments of power.

Other early-1980s writers drawn into feminist theatre included Jennifer Claire, whose *The Butterflies of Kalimantan* (1983) explored sexual angst in inner-city artistic circles, in a work that looks now like an intercultural dispute between straight women and gay men; and Sue Ingleton who created the character of Bill Rawlings, an ocker male suddenly surprised to find himself pregnant. This was written for the satirical ABC television show, *Australia: You're Standing In It* (1983–84), as was the subversively comic character, Sheila Shit, a gender-inversion of the aggressively obscene male comedians, such as Rodney Rude and Gary Who, who were popular at the time. Her play *The Passion ... and its Deep Connection with Lemon Delicious Pudding* (1995) is a sprawling feminist extravaganza about the personal and spiritual journey of a mother figure named Silver, bringing together scenes of her trapped domesticity, her wild eroticism, her anger and disgust at patriarchal sexual oppression and her communion with the various ancestral and goddess figures who appear to her.

Suzanne Spunner's *Running up a Dress*, produced by the Home

BELONGING

Cooking Theatre Company in Melbourne in 1986, reclaims domestic women's business and turns it into a celebration of the relationships between mothers and daughters. *Running up a Dress* is a rich collection of scenes, texts, speeches and images that brings together dressmaking and motherhood in sensual, physical detail. It relishes detail, the pattern, the cutting, the feel of the cloth, the fitting and the sewing, and relates these to the emotional and physical ties between mothers and daughters—loving, caring, resenting; birthing, feeding, bleeding. In Act One, titled 'My Mother Made Me a Daughter', the making of the dress is interspersed with the attitudes of a daughter growing up and interacting with her mother. In Act Two, 'My Baby Made Me a Mother', the daughter, now grown up, dwells on the experiences of becoming a mother. The work is partly about the cuts and blemishes that have to be made on the cloth/body in order to create a beautiful dress/child. In *Dragged Screaming to Paradise* (1988), a one-woman show, based on Spunner's own experience, a woman speaks of her horror at the thought of moving to Darwin from Melbourne when her husband's work takes them there, and then her eventual acceptance and love of the place. Like so many works in this chapter, it could be grouped elsewhere—it's a story of (internal) migration, about feeling exiled and then coming to terms with calling a new place home.

Materialist feminism first found its voice in the early 1980s in the work of working-class women playwrights, such as the undervalued Doreen Clarke, whose plays have feisty battling women, celebrating their struggle and their grim triumphs. In *Bleedin' Butterflies* (1980) a group of fiercely independent wives struggle to survive and look after their kids and their drunken loser husbands in a riverside camp during the 1930s Depression. *Roses in Due Season* (1978) is a tough comic drama about a family of women and their struggles with an alcoholic patriarch. *Farewell Brisbane Ladies* (1981) is a farcical odd-couple comedy about two retired and bickering prostitutes who eventually, in a joyously triumphant ending, decide to strike out on their own. They become independent madams in charge of a brothel, owning and controlling the means of production in their particular industry. These plays brought a new underclass perspective to women's drama that

12. IDENTITY AND COMMUNITY

was not matched until the 1990s with the plays of Debra Oswald and Katherine Thomson.

A wide range of feminist theatrical practices emerged over the years, based on a variety of theoretical models for dealing with the performance of identity. Judith Butler's highly influential *Gender Trouble*, which deconstructed fixed ideas of gender and argued that gender was performed—individually, socially and culturally—had a huge impact on feminist theatre in the 1990s, not least because it offered a way of theorising and making feminist (and for that matter queer) performance that the theatre already understood.[7] It also had implications for understanding the interactions between form, genre and the performative construction of identity in many earlier and subsequent alternative theatres of resistance and transgression. Some of these theatres fall outside the range of this book, including the work of a wide range of contemporary performance ensembles and individual performance artists, as well as non-representational physical theatre forms and genres, including cabaret and women's circus.[8]

Two later plays that might be called 'women's theatre' are Jan Cornall's *At the Crossroads* (1998), about four women from different backgrounds who come together for a community meeting; and Merilee Moss's *Empty Suitcase* (1993), which intersperses domestic scenes of three contemporary women flatmates with the stories of pioneering women travellers: Isabelle Eberhardt, who lived and travelled in the Sahara as an Arab man;[9] Beryl Markham, the first person to fly across the Atlantic from east to west; and Alexandra David-Néel, who travelled in Tibet until a late age. The plays were produced and toured by Canberra's Women On A Shoestring Theatre Company in the late 1990s. By this time the category had begun to break down. Rachel Fensham and Denise Varney argue that there was a revolution, at least a Guattarian 'molecular' one, in the 1990s, when women playwrights and other theatre practitioners started to be influential in mainstream theatre.[10] These playwrights, including Beatrix Christian, Hannie Rayson, Joanna Murray-Smith, Tobsher Learner, Katherine Thomson, Debra Oswald, and Hilary Bell are discussed in the last two chapters, as is the innovative work of Jenny Kemp, who did more than any writer to forge a new poetic women's theatrical aesthetic in Australia.

BELONGING

Gay and Lesbian Theatre

A similar seepage between mainstream theatre and the identity politics of the 1970s and 1980s occurred in gay and lesbian theatre. As in the case of the women's theatre movement it involved a lot of strategic essentialism. Peter Kenna, Nick Enright and Michael Gow became major figures, writing gay into the mainstream. Other playwrights worked within their communities.

In both women's and gay theatre, the way that sexuality was presented and the body was performed, contested or subverted the eroticised body presented in the mainstream media. This meant that behind all the arguments about cultural separatism, there were important issues of audience voyeurism. As the popularity of the annual Sydney Mardi Gras parade grew in the late 1980s and 1990s—it was televised from 1994—there was much debate about opening up the sexualised carnival to the gaze of the general public, especially in the 1990s, when groups of heterosexual men started turning up at the big community dance party that followed the parade.

In the 1980s there was a thriving underground lesbian theatre in Sydney,[11] although a number of playwrights including Sandra Shotlander, Margaret Fischer, Alison Lyssa and Eva Johnson were also part of feminist identity groupings and, in Johnson's case, Indigenous as well. Lyssa's *Pinball*, first produced in 1981 as part of Nimrod's Women and Theatre Project, and Johnson's *What Do They Call Me?* were both published in the first mainstream anthology of gay and lesbian plays, while *Murras*, an earlier play by Johnson, was included in a collection of Aboriginal plays.[12] As in the case of the 'multicultural' plays of the 1980s and 1990s, different works move between different, overlapping cultural formations, blurring the boundaries between them and disrupting the old simple taxonomies of otherness.

Shotlander's plays are lesbian appropriations of mainstream genres. *Framework* (1983) is a witty formulaic love story, full of recognition humour, about Lee, a 40-something woman in the throes of a divorce, who meets an Australian woman, Iris, in an art gallery in New York and has an affair with her. Iris returns to Australia to her Australian partner Penny, but eventually commits to Lee. *Blind Salome* (1985) is more self-

12. IDENTITY AND COMMUNITY

consciously based in feminist theory and myths, attacking the Jungian idea of the animus. Chris, a sexist old Freudian psychiatrist, tries to help Phillip and Bernice, who are a couple, and Bernice's sister Della. After lots of interplay, including some love-triangle complications, Phillip leaves and the women become stronger without him. *Is That You Nancy?* (1991) is a collage of telephone conversations, based around the dramatic conceit of having Gertrude Stein make calls to powerful public women. The calls are interspersed with other characters talking on the phone about lesbian couples they know, and trying to arrange to have quality time together to talk about their relationships.

Also laced with lesbian recognition humour is Margaret Fischer's *The Gay Divorcee* (1990), a simple monodrama about the hurt and struggle of going through a divorce. The story is framed by a Jewish 'Grandma Mermaid', who tells the story of her daughter's adventures in the human world and her eventual return to the winds over the sea. The main character, the daughter Gretel, goes through hell when her partner Rita, whom she mothers like a Jewish momma, wants out and starts an affair with Sarah, a woman from Sydney. Produced by Vitalstatistix Theatre Company in Adelaide, the work was a great performance vehicle for Fischer herself.

Alison Lyssa's *Pinball* (1981) is a classic feminist new-form drama, about a mother, Theenie, and her partner, Axis, who battle to keep shared custody of Theenie's beloved son. Theenie faces a vindictive, homophobic custody suit brought by her son's father, Sylvester, a decent but weak man who is manipulated by his evil new wife and goaded on by Theenie's equally evil brother. The play is full of cartoon villains, and has a heroine named Vandelope, an 'anarcho-lesbian bicyclist' who helps Theenie by painting graffiti on Sylvester's wall, organising demonstrations outside the court, and generally mucking up in an exultantly activist way. The domestic and interpersonal scenes are exuberantly non-realistic, and outside them there are some crazy theatrical effects. Insofar as there is a 'real' world in this extravagant story, Theenie loses her son, but there is also an alternative fantasy ending.

Lyssa's *The Boiling Frog* (1982) is a polemical play, with songs and dance, about a group of women struggling through four centuries in

BELONGING

search of a clean place to live, safe from the advance of a dirty world and its technologies: a seventeenth-century plague, eighteenth-century coal mines and twentieth-century nuclear power plants. At each crisis they are driven away. Two male representatives of the twentieth-century military-industrial complex enter and freeze them in a tableau of a famous painting that is stashed away in underground bunkers in the face of the coming nuclear disaster. At the end the group is machine-gunned from a helicopter, but, as they form the last tableau, they rebel, refuse to be locked away, and sing a triumphant song of survival.

Australia's first openly gay male play was Martin Smith's *Love Has Many Faces*, which provoked a brief storm of media controversy in 1970 because a throwaway joke suggested, according to the contemporary press, that Captain Cook (whose Australian bicentennial it was that year) had been homosexual.[13] The Gay Theatre Company operated in Sydney between 1979 and 1982, and its productions included *Writer's Cramp*, by Barry Lowe, whose other plays made up the repertoire of Hullabaloo Theatre Company in the early 1980s. The Sydney Gay (from 1989, Gay and Lesbian) Mardi Gras started in 1978 as a political protest march and grew to become a major mainstream cultural institution, with an associated arts festival that introduced the work of playwrights such as Timothy Conigrave and Alex Harding.

Harding's *Blood and Honour* (1990) is famous as Australia's first AIDS play, although that has since become yet another problematic label.[14] Part polemic, part carnivalesque celebration and part human story, it tells the story of Colin, dying of AIDS-related illnesses, and his Asian lover Michael. Colin's mother, a well-known actress with a wild past and a strong political activism that has ruined her career, presides sympathetically over it all. Dealing with public homophobia and racism, the official neglect and the personal confusion that conspired to make the lives of people living with AIDS even more hideous than the virus itself had already done, it remains a powerful document of the first wave of AIDS awareness in the 1980s.

In *Only Heaven Knows* (1988), a play with songs rather than a full musical, a young playwright comes to Sydney to join its burgeoning bohemian gay scene during World War II. Later, to escape the anti-

12. IDENTITY AND COMMUNITY

gay conservatism of the Menzies years—he cannot even kiss his lover good-bye, for fear of being arrested—he sails to England to pursue a theatrical career. Presiding over the action is a new theatrical ghost, Lea Sonia, an American drag performer on the Tivoli Circuit, who died in 1943 when pushed under a tram by an American serviceman. Her mischievously high camp spirit haunts the show.

Christopher Maver's *The Girl in the Lime Green Bikini* (2002) is a celebration with a similar intention but very different in tone and style, which looks at forty years of gay culture in Brisbane, secret and then out. Maver wrote it as a solo show for himself—presenting a bold range of wild characters from the past and present, interspersed with autobiographical material in narrative and on slides. Among other things it covers the attacks on gays mounted by the conservative Bjelke-Petersen government in Queensland, desperate to divert public attention from the Fitzgerald enquiry into public corruption.

Timothy Conigrave died of an AIDS-related illness in 1994, two years after the death of his long-term partner John Caleo. Following the success of his memoir, *Holding the Man*, his plays, *Thieving Boy* and *Like Stars in My Hands* (both 1997), were produced and published posthumously, in versions edited by Tony Ayres. *Like Stars in My Hands* is a simple and moving account of the last stages of a loving relationship in which one partner is dying and the other caring for him. The central character Simon is angry and petulant as his body fails him, but after an initially jealous reaction he blesses his partner Marcello's new relationship with their mutual friend Jimmy. The play brings together the physicality of Simon's illness and his spiritual yearnings, as he communes with the Hindu god Ganesh and contemplates death. *Thieving Boy* traces, over the course of a day, the journey of a young man temporarily released from jail to visit his dying, distant, father, and his ultimately successful attempt to re-establish his loving relationship with his boyfriend and to integrate that relationship into what is left of his family. It ends with an understated image of intimacy between the two lovers not unlike the tender images in the plays of Jim McNeil. Both plays are theatrically lyrical celebrations of what Patrick White, in his similarly visceral/spiritual plays, called 'loving-kindness'. Tony Ayres' own play, *The Fat Boy* (2003), also has sudden outbursts of tenderness, but they emerge out of a much wilder story. Its central character Trevor is self-absorbed and obsessed with finding sex. After a series of plot developments in which the characters keep meeting in provocatively absurd recombinations, he finds instead a kind of love.

More recently, in 2006, Conigrave's *Holding the Man* found a substantial audience in a stage adaptation by Tommy Murphy which premiered at Sydney's Griffin Theatre. Murphy's 2005 play, *Strangers in Between*, told an unexpectedly happy story about a young boy leaving the country town he grew up in, to find welcome and companionship in the supposedly dangerous city.

Community Theatre

The Community Theatre and Art-in-Working-Life movements in the 1980s brought together many issues of identity politics. They also harked back to political theatre traditions from the 1920s and 1930s, when Katharine Susannah Prichard and others were writing agitprop scripts for performances at strikes and Communist party rallies; and to the counter-cultural street and guerrilla theatre that ushered in the New Wave, including neo-agitprop pieces protesting nuclear proliferation and the war in Vietnam. Mixed with social realist styles, the theatrical vocabulary of neo-agitprop was used to tell new stories about society's marginalised.

The forerunner was the Popular Theatre Troupe, a political theatre company started in 1974 by Richard Fotheringham, with the support of visiting English community theatreworker Albert Hunt. It had its local theatrical roots in the New Wave and its political roots in the revolutionary theatre of the early twentieth century. It made its reputation with Fotheringham and Hunt's *The White Man's Mission* in 1975, and *Fallout and Follow Me* in 1977, also by Fotheringham, a short piece about uranium mining, nuclear warfare and the nuclear power industry portrayed as a mock-heroic battle: Rio Tinto Zinc, General Electric and Westinghouse are beleaguered corporations struggling, as if in the trenches or the jungle, against the dark forces of scientific fact and concerned public opinion. Naturally, on the stage they win—as, indeed, they did in reality.[15]

12. IDENTITY AND COMMUNITY

The Community Theatre movement was as broad in its rhetoric as in much of its practice. The companies who were gathered together in its name aimed to speak from the margins, as if the margins were a single territory inhabited by a family of united, or at least interconnected, minorities. 'Community' was most often defined in terms of ethnicity, geography or workplace, but there were also projects that aimed to create their own communities.

One of best known was a series of projects undertaken in Logan City by the Brisbane-based Street Arts Community Theatre Company. Logan City was part of a suburban sprawl on the highway between Brisbane and the Gold Coast that grew alongside commercial property development from the 1970s under the conservative government of Premier Joh Bjelke-Petersen (1968–87). A large-scale community-participation project *The Logan City Story*, with writer P. P. (Pat) Cranney, took place in 1984.[16] Street Arts returned to Logan City in 1989 and 1990 to create *Charged Up*, a show about young men roaming the streets in the area; and *Raise the Roof*, about young people looking for a place to call home. Hugh Watson's account of his research and personal involvement in these latter two projects offers a rich documentary record of the working practices of the community theatre movement.[17]

In *Raise the Roof* (1990) Kerri, a rebellious teenager, leaves home haunted by a secret, guilty feeling that she is somehow responsible for the crises in her life, even though she is the victim. She blames herself for the death of her Child Guidance Officer, who had a heart attack, and she believes the dog that accompanies her is his reincarnation. She ends up at a hangout where she finally learns that none of it is her fault. Watson also wrote *A Few Short Wicks in Paradise* (1985) for Order by Numbers, another Brisbane community-theatre company. An angry protest show about political and social repression during the Bjelke-Petersen years, it looked at, among other things, how the poor were cleared out of South Brisbane to make way for the development of the Expo 88 site.

Both Popular Theatre Troupe and Street Arts were influenced by 1960s counter-culture performance groups such as Joan Littlewood's Theatre Workshop and John McGrath's 7:84 in the UK and Luis Valdez's

BELONGING

El Teatro Campesino and Peter Schumann's Bread and Puppet Theatre in the USA, noted above. But, as David Watt, a prolific chronicler of the community-theatre movement, points out, there was a distinction between the Marxist protest theatre of the Popular Theatre Troupe and the grassroots community involvement of Street Arts.[18]

Apart from these two companies, the best-known early community-theatre companies were Adelaide's Junction Theatre, Melbourne's Theatre West, Sydney's Sidetrack Theatre (later the Sidetrack Performance Group) and Death Defying Theatre (later Urban Theatre Projects). Other documented community theatre projects include FILEF's *Nuovo Paese*, in Sydney's Italian suburb of Leichhardt, and Graeme Dunstan's *Project Ghostfisher*. The latter reclaimed what had become a violent New Year's Eve tradition of car-burning and street rioting in Minto, a Housing Commission estate south of Sydney. The project included the ritualised burning of a sculpture made up of sixteen derelict cars, with community-produced monster masks thrown onto the pyre.[19]

A range of other initiatives worth mentioning here includes the experiments by the National Theatre of the Deaf, which mixed iconic sign language, theatrical mime, Auslan (the formal sign language of the deaf in Australia), spoken language and music. They explored the physical language of the theatre in ways that dance-based physical theatre and 'contemporary performance' movements from the late 1980s should have noticed, but didn't. Neil Cameron created large-scale community performance work, including the climactic fire event that for many years closed the annual Woodford Folk Festival in Queensland.[20] Big hART, an activist community cultural-development company of artists founded in 1992 by Scott Rankin and John Bakes in Tasmania, continues to work in theatre, film, television and other arts projects. One of their projects is *Ngapartji, Ngapartji* ('I give you something, you give me something'), a series of performances with a related cultural action program, especially on the internet. Originating in Alice Springs, but performed across the country, it aims to teach the Pitjantjatjara language to a wider Australian community.

There is much blurring of categories—of community and of performance form—in all this work, and most of it lies beyond the

12. IDENTITY AND COMMUNITY

scope of this book. It is a neglected area of study, in which Richard Fotheringham, Noëlle Janaczewska, Hugh Watson, Therese Collie, Patricia Cornelius and Paul Brown are significant writers. The major writers in the community-theatre movement, however, alongside John Romeril, are Pat Cranney, Graham Pitts and Errol O'Neill. Pitts is a dedicated writer whose plays, with the exception of *Emma*, have not been published. The work of both Pitts and O'Neill harks back to the agitprop tradition of Katharine Susannah Prichard and Betty Roland, and the later social realist work of Mona Brand. The early communist writer Jean Devanny appears as a character in O'Neill's *Popular Front*.

Popular Front (1986) is the third part of a trilogy about the labour movement in Queensland. It consists of *On the Whipping Side* (1991), about the 1891 shearers' strike (a much better play than Vance Palmer's *Hail Tomorrow*, on the same subject); *Faces in the Street* (1983), about the 1912 general strike in Brisbane; and *Popular Front*, about the labour movement in Queensland between 1930 and 1950, and loosely based on the career of Fred Paterson, the only Communist Party candidate ever elected to an Australian Parliament. All these plays mix historical with fictional characters, in plots that try to humanise and individualise their political narratives. The legendary William Lane, for instance, and his excursion to set up a utopian socialist community in Paraguay, are treated much less sympathetically than in *Hail Tomorrow* or George Hutchinson's *The Ballad of Billy Lane*.

Aftershocks (1991) is a verbatim theatre report on the Newcastle earthquake a year earlier. It was written by Paul Brown in conjunction with the Newcastle Workers' Cultural Action Committee who presented it in association with the local Hunter Valley Theatre Company, in Newcastle, NSW. As in the case of Nick Enright's *A Property of the Clan*, produced in the same city less than a year later, there was some concern about big-city appropriation when these regional community shows were produced in metropolitan centres by mainstream companies (Company B and the Sydney Theatre Company, respectively.)

Feminist, gay and lesbian, working-class and community-theatre were categories of identity-based work that overlapped in the 1980s

BELONGING

because they represented cultures that intersected, especially at the personal level. Any one person might be a member of any combination of several of them. There have always been wealthy middle-class gay men, professionally successful lesbians, working-class heterosexual women and underclass white men. On the intracultural level there are obvious differences within even the most precisely defined categories. There are many ways of being female or gay or poor. Even so, theatre and drama were characterised by a complex negotiation of difference which produced a tension between, on the one hand, the desire to close ranks and celebrate community and, on the other, the desire to speak back to the centres of mainstream power. The stirrings of dissent in the MWTG collective over women-only nights in the 1970s were repeated many times in different companies during the ensuing twenty years. These issues were debated most fiercely in relation to immigrant/multicultural drama, where the overt markers of language and physical appearance helped initially to define difference. It starts in the ghetto.

13
IMMIGRANTS AND EXILES

The ghetto and the community

The first step taken by any new identity-based group is to establish a closed community. It might be defined by class, gender, sexuality, homeland, ethnicity or diaspora, but once there it clearly demarcates the in-group from the out-group. These politically-defined communities later become microcosmic mainstreams of their own. When their work is accepted, it can be hegemonically neutralised as yet another voice in the culinary model of pasta-and-pesto multiculturalism. But in the early stages such cultural ghettos operated as strategic cells of resistance.[1]

The word 'ghetto' was first used in the Australian theatre to refer to the Old Tote Theatre's 1968 Australian Play Season when, in the Anglophile theatrical culture of the time, all local playwriting was seen as marginalised. By the 1980s, when the idea of 'Australian' had fragmented, some playwrights looked to their community bases and there was a brief time of conscious ghetto-formation. Much early feminist, and gay and lesbian theatre was produced in and for the communities of interest, in a culture of consciousness-raising and solidarity.

The issues were much more overt in the ethnic/ multicultural theatre, however, where 'ghetto' had a particular resonance, and

BELONGING

where language clearly distinguished the ghetto from the mainstream. 'Mainstream' theatre was for monolingual English-speaking audiences who, in turn, were excluded from the ethnic theatre that, in the case of Italian and Greek communities at least, had been thriving for decades.[2] In 1985, Pino Bosi distinguished between 'ethnic' arts, meaning work produced within and for a particular language group, and 'multicultural' arts, meaning cross-over work in which the interests and expressions of those groups and their new Australian contexts intersect.[3] In the same year George Michelakakis argued in the Greek-language press that Australian Greek-language theatre was producing generic conservative plays and that the 'only true migrant theatre is to be found outside the "ghetto"'.[4]

One of the playwrights Michelakakis identified as 'outside the "ghetto"' was community-theatre writer/director Tes Lyssiotis, who spoke for many writers and artists in the heyday of the community arts movement and the politics of multiculturalism when she said, 'I don't want to be labelled as 'multicultural', I want to be regarded as an artist, and the fact that I am working on things to do with migrants is irrelevant'.[5] This became a big issue in the identity-based arts movements, particularly when groups of artists who had united for politically strategic reasons in the 1980s went their separate ways in the 1990s. Today few writers identify exclusively with the cultural groups in which they began. True 'migrant theatre' became a generational issue, between the first-generation migrants and their children. A classic image of this new form of outsidership, parodied in the mockumentary opening sequence of the 1999 film *The Wog Boy*, was the Greek kid with garlic salami isolated in a school playground full of Anglo kids with vegemite and cheese sandwiches.

All the identity-based theatres processed such images. Once upon a time lesbians were solidly built women with hairy legs who had social consciences and spent a lot of time walking their dogs. Gay men were effete, had style and money, and spent a lot of time decorating their apartments. Young Italian or Greek men had hairy chests, wore gold jewellery and drove hotted-up purple Holden Monaros, their raging machismo controlled only by their domineering mothers. These and other stereotypes were contested in the theatre in the 1980s, and then

13. IMMIGRANTS AND EXILES

reclaimed and ironically celebrated in the 1990s by new generations of feminine lesbians, macho gay men and sensitive new-age Italians and Greeks.

Down Under the Thumb and *Out From Under*, were two multicultural community theatre shows devised by Sidetrack Theatre in the early 1980s that featured a nuclear family in which each member spoke a different language, depending on the language of the performer.[6] The effect was culturally non-specific, but the tactic managed to celebrate ethnic diversity while at the same time creating a generalised community of otherness. These shows, together with *Kin* (1987), anticipated the proud appropriation of the term 'wog' and turned it into a brand.

Kin, a collection of interwoven stories, toured in 1988 and played to school and community audiences. It looked at the difficulties faced by Greek, Pakistani and Italian migrants adjusting to their new country, dealing with their Australian-born children and going back home to discover that home wasn't there any more.[7]

The 'wog' brand was popularised by the extraordinary commercial success of the 1987 stage revue *Wogs Out of Work*. This was expanded in the follow-up show *Wogarama*, which added a Vietnamese-Australian comedian, Hung Le, and an Aboriginal, Denise Kickett. The stage shows went on to become the television series, *Acropolis Now* (1989–92) which took the ethnically-mixed family of the Sidetrack shows and turned it, more realistically for television, into a mixed group of ethnic characters operating a café. In addition to Simon Palomares, the café's gentle Spanish-Australian manager, it produced such stars as Mary Coustas, with her wog-sheila character Effie, and Nick Giannopoulos, star and producer of *The Wog Boy*.

In 1994, looking back on the rather brief history of multicultural arts in Australia to that time, Sneja Gunew wrote of the difficulties of defining multiculturalism. If defined in terms of migration, it references an old world that recedes with each generation; if defined in terms of ethnicity, it locks migrants into a fixed cultural formation outside the mainstream and outside history.[8] In both cases the result is the creation of a cultural space from which migrants—and, if we extend her point, other marginalised groups discussed in the previous chapter—can never escape. Both definitions introduce a myth, of homeland or of ethnicity, and the only escape is an appeal to highly problematic notions such as 'authenticity'.

Such appropriations of the old stereotypes were at first mainly comic, in the manner of Reg Livermore's subversions. But some theatre companies in the early 1980s brought together marginal groups to create a kind of generic otherness—different ways of being different, presented as if they were the same.

Ethnicity and multiculturalism

The first serious explorations of the immigrant experience in Australia—including what Con Castan calls the 'full cycles of migration',[9] in which migrants move back and forth between two homelands, unable to settle comfortably in either—were novels about English settlers.[10] The drama has no equivalent to Henry Kingsley's mid-nineteenth-century novels, Henry Handel Richardson's *The Fortunes of Richard Mahony* trilogy, set in the late nineteenth century (and dramatised by Michael Gow in 2002), and Martin Boyd's Langton tetralogy, published between 1952 and 1962. Tom Rothfield's 1939 *Jam Tomorrow*, comes closest, a play in which a suffering family of English settlers face social and legal discrimination in a way that anticipates the racism depicted in later non-Anglo migrant dramas. Mary Gage's terse one-acter, *The New Life*, written much later, in 1974, presents the feelings of loss and alienation of an English migrant as a type of domestic neurosis.

But it was non-Anglo writers who brought the experience of immigration to the fore. There were three waves of postwar immigration—from Southern, Central and Eastern Europe in the 1950s and 1960s, from South-East Asia in the 1970s and from the Middle East in the 1980s. (In the late 1990s and early 2000s a new wave of immigrants came, escapees from wars in Iran, Iraq, Afghanistan, Somalia and Sudan. At the time of writing they too had begun to produce a theatre of their own, largely in response to the refugee crises of the early twenty-first century.)

The first playwright in this group was Theodore Patrikareas, who migrated to Australia in 1958 and wrote in Greek about postwar

13. IMMIGRANTS AND EXILES

migrant experience. His first two plays, *The Promised Woman* and *The Uncle from Australia*, date from the early 1960s and were successful for many years in both Greece and in the Australian Greek community. *The Promised Woman* was filmed in Australia in 1974 and *The Uncle from Australia* produced for television in Greece the same year.[11] Patrikareas returned to Greece in 1973, and wrote a third play, *The Divided Heart*, in 1989. All three plays have been translated into English and were published in 2000, when Sydney's Sidetrack Performance Group revived *The Promised Woman*. The trilogy covers Castan's 'full cycle'—migration, return and remigration—and is written in a generic popular style by a first-generation Greek-Australian who remained proudly Greek, but who wrote in detail about the complexities implied by the hyphen in the label.

The Promised Woman (1963) portrays a group of mostly Greek migrants living in a boarding house. They are one step further into Australian society than a Displaced Persons' camp or a Detention Centre for asylum seekers, the settings for several plays of the early 2000s—but it is still a border space. Some will make new lives in a new country; others will fall by the wayside and live permanently on the margin, and many will yearn for their homeland. The play's two Anglo-Australian characters are the aliens, an exotic couple in a play that exemplifies a common postwar migrant experience—arriving in expectation of a free land of opportunity, only to be met with racism and social marginalisation.

The play also celebrates the economic liberation migrants found in their new country, something Patrikareas does more elaborately in later plays. Nick, the owner of the boarding house in Sydney's innercity suburb Newtown, is an old Greek who has been battling in his new country for many years and has finally acquired some property. His ailing wife Helen yearns to return home before she dies, but doesn't make it. Like a lot of boarding-house dramas, going back to Gorky's *The Lower Depths* and O'Neill's *The Iceman Cometh*, the action brings together a motley collection of individuals with different stories. A good realistic comedy-drama, at its centre is Antigone, who is brought from Greece as a bartered bride by Tellis, an arrogant and finally violent young man, who rejects her when she turns out to be much older

BELONGING

than her photo suggests. She decides to stay and, after much incident involving the other boarders and their individual hopes and dreams, makes an independent life for herself in this strange new country.

The Uncle From Australia (1964) is a Plautine comedy which continues the story with different characters, and in a livelier and more comic style. Jimmy is a successful migrant who runs a café that is continually being trashed offstage by bodgies. When he returns to Greece he does not want his family there to know that he is now rich. But after a ploy manipulated by a servant-trickster figure, Nicholas, Jimmy eventually parts with some of his money in order to allow his niece Katerina to marry for love.

The Divided Heart (1992), written long after Patrikareas had himself returned to Greece, treats the issue of return to the homeland more seriously, though still in a popular style, if now sentimental rather than comic. Alex is another long-term migrant who decides to go back permanently with his wife Helen, taking, against their wishes, two of his three adult children, who have made good lives in Australia. Nonetheless, out of family loyalty and respect for the patriarch, they agree to return to Greece—where they become an isolated small family, refugees in their own homeland, struggling to deal with family and political events in an old world that they no longer understand.

The Promised Woman, under its original title *Throw Away Your Harmonica, Pepino*, was one of the first plays to deal with the Australian experience from a migrant point of view. At least since Esson's *The Sacred Place* in 1919, plays by Anglo-Australians have included immigrant characters, among them Sydney Tomholt's *Anoli the Blind*, Jean Devanny's *Paradise Flow*, Oriel Gray's *Sky Without Birds*, Richard Beynon's *The Shifting Heart*, Mona Brand's *Pavement Oasis*, Marjorie McLeod's *Horizons*, Anthony Coburn's *The Bastard Country* and Peter Kenna's *An Eager Hope*. But in most of these, and others such as Jean Oliver's *Pay Cisca Manetti*, Bec Robinson's *Dark, Out There* and Eunice Hanger's *Flood*, the migrant characters are outsider figures and their experience is peripheral to the main action. In some cases they provide colour, in others they are presented in stereotypical ways. Whichever the case, immigrants are reinscribed as

13. IMMIGRANTS AND EXILES

marginal, despite sympathetic accounts of the harshness of their life and their struggles with racist Australian communities.[12]

Patrikareas was the first writer to represent established Australian rural and urban society as alien from an immigrant perspective, and to mark whiteness as an ethnicity. However, the plays did not appear together until 2000, when they were published as *Antipodean Trilogy*. This was after the impact of two second-generation trilogies about migration and return, written by Tes Lyssiotis and Janis Balodis.

Tes Lyssiotis founded the Melbourne-based Filiki Players in 1984, and in 1985–87 they toured a successful production of her play *The Journey*, a Brecht-influenced musical saga of immigration. In 1990 she produced one of the most influential early bilingual plays about the immigrant experience, *The Forty Lounge Café*. This became the central play in another trilogy of migrant plays, framed by *A White Sports Coat* (1988) and *Blood Moon* (1993), published together in 1996.[13]

In *A White Sports Coat*, the Daughter, in the last stages of pregnancy, is trying to finish the last scene of a play that sketches the material of the later plays. She checks on her sleeping son, and on her typewriter creates the characters of her mother, father and others in the subsequent plays, including the feuding sisters in Greece who feature in *Blood Moon*.

The Forty Lounge Café is based on the experiences of one of the greatest migrant characters in Australian drama, Eleftheria. Consigned to an orphanage by her family in Greece, Eleftheria is sent to Australia as a bartered bride, and marries a stranger, Vassili. She works a long life in the family business, the Forty Lounge Café, serving ham, eggs and chips to the passing white Aussie coach trade. Intercut are scenes from her Greek village childhood, the orphanage, and her lonely life as an outsider in Australia. A central image is her glory box, which comes to represent all her personal and cultural past. There is a great richness in the evocation of her traditions and the earthly sensuality of women's business: the girls in the orphanage dreaming of love, the grown Eleftheria's experience of childbirth, and the experiences, of men, that she and her friend Sonia share.

Eleftheria's lively daughter Toula copes well in a new world in which Eleftheria herself will never feel at home. When Vassili dies, Eleftheria

BELONGING

grieves passionately—a grief accentuated by the loss of her family and her homeland. Toula takes over the business and Eleftheria returns to Greece to retrieve, from her sister Aspasia, a Black Madonna icon that she cherished as a child.

This journey is the subject of *Blood Moon*. The characters are renamed but are clearly the Greek village family that threw Eleftheria out all those years ago. She has become Katina. Her sisters feel her life in Australia has been successful, but she finds it incomplete as she grieves for her lost past. It is a passionate and feverish play, as the four sisters gather, ten years after their mother's death, to divide her possessions. They have small pieces of land, uneven in size, but their brother and his wife, who never appear, have the house. As they squabble over special little things they thought they were promised, much emerges about their conflict over men, the tragedies of their lives, and especially their competitive struggle for their mother's love and approval. By the end we know that these four will never be a family again, and that, in both countries, the world that bred them is lost and gone.

Janis Balodis's *Ghosts* trilogy (*Too Young for Ghosts*, *No Going Back* and *My Father's Father*) is the greatest and most ambitious of all the Australian family sagas. It brings together the tropes of exile, dispossession, loss and longing that pervade so much of twentieth-century Australian playwriting, and presents them in an epic but intensely personal sequence of plays that spread out over two continents and 150 years of Australian and European experience. It explores—often harshly, sometimes comically and always with a detached but concerned interest—the passions and struggles of people who have been exiled to Australia, tried to feel at home here and unsuccessfully tried to go back. Almost incidentally, the third play relates these issues to the dispossession of Indigenous people. The trilogy draws all its characters into its central anguish: how do we learn to belong in a new place? In spite of its title, the first play is full of ghosts—who swarm the stage by the end of the third play, outnumbering, although perhaps comforting, the living.

Each of the plays can stand alone, and that is how they have been produced, but the work is a complete dramatic trilogy that has never

13. IMMIGRANTS AND EXILES

been given the large-scale production it deserves. It is dramaturgically complex and theatrically demanding, witty, passionate and wise, with a cast of tough characters who deserve to be as well-known as Olive, Roo, Nancy, Barney and Pearl in the *Doll* trilogy.

The plays interweave multiple stories set in different times. Underlying them is the mad visionary explorer Ludwig Leichhardt, who in three unsuccessful expeditions in 1845–46, the last ending in his death, attempts to appropriate the country by tramping across it and mapping it. In the first play he drags his exhausted and starving men behind him and carves his mark, 'L1845', in trees, like a decrepit old dog pathetically marking lamp posts. His companion Gilbert, a precise scientist, plods along behind him, focusing on the details, collecting specimens and painstakingly recording them, trying to understand the land in a different way. When the two young men who accompany them disturb a native camp and rape two of the women, the explorers' party is attacked. Gilbert is killed, perhaps by the rabid Leichhardt. The ghosts of Leichhardt and Gilbert haunt the next two plays. In *No Going Back* Leichhardt is driving his men to an even larger disaster. By *My Father's Father* he is dying in the desert, tended by his increasingly rebellious Aboriginal guide, Brown.

The Leichhardt scenes frame the main action of the trilogy, which is the story of a group of Latvian refugees who come together in a refugee camp in Stuttgart after World War II and emigrate to Australia. Otto and Lydia, a respectable middle-class couple dispossessed by the war, eventually make a materially successful life for themselves. In the first play, Karl and Ilse, who are much tougher, fight with each other as they are drawn together by their desperate situation and by a comic urgency, tempered by an odd kind of animal love, to mate and survive. By the third play they have become old survivors, weary but enduring.

The three central characters of the trilogy are Ruth, her new man Leonids and her war-scarred husband Edvards, back from the dead. In the first play Ruth and Leonids die after fleeing down a flooded river in order to be together, but they continue to haunt the other characters, until Edvards, after grieving for Ruth for more than forty years, finally dies in his new old land.

BELONGING

In *Too Young for Ghosts* (1985) these characters arrive in the same part of far north Queensland where Leichhardt and Gilbert got lost a hundred years before. They face a postwar immigrant struggle, in hideous corrugated-iron huts, the men working it hard and the women trying to support them, but becoming increasingly alienated. In their struggle to come to terms with this alien new country, they leave a few ghosts.

In *No Going Back* (1992) we meet them three decades later, settled now with grown-up children, but haunted by their past. They still feel Australia to be a place of exile, yet are conscious that they cannot, and do not want to, return to their homeland. On an Aussie family camping trip in the place where they started their hard-fought new life, they are haunted by the ghosts of Leichhardt and his second team, and they meet Brown, the mysterious Aboriginal who becomes the dying Leichhardt's companion in the third play.

In *My Father's Father* (1996), after Edvards's death and using his money, Karl and Ilse return late in life with their son Armand to Latvia. There they re-encounter their lost family and the European traditions from which they were torn away by the war and for which they have been grieving ever since. In a powerful sequence of scenes, the rituals of their old and new lives and worlds finally come together: home, they discover, is where your loved ones have died, because ghosts are tied to places not people. They have started to belong to Australia now that enough of their family have died there. Armand, at the end of the first play a new-born baby, and in the second a troubled young man uncertain of where he belongs, has become by the third a culturally diffident family son—a photographer recording the lives of his troubled family.

After *Too Young for Ghosts*, but before completing the trilogy, Balodis wrote *Wet and Dry* (1986), which depicts complex interactions between two couples in their struggle to love each other and to have children. The play uses the medicalisation of conception and childbirth as a metaphor for the isolation between people; and a secret coupling and successful birth as a metaphor for people coming together and finding warmth. It has a cool, intellectual surface—comic, but not celebratory—masking a buried yearning for closeness. The play

13. IMMIGRANTS AND EXILES

evocatively exploits the imagery of its title in scenes that move from the ocean cliffs of Sydney to the Northern Territory desert, and from hospital wards to tropical Darwin beaches. Everywhere in its settings there are fences, which the characters mostly manage to cut through.

Balodis has also worked closely as a dramaturg with Michael Futcher and Helen Howard, founders of Brisbane's Matrix Theatre, which produced their *A Beautiful Life*, discussed below, and, in 2005 *The Drowning Bride*, another great and complex play about Latvian migrants in the New World tormented by their war experiences. The play is based on a true story told to the authors by Brisbane painter Elise Parups.

Ellen is a young Brisbane artist who, after the death of her Latvian grandmother Sarmitte, travels to Pittsburgh to meet her grandfather, Valdis, a cruel old man with a secret past who is dying of a heart condition. He has sponsored Zenta, a Latvian relative, to come to the States to take care of him and he now tyrannises her. Zenta, who is pretty and sexy, is trying to get a man so that she can stay in America and Valdis sees her as a whore. Eventually, driven by need, that is what she tries to become.

Ellen's message to Valdis from the dying Sarmitte is that she loves and forgives him. Zenta gives Ellen a mysterious letter that Valdis sent Sarmitte at the end of the war, organising her escape, even though they were separated by then. He has written 'A life for a life' and she has sent it back to him with the message 'I did it because I loved you. We are still alive'. Ellen wants to find out what happened, and so do we.

As the play unfolds, we learn about their wartime relationship with Brandt, a sinister German officer who has power over them both. Valdis, who collaborated with the Germans to protect his family, took part in a massacre in which 25,000 Jews were shot. Brandt, who ordered the massacre, lusts after Sarmitte and pursues her. When Valdis is arrested as a spy she submits to Brandt in return for her husband's life. But Brandt, unconvinced by her pretence, is not satisfied and rapes her

Overleaf: Lee McGuiness as Laura in the 1986 Darwin Theatre Company production of Wet and Dry. *(Photographer: Jude Swift)*

BELONGING

in front of Valdis. This terrible secret has kept Sarmitte and Valdis estranged for fifty years.

As Ellen, watched over by her increasingly estranged fiancé Matt, drags these revelations out of Valdis, she is drawn back into her own grief and guilt about Sarmitte. While Ellen was away and in bed with Matt, Sarmitte, at the age of 80, was raped again and died of the injuries. In the final confrontation between Ellen and Valdis, some of her guilt is absolved but none of his. Ellen and Matt meet in Brisbane at the end. There is a truce between them, and the possibility of a new beginning. It is an extraordinarily powerful play.

A handful of other plays have explored the great issues of dispossession and longing in the immigrant experience. Tom Petsinis's *The Drought* (1994) is a grim folk-tragedy in which an exile returns to his homeland with terrible consequences. Back in his Macedonian village after twenty unsuccessful years in Australia, Vangel has lost touch; his mother has died after a long time grieving his loss, and he wants to make amends. The village is ravaged with drought, which has resonances for Vangel, who worked in dry desert mining towns in Australia. The ensuing story, of love and misunderstanding, ends like a classical Greek tragedy, with a ritual mourning by a chorus of village women and a Cassandra-like old gypsy woman. Strongly lyrical, the play is filled with yearning for a homeland forever lost.

Antonietta Morgillo's *The Olive Tree* (1990) is a bilingual play, a family tragedy about three generations of women caught between two worlds. As Fran comes to understand the sufferings of her grandmother Rosa, it helps her to understand her disturbed and difficult mother Belinda who has committed suicide. The play depicts traditional Italian culture as oppressive, something to be escaped. Angela Costi's *Panayiota* (1997) shows, in a series of memory scenes, the concerns and hopes of three second-generation women, with Cypriot-Greek, Greek-Macedonian and Italian parents. It revolves around Lisa Harris, who has changed her name from Athena Harismiriadis and who rejects, to the very end, her traditionally assigned role.

Mary is an early play by Hannie Rayson, a highly successful Anglo-Australian writer of the 1990s and 2000s, whose work is discussed in Chapter 15. A typical feel-good 1980s multicultural drama, the script

13. IMMIGRANTS AND EXILES

is a document of its time, about three generations of Greek women as the family move to Doncaster from the predominantly Greek Melbourne suburb of Richmond and find they are the only wogs in their street. The play compares the effects of different cultural backgrounds on the ways mothers give or don't give independence to their teenage daughters, and ends happily in friendship and mutual understanding.

Emma Celebrazione! (1991), based on Emma Ciccotosto's *Emma—A Translated Life*, did for cooking what Suzanne Spunner's *Running Up a Dress* did for sewing. A celebration of culturally traditional women's business, it is the only published script by the community-theatre writer Graham Pitts, who would loom a lot larger in a history of Australian theatre than he can in this history of playwriting. Like John Romeril, but even more so, he has been self-effacing as a playwright but extraordinarily prolific. *Emma* is a first-generation story, celebrating the life, culture and memories of Ciccotosto, who migrated from Italy in 1939 and struggled to come to terms with the new Anglo-Australian culture into which she was thrown. Originally produced in 1991 by Deckchair Theatre in Fremantle, Western Australia, with the Italian community women's choir Le Gioie delle Donne (The Joys of the Women), this glorious show played throughout Australia and, translated into Italian, in Italy as well.[14] As Emma cooks a wedding feast onstage for the audience, she is visited by figures from her lost life: Peter, her difficult yet beloved, basically decent husband, a gambler wanting to be the *padrone* of his household but not up to it; Peter's mother, her dreadful mother-in-law, Concetta, who mocks her cooking, and complains her way through their lives together, a terrible woman but with an aggrieved sense of dignity we come to respect; and Emma's mother Marianina and her elder brother Domenico, who transport her in her memories back to her childhood in Abruzzi.

The play is all about the baggage that people bring with them when they change countries, the ghosts of the past, the weight of culture and memory, and the importance of cooking for the people you love. Emma spends the play getting *la melanzane* (eggplant) right, because, she says, *melanzane* makes a meal and meals make a family. The choir were a powerful presence in Deckchair's production, not only for their

BELONGING

songs, but because the singers themselves shared something of Emma's experience.

Valentina Levkowicz's *Svetlana in Slingbacks* (2000) is a bittersweet coming-of-age play, with flashbacks and scenes from the fantasy life of a collection of crazy characters who are disconnected yet trapped in a family structure, each with their own nightmares, memories and fantasies, and unmet needs.

Svetlana, or Sveta, is a chubby 12-year-old girl growing up in a family of Russian immigrants who fled Stalin during the war. The play is set in the 1960s, when satellites were all the rage and, like Lewis in Louis Nowra's *Summer of the Aliens*, Sveta is obsessed with aliens. Her fantasy alien, Zorgon, is like a secret friend who keeps promising to take her away. Her father Boris, a hard-working family man, is strict and insensitive. Her mother Luda is tormented by paranoid fantasies, many of which relate to her experiences fleeing the KGB. During the course of the play she breaks down and is given a lobotomy which leaves her institutionalised, apparently a vegetable. Sonya is her daughter, half-sister to Sveta, a rebellious and beautiful, very 1960s, university student. After many fights with Boris, and in disgust that he authorised Luda's lobotomy, Sonia leaves home, probably, we think, to be estranged forever. Poor little Sveta is left behind to look after a father who doesn't understand her. It's a grimmer play than *Summer of the Aliens* but, like it, blackly comic.

These plays are connected to the wave of European migration that followed World War Two and the Cold War division of Europe. The next wave, following the end of the war in Vietnam, consisted of 177,000 Indo-Chinese refugees, but is not nearly so well represented in the repertoire. Not one of them himself, Duong Le Quy came to Australia later, in the mid-1990s, and wrote *Market of Lives*, *Meat Party* and *A Graveyard for the Living*. These do not constitute a trilogy, but, published together in 2002, are related in their concern with the aftermath of the war and the scars it left on the Vietnamese people. Nor are they migrant dramas—all are set in Vietnam—but they include Australian characters and address indirectly the need for reconciliation with postwar Vietnam.

13. IMMIGRANTS AND EXILES

Binh Duy Ta's *The Monkey Mother* (1998) is a lyrical script for a dance and music work about the experience of having no cultural centre or anchoring point. The Monkey Mother is a spirit in a mythic Forest, who adopts a baby washed up by the sea and, against the advice of the spirit of the Forest, decides to nurture him. The Forest is napalmed, but the baby escapes and becomes a Young Man who meets an Anglo Young Woman and falls in love with her. Their relationship has a crisis point when the Young Woman wants to take him from the Forest, back to Australia. In Australia, the Monkey Mother is reduced, becoming an old mother who dies just as the Young Woman is giving birth to an Australian-Vietnamese child. All these evocations of traditional Vietnamese, wartime Vietnamese and immigrant Australian-Vietnamese experiences are blurred and fluid, so that none is a reference point for any of the others. It is not a hybrid work but one in which everything between cultures is in flow.

Wild Rice (1997), by Huong Nguyen, Phi Hai, Pat Rix and Geoff Crowhurst, is a classic immigrant story, like the earlier Italian and Greek ones. Sonny, a teenaged boy with childhood memories of fleeing Vietnam by boat, is now resisting his stern, traditional father, who cannot accept the independence that growing up in Australia has given his children. A Chorus of young people enact memory scenes of being in the boats. In the Australian present Sonny runs away from home and lives with a friend Steve. When forced to leave, he plans to move into a squat, and seems to be on a downward path, but he is persuaded to go home, where he achieves an uneasy reconciliation with his family.

One of the most evocative works about fluidity between cultures is Noëlle Janaczewska's *The History of Water* (1992). It explores shifting experiences of identity and rootedness through the languages and memories of Kate and Ha, two estuarine figures for whom, as in *The Monkey Mother*, movement is more important than place. Kate is a photographer who, dissatisfied with trying to capture stories, locations and scenes, has decided to photograph only water. She remembers a typical Australian childhood in Perth, on beach holidays, but never quite learning to swim; she is haunted by memories of grim tidal mudflats in England when, as a terrified 8-year-old, she was taken to visit poverty-stricken relatives living in a space between land and sea

BELONGING

with no flowing water; and she recounts her experiences of her hopeful journey to Vietnam, a land as wet as Australia is dry. Ha is a translator who remembers her childhood beside great peaceably flooding rivers, in which she caught fish. She is comfortable between cultures, and fascinated by the way her two languages reflect her two lives: a youth she experiences in Vietnamese and an adulthood in English. Gradually she discovers that her two languages and the lives they express 'seep into each other like a watercolour painting left out in the rain' (p. 32).

Kate and Ha are brought together by their different experiences of language and memory, especially by their different accounts of the mysterious disappearance of a man from a ferry crossing an unnamed stretch of water that could be in either country. They both seem to have been close to him and to have been profoundly affected by his failure to cross the water. Yet the relationships are never made explicit—he may not even be the same man. It is a vivid work, full of measured reflection, sensual language, and projected images. In the performance water drips, is poured and gushes, completing an intricately developed metaphor of water as the medium in which cultural and personal differences are reflected and perhaps dissolved. At the end the two performers invite the audience to join them in the foyer for a drink.

Janaczewska's *Blood Orange* (1993), produced in both a community celebration version and a schools touring version by western Sydney's Death Defying Theatre, draws on the experiences of teenage girls and young women from many different backgrounds—including Arabic, Italian and Vietnamese—to explore issues of body-image and sexuality.

New waves of immigrants came from the Middle East in the 1980s in the aftermath of the war in Lebanon; and from Afghanistan, Iraq, Iran and ravaged African countries such as Somalia and Sudan, in the 1990s. The Lebanese have not been much represented in the theatre, but have become a major group portrayed by the media as tribal and joked about in popular comedy. The later refugees are represented in an extraordinary resurgence of political theatre, from 1999 to 2005, produced in response to the Liberal Government's policies of detainment and forced deportation of asylum-seeking refugees. Few of these plays are yet in print, but in all of them the shifting space between cultures became fixed again in harsh and hard spaces hidden

13. IMMIGRANTS AND EXILES

away behind fences topped with razor wire, as outback detention centres became the new dead heart of the Australian imaginary in the of the early twenty-first century. Nick Enright's *Country Music* has one of these fences looming over a classic country town straight out of the old bush sagas.

Among the first and strongest plays about the experience of this new wave of refugees is Michael Futcher and Helen Howard's *A Beautiful Life*, based on the reminiscences of an Iranian-Australian they knew in Brisbane, and also on the 1992 protest raid on the Iranian Embassy in Canberra, documented in Barbara Chobocky's film *The Raid*.[15]

In the prologue, the main character Hamid conjures his son Amir to tell the story. The boy does so, starting with the raid and a confrontation, tense with unknown significance, in which one of the protesters stops another from killing an embassy official. The rest of the play unpacks that moment. The trial of Hamid, the first protester, Kamran, the second, and Hamid's wife Jhila is interspersed with Hamid's experiences in Ayatollah Khomeini's Iran from which he and his family have fled for their lives. Hamid, a simple man caught up in terrible events, is now frustrated. He despairs at not being allowed to tell his story to the Australian people or their courts and is confused, and sometimes angry, at their uncaring prejudice. The story of the trial, and Hamid's conflicts with his Australian lawyers, is intercut with the gradually revealed horrific details of his earlier imprisonment, torture and trial in Iran.

Eventually he tells his secret. Kamran, now mentally disturbed, was his supporter when they were imprisoned in Tehran. Their torturer in prison, a guard they called 'Hassan Gestapo', is the embassy official Ahmad. Hamid prevented Kamran from killing Ahmad during the raid but Ahmad, who provoked the riot for political reasons, now accuses him of being a 'terrorist'. The crucial event that haunts Hamid was when Ahmad made him watch the killing of three prisoners and then the torture (it seems to include a castration) of Kamran with a broken bottle. Tormented with guilt for failing to kill Ahmad when he had the chance, Hamid has also stopped Kamran killing him at the embassy. He is incapable of killing, which makes the charge of 'terrorism' against him hideously ironic.

BELONGING

In the end, unable to contain his anger in front of the jury, Hamid is convicted. But, given his experiences, he does not find the sentence is too hard. Offered the opportunity to challenge the verdict (one juror is found to be prejudiced), he can face no more Australian justice: 'I can endure one year in an Australian jail, okay?' (p. 101). After what we have seen we know that he can. As he is led away, he tells Jhila and Amir, 'In my head I practise living beautiful life for when we are home'. Which, by now, means Brisbane.

Many of these plays, whatever their cultural background, have stern fathers and long-suffering mothers, and rebellious children looking for a new life. In this they resemble the old bush-city plays, and generational family dramas everywhere. The multicultural theatre in the last three decades of the twentieth century picked up the theatrical and dramatic conventions of their different times: the traditions of Australian realism and its lyrical and expressionist variations, the eclecticism of the New Wave, the Brechtian techniques of 1980s community and political theatre, and the new physical theatre forms and styles and the direct performance approach of the post-dramatic theatre in the 1990s. These conventions were used to explore issues of otherness and marginalisation, and their continuity with old traditions suggests that we still live in a continent full of exiles. Their breaking down of barriers and their new inter- and trans-cultural fluidity of identity and place, still have practical political implications today.

The communities discussed in this chapter adopted a common ground for strategic political or cultural reasons, and it is good to remember the differences within them. But for one group of Australians the differences were profound, and almost completely occluded by two hundred years of colonisation. Many Aboriginal theatre artists in the 1980s and 1990s wanted no part of multiculturalism and objected to being 'ethnicised'.[16] As descendants of the first people they had a spiritual and philosophical relationship with this continent, and their own creation story and cosmology. They were subjected to a unique dispossession.

14
ABORIGINAL THEATRE

Kevin Gilbert's *The Cherry Pickers*, written in 1968, before the ocker New Wave started, anticipated many of the issues that were to be raised in the debates over identity politics in the 1980s. Originally workshopped at the Mews Theatre, Sydney, in 1971, with an all-Aboriginal cast as Gilbert insisted, the play was the forerunner of a great body of work by Indigenous playwrights. It follows Zeena, a lively young woman caught between old and new worlds, as her man Tommlo tries to take her back to what he sees as an 'authentic' tribal life away from the white oppressors. He wants her to take off her white clothes and dance naked with him around the sacred tree—ironically, a European cherry tree that is the source of their income as itinerant fruit-pickers—but, forced to retreat into an originatory myth of cultural authenticity, she rebels:

> This—this is an anachronism! The truths from the beginning of time—the truth of two hundred years ago can't be given rebirth and become the truth applicable to today! [...]
> We must hold to a truth only until such time as we can think it out and then supersede it by a higher truth. (pp. 63–4)

By 'a higher truth', Zeena seems to mean what we would now call a hybrid culture. Her fear of Tommlo's plan to return to his origins anticipates many later debates about cultural authenticity.

BELONGING

Before Gilbert, starepresentations of Aboriginal characters had all been written by whites. Indigenous Australians first appeared on the Australian stage in nineteenth-century melodrama as 'Jacky-Jacky' figures in what were essentially localisations of a stock type of the genre—the wily servant with the heart of gold who is instrumental in saving the day. In the first half of the twentieth century white liberal playwrights attempted to present the struggles and fate of Aboriginal people with sympathy, although today their understanding of what it is to be Indigenous often comes across as naïve.

But in the years after the first production of *The Cherry Pickers*, Aboriginal playwrights Robert Merritt and Gerald Bostock (with his *Here Comes the Nigger* in 1977) pioneered a new drama of Indigenous experience. Merritt's *The Cake Man* (1975) introduced the plays of Aboriginal mission life that Jack Davis took into the mainstream. Both writers reversed the bush-hut staging tradition so that the fringe-dwelling black characters who had turned up at the doors of white pioneers in the plays of Vance Palmer, George Landen Dann and Katharine Susannah Prichard were now the focus of attention. The sets represented houses teeming with Aboriginal life, with occasional intrusions by white bureaucrats and social workers, the new outsiders. The productions also included a wide range of non-realistic effects—songs, narrations, comedy routines and most powerfully, in Jack Davis's *Barungin*, a magnificent final litany of the names of the dead, like a chorus from Aeschylus.

The Cake Man was written in Bathurst jail, where Merritt met playwright Jim McNeil and he dedicates the published script to 'brother Jim' with a short poem.[1] It opens with an allegorical first-contact scene in which a savagely hypocritical Priest, Soldier and Civilian interrupt an idyllic family scene. They kill the man and take away the woman and child. These figures then transform into characters on a mission settlement outside Cowra in central western New South Wales, where Merritt grew up.

The family—Ruby, Sweet William and their 11-year-old son Pumpkinhead—now struggle in extreme poverty. Pumpkinhead pinches coal for his mum and dreams of the Cake Man, a figure in a story Ruby tells him, who was sent by Jesus to bring cake to the Koori kids, but who was blinded by bad men and unable to find them. The

14. ABORIGINAL THEATRE

baby has infected eyes which Pumpkinhead washes for him, scornful of his drunken father. Ruby reads her Bible and quietly grieves for William, a drinker who dreams of going to Sydney to work and buy them all a big red house with electricity.

The Priest and the Soldier have become the smarmily patronising Mission authority figures—the Manager and Inspector—but the Civilian, nastily racist and aggressive at first (especially when he catches Pumpkinhead stealing his coal), has an abrupt change of heart when he visits the family and sees their poverty. He gives them a box of supplies, and so, at least to Pumpkinhead, becomes the lost Cake Man.

The central character, however, is the black man from Scene 1, who becomes Sweet William. His alienation and confusion about what is expected of him and how he can support his family draw together the threads of black traditional culture and the post-invasion white world that the play weaves together. Early on, Sweet William has a monologue in which he presents as a comically drunken, knowing but self-mocking fool, a character that was to become familiar in later Aboriginal plays, especially those of Jack Davis. He asks the question that haunts him, 'What you want from me that I got?' (p. 13), and tells a Dreamtime story of how the curlew tricked the emu into cutting off his own wings. When Sweet William finally gets to Sydney, he is immediately arrested while innocently standing outside a pub after a brawl. In an epilogue he tells us of his mysterious encounter with a spirit figure, the eurie-woman, who leads him to stop questioning what whites want of him and to search instead for a different, Aboriginal, reality that is finally his own.

The Cake Man was the first in a series of plays in which the lived experience of black Australians was represented in family scenes rendered more or less realistically, but framed by theatrical and dramaturgical effects that broadened the perspective. It was as if black playwrights were saying that while white realism might adequately represent the experience of white society, to tell the full story they needed their own stories, dances, songs and ironic subaltern humour. A sudden turning to the audience became the great feature of the family plays of Jack Davis and eventually became the main style of late twentieth-century Aboriginal theatre.[2]

BELONGING

Jack Davis and black theatre in the 1980s and 1990s

Jack Davis's first play, *Kullark*, was produced in 1979. He was 61 and had already had a long and distinguished career as an activist and an influential cultural and community policy worker, writer, editor and poet. He wrote for both black and white audiences. One of the most astonishing things about his writing for the stage, and about a great deal of other black theatre at the time, considering the terrible events the writers were dealing with, was its apparent goodwill towards white people.

Davis dealt with the facts of the nineteenth-century war between the Indigenous population and the white invader-settlers, and with the later missionary and government oppression that is the socio-political context for the lives of his characters. Yet on the surface his plays look like warmly realistic family comedy-dramas in the European tradition, inviting understanding and empathy. Perhaps in appropriating this form he was being slyly civil towards the colonisers, or perhaps genuinely reconciliatory. In either case his plays eased black issues into the white middle-class theatre, as well as into the secondary and tertiary education systems where they found new audiences.

Davis wrote sympathetic representations of Nyoongah family life in fringe communities, including frank scenes of drunkenness and neglect, but always set in the context of their historical and social preconditions. He introduced characters—black and white—who moved between two cultures, were educated in both and who cared for the people who lived under appalling social conditions imposed by a colonising system. This system he usually represented, if at all, by a few bad individual characters, or by historical documentary means. He included savage scenes of white oppression, but never called for revolutionary resistance.

His interest in reconciliation is most obvious in his plays for children, *Honey Spot* and *Moorli and the Leprechaun*. *Honey Spot* (1985) explores in a sentimental tone the initial suspicion and then growing friendship between a black boy and a white girl who come to understand each other through dance. A classic reconciliation play,

14. ABORIGINAL THEATRE

it anticipates, in simple terms, the hybridisation of black and white art forms, when the boy and the girl, with the help of their families, make a collaborative dance-work that brings together their different traditions.

The theme carries through to one of his last plays, *In Our Town* (1990), which deals with the challenge to a friendship between two returned soldiers, one black and the other white. Although they fought together in World War Two, David Millimurra and Larry Moss find that back home deep-seated racism drives them apart, especially when David falls in love with Larry's sister Sue. It is a Romeo and Juliet story without the tragic conclusion. David and Sue re-unite at the end, rather awkwardly, and return to their town to fight racism.

Davis's major plays together make up a series of integrated family sagas, a postcolonial counter-narrative spanning more than fifty years of race relations in Western Australia. *Kullark* reaches back to first contact in the 1830s, and the establishment of the Swan River settlement that became Perth. The families are the Yorlahs (in *Kullark*), the Wallitches (in *The Dreamers* and *Barungin*) and the Millimurras (in *No Sugar* and *In Our Town*), but their experiences overlap to such an extent that they can be seen as one extended family. The plays revolve around three key historical moments: the forced removal of the Indigenous population of Northam to the Moore River Native Settlement during the early years of the Depression (*Kullark* and *No Sugar*); the return of Aboriginal soldiers after World War Two and the racism they faced back in their country towns (*Kullark* and *In Our Town*); and the contemporary (1980s) settings of the plays when the families face challenges from a new interaction with white Australia, especially the land-rights movement and the oppression of deaths-in-custody (*Kullark, The Dreamers* and *Barungin: Smell the Wind*). The plays achieve a grand dramatic rewriting of the official white version of Western Australian history, putting the Nyoongah experience into the foreground.

Kullark (1979) laid the groundwork. Originally a theatre-in-education piece, it mixes documentary and dramatic techniques to portray the narratives and memories that are dealt with more fully in the later plays. A sub-plot in the first half is a docu-drama account of

BELONGING

early 1830s wars in the Pinjarra area near the Swan River, in which the white pioneer Captain Stirling struggles against Yagan, the resistance guerrilla fighter. Yagan is defeated and decapitated, his head smoked in a tree stump for three months and sent to England as a scientific curiosity. Another sub-plot in the second half tells the story of the removal in 1931 of the Northam mob of Aborigines to the Moore River Settlement.

The major story running through the entire play concerns a contemporary family, Alec and Rosie Yorlah, and their son Jamie, who is studying to be a teacher. The play opens just after a funeral and sets up Rosie's fierce determination, as Alec and his cousins drink, to keep the family together. She is the tough matriarch, a Nyoongah version of the battling bush mum, dealing with the wild behaviour of her husband and his cousins, and struggling each morning to get her kids off to school.

When Jamie returns from his studies he is involved with the land rights movement and with Lyn, a sympathetic white woman, which creates tension with his father. Lyn, the first of Davis's many sympathetic characterisations of white people, is friendly and wants to help. But when Jamie is arrested in a pub brawl and she offers assistance, Alec insists he will bail out his son. Eventually Jamie is given a good behaviour bond and that part of the play ends with a cautious optimism. So, too, does the flashback story of young Alec, who returns from the war and moves his family from the reservation into an old farmhouse, in anticipation of the plot of *In Our Town*.

The Dreamers (1981) introduces the Wallitch family. Framing their domestic struggles is a vision of a traditional dancer and glimpses of a family, a traditional tribal group who are seen walking silhouetted in the distance, always moving on. When they reappear in Act 2 they have been forced from their land.

Dolly is another matriarchal figure who rules the extended family, coping with a collection of squabbling children and drunken men. Old Uncle Worru is sick and dying, but he carries the past with him, although the stories and traditions are decayed by the endless flagons of port and the fighting. He opens the play with a poem lamenting the loss of the old days and ways. At the end, when he dies, Dolly delivers a poem remembering him as a young proud warrior.

14. ABORIGINAL THEATRE

Dolly's husband Roy and his cousin Eli spend most of the play drinking and neglecting the kids. Meena and Shane are like kids anywhere, loyal to Uncle Worru, but looking now to their own lives—Shane to his footie and Meena to her schoolwork in Act 1 and to her new boyfriend in Act 2. Other characters are an older son, Peter, who gets into trouble in a stolen car and is in jail in Act 2; the respectable and helpful cousin Robert who is a legal aid officer; and Darren, a *wetjala* (white) friend of the young children, who makes a brief appearance.

A powerful sense of loss and a spirit of bittersweet comedy pervade the play. The climax is a drunken fight over a poker game, during which Uncle Worru, sick in bed, falls and is taken to the white hospital that he dreads. He dies just before his planned—and longed-for—visit to the traditional Nyoongah doctor.

No Sugar (1985), Davis's best-known play, tells in detail the story of the forced transfer in 1931 of the poor but independent Northam Aboriginal community, represented here by the Millimurra family (and in *Kullark* by the Yorlahs), to the tightly controlled and oppressive Moore River Settlement. It includes representations of the historical figures A. O. Neville, the coldly bureaucratic WA Chief Protector of Aborigines, based in Perth, and N. S. Neal, the corrupt and violent Superintendent at Moore River, who preys sexually on the black girls and beats them when they won't comply. Originally produced for the Festival of Perth in an outdoor, ambulatory staging, in which the audience's movements reflected those of the dispossessed Aborigines, the play deals with the Millimurras's struggle to stay together as a family in the face of their treatment—sometimes intrusively officious, sometimes vicious and cruel, sometimes simply neglectful—by white authorities.

The Millimurras are the matriarch Milly, her husband Sam and her children Joe, Cissie and David. The family also includes Jimmy Munday, Milly's angry and wild brother, and their mother Gran, who represents their broken links with a traditional past. In the central

Trevor Parfitt as Eli, Wayne Bynder as Robert, Jack Davis as Worru and Michael Fuller as Roy in the 1982 Swan River Stage Company production of The Dreamers.

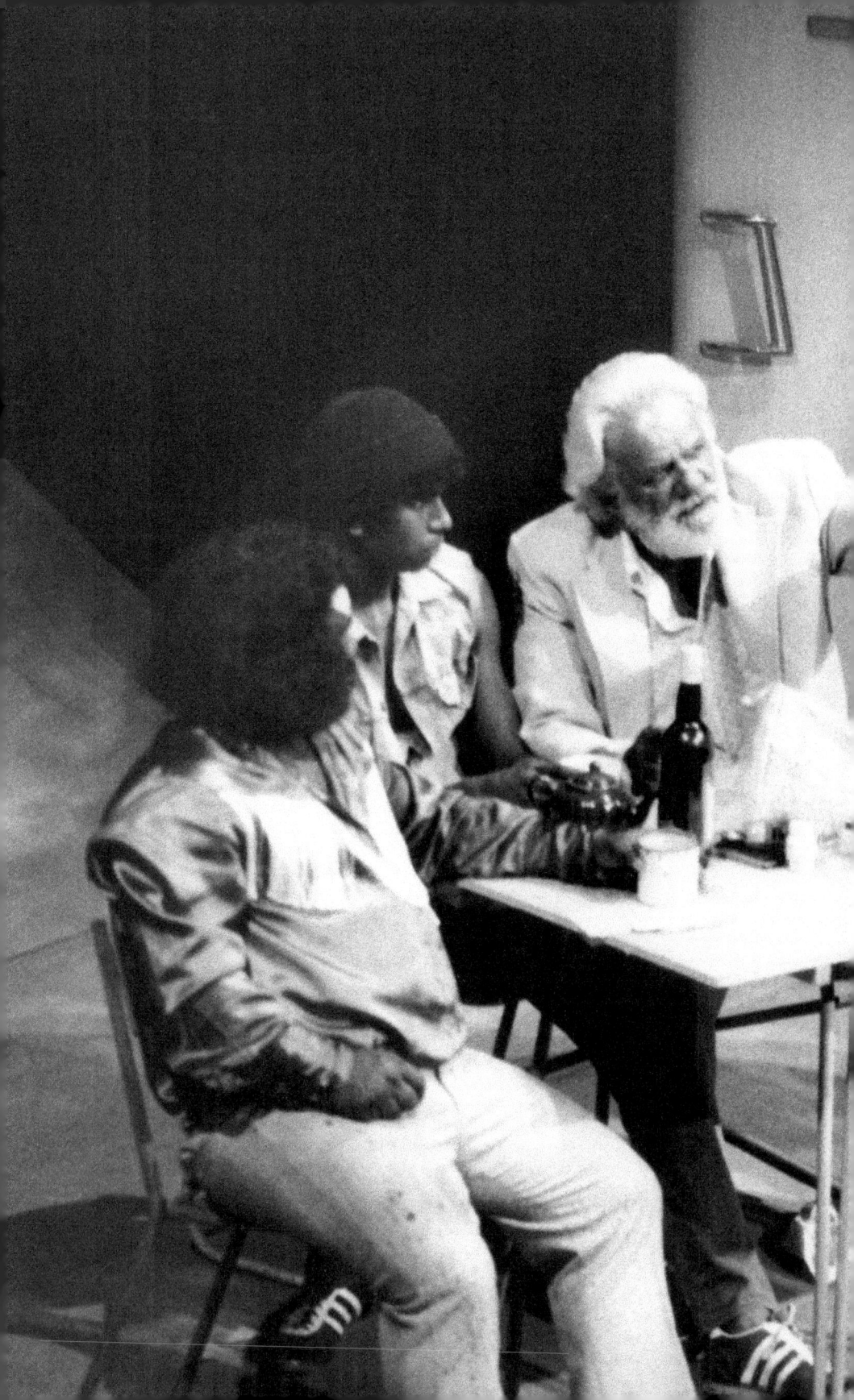

BELONGING

romance Joe falls in love with Mary, a Kimberley woman he meets at the settlement, and he flees with her when she is threatened and beaten by Neal. They are captured and returned several times, but Joe's determination to escape, and his willingness to spend time in jail every time he is brought back, eventually work, as a form of non-compliant protest, and the couple are finally allowed to leave Moore River and return to their country at Northam.

Capturing them each time is the black tracker Billy Kimberley, who works for Neal. Caught between two worlds, he has vivid memories of the massacre of his own people, told in a moving scene after a corroboree (Act 2, Scene 6). Neal's wife, the matron at Moore River, wearily aware of her husband's transgressions, is sympathetically portrayed.

In the climactic scene that gives the play its title, the black characters undermine an Australia Day celebration in a classic moment of trickster subversion, singing their own words to the hymn 'There is a Happy Land':

> There is a happy land,
> Far, far away.
> No sugar in our tea,
> Bread and butter we never see.
> That's why we're gradually
> Fading away. (p. 98)

Barungin: Smell the Wind (1988), the toughest of Davis's plays, deals with the issue of black deaths in custody. It returns to the Wallitch family eight years on. Although the dates of the settings and the ages of the characters in the two plays don't quite add up, the spirit is of a new generation.

Dolly is now Granny Doll, the old woman of the family, like Gran in *No Sugar*. She still worries about her troublesome brood, but is past being able to do much except offer wisdom. Meena is grown up and married to Arnie, who is in jail. She is having an affair with a cousin of the family, the wild Peegun. Her brother Peter, who was in jail at the end of *The Dreamers*, is still rebellious and again in jail, but he has been released and pledges to get a job. Meena and Arnie's kids are Little Doll and Micky. Little Doll is a capable 12-year-old, bright and lively, as her mother was when she was young. Robert, Dolly's respectable

14. ABORIGINAL THEATRE

nephew from *The Dreamers*, is now devoutly religious, and tries to help them all. Micky is a troubled 14-year-old, drinking with his mate Slugger and secretly stealing stuff and hiding it under the house. When Peegun finds the stolen goods he hides them in the boot of his car, but when Peter drives Little Doll to her swimming carnival, it is searched by the police. Peter is arrested and dies in jail, after a savage beating.

The play opens with the funeral of Eli, the drunken uncle from *The Dreamers*. Towards the end of the play, at a Rotary Club dinner, Robert gives a speech in which he recounts some of the stories from *Kullark*—the massacres and individual murders committed by the early settlers, referring to Rottnest, the prison island now a holiday resort for the *wetjalas*, as the Aboriginal Auschwitz. After Peter's death is revealed, Meena recites the names of all the Aboriginal deaths in custody from 1833, when settlement in Western Australia began, to 1988, when the play was written. It is a grim and powerful conclusion.

Davis was a much-loved writer/actor/activist: he played Uncle Worru in the original production of *The Dreamers* and Billy Kimberley in *No Sugar* when it toured to the Expo 86 World Theatre Festival in Vancouver. He did more than anyone to put Aboriginal issues onto the stage, and inspired a generation of black writers.

One of these was Richard Walley, a director and performer whose *Coordah*, a rambling comedy with a bitter edge, tells of Aboriginal life in a small town. In the secondary story, set in 1940, June, a well-meaning journalist, befriends Koolbardi, a white-educated Aboriginal man, and persuades him to reveal some secret men's business which she publishes in a magazine story, with disastrous results. The main story is contemporary and concerns the shambolic attempts of a bunch of cheerful drunks, led by the irrepressible Nummy—a trickster figure—to put together a corroborree for the annual town ball. Treb and his wife Elly are capable Aboriginal community leaders, but their attitude towards the others is indulgent, and Treb turns out to be a bit of a lair himself.

After one antic too many, Nummy is prohibited from performing. He gets drunk and disrupts the ball by turning on the fire sprinkler system and drenching the assembled whitefellas. Afterwards he is knocked over by a hit-and-run driver and spends a week in hospital

BELONGING

in a coma. The culprit turns out to be a farmer from whom he has been stealing sheep, one of which, a prize ram worth $35,000, Nummy killed at the beginning of the play and cut up for a feed. Discharging himself from hospital, he returns to the bush meeting place where they used to rehearse, accompanied by the simple-minded Ginna, his *coordah* (brother, or mate). He falls off his log and Ginna sits loyally by him as he lies still on the ground. We assume that he has died. Though awkwardly written, it could still work as a subversive comedy.

Bob Maza's *The Keepers* (1988) is a much tougher play—a saga of black-white relations from first contact to Federation. The first contact is between two decent families: Scottish Christian settlers James and Elizabeth Roeburne, and Boandik Indigenes Koonawar and Mirnat. In the face of the horrors of the frontier war between the blacks and the whites, they manage to form a bond, partly through their two babies. When James and Koonawar are killed by an armed white mob, Elizabeth and Mirnat team up and live together with the Boandik for five years before moving to the city with their sons to set up Clarendon, a school for young black women.

The boys grow up together, all but brothers. Elizabeth's Michael thinks of himself as part Boandik and Mirnat's son Daniel is fascinated by getting on in white society. The climax comes when Daniel discovers hospital reports of strychnine poisonings of Aborigines. He rebels, getting angry for the first time, and goes on a rampage of grief and bitterness, smashing windows in the town and setting fire to the white tennis club he's tried so hard to join. Lillipa, a young black woman whom Michael has befriended, finds Daniel drunk in a laneway and, although she is a virgin, offers herself to him in an attempt to draw him away from the rabid white mob that is pursuing him. He scorns her, calling her a whore, and she leaves. Then Michael appears and Daniel rails against him too, until he realises that Michael has been stabbed by the mob, who think of him as a 'nigger lover'. Daniel is remorseful. They face the approaching white vigilantes together and are killed.

In a coda we see Elizabeth and Mirnat again, by now very old women, giving speeches at the Federation celebrations—Mirnat asserting with quiet dignity that you cannot own the land, you can only be its keepers. It is a strong play, melodramatic and passionate.

14. ABORIGINAL THEATRE

The first woman Aboriginal playwright was Eva Johnson, a feminist and activist whose play *Murras* (1988) is a non-realistically condensed drama tracing an Aboriginal family moving from the fringe of a small town to the city in the early 1970s. It deals with an important transition, as it charts the loss of the old traditions and the rise of Aboriginal activism, especially in the character of the young boy Wilba, who grows up to become an activist in the land rights movement. In a sudden revelation towards the end we learn that the daughter of the family, Jayda, has been sterilised by white doctors. The title *Murras* means 'hands': the strong hands that Charlie, the patriarch, once used to carve the totems of the group before alcoholism killed him; and the fists that Wilba clenches as an angry young rebel. The family scenes are punctuated by a dancer who plays the traditional Mimi Spirit, performed in the original production by Stephen Page. Nothing Jack Davis ever wrote approaches the naked anger of this play. Johnson also wrote and performed *What Do They Call Me?*, three interconnected monologues in which an alcoholic mother and the two daughters who were taken from her—one now a middle-class woman brought up as white and the other a radical activist lesbian—tell their stories and belatedly connect with each other.

The greatest success of Aboriginal theatre, after Davis and partly with his encouragement, was Jimmy Chi's musical *Bran Nue Dae* (1990)—a 'spiritual/rock/reggae opera'[3]—which grew out of songs that Chi had been writing and performing with his band Kuckles since the early 1980s. It is a joyously rambunctious celebration of Indigenous and multicultural life in the northern Western Australian town Broome—part travelling road show, part religious revivalist meeting and a gloriously theatrical celebration of Aboriginality. It is about reconciliation, redemption and the happy discovery that Australia has a black heart.

The story centres on Willie and Rosie, a pair of impossibly naïve young lovers. Sent off to school in Perth, Willie is expelled by the tyrannical, but comically unthreatening Father Benedictus for stealing Cherry Ripes and Coke from the canteen fridge and handing them out to his friends. Out on the street, destitute and anxious to get back to Broome, he meets an old park-dweller named Tadpole. After a

BELONGING

near-miss road accident they team up with a hippie named Marijuana Annie and her comic German backpacker lover Slippery. Together they drive the 1,500 miles to Broome—a journey home, towards self-discovery. Willie becomes a man twice: once when he undergoes a very contemporary rite of Aboriginal initiation by spending a proud night in jail, and then again when he finally gets to 'pook' Rosie.

After Broome the characters travel on to Lombadina in the Djarundin Hills—'our country'. Almost everyone turns out to be Aboriginal, in a grand happy parody of the endings of sweet white American musicals. Willie's mother Auntie Theresa is discovered also to be Slippery's mother ('Ich bin ein Aborigine!!', crows Slippery with delight, after his initial suspicion and fear of the whole native, tribal thing (p. 71)). Father Benedictus, who magically turns up in Lombadina dispensing Cherry Ripes, turns out to be the incidental father. Tadpole turns out to be Auntie Theresa's long-lost lover and therefore Willie's father. Marijuana Annie, with comic abruptness, reveals herself to be an Aborigine too, stolen from her mother when she was young.

The show finishes with an extravagant, parodic, yet sincere, celebration of Christian Aboriginality, singing the title song: 'On the way to a Bran Nue Dae/ Everybody everybody say ...' (p. 84). It has lots of humour, dancing and singing in a splendid appropriation of white music-theatre traditions. In its many tours the exuberant chorus of black singers and dancers were its real stars.

Another musical play, Roger Bennett's *Funerals and Circuses* (1992), also explores black-white relations in a small town but, as the title suggests, with a much starker juxtaposition of the grim and the cheerful, in style as much as in content. In an inversion of Dorothy Hewett's *The Man From Mukinupin*, the dark side of town is in this case the white area. Like Davis's *No Sugar*, it was first done as a promenade production with the audience moving from location to location. Again, everyone is related to everyone else.

After an opening pub scene in which a rascally Aboriginal trickster Joseph gets himself barred by a racist white bouncer Kev, the action moves into a chapel for the wedding of Ben, an artist and Aboriginal elder, to Nona, the white daughter of the local cop, Graham. The town setting for the ensuing scenes clearly demarcates the whites on one

14. ABORIGINAL THEATRE

side of the street and blacks on the other. During a night of wedding partying and romancing, a feeling of foreboding begins to grow. A young black boy goes missing and Ben's young daughter Jessie goes off to the bush to grieve for her birth mother. The following morning the town wakes up to find that the boy's body has been found, supposedly accidentally drowned but in fact murdered.

After interval a cheerful talent night, in which the audience are invited to participate, is interrupted by the boy's funeral procession. The tension leads to violence and Joseph is arrested. In the bush away from town Jessie is brutally raped by three hooded KKK figures, one of whom turns out to be Kev. Nona appeals to her father to do something to stop the violence, as Joseph rushes back to town to kill Kev. The others follow and find Kev barricaded in his mum's store. He shoots himself, and so, perhaps, the tensions are resolved. The play ends with the town waking up again, as it did after the wild post-wedding party night, when all the violence began. The songs by Paul Kelly, who played a role in the original production, were a large part of the show's appeal. It has an odd stylistic mix—full of life and death, light and dark.

A new generation of Aboriginal writers and performers emerged in the second half of the 1990s, spurred in part by the political events of the times and the reports of the Wootten Royal Commission into Aboriginal Deaths in Custody and *Bringing Them Home*, the report of the Wilson Inquiry in 1997 into what came to be known as the Stolen Generation.[4] The new work was also prompted by new post-realist forms of theatre and, in particular, by the 1997 Festival of the Dreaming, the first of a series of arts festivals funded by the Sydney Organising Committee of the Olympic Games in the lead-up to the 2000 Olympics. The Festival was directed by Rhoda Roberts, who picked up Brisbane's Kooemba Jdarra production of *The 7 Stages of Grieving*, by Wesley Enoch and Deborah Mailman, and put it together with newly commissioned shows—Leah Purcell's *Box the Pony*, Deborah Cheetham's *White Baptist Abba Fan* and Ningali Lawford's *Ningali*—to make up a highly successful program of solo performances called *Wimmin's Business*. Other productions at Roberts's festival included Roger Bennett's *Up the Ladder*, about Aboriginal tent-show

BELONGING

boxers, and white writer Julie Janson's *Black Mary*, about the black partner of legendary white bushranger Captain Thunderbolt.

Box the Pony (1997) was a virtuoso show about Purcell's upbringing in the country town of Murgon in rural Queensland, 'up'ome'der'. Purcell, who started out in *Bran Nue Dae* and subsequently became a television presenter, actor, singer and writer, wrote the script with Big hART's Scott Rankin. She presents as a proud black chick from the sticks who has made it in the big city and tells the story of her abused friend Steff.[5] The show is a mixture of comic storytelling, direct audience address and thumbnail performance portraits of a great range of characters from both their stories.

Although told in Purcell's cheerfully assertive comic style, Steff's story is increasingly harrowing, as she boxes a punching bag that stands in for all the people who have abused her. She has an alcoholic mother and is surrounded by rough men and boys, from whom she learns fighting, boxing, drinking and sex. When her mother dies, her abusive boyfriend, the father of her baby Jess, moves in and regularly bashes her. She flees and hides, and starts to work overtime as a packer at the local abattoir to save petrol money to get away. The boyfriend, seeking revenge, has her beloved pony killed and sends its cut-up flesh down the conveyer belt to her on the meat-packing line, for a different sort of boxing. Despairing of her old life, she flees again. With Jess in her car, she decides to crash into a tree and kill them both, but at the last minute has a vision of her grandfather's horse and decides to battle on. At this point we realise that Steff is in fact Leah, and the proud confident woman that Purcell has become is telling her own story.

Tammy Anderson's *I Don't Wanna Play House* (2002) is a solo show in a similar style, in which Anderson played a range of characters from her past, starting when she was eight, with an abusive alcoholic white stepfather and several comic bittersweet upheavals, each of which ends in them returning to Nan's house.

The most influential solo Indigenous woman's show is Deborah Mailman and Wesley Enoch's *The 7 Stages of Grieving* (1995). In his introduction to the published script, Enoch writes that it was modelled on Elizabeth Kübler-Ross's Five Stages of Grief (p. 15). Mailman played an Everywoman figure, grieving for and celebrating all that her

14. ABORIGINAL THEATRE

people and her family had lost since white invasion. Extensive tours and revivals, and the education syllabuses, have given this extraordinarily powerful piece considerable exposure.

The set of the original production was a red-earth grave in the middle of a great circle of black powder surrounded by a thin ring of white. Mailman was dressed in a simple white slip which, during the course of the show, became coloured by earth and dust. Over the grave, suspended by seven ropes, there was a block of ice, which slowly melted, dripping onto the earth like falling tears.

In the performance a series of memories, projections and vivid stage images lead through the seven stages of Aboriginal experience: Dreaming, Invasion, Genocide, Protection, Assimilation, Self-Determination and Reconciliation. The play opens with The Woman wailing in grief as, one after another, words of emotion are projected onto a screen, ending with 'I feel nothing'. She performs a smoking ceremony and tells the story of her Nana's death and how the mob gathered together to celebrate her life and mourn. She introduces a suitcase full of old photographs, some of which are projected. She tells us how she is preparing to grieve for her battling father. The European alphabet is projected on her dress, which she takes off in an attempt to scrape off the letters, but they continue to flicker over her body. She recites an invasion poem and delivers a stand-up routine about being black and proud, but harassed.

She returns to Nana's funeral and tells the story of Aunty Grace, who married a white man and has been in England for fifty years. Aunty Grace came back but she didn't cry, aloof and distant now from the mob. But on their way to the airport Mailman's persona visits the grave with her, and Grace, crying at last, empties the suitcase and starts to fill it with red earth.

The Woman tells the story of the death in custody of Daniel Yocke and the silent grieving protest march afterwards. Then, in the most powerful scene of the performance, she tries to explain traditional Aboriginal kinship patterns using handfuls of earth, sweeping them away to show the devastation that is caused when you take away the children. She tells the story of her brother, having a hard, shamed time of it. The performance arrives at the last stage, Reconciliation, with a

BELONGING

great deal of uncertainty and ambivalence. The Woman's last words are, again, 'I feel nothing'.

In his introduction to the published text Enoch reflected on the Davis tradition:

> Historically, Indigenous writers have focused on appropriating the western forms of theatre to create the drama, incorporating the elements of dance, advanced metaphor and use of language to highlight the writing's Aboriginality. An over-reliance on character and the denial of abstraction has often created a situation where the writing is perceived as unsophisticated and/or primarily issue-based, outside of artistic scrutiny. *The 7 Stages of Grieving* wishes to challenge this history. (p.15)

The 7 Stages of Grieving was the first great Aboriginal work to mix traditional and contemporary arts to create a new culturally hybrid form of performance. Later Enoch wrote the musical play *The Sunshine Club*, about an Aboriginal dance hall, and produced another musical written by Tony Briggs, *The Sapphires*, about an Indigenous band that toured the battlefields of Vietnam in the late 1960s. These happy works with a serious edge, in the style of *Bran Nue Dae*, were followed by the Indigenous appropriation of a Greek classic, *Black Medea*, reworking Euripides' tragedy and making Medea an Aboriginal woman who has betrayed her people and her traditions for the sake of a violent and abusive urbanised black Jason. In Enoch's version she kills her son not out of revenge, but to prevent him from becoming like his father.

By the late 1990s, with growing public debates about the Stolen Generation and the Reconciliation movement, Aboriginal playwriting was established and influential. Jane Harrison's *Stolen* (1998), originally developed and produced by the Ilbijerri Aboriginal and Torres Strait Islander Theatre Co-operative, was taken up by Playbox Theatre in Melbourne and toured widely. Based on extensive interviews with people who had been stolen from their families, it is a moving, quasi-documentary drama that follows into adulthood the lives of five of them, exploring their traumas and, in a few cases, their victories. It has had a long life as a school text.

The title of Dallas Winmar's *Aliwa!* (2002) means 'Watch out!', a cry of mothers when the police came to take their children away.

14. ABORIGINAL THEATRE

The play is about the Nyoongah family of Jack Davis and his sister Aunty Dot Collard, who was played by Mailman, but who appeared as herself in Neil Armfield's 2001 production, commenting sardonically from the sidelines. The family struggles to stay together as they battle against the intrusive and oppressive 'protection' offered by the white bureaucrats who try to implement the government's policy of assimilation. The play is a joyful, mischievous celebration of memories of black family and community life, as was John Harding's earlier family comedy-drama, *Up the Road* (1991), about the emotional and cultural distance that separates an urban black bureaucrat from his country-town family when he returns after ten years to attend the funeral of his beloved Uncle. *Up the Road* is awkwardly written, but it was given an extraordinarily lively and joyously stirring production by Armfield which turned the performers' onstage cheerfulness into a celebration of Aboriginal survival.

Andrea James's *Yanagai! Yanagai!* (2003) is a passionate play that reclaims traditions in a magic realist style. It is ostensibly about the failed 2002 land rights claim of the Yorta Yorta people on the Dhungula (the Murray River) but its reach goes well beyond contemporary history. Like *The 7 Stages of Grieving*, it is a hybrid work, telling in intercut scenes a magical story of a traditional woman/warrior, Munarra, who is sent from the skies to heal her land which has been desecrated by the white invaders. These are represented by the sinister, ghostly, comic-savage figure of Sir Edward Curr, an early 'pioneer' whom Munarra pursues like a reluctantly avenging angel and eventually traps.

Meanwhile Lyall, a young urban black activist, seeks out Uncle, an elder. Uncle just wants to fish in Dhungula, but Lyall thinks he can use his memories in the Yorta Yorta claim he is fighting in the white courts. Uncle remembers when he swam the river as a child with his sister Mae to escape the black Welfare cars sent to take them away. Mae was swept away by the river. They lose the court case because there is no paper-trail for their claim. At the end Munarra returns to the river to assert the presence of her people.

In early 2002 Iljiberri and Playbox produced a festival of Indigenous theatre, *Blak Inside*, which included Anderson's *I Don't Wanna Play House*, Maryanne Sam's *Casting Doubts*, about issues of the

BELONGING

authentic 'look' of Aboriginal actors in the film industry and Tracey Rigney's *Belonging*, about, among other things, black-white issues in the relationship between a pair of school friends. The season also included Jadah Milroy's *Crow Fire*, John Harding's *Enuff* and Richard J. Frankland's *Conversations with the Dead*.

Like *Up the Road*, *Crowfire* is about the conflicts between urban and bush Aboriginality, but done here from a city perspective. It centres on the relationship between a disillusioned Aboriginal Affairs bureaucrat, Dayna, and her scornful activist boyfriend, Tony. Dayna is inspired by her Dreaming spirit, Crow, and she roams the streets dressed as him. Meanwhile Yungi, a traditional man from the desert, has come to the city seeking help for his community, but he gets into heroin (represented by the White Lady, also a symbol of the city) and dies without returning. The white characters are Wallace, a disillusioned banker yearning for something more out of life, and his politician wife Sharon, drinking heavily and struggling to battle on professionally. Their lives all cross as they move about the city. In the end Dayna goes off to the desert to try to help her people and Tony stays behind, having lost her.

Harding's *Enuff* was the first play to confront the mystery in Aboriginal politics as to why, aside from the frontier wars of the early nineteenth century, represented by Yagan in Davis's *Kullark*, there has never been any violent resistance movement. The play is set in 2028 and imagines a savage black revolution led by cynical international mercenaries who suddenly abandon their Aboriginal recruits when the going gets tough. A confused play, it is nonetheless boldly conceived.

Conversations with the Dead is a passionate, anguished and personal work by Richard J. Frankland, who was a senior advisor to the 1988 Royal Commission into Aboriginal Deaths in Custody. The play centres on Jack, a young Aboriginal man who suddenly finds himself working for the Commission investigating the deaths. He talks to bereaved families and then, as he gets drawn into the whole whitefella business of the inquiry, tries to intervene and prevent further deaths. He loses his family and is branded a collaborator as he internalises the pain of his people, in what he learns to call 'cases'. In his despair he gets violently drunk, lashes out at white strangers and cuts himself. He

14. ABORIGINAL THEATRE

becomes a conduit for the ninety-nine human stories investigated by the Commission—the dead with whom he is having the conversations. The published script is rambling and difficult to read, but Wesley Enoch's 2003 production for Company B concentrated it into a tight 90 minutes.

The *Blak Inside* season, for all its faults, revealed a new sensibility in Aboriginal playwriting—especially a new interest in what Enoch was later to call 'black on black' issues, in which the solidarity of the first wave of black writing was set aside and writers began to explore differences and problems within the previously homogenous conception of what it meant to be part of the Aboriginal 'community'.[6]

The development of a strong voice in Aboriginal drama can be traced through the titles. In the languages *kullark* means 'home', *barungin* means 'smell the wind' and *coordah* means 'brother'. *Aliwa!* means 'watch out!' and *yanagai!*—supposedly the first recorded word spoken to white men by the Yorta Yorta people—means something close to 'fuck off!'. And, like 'fuck off!' everywhere, it could be made to mean, 'tell me why you're here, let's talk'.[7]

White writers

Katharine Susannah Prichard, Vance Palmer and George Landen Dann were notable among the early white playwrights who dealt with black-white relations, and their work has been discussed above. Later works include three linked one-act plays about Truganini, said to have been the last 'full-blood' in Tasmania, written by Bill Reed in 1970; and Thomas Keneally's *Bullie's House*, a tough drama of black-white confrontation, staged at the Nimrod in 1980. The latter concerns a traditional man living on an island mission who, in a gesture of potlatch, exposes sacred objects, the *ranga* of his people, to white officials. He expects his gift to be reciprocated with the gift of European knowledge, represented for him by the treasures of the British Museum. Too late he learns that imperial authority doesn't reside in a box of books.

David Malouf's *Blood Relations* (1987) is a fine and extravagantly conceived version of *The Tempest*, a classic postcolonial retelling of Australian and European myths full of ambivalence and ghosts. The

BELONGING

patriarch Willy McGregor was a young boy when he left the Greek island where he was born to come to the world's biggest island but furthest outpost. Now 73 and a wealthy businessman, he lives reclusively on the wild northern coast of Western Australia in a house crowded with ancient, but still not unpacked, crates from his homeland. Also in his retreat are his housekeeper Hilda, his half-Aboriginal son Dinny and his daughter Cathy. The crates turn out to contain stones from the wall that hemmed him in as a child on his Greek island. Like many migrants he has, in this case literally, carried his prison with him from the other side of the world.

White writing about Indigenous issues began to fall away during the Davis years, however, as a sensitivity about authenticity and a feeling that black writers should be allowed to tell their own story came to the fore. In the early 1990s a number of white writers returned to these themes, not to speak on behalf of Indigenous people, as had the writers of the 1930s and 1940s, but to explore black-white relationships. Like many of the early plays, Eric Earley's *The Custodians* (1993) is set in a small country town with a large Aboriginal population and a mission. It is a good piece of socialist activist realism. The central character, Maria Giotto, a policewoman who has faced discrimination in her city career because of her ethnicity, volunteers for a posting in a racist town after the Aboriginal women elders request a woman constable. She befriends Paul, a bitter young Aboriginal man who, after a drunken brawl in the local pub, is beaten up by one of her police colleagues and dies in jail. The play ends with an order from the central authorities to cover it up.

Ned Manning's *Close to the Bone* (1991), a family saga about the stolen generation, was reworked in his later play *Luck of the Draw* (1999). It spans forty-six years, from 1944, when the central character Annie is taken from her war-hero Aboriginal father as a young child, till 1990, when Annie, mentally unbalanced by her terrible experiences, is movingly reunited with her daughter, Pearl. Pearl, also stolen, has grown up in the city and become a successful lawyer.

Martin Buzacott's *Kingaroy* (1994) is a bizarre, carnivalesque version of the old station-dramas. Rhett and Mercy live together on their horse-breeding property. Rhett has invited onto his land the local

14. ABORIGINAL THEATRE

rodeo championship, which takes place offstage during the play. He is a former Country and Western singer; part Aboriginal, but he doesn't like to talk about that; and also a Vietnam veteran with an alarming collection of guns. He seems to be preparing to use these on a crowd of religious fundamentalists who have gathered outside his homestead to protest his relationship with Mercy. Since they believe Mercy to be his daughter, they see this as incest.

Various strange characters arrive, including Waylon, an Aboriginal rodeo star, and Mrs Highfields, his partner (apparently) and manager. Charlotte Cooyar is a respectable local woman sent to negotiate by the leader of the religious protesters, Miss Lumley. During the course of the play, however, she is converted to their wild ways, and falls in love with Doctor Eddy, a weird doctor who narrates the play at the opening of each act. Like Rhett, he is a Vietnam veteran, and the two of them briefly join forces to scare away the protesters by shooting at them.

As in *Bran Nue Dae*, but in a much darker tone, it turns out in the end that nearly everyone is related: Mercy is, in fact, Rhett's daughter, the result of a drunken one-night stand many years earlier and her mother turns out to be Mrs Highfields, then a Sister in a strict local convent out on a drunken spree. Miss Lumley turns out to be the former Mother Superior of the convent, whose lies have forced the family apart. And Waylon is the son of Mrs Highfields and Rhett— she had twins. The ending is a grand and crazy family reunion and reconciliation.

Several other plays explore the workings of the legal system. Rodney Hall's *A Return to the Brink* (1999) is a political drama about the court case that followed the notorious Myall Creek massacre of blacks in the 1830s. Tony Strachan's *State of Shock* (1986) is based on the story of Alwyn Peter, who murdered his girlfriend, but was eventually released after basing his defence on the appalling conditions he faced when he was removed from his land to a mission. In the play Eddie Thomas and his girlfriend Doreen dream of leaving the Cheka Aboriginal Reserve in far north Queensland—either to return to their traditional land or, Doreen's preference, to go down to Brisbane, where they might have a fridge. Eddie's grandmother, Mrs Jenny Bob, is Chair of the Cheka Aborigine Council and a local activist. She has

BELONGING

the ear of Bernie O'Connor, a white public servant based in Brisbane, who comes up to the Cape country regularly, partly because he wants to run for Parliament and partly, it emerges, because he likes the young black women. Eddie is a disturbed and violent man, and at the end of Act 1, in a fit of drunken jealousy provoked by O'Connor, he kills Doreen.

In Act 2 we learn of the campaign mounted for his defence. He is silently grieving in prison and wants to be punished. Jenny Bob visits him and in their imaginations they fly over their land, seeing the abject condition of their people. Eddie decides to cooperate. We learn at the end that the appeal has been successful, and Eddie is rehabilitated.

Though a rather messily structured play, it is passionately written and strong, not only in its material, but also in its desire to educate and reform. Following its Company B production in 1989, it had a success as a theatre-in-education piece with Toe Truck Theatre, and again, in 1999, in a production by the Riverina Theatre Company that toured to Adelaide and Sydney.

Strachan's earlier play, *Eyes of the Whites* (1981), is one of the few Australian plays about Papua New Guinea. (A later one was Adam May's *Rising Fish Prayer* in 1993.) It is a powerful piece of realism about Australian colonialism in PNG on the verge of independence, with big-business interests about to move in and take over where the official government control is about to leave off. In the climactic scene, Yulli, the Nigerian World Health Organisation representative, disarms Peter, the angry nationalist Pangu Pati candidate, and prevents him from killing Tom, the representative of Australian imperialism. 'Don't destroy your own future', he says. 'Train your anger. Don't kill him, replace him' (p. 54).

Nicholas Parsons's *Dead Heart* (1993) is a compellingly written play—a tough drama about race relations in an isolated settlement west of Alice Springs, ruled over spiritually by Poppy, an old Aboriginal man. Its central concern is the struggle between 'blackpalla' and 'watpalla' law as Poppy does battle with Ray, the white policeman. Ray, who initially allows traditional punishments, changes his tune when an Aboriginal teacher's aide is killed because he has taken his white mistress to a sacred site. Ray, rightly, suspects the killer to be a

14. ABORIGINAL THEATRE

traditional desert-living young man who has been egged on by Poppy. He arrests the young man, but he escapes and Ray, a bit deranged by now, chases him into the desert where he disappears. Ray is destroyed and the settlement abandoned in a flurry of media attention. Poppy, who has been telling the whole story to two mysterious black men over a game of cards, has won—whether as a trickster or a shaman we never really know.

The dramatic representation of Indigenous Australians has changed to an extraordinary extent since the English invasion—from the stereotypes of the nineteenth-century melodrama; via the sympathetically portrayed outsider figures of the mid-twentieth-century drama, written mostly by middle-class white authors; to the upsurge of Indigenous writers and performance makers since the mid 1970s. The key political issues have been about authority and authenticity. As in the cases of the dramas of identity politics, we can ask: who has the right to speak, on behalf of whom? The remarkable change in Aboriginal theatre, from the more or less realist comedy-dramas of the 1970s to the eclectic and sophisticated performance styles of the 1990s and early 2000s, has been one of the great success stories of the Australian drama.

15
PLAYWRIGHTS IN THE 90S

'Australian Drama' as a cohesive idea emerged at the beginning of the twentieth century, was institutionalised by advocates, notably Leslie Rees, in the middle years, and reinvented during the New Wave. It was challenged during the rise of identity and community-based drama in the 1980s, and by the end of the century it had all but died. The playwrights who rose to prominence in the 1990s include some of the best of the century. However, while for convenience they may be placed into groups—as they are here—there were no more new waves. Amidst debates about globalised culture and new cultural flows, playwrights stopped coalescing around discourses of nationhood or identity, although in many cases their work can be linked back to the genres, traditions and tropes already discussed. For most of the 90s, until political changes and events at the turn of the century brought them together, Australian playwrights no longer shared a sense of common purpose.

A new group of women playwrights, including Hannie Rayson, Tobsha Learner and Joanna Murray-Smith, wrote about middle-class professional women's experience, but not exclusively, and certainly not as part of a movement or program. Debra Oswald and Katherine Thomson wrote dramas of working-class experience which had their roots in the social realism of some mid-century plays.

BELONGING

There was a resurgence in verbatim theatre, including Alana Valentine's *Run Rabbit Run* (2004), about the struggles of a Sydney Rugby League club against the commercialisation of their sport. In *Parramatta Girls* (2007), Valentine used verbatim research to create a documentary drama. The play told the stories of women incarcerated in the notorious Parramatta Girls Home in Sydney who return for a reunion, and finally find some peace.

There was also a revival of the bush-gothic dramas at this time, including Kathryn Ash's *Flutter* (2004), a brooding magical thriller set in far north Queensland. It is a genre that dates back to Esson's *Shipwreck*, was nodded at by Anthony Coburn and Alan Seymour (in *The Bastard Country* and *Swamp Creatures*, respectively) and developed by Beatrix Christian in the 1990s.

In fact Christian's epic drama of colonisation, racism and incest, *The Governor's Family*—which has never been revived or published since its premiere in 1997—is one of the most unjustly neglected plays of the 1990s. Her earlier play *Blue Murder* (1994), a surreal urban gothic poetic drama based on the Bluebeard story and full of powerful Freudian imagery and myth, is one of the best plays about female desire and subjugation written in Australia. Christian has also written *Fred* (1998) and *Old Masters* (2000), both of which had mainstream success; and the screenplay for the award-winning 2006 film *Jindabyne*.[1]

Hilary Bell's *Fortune* (1993), a wild play about Chang, an 11-year-old Chinese giant kept as a slave and exhibited as a freak around the goldfields in the 1860s, is another savage revisiting of the colonial legend. Chang is the only Australian-born character in the play and at the end he transcends the brutality of his experience and seems to have found a way to go on. Bell's *Wolf Lullaby* (1996) is a dark drama about a 9-year-old girl, haunted by a Wolf-figure, who may or may not have murdered a small child, and the ramifications this has for the way in which adults—especially, in this case, her parents—think about childhood. Both Christian and Bell bring an extraordinarily vivid theatrical imagination to their reconceptualisation of national and personal myths and stories.

As Rachel Fensham and Denise Varney argue, women playwrights joined the mainstream in the 1990s, but other developments also

15. PLAYWRIGHTS IN THE 90S

contributed to the new tenor of Australian theatre. Michael Gurr produced a fine series of political human dramas. In Melbourne Andrew Bovell and Daniel Keene wrote with savagery about the experience of a new urban underclass created by the new cold-hearted economic times.

Given this, it may seem odd to talk of the decline of the playwright, but the profession has faced a number of pressures. Like all artsworkers, playwrights suffered in the 1990s when economic rationalism was suddenly and irrationally imposed on mainstream theatres. Many theatre companies lost a battle they should never have fought when they accepted that they were part of an 'industry'. This forced them increasingly to share productions and led them, inevitably, to 'downsize', if they could not find non-government sponsorship. For playwrights, downsizing meant smaller casts, narrative constraints and fewer expressive opportunities.

Artistic Directors and Festival Directors exercised a new dominance as did a new generation of directors and designers. At its best this has led to exciting new work by a handful of auteurs inspired by the extraordinary work of Barrie Kosky, and by new models of theatre-making in which the playwrights became members of creative teams. For fifteen years, until 2005, when it was renamed the Malthouse after its venue, Melbourne's Playbox Theatre had produced only new Australian plays. Under the direction of Michael Kantor the company redefined the idea of 'a new Australian work' to include Australian revisionings of classic texts, not necessarily dramatic ones. In a similar vein, Barrie Kosky's eight-hour epic *The Lost Echo*, based on stories from Ovid and including, almost incidentally, a complete production of Euripides' *The Bacchae*, was a triumph for STC in 2006. It remains one of the most important and influential productions of the new century.

In short, as the old art-form divisions were challenged by new cultural formations and, particularly, by new non-text-based performance forms in the 1990s, playwrights became less important in Australian theatre. With the rise of physical approaches to performance-making, for instance, the writer, where there is one, contributes text in a process led by other creative collaborators. Such work lies outside the scope of this book, however, and two examples will have to serve here.² In both cases texts and related documents are published, along with some commentary, in Richard James Allen and Karen Pearlman's 1999 anthology *Performing the Unnameable*, which includes samples and some texts of a wide range of performance work.³

The first is from The Sydney Front, whose influential productions between 1986 and 1993 explored relationships of desire and power using the interaction between performers and spectators. Their *First and Last Warning* engaged its audience directly in the experience of being in the space. It started with a double segregation of the audience, first into men and women, and then into an 'elite', who paid extra in order not to have to take their clothes off, and an 'ordinary', which had to change into black nylon slips. The performers, who were similarly dressed, performed a number of actions that gradually drew the audience into negotiations of power, culminating in the building of a wall of cardboard boxes between the 'elite' and the 'ordinary'. Other Sydney Front productions, such as *Don Juan* and *The Pornography of Performance*, also explored and exploited a mutual gaze between performer and spectator, partly about desire and partly about power.⁴

The second example is Josephine Wilson and Erin Hefferon's *The Geography of Haunted Places* (1994), a complex performance drawing on eighteenth-century exploration and nineteenth-century anthropology, filtered through postcolonial perspectives on the appropriation of the New World and relating its images to the economic imperatives of colonisation. Hefferon's performance played games with the audience, personifying and eroticising imperialism, turning the nineteenth-century scientific museum collection of specimens, all killed and stuffed, into something akin to a child's enthusiasm for the soft toys in her bedroom.

Jenny Kemp

A writer whose work bridges the worlds of theatre and contemporary performance is Jenny Kemp, a director, theatrical auteur and teacher who has done more than any other theatre-worker to reconfigure the aesthetic and formal ways in which the Australian theatre has

15. PLAYWRIGHTS IN THE 90S

presented the subjectivity of women. Her work is a poetic, visual and (with composer Elizabeth Drake) musical theatre of interiority, in which the effects of story and social realism are subsumed in a multi-register series of texts, images and scenes as women's inner worlds are performed. It dwells on domestic detail, with a non-linear narrative style that draws in memories, dreams and myths.

Kemp divides the inner life of her women characters among several stage figures, numbered or defined in performance by simple dress signs. *Call of the Wild* (1989), for example, includes Woman in Green Skirt, Woman in Pale Hat and others. They are all aspects of a single performed subject, split theatrically. Even more than with most playwrights, it is impossible to separate the written text from the complete performance.[5]

Remember (1993) explores the inner experience of a woman named Moderna, who has been violently raped. Moderna has two stage presences: Moderna One, who is in hospital recovering from her physical and psychological injuries, and Moderna Two, a figure who enacts her memories, in a vast Strindbergian house with rooms that are compartments of her mind. There are other figures who perform her dreams, and perhaps the mythic consciousness of her womanhood, but everything that happens on stage is filtered through Moderna. The work revolves around a persistent act that is performed jointly by Moderna One and Moderna Two—shooting her rapist with the gun he used to rape her. It is never clear whether this is a memory or a dream, but at the end the gentleness of her relationship with her patient man, Jack, perhaps brings peace.

The Black Sequin Dress (1996) is a collage of swirling theatrical impressions around the events of a single evening. A Woman, played in four different personas, gets up in the night, puts on a black sequin dress and travels by train into the city to go to a night-club. She walks in, then slips and falls. A Waiter helps her up, leads her to a table and gives her a glass of water. She stays there for a little while.

In terms of everyday incident, this is all that happens, but the work stages, again in a surrealist style, resonances of these events. A vivid sequence of images, scenes and encounters explores the Woman's subjective experience and the interconnections between her inner life

BELONGING

and the outer world. There are childhood memories of her mother lying, fallen, on the lino in the kitchen; fantasy conversations with the Waiter, increasingly erotically charged; memories of a Man she has perhaps met on the train, or maybe has known for a long time, or might have dreamt; and a narrative of Undine, probably another version of the Woman, who walks through a desert landscape into wooded country and finally into the city.

The Woman's entrance into the nightclub is enacted nine times. Each has a different context and different emotions, and the formal enactment sets off new scenes like ripples in a pond. A key metaphor is Brownian motion—the complex behaviour of moving molecules interacting in a fluid. This becomes an image for the apparently chaotic ways in which everything we experience in the exterior world is accompanied by an interior monologue made up of a complex interplay of previous impressions and desires.

The Woman's journey to the nightclub and back also has a mythic dimension. Some of the ripple scenes evoke a journey across the River Styx into the Underworld. Towards the end of the work there is a revolt, and perhaps a resolution, as the Woman sees the realities of her brick-walled suburban life in a new way and appears to accept something inside her self. She is ovulating. 'The inside was the outside, she remembered' (p. 55). In the final re-enactment of her entrance into the nightclub she does not fall.

Still Angela (2002) also has four actors performing one woman, this time Angela at different ages. This work is like a development of Undine's journey, but in the opposite direction. A suburban woman, with memories of her childhood and experiences as an adult, embarks on a train journey into the desert. Scenes from her suburban life with her husband are played out, as the three adult Angelas bring their different responses and inner thoughts to their daily life. There is another seductive Waiter, this time on the train, and mysterious men from Angela's past or from her fantasies—we cannot say which, or rather, we are invited to choose. A Child version of Angela, performed by a dancer with a voice-over, haunts the piece. The metaphor this time is a chess game. *Still Angela* is a more ambiguous work than *The Black Sequin Dress*, but Angela's sensual and excited return from the

15. PLAYWRIGHTS IN THE 90S

desert at the end, to a carnival fortieth birthday party, feels like a kind of triumph.

Kemp uses new forms and explores a different subjectivity, but she picks up and transforms the Patrick White tradition of infusing mundane life in the suburbs with an emotional spirituality. As the stolidly earthbound Landlord says, in White's *The Ham Funeral*, written in 1947, 'This table is love, if you can get to know it'.

Hannie Rayson

Hannie Rayson is a much more traditional playwright of ideas, increasingly taking part in public discussion of political issues, but she started out as a naturalistic dramatist of middle-class mores. In the mid-1980s she was sometimes referred to as a female David Williamson, to the annoyance, apparently, of both. Even though she has written some of the most interesting scenarios of the late-twentieth-century drama, her characters are often functional, like Williamson's, serving a satirical or issue-based dramaturgy that is driven by argument and, especially, by plot. Her three most successful plays are *Hotel Sorrento*, *Life After George* and *Inheritance*.

Her first published play, *Mary*, a solidly researched contribution to the multicultural theatre of the mid-1980s, has already been discussed. Her next, *Room to Move* (1985), is a light comedy that looks at the earnest, but mostly inadequate, response of decent men to feminism, in which a number of men find that, like their women, they have what Betty Friedman called a 'problem without a name'. When an elderly, motherly widow, Peggy, skips a generation and takes in a young man as a boarder, it provokes a series of crises in the marriages of her grown-up children. The play tries to link social issues to individual stories, something that soon became the author's trademark.[6]

Hotel Sorrento (1990) was Rayson's first mainstream success, a thoughtful survey of Australian intellectual and cultural life in the 1970s and 1980s, told through the concerns and feelings of interesting and affecting characters. It deals with many of the issues of the cultural cringe and Australian nationalism already raised in this book.

BELONGING

Hilary lives with Wal, her father, and Troy, her 16-year-old son, in the old family home in Sorrento, a seaside Victorian town. Her sister Meg is a successful novelist who lives in London with her very English husband Edwin. Meg's new book *Melancholy* has just been short-listed for the Booker Prize. The youngest sister, Pip, a successful advertising executive who lives in New York, has returned to Australia on a business trip. When Meg decides to visit home, the three sisters are reunited after many years.

Unconnected to the family are Marge and Dick from Melbourne who occasionally spend weekends at Marge's holiday house in Sorrento. They are not lovers but old friends. Marge has read and been profoundly affected by *Melancholy*. Dick is a cynical old leftie who edits a serious newspaper and writes articles about Australian politics and society.

At first, scenes from these separate worlds are intercut but gradually they merge. At the end of Act 1, while swimming with Troy, Wal dies unexpectedly in the sea. Suddenly everything is up in the air.

The three sisters have unfinished business concerning Hilary's husband, who was killed when his car crashed into a tree. It emerges that he was having an affair with Pip, and that Meg also loved him. Could it be that he committed suicide? Troy, in particular, is trying to unravel the secrets of his troubled family. Amid this, there is a great deal of discussion about issues of the Australian colonial mentality and the need for independence from England.

The ending is moving, as revelations tumble out. The three sisters have never talked about the things that matter most deeply to them, but they appear in Meg's highly personal book which is based in the lives of the family. It is a neat play in which personal dramas throw up issues of belonging, yearning, alienation and loss—migrant issues translated into a drama of middle-class Anglo-Australian professional expatriates.

Falling from Grace (1994) is a well-crafted, highly contrived drama about Brock, Susannah and Maggie, three friends who work together on a magazine. Brock, the features writer, is happily married and pregnant. She wants to publish an article on a pioneering new drug to treat pre-menstrual syndrome which Miriam, an idealistic medical

15. PLAYWRIGHTS IN THE 90S

researcher, has developed. However Susannah, the magazine's editor, holds the story over when her ex-husband, a doctor, claims that the drug produces thalidomide-like birth defects. When it turns out that Susannah is having an affair with Miriam's husband, the personal and moral issues become intricately entangled. They are resolved, finally, when sub-editor Maggie, a comically bitter and witty single mother, leaks the scandal to the tabloid press. This brings them together in a celebration of women's friendship, just in time for the birth of Brock's baby. The happy sisterhood gathered around the birthing table makes for a bleak ending as, uncaringly, they leave the visionary Miriam's career and marriage in tatters.

In 1996, together with Andrew Bovell, Rayson wrote *Scenes from a Separation*, in which two characters tell different versions of the end of their marriage. The first half is Mathew's version, written by Bovell, and the second half Nina's, written by Rayson. Although there are other, offsider characters—family and new lovers—the focus remains fixed on Mathew and Nina. They continue to love each other, as they struggle to figure out what they want for themselves and what they are prepared, or not prepared, to do for each other. There is a neat, slightly tricky, repetition of key scenes, when Nina gets to rewrite some of the contentious moments. The play is written as an open narrative into which audiences can insert their own experience. STC produced a revised version in 2004.

Competitive Tenderness (1996) is a wild, rather elaborately plotted, satirical farce about local council corruption and the effects of a tough new economic-rationalist management style on a pleasantly shambling bunch of council workers. In an odd way it harks back to Buzo's *The Front Room Boys* and *Tom*, but without the frightening absurdist undertone. Dawn Snow, a Thatcherite character who claims to have made her name reforming the Ugandan police service, is appointed CEO of the city of Greater Burke. There she meets and tries to tame a crazy collection of characters, some with visions of what should be done for the community and others with visions of what should done for themselves. She tries to institute a new regime, but there is considerable trickster resistance and mayhem, partly prompted by Delia, the canny receptionist. Dawn has a comic

BELONGING

affair with the incompetent Mayor, Brian Guest, and tries to bring in the local Macedonian smallgoods manufacturer Dragi Smilevski to support her 'reforms'. There are machinations over the sale of the Neighbourhood Centre, and with the corrupt Minister for Local Government, Kimble Farkley, and others. There is a lot of mad business with a savage pit-bull terrier, owned by Dawn, and lots of running in and out of doors and hiding in cupboards. It all ends in chaos, but with Dawn rising.

Rayson's most complex play is *Life After George* (2000), another carefully plotted human drama in which emotions ebb and flow within a group of characters, each of whom represents an idea and a cultural era. It focuses on three women, each the 'it' girl of her generation, and a fourth, the neglected daughter of a 'great man'. In telling this story it raises, again, issues of the social and cultural impact of economic rationalism—in this case, on universities.

As the play opens, Peter George, a world-famous intellectual and old-fashioned liberal rebellious academic, has recently died. His three wives, his daughter and his best friend from way back gather during the lead-up to his funeral. We meet the women through a sequence of interconnected addresses to the audience, flashbacks and present scenes. His first wife, Beatrix, is old-school, an artist, pre-feminist, whom he dragged to Melbourne from Europe and then left. She has her own life now, content to put the past behind her, but drawn reluctantly back into it by George's death. He left Beatrix for his second wife, Lindsay, once his radical-feminist PhD student, but now a tough careerist academic in the new corporatised world of university management. His third wife, Poppy, is a new-generation post-feminist, who grieves sincerely and passionately for him, but is excluded, now that he is dead, by the weight of the past and the older women. We also meet Ana, his daughter, who in her own tortured way has carried on his vision by dropping out and denying her talent as a musician. We don't meet David, the estranged son who is on a personal mission of his own in India. The best friend Duffy, a gentle amiable character, is the conduit by which the women communicate.

Duffy provides the background to the mystery aspect of the plot. George has died in a plane crash flying Duffy's plane to their

15. PLAYWRIGHTS IN THE 90S

jointly-owned retreat on Flinders Island. The key revelations—each of which prompts the four women to some radical re-evaluation—are that when he died he was with a woman, and that the woman was not, as everyone assumed, yet another young lover, but a long lost daughter. The daughter's mother is Lindsay, who adopted the baby out and never told George. The revelation that George met her and took her to his special island, suggests to them that he wasn't the individually neglectful person they believed. There is an echo of Frank from Williamson's *Travelling North*: 'While I've always loved mankind in general, I have been less than generous to some of those I've been involved with in particular'.[7] Somehow the knowledge that George has been kind to this unknown woman provides comfort for the rest of them, especially Ana, who praises and forgives him at the funeral, and finally plays a piece she has composed on the piano—something she had never dared to do while he was alive.

The play is one of a number of works that celebrate the life of a cranky, unreformed, difficult, talented, visionary man who made life tough for those around them. As well as *Travelling North*, there are Williamson's *The Great Man*, Tobsha Learner's *The Glass Mermaid* and De Groen's *Wicked Sisters*. But *Life After George* is also about the difficulty of sustaining idealism, and it has a grudging respect for those old bastards who do this. We are invited to accept George for what he was, and perhaps forgive him.

Inheritance (2003) is a bush family saga in the tradition of those of the 1930s and 1940s, but contemporary in its politics and its treatment of the problems facing rural Australians. It explores the difficulties that rural Australia faced in the 1990s and links these with the rise of right-wing populist politicians such as Pauline Hanson. In some ways it is about the end of the tradition it celebrates.

Two households occupy the Allandale station. The old rural problem, that dividing a property makes it unviable, means that inheritance is always a source of conflict. Dibs and Girlie are old women, battling on. Inheritance in their family has always been matrilineal and Dibs is now legally the owner of Allandale, as a result of a coin toss many years ago when the two were 18. Both had wanted to get off the land, but knew, when their father hanged himself, that one of them had to stay.

BELONGING

Dibs heads the Hamilton family, although old man Farley—now demented, but clinging to old ideas of the traditional station life—remains theoretically the patriarch of the household and the station owner. The Hamilton children are William, a gay restaurateur who moved to the city, and who now wants Dibs to sell the farm and put the money into a boutique vineyard for him and his partner; and Julia, divorced, with a citified 19-year-old son who hates having to visit his country family and is outraged by their racism and violence. The most important member of the family is Dibs's adopted Aboriginal son Nugget, who looks after Farley and works the land.

In another house on the property are the Delaneys, led by Girlie, who lost the toss and is now landless. Her hard-working son Kyle is a violent, troubled man who copes by drinking. He has two daughters and a wife Maureen—a conservative, racist battler type, self-centred and on the make. Maureen hates her husband's loser streak and becomes a political, Pauline Hanson-like figure by the end.

The action takes place in a complex series of scenes in which the contemporary story is intercut with what happened long ago. When Farley dies, things come to a crisis. Kyle needs the property to keep going; Nugget deserves the property because he too has worked hard on it. It turns out that Nugget is Farley's natural son and in a new will Farley has left him the property.

In the play's climax Dibs finds and tears up the will and, while she and Girlie are away on a holiday, Kyle goes mad with despair. After a succession of terrible encounters with the young people in the play, he hangs himself, just as his grandfather had. At the same time, Dibs and Girlie are legally transferring the property to him, on the principle, from Brecht's *The Caucasian Chalk Circle*, that the land should go to whoever works it best. On that principle it should really be Nugget, but Dibs is unable to give the property to her husband's bastard son. Because Kyle is dead, his wife Maureen inherits the property. In a bitter epilogue a year later it turns out that she has sold it to finance her successful election campaign as a right-wing independent. The whole inheritance is in ruins and everything crumbles.

15. PLAYWRIGHTS IN THE 90S

Inheritance is a strong play about rural bigotry and suffering—bush melodrama pushed along by some tough characters, but with its action still primarily driven by plot.

Two Brothers, which caused a media controversy when it was first staged in 2005, is a political thriller about two brothers, a right-wing politician and a left-wing director of a charitable organisation, who seemed to bear a resemblance to the public figures Peter and Tim Costello.[8] It draws on the politics of the refugee crisis, especially the sinking of the 'SIEV X' in 2001, in which 353 asylum-seekers drowned. In the play one survivor, Hazam Al Ayad, embodies the story.

Tom, the brother with the social conscience, takes up Hazam and the refugees' cause and tries to lobby his brother, Eggs. It turns out that Eggs, who wants to be Prime Minister, has been instrumental in the tragedy, ignoring, as the responsible Minister, a message about the ship's distress, and ordering the Navy to turn away and leave it to sink. He has also killed Hazam one terrible night at the family's beach house. Hazam was given refuge there by Tom, but this was unknown to Eggs who thought he was an intruder.

After a great deal of family conflict and political chicanery, Eggs wins when he blackmails Tom into giving up his struggle. The right-wing media support Eggs, and the politics of fear and paranoia win out over compassion and justice. Eggs becomes Prime Minister, mouthing platitudes and telling lies in his victory speech. It is a viciously bleak conclusion to a political play that occupies similar territory to that of the political thrillers of Stephen Sewell.

Joanna Murray-Smith

Joanna Murray-Smith's work is built on ambiguity. Her characters confront each other intensely and intimately, but always in an impressionist whirl of mystery. Who did what, exactly, to whom? Her plays, full of middle-class professional anxiety, reflect the confusions of individuals in the 1990s, just as the plays of Katherine Thomson and Debra Oswald, full of underclass survivors, reflect social injustices of the period. Murray-Smith writes beautifully lyrical dialogue for characters who are theatrically articulate and contemplative, but elusive—not quite there, not quite honest.

BELONGING

Atlanta (1990) is about a group of young professionals who believe themselves to be on top of life in their own ways. But, as the play's complex non-linear narrative develops, they become obsessed with the death of Atlanta, the depressed outsider of their circle. Atlanta feels special because she was conceived while the spacecraft Atlanta passed overhead. But her Polish mother is the only Holocaust survivor in her family and is haunted by its memories. Because of this Atlanta can never feel at home in the matey world of her friends. At the beach house which, in the spirit of the movie *The Big Chill*, holds so many happy memories for the group, she drowns. At first we think it might be suicide, but then a letter turns up. It might still be suicide, but at least she pretends that it is not.

This was the first of Murray-Smith's many plays about mysterious, troubled women. In *Flame* (1994), a woman calls back to life the ghost of her dead husband who was killed in a car crash. She wants to tell him that during the last year of their life together she was having an affair and that his death brought her release. She has summoned him in order to send his spirit away, so that she can stop pretending to grieve.

Honour (1995) is a highly-strung play about a successful middle-aged man, Gus, who leaves his wife of 32 years, Honor, for a much younger woman, Claudia. It is an old middle-class theme, executed with great simplicity and nuanced, allusive, spare dialogue in a series of two-handed scenes between Gus and Claudia, Gus and Honor, Honor and their daughter Sophie and all the other combinations. Each of the characters has their strength, their point-of-view and their particular vulnerability. The play has an odd detachment as it explores their emotions, as if asking broad questions about love and honour as part of a social work case-study.

Murray-Smith's other plays in the 1990s were unashamedly case-studies—little dramatic experiments in confrontation. *Love Child* (1993) is a classically simple and intense confrontation between a young woman Billie, who was adopted out at birth, and her birth mother Anna, whom Billie has finally found. It is a story of two women from different times who don't understand each other's worlds.

Billie is a young soap star in comically crass shows with titles like

15. PLAYWRIGHTS IN THE 90S

Supermodels and *Taxidrivettes*. She is upfront, needy, asking for what she wants, uneducated from Anna's point of view but bright and sharp. Anna is a stitched-up film editor of nature documentaries, living in a sterile designer apartment. She is reserved and self-protective, a proud feminist from the 1960s and 1970s who fought for women's rights but doesn't seem to have made much of a life for herself. Her husband, a famous writer, left her because she didn't want children.

The play develops in a schematic sequence of encounters between the two women, until Billie eventually breaks down Anna's defensive walls and Anna crumbles, confessing the emotions that she has held in for so long. At this point Billie says that she is not Anna's birth daughter at all. But in their new intimacy they have found something in each other and it doesn't matter. In a gentle coda Anna visits Billie some time later and they go to the movies together. The play suggests that, while people might want to know their pasts, they will find in the present what they need; that memory, desire and intimacy are fluid and that factual details don't matter. And as in all Murray-Smith's plays we're never quite sure what the facts are.

Redemption (1997) is a meeting between two people after the death of another. Jacob, a musician who was adored and special, has been murdered by a kid on the street. Edie, his ex-wife, is a beautiful, chic woman who has come back from France for the funeral. Sam, his brother, arrives and they confront each other in Jacob's apartment. It turns out that Edie left Jacob after an affair with Sam, and that Sam stopped seeing his brother. Now that Jacob is dead they can rediscover each other. They remember what they were and fall into each other's arms.

Nightfall (1999) is even more like a behavioural case-study. Edward and Emily wait yearningly for their long-lost daughter, Cora. Instead, Kate, who might be Cora's therapist specialising in recovered memory, turns up. A tough and unsympathetic woman, Kate seems to know everything about them and Cora, and gradually wears them down. Eventually she says that Cora won't see them until Edward admits that he sexually abused her after he lost his job. Emily is so desperate to see Cora again that she provokes Edward into saying that he did. We have no idea whether he is guilty or not but Kate's manipulation and Emily's

BELONGING

vulnerability gradually herd him into his 'confession'. At the end Kate, in triumph, beckons the waiting Cora into the house.

Rapture (2002) probes the longstanding friendship of three successful professional couples who have shared a lot, especially many glowing dinner parties. The play is set on the first night back for Henny and Harry, one of the couples, who have been away since their beautiful house burnt down seven months earlier. No one knows where they went, but it is assumed that they were overseas. It turns out that they were holed up in a luxury hotel, where they had a spiritual epiphany and have been utterly changed. Their new faith is highly confronting for the others and during the evening not only the friendships, but the marriages are tested, as Henny and Harry challenge the others to make a spiritual leap forward.

Bombshells (2002), written as a virtuoso vehicle for the performer Caroline O'Connor, consists of six monologues by women: a frantic oppressed housewife who blames herself for her unhappiness; an abandoned cactus-fancier wife, pathetic and funny; a bitchy teenage girl obsessed with herself and her performance in the school Talent Night; a bride who realises at the crucial 'I do' moment that everything she has dreamed of is wrong; an older woman, with a neat and tidy widow's life, who has an exultant sexual encounter with the young blind man she reads to; and, finally, an American singer with a terrible life on the comeback, singing gloriously about the fundamental importance of avoiding men. The tone, at first desperate, becomes gradually more positive and is grimly triumphant as the show reaches its conclusion.

In 2006 Murray-Smith wrote *The Female of the Species*, a farcical comedy about second-wave feminism, based around a home-invasion incident that Germaine Greer had experienced, and speculating, in the manner of the 'great man' plays of Williamson, Rayson and De Groen, about the influence of a great woman.

Tobsha Learner

Before she turned to novels, Tobsha Learner explored middle-class individualism in plays that were vaguely impressionist and obscurely erotic. *Wolf* (1992) is a saga charting three decades in the life of Daniel

15. PLAYWRIGHTS IN THE 90S

Lupus, a man who would have been called a mad rooter during the New Wave. The play presents his sexual predation in almost spiritual terms, as he grows from a randy schoolboy in the 1950s to become a hippie student in the 1960s, an artist and teacher of nubile students in the 1970s and a dirty old man in the 1980s. Between scenes he presents and represents the wolf's side of the Little Red Riding Hood story. The kitchen table on and under which he ravishes his women has legs that end in wolf's feet. As his sexual career nears its end, just before he dies, the table starts to seep blood.

More light-hearted is *Miracles* (1992 under the title *Miracle*, then revived in 1998), a fable-like celebration of self-acceptance and self-reliance, in which a woman, Immaculata, who has worked meekly for many drab years as a checkout operator in a small suburban supermarket, is visited by what she takes to be the voice of God, an Italian woman like herself, speaking through her cash register. She is guided through her hesitant acceptance of sainthood by a mysterious Aboriginal woman named Pearl, an avatar of kindly Aboriginal spirits. The local church and the police are outraged when Immaculata starts to perform miracles and to acquire a following among the local halt and lame. By the end the voice of God has become her own voice. She throws off her self-doubt, realises that she is the only one with authority over her soul and starts wearing colourful clothes instead of her usual black. She also accepts the attentions of the eccentric local failed businessman who has been courting her, and goes off to a party in her honour. Like Patrick White's avatars in *Signal Driver*, Pearl moves on to another location that requires her attention.

The Gun in History (1994) is a short play in which three women engage sexually and violently with three strange men. Each encounter involves a Luger originally stolen from a dying German soldier during World War Two. The first woman cleans it before making love with the soldier who stole it. The second woman leaves her man, returned from the Korean War, and he uses it to shoot himself. In the third scene a big-shot criminal-lawyer husband has acquired it for his collection and uses it to shoot a housepainter who has had sex with his trophy wife. As in all Learner's writing the action is enigmatic but the imagery is obvious.

BELONGING

The Glass Mermaid (1994) is a lyrical play about Sara, who is grieving for the loss of her husband Karl, a great philosopher who killed himself at their beach house by walking into the sea. He always spoke of the Song of Songs, the sound behind existence—which he interpreted, perhaps figuratively or perhaps literally because he seems to have been a bit crazy, as the mermaid's song.

Now, a year later, Sara has returned to the beach house for the first time. She reconnects with her daughter Cassandra and also with her neighbours, Julian and Kristin, who were intimately involved with Karl. Cassandra is revolted when her mother takes a young lover, Janko, but later is strangely drawn to him. Janko is a male escort who has mistaken the house number of his client. At first Sara throws him out, but she calls him back, wanting him to stand for Karl in her erotic memories. Janko has fled the war in Bosnia-Herzegovina after his wife and child were murdered by neighbours. During their relationship Sara lets go of Karl and Janko manages to start dreaming of his lost family again and so let them go. All this and more emerges gradually, as the memories are dredged up and carried down to the beach where Karl drowned.

Witchplay (1987) is a solo opportunity for a virtuoso performer to play many roles, principally Batcha, an old Jewish survivor of Auschwitz, who supplements her social security payments by working as a fortune-teller and medium. Narelle comes to communicate with her mother Maureen, who has died in an accident with a hair-dryer. In the play Batcha channels a string of other characters from different times. At the end she dies of a heart attack, remembering Auschwitz and her beloved Jacov, who died there. An inexplicable pet rabbit that she keeps in a child's dolls' house comes over and sniffs her body. It is an intense piece—evoking the long history of male fear of female sexuality and the resulting violence, channelled through an extraordinary character, with her memories of the camp and her grief at her loss—that is full of oddly banal moments and revelations.

Around the turn of the century political conditions in Australia threw up a series of crises and events that did seem to bring playwrights together. Hilary Glow, in her book *Power Plays*, writes about their response to the stalled debate about reconciliation, and to the retreat,

15. PLAYWRIGHTS IN THE 90S

under the Howard Liberal Government, from a commitment to multiculturalism. She singles out three 'critical incidents' in particular: 'the attack on the World Trade Centre on September 11, 2001; the anti-globalisation movement in the face of the domination of neo-liberalism; and the crisis over the detention of refugees.' She argues convincingly that, although 'the national cultural project faltered through the 1990s,' there was still nevertheless a new kind of 'critical nationalism' in the writers' response to those events, something about the nation as an entity that was, she says, referring to a phrase of Ghassan Hage's, worth 'caring about.'

We have seen some of this in the work of the multicultural and Indigenous playwrights discussed in Chapters 13 and 14. But as the effects of economic rationalism began to bite another series of plays emerged—plays that were interested, like so many from the beginning of the twentieth century, in issues of class.

16
THE END OF THE TWENTIETH CENTURY

The 1990s was a bad decade for the poor, the inarticulate and the outcast. Katherine Thomson and Debra Oswald, and, in different ways, Michael Gurr, Andrew Bovell and Daniel Keene, all addressed this.

Katherine Thomson

Katherine Thomson is one of the great observers and recorders of the lives and struggles of marginalised people, people depicted in her plays as always extraordinary and sometimes heroic. Her plays are beautifully crafted, conventionally formed dramas full of humour in which individual lives are placed firmly in their social context. She captures a period when, amidst the triumphalist rhetoric and social chaos of late-twentieth-century global capitalism, many people's lives went belly up.

In *Barmaids* (1991) Nancy and Val rule their hotel, which includes the audience, with a worldly wisdom about their customers' needs that doesn't quite help them to manage their own. The play celebrates an old-fashioned Australian pub that is a close-knit community until it is fragmented by the arrival of new absentee owners and their accountants. We get to know a range of unseen colourful characters through the lively incidents and stories Nancy and Val tell.

BELONGING

Diving for Pearls (1992) is the first of the great working-class dramas of the 1990s, a decade in which a generation of working people were betrayed by the companies that employed them and by the governments that were supposed to be protecting them. It is set in an industrial city very like Wollongong, NSW, where long-serving steelworkers were retrenched by the thousands, and found themselves with no support, no resources, unable to fight their way out.

Barbara is a battler, living by herself in a boarding house after leaving her husband. Her intellectually backward but lively daughter Verge (Virginia) lives in the nearby metropolitan city with Marj, Barbara's upwardly mobile sister. Den, a shy and lonely labourer in the local steelworks, loves Barbara and eventually persuades her to move in with him. He pays for her expensive course in self-improvement—deportment, elocution, things she will never be good at—because she dreams of getting a job in the new flash resort hotel that is being built on the peninsula.

Verge turns up and the three of them make a desperate family. Den is a decent bloke who puts up with a lot, but the house he lives in is actually owned by his sister Jennie whose husband Ron is a management consultant. Ron is called in by the government supposedly to save the steelworks but, as it turns out, without knowing it, actually to prepare it for privatisation.

Barbara doesn't get her job, Den gets retrenched, Verge goes back to Marj temporarily. These characters are used, then rendered useless, and they know it. Yet there is a suggestion that they might make a go of it, in particular Verge and Den and perhaps even Barbara. As Peter Kenna's Martin Cassidy put it in *A Hard God*, they just stumble on with God's love raining down on them like thunderbolts.

Thomson's next play, *Navigating* (1997), has in Bea one of the great characters of Australian drama. It tells the story of a fight against corruption in a small town, but stands for many broader national battles and remains topical.

Bea is a 49-year-old woman who lives with her younger sister Isola. After many years away they have returned to the town in the midst of a controversy about a proposed new private prison. The town badly wants the work and service opportunities. Bea is anonymously sent

16. THE END OF THE TWENTIETH CENTURY

details of the corrupt dealings of the wealthiest local businessman Peter Greig. In all innocence she takes them to Ian Donnelly, a supposedly upright and worthy local businessman and town councillor. Bea doesn't know that he is fact having an affair with Isola. The gormless editor of the local newspaper, Brent, is in love with Isola but she spurns him.

Another part of the set-up is that Bea and Isola are daughters of a skipper who killed himself thirty-five years earlier rather than face an inquest into the deaths of twenty-eight local children who were drowned when his ship capsized on a sandbank. He was taking them for a picnic on an island. The official verdict was a freak wave.

When Bea discovers and then struggles to tell the truth of the wreck, she is ostracised from the community and her life is threatened. But she is rescued and goes on a healing boat journey to the site of the disaster. At the end there is a feeling of peace, a release, and an implication that somehow or other Bea will keep on fighting. It is a good strong social issues play, the sort that the red witches used to write in the 1940s and 1950s.

Like Rayson's *Inheritance*, Thomson's *Wonderlands* (2003) harks back to the outback dramas of the 1930s and 1940s, lamenting, as did plays by Vance Palmer and George Landen Dann, that the early opportunities for cooperation between white settlers and black owners of the land collapsed in the brutal processes of invasion and pastoral development. An old agreement between a white station owner and her Aboriginal head stockman to hand the land back to him and his people becomes evidence in a bitter land-rights dispute many years later. Estrangements within the modern white family ironically parallel the dislocation that the black characters have suffered. The play is about what might have been, if well-meaning, sympathetic pastoralists had prevailed in the long battle between blacks and whites. Its story is brutal, because, of course, they didn't.

Harbour opened the new Sydney Theatre in Walsh Bay in 2004. Like the Wollongong of *Diving for Pearls* but on a much larger scale, Walsh Bay, an area long associated with working-class struggle, was undergoing upmarket development. *Harbour* is a fine drama of battlers, set during the industrial dispute between Patrick Stevedores and the Maritime Union of Australia in 1998, when balaclava-clad

BELONGING

'security guards' confronted striking workers at picket lines a few hundred metres down the road from the expensive new harbourside developments and, for that matter, from the theatre in which the play was being performed. The play is based around the family of an old unionist, Sandy, who is shocked and baffled to find that in this savage new business-managed world he and his working mates are somehow standing in the way of that mysterious beast 'the economy', which he thought he'd been supporting all his working life.

Debra Oswald

The characters in Debra Oswald's *Gary's House* (1996), one of the finest underclass dramas of the 1990s, try to survive outside the notorious 'economy'. Gary and his desperately needy but feisty and aggressive young wife, Sue-Anne, have fled from the new corporatised world that has no need or room for them. Gary, brimming with barely contained rage, is defiantly building them a house in the bush. Like Den in Thomson's *Diving for Pearls*, he is offering this gift of retreat to the difficult woman he wants to love, but he doesn't fully own the land and his sister, a successful city corporate type, wants to sell it out from under him.

When Christine, the sister, turns up, there is a series of bitter encounters, in which the terrible events of their past are dragged up. Sue-Anne leaves and Gary shoots himself, in a shocking conclusion to the first half. Sue-Anne returns, with Gary's baby, only to run off with the gormless but devoted young local man who has loved her from afar. After Gary's death Christine mellows and falls in love with Dave, a shiftless loner on the neighbouring property. She decides to leave her business life behind and finish building Gary's house. There is a glorious moment at the end when Christine, pregnant to Dave, takes Sue-Anne's baby to the door of the finally completed house and finds the ghost of Gary there. She gives him his child to hold.

Oswald's first success was *Dags* (1985), a classic coming-of-age play about a 16-year-old girl who thinks she's ugly and has no friends. To us, she is clearly much cleverer than the spunkrats and princesses who play bitchy social games in the playground. She has a crush on

16. THE END OF THE TWENTIETH CENTURY

the best-looking guy in school, Adam, and puts up with his constant consultations about his problems with his girlfriend, the best-looking girl. Eventually her triumph is not that she gets him, but that she rejects him. Another, much later, play for young people was *Skate* (2003), about a group of skateboarders in a country town fighting to get a skatepark. One of them, Corey, the son of the 'trash' family in town, is killed half-way through by his violent stepfather. Everyone is devastated. The fight for the park seems to have been lost, until two of the main characters, Zac and Lauren, are united in their grief and the campaign ends in success.

Sweet Road (2000) is an odd on-the-road fantasy in which the characters keep soliloquising, not quite talking to us, but figuring things out for themselves. The play is patterned by their journeys and the staging involves a lot of cars and driving. A flood temporarily isolates and then brings the characters together in different ways. The work has a mythic quality but also depicts a familiar outback Australia, full of caravan parks, country towns, servos, dusty and then muddy highways, dry salt lakes, and flooded rivers.

It opens with Jo, an orderly suburban housewife, childless, worrying about her husband and about the girl at their work who is pregnant. Stopping at lights, she sees her husband kissing the same girl in a car. He sees her. She twigs, and drives off blindly out into the desert, a great parched expanse dotted with lonely characters.

There's Andy, a permanently manic no-hoper, full of mad unrealistic dreams, driving with his wife Carla and their two kids to some crazy hope of a job in Murwillumbah. His mania includes a gambling addiction and he loses most of their cash stash, but then gets a job from a guy in the TAB delivering irrigation equipment to a dope plantation. Stopping at a servo they pick up a loser Curtis who, convinced they've got money, tries to rob them at knifepoint. Carla scares him off but it is all too much. She takes the kids and leaves Andy with the car by the side of the road as the rain starts.

There's also Michael, a lonely soft-drink deliverer, always on the road, haunted by the death of his baby son in a car crash in which he was the no-fault driver. Jo picks up Yasmin, a hitchhiker who is completely hyped up with love for a boyfriend she's going to visit

BELONGING

on the Queensland oil fields. And there's Frank, an elderly man who had been planning the standard grey-nomad campervan tour of the country, except that his wife died of cancer before they got round to it. Completely at a loss, he's doing the trip anyway. Frank meets Andy and Carla at a caravan park and, after the flood, he meets up with Carla and the kids. He decides he wants to go solo canoeing on the newly running rivers and she drives his van to a rendezvous point. There he decides to canoe all the way back to Adelaide, so he gives her the van, signing the papers and everything, and sets off. She picks up Andy, who is still stranded in the broken-down car in the rain. They are reconciled and drive on together to God knows where.

Meanwhile Jo, having crashed her car in the wet, is picked up by Michael the soft-drink deliverer. Waiting in the flood through the night, they share stories and Michael finally comes out of himself. They make love. Afterwards she tells him to go back to his family. She also finds, in the pocket of hubby's sailing jacket, a bank card to a secret account. She guesses his PIN and manages to withdraw enough money to take off on her own. After Michael has left she finds that she is at last pregnant. She uses the money to get another car and head off to have her baby and make a new life for herself.

The play has a fairy-tale quality and a great epic resonance of many old bush stories. Bad things happen to nice people, but society's losers somehow get by because in this play they have a kind of radiance.

Mr Bailey's Minder is another play in which hurt and damaged people find each other. A tough desperado young woman, recently released from prison, gets a job minding a cruel old alcoholic, a famous painter now on the skids. She is caught between the middle-class world of his bitchy but finally repentant daughter and a new world offered by a simple, good man, an honest carpenter who comes to work in the house. Like all Oswald's plays, it is funny and tender.

Michael Gurr

Michael Gurr is a complex chronicler of social, political and moral problems. A Melbourne-based playwright who hasn't had the recognition outside his home city that he deserves, he started writing

16. THE END OF THE TWENTIETH CENTURY

a series of absurdist dramas and farces in the 1980s, and became one of the most prolific political playwrights of the 1990s with his major plays, *Sex Diary of an Infidel, Underwear, Perfume and Crash Helmet, Jerusalem, Crazy Brave, The Simple Truth* and *Julia 3*.

In some ways he is an old-fashioned, almost Shavian, playwright of ideas, but his interest in how the world could be changed—in the face of left-wing despair after thirty years of ineffectual liberal activism—puts him in tune with the specific debates of his times. Not as wild as Sewell, he nevertheless has a similar mixture of compassion and intellectual detachment that allows him to ask hard questions. *Underwear, Perfume and Crash Helmet* is such a savage account of how the new right has infected the left that there seems to be no human way out. His subsequent plays explore seriously a number of extreme solutions, of the sort that must have occurred to even the most liberal of well-meaning social reformers. The arguments are never straightforward, but are responses to the basic question of all post-New Wave activists: what on earth is to be done?[1]

The early plays, *Magnetic North* (1983) and *Imitation Real* (1981), are absurdist comedies. The first is set in a bathroom in which three people arrive with very different ideas of where they are and what is outside. It is a simple piece, but surprising and funny. The second, also very funny, shows three people—a real estate agent and two of his tenants—living media-driven fantasy lives and ends with them pathetically planning a great new future for themselves.

What You Wanted (1983) is an Ortonesque farce about Max, a doctor who, in experimenting with a new cancer cure, has killed five of his patients. He now lives in hiding, posing as a blind cripple on social security. He has picked up Mary in a singles bar and she's still there the next morning when the gardener arrives. There are lots of complications and disguises, including the arrival of a Social Security inspector and an AMA investigator who has tracked Max down. By the end all the outsiders have been killed, Mary has left and Max starts to bury his latest collection of bodies in the garden.

The first of Gurr's overtly political dramas was *A Pair of Claws* (1983), about the nexus between private and public life and between morality and expediency. Simon, the son of Presley Swift, a distinguished

BELONGING

conservative lawyer and diplomat, is about to run for Parliament, when details emerge of a party his father attended many years earlier. At the party, following an argument with Presley, a call-girl fell from a balcony and, to avoid scandal, was left on the lawn, where she died. Presley's wife Sylvia has always known about this and been quietly supportive. However, to have any chance of being elected, Simon must denounce his father. At the end of the play the story breaks and Presley and Sylvia go off to face the press. It is a complex play in which the personal and political interconnect in ways that show each affecting and infecting the other. The relationship between Presley and Sylvia—loving and loyal but deeply compromised—is particularly well handled. So, too, are the troubled responses of Simon and a humble old family friend, Frances, who is treated as something of a pet, but who is outraged by what she discovers.

Sex Diary of an Infidel (1992) is the first of a terrific series of political thrillers about personal responsibility in a corrupt world and the difficulty of acting for change.

Jean is a journalist who has written an award-winning story on Tony, once a street-living, drug-addict male prostitute, but now, apparently, reformed. With her lover Martin, a photographer, she goes to the Philippines to do a story on sex-tourism—not just to expose the fact of it, but to use it, high-mindedly in her case, as a metaphor for the Western exploitation of developing countries.

There is a split narrative. Jean and Martin find their way through the sex-industry in Manila—meeting Toni, a transexual prostitute who works for Max, an Australian businessman and pimp. Meanwhile, back in Melbourne, Jean's sister Laura is minding her flat, and meets Tony when he breaks into it.

But there many surprising reversals in a narrative that embroils all the characters in moral, political and personal complications. Jean turns out to know Max. When Tony rings her, she flies back to Melbourne, alarmed that he has invaded her flat. Max gives her a package of heroin to take with her. It turns out that she has invented Tony's life, for her award-winning story, and to avoid exposure she gives him the heroin and flies back to Max. They disappear together into some criminal world. Jean is one of Gurr's many apparently decent left-liberal

16. THE END OF THE TWENTIETH CENTURY

characters who turn out to be utterly compromised and desperately corrupt, like Caroline in *Underwear, Perfume and Crash Helmet* and Julia in *Julia 3*.

Meanwhile we see a nice, if odd, love affair develop between Laura and Tony and a friendship between Martin, left behind in Manila, and Toni. Toni has always wanted to save enough money to get to Hong Kong for his sex-change operation. But he has family and, for the sake of his brother, who is a communist insurgent, he goes to throw a Molotov cocktail in a protest against the Americans. Martin accompanies him. Toni is burned in the face. At the end we discover that he has abandoned his transgender ambitions to become an insurgent, fighting, rather inexpertly, in the jungle. He wanted to be a woman so as to attract the love of men. At the end he finds the love he wants.

There are other complications, in this thoughtful, strong play. The effect is of a group of confused people—some decent and others, with guilty secrets, who would like to be—struggling to make a life and do good in the world, and, in their failure, drifting apart.

Underwear, Perfume and Crash Helmet (1994), a tough drama about nasty people, evokes a world of poverty and social decline under threat from the new political, economic and religious fundamentalism of the 1990s. It is set on the eve of the 1994 Federal election, after twelve years of Labor government, in the camp of the conservative coalition, and tells an imagined story of their last election campaign.

Caroline is the recent widow of a conservative politician. Her younger brother, Nicholas, is a shiftless musician who starts out supporting her as she grieves, but who ends up baffled and alienated by her retreat from compassion and her embrace of the new world order.

Blair is part of a conservative think-tank that is working to help the conservative coalition. She invites to Melbourne a distinguished international neo-con speaker named Lionel, who has a sinister personal assistant named Patrick. When the election is called, Caroline is persuaded to stand in her husband's old seat, and Lionel and Patrick help out.

One night Patrick and Nicholas go partying and pick up Michelle, a mentally disturbed street kid who lives under a grate in the park. We

BELONGING

have seen her setting fire to bins in the park and throughout the play we hear her theories about the aliens who will have sex with her and then take her away to happiness. The bins are her beacons, attracting them to her. Patrick, whose perversions have already been hinted at, plays along with her, takes her under the grate and rapes her. She believes he is the leader of the aliens. Nicholas holds back.

The conservatives lose the election, but Caroline wins her seat. Nicholas meets Michelle again and realises the nature of her disturbance. He asks whether it was her father who first abused her, but she cannot answer. Patrick turns up later, as she expected, and promises that the time for lift-up to a better universe has come. He sprinkles her with kerosene and is about to set fire to her but, with some sense intact, she wants the password for escape. When he doesn't have it, she runs away. He pours the rest of the kerosene into the grate and when Nicholas arrives he tells him that she is down there and sets fire to it. ('Show me who you actually are. Will you save your friend or warm yourself by the fire?' p. 69) Nicholas shows who he is by rushing, apparently self-destructively, into the fire to save her. It is a savage scene, emblematic of moral questions facing us all: how much are we prepared to sacrifice personally to do what we like to say in public is 'the right thing'?

Nicholas risks his life and is badly burnt, but recovers. Lionel and Patrick go off to rampage in other parts of the world and Caroline goes to Canberra. In the final scene we see Michelle waiting for lunch outside a shelter, and telling us in poetic terms of the simple joys of being fed and helped. The title comes from three oddly tender images in her final speech. The perfume is the smell of gravy when you are hungry. It's a terrific play, committed and powerful.

Jerusalem (1996) is set after the conservative victory in 1996, and is told from the point of view of decent hard-working people who struggle to improve the world from within the system.

Three groups of characters are involved in interconnected stories. The first group is led by Vivien, who runs a vaguely Christian prisoner support group with the help of Maureen and Malcolm. Their main case is a disturbed young woman named Amy, who was in a religious evangelical group and killed her two babies so that they could be with God. The second group is led by Vivien's ex-husband Cameron, a

16. THE END OF THE TWENTIETH CENTURY

Labor backbencher who is good at the basic electorate work of helping constituents in trouble, but not good at internecine party politics. His office staff includes Jocelyn, an honest party worker who supports him to the hilt; and Adrian, a new-Labor go-getter who eventually defeats him and wins pre-selection for his seat. The third group is Oliver (Vivien and Cameron's son) and his girlfriend Nina, who are travelling in Egypt. At the end of Act I Nina is raped in a Cairo market and Amy, released on parole, steals a baby.

The interconnections are many. Vivien and Cameron, long-separated (Cameron has a pregnant new wife, Kate), have another fling together. Maureen discovers that she has a serious cancer and tells Vivien, who supports her. Cameron tries to help Amy, re-imprisoned in a secure ward of a psychiatric hospital, but he is rapidly losing power and influence. Oliver and Nina get home from Cairo, but Oliver leaves her, riddled with guilt that he left Nina in the market where she was raped. When Kate, whom we never meet, gives birth at the end there is a sense of renewal, but also of the failure of quiet reform and good works. The plot is beautifully crafted, the characters are complex and multi-layered and the dialogue is full of ideas and nuances. The play brings together the political and the personal to explore the moral—in Gurr's hands not the passionate quest that it is in Sewell's, but a weary yearning for basic human decency.

In *Crazy Brave* (2000) Gurr turned to explore another solution to the problem of how to change the world: interventionist, culture-jamming activism.

An ineffectual group of inner-city rebels—Alice, Paul and Deborah—do comical public protests such as pretending to be traffic controllers diverting an arriving audience away from the venue of a Norman Schwarzkopf lecture, and throwing gladbags full of vomit at dignitaries at a museum opening. They are infiltrated by a serious activist terrorist, Jim, who sets them up to explode smoke bombs at a big business charity lunch. This story is intercut with meetings between Nick, a radio journalist, and Harold Hoffman, an old left-wing lawyer about whom Nick is doing a documentary. Harold is an activist from a different world, once a legend but now living in poverty and obscurity.

BELONGING

Alice, it turns out, knows Harold from his favourite café. She also turns out to be Nick's wife, but she disappeared abruptly some time ago to pursue her revolutionary activities. She is now living poorly and working by day as a packer in a frozen-food factory. Nick still cares. He breaks into her flat to see how she's living and finds Jim's bomb-making equipment and floor plans of the venue. He doesn't know whether to tell the police.

Paul and Deborah, comic figures, are too soft for Jim's brand of terrorism. More interested in each other, they back out of the smoke-bombing raid. But Alice has become deeply involved and goes ahead with it single-handedly. The bombs Jim supplies turn out to be real ones, of course, and several people are badly injured. Alice ends up in jail, with Jim having mysteriously disappeared. After the event she can't understand that the revolution hasn't happened—she seems to have gone crazy brave. Nick stands by her and Harold tells the story of the one time when he thought change was really going to happen—when he felt he did some good—a simple story about a poor woman and a loaf of bread. It is a very small victory, but perhaps that is all that can be expected.

Crazy Brave, with its zealous urban terrorists, was written before 'terrorism' became a political buzz-word and the events of the early twenty-first century were to make the play's take on terrorism seem a bit quaint.

The Simple Truth (2002) is not based overtly in political events, but is a contemporary morality play in which the ground is always shifting. In it Gurr, having found his voice, returns to the simpler style of his early plays. A woman who claims to have killed her husband is being interviewed at a police station by a doubtful police officer. It is never clear whether or not she has committed the crime to which she is supposedly confessing. The policeman's attitude, as he reveals his own insecurities, is equally ambiguous, as they are drawn together at a personal level. As they sink into each other, the death of her husband retreats into the background.

Julia 3 (2004) was (at the time of writing) Gurr's latest study of the ethical compromises involved in activist intervention—a fine play, wordy, political but with a classically simple mise-en-scène and a brooding human dimension to its action.

16. THE END OF THE TWENTIETH CENTURY

Julia is a grand, disturbed character, the wife of a very wealthy businessman who has put her in charge of his philanthropic trust. For much of the play she is telling us her story: she has dismissed the advisory panel of experts who once helped her choose worthy projects and has concentrated on three men whose work she has funded—Charlie, a young writer; Joe, a cancer researcher; and Leon, an art fraud investigator—all of whom she has also taken as lovers. Now her husband has died of cancer and she has brought these three together for the funeral. The action intercuts her meetings with them six months previously, when she was toying with them, and scenes of their meeting each other now, squabbling like puppies. As it progresses she tells us, chillingly, of the new use she has found for her husband's money.

In her addresses to the audience she speaks, in an oddly detached way, of her response to the horrors and crimes of the contemporary world—the disasters she reads about in the newspapers, and the way developing world poverty and suffering can be sheeted back to the faceless figures of globalised capitalism. But her outrage takes on a personal dimension when she tells us of an 8-year-old girl from the developing world whose education her husband had sponsored, and whom he sexually abused when he visited. On discovering this, in photos her husband kept, she wrote to the girl's guardian and sent money. She was drawn into the guardian's plan to target for assassination selected individuals whose role in multinational corporate capitalism had led to the abuse and death of people such as his innocent daughter. Julia has started funding this international terrorist campaign out of the money that her husband meant for the arts and for elite medical research into Western health problems of the wealthy. It is an extraordinarily confronting play, about terrorism as a savage revenge for great wrongs and the moral compromise of the people who undertake it, especially when they are privileged, personally hurt, complicit representatives of the system against which the real terrorists are acting.

At the end of the play Julia's three men are revealed as pathetically ineffectual, unlike the mysterious Osama Bin Laden-like figure she has begun supporting. As the three men throw flowers into her husband's

BELONGING

grave, Julia recounts the assassinations around the world that she has paid for, and that have given her life a new sense of purpose.

Julia is a very dark figure, in her elegance and her strangely detached interest in the horrors of the modern world. The personally vengeful side of her behaviour is like Claire Zachanassian's mission back to her home town in Friedrich Dürrenmatt's *The Visit*; and the moral challenge her actions provoke is no less confronting.

Andrew Bovell

Andrew Bovell is an eclectic and powerful writer and a dramaturgically sophisticated craftsman whose best plays of the 1990s, including *Speaking in Tongues*, have complex multiple narratives and an eerie mystery. His 2001 play *Holy Day* is one of the toughest dramas ever written about the frontier war fought between the early colonisers and the Indigenous population. One of his early unpublished plays, *The Ship of Fools* (1987), anticipated the strength and complexity of his later work, but his other early plays were mostly more straightforward.

After Dinner (1988) is a farcical comedy set in a pub bistro on a Friday night in which a table of girls from one workplace is next to a table of boys from another. The play has the structure of a drunken Friday night out, beginning quietly as the girls get to know each other and start chatting with the boys, and then degenerating into wild behaviour and drunken sexual confessions as the evening wears on. His play for the Melbourne Workers' Theatre in the same year, *The Ballad of Lois Ryan*, is a simple social-realist community theatre piece, with songs by Irine Vela, about a woman who dies in an industrial accident. The framing scenes suggest that we should think of Lois's death as an industrial not a personal issue.

Speaking in Tongues (1996) is more complex, a bringing-together of separate narratives that he first devised for other plays, including his one-acter *Like Whiskey on the Breath of a Drunk You Love* (1992). The full-length play became, in 2001, an AFI award-winning movie, *Lantana*. It is partly a detective mystery, partly a love story about trust and fidelity. The characters are all confused and yearning for something: they think they know what's happening, what they have

16. THE END OF THE TWENTIETH CENTURY

and what they want, but they are continually proved to be wrong. In an intricate action they all turn out to be connected with one another. The play is constructed in three parts in which nine characters are brought together in a series of interlinked dramatic quartets.

In the first part, four people go out, lonely, to a bar, pick up someone and take them back to a cheap hotel room. The four are two couples, and each picks up their one-night-stand from the other couple in a sort of inadvertent partner-swapping. One of the new pairs goes through with it, the other doesn't. When the infidelities are discovered, the established couples separate, come back together, and then throw to the next part of the play by telling stories of things they have seen while they were out alone. These include a man hurling a woman's shoe into the bushes and another man, who is desperately unhappy and seems to have drowned himself, wearing a distinctive pair of brown shoes.

The second part, in which the mystery element takes over, picks up on these last two events. A woman, Valerie, stranded when her car breaks down on a lonely road, keeps calling her husband and getting their answering machine. Eventually she is picked up by a passing car, but doesn't make it home. The driver is seen throwing a shoe into the bushes—has he killed her? The police think so, partly because the women from the first part have seen him and dobbed him in. Neil, the man with the distinctive brown shoes, writes desperately lonely love letters to Sarah, his lost love, who is one of Valerie's patients. It turns out that Valerie was terrified and fled into the bushes, where she died in an accidental fall. Neil, who turns out to be a workmate of Nick, the man who threw the shoe into the bushes, recounts all this in his love letters, before he dies.

In the third part, these fragmented pieces of narrative start to come together. We finally meet Valerie's husband John. He has been having an affair with Sarah and it turns out he was at home all the time, listening to his wife's increasingly desperate messages on the answering-machine, but doing nothing. He admits at the end that he knew she would never come home.

It is an extraordinarily complicated series of stories. The connections and re-incorporations of the narrative become a metaphor for the

BELONGING

hidden links between people and so a metonym for all the things that we don't do for each other. The overriding mood is one of missed connections, lost opportunities and thoughtless betrayals that have large consequences, and the yearnings that underlie all these. In the theatre the action is dominated by the insistent beeps of the answering-machine, which come to represent all failures in communication.

Before *Lantana*, Bovell used and developed these stories in his contribution to *Confidentially Yours* (1998), a remarkable collection of monologues written for Melbourne performer Deirdre Rubenstein by Janis Balodis, Nick Enright, Michael Gurr, Daniel Keene, Joanna Murray-Smith and Debra Oswald, as well as Bovell.[2] Bovell also collaborated in the writing of *Who's Afraid of the Working Class?*, discussed below, a wild, angry and bold series of theatrical responses from Melbourne Workers' Theatre to the new economic-rationalist policies of the 1990s.

Holy Day (2001) is a savage story of the frontier war between blacks and whites in the mid-nineteenth century, a play about colonisation such as those written from the 1920s to the 1950s.

Nora is a tough middle-aged woman who runs the Travellers' Rest, a shanty on the fringes of white settlement, with the help of her 'adopted' half-caste daughter, Obedience. Three travellers arrive: an extraordinarily brutal convict, Goundry; a mute boy/man Cornelius; and Epstein, a Jewish ex-convict who is vaguely decent, but who travels with them for safety in this dangerous territory. It seems there has been a sort of lull in the war, but this is disrupted when a missionary's wife, Elizabeth, arrives with a story that her baby has been stolen and her husband is missing. A nearby landowner, Wakefield, is called in and the search for a culprit begins.

The details emerge gradually, each more terrible than the last. Goundry wants Obedience, but to protect her Nora takes him to bed and satisfies him, for a while. He has been keeping Cornelius as a sex slave, after murdering his parents and cutting out his tongue so that he cannot tell the story. Epstein, who has turned a blind eye to this, feels guilty for having done nothing. A mysterious young black woman, Linda, hovers around wanting food. When it is discovered that she has the missing baby's shawl, she is captured, savagely beaten and chained

16. THE END OF THE TWENTIETH CENTURY

to a tree. She refuses to talk, until she learns that the local tribe are about to be massacred by a party of vigilantes led by Goundry. She makes a false confession in order to save them and hangs herself, but they are massacred regardless. It turns out that the missionary's wife has killed her own baby.

The final betrayals are all by the white invaders. The supposedly decent settler Wakefield takes Elizabeth in, knowing but not acknowledging what she has done. Nora and Goundry, enemies from the beginning, make a hideous pact. He gets back his boy Cornelius and she gets back her stolen child, Obedience, but only after Obedience has been raped by Goundry and, like his boy, has had her tongue cut out so that she can never tell the truth.

The play has all the elements of the pioneering bush plays, with a touch of ancient Greek tragedy, done with a new brutality. It is a kind of anti-ancestor-drama, dark and disturbing. It is a frankly 'black armband' vision of the past, leaving us feeling that we can never again hold up our heads until we have somehow expiated the crimes on which our nation is built.

Daniel Keene

Daniel Keene is the most important Australian playwright in the transition between the twentieth and twenty-first centuries. He started out in the early 1980s with plays at La Mama Theatre, Playbox and Tide Theatre Company, including the very successful *Cho Cho San*, which toured Australia in 1984. From 1997 to 2002 he produced a series of short plays for the laboratory-like Keene/Taylor Theatre Project (KTTP), working with director Ariette Taylor and a group of actors to explore a new kind of intimate, socially contextualised theatre about bruised and fleeting encounters between often damaged characters who exist outside the mainstream of middle-class society. He has been widely produced in the United States and Europe, especially France, where he has become a significant playwright, in translations by Séverine Magois, and where he has had several commissions.

Although he has won many awards, he has not had the theatrical impact in Australia that he deserves. In an interview with Marcel

BELONGING

Delval, one of his European directors, he said, 'Australia has always been and remains an eternal purgatory for anyone who thinks; it is hell for anyone who acts upon what they think'.[3] Like director Barrie Kosky, but with a very different style, he is the most recent of the many escapees from Australian colonial philistinism, a successful centennial bookend to Louis Esson. Esson, who wanted to escape, went to France then Oxford then Dublin, but was driven back to Australia where he died of artistic thirst trying to write about the bush. Keene is the first truly post-nationalist Australian playwright with a global audience. His contribution to KTTP, more than thirty short plays, is represented in the English-language published repertoire by *To Whom It May Concern, and other plays* and *Terminus and other plays*. More of his plays have been published in French than in English, in translations by Magois.[4]

Cho Cho San, with music by Dalmazio Babare and Boris Conley, is based on the Madame Butterfly story, using actors, dancers and puppets. It is a tragic, post-colonial version, in which Pinkerton becomes a drunken Yankee sea-captain sitting trashed in a bar and buying Butterfly from her Mama San like a prostitute. Butterfly is played by a puppet. An actor plays the bitter, derelict Cho Cho San three years later, as she waits for Pinkerton to return.

Back in New York and married, the memory of Butterfly haunts Pinkerton. She is the exotic Oriental Other, and when he hears about the child she bore, he goes back to reclaim the boy. His new American wife comes with him and tells Cho Cho San what Pinkerton intends to do, while he himself is prowling the bars, perhaps torn, certainly unable to face it. Pinkerton bursts in at the end, only to find that Cho Cho San has killed both her child and herself. The piece has a grand, simple emotional line, and Keene's script and lyrics are poetic and haunting.

All Souls is set on Walpurgisnacht, when the spirits of the dead come back to visit the living. Our spirit is Phillipa, an old street-dwelling woman who wanders in the night, chanting, singing, telling fragments of her story and conjuring up three stories of the darkened city.

They are the stories of three couples: Frank and Gina, whose marriage has gone stale, at least for Gina, but who have two young children and are struggling to stay together; Angela and Joe, in hospital

16. THE END OF THE TWENTIETH CENTURY

on the eve of Angela's cancer operation, which she might not survive; and Sylvia and Rosie, a tattooist and her client, both lonely, who come together over bottles of vodka.

Phillipa appears briefly outside each of their windows and they hear her. Something happens for each of them, as if, after a moment of stillness in their lives, they are suddenly able to move on. Frank and Gina put their children in the pram and go for a long walk through the night; Joe gets drunk and returns to Angela in hospital and they talk in a way they haven't before as he falls asleep beside her; Rosie tells Sylvia her story and Sylvia invites her to stay and they kiss. Each resolution is eloquent and moving—small changes in insignificant, but valuable, lives.

Phillipa's interspersed faltering memories are of the baby she had to give away, the man who left her to drink himself to death, her Mumma who cried all the time in her room for grief over a lost son, and her Dadda, who took her into the cupboard under the stairs and did things to her that their God couldn't see and that he made her promise not to tell.

At the end dawn comes, the others are redeemed, and Phillipa disappears back to wherever spirits go after their one night of the year.

Keene's short plays are classic works in the formal sense of the word: they distil great emotions and large social contexts into simple and profoundly moving pieces driven by the passions and longings of characters who on the surface can sometimes scarcely say what it is they want. In a note on the cover he ironically describes *To Whom It May Concern and other plays* as 'A Little Bumper Book of Plays'. They are in fact works with huge resonance and, like the short plays of Samuel Beckett, the playwright with whom he has most in common, they can be read as short lyrical prose pieces, highly theatrical in their conception.

The title play, for example, *to whom it may concern*, is a series of glimpses of a dying old man leading his middle-aged, intellectually disabled son around the city, talking to him as he looks for something to do with him, somewhere to place him when he goes into hospital to be cared for during his last weeks.[5] He tries to contact a long-estranged

BELONGING

brother, but there is nothing left there. He takes his son to a beach and encourages him to swim out into the ocean, but the man/boy is frightened and so he takes him home. At the end they sit briefly on a bench outside the hospital, as the father's appointment time passes, and then they go home again. The son never speaks. The mood of alienation is devastating, but there is a humanness underneath—a sense of all that has been yearned for and lost—that is uplifting. It is a modern tragedy reduced, in the sense of being boiled down and concentrated.

A glass of twilight is an encounter between a lonely travelling salesman and a destitute young man whom he picks up in a bar. The salesman tries to turn a commercial sexual encounter into a genuine intimacy, eventually with a kind of guarded, desperate success. *Neither lost nor found* does something similar. A birth mother meets her daughter who has been fostered. In the course of several briefly glimpsed moments, she struggles to get close to her. In *untitled monologue*, a lonely young man who has moved from the bush to the city to find work writes home to his father, never getting a reply. We watch as he slides into dereliction and we grieve for him, with the classic Aristotelian pity and terror, as in his confused way he reveals his violence against a young woman he meets in a pub.

In *night, a wall, two men*, two comically obscene homeless drunks meet each week and form a bond in the face of their social abjection and personal and philosophical despair. Again, the mood is Beckettian ('You crawl out of your old mum and into your fucking grave.' [p. 93]) They are like Didi and Gogo, but without the hope of a Godot arriving. Eventually they escape into dreams, away from their grim lives:

> you're walking down a street a street you used to know and
> you see every fucking house on that street you know every
> house and who lives in every house and you don't feel
> hungry any more because you're not there you're not there
> feeling hungry not feeling like you're being eaten alive by
> your own guts sitting in your flop or on the street or up
> against a wall somewhere with the cold tearing through you
> like you were made of paper you're not there any more
> you're away in your in your own mind you're somewhere
> fucking else [p. 94]

16. THE END OF THE TWENTIETH CENTURY

So, perhaps with this vision they don't need a Godot. Perhaps it's enough to be, in your own, addled mind, 'somewhere fucking else'.

Kaddish is a brief monologue by a widower whose sudden grief for his dead wife can scarcely be expressed, surprising himself, in its sudden violence, as much as it does us. *The violin, the first train* and *the rain* are three plays about the Nazi holocaust, in each case using an image/memory of the trains that took the Jews to the camps. *The violin* briefly captures the moment of arrest and leaving the old culture behind. *The first train* is a monologue in which a middle-aged man mending broken and dirty children's shoes tells us a story, narrated from the point of view of a little boy, of his mysteriously anxious mother, and of a train that arrives with sudden shouting, fires in the night and breaking glass, as on Krystallnacht. His mother runs away with him and hides him in a box of straw in a laneway and says 'Wait here till I come back for you'. He hears the train go away again and the town return to silence, as if emptied. The play ends there, but we assume that she never returned and that the cobbler is the boy, survived, grown up and still mending children's shoes, from a pile, out of a deep grief.

The greatest in this series of plays is *the rain*, originally performed by veteran Melbourne actor Patricia Kennedy and later by Helen Morse. An old woman remembers when people boarding a train kept giving her things, as she stood in a field and watched them go, things that they weren't permitted to take on the train, things that she filled her house with and kept for them, in case they ever came back, which they never did. She tells us of her house filling with these traces. Framing the play is the story of the small boy who gave her a bottle of rain—water he collected from runoff of the house from which he has been taken. 'The rain belongs to God I've kept it for him', he says. She promises to keep it for when the boy comes back, and she has kept that promise. He never does come back, of course, and we assume he has been killed in the gas chambers. But, as in all Keene's plays, there is redemption in the conclusion. As he was taken away to the train, the

Overleaf: Dan Spielman and Robert Menzies in the 2002 Playbox production of Half and Half. *(Photographer: Jeff Busby, held by the Arts Centre in the Performing Arts Collection, Melbourne, Playbox Collection)*

BELONGING

boy said that he'd be back to collect the rain and this has kept the old woman going.

Terminus is a bleak, lyrical, full-length play about loneliness and alienation in a modern city where a group of characters interact and lapse back into aloneness. The settings include a train, a bar, a hotel room, a police station, a brothel, a street and an aviary at the zoo. Between these isolated spaces the characters move, sometimes coming together in moments of contact, sometimes just sitting alone, remembering, wondering, absorbed in their thoughts.

The scenes move fluidly. Behind them is a loose story with five strands, all tied to a man, John. At the beginning John strangles a solitary 15-year-old boy on the train and takes the boy's yellow bird to a cheap hotel. There he rents a room from a lonely drunken Clerk—who makes a brief pass at him and later gets drunker and reveals his hurt at the loss of his boyfriend. Two alienated policemen investigate the murder, and arrest an innocent, derelict street prophet, who can only speak of the angels who inhabit his inner world. John finds the boy's sister, Johanna, and starts a relationship with her which is sexual but also oddly tender: he says he will teach her to cry, to grieve, and eventually he does. He also has a relationship with a prostitute, which is not sexual—to her confusion he just wants to talk. When he fails to make contact with her, he strangles her, meaninglessly, as he had earlier strangled the boy.

All these threads, and others, are interwoven in scenes of great theatrical and lyrical beauty, and a deep humanity, brought together in the Terminus Bar, where people sit alone, speaking into the void, not communicating with each other. John, the bird and the sound of a passing night train are a haunting connection. There is a redemption in John's savage journey as the ghosts of the boy and the prostitute return to follow him. At the end he is back in the train with Johanna, and the ghosts are in the carriage with them. The final image is the four of them together, each alone but connected. It is a very powerful play about the ache of the heart in a mean city, much like *All Souls*, but more haunted.

The eyes is a creepy encounter between two middle-aged men on a park bench, as the twilight fades, and one tells the other of his

16. THE END OF THE TWENTIETH CENTURY

violation of a young girl. *River* is another bleakly tender play about a father and son, like *to whom it may concern*, but in this case told from the boy's point of view. *The fire testament* is a post-nuclear-apocalypse monologue by a survivor who speaks savagely, but wants gentleness.

Half and Half, which was first produced in 2002 as one of the last of the KTTP seasons, is one of the most beautiful, haunting plays ever written in Australia and it ushers in a whole new style of allusively spare, powerfully evocative playwriting that no other Australian playwright does as well.

Two half-brothers meet in their mother's old house, when Luke, who has been away for ten years, suddenly and mysteriously returns. It is the house where they spent their childhoods and Ned, twenty years younger, has stayed on there, after nursing his mother through her final illness. The relationship between them is as much a father–son one as a brotherly one. Their different fathers have both been terrible.

At the beginning they are scarcely able to speak to each other: their interactions are full of riddles, games and evasions, as they spar with one other. Despite a lot of aggressive distance and unfinished business, as the play progresses they open up and, literally, regrow their lost past.

Luke goes to their mother's grave and brings back leaves and plants and earth. He spreads them on the kitchen table around which they used to sit. It becomes their mother's garden, which they never played in together. Gradually Ned joins in and the whole kitchen becomes verdant, their past recovered. All it needs is rain. From his last trip to the cemetery Luke brings back their mother's bones and buries them in the new earth. Their kitchen becomes a green paradise. The two of them recover their memories of her and their lost relationship with each other. The third act is full of birdsong. At the end of the play they seem reunited. A storm comes into their kitchen and the rain starts to fall.

It is a miraculous play about reconciliation, with two estranged characters who find solace in each other after a struggle. It is also about the classic Australian breaking of the drought. Perhaps Ned and Luke have died and been reborn. Perhaps they are ghosts.

Certainly, as in the work of all the Australian playwrights of the twentieth century, they are yearning to belong.

CONCLUSION

In this account, 1912 is the starting point for twentieth-century Australian playwriting, a symbolic transition year in which Bert Bailey's stage adaptation of On Our Selection and Louis Esson's The Time is Not Yet Ripe both first appeared. Bailey's show, with its roots in nineteenth-century melodrama, transformed a series of bush yarns into a successful commercial product. Esson's work written in a relatively recent middle-class form, was searching for a non-commercial and non-formulaic nationalist drama—an original, fresh drama based in the imagined construction of a new world.

Esson's repudiation of Arthur Adams, discussed in Chapter One, represents the first struggle in Australia between nationalist and genre-based drama. Esson and his successors won this struggle in the histories, if not always in the theatres. Since the late 1960s, the continuing rebellion against 'naturalism', while often couched as a critique of realist dramatic representation, also reflected the New Wave rejection of genre writing. This is true even where, as in the case of David Williamson, who has been the object of the strongest critiques, the precise genre being attacked was not clear. This book has tried to reclaim the importance of the genre playwrights from Adams through the Red Witches of the 1930s and 1940s, the bush and urban realist playwrights of the 1940s and 1950s and the work of their

BELONGING

descendants in the 1980s and 1990s. Today genre playwriting is being revisited. As the film and television industries know, and as Williamson and his theatre producers know, audiences like genre, and good writers can do interesting things with it. It refuses to die.

Since the 1990s even the most radically post-dramatic performance works have, perhaps unconsciously, drawn on the aesthetic, cultural and social traditions of the rapidly vanishing twentieth century. The Sydney Front's *First and Last Warning* refers to, and transgresses, traditions of violent family drama. *The Geography of Haunted Places* is like a parodic recapitulation of the great themes of heroic historical pageants since the mid-nineteenth century. *Politely Savage* (2005), an installation piece that was performed with puppets by a company called My Darling Patricia (named for a long-lost love letter found in a 1950s vanity case), starts in a retro vision of a 1950s cocktail party and travels backwards. Using ghosts in a series of startling images, it explores the small country town and bush-gothic tradition that Australian theatre, in all its forms and genres, has been constructing for more than a hundred years. Its final image shows the drowned bodies of women who rise up after a flood and escape from their old bush hut into an imagined open paddock full of long grass. It is a new-form expression of the old realist drama's constant search for belonging.

This interest in the old forms and tropes can also be seen in a new series of plays exploring the past, especially historical family sagas; as well as an upsurge of political writing, partly in response to the radically conservative agenda of the Howard government; and through a continuation of the observational comedy/drama of contemporary middle-class manners and society, dating back to *The Time is Not Yet Ripe* and perfected by Williamson, Hannie Rayson and others. Tony McNamara, for instance, has produced a series of plays—*The John Wayne Principle*, *The Virgin Mim*, *The Unlikely Prospect of Happiness* and *The Give and Take*—in which the moral challenge of trying to lead a good life in the glittering world of modern corporate Sydney is explored in a style so light it is almost mocking. A younger writer who has dealt directly with the moral vacuum of contemporary urban life is Brendan Cowell. In *Morph* a mismatched pair thrown together by a mysterious offstage manipulator, play out childish, media-generated, self-obsessed fantasies of middle-class coupledom.

CONCLUSION

There has, nevertheless, been a shift in attitude. The simple nationalist quest has ended. Some playwrights who started out in the 1990s and became prominent in the early years of the new century revisited old forms and themes but the best new plays are being produced by writers who for the most part appear to be unattached to the old dreams, or in some cases despairing of them.

They are still connected with the past, of course. There was an extraordinary resurgence of hard-edged underclass drama, in the tradition of Daniel Keene, but influenced by the 'in-yer-face' drama of English and Irish writers such as Sarah Kane, Patrick Marber, Martin McDonagh and Mark Ravenhill, whose plays had a lot of influence in Australia in the 1990s. A great deal of this came out of Melbourne.

One of the first was the Melbourne Workers' Theatre's *Who's Afraid of the Working Class?* (1998), an interconnected collection of savage studies of the alienation of contemporary urban life, with scene-sequences written by Andrew Bovell, Patricia Cornelius, Melissa Reeves, Christos Tsiolkas and with music by Irine Vela. The structure is a theatrical collage of stories of lonely people doing it hard, with sudden points of contact between them, especially at the end.

The lynchpin of the show is Bovell's stark sequence, 'Trash'. In this a young girl, Stacey, goes out into the city to find her 15-year-old brother, who has fled their violent home and now works as a street prostitute. She has her first period while hanging out with him on his beat trying to persuade him to come home, and has no idea why she is suddenly bleeding. Huddling together with a candle for warmth and comfort they are burnt to death, and literally fused together, when they try to find shelter for the night in a charity clothes bin. It is one of the most powerful images in recent Australian drama.

A most interesting writer in this vein is Raimondo Cortese, whose 1997 play *Features of Blown Youth* is a version, suitable for the new economic times and social conditions, of the grim doss-house allegories of a tradition going back to Maxim Gorky and Eugene O'Neill. In the 1960s and 1970s there was a flurry of similarly grim dramatic visions, in which houses full of social outcasts come to metonymise the social and economic conditions of their times. These include John Romeril's *I Don't Know Who to Feel Sorry For* and *Bastardy*, Ron Blair's *Last Day in Woolloomooloo* and Barry Dickins's *The Fools' Shoe Hotel* which

BELONGING

gleefully pushes the genre to the brink of nonsense. *Features of Blown Youth* is a superb example of the genre, an allegory of privatisation with a collection of socially outcast characters occupying a share-house. So caught up are they in their personal obsessions—finding sex, doing drugs and making money—they fail to notice that a sinister mercenary outsider named Strawberry is turning their house into a brothel for his own profit. Only one character manages to escape.

Cortese's *St Kilda Tales* (2001), set in a pub very like the famous Esplanade Hotel in the Melbourne suburb of the title, with a group of desperately lonely characters, and his collection of twelve short plays, *Roulette* (2005), document the human effects of economic rationalism with a shocking bleakness. In his work the dialogue, and the action that underpins it, grows out of encounters between the characters. It has a situation but no plot or goal to drive it, just the crackling of the moment between people. The writer and director are intended to be invisible.[1] Like the supposed 'super-naturalism' of the early Romeril and other New Wave writers whose work was produced at La Mama thirty years previously, when it works it has the effect of an intense immediacy, a kind of unconscious communion between actors and audiences.

Another group of writers of the new millennium includes Brendan Cowell, Ian Wilding, Reg Cribb, Ross Mueller and, strongest of all, Ben Ellis. Ellis's plays are savagely satirical, overtly political and theatrically and dramatically grotesque. He is the first writer of the new generation to directly confront the gap between the baby-boomers and their grown-up children. In *Post Felicity* (2002) a boomer couple, James and Madeleine, have been told by a hospital that their daughter Felicity has killed herself. They seem strangely unconcerned, very confused and disengaged. If Cortese's antecedents are the underclass dramas of the realist tradition then Ellis's are in the tradition of the anti-realist avant-garde of the early twentieth century and the absurdists. *Falling Petals* (2003) is a marvellous dystopian nightmare which offers a chilling and bleak vision of the consequences of the boomers' coolly distant legacy to their children, and their children's resulting alienation. *These People* (2003), his response to the refugee crisis of the early 2000s, is a darkly farcical charade based in a parody of a xenophobic Australian suburban family, with echoes of the early Barry Humphries and Patrick White.

CONCLUSION

Angela Betzien, Kathryn Ash and Stephen Carleton have revisited old Australian myths in a gothic style. Betzien's *Children of the Black Skirt* (2003) tells, for young audiences, a splendidly eerie ghost story about the lost-child tales that have haunted so much Australian popular mythology, and links them with the stolen generation of Aboriginal children (as did Bovell's *Holy Day*). Ash's *Flutter*, already mentioned, is a twenty-first century revisiting of the old station dramas. Carleton's *Constance Drinkwater and the Final Days of Somerset* (2006) is a strong melodrama with a brooding atmosphere and some very strange characters, set in Far North Queensland in the late nineteenth century, about a dying settlement full of dark secrets about the dispossession of the Indigenous people.

Many other dramatists of the new millennium have revisited the past. Kate Mulvany's moving play *The Seed* (2007) tells a personal story about her father, a Vietnam war veteran, and her grandfather, a supposed IRA hero who turns out to be something else. Melissa Reeves's *The Spook* (2004) is a comic yarn about an innocent boy caught up in the Cold War paranoia of the 1960s. Sven Swenson's *Vertigo and the Virginia* (1999) is a small-town drama, such as might have been written by Gwen Meredith, but it takes the genre and transforms it, with a double narrative, into a work about how memories make us—especially perhaps very dark ones. It is centred around the flooding of the NSW town of Adaminaby during the construction of the Snowy River hydroelectric scheme by 100,000 immigrant workers. In the play one of them has a terrible past from World War II, as no doubt many did in life.

In the early twenty-first century the most exciting theatre in Australia was being created by a new generation of auteur directors. Barrie Kosky's eight-hour production *The Lost Echo* (2006) has already been mentioned. Based on the Roman poet Ovid's *Metamorphoses*, using texts by Tom Wright, it told Ovid's stories of the conflicts between violent predatory gods and suffering defiant humans in terms that resonated morally and politically with twenty-first century conflicts. It was also thrillingly staged, with a viscerality that was relatively new in Australian theatre.

Wright also wrote the script for Kosky's 2008 production of *The Women of Troy* for the Sydney Theatre Company, recasting Euripides' play in terms of the wars that are still going on in the part of the world the Greeks knew. He adapted, for the STC in early 2009, eight of Shakespeare's history plays in a new version of *The War of the Roses*, for a production by Benedict Andrews.

Wright's work with Kosky and Andrews provides a new model for the role of the playwright in Australian theatre. When Michael Kantor took over the former Playbox Theatre in Melbourne in 2004, renaming it Malthouse after its venue, he signalled a shift away from a play-based definition of 'new work'. The new interest in the classics perhaps represents, in a new generation, the latest turn in the great cycles between nationalism and internationalism.

At the end of the previous chapter I suggested that Daniel Keene may well be Australia's first post-nationalist playwright. More generally, in the early twenty-first century, amid the complexities of globalisation and postcolonialism, nationalist cultural projects are on the wane. This is beyond the interplay between nationalist and internationalist influences that characterised Australian playwriting throughout the last century.[2] Australian playwriting and theatre are now part of a wider world. There is no going back to old island simplicities.

As I said at the beginning, this book is an account of twentieth-century Australian drama, not theatre. While it records traces of theatre left by the scripts, it does not even begin to explore the heart of theatre—the palpable experience of it in the space.

But it is my love of that experience that has lead to my love of plays, not the other way round. Very few people read plays for fun, or want to write about them, unless they have first been excited in a theatre. Many of the plays discussed in this book I haven't seen. My biggest regret is that I have not been able to write here about more of the experiences I have had sitting in an audience, which I have been doing for more than forty years.

So I'd like to conclude with a personal example of a wonderful experience of a theatrical transformation of a written text. In 2004 the State Theatre Company of South Australia produced a stage adaptation of Robert Dessaix's epistolary novel, *Night Letters*, in which a man named Robert, dying of an AIDS-related illness, flees his life in Melbourne and travels to Europe where, amidst floating stories from

CONCLUSION

the past and experiences in the present, he searches for a way to go back home.

The story, in the novel and the play, is haunted by memories of the old colonising world: a courtesan in old Venice, when the gorgeous palaces and cloud-capped towers were all new and fresh, is savagely brutalised at the end; a Russian aristocrat leaves her good husband for a dangerous new love; and in the modern time a stolid German professor who comes to tourist Venice every year to indulge in secret fantasies. Meanwhile Robert travels around Europe, with its crowded corruption, petty restrictions and suffocating past.

In their theatrical transformation writer Susan Rogers and director Chris Drummond did something with the layers of the book that mere writing cannot do. All the characters were on stage, occupying the same space, but in different stories. As Robert sat writing his letters, framed as if in a painting, and moved about his hotel and out into the back streets of Venice, the characters from his past moved with and around him. In the theatre ghosts are never ethereal, they are always present, bodies on stage.

It was performed in the old Queen's Theatre in Adelaide, a once grand, now decrepit, theatre with ghosts of its own. Threaded through this haunting, and haunted, production was the straightforward, naturalistic story of Robert's crisis with his partner Peter, as he flees from the support of his friends to the Europe of his dreaming. At the end he returns home. He is dying. Peter is preparing for a new life without him, but they are both still looking for an exultation based in being there in a place. Of belonging.

ENDNOTES

Introduction

1. See Richard Waterhouse, *From Minstrel Show to Vaudeville: The Australian Popular Stage, 1788–1914*, UNSW Press, Sydney, 1990.
2. Harold Love, 'Chinese Theatre on the Victorian Goldfields, 1858–1870', *Australasian Drama Studies*, vol. 3, no. 2, 1985, pp. 45–86.
3. Richard Fotheringham, *In Search of Steele Rudd*, University of Queensland Press, St. Lucia Qld, 1995, pp. 46–7.
4. Louis Nowra, *The Golden Age*, Currency Press, Sydney, 1989, pp. 76, 77.
5. Geoffrey Milne, *Theatre Australia (Un)limited*, Rodopi, Amsterdam, 2004.

Chapter One: The turn of the century

1. The Real Australia (1907), quoted in *The Australian Stage: A Documentary History*, Harold Love (ed.), UNSW Press, Sydney, 1984, p. 145.
2. Pamela Heckenberg and Philip Parsons, 'The Struggle for an Australian Theatre 1901–1950: Summary of Theatrical Events', in Love (ed.), p. 127.
3. John Andrews, 'Melbourne Theatre, 1929–1945: Recession and Response' unpupblished manuscript, 1979, p. 7, held in State Library of Victoria, Latrobe Library, MS 10884.
4. Richard Waterhouse, *Private Pleasures, Public Leisure: A History of Australian Popular Culture since 1788*, Longmans, Melbourne, 1995, p. 175.
5. Victoria Chance, 'George Sorlie', in *Companion to Theatre in Australia*, Philip Parsons with Victoria Chance (eds.), Currency Press, Sydney, 1995, pp. 534–5.

BELONGING

6 Vance Palmer, *Louis Esson and the Australian Theatre*, Georgian House, Melbourne, 1948, p. 40.
7 J. C. Williamson Papers, Box 2071, held in State Library of Victoria, Latrobe Library, MS 10052. For an account of the Abbey tour, see Peter Kuch, 'The Abbey Irish Players in Australia, 1922', in *The Irish Theatre on Tour*, Nicholas Grene and Christopher Morash (eds), Carysfort Press, Dublin, 2005, pp. 69–88.
8 See Dennis Carroll, *Australian Contemporary Drama* (rev. ed.), Currency Press, Sydney, 1995, pp. 7–8.
9 George Darrell, *The Sunny South*, Currency Methuen, Sydney, 1975.
10 Margaret Williams, *Australia on the Popular Stage, 1829–1929*, Oxford University Press, Melbourne, 1983, p. 177.
11 Williams, pp. 208–9.
12 Williams, p. 223.
13 Williams, p. 235.
14 See Terry Sturm, 'Drama', in *The Oxford History of Australian Literature*, Leonie Kramer (ed.), Oxford University Press, 1981, p. 209. See also Richard Fotheringham, *In Search of Steele Rudd*, University of Queensland Press, St. Lucia Qld, 1995.
15 A neat short account of the family history, over the ten books, is given in 'Rudd Family', in William H. Wilde et al (eds), *The Oxford Companion to Australian Literature*, Oxford University Press, Melbourne, 1985, pp. 602–3.
16 See Fotheringham's *In Search of Steele Rudd* for an excellent account of Davis's double life.
17 Helen Musa discusses the authorship of the play in her introduction to Bert Bailey, *On Our Selection*, Currency Press, Sydney, 1984. See also Richard Fotheringham, 'On Our Selection', in Parsons and Chance (eds), pp. 417–18.
18 Fotheringham, *In Search of Steele Rudd*, p. 124.
19 See Andrew Pike, 'Dad and Dave in the Cinema', in Bailey, pp. 62–9.
20 *Smith's Weekly*, 4 September 1931, quoted by Pike, p. 63.
21 Williams, pp. 281–2.
22 Introduction to Betty Roland, *The Touch of Silk* and *Granite Peak*, Currency Press, Sydney, 1988, p. xii.
23 Love, p. 133.
24 Leslie Rees, *A History of Australian Drama. Vol. I. The Making of Australian Drama from the 1830s to the late 1960s*, Angus & Robertson, Sydney, 1978, Ch. VI; and 'Stargazer' (pseud.), 'The Australian Play', *Lone Hand*, May 1907, p. 104. A comprehensive account of the campaign is given in Virginia Kirby-Smith, 'The Development of Australian Theatre and Drama, 1788–1964', unpublished PhD dissertation, Duke University, 1969, Ch. IV. There is a copy in the Mitchell Library, State Library of NSW. See also Michelle Arrow, *Upstaged: Australian Women Dramatists in the Limelight at Last*, Currency Press, Sydney, 2002, pp. 27–38.
25 Harold Bowden, quoted by Viola Tait, *A Family of Brothers: The Taits and J. C. Williamson: A Theatre History*, Heinemann, Melbourne, 1971, p. 215.

ENDNOTES

26 See Kirby-Smith, pp. 73–8 for a discussion of the debate about the commercial repertoire. The response to the Achurch tour is discussed in Deborah Campbell, 'A Doll's House: The Colonial Response', in *Nellie Melba, Ginger Meggs and Friends: Essays in Australian Cultural History*, Susan Dermody et al (eds), Kibble Books, Malmsbury, 1982.
27 Allan Ashbolt, 'Courage, Contradiction and Compromise: Gregan McMahon, 1874–1941', *Meanjin*, 37, 1978, p. 332.
28 Tait, p. 252.
29 Tait, p. 277.
30 Quoted by Kirby-Smith, p. 438, but see also Ch. VI, 'The Development of "Repertory", "Art" and "Little" Theatre', pp. 203–67.
31 Kirby-Smith, *passim*, particularly Ch. IX. See also Arrow, Ch. 3. For a detailed first-hand account of the Little Theatre movement in Adelaide, see Thelma Afford, *Dreamers and Visionaries: Adelaide's Little Theatres From the 1920s to the Early 1940s*, Currency Press, Sydney, 2004.
32 Allan Ashbolt, *Focus*, February 1948, pp. 26–9, quoted in Love, pp. 158–61.
33 Heckenberg and Parsons, p. 132.
34 Sir Paul Haluck, *Mucking About: An Autobiography*, Melbourne University Press, Melbourne, 1977, pp. 150–2, in Love, p. 177.
35 Alice Grant Rosnan, *Lone Hand*, 1 November 1909, quoted in Love, pp. 153–6.
36 Dennis Douglas and Morgan M. Morgan, 'Gregan McMahon and the Australian Theatre', *Komos*, no. 2, 1969, p. 59 and no. 3, 1969, p. 130.
37 Andrews, p. 25.
38 See Douglas and Morgan, p. 129. The original reference is to *Society*, 1 April 1922, pp. 12–14.
39 Allan Ashbolt summarised his argument in retrospect in Woolacott (ed.) *Playwriting*, Currawong Publishing, Sydney, 1942, pp. 173–4.
40 Arthur H. Adams, *The Forty Thieves*, Williamson and Musgrove, Melbourne, 1899. There is a copy in the State Library of Victoria, Latrobe Library.
41 For Adams' plays, see *Three Plays for the Australian Stage*, William Brooks, Sydney, 1914, and, for Esson's reactions, *Ballades of Old Bohemia*, Hugh Anderson (ed.), Red Rooster Press, Melbourne, 1980, p. 227.
42 Adams, *Three Plays*, p. 3.
43 'The Australian Drama', *Lone Hand*, 1 December 1908, p. 236.
44 See Richard Fotheringham's entry on him in Parsons and Chance, p. 24. Fotheringham writes on *Gallipoli Bill* with genuine enthusiasm.
45 Esson, *Ballades*, pp. 223–4.
46 Esson, *Ballades*, p. 227.
47 Arthur H. Adams, *The Knight of the Motor Launch*, NSW Bookstall Company, Sydney, 1913.
48 Esson, *Ballades*, p. 226.
49 Louis Esson, *The Time Is Not Yet Ripe*, ed. Philip Parsons, Currency Press, Sydney, 1973, pp. xiii, xiv.
50 See Sturm, p. 214.
51 Esson, *The Time Is Not Yet Ripe*, p. xi.
52 Palmer, p. 27.

53 See Peter Fitzpatrick, *Pioneer Players: The Lives of Louis and Hilda Esson*, Cambridge University Press, Melbourne, 1995.

Chapter Two: Bush and city

1 Letter to Leslie Rees, in *Letters of Vance and Nettie Palmer 1915–1963*, ed. Vivian Smith, National Library of Australia, Canberra, 1977, p. 162.
2 Quoted by T. Inglis Moore, *Social Patterns in Australian Literature*, Angus & Robertson, Sydney, 1971, p. 145.
3 Quoted by Helen Gilbert, *Sightlines: Race, Gender, and Nation in Contemporary Australian Theatre*, University of Michigan Press, Ann Arbor MI, 1998, p. 239.
4 See Paul Makeham, 'Framing the landscape: Prichard's *Pioneers* and Esson's *The Drovers*', *Australasian Drama Studies*, no. 23, April 1993, and Jane Goodall, 'Some rooms in outer space', *Australasian Drama Studies*, no. 19, October 1991.
5 Graeme Davison, 'Sydney and the Bush: An Urban Context for the Australian Legend', *Historical Studies*, vol. 17, no. 71, 1978, pp. 191–209.
6 Introduction to H. G. Kippax (ed), *Three Australian Plays*, Penguin, Ringwood, 1963, p. 13. See also Hugh Hunt, *The Making of Australian Theatre*, F. W. Cheshire, Melbourne, 1960, p. 17.
7 Margaret Williams, *Drama*, Oxford University Press, Sydney, 1977, p. 21.
8 Williams, pp. 14–15.
9 Quoted by Vance Palmer, *Louis Esson and the Australian Theatre*, Georgian House, Melbourne, 1948, p. 49.
10 Louis Esson, *Ballades of Old Bohemia*, ed. Hugh Anderson, Red Rooster Press, Melbourne, 1980, p. 176.
11 Palmer, p. 3. Esson tells the story slightly differently in *Ballades of Old Bohemia*, p. 174.
12 Esson, *Ballades*, p. 184.
13 See Palmer, p. 41.
14 Palmer, p. 27.
15 Esson, *Ballades*, p. 187.
16 See David Walker, *Dream and Disillusion: A Search for Australian Cultural Identity*, Australian National University Press, Canberra, 1976; John McCallum, 'Something With a Cow In It: Louis Esson's Imported Nationalism', *Overland*, no. 108, September 1987, pp. 6–13; John McCallum, 'Irish Memories and Australian Hopes: William Butler Yeats and Louis Esson', *Westerly*, no. 2, June 1989, pp. 33–40; and Peter Fitzpatrick, *Pioneer Players: The Lives of Louis and Hilda Esson*, Cambridge University Press, Melbourne, 1995.
17 Fitzpatrick, p. 183.
18 Palmer, pp. 90–1.
19 See Philip Parsons' introduction to Esson, *The Time Is Not Yet Ripe*.
20 Esson, *Ballades*, pp. 306–09.
21 Introduction to Louis Esson, *The Southern Cross and Other Plays*, Robertson and Mullens, Melbourne, 1946, p. xi.
22 Introduction to Esson, *Southern Cross*, p. xii.

ENDNOTES

23 *Hal's Belles*, for example, was produced at the Middle Park Repertory Theatre, Melbourne, in 1945, with Frank Thring in the leading role. The play is quite fun. There is a copy in State Library of Victoria, Latrobe Library, Melbourne Repertory Theatre Papers, MS 9758.
24 Palmer, p 50. The Tomholt comment is written in the margin of Tomholt's copy of Palmer's book, in the possession of the author.
25 Smith, p. 18.
26 Introduction to Louis Esson, *Plays 1: Terra Australis*, Five Islands Press, Wollongong, 1999, p. 12.
27 The quotation is in *The Campbell Howard Annotated Index of Australian Plays 1920–1955*, ed. Jack Bedson and Julian Croft, University of New England Press, Armidale, 1993, p. 309.
28 Introduction to Katharine Susannah Prichard, *Brumby Innes and Bid Me To Love*, Currency Press, Sydney, 1974, p. xxviii.
29 *The Forerunners* is the title of the Eureka play by Davidson in the Campbell Howard Collection, where it is dated 1925. L. L. Woolacott, *Playwriting*, Currawong Publishing, Sydney, 1942, p. 177, refers to the play as *Eureka Stockade*. However, Leslie Rees, *The Making of Australian Drama: A Historical and Critical Survey from the 1830s to the 1970s*, Angus & Robertson, Sydney, 1973, p. 172, says that a 'turgid' Eureka play by Davidson did win a Triad competition.
30 'Notes on the Aborigines in *Brumby Innes*' in Prichard, p. 102.
31 Letter from Katharine Susannah Prichard to Vance Palmer, quoted in the Preface to *Brumby Innes*, p. ix.
32 See Kay Schaffer, *Women and the Bush: Forces of Desire in the Australian Cultural Tradition*, Cambridge University Press, Melbourne, 1988.
33 See, for example, Helen Thomson, 'Gardening in the Never-Never: Women Writers and the Bush', in *The Time To Write: Australian Women Writers 1890–1930*, ed. Kay Ferres, Penguin, Ringwood, 1993; and Susan Sheridan, *Along the Faultlines: Sex, Race and Nation in Australian Women's Writing*, Allen & Unwin, Sydney, 1995.
34 See Schaffer, pp. 70–3.

Chapter Three: Settling the land

1 A. D. Hope, 'Standards in Australian Literature', *Current Affairs Bulletin*, 19 (26 November 1956), p. 40.
2 See Bedson and Croft (eds); and *Australian Drama Productions, 1950–1969*, ed. by Alrene Sykes, University of Queensland Library, Brisbane, 1984.
3 Bedson and Croft, p. 356.
4 Betty Roland, *The Eye of the Beholder*, Hale & Iremonger, Sydney, 1984 and Betty Roland, *An Improbable Life*, Collins, Sydney, 1989.
5 Michelle Arrow, *Upstaged: Australian Women Dramatists in the Limelight at Last*, Currency Press, Sydney, 2002, especially Ch. 4.
6 See Susan Pfisterer and Carolyn Pickett, *Playing with Ideas: Australian Women Playwrights from the Suffragettes to the Sixties*, Currency Press, Sydney, 1999.
7 See Frances de Groen, 'Dymphna Cusack's *Comets Soon Pass*: The genius

and the potato wife', in *Wallflowers and Witches: Women and Culture in Australia 1910–1945*, ed. Maryanne Dever, University of Queensland Press, St. Lucia Qld, 1994. De Groen discusses Cusack's attempts to resist her romantic inclinations, referring to her affair with Xavier Herbert, the model for Jason Denver in *Shoulder the Sky*.

8   Leslie Rees, *A History of Australian Drama. Vol. I. The Making of Australian Drama from the 1830s to the late 1960s*, Angus & Robertson, Sydney, 1978, p. 192.
9   See Sue Cullen, 'Australian theatre during World War One', *Australasian Drama Studies*, no. 17, 1989, pp. 157–81.
10 See Pfisterer and Pickett, pp. 72–7 and Vic Lloyd, 'Dymphna Cusack's *Morning Sacrifice*', *Australasian Drama Studies*, no. 10, 1987, pp. 71–2.
11 Rees, p. 163. Rees gives details of the controversy, pp. 162–5.
12 Philip Parsons with Victoria Chance (eds.), *Companion to Theatre in Australia*, Currency Press, Sydney, 1995, p. 182.
13 See Arrow, Ch. 6.
14 See Bedson and Croft, pp.42–3 and Rees, pp. 203–5.
15 See 'Authors Preface' and Doris Fitton, 'A Protest Against Bureaucracy', in Sumner Locke Elliott, *Rusty Bugles*, Currency Press, Sydney, 1980, pp. vii–xiii. An account of the banning of the play is given in the same volume, pp. xiv–xxxi, and also in Rees, pp. 459–464.

Chapter Four: Into the city

1   John Clarke, *A Dagg at my Table: Selected Writings*, Text Publishing, Melbourne, 1998, pp. 29–30.
2   Leslie Rees, *Hold Fast to Dreams: Fifty Years in Theatre, Radio, Television and Books*, Alternative Publishing Cooperative, Sydney, 1982, p. 200.
3   For instance, *Brumby Innes* which won its prize in 1927, wasn't published until 1940 or produced until 1973.
4   H. G. Kippax, 'Australian Drama Since "Summer of the Seventeenth Doll"', *Meanjin*, no. 23, September 1964, pp. 223–39, reprinted in Peter Holloway, *Contemporary Australian Drama* (rev. ed.), Currency Press, Sydney, 1987, p. 229.
5   Kevon Kemp, *Bulletin*, 18 August 1962, quoted in Virginia Kirby-Smith, 'The Development of Australian Theatre and Drama, 1788–1964', unpublished PhD dissertation, Duke University, 1969, p. 606.
6   See Leslie Rees, *A History of Australian Drama. Vol. I. The Making of Australian Drama from the 1830s to the late 1960s*, Angus & Robertson, Sydney, 1978; Kippax; and Kirby-Smith; and also Davison, Cherry, Hibberd and Hooton, in Holloway. See also Peter Fitzpatrick, *After the Doll: Australian Drama since 1955*, Edward Arnold, Melbourne, 1979; John McCallum, 'The *Doll* and the Legend', *Australasian Drama Studies*, vol. 3, no. 2, 1985; and Kerryn Goldsworthy, 'Is It a Boy or a Girl? Gendering the Seventeenth Doll', *Southerly*, vol. 55, no. 1, 1995.
7   George Molnar, *Sydney Morning Herald*, 14 January 1956, p. 6.
8   An account of the initial response is given in Rees, *History*, pp. 465–75.
9   Introduction to H. G. Kippax (ed), *Three Australian Plays*, Penguin, Ringwood, 1963, p. 17.

ENDNOTES

10 McCallum, pp. 33–44.
11 Jennifer Palmer, *Contemporary Australian Playwrights*, Adelaide University Union Press, Adelaide, 1979, p. 39.
12 Anne Summers, *Damned Whores and God's Police: The Colonisation of Women in Australia*, Penguin, Ringwood, 1975, pp. 43–4.
13 See McCallum; and Goldsworthy.
14 Palmer, p. 44.
15 Hugh Hunt, *The Making of Australian Theatre*, F. W. Cheshire, Melbourne, 1960, p. 17.
16 Eunice Hanger, introduction to Ray Mathew, *A Spring Song*, University of Queensland Press, St. Lucia Qld, 1961, p. 9. An excerpt from this is in Holloway, pp. 195–202.
17 See Kippax, introduction to *Three Australian Plays*, p. 17 and 'Australian Drama Since "Summer of the Seventeenth Doll"'. The plays are in the Hanger Collection of Australian Playscripts at the Fryer Library, University of Queensland.
18 P. H. Davison, 'Three Australian Plays: National Myths Under Criticism', *Southerly*, no. 2, 1963, and in Holloway, pp. 203–22.
19 Kippax, introduction to *Three Australian Plays*, pp. 12–14, 19–20 and Hunt, p. 17.

Chapter Five: Patrick White

1 Alex Buzo, *The Young Person's Guide to the Theatre and Almost Everything Else*, Penguin, Ringwood, 1988, p. 67.
2 Key critical sources from the first period are: R. F. Brissenden, 'The Plays of Patrick White', in Peter Holloway, *Contemporary Australian Drama* (rev. ed.), Currency Press, Sydney, 1987; J. F. Burrows, 'The Four Plays of Patrick White', *Australian Literary Studies*, vol. 2, no. 3 June 1966; Roger Covell, 'Patrick White's Plays', *Quadrant*, vol. 8, no. 1, April/May 1964; J. R. Dyce, *Patrick White as Playwright*, University of Queensland Press, St. Lucia Qld, 1974; T. Herring, 'Maenads and Goat-Song: The Plays of Patrick White' in *Ten Essays on Patrick White*, ed. G. A. Wilkes, Angus & Robertson, Sydney, 1970; and H. G. Kippax, 'Razzle-Dazzle Over Dog Pack', in Holloway. For other references see May-Brit Akerholt's 'Bibliographical Note' in Patrick White, *Collected Plays I*, Currency Press, Sydney, 1993, pp. 357–61 and her book, *Patrick White*, Rodopi, Amsterdam, 1988, pp. 199–206. See also Dennis Carroll, *Australian Contemporary Drama* (rev. ed.), Currency Press, Sydney, 1995; Peter Fitzpatrick, *After the Doll: Australian Drama since 1955*, Edward Arnold, Melbourne, 1979; and Leslie Rees, *A History of Australian Drama. Vol. I. The Making of Australian Drama from the 1830s to the late 1960s*, Angus & Robertson, Sydney, 1978.
3 David Marr, *Patrick White: A Life*, Random House, Sydney, 1991. See Chapter 19.
4 Quoted in Carroll, p. 158.
5 See her introduction to White, *Plays 1*, p. 8.
6 A plot summary of *Return to Abyssinia* is in Marr, pp. 174–5.
7 Marr, Chapter 19.
8 See Carroll, pp. 134–5.

9. Carroll can be taken as representative of the former and Brissenden of the latter.
10. See Akerholt, *Patrick White*, p. 172, for a description of Ken Wilby's set in Adelaide 1983.
11. The hero of Michael Boddy and Bob Ellis's *The Legend of King O'Malley*, discussed in Chapter 7.
12. Marr, p. 631.
13. See Marr, Chapter 29, which takes its title from the play and Akerholt, *Patrick White*, pp. 193–198.
14. Neil Armfield, 'About Signal Driver', in the program for the 1983 production for the Queensland Theatre Company.

Chapter Six: Playwrights in the 60s

1. Dorothy Hewett, *Bobbin' Up*, Virago, London, 1985. Her later novels are *The Toucher*, McPhee Gribble, Melbourne, 1993, and *Neap Tide*, Penguin, Ringwood, 1999.
2. Observered by the actor Carmel Dunn, who was Playreader for Melbourne Theatre Company at the time. This and the next two quotations are from Kristen Williamson's introduction to Dorothy Hewett, *Collected Plays I*, Currency Press, Sydney, 1992.
3. See Margaret Williams, *Dorothy Hewett: the Feminine as Subversion*, Currency Press, 1992, pp. 123–5.
4. Dorothy Hewett, 'Creating Heroines in Australian plays', *Hecate*, no. 2 1976, p. 74.
5. Hewett's first husband, Communist lawyer Lloyd Davies, whom she had married in 1945, sued her for defamation over material in the poem and play.
6. John Higgins, in the London *Times*, quoted in the *Sydney Morning Herald*, 29 April 1978.
7. See, for example his prefatory note to 'Sandy Soldiers On' in Barry Humphries, *The Life and Death of Sandy Stone*, Macmillan, Sydney, 1990, p. 91.
8. Barry Humphries, *A Nice Night's Entertainment*, Currency Press, Sydney, 1981, p. 115. The quotation from Big Sonia is on p. 106.
9. Collin O'Brien and Barry Humphries, 'Sandy's Australia', in Humphries, *Sandy Stone*, pp. xiii, xlii.
10. Humphries, *Sandy Stone*, p.92.
11. O'Brien and Humphries, p. xxxv.
12. John Sumner, *Recollections at Play: A Life in the Australian Theatre*, Melbourne University Press, Melbourne, 1993, throughout, but see especially pp. 219, 230ff, and 263.
13. Sumner, p. 110.
14. See, for example, Jack Hibberd, 'How Marvellous Melbourne Came To Life', *Theatre Australia*, vol. 2, no. 4 August 1977, pp. 36–7.

Chapter Seven: The New Wave

1. See Max Harris, *Ockers: Essays on the Bad Old New Australia*, Maximus Books, Adelaide, 1974.
2. Jim Davidson, 'Interview [with John Romeril]', in *Contemporary Australian*

ENDNOTES

    Drama, ed. by Peter Holloway, Currency Press, 1981, p. 376.

3   Julian Meyrick, *See How It Runs: Nimrod and the New Wave*, Currency Press, Sydney, 2002. See also Meyrick's *Trapped by the Past: Why Our Theatre is Facing Paralysis*, Platform Papers No. 3, Currency House, Sydney, 2005 and Gabrielle Wolf, *Make It Australian: The Australian Performing Group, the Pram Factory and New Wave Theatre*, Currency Press, Sydney, 2008.

4   For accounts of the National Theatre debate see Stephen Alomes, 'The search for a National Theatre', *Voices*, Spring 1993, and Donald Batchelor, 'Political manoeuvring behind the scenes: the development of the national theatre idea in Australia during the 1940s', *Australasian Drama Studies*, no. 40, 2002, pp. 58–73.

5   Meyrick, *See How It Runs*, p. 64.

6   Peter Brook, *The Empty Space*, Methuen, London, 1968.

7   See Graeme Blundell's introduction to *Four Australian Plays*, Penguin, Ringwood, 1970, also Elizabeth Jones et al, *La Mama: The Story of a Theatre*, McPhee Gribble & Penguin, Ringwood, 1988.

8   Jack Hibberd, *Squibs: A Collection of Short Plays*, Phoenix Publications, Brisbane, 1984, p. 22.

9   See Tim Robertson, *The Pram Factory: The Australian Performing Group Recollected*, Melbourne University Press, Melbourne, 2001.

10   See the appended lists in Jones et al; Robertson; and Meyrick, *See How It Runs*.

11   Meyrick, *See How It Runs*, pp. 207, 209. The figures include revivals as well as premieres, and short works that were part of a program and street theatre pieces.

12   See Adrian Kiernander, 'John Bell and a post-colonial Australian Shakespeare, 1963–2000', in *O Brave New World: Two Centuries of Shakespeare on the Australian Stage*, ed. John Golder and Richard Madelaine, Currency Press, Sydney, 2001, pp. 236–55.

13   See Steve Capelin, *Challenging the Centre: Two Decades of Political Theatre*, Playlab Press, Brisbane, 1995.

14   See Wolf, and for a broad survey, Geoffrey Milne, *Theatre Australia Unlimited: Australian Theatre since the 1950s*, Rodopi, Amsterdam, 2004.

15   See Barry Oakley, *The Great God Mogadon and Other Plays*, University of Queensland Press, St. Lucia Qld, 1980, p. viii.

16   See Peter Batey's glowing account of its theatrical effectiveness in his introduction to the published script, in the Play List of this book.

17   Margaret Williams, introduction to John Romeril, *A Stretch of the Imagination*, Currency Press, Sydney, 1973, p. iii.

18   For book-length studies of Hibberd's work, see J. D. Hainsworth, *Hibberd*, Methuen, Sydney, 1987 and Paul McGillick, *Hibberd*, Rodopi, Amsterdam, 1988.

19   See D. J. O'Hearn's introduction to Jack Hibberd, *Squibs*, Phoenix Publications, Brisbane, 1984, pp. 6–7. The seven short pieces in this volume are not listed individually in the Play List in this book.

20   Hibberd, *Squibs*, p. 4.

21   In the late-1980s a well-publicised American show, *Tony and Tina's*

Wedding, based on the same idea, opened in Sydney and bombed. It was like a version of *Dimboola* without jokes.
22. Hibberd, *Squibs*, p. 2. See also the introduction to Jack Hibberd, *A Country Quinella: Two Celebration Plays*, Penguin, Ringwood, 1984, n.p.
23. Hibberd, *A Country Quinella*, n.p.
24. See the revised introductions to *A Stretch of the Imagination* by Jack Hibberd and Margaret Williams to the second edition, published by Currency Press, Sydney, 1977. The script is unrevised.
25. Hibberd's introduction to the 1973 edition of *A Stretch of the Imagination*, pp. v and 24.
26. See Lisa Jacobson, 'The ocker in Australian drama', *Meanjin*, vol. 49, no. 1, 1990, pp. 137–47.
27. Introduction to Hibberd, *A Stretch of the Imagination*, 1973 edition, p. iii.
28. In 2008 Romeril received the Patrick White Award, which is given to a writer who has been highly creative over a long period but whose body of work has not been as widely recognised as it deserves.
29. Gareth Griffiths (ed.), *John Romeril*, Rodopi, Amsterdam, 1993, p. 196.
30. Davidson, p. 376.
31. Davidson, p. 380.
32. 'Afterword' to Barry Oakley, *The Feet of Daniel Mannix*m Angus & Robertson, Sydney, 1975 and Davidson, p. 376.
33. Quoted by David Watt in Griffiths, p. 106.
34. See Graeme Blundell's account of this incident in the film *Pram Factory*, directed by Anna Grieve and James Manché, Film Australia, 1994.
35. Introduction to John Romeril, *I Don't Know Who to Feel Sorry For*, Currency Press, Sydney, 1973, p. 16.
36. John Romeril, 'A note from the playwright', in *Love Suicides*, Currency Press, Sydney, 1997, n.p.
37. Bob Ellis, 'Go out and write an Australian play (It's not hard)', *Bulletin*, October 1970, pp. 43–4. The earlier historical plays include George Landen Dann's *Caroline Chisholm*, Vance Palmer's *Hail Tomorrow* (the 1890s shearers' strike), Leslie Haylen's *Blood on the Wattle* (the Eureka stockade), Max Afford's *Awake My Love* (Colonel Light and the founding of Adelaide), Catherine Shepherd's *Jane, My Love* (Sir John Franklin in colonial Tasmania), Kylie Tennant's *Tether a Dragon* (Alfred Deakin) and George Farwell's *The House That Jack Built* (the Rum Rebellion). More recent plays about Australian history and historical figures, not mentioned elsewhere, include Ralph Peterson's *The Third Secretary* (the Petrov affair), Roger Pulvers' *Yamashita* (the Japanese General in World War Two, but, like Romeril's Japanese plays, with wider resonances than the historical interest), Therese Radic's *A Whip Round for Percy Grainger* and *Peach Melba*, George Hutchinson's *Henry and Peter and Henry and Me* (Louisa Lawson), John O'Donoghue's *Essington Lewis: I Am Work* (the founder of BHP) and *Abbie and Lou, Normie and Rose* (Louis Stone and Norman Lindsay and their wives), Rodney Hall's *A Return to the Brink* (the Myall Creek massacre) and Bille Brown's *Bill and Mary* (Mary Gilmour and William Dobell).
38. See Margaret Williams, *Australia on the Popular Stage, 1829–1929*, Oxford University Press, Melbourne, 1983. A script of Dampier's play is in the State Library of New South Wales, Mitchell Library, MS B753.

ENDNOTES

39   Guy Rundle, *Your Dreaming*, Pluto Press, Sydney, 2002.
40   See Jack Hibberd's introduction to his *Three Popular Plays*, Outback Press, Melbourne, 1976.
41   See Robertson, pp. 77–84.
42   See Capelin.

Chapter Eight: David Williamson

1   On Williamson, see Peter Fitzpatrick, *Williamson*, Methuen, Sydney, 1987; Ortrun Zuber-Skerritt (ed.), *David Williamson*, Rodopi, Amsterdam, 1988 and Brian Kiernan, *David Williamson: A Writer's Career*, (rev. ed.), Currency Press, Sydney, 1996.
2   Delivered at the Seymour Centre, Sydney on 9 October 2005, available at http://currencyhouse.org.au/documents/ch_d_parsons2005_david_marr.pdf (accessed 10 December 2008).
3   Katharine Brisbane, introduction to David Williamson, *Collected Plays 1*, Currency Press, Sydney, 1986, p. xvii.
4   Robyn Nevin, 'A Classic Text', in David Williamson, *After the Ball*, Currency Press, Sydney, 1997, p. xii.
5   Philip Parsons, 'This World and the Next', in David Williamson, *Travelling North*, Currency Press, Sydney, 1980, p. xiv.
6   See Katharine Brisbane's introduction to *Siren*, Currency Press, Sydney, 1991, pp. ix–xiv.
7   David Williamson, introduction to *After the Ball*, Currency Press, Sydney, 1997, p. viii.
8   The correspondence, in the weekly *Nation Review*, was republished in *Days of Wine and Rage*, ed. Frank Moorhouse, Penguin, Ringwood, 1980. The film Colin has just written at the opening of *Emerald City* is called *Days of Wine and Whitlam*.
9   See David B. Moore and John M. McDonald, 'The Theatre of Everyday Conflict', in Williamson, *Two Plays:* Corporate Vibes *and* Face to Face Currency Press, Sydney, 1999, pp. 69–72.
10   The London version of the play was published by Faber and Faber in 2002.

Chapter Nine: Playwrights in the 70s

1   Their plays, where published, are listed in the Play List.
2   Alex Buzo, Jack Hibberd, John Romeril, *Four Australian Plays*, Penguin, Ringwood, 1970.
3   Alex Buzo, 'The day of the playwright', Theatre Quarterly, no. 26, 1977, pp. 71–3.
4   See Margaret Williams, 'Mask and Cage: Stereotype in Recent Drama', in Contemporary Australian Drama (rev. ed.), ed. P. Holloway, Currency Press, Sydney, 1987, pp. 327–33.
5   For details, see Leslie Rees, *The Making of Australian Drama: A Historical and Critical Survey from the 1830s to the 1970s*, Appendix VIII, Angus & Robertson, London and Sydney, 1973, pp. 489–91.
6   John McCallum, *Buzo*, Methuen Australia, Sydney, 1987, pp. 106 n.6 and

	138–47, also Alex Buzo, *Martello Towers*, Currency Methuen, Sydney, 1976, pp. 70–2.
7	Introduction to Buzo, *Martello Towers*, pp. xi–xiv.
8	Elizabeth Perkins, *The Plays of Alma De Groen*, Rodopi, Amsterdam, 1994.
9	Alma De Groen, *Wicked Sisters*, Currency Press, Sydney, 2003, p. xiii.
10	See Rémy Davison, 'Outside looking in: an interview with Ray Mooney', *Australasian Drama Studies*, no. 28, 1996, p. 57.
11	See Nadia Fletcher, 'Reg Livermore: a laugh in the wilderness', *Australasian Drama Studies*, no. 26, 1995, pp. 4–21. Some of the scripts are published in Livermore's splendidly produced *Chapters and Chances* (styled as a 'Souvenir Program of a Life in Theatre') Hardie Grant Books, Melbourne, 2003.
12	Fletcher, p. 17.

Chapter Ten: The new internationalism

1	Jack Hibberd, 'Proscenium-arch blues', in *Contemporary Australian Drama* (rev. ed.), ed. Peter Holloway, Currency Press, Sydney, 1987, p. 126. See also *Theatre Quarterly* 26, Summer, 1977 and Peter Fitzpatrick's account of the 'forebodings' in 'After the Wave: Australian drama since 1975' in *New Theatre Quarterly*, no. 5, February 1986, pp. 55–6.
2	See D Carroll, *Australian Contemporary Drama* (rev. ed.), Currency Press, Sydney, 1995; Peter Fitzpatrick, *After* The Doll: *Australian Drama since 1955*, Edward Arnold, Melbourne, 1979; Leonard Radic, *The State of Play: The Revolution in the Australian Theatre since the 1960s*, Penguin, Ringwood, 1991; and John McCallum, 'The World Outside: cosmopolitanism in the plays of Nowra and Sewell', in Holloway (ed.).
3	See Jeremy Ridgeman, 'Interview: Louis Nowra, Stephen Sewell and Neil Armfield talk to Jeremy Ridgeman', *Australasian Drama Studies*, no. 2, 1983, pp. 105–23.
4	Quoted by Sheridan Morley, 'Drama in history', *Sydney Morning Herald*, 11 October 1980.
5	This was in part because of a disillusionment with the critics who found his work too large, and theatre producers who were consequently, he said, too frightened to put them on. See his interview with Mary Ann Hunter, *Australasian Drama Studies*, no. 14, April 1989, pp. 35, 38–9. The main secondary source on Sewell is Peter Fitzpatrick, *Stephen Sewell: The Playwright as Revolutionary*, Currency Press, Sydney, 1991.
6	Quoted by Michael Morley, 'Trotsky Cassidy & dancing giants', *The National Times*, 7–13 October 1983, p. 31.
7	Ridgeman, p. 112.
8	Brecht, 'The Popular and the Realistic', in *Brecht on Theatre*, ed. John Willett, Eyre Methuen, London, 1973, pp. 109, 112.
9	Ridgeman, p. 115.
10	The main secondary sources are Veronica Kelly (ed.), *Nowra*, Rodopi, Amsterdam, 1987; and Veronica Kelly, *The Theatre of Louis Nowra*, Currency Press, Sydney, 1998.
11	Louis Nowra, 'Introduction' to *Inner Voices*, Currency Press, Sydney, 1977.

12 Nowra has said, oddly, that this was the play that suffocated him and that provoked an epiphany in which he determined to become more human. See his *Shooting the Moon: A Memoir*, Picador, Sydney, 2004, pp. 46–7.
13 See Helen Gilbert, 'Monumental moments: Michael Gow's *1841*, Stephen Sewell's *Hate*, Louis Nowra's *Capricornia* and Australia's Bicentenary', *Australasian Drama Studies*, no. 24, 1994, pp. 29–45.
14 See Nowra, *Shooting the Moon*, p. 101.
15 There is a two-year gap in the dates and ages. Lewis is 14 in 1962 and 21 in 1971 but it is clearly the same character.
16 One of the scenes, 'The Price of Prayer' (Scene 9 of the published script of *The Jungle*) was produced by itself as part of an evening of one-act plays by the Sydney Theatre Company in January 1995.
17 See Geoffrey Milne, *Theatre Australia (Un)limited: Australian Theatre since the 1950s*, Rodopi, Amsterdam, 2004, Section 4 and Epilogue.

Chapter Eleven: Playwrights in the 80s

1 Steve J. Spears, 'The Elocution of Benjamin Franklin', in *Drag Show* Currency Press, Sydney, 1977, p. 107.
2 One of the original Mo's comic devices was a splutter that turned 'recitation' into 'resuscitation'. One of his great sketches was a continually interrupted attempt to recite 'The Green-Eyed Idol of the Little Yellow God', and Spears's Mo keeps attempting to recite a similar poem in the play. Spears's title also alludes parodically to Peter Brook's then famous production of Peter Weiss's *The Persecution and Assassination of Jean Paul Marat as Performed by the Inmates of the Asylum at Charenton Under the Direction of the Marquis de Sade*, known more familiarly as *Marat/Sade*. A later project in the same style was the Aboriginal author Mudrooroo's play *The Aboriginal Protesters Confront the Declaration of the Australian Republic on 26 January 2001 with a Production of The Commission by Heiner Müller*, published in *The Mudrooroo/Muller Project: A Theatrical Casebook*, ed. by Gerhard Fischer, UNSW Press, Sydney, 1991. In the spirit of all these works this is the longest endnote in this book.
3 It is reproduced on the cover of Julian Meyrick, *See How It Runs*, Currency Press, Sydney, 2002.
4 Philip Parsons and Victoria Chance (eds), *Companion to Theatre in Australia*, Currency Press, Sydney, 1995, p. 190.
5 Elephant: 'I'm a lot bigger than you.' Mouse: 'But I've been sick!' See *One Woman Shoe*, p. 52; *Lennie Lower*, p. 9 and *The Golden Goldenbergs*, p. 13. Publication details in Play List.
6 In the first version, published in 1979 by Currency Press and *Theatre Australia* in their 'New3 Writing' series. The version published later in Bruce Parr (ed.), *Australian Gay and Lesbian Plays*, Currency Press, Sydney, 1996 has a slightly different ending.
7 See Anne Pender and Susan Lever (eds), *Nick Enright: An Actor's Playwright*, Rodopi, Amsterdam, 2008.
8 Personal communication, 1996.
9 Peter Kingston, in his introduction to Michael Gow, *Europe/On Top of the World*, Currency Press, Sydney, 1987.

BELONGING

Chapter Twelve: Identity and community

1. David Watt, 'The Popular Theatre Troupe and Street Arts: Two Paradigms of Political Activism', in Capelin (ed.), *Challenging the Centre: Two Decades of Political Theatre*, Playlab Press, Brisbane, 1995, pp. 13–33. See also Alan Filewood and David Watt, *Workers' Playtime: Theatre and the labour movement since 1970*, Currency Press, Sydney, 2001.
2. See, for example, Tony Mitchell, '"Going to the Source": Tes Lyssiotis talks to Tony Mitchell', *Australasian Drama Studies*, no. 12/13, 1988, p. 12.
3. See Sneja Gunew and Fazal Rizvi (eds), *Culture, Difference and the Arts*, Allen & Unwin, Sydney, 1994, pp. 1–3.
4. See Tim Robertson, *The Pram Factory*, Melbourne University Press, Carlton South, 2001 for a vivid personal account of the inner workings of the APG collective. See also Anna Grieve's documentary film, *Pram Factory*, Film Australia, 1994.
5. Peta Tait, *Original Women's Theatre: The Melbourne Women's Theatre Group 1974–77*, Artmoves, Melbourne, 1993, pp. 45–6.
6. By the time it came to be published a play of that name by Harold Pinter had opened and when Pinter refused to change his title Compton had to change hers. See Katharine Brisbane, Introduction to *Plays of the 70s Volume 3*, Currency Press, Sydney, 2001, p. vi.
7. Judith Butler, *Gender Trouble*, Routledge, New York, 1990.
8. Peta Tait, *Converging Realities: Feminism in Australian Theatre*, Currency Press and Artmoves, Sydney, 1994; Introduction to Peta Tait and Elizabeth Schafer, *Australian Women's Drama: Texts and Feminisms*, Currency Press, Sydney, 1997.
9. Stephen Sewell wrote the screenplay for a movie, *Isabelle Eberhardt*, released in 1992.
10. Rachel Fensham and Denise Varney, *The Dolls' Revolution : Australian theatre and cultural imagination*, Australian Scholarly Publishing, Melbourne, 2005 pp. 1–45. See p. 13.
11. See Jai Greenaway, *Political Acts: Lesbian Theatre in Sydney*, Amazon Desktop Publishing, Sydney, 1990.
12. Bruce Parr (ed.), *Australian Gay and Lesbian Plays*, Currency Press, Sydney, 1996; and *Plays From Black Australia*, Currency Press, Sydney, 1989.
13. Stephen Dunne, 'As Many Pearls As Possible: Gay Theatre in Sydney', unpublished BA (Hons) dissertation, University of Technology, Sydney, 1991. pp. 30–6.
14. See Parr, p. 25.
15. The story of Popular Theatre Troupe is told by one of its key artists, Errol O'Neill, in Steve Capelin's book, *Challenging the Centre*, Playlab Press, Brisbane, 1995, the principal documentary source for the extraordinary flourishing of protest theatre in Queensland during the years of the Bjelke-Petersen government.
16. John Stanwell and Anne Jones, 'The Logan City Story', in Richard Fotheringham, *Community Theatre in Australia*, Currency Press, Sydney, 1992, pp. 79–88.
17. H. Watson, '"All 4114 All": Writing For Street Arts in Logan City', in Capelin, pp. 159–69. 4114 is Logan City's postcode.

ENDNOTES

18 See Watt in Capelin; and David Watt and Graham Pitts, 'Community Theatre as Political Activism: Some Thoughts and Practices in the Australian Context', in *Community and the Arts*, ed. Vivienne Binns, Pluto Press, Sydney, 1991.
19 These projects are documented in Fotheringham's *Community Theatre in Australia*. This anthology of reports from the artistic coalface also includes accounts of early Aboriginal theatre; regional companies such as the Murray River Performing Group, in Albury/Wodonga, on the NSW/Victorian border; the new form of rough cabaret initiated by Newcastle's Castanet Club; and an account by Nicky Bricknell of the various state Deaf theatre companies that eventually became the National Theatre of the Deaf, now based in Sydney.
20 See his book *Fire on the Water*, Currency Press, Sydney, 1993.

Chapter Thirteen: Immigrants and exiles

1   See Sneja Gunew and Fazal Rizvi (eds), *Culture, Difference and the Arts* Allen & Unwin, Sydney, 1994.
2   See Tony Mitchell, 'Italo-Australian theatre: multiculturalism and neo-colonialism' *Australasian Drama Studies*, no. 10, 1987, pp. 31–48; and Con Castan, 'Greek-Australian Plays', *Australasian Drama Studies*, no. 12/13, 1988, pp. 17–33 for lists and discussions of plays written in Australia in Italian and Greek.
3   Pino Bosi, 'Making a Distinction between "Ethnic" and "Multicultural"', *Writing in Multicultural Australia 1984: An Overview*, Australia Council, Sydney, 1985.
4   Quoted in Castan, pp. 18–19.
5   Tony Mitchell, 'Going to the Source': Tess Lyssiotis talks to Tony Mitchell, *Australasian Drama Studies*, no. 12/13, 1988, p. 14.
6   *Out From Under* was published and is in the Play List with the author as Sidetrack Theatre.
7   See Tom Burvill, 'Sidetrack's *Kin*: intervening in multiculturalism', *Australasian Drama Studies*, no. 12/13, 1988, pp. 59–71.
8   Gunew, S. and Rizvi, F. (eds), *Culture, Difference and the Arts*, Allen & Unwin, Sydney, 1994, pp. 4–5.
9   Castan, pp. 18–19.
10 See Introduction to Theodore Patrikareas, *Antipodean Trilogy: Three Greek Australian Plays*, RMIT University Greek Archive Publications, Melbourne, 2000, pp. iii-v.
11 Patrikareas, pp. 213–14.
12 Tony Mitchell discusses some of them in 'Italo-Australian theatre: multiculturalism and neo-colonialism'.
13 See Carolyn Pickett, 'A Greek-Australian Drama', in Tes Lyssiotis, *A White Sports Coat and Other Plays*, Currency Press, Sydney, 1996, p. 7.
14 See Emma Ciccotosto and Michael Bedworth, *Emma: A Recipe for Life* Fremantle Arts Centre Press, Fremantle, 1995.
15 Film Australia, 1994.
16 See, for example, Henrietta Fourmile, 'Aboriginal arts in relation to multiculturalism', in Gunew and Rizvi, pp. 69–85.

BELONGING

Chapter Fourteen: Aboriginal theatre

1. Adam Shoemaker, *Black Words, White Page: Aboriginal Literature, 1929–1988*, University of Queensland Press, St Lucia, 1989, p. 242; Robert Merritt, *The Cake Man*, Currency Press, Sydney, 1983, p. 1.
2. A comprehensive account of contemporary Indigenous theatre is given in Maryrose Casey, *Creating Frames: Contemporary Indigenous Theatre* University of Queensland Press, St Lucia, 2004.
3. Peter Bibby's Introduction to Jimmy Chi and Kuckles, *Bran Nue Dae* Currency Press and Magabala Books, Sydney and Broome, 1991, p. vi.
4. Aboriginal and Torres Strait Islander Social Justice Commission, *Indigenous Deaths in Custody 1989–1996*, Aboriginal and Torres Strait Islander Commision, Canberra, 1996; and Human Rights and Equal Opportunities Commission, *Bringing Them Home: Report of the National Inquiry into the Separation of Aboriginal and Torres Strait Islander Children from Their Families*, Australian Government Publishing Service, Canberra, 1997.
5. Purcell later published a series of talks with other successful Indigenous women, later filmed, *Black Chicks Talking*, Hodder, Sydney, 2002.
6. Program to *Black Medea*, Company B Belvoir, April 2005.
7. Wayne Atkinson, 'Elder Introduction', in Andrea James, *Yanagai! Yanagai!*, Currency Press, Sydney, 2003.

Chapter Fifteen: Playwrights in the 90s

1. For a discussion of Christian's work see Laura Ginters, 'Violating the Past: Beatrix Christian', in Fensham and Varney (eds), *The Dolls' Revolution: Australian theatre and cultural imagination*, Australian Scholarly Publishing, Melbourne, 2005.
2. For scholars and practitioners who have written about this work see Veronica Kelly (ed.), *Our Australian Theatre in the 90s*, Rodopi, Amsterdam, 1998; and Peta Tait (ed.), *Body Show/s: Australian viewings of live performance*, Rodopi, Amsterdam, 2000. Other essays have been published in the journal *Australasian Drama Studies* and in the journal *RealTime*.
3. Allen, R. and Pearlman, K. (eds), Performing the Unnameable: An anthology of Australian performance texts, Currency Press, Sydney, 1999. This anthology includes work by individual artists Jenny Kemp, Richard Murphet, Lyndal Jones, Josephine Wilson and Margaret Cameron, companies such as Virginia Baxter and Keith Gallasch's Open City, Don Mamouney's Sidetrack Performance Group, David Williams and Barry Laing's Ek-Stasis Theatre Collective, Teresa Crea's Doppio Teatro, the Kinetic Energy Theatre Collective, Entr'Acte, the All Out Ensemble and the physical theatre company Legs on the Wall.
4. See Kerrie Schaefer, 'Staging Seduction: The Sydney Front and the postmodern geography of theatre's bodies and spaces', in Tait (ed.), *Body Show/s*.
5. Fensham and Varney give a detailed account of Kemp's major works, discussing the interplay of signs in them and exploring her staging and dramaturgy, pp. 64–108.
6. Hilary Glow gives a good detailed discussion of Rayson as a political

ENDNOTES

    playwright in *Power Plays: Australian Theatre and the Public Agenda*, Currency Press, Sydney, 2008.
7   David Williamson, *Travelling North*, Currency Press, Sydney, 1980, p. 56.
8   For a discussion of the media controversy, see Glow, pp. 155–9
9   See Glow, throughout, but see especially pp. 183–6.

Chapter Sixteen: The end of the twentieth century

1   See Michael Gurr's memoir, *Days Like These*, Melbourne University Press, 2006, throughout, but especially p. 284.
2   *Confidentially Yours* is listed in the Play List under Balodis, the first author alphabetically. Bovell's contribution is two monologues that amplify the action of his *Speaking in Tongues*.
3   '22 Questions', http://danielkeene.com . Accessed 10/12/2008
4   The volumes published in French, not listed in the Play List, include *Vive le marie*, Gallimard, Paris, 1992; *Silence compris terminus*, Théatrales Eds, Paris, 1999; *Douze pièces courtes*, Théatrales Eds, Paris, 2001; *Le marche d'architecte*, Théatrales Eds, Paris, 2002; *Cinq hommes suivi de Moitié-moitié*, Théatrales Eds, Paris, 2003; *Une heure avant la mort de mon frère*, Lansman Eds, Morlanwelz, 2004; *Paradise*, Théatrales Eds, Paris, 2004; *Avis aux intéressés*, Théatrales Eds, Paris, 2004; *Pièces Courtes*, Théatrales Eds, Paris, 2005; and *Pièces Courtes T2*, Théatrales Eds, Paris, 2007.
5   These plays are published without capitalisation, punctuation or character names in the dialogue—leaving them open for the actors but also, once you get used to it, for readers.

Conclusion

1   Adriano Cortese, 'Director's Note', in Raimondo Cortese, *Roulette*, Currency Press, Sydney, 2005, p. viii.
2   Dennis Carroll, *Australian Contemporary Drama* (rev. ed.), Currency Press, Sydney, 1995.

PLAY LIST

This is a list of published twentieth-century Australian plays. It also includes those unpublished ones and those from the twenty-first century that are mentioned in the text. The entries take the form:

Playwright *Title* Date of publication or date in archive (Date of first production) Publication or archive details (First production details)

The publication details are of the most recent edition. No details usually means that no publication or production took place, but it might mean that I haven't got the information. Corrections and additions should be sent to j.mccallum@unsw.edu.au.

Abbreviations
ATYP – Australian Theatre for Young People, Sydney
A&R – Angus and Robertson
APG – Australian Performing Group, Pram Factory, Melbourne
Currency – Currency Press, Sydney
QPAC – Queensland Performing Arts Centre, Brisbane
QTC – Queensland Theatre Company, Brisbane
La Boite – La Boite Theatre, Brisbane
La Mama – La Mama Theatre, Melbourne
MTC – Melbourne Theatre Company
Playbox – Playbox Theatre, CUB Malthouse, Melbourne

BELONGING

Playlab – Playlab Press, Brisbane
STC – Sydney Theatre Company
UQP – University of Queensland Press
VAC – Victorian Arts Centre
Yackandandah – Yackandandah Playscripts, Montmorency, Victoria

Acworth, Elaine *Composing Venus* 1995 (1994) Currency (QTC, 17 February)
Adams, Arthur H. *Doctor Death* 1909 *The Lone Hand*, 5/27 1909: 257–68.
―― *The Forty Thieves* 1899 (1899) Williamson and Musgrove, Melbourne; 1899 (Williamson and Musgrove, Her Majesty's Theatre, Sydney)
―― *Galahad Jones* 1914 In *Three Plays for the Australian Stage*. William Brooks, Sydney
―― *Mrs Pretty and the Premier* 1914 In *Three Plays for the Australian Stage*. William Brooks, Sydney
―― *The Wasters* 1914 (1910) In *Three Plays for the Australian Stage*. William Brooks, Sydney (Adelaide Literary Theatre, 27 August)
Adkin, Paul *The Jack and Jill Story* 1981 (1981) Australian Nouveau Theatre, Melbourne (La Mama)
Afford, Max *Awake My Love* 1974 (1947) In *Mischief in the Air: Radio and Stage Plays*. UQP (Independent Theatre, Sydney, 4 September)
―― *Consulting Room* 1974 (1978) In *Mischief in the Air: Radio and Stage Plays*. UQP
―― *Lady in Danger* 1974 (1942) In *Mischief in the Air: Radio and Stage Plays*. UQP, (Independent Theatre, Sydney, February)
―― *Lazy in the Sun* 1974 (1951) In *Mischief in the Air: Radio and Stage Plays*. UQP
―― *Mischief in the Air* 1974 (1944) In *Mischief in the Air: Radio and Stage Plays*. UQP (JC Williamson Ltd, Theatre Royal, Sydney, June)
Allayialis, Toni *My Of-Course Life* 2004 (2004) Playlab (Just Us Theatre Ensemble and QPAC, Cairns, Queensland, 10 September)
Allen, David *Cheapside* 1985 (1984) Currency (MTC, Athemaeum 2, 5 June)
―― *Gone With Hardy* 1978 (1978) *Theatre Australia*, 3,4:39–44 and 3,5:35–39 (MTC, 21 September)
―― *Karen* 1982 In *One Act Plays: Series 2*, edited by David Allen. Heinemann Educational, Richmond, Victoria
―― *Modest Expectations* 1990 (1990) Currency (Playbox, 2 November)
―― *Upside Down at the Bottom of the World* 1981 (1979) Heinemann Educational, Richmond, Victoria (Nimrod Theatre Downstairs, 8 August)
Anderson, Tammy *I Don't Wanna Play House* 2002 (2002) In *Blak Inside: 6 Indigenous Plays from Victoria*. Currency (Ilbijerri Aboriginal and Torres Strait Islander Theatre Cooperative and Playbox, 25 April)
Antill, John Macquarie and Rose Antill-De Warren *The Emancipist* 1936 A&R
Archer, Robyn *Cafe Fledermaus* 1990 (1990) Currency (Playbox, 28 May)
Armstrong, Millicent *As The Moon Sets* 1958 Campbell Howard Collection, University of New England, Armidale, NSW

PLAY LIST

—— *At Dusk* 1937 (1938) In *Best Australian One-Act Plays*, edited by William Moore and T. Inglis Moore. A&R (Sydney Drama Society, 23 July)

—— *Drought* 1958 (1924) In *Plays in One Act*. Edwards and Shaw, Sydney (The Playhouse, Melbourne, 24–25 June)

—— *Fire* 1923 Campbell Howard Collection, University of New England, Armidale, NSW

—— *Goblin Gold* 1932 Campbell Howard Collection, University of New England, Armidale, NSW

—— *Nina* 1936 Campbell Howard Collection, University of New England, Armidale, NSW

—— *Penny Dreadful* 1958 (1961) In *Plays in One Act*. Edwards and Shaw, Sydney (Arrow Theatre, Melbourne, 8 August)

—— *Thomas* 1958 (1959) In *Plays in One Act*. Edwards and Shaw, Sydney, 1958d (Armidale Theatre Club, Armidale, NSW)

Aronson, Linda *Dinkum Assorted* 1989 (1988) Currency (STC and MTC, Drama Theatre, Sydney Opera House, 1 June)

—— *The Fall Guy* 1977 (1977) *Theatre Australia*, 2,2:35–46 and 2,3:35–41 (MTC, 29 March)

—— *Reginka's Lesson* 1989 (1986) Currency (The Stage Company, Adelaide Festival Centre, 29 May)

Ash, Kathryn *Bag O' Marbles* 2002 (2002) Playlab (Just Us Theatre Ensemble, Cairns, Queensland, 31 May)

—— *Flutter* 2004 (2004) In *From the Edge: Two Plays from Northern Australia*, edited by Anne Harris. Playlab (Just Us Theatre Ensemble, Cairns, Queensland. 8 May)

Ash, Kathryn, Stephen Carleton, Gail Evans, and Anne Harris *Surviving Jonah Salt* 2004 (2004) In *From the Edge: Two Plays from Northern Australia*, edited by Anne Harris. Playlab (Just Us Theatre Ensemble, Cairns, Queensland, 30 July)

Aston, Manuel *Clay Soldiers* 1991 (1990) Big Hand Theatre Company, Sydney (Big Hand Theatre Company, Stables Theatre, Sydney. 21 June)

—— *Fossils!* 1995 (1993) Currency (Theatre South, Bridge Theatre, Wollongong, 23 October)

—— *When the Bough Breaks* 1992 (1992) Big Hand Theatre Company, Sydney (Big Hand Theatre Company, Stables Theatre, Sydney, 14 May)

Atkinson, E. J. Rupert *The Dead Man's Ghost* 1925 Edward A. Vidler, Melbourne

—— *Each Man a Multitude* 1923 Edward A. Vidler, Melbourne

—— *A Nocturne* 1919 Edward A. Vidler, Melbourne

—— *Ten Years' Remorse* 1923 Edward A. Vidler, Melbourne

Atkinson, L. V. *Divided They Fall* 1953 Gaythorne Publications, Brisbane

Austin, Ian *Down Came a Jumbuck* 1983 (1983) In *Down Came a Jumbuck and other One-Act Plays*. Playlab

—— *Duchess on Thursday* 1983 (1969) In *Down Came a Jumbuck and other One-Act Plays*. Playlab

—— *Elizabeth the Third* 1983 (1976) In *Down Came a Jumbuck and other One-Act Plays*. Playlab

BELONGING

────── *Over My Dead Body* 1983 (1978) In *Down Came a Jumbuck and other One-Act Plays*. Playlab
────── *Sex and Other Frustrations* 1987 (1985) Playlab (Buderim Amateur Theatrical Society, Buderim, Queensland, 18 October)
────── *Two Men in Buckram* 1978 (1966) In *3 Queensland One-Act Plays for Festivals*. Playlab (Warana Drama Festival, Rialto Theatre, Brisbane, 1 October)
────── *The Un-Cucumber Man* 1983 (1965) In *Down Came a Jumbuck and other One-Act Plays*. Playlab
Ayres, Tony *The Fat Boy* 2003 (2003) Currency (Playbox, 9 April)
Bailey, Bert *On Our Selection* 1984 (1912) Currency (Kings Theatre, Melbourne)
Bakaitis, Helmut *The Incredible Mind-Blowing Trial of Jack Smith* 1973 (1971) Heinemann Educational, Melbourne (PLC Burwood, 21 June)
Balodis, Janis *My Father's Father* 1997 (1996) In *The Ghosts Trilogy*. Currency (MTC, The Fairfax, Victorian Arts Centre, 1 March)
────── *No Going Back* 1997 (1992) In *The Ghosts Trilogy*. Currency (MTC, Russell Street Theatre, 16 July)
────── *Perfect Skin* [Adapted from the novel by Nick Earls] 2006 (2006) Currency (La Boite Theatre, Brisbane, 19 May)
────── *Too Young For Ghosts* 1997 (1985) In *The Ghosts Trilogy*. Currency (MTC, Studio, Victorian Arts Centre, 4 July)
────── *Wet and Dry* 1991 (1986) Currency (Darwin Theatre Group, Brown's Mart Theatre, October)
Balodis, Janis, Andrew Bovell, Nick Enright, Michael Gurr, Daniel Keene, Joanna Murray-Smith and Debra Oswald *Confidentially Yours* 1998 (1998) Currency (Playbox, 11 November)
Barclay, Edmund *Murder in the Silo* 1937 In *Best Australian One-Act Plays*, edited by William Moore and T. Inglis Moore. A&R
Barnard Eldershaw, M. *The Watch on the Headland* 1961 In *Eight One-Act Plays*. Thomas Nelson and Sons, Melbourne
Barnett, Christopher *Basket Weaving for Amateurs* 1984 (1981) In *Last Days of Th World* [sic] *and other texts for theatre*. Rigmarole Books, Melbourne (Roundspace Gallery, Adelaide, 19 March)
────── *Selling Ourselves For Dinner* 1982 (1982) All Out Ensemble, Adelaide (Adelaide Festival, Rundle Mall Car Park, March 10)
────── *Th Last Days of Th World* [sic] 1984 (1982) In *Last Days of Th World* [sic] *and other texts for theatre*. Rigmarole Books, Melbourne (Reconnaisance Gallery, Melbourne, 11 September)
────── *Ulrike Meinhof Sings* 1984 In *Last Days of Th World* [sic] *and other texts for theatre*. Rigmarole Books, Melbourne
Barrett, Richard *The Heartbreak Kid* 1988 (1987) Currency (Griffin Theatre Company, Stables Theatre, Sydney, 29 July)
Bates, Vanessa *Darling Oscar* 1998 (1994) In *Sydney Theatre Company: Plays 1*, edited by John Senczuk. Five Islands Press, Wollongong (STC New Stages, Wharf 2, 27 August)

PLAY LIST

Baxter, Virginia and Keith Gallasch *Tokyo Two: A Tourist Thriller* 1993 (1992) *Canadian Theatre Review*, 74:54–72 (The Performance Space, Sydney, 18 June)
—— *What Time is This House* 1992 (1985) Australasian Drama Studies Association, Sydney (Adelaide)
Beaton, Hilary *No Strings Attached* 1994 (1994) Playlab (La Boite, 8 September)
Becher, Alan and David Britton *The Newspaper of Claremont Street* 1991 (1990) Currency (Festival of Perth, Dolphin Theatre, Perth, 18 February)
Bedford, Eric *The Pendulum* 1932 Australasian Press Agency, Sydney
Beeby, George S. *The Banner* 1923 In *Concerning Ordinary People: Six Plays*. Gordon & Gotch, Sydney
—— *Dregs* 1923 (1933) In *Concerning Ordinary People: Six Plays*. Gordon & Gotch, Sydney (Sydney Theatre Guild, Ingersoll Hall, 21 October)
—— *In Quest of Pan* 1924 Tyrrells Limited, Sydney
—— *One Touch O' Nature* 1923 (1923) In *Concerning Ordinary People: Six Plays*. Gordon & Gotch, Sydney (Sydney Players' Club)
—— *The Point o' View* 1923 (1925) In *Concerning Ordinary People: Six Plays*. Gordon & Gotch, Sydney (Sydney Players' Club, 11 July)
—— *Potter and Clay* 1923 In *Concerning Ordinary People: Six Plays*. Gordon & Gotch, Sydney
—— *Still Waters* 1923 (1924) In *Concerning Ordinary People: Six Plays*. Gordon & Gotch, Sydney (The Playbox Society, St James' Hall, Sydney, April)
Behenna, Craig *Calvin Mollycoddle* 1985 (1985) In *Troupe's Young Playwrights Season: seven plays written by young South Australians*. Currency (Troupe, The Old Unley Town Hall, Unley, South Australia, 11 May)
Bell, Hilary *Fortune* 1995 (1993) Currency (Griffin Theatre Company, Stables Theatre, Sydney, 30 April)
—— *Wolf Lullaby* 1997 (1996) Currency (Griffin Theatre Company, Stables Theatre, Sydney, 23 April)
Bennett, Roger *Funerals and Circuses* 1995 (1992) Currency (Magpie Theatre, Theatre 62, Adelaide, 3 March)
—— *Up the Ladder* 1997 (1990) Playlab (Tandanya Aboriginal Cultural Centre)
Benyon, Lissa *Love Seen in Laundromat* 1994 (1994) In *Passion: Six New Short Plays by Australian Women*, edited by Ros Horin. Currency (Griffin Theatre Company, Stables, Sydney, 27 October)
—— *The Margarine Conspiracy* 1985 (1985) In *Shorts at the Wharf*. Vol.2. Currency (STC, The Wharf, 9 March)
Benzie, Tim *Personal Fictions* 1997 (1994) *Australasian Drama Studies*, 31:129–74. (Pandemonium Theatre, Avalon Theatre, Brisbane, 29 June)
Betzien, Angela *Children of the Black Skirt* 2005 (2003) Currency (Real TV, in association with the Queensland Arts Council)
—— *Hoods* 2007 (2006) Currency (Sydney Opera House Studio, 8 May)
Bews, Samantha *So Wet* 2000 (2000) In *Inside 2000*. Currency (Playbox, 12 April)
Beynon, Richard *Epitaph For Two Faces* 1964 In *Next Act!*, edited by Richard Beynon and H. G. Fowler. A&R

BELONGING

—— *The Shifting Heart* 1960 (1957) A&R (Elizabethan Theatre, Sydney, 4 October)
—— *Summer Shadows* 1986 (1986) Currency (Playbox Theatre Company, Melbourne, 16 September)
Bierwirth, Judy *Alive and Kicking* 1991 (1991) Currency (Playbox, Melbourne, 4 May)
Bishop, Robyn *Only the End* 2005 (2005) *In Only the End and Shakespeare and the Dark Lady of the Sonnets: Two plays*. Currency (La Mama at the Carlton Courthouse, 20 April)
Blair, Ron *A Place in the Present* 1985 (1977) In *Popular Short Plays for the Australian Stage Volume 1*, edited by Ron Blair. Currency (State Theatre Company of South Australia, 23 June)
—— *The Christian Brothers* 2001 (1975) In *Plays of the 70s Volume 3*, edited by Katharine Brisbane. Currency (Nimrod Theatre, Sydney, 1 August)
—— *Flash Jim Vaux* 1990 (1971) Yackandandah (Nimrod Street Theatre, Sydney, April 29)
—— *Last Day In Woolloomooloo* 1983 (1979) APCOL/Nimrod, Sydney (State Theatre Company of South Australia, 30 November)
—— *Mad Bad and Dangerous to Know* 1976 (1976) *Quadrant*, 20.10(October):15-21 (Nimrod Theatre Downstairs, 12 March)
—— *Marx* 1983 (1978) Currency (South Australian Theatre Company 1 June)
—— *President Wilson in Paris* 1974 (1973) Currency Methuen, Sydney (Nimrod Theatre, Sydney, 7 February)
Blake, Leila *Prey* 1978 (1973) In *Can't You Hear Me Talking to You?: Eight Short Plays about Lovers and Others*, edited by Alrene Sykes. UQP (Q Theatre, AMP Theatrette, Sydney, 15 May)
Blewett, Dorothy *Quiet Night* 1941 (1941) Australasian Publishing Company, Sydney (Dramatists' Club Players, Little Theatre, South Yarra, 8 March)
—— *The First Joanna* 1948 (1948) Campbell Howard Collection, University of New England, Armidale, NSW (Adelaide Repertory Theatre, 28 August)
Bobis, Merlinda *Ms Serena Serenata and Beaut, Luv* 1995 *Australasian Drama Studies*, 27: 87–122
Boddy, Michael and Bob Ellis *The Legend of King O'Malley* 1998 (1970) In *Plays of the 70s Vol 1*, edited by Katharine Brisbane, Currency (Jane Street Theatre, Sydney, 11 June)
Bol, Lorna *Treadmill* 1978 (1977) Playlab (La Boite, 1 April)
Bond, Graham and Jim Burnett *Boy's Own McBeth: a really rotten tragedy* 1980 (1979) Currency (Dunsinane Enterprises, Kirk Gallery, Sydney, 11 July)
Bostock, G. L. *Here Comes the Nigger* 1977 Meanjin, 36: 479–93 [extract].
Bourne, Suzy *George and the Goonybird* 1985 (1985) In *Troupe's Young Playwrights Season: seven plays written by young South Australians*. Currency (Troupe, The Old Unley Town Hall, Unley, South Australia. 11 May–1 June)
Bovell, Andrew *After Dinner* 1989 (1988) Currency (La Mama, 20 April)
—— *The Ballad of Lois Ryan* 1990 (1988) *Australasian Drama Studies*, 17:85–116. (Melbourne Workers' Theatre)
—— *Holy Day* 2001 (2001) Currency (State Theatre Company of South Australia, The Playhouse, Adelaide Festival Centre, 21 August)

PLAY LIST

———— *Speaking in Tongues* 1998 (1996) Currency (Griffin Theatre Company, Stables Theatre, Sydney, 6 August)
Bovell, Andrew and Hannie Rayson *Scenes From a Separation* 1996 (1995) Currency (MTC, Fairfax Theatre, Victorian Arts Centre, 15 November)
Bovell, Andrew, Patricia Cornelius, Melissa Reeves, Christos Tsiolkas, and Irine Vela *Who's Afraid of the Working Class?* 2000 (1998) In *Melbourne Stories: Three Plays*. Currency (Melbourne Workers' Theatre. Victoria Trades Hall. 1 May)
Bower, Humphrey *Natural Life* 1998 (1998) Currency (Playbox, 25 March)
Braddon, Russell *Naked Island* 1961 (1960) Evans Brothers, London (Arts Theatre, London, 29 September)
Bradhurst, Jane *Duet* 1987 (1984) In *Three One-Act Plays*. Playlab (Canberra Playhouse, 9 June)
————*Quartet* 1987 In *Three One-Act Plays*. Playlab)
———— *String Trio* 1976 (1975) In *Three One-Act Plays*. Playlab (Women's Theatre Group, Pram Factory, Melbourne. October)
Bradley, Belinda *Polly Blue* 2000 (1995) In *Melbourne Stories: Three Plays*. Currency (La Mama at the Courthouse, November [under the title *A Quiet Life*])
Bradley, John *Irish Stew* 1980 (1979) In *Three Political Plays*, edited by Alrene Sykes. UQP (La Boite, 2 February)
Bradshaw, Richard *Bananas* 1976 (1975) In *The Guerilla/Bananas and The Fourth Wall*. Currency Methuen, Sydney (Sheridan Theatre, Adelaide, 31 July)
Brand, Mona *Barbara* 1969 (1966) In *Here Under Heaven: Three Plays*. The Wentworth Press, Sydney (New Theatre, Sydney)
———— *Better a Millstone* 1965 In *Plays*. Progress Publishers, Moscow
———— *The Clearing House* 1989 (1995) New Theatre Publications, Clifton Hill, Victoria (Mitcham Repertory Group, the C. Healy-J.Wilson Memorial Theatre, Whitefriars College, Donvale 25 May)
————*Flood Tide* 1955 Campbell Howard Collection, University of New England, Armidale, NSW
———— *Flying Saucery* 1981 (1970) In *Flying Saucery, and Other Plays For Young People*. APCOL, Sydney (New Theatre, Sydney, 20 June)
———— *The Ghost of Grey Gables* 1981 (1972) In *Flying Saucery, and Other Plays For Young People*. APCOL, Sydney (The Holiday Theatre, Wesley Auditorium, Sydney, 15 December)
———— *Here Comes Kisch!* 1983 (1982) Yackandandah (Australian National Playwrights Conference, Canberra,)
———— *Here Under Heaven* 1999 (1948) In *Tremendous Worlds* edited by Susan Pfisterer. Currency (New Theatre, Melbourne, May)
———— *No Strings Attached* 1965 (1958) In *Plays*. Progress Publishers, Moscow (New Theatre, Sydney, 4 October)
———— *Our 'Dear' Relations* 1969 In *Here Under Heaven: Three Plays*. The Wentworth Press, Sydney
———— *Pavement Oasis* 1958 Campbell Howard Collection, University of New England, Armidale, NSW
———— *Strangers in the Land* 1965 (1952) In *Plays*. Progress Publishers, Moscow (Unity Theatre, London, 20 November)

BELONGING

────── *The Three Secrets* 1981 (1980) In *Flying Saucery, and Other Plays For Young People*. APCOL, Sydney (New Theatre, Sydney, 7 January)
Brereton, John Le Gay *So Long Mick!* 1931 (1931) A&R (Fellowship of Australian Writers, St James Hall Sydney, 21 August)
────── *Tomorrow* 1919 A&R
Brereton, John Le Gay and H. M. Green *The Temple on the Hill: A Mask* 1928 (1928) The Australian Medical Publishing Company Ltd, Sydney (Sydney University,)
Brodney, Spencer *Rebel Smith* 1925 (1925) Siebel Publishing Company, New York (Pioneer Players, Melbourne)
Broinowski, Anna *The Gap* 1995 (1993) Currency (Sydney Asian Theatre Season, Belvoir St Theatre, Sydney, June)
Brooksbank, Anne and Bob Ellis *Down Under* 1977 (1975) A&R & Melbourne (The Stables, Sydney, 3 September)
Brown, Bille *Bill and Mary* 2004 (2002) Phoenix Education, Melbourne (QTC, 12 August)
Brown, David *Eating Ice Cream With Your Eyes Closed* 2004 (2004) Playlab (QTC and Hothouse Theatre, QPAC, 5 August)
Brown, Frank and Louis Esson *Mates* 1999 (1923) In Louis Esson, *Plays 1: Terra Australis* Five Islands Press, Wollongong, NSW (Pioneer Players, Melbourne, August)
Brown, Paul *Aftershocks* 1993 (1991) Currency (Newcastle Playhouse, presented by the Workers' Cultural Action Committee with the assistance of the Hunter Valley Theatre Company, 12 November)
Brown, W. Jethro *Who Knows?* 1923 The Hassell Press, Adelaide [the most ludicrously incompetent play published in Australia in the 20th century]
Burrell, Donald *Baby, Cradle and All* 1994 four W Press Booranga, The Riverina Writers Centre, CSU, Wagga Wagga, NSW
Buzacott, Martin *Kingaroy* 1996 (1994) In *Kingaroy and Milo*. Currency (Royal QTC, Cremorne Theatre, QPAC, 16 July)
Buzo, Alex *Big River* 1985 (1980) In *Big River/The Marginal Farm*. Currency (MTC, Arts Theatre, Adelaide, 7 March)
────── *Coralie Lansdowne Says No* 1999 (1974) In *Plays of the 70s Volume 2*, edited by Katharine Brisbane. Currency (Nimrod Street Theatre Company at Theatre 62, Adelaide, 9 March)
────── *The Front Room Boys* 1998 (1969) In *Plays of the 60s Volume 3*, edited by Katharine Brisbane. *Currency* (Australian Theatre Company, Arts Lab, Sydney, 9 October)
────── *Macquarie* 1971 (1971) Currency (MTC (Workshop Production, Normanby Road,)
────── *Makassar Reef* 1979 (1978) Currency (MTC, Russell Street Theatre, 31 August)
────── *The Marginal Farm* 1985 (1983) In *Big River/The Marginal Farm*. Currency (MTC, Russell Street Theatre, 2 November)
────── *Martello Towers* 1976 (1976) Currency Methuen, Sydney (Nimrod Theatre, Sydney, 30 April)
────── *Norm and Ahmed* 1999 (1968) In *Plays of the 60s Volume 2*, edited by Katharine Brisbane. Currency (Old Tote Theatre Company, 9 April)

PLAY LIST

—— *Pacific Union* 1995 (1995) Currency (Playbox, 19 September)
—— *Rooted* 1973 (1969) In *Three Plays*. Currency Methuen, Sydney (Stage, Childers Street Hall, Canberra and Jane Street Theatre, Sydney, both 14 August)
—— *The Roy Murphy Show* 1973 (1971) In *Three Plays*. Currency Methuen, Sydney (Nimrod Street Theatre, Sydney. 1 July)
—— *Tom* 1975 (1972) A&R (MTC, Russell Street Theatre, 21 November)
Callaghan, Stacey *still raw* 1997 (1994) *Australasian Drama Studies*, 31:179–99. (National Lesbian Confest, Brisbane, July)
Cameron, Margaret *Bang! A Critical Fiction* 2001 (2001) In *Inside 01*. Currency (Playbox, 6 June)
—— *Knowledge and Melancholy* 2001 (2001) In *Inside 01*. Currency (Playbox. 20 June)
Cameron, Matt *Ruby Moon* 2003 (2003) Currency (Playbox. 30 July)
—— *Tears From a Glass Eye* 1998 (1998) Currency (Playbox. 27 May)
Carleton, Stephen *Constance Drinkwater and the Final Days of Somerset* 2006 (2006) Playlab (QTC, 13 July)
Carroll, Kathleen *Office Interlude* 1944 (1940) In *Six Australian One Act Plays*. Mulga Publications, Sydney (Chelsea Dramatic Group, Sydney, 31 January)
—— *Saturday* 1940 (1940) Campbell Howard Collection, University of New England, Armidale, NSW (Perth Repertory Society, Perth, 18 September)
Cathcart, Sarah and Andrea Lemon *The Serpent's Fall* 1988 (1987) In *Steal Away Home and The Serpent's Fall*. Currency (La Mama, 17 June)
Cazouris, George *Almost a Divorce* 1988 In *Greek Voices in Australia: A Tradition of Poetry, Prose and Drama*, edited by George Kanarakis. ANU Press, Canberra
Cerini, Angus *Seven Days of Silence* 2001 (2001) In *Inside 01*. Currency (Playbox, 20 June)
Charles, Shaun *Last Drinks* 2006 (2006) Playlab (La Boite, 17 August)
—— *Rio Saki and Other Falling Debris* 2006 (1999) Playlab (La Boite, 2 September)
Chi, Jimmy and Kuckles *Bran Nue Dae* 1991 (1990) Currency; Magabala Books, Broome (Bran Nue Dae Productions and the Western Australian Theatre Company, Octagon Theatre, Perth, Festival of Perth February)
Christian, Beatrix *Blue Murder* 1994 (1994) Currency (Company B, Belvoir St Theatre, Sydney, 5 April)
—— *Fred* (1998) (STC, Wharf 1)
—— *The Governor's Family* 1997 (1997) Script supplied by the author (Company B, Belvoir St Theatre, Sydney 1 May)
—— *Old Masters* 2000 (2001) Script supplied by the author (STC, Wharf 1, 17 October)
Christie, William *Under Mulga Wood* 2004 (2003) Mumford and More, Camperdown, NSW (Northbridge Bowling Club, Sydney, November 3 [rehearsed reading])
Claire, Jennifer *The Butterflies of Kalimantan* 1983 (1982) Currency (STC, Stables Theatre, Sydney, 1 October)
Clark, Almon *Nymphs and Fauns: Four Plays* 1929 Edward A. Vidler, Melbourne

BELONGING

Clark, Bruce *King MacBee and the Walking Trees* 1984 (1982) Playlab
Clarke, Doreen *Bleedin' Butterflies* 1982 (1980) In *Roses in Due Season/Bleedin' Butterflies*. Currency (Troupe, at the Red Shed, Adelaide, 3 September)
—— *Farewell Brisbane Ladies* 1980 (1981) Yackandandah (State Theatre Company of South Australia, Theatre 62, June)
—— *Roses in Due Season* 1982 (1978) In *Roses in Due Season/Bleedin' Butterflies*. Currency (Troupe, at the Red Shed, Adelaide, 28 September)
Clarke, Rebecca *Unspoken* 2006 (2005) Currency (Old Fitzroy Theatre, Sydney, 21 April)
Cleven, Vivienne *Bitin' Back* 2007 (2005) In *Contemporary Indigenous Plays*. Currency (Kooemba Jdarra Theatre Company, Brisbane, 5 July)
Coburn, Anthony *The Bastard Country* 1963 (1959) Evans Brothers, London (The Trust Players, Elizabethan Theatre Newtown, Sydney)
Coleman, Elizabeth *It's My Party (And I'll Die If I Want To)* 2003 (1993) In *Secret Bridesmaids' Business and It's My Party (And I'll Die If I Want To)*. Currency (La Mama, 31 March)
——*Secret Bridesmaids' Business* 2003 (1999) In *Secret Bridesmaids' Business and It's My Party (And I'll Die If I Want To)*. Currency (Playbox, April 14)
——*This Way Up* 2002 (2001) Currency (Playbox, 21 November)
Collie, Therese *Goin' to the Island* 2002 (1999) In *Only Gammon: Three Plays from Kooemba Jdarra*. Playlab (Kooemba Jdarra, Brisbane, 7 September)
—— *Out of the Blue (A Jailbird's Story)* 1995 (1991) In *Challenging the Centre: Two Decades of Political Theatre*, edited by Steve Capelin. Playlab (Street Arts Community Theatre Company, Brisbane, 27 February)
Collie, Therese and Nadine McDonald *Binni's Backyard* 2002 (2000) In *Only Gammon: Three Plays from Kooemba Jdarra*. Playlab (Kooemba Jdarra, Brisbane, 24 October)
Collings, Paul *Churchyard* 1978 (1974) In *2 Queensland One-Act Plays for Festivals*. Playlab (La Boite, March)
Compton, Jennifer *Barefoot* 1994 (1994) In *Passion: Six New Short Plays by Australian Women*, edited by Ros Horin. Currency (Griffin Theatre Company, Stables, Sydney, 27 October)
—— *The Big Picture* 1999 (1998) Currency (Griffin Theatre Company, Stables Theatre, Sydney, 17 October)
—— *Crossfire* 2001 (1975) In *Plays of the 70s Volume 3*, edited by Katharine Brisbane. Currency (Nimrod Theatre, Sydney, 28 March)
—— *They're Playing Our Song* 1978 (1975) In *Can't You Hear Me Talking to You?: Eight Short Plays about Lovers and Others*, edited by Alrene Sykes. UQP (Nimrod Theatre, Sydney, 20 June)
Condello, Enzo *Shakespeare and the Dark Lady of the Sonnets* 2005 (2003) In *Only the End and Shakespeare and the Dark Lady of the Sonnets: Two plays*. Currency (Melbourne Writers' Theatre at the Carlton Courthouse, 5 December)
Conigrave, Timothy *Like Stars in My Hands* 1997 (1997) In *Thieving Boy and Like Stars in My Hands*. Currency (Playbox, 22 July)
—— *Thieving Boy* 1997 (1997) In *Thieving Boy and Like Stars in My Hands*. Currency (Playbox, 22 July)

PLAY LIST

Conn, Linda *Song of the Women* 1981 Hexagon Press
Cook, Kenneth *Stockade* 1975 (1971) Penguin, Ringwood, Victoria (Independent Theatre, Sydney 13 March)
Cornall, Jan *At the Crossroads* 2004 (1998) *In At the Crossroads and Empty Suitcases*. Ginninderra Press, Canberra (Women on a Shoestring Theatre Company, Canberra)
Cornelius, Patricia *Lily and May* 1987 (1986) Currency (La Mama, 18 September)
—— *Love* 2006 (2005) Currency (Hothouse Theatre, Wodonga, Victoria, 27 October)
Cortese, Raimondo *Features of Blown Youth* 2000 (1997) In *Melbourne Stories: Three Plays*. Currency (Ranters Theatre in association with the Melbourne International Festival, Spencer Street Power Station, 18 October)
—— *Inconsolable* 1997 (1996) In *The La Mama Collection: Six Plays for the 1990s*, edited by Liz Jones. Currency (Ranters Theatre Company, La Mama, 11 September)
—— *Roulette* 2005 (1996–2005) Currency (Ranters Theatre, at La Mama [The twelve short plays opened at different times—dates and productions are listed in the book])
—— *St Kilda Tales* 2001 (2001) Currency (Ranters Theatre and Playbox, 15 May)
Costi, Angela *Panayiota* 1998 (1997) *Australasian Drama Studies*, 32:77–108. (Knockknock Theatre, Brunswick Mechanics Institute, Melbourne, June)
Cotterill, Ken *Perfect Murder* 1993 (1989) Playlab (Mareeba Repertory Society, 13 October)
—— *Rachel* 2002 (1995) Ancient Mariner Publication, Mareeba, Queensland; 2002 (Atherton Performing Arts. 24 November)
—— *Re-electing Roger* 1989 (1986) Playlab (Mareeba Repertory Society, 21 November
Cousins, John *The Inspector* 1987 (1987) Currency; 1987 (Harvest Theatre Company, Middleback Theatre, Whyalla, NSW, 29 May)
Cove, Michael *Duckling* 1978 (1973) In *Can't You Hear Me Talking to You?: Eight Short Plays about Lovers and Others*, edited by Alrene Sykes. UQP, 1978 (Q Theatre, AMP Theatrette, Sydney, 12 June)
—— *Family Lore* 1985 (1976) In *Popular Short Plays for the Australian Stage Volume 1*, edited by Ron Blair. Currency (Theatre Foray, Armidale, NSW, 12 August)
——*The Gift* 1977 (1976) *BIALA* 2:11–59. (Stables Theatre, Sydney, 10 June)
Cowell, Brendan *Morph* 2004 (2003) Currency (STC, Wharf 2, November)
Crawford, Jim *Rocket Range* 1947 (1947) Campbell Howard Collection, University of New England, Armidale, NSW (New Theatre, Sydney, 14 March)
—— *Welcome Home* 1947 (1947) Campbell Howard Collection, University of New England, Armidale, NSW (New Theatre, Sydney, 14 March)
Crea, Teresa *Preludes to an Exile* 1999 (1996) In *Performing the Unnameable: an anthology of Australian performance texts*, edited by Richard James Allen and Karen Pearlman. Currency (Doppio Teatro, Adelaide Festival)

BELONGING

Creyton, Barry *Double Act* 1988 (1987) Currency (Ensemble Theatre, Sydney, 19 September)
Cribb, Reg *The Return* 2003 (2001) Currency (Griffin Theatre Company in association with Riverina Theatre Company, at the Stables)
Cronin, Bernard *Stampede* 1937 In *Best Australian One-Act Plays*, edited by William Moore and T. Inglis Moore. A&R
Crowley, Anthony *The Frail Man* 2004 (2004) Currency (Playbox, 28 April)
Cunnington, L. L. *The Cudgewa Outlaw* 1933 The Australian Theatre Society, Sydney
Curtis, Allan *Kabbarli* 1985 (1983) Heinemann Educational, Richmond, Victoria (Studio Sydney, Rex Hotel, Potts Point, 20 September)
Cusack, Dymphna *Anniversary* 1935 Campbell Howard Collection, University of New England, Armidale, NSW
—— *Comets Soon Pass* 1943 (1943) In *Three Australian Three Act Plays*. Australasian Publishing Company, Sydney (Perth Repertory Theatre, October.)
—— *Eternal Now* 1946 Campbell Howard Collection, University of New England, Armidale, NSW
—— *The Golden Girls* 1955 (1955) Deane, London (Kidderminster Repertory)
—— *His Honour Comes to Tea* 1933 (1934) Campbell Howard Collection, University of New England, Armidale, NSW (Sydney Players Club, St James Hall, 13 September [under the title *The Legal Point of View*])
—— *Morning Sacrifice* 1999 (1942). In *Tremendous Worlds* edited by Susan Pfisterer. Currency (Repertory Theatre, Perth, 8 October)
—— *Pacific Paradise* 1991 (1955) Australasian Drama Studies, St Lucia (New Theatre W.W.F. Hall, Sydney, 3 December)
—— *Red Sky at Morning* 1942 Melbourne University Press, Melbourne
—— *Shallow Cups* 1934 (1933) In *Eight Plays by Australians*. The Dramatists' Club, Melbourne (Pakie's Club, Sydney 20 September)
—— *Shoulder the Sky* 1945 In *Three Australian Three Act Plays*. Australasian Publishing Company, Sydney
Dal-Bosco, Andrew *Eliot Loves Diana* 1989 (1985) Yackandandah (National Institute of Dramatic Art, Sydney, October)
Daly, Timothy *The Don's Last Innings* 1985 (1982) In *Popular Short Plays for the Australian Stage Volume 1*, edited by Ron Blair, Currency (State Theatre Company of South Australia, Playhouse, Adelaide, 26 November)
—— *Kafka Dances* 1994 (1993) Currency (Griffin Theatre Company, The Stables Theatre, Sydney, 7 July)
Dann, George Landen
—— *Caroline Chisholm* 1943 Mulga Publications, Sydney (Brisbane Repertory Theatre, 28 September 1939 [under the title *A Second Moses*])
—— *Fountains Beyond* 1944 (1942) The Australian Publishing Company Ltd, Sydney (New Theatre, Sydney, 28 January)
—— *How Far Returning* n.d. Campbell Howard Collection, University of New England, Armidale, NSW

PLAY LIST

―――― *In Beauty It Is Finished* 1931 (1931) Campbell Howard Collection, University of New England, Armidale, NSW (Brisbane Repertory Theatre, 16 July)

―――― *No Incense Rising* 1937 (1937) Campbell Howard Collection, University of New England, Armidale, NSW (Independent Theatre, North Sydney, November)

―――― *Ring Out Wild Bells* 1958 (1958) Campbell Howard Collection, University of New England, Armidale, NSW (Twelfth Night Theatre, Brisbane, July)

Darrell, George *The Sunny South* 1975 (1883) Currency Methuen, Sydney; 1975 (Prince of Wales Opera House, Melbourne, 31 March)

Davidson, E. Coulson *The Forerunners* 1925 Campbell Howard Collection, University of New England, Armidale, NSW

―――― *Just Mum* 1919 (1919) Campbell Howard Collection, University of New England, Armidale, NSW (Australian National Theatre Company, Princess Theatre, Melbourne, 30 December)

Davies, Paul *Full House/No Vacancies* 1989 (1989) Currency (Theatreworks, at the 'Linga Longa', St Kilda, Melbourne, 3 April)

―――― *Storming St Kilda by Tram* 1991 (1982) Currency (Theatreworks, on the no. 42 tram route [under the title *Storming Mont Albert by Tram*])

Davis, Jack *Barungin: Smell the Wind* 1989 (1988) Currency (Playhouse, Perth, 10 February)

―――― *The Dreamers* 1989 (1981) In *Plays From Black Australia*. Currency (Swan River Stage Company, Dolphin Theatre, Perth, February 2)

―――― *Honey Spot* 1987 (1985) Currency (Come-Out Festival, Ardrossan Area School, South Australia, 29 April)

―――― *In Our Town* 1992 (1990) Currency (Marli Biyol Company and the Western Australia Theatre Company, Playhouse, Perth, 22 October)

―――― *Kullark* 1982 (1979) In *Kullark and The Dreamers*. Currency (TIE team of the National Theatre Company, Titan Theatre, Perth, 21 February)

―――― *Moorli and the Leprechaun* 1994 (1989) Currency (WATC/Marli Biyol Theatre Company, WA Academy, Perth, 28 June)

―――― *No Sugar* 1986 (1985) Currency (Playhouse Company, the Maltings, North Perth, 18 February)

Davis, Stephen *Juice* 1998 (1997) Playlab (Cremorne Theatre, QPAT Complex, Brisbane. 17 October)

Dawson, Steven *The Art of Being Still* 1991 (1991) Wingandaprayer Publications, Sydney; 1991 (Stables Theatre, Sydney, 7 August)

De Groen, Alma *The After-Life of Arthur Cravan* (1973) (Jane Street Theatre, Sydney, June)

―――― *Available Light* 1994 (1994) LiNQ, 20,1:5–25. (Belle Tournure Theatre Collective, Upstairs Theatre, Townsville, 24 March [Act 1 only])

―――― *Chidley* 1976 (1976) *Theatre Australia*, 1,6: 22–34. (Hoopla Productions, Melbourne 15 December)

―――― *The Girl Who Saw Everything* 1993 (1991) Currency (MTC, Russell Street Theatre, 11 November)

―――― *Going Home* 1983 (1976) In *Vocations/Going Home*. Currency (MTC, St Martin's Theatre, 11 March)

BELONGING

——— *The Joss Adams Show* 1998 (1972) In *Plays of the 70s Vol 1*, edited by Katharine Brisbane. Currency, 1998 (APG, 28 September)
——— *Perfectly All Right* 1977 (1973) In *Going Home and Other Plays*. Currency (Theatre-Go-Round, touring company of the South Australian Theatre Company, Sheridan Theatre, Adelaide 15 May)
——— *The Rivers of China* 1988 (1987) Currency (STC, Wharf Theatre, Sydney, 9 September)
——— *The Sweatproof Boy* (1972) (Nimrod Theatre, Sydney)
——— *Vocations* 1997 (1982) In *Australian Women's Drama: Texts and Feminisms*, edited by Peta Tait and Elizabeth Schafer. Currency (MTC, Russell Street Theatre, 24 August)
——— *The Woman in the Window* 1999 (1998) Currency (MTC, The Fairfax, Victorian Arts Centre, 28 February)
——— *Wicked Sisters* 2003 (2002) Currency (Griffin Theatre Company, Stables Theatre, Sydney, 5 April)
de Guerry Simpson, Helen *A Man of His Time* 1923 A&R
Deamer, Dulcie *Easter* 1937 In *Best Australian One-Act Plays*, edited by William Moore and T. Inglis Moore. A&R
Dean, Philip *48 Shades of Brown* 2001 (2001) Currency (La Boite Theatre at the Roundhouse Theatre, Kelvin Grove, Brisbane, 3 May)
——— *After January* 2000 (2000)) Currency (La Boite, 24 January)
——— *Long Gone Lonesome Cowgirls* 1995 (2005) Currency (La Boite, 15 July)
——— *Zigzag Street* 2004 (2004) Currency (La Boite, 19 February)
Deane, Adam *Storm Water Drain* 1985 (1985) In *Troupe's Young Playwrights Season: seven plays written by young South Australians*. Currency (Troupe, The Old Unley Town Hall, Unley, South Australia, 11 May)
Decent, Campion *Baby X* 2000 (2000) In *Inside 2000*. Currency (Christine Dunstan Productions, Sydney Gay and Lesbian Mardi Gras, Belvoir St Theatre, Sydney, 24 February)
Denver, Simon and Ian Dorricott *Man of Steel* 1978 (1977) Playlab (Middle Stagers, La Boite, 26 November)
Devanny, Jean *Paradise Flow* 1985 Hecate Press, St Lucia
Diamond, Dick *Reedy River* 1989 (1953) Currency (New Theatre, Melbourne, 11 March)
Dickins, Barry *A Dickins' Christmas* 1992 (1992) Currency (Playbox, Melbourne, 30 November)
——— *The Banana Bender* 1981 (1980) In *The Banana Bender/The Death of Minnie*. Currency (La Mama, 4 April)
——— *Beautland* 1985 (1985) Currency (State Theatre Company of South Australia, Playhouse, Adelaide Festival Centre, 4 May)
——— *The Bridal Suite* 1985 (1979) In *The Bridal Suite and Mag and Bag*. Currency (La Mama, Feb-March)
——— *The Death of Minnie* 1981 (1980) In *The Banana Bender/The Death of Minnie*. Currency (Playbox Theatre Upstairs, Melbourne, 10 July.)
——— *The Fools' Shoe Hotel* 1987 (1978) Yackandandah (APG, 15 August)
——— *The Golden Goldenbergs* 1987 (1981) In *Short Plays for the Australian Stage Volume 1*, edited by Leonard Radic. Yackandandah (Playbox Theatre, Melbourne, 5 August)

PLAY LIST

—— *Green Room* 1993 (1985) Yackandandah (La Mama, April)
—— *Insouciance* 2001 (2001) In *Insouciance and The Prodigal Son*. Currency (Playbox, 25 July)
—— *Lennie Lower* 1982 (1982) Currency (Playbox Theatre, Melbourne, 18 February)
—— *Mag and Bag* 1985 (1978) In *The Bridal Suite and Mag and Bag*. Currency (La Mama, Melbourne, May [under the title *The Horror of Nature Strips*])
—— *One Woman Shoe* 1984 (1981) Yackandandah (La Mama, 2 July)
—— *Remember Ronald Ryan* 1994 (1994) Currency (Playbox, 21 September)
—— *Royboys* 1987 (1987) Currency (Playbox Theatre, The Studio, VAC, Melbourne. March 1987)
Drake-Brockman, Henrietta *Dampier's Ghost* 1937 In *Best Australian One-Act Plays*, edited by William Moore and T. Inglis Moore. A&R, 1937
—— *The Man From the Bush* 1934 (1932) In *Eight Plays by Australians*. The Dramatists' Club, Melbourne (Playbox Theatre, Perth)
—— *Men Without Wives* 1938 (1938) Patersons Printing Press Ltd, Perth (Sydney Players Club, 30 April)
Dugon, Nora *Can't You Hear Me Talking to You?* 1978 (1974) In *Can't You Hear Me Talking to You?: Eight Short Plays about Lovers and Others*, edited by Alrene Sykes. UQP (Q Theatre, Adelaide, April)
—— *The Waiting Room* 1984 (1982) In *Malice, Menace and Malevolance: 3 Sinister One-Act Plays*. Playlab, 1984 (Salamanca Arts Festival, Hobart, November)
Duncan, Catherine *Sons of the Morning* 1946 (1945) Mulga Publications, Sydney (New Theatre, Melbourne, 21 April)
Dwyer, Jill *Annie Storey* 1985 (1974) Yackandandah (MTC, St Martin's Theatre, January)
Earley, Eric *The Custodians* 1993 (1993) Currency (Canberra Theatre Trust, The Playhouse, Canberra, 4 September)
Elisha, Ron *Choice* 1994 (1994) Currency (NSW State Theatre Project, The Playhouse, Newcastle. 2 March)
—— *Einstein* 1986 (1981) Penguin, Ringwood (MTC, April)
—— *Esterhaz* 1990 (1990) Currency (Playbox, Melbourne. 16 November)
—— *The Goldberg Variations* 2000 (2000) Currency (Playbox, 24 May)
—— *Impropriety* 1993 Yackandandah
—— *In Duty Bound* 1983 (1979) Yackandandah (MTC, Athanaeum Theatre, 24 September)
—— *The Levine Comedy* 1987 (1986) Yackandandah (MTC, Russel St Theatre, Melbourne, 5 November)
—— *Pax Americana* 1990 Yackandandah
—— *Safe House* 1989 (1989) Currency (Playbox Theatre, Anthill Theatre, Melbourne, 17 May)
—— *Two* 1985 (1983) Currency (Hole in the Wall Theatre, Perth, 3 August)
Locke Elliott, Sumner *Buy Me Blue Ribbons* 1952 (1951) Dramatists Play Service Inc, New York (Empire Theatre, New York, 17 October)
—— *Interval* 1942 (1939) Melbourne University Press, Melbourne (Independent Theatre, North Sydney, 1 April)

BELONGING

———— *Rusty Bugles* 1980 (1948) Currency [revised edition] (Independent Theatre, North Sydney, 21 October)
Ellis, Ben *Falling Petals* 2003 (2003) Currency (Playbox, 2 July)
———— *Post Felicity* 2002 (2002) In *Svetlana in Slingbacks and Post Felicity*. Currency (Playbox, 23 April)
———— *These People* 2003 (2003) Currency (STC, Wharf 2, September 16)
Ellis, Bob and Robin McLachlan *A Man of Substance* 2005 (2004) Currency (Ponton Theatre, Charles Sturt Unhiversity, Bathurst, NSW, 6 August)
———— [See also Boddy and Brooksbank]
Emmerson, Darryl *Earthly Paradise* 1991 (1991) Currency (Playbox 8 June)
———— *The Pathfinder* 1988 (1986) Currency (The Australian Contemporary Theatre Company, Melbourne, 23 September)
Enoch, Wesley *Black Medea* 2007 (2000) In *Contemporary Indigenous Plays*. Currency (Blueprints, STC, Wharf 2, 19 August)
Enoch, Wesley and Deborah Mailman *The 7 Stages of Grieving* 1996 (1995) Playlab (Kooemba Jdarra, Metro Arts Theatre, Brisbane, 13 September)
Enright, Nick *A Man With Five Children* 2003 (2002) Currency (STC, Wharf 1, 4 January)
———— *A Property of the Clan* 1994 (1992) Currency (Freewheels Theatre-in-Education Company, Newcastle, 14 August)
———— *Blackrock* 1996 (1995) Currency (STC, Wharf 1, 30 August)
———— *Country Music* (2002) (National Institute of Dramatic Art, Parade Theatre, 17 July)
———— *Daylight Saving* 1990 (1989) Currency (Ensemble Theatre, Sydney, 21 September)
———— *Good Works* 1995 (1994) Currency (Q Theatre, Penrith, NSW, 29 July)
———— *Mongrels* 1994 (1991) Currency (Ensemble Theatre, Sydney. 7 November)
———— *On the Wallaby* 1982 (1980) Currency (State Theatre Company of South Australia, The Playhouse, Adelaide Festival Centre, 4 July)
———— *The Quartet from Rigoletto* (1995) (Q Theatre, Penrith, NSW, 17 March)
———— *Spurboard* 2001 (1999) Currency (Australian Theatre for Young People, Wharf 2 Sydney, 4 November)
———— *St James Infirmary* 1993 (1992) Currency (Q Theatre, Penrith, NSW. 14 February)
———— *The Venetian Twins* 1996 (1979) Currency (Nimrod Theatre for the STC, Opera House Drama Theatre, Sydney, 26 October)
Enright, Nick and Terence Clarke *Summer Rain* 2001 (1983) Currency (National Institute of Dramatic Art, Parade Theatre, Sydney, 19 October)
Enright, Nick, Justin Monjo, and Tim Winton *Cloudstreet* 1999 (1998) Currency (Company B Belvoir and Black Swan Theatre, Berth 9, Darling Harbour, Sydney, 3 January)
Epstein, June *The Nine Muses [and other plays]* 1951 Robertson & Mullens, Melbourne
Esson, Louis *Australia Felix* 1999 (1991) In Louis Esson, *Plays 1: Terra Australis*, edited by John Senczuk. Five Islands Press, Wollongong (Griffin Theatre Company, Sydney, 3 January)

PLAY LIST

——— *The Bride of Gospel Place* 1946 (1926) In *The Southern Cross and Other Plays*. Robertson and Mullens, Melbourne (Pioneer Players, Melbourne, June)
——— *Dead Timber* 1999 (1911) In Louis Esson, *Plays 1: Terra Australis*, edited by John Senczuk. Five Islands Press, Wollongong (Melbourne Repertory Theatre, 13 December)
——— *Digger's Rest* 1922 (1922) Campbell Howard Collection, University of New England, Armidale, NSW (Pioneer Players, April)
——— *The Drovers* 1999 (1923) In Louis Esson, *Plays 1: Terra Australis*, edited by John Senczuk. Five Islands Press, Wollongong (Pioneer Players, Melbourne, 3 December)
——— *Lachryma Christi* 1937 Campbell Howard Collection, University of New England, Armidale, NSW
——— *Mother and Son* 1999 (1923) In Louis Esson, *Plays 1: Terra Australis*, edited by John Senczuk. Five Islands Press, Wollongong (Pioneer Players, Melbourne,)
——— *Shipwreck* 1999 (1984) In Louis Esson, *Plays 1: Terra Australis*, edited by John Senczuk. Five Islands Press, Wollongong (UNE, Armidale, September [rehearsed reading])
——— *Terra Australis* 1999 In Louis Esson, *Plays 1: Terra Australis*, edited by John Senczuk. Five Islands Press, Wollongong
——— *The Quest* 1999 In Louis Esson, *Plays 1: Terra Australis*, edited by John Senczuk. Five Islands Press, Wollongong
——— *The Sacred Place* 1980 (1912) In *Ballades of Old Bohemia*, edited by Hugh Anderson. Red Rooster Press, Melbourne (Turn Verein Hall, Melbourne, 15 May)
——— *The Southern Cross* 1946 (1930s) In *The Southern Cross and Other Plays*. Robertson and Mullens, Melbourne (Workers' Art Guild, Perth)
——— *The Time Is Not Yet Ripe* 1973 (1912) Currency Methuen, Sydney; 1912 (Melbourne Repertory Theatre, 23 July)
——— *Vagabond Camp* 1999 In Louis Esson, *Plays 1: Terra Australis*, edited by John Senczuk. Five Islands Press, Wollongong
——— *The Woman Tamer* 1980 (1910) In *Ballades of Old Bohemia*, edited by Hugh Anderson. Red Rooster Press, Melbourne (Turn Verein Hall, Melbourne, 5 October)
Esson, Louis and Frank Brown *Andeganora* 1937 (1938) In Louis Esson, *Plays 1: Terra Australis*, edited by John Senczuk. Five Islands Press, Wollongong (Sydney Drama Society, Little Theatre, Sydney, 23 July)
——— *Mates* 1999 (1923) In Louis Esson, *Plays 1: Terra Australis*, edited by John Senczuk. Five Islands Press, Wollongong (Pioneer Players, 16 August)
Euclid, James *Trial of the Gadfly, and other plays* 1997 Strawberry House Publishers, Townsville Qld
Evans, Chad E. *A Woman for Hanging* 1990 (1988) Woodall Holdings, Sydney (Guild Theatre, Sydney)
Evans, Daniel *Opening a Fuzzwollop's Frame of Mind* 2002 (2001) Currency (Synergy Theatre Company, Brisbane Arts Theatre as part of Brisbane Festival of the Arts, 26 August)

BELONGING

Farwell, George *The House That Jack Built* 1970 Heinemann Educational, South Yarra, Victoria

Fein, Yvonne *On Edge* 1992 (1988) CIS Publishers, Melbourne (Saltpillar Theatre, for the Jewish Arts Festival, Melbourne)

Fenn, Cheryl *And the Villain Was a Lady* 1984 (1980) Yackandandah (King and Ovens Performing Group, Melbourne, 22 November)

Fennessy, Aidan *Chilling and Killing My Annabel Lee* 1999 (1999) Currency (Playbox)

Fetter, Delia *Hypothalaemia* 1998 (1993) In *Sydney Theatre Company: Plays 1*, edited by John Senczuk. Five Islands Press, Wollongong (STC, 24 October [rehearsed reading])

Fischer, Margaret *The Gay Divorcee* 1996 (1990) In *Australian Gay and Lesbian Plays*, edited by Bruce Parr. Currency (Vitalstatistix Theatre Company, Old Lion Theatre, Port Adelaide, 6 October)

Fitzjohn, Eric *Truscott* 1984 (1982) In *Malice, Menace and Malevolance: 3 Sinister One-Act Plays*. Playlab (Playlab, the Warana and Commonwealth Festival of Drama, at the Brisbane Arts Theatre. September)

Flanagan, Martin and Bruce Myles *The Call* 2004 (2004) Currency (Playbox, 16 October)

Flanagan, Nicholas *Burning Time* 1996 (1996) Currency (Playbox and Black Swan Theatre Company, Melbourne, May 22)

Fleming, Justin *Burnt Piano* 1999 (1999) In *Burnt Piano and Other Plays*. Five Islands Press, Wollongong (Company B, Belvoir St Theatre, Sydney, 9 March)

—— *The Cobra* 1998 (1983) In *Sydney Theatre Company: Plays 1*, edited by John Senczuk. Five Islands Press, Wollongong (STC, Drama Theatre, Sydney Opera House, 5 October)

—— *Hammer* 1999 (1981) In *Burnt Piano and Other Plays*. Five Islands Press, Wollongong (Ensemble Theatre, at the Phillip Theatre, Sydney, 13 January)

—— *Harold in Italy* 1999 (1989) In *Burnt Piano and Other Plays*. Five Islands Press, Wollongong (STC and the One Extra Company, Drama Theatre, Sydney Opera House, 22 July)

—— *Indian Summer* 1999 (1982) In *Burnt Piano and Other Plays*. Five Islands Press, Wollongong (Ensemble Theatre, at the Phillip Theatre, Sydney. 5 January)

—— *The Nonsense Boy* 1999 (1992) In *Burnt Piano and Other Plays*. Five Islands Press, Wollongong (the Rep Theatre, Newtown, 31 January)

Fools Gallery Theatre Company *Standard Operating Procedure* 1982 (1980) Cafe Press, Canberra (Fools Gallery Theatre Company, Canberra, 25 September)

Foran, Barney and Bob Sharp *Come Hell or High Water* 1988 (1988) Currency (Alice Springs Theatre Group, Araluen Arts Centre, Alice Springs, 13 April)

Forde, Margery *Snapshots from Home* 1997 (1995) Playlab (Cremorne Theatre, Queensland Performing Arts Complex, 16 November)

—— *X-Stacy* 1999 (1998) Currency (La Boite, 16 July)

PLAY LIST

Forde, Margery and Michael Forde *Milo's Wake* 2002 (2000) Currency (La Boite, 17 August)
────── *Way Out West: Legends and Larrikins* 2001 (2001) Playlab (Queensland Performing Arts Trust and La Boite Theatre 6 May)
Foster, Lynn *There is No Armour* 1945 (1939) Mulga Publications, Sydney (Independent Theatre, North Sydney, 1 July)
Fotheringham, Richard *Fallout and Follow Me* 1995 (1977) In *Challenging the Centre: Two Decades of Political Theatre*, edited by Steve Capelin. Playlab (Popular Theatre Troupe,)
────── *Hell and Hay* 1984 (1982) Playlab (La Boite, March)
Fotheringham, Richard and Albert Hunt *The White Man's Mission* 1995 (1975) In *Challenging the Centre: Two Decades of Political Theatre*, edited by Steve Capelin. Playlab, 1995 (Popular Theatre Troupe)
Francis, Gordon *God's Best Country* 1987 (1987) Currency (Western Australian Theatre Company, 3 February)
Frankland, Richard J. *Conversations with the Dead* 2002 (2002) In *Blak Inside: 6 Indigenous Plays from Victoria*. Currency (Ilbijerri Aboriginal and Torres Strait Islander Theatre Cooperative, Playbox Theatre and La Mama at the Carlton Courthouse, 13 February)
Franklin, Miles *No Family* 1937 In *Best Australian One-Act Plays*, edited by William Moore and T. Inglis Moore. A&R
Franklin, Miles and Dymphna Cusack *Call Up Your Ghosts* 1945 (1945) In *The Penguin Anthology of Australian Women's Writing*, edited by Dale Spender, Penguin, Ringwood (New Theatre, Melbourne, October)
Fraser, William *Blood* 1984 (1979) In *Malice, Menace and Malevolence: 3 Sinister One-Act Plays*. Playlab (Camerata Theatre Group, Brisbane, November)
Fry, Garry *Lockie Leonard Scumbuster* 2000 (1998) Currency (Theatre South, Wollongong, 7 July)
Futcher, Michael and Helen Howard *A Beautiful Life* 2000 (1998) Currency (Matrix Theatre Company and La Boite, 27 August)
────── *Citizen Jane* 2002 (2002) Playlab (Queensland Arts Council, 6 June)
────── *The Drowning Bride* 2005 (2005) Currency (La Boite Theatre Company, Roundhouse Theatre, Brisbane. 2 June)
Gage, Mary *My Name Is Pablo Picasso* 1984 (1982) Currency; Australian National Gallery, Canberra (Hole-in-the-Wall Theatre, Perth, January)
────── *The New Life* 1977 (1974) In *The New Life/The Foreman*. Currency, 1977 (Playhouse, Perth, 30 April)
Gallagher, Jodi *Elegy* 2000 (2000) In *Inside 2000*. Currency (Playbox, 5 April)
Garner, Bill and Sue Gore *The Ishmael Club* 2004 (2003) Currency (Commonplace Productions, Trades Hall, Melbourne, 26 August)
Gencer, Gün *Hard Rain* 1985 *Outrider*, 3:59–87
George, Emily *The Collective Meeting* 1986 Dykebooks, Melbourne
George, Rob *Sandy Lee Live at Nui Dat* 1983 (1981) Currency (Stage Company, the Space Theatre, Adelaide Festival Centre, 26 November)
Gilbert, Kevin *The Cherry Pickers* 1988 (1971) Burrambinga Books, Canberra (workshopped at the Mews Theatre Workshop, Sydney and produced shortly after at Nindethana Theatre, Fitzroy, Victoria)

BELONGING

Giles, Mike *Rest and Recreation* 1983 (1973) In *Seven One-Act Plays*, edited by Rodney Fisher. Currency (Canberra Repertory Society, Workshop Theatre, Riverside, 9 February)

Glyn-Daniel, Marya *Gulf Country* 2000 (2000) Ginninderra Press, Canberra (the players company [sic] at the UCU Theatre, University of Canberra, 23 February)

Goldsmith, Frank H. *Batavia Ahoy!* 1946 In *Treasure Lies Buried Here*. C H Pitman, Perth

Golvan, Colin *An Evening with Shalom Aleichem* 1990 (1989) In *Eichmann in Haifa and An Evening with Shalom Aleichem*. Yackandandah (Phoenix Theatre, Melbourne)

—— *Eichmann in Haifa* 1990 (1988) In *Eichmann in Haifa and An Evening with Shalom Aleichem*. Yackandandah (MTC, Athanaeum 2, 29 March)

—— *The Tramp's Revenge* 1985 (1984) Yackandandah (Playbox Theatre, Melbourne, May 31)

Goodall, Julie *Texas, Queensland* 1997 (1993) In *The La Mama Collection: Six Plays for the 1990s*, edited by Liz Jones. Currency, (La Mama, 17 November)

Gorman, Clem *A Fortunate Life* 1987 (1984) Currency (MTC, Playhouse Theatre, Victorian Arts Centre, 26 June)

—— *A Manual of Trench Warfare* 1996 (1978) In *Australian Gay and Lesbian Plays*, edited by Bruce Parr. Currency (State Theatre Company of South Australia, Playhouse, Adelaide Festival Centre, 8 September)

—— *A Night in the Arms of Raeleen* 1983 (1981) In *A Night in the Arms of Raeleen/The Harding Women*. Currency (Playbox Theatre, Melbourne, 7 October)

—— *The Harding Women* 1983 (1981) In *A Night in the Arms of Raeleen/The Harding Women*. Currency (The Stage Company, the Space Theatre, Adelaide Festival Centre, 4 June)

—— *The Last Night-Club* 1985 Yackandandah

—— *The Motivators* 1983 (1983) Yackandandah (Threshold Theatre Company, Stables Theatre, Sydney 23 November)

Gow, Michael *1841* 1988 (1988) Currency (State Theatre Company of South Australia, Playhouse, Adelaide Festival Centre, 3 March)

—— *All Stops Out* 1991 (1989) Currency (Australian Theatre For Young People, Rocks Theatre, Sydney, July)

—— *Away* 1988 (1986) Currency (Griffin Theatre Company, Stables Theatre, Sydney, 7 January)

—— *The Fortunes of Richard Mahony* 2002 (2002) Currency (QTC, Brisbane Powerhouse, 12 September)

—— *Europe* 1987 (1987) In *Europe/On Top of the World*. Currency (Griffin Theatre, Stables Theatre, Sydney, 27 January)

—— *Furious* 1996 (1990) In *Australian Gay and Lesbian Plays*, edited by Bruce Parr. Currency (STC, Wharf Theatre, 6 November)

—— *The Kid* 2008 (1983) Currency (Winter Theatre, Fremantle, Western Australia 25 August)

—— *On Top of the World* 1987 (1986) In *Europe/On Top of the World*. Currency (STC, Wharf Theatre, 26 August)

PLAY LIST

—— *Sweet Phoebe* 1995 (1994) Currency (STC, Wharf Theatre, 2 November)
—— *Toy Symphony* 2008 (2006) Currency (Company B Belvoir, Belvoir St Theatre, Sydney, 14 November)
Graham, Gordon *The Boys* 1994 (1991) Currency (Griffin Theatre Company, Stables Theatre, Sydney, 28 February)
—— *Demolition Job* 1984 (1980) Yackandandah (MTC, Athenaeum II)
—— *Four Colour Job* 1978 (1976) In *Can't You Hear Me Talking to You?: Eight Short Plays about Lovers and Others*, edited by Alrene Sykes. UQP (Civic Centre, Cairns, 5 October)
—— *Innocent Bystanders* 1985 (1975) In *Popular Short Plays for the Australian Stage Volume II*, editor by Ron Blair. Currency (Royal Court Upstairs, London, 5 January)
Gray, Christine *Talk and Trivia* 1978 *BIALA*, 3 1:36–58
Gray, Oriel *Burst of Summer* 1959 (1960) In *Plays of the 60s Volume 1* edited by Katharine Brisbane, Currency (The Little Theatre, Sydney, 20 February)
—— *Drive a Hard Bargain* 1958 (1957) Tasmanian Adult Education Board, Hobart (Hall, Ballarat, October)
—— *Lawson* 1989 (1943) Yackandandah [revised edition] (New Theatre, Sydney, 10 October)
—— *Sky Without Birds* 2007 (1952) In *Plays of the 50s Volume 1*, edited by Katharine Brisbane Currency (New Theatre, Sydney, 22 March)
—— *The Torrents* 1996 (1956) Currency (New Theatre, Adelaide, Stow Hall, 9 August)
Green, Cliff *Cop Out!* 1983 (1977) Yackandandah; (MTC, Russell Street Theatre, 22 November)
Grossetti, Adam *Mano Nera* 2005 (2005) Playlab (QTC, 6 June)
Grover, Montague *"Gib It Tshillin"* 1937 In *Best Australian One-Act Plays*, edited by William Moore and T. Inglis Moore. A&R
Gunzburg, Darrelyn *Hiccup* 1989 (1989) Currency (The Playhouse, Perth, 14 June)
—— *Behind the Beat* 1992 (1990) Currency (Multicultural Youth Theatre, The Parks Arts Complex, Adelaide, 20 February)
Gunzburg, Darrelyn, Ollie Black and Margaret Fischer *A Touchy Subject* 1989 (1987) *Australasian Drama Studies*, 14 65-104 (Vitalstatistix, Parks Community Centre Theatre 1, Adelaide, 3 July)
Gurr, Michael *A Pair of Claws* 1983 (1983) Yackandandah (MTC, Athenaeum Theatre, 20 July)
—— *Crazy Brave* 2000 (2000) Currency (Playbox, 28 June)
—— *Dead to the World* 1986 Yackandandah
—— *Imitation Real* 1983 (1981) In *Magnetic North and Imitation Real*. Yackandandah (Miscaste Theatre Group, ICI Theatre, Melbourne)
—— *Jerusalem* 1996 (1996) Currency (Playbox, 24 July)
—— *Julia 3* 2004 (2004) Currency (Playbox, 8 September)
—— *Magnetic North* 1983 (1983) In *Magnetic North and Imitation Real*. Yackandandah (MTC, Athenaeum Theatre, 1 February)
—— *Sex Diary of an Infidel* 1992 (1992) Currency (Playbox, 27 June)
—— *The Simple Truth* 2002 (2002) Currency (Playbox, 11 September)

BELONGING

───── *This and That* 1988 In *What You Wanted and This and That* Yackandandah

───── *Underwear, Perfume and Crash Helmet* 1994 (1994) Currency (Playbox, 12 July)

───── *What You Wanted* 1988 (1983) In *What You Wanted and This and That*. Yackandandah (MTC Play Reading)

Gurr, T. Stuart and Varney Monk *Collits' Inn* 1990 (1932) Currency; Australasian Drama Studies, St Lucia (Savoy Theatre, Sydney 5 December)

Haenke, Helen *The Bottom of a Birdcage* 1978 (1976) Playlab (The Burly Griffin Incinerator Theatre, Ipswich, Queensland, 3 March)

───── *Firebug* 1978 (1974) In *3 Queensland One-Act Plays for Festivals*. Playlab (Murrumba Theatre Company, at Warana One-Act Drama Festival)

Hall, Rodney *A Return to the Brink* 1999 (1999) Currency (Playbox, 23 October)

Hamilton, Ron *The Spiders* 1970 (1965) In *6 One-Act Plays*, edited by Eunice Hanger. UQP (St James Players, Townsville)

───── *Vacancy* 1978 (1976) In *2 Queensland One-Act Plays for Festivals*. Playlab, 1978 (St James Players Townsville [rehearsed reading])

Hanger, Eunice *2D* 1978 In *2D and Other Plays*. UQP

───── *Flood* 1978 (1955) In *2D and Other Plays*. UQP (Twelfth Night Theatre, Brisbane, 19 October)

───── *The Frogs* 1978 In *2D and Other Plays*. UQP

Harding, Alex *Blood and Honour* 1996 (1990) In *Australian Gay and Lesbian Plays*, edited by Bruce Parr. Currency (Sydney Gay and Lesbian Mardi Gras, Belvoir St Theatre Downstairs, 8 February)

───── *Only Heaven Knows* 1989 (1988) Currency (Griffin Theatre Company, Stables Theatre, Sydney)

Harding, John *Enuff* 2002 (2002) In *Blak Inside: 6 Indigenous Plays from Victoria*. Currency, 2002 (Ilbijerri Aboriginal and Torres Strait Islander Theatre Cooperative and Playbox. 5 February)

───── *Up the Road* 1997 (1991) Currency (Ilbijerri Aboriginal and Torres Strait Islander Theatre Cooperative, Melbourne,)

Hardy, Frank *Faces in the Street* 1988 (1988) Stained Wattle Press, Sydney (Everest Theatre, Sydney, 16 January)

───── *Mary Lives!* 1992 (1992) Currency (Playbox, Melbourne, June 6)

Hardy, Jonathan *Jungfrau* 1997 (1997) Currency (Playbox, 3 June)

Harmer, Wendy *Backstage Pass* 1991 (1990) Currency (Toe Truck Theatre, Marist Brothers High School, 19 February)

───── *What is the Matter with Mary Jane?* 1996 (1995) Currency (STC, New Stages, Wharf 2, 3 March)

Harrison, Jane *Rainbow's End* 2007 (2005) In *Contemporary Indigenous Plays*. Currency (Ilbijerri Theatre Co-operative, Melbourne, 18 February)

───── *Stolen* 2006 (1998) Currency [revised edition] (Ilbijerri Aboriginal and Torres Strait Islander Theatre Co-operative and Playbox, 21 October)

Harvey, Anne *I'll Be In On That* 1991 (1975) Yackandandah (Tasmanian Theatre Company's Theatre in Education team)

Harvey, Joan *The Hidden Valley* 1936 In *Five Plays by Australians*. Dramatists' Club of Australia, Melbourne

PLAY LIST

Hawley, Suzanne *Mummy Loves You Betty Ann Jewel* 1988 (1984) Currency (Sailors Home Theatre, The Rocks, Sydney, 2 May [under the title *Hitler Had a Mummy Too*])

Hayball, Doris *The Grotesque* 1934 (1932) In *Eight Plays by Australians*. The Dramatists' Club, Melbourne (Pakie's Club, Sydney, 26 November)

Hayhow, David *Ancient Enmity* 2001 (2001) In *Inside 01*. Currency (Playbox. 27 June)

Haylen, Leslie *Two Minutes Silence* 1933 The Macquarie Head Press, Sydney

—— *Blood on the Wattle* 1948 A&R

Haywood, Claire *Table for One* 1995 (1993) Currency (Hunter Valley Theatre Company, Newcastle Playhouse, 14 July)

Herbert, Bob *A Man of Respect* 1977 *BIALA*, 2: 60–81

—— *Brer Rabbit and the Magic Lolly Cave* 1989 (1986) Currency (New England Theatre Company, Arts Theatre, UNE, Armidale. 9 July)

—— *No Names... No Pack Drill* 1980 (1979) Currency (New England Travelling Playhouse, Arts Theatre, UNE, Armidale NSW, 12 May)

Herbert, Bob and Allan McFadden *The Last Wake at She-Oak Creek* 1988 (1986) Currency (The Stables Theatre, Sydney, 3 October)

Herbert, Kate *Dirty Laundry* 2003 (2003) In *Moon Babies and Dirty Laundry*. Currency (La Mama, June 3)

—— *Hit and Run* 2001 (1995) Currency (La Mama at the Carlton Courthouse Theatre, 18 July)

Heron, Sarah *Doctor What and the attack of the Darlings* 1985 (1985) In *Troupe's Young Playwrights Season: seven plays written by young South Australians*. Currency (Troupe, The Old Unley Town Hall, Unley, South Australia, 11 May)

Hewett, Dorothy *The Beautiful Mrs Portland* 1976 *Theatre Australia*, 1,4:27-32; 1,5:26–31

—— *Bon-Bons and Roses for Dolly* 1976 (1972) In *Bon-Bons and Roses for Dolly and The Tatty Hollow Story*. Currency Methuen (National Theatre Company, Playhouse, Perth, 4 October)

—— *The Chapel Perilous* 1997 (1971) In *Australian Women's Drama: Texts and Feminisms*, edited by Peta Tait and Elizabeth Schafer. Currency (New Fortune Theatre, Perth, 21 January)

—— *The Golden Oldies* 1981 (1977) In *The Golden Oldies and Susannah's Dreaming*. Currency (Hoopla Productions, Grant Street Theatre, Melbourne, 19 January)

—— *Golden Valley* 1985 (1981) In *Golden Valley and Song of the Seals*. Currency (Magpie Company, Playhouse, Adelaide Festival Centre, 8 May)

—— *Joan* 1984 Yackandandah

—— *The Man From Mukinupin* 1979 (1979) Currency; Freemantle Arts Centre Press, Perth [revised edition: Currency, 1980] (National Theatre Company, Playhouse, Perth, 31 August)

—— *Mrs Porter and the Angel* 1992 (1969) In *Collected Plays Volume 1*. Currency (PACT Theatre, Sydney, 18 May)

—— *Nowhere* 2001 (2001) Currency (Playbox, 17 October)

—— *Pandora's Cross* 1978 (1978) *Theatre Australia*, 3,2:33–40; 3,3:33–40:33–39 (Paris Theatre, Sydney, 29 June)

BELONGING

———— *Song of the Seals* 1985 (1983) In *Golden Valley and Song of the Seals*. Currency (Magpie Company, Playhouse, Adelaide Festival Centre, 6 May)
———— *Susannah's Dreaming* 1981 (1980) In *The Golden Oldies and Susannah's Dreaming*. Currency (2NURFM, Newcastle, 16 October)
———— *The Tatty Hollow Story* 1992 (1974) In *Collected Plays Volume 1*. Currency (Sydney University Women's College, 29 August [rehearsed reading])
———— *This Old Man Comes Rolling Home* 1999 (1967) In *Plays of the 60s Volume 2*, edited by Katharine Brisbane. Currency (University Drama Society, New Fortune Theatre, UWA Perth, 11 January)

Hewett, Robert *The Adman* 1991 (1991) Currency (Playbox, Melbourne, 20 July)
———— *Goodbye Mrs Blore* 2000 (2000) Currency (HIT Productions, Darebin Arts and Entertainment Centre, Melbourne, 29 April)
———— *Gulls* 1984 (1983) Currency (MTC, Russell Street Theatre, 1 March)
———— *Waking Eve* 1997 (1997) Currency (Playbox, 5 April)

Hibberd, Jack *A Knotty Problem* 1984 In *Squibs: A Collection of Short Plays*. Phoenix Publications, Brisbane
———— *A League of Nations* 1984 In *Squibs: A Collection of Short Plays*. Phoenix Publications, Brisbane
———— *A Stretch of the Imagination* 2000 (1972) In *Selected Plays* Currency (APG, 8 March)
———— *A Toast to Melba* 1976 (1976) In *Three Popular Plays*. Outback Press, Melbourne (Australian Performing Group, Theatre 62, Adelaide, 6 March)
———— *Asian Oranges* 1984 In *Squibs: A Collection of Short Plays*. Phoenix Publications, Brisbane
———— *Captain Midnight VC* 1984 (1973) Yackandandah (MUST Kaleidoscope country tour, Victoria)
———— *Commitment* 1984 (1968) In *Squibs: A Collection of Short Plays*. Phoenix Publications, Brisbane (Saturday Morning Club, MTC, Russell Street Theatre 25 July)
———— *Death Warmed Up* 1984 *Scripsi*, 2:4:203–14
———— *Dimboola* 2000 (1969) *In Selected Plays*. Currency (Australian Performing Group, La Mama, 6 July)
———— *Glycerine Tears* 1982 *Meanjin*, 41:509–22
———— *Just Before the Honeymoon* 1984 (1967) In *Squibs: A Collection of Short Plays*. Phoenix Publications, Brisbane (La Mama, 24 September)
———— *The Les Darcy Show* 1976 (1974) In *Three Popular Plays*. Outback Press, Melbourne (Drama Centre, Flinders University, Adelaide, March)
———— *Liquid Amber* 1984 (1982) In *A Country Quinella: Two Celebration Plays*. Penguin, Ringwood (Murray River Performing Group, Albury-Wodonga, 24 February)
———— *Memoirs of a Carlton Bohemian* 1977 (1977) *Meanjin*, 36:298–305. (La Mama, August)
———— *Mothballs* 1980 *Meanjin*, 39:4:560–73
———— *No Time Like the Present* 1984 (1968) In *Squibs: A Collection of Short Plays*. Phoenix Publications, Brisbane (Architecture Theatre, University of Melbourne, April 17)

PLAY LIST

—— *O* 1984 (1967) In *Squibs: A Collection of Short Plays*. Phoenix Publications, Brisbane (La Mama, 24 September)

—— *Odyssey of a Prostitute* 1985 *Outrider*, 2.1:87–154

—— *One of Nature's Gentlemen* 1976 (1968) In *Three Popular Plays*. Outback Press, Melbourne (Architecture Theatre, University of Melbourne, April 17)

—— *The Overcoat* 1977 (1976) In *The Overcoat, Sin: Two pieces of Music Theatre*. Currency (APG, 11 November)

—— *Peggy Sue* 1982 (1974) Yackandandah (APG)

—— *The Prodigal Son* 2001 (1997) In *Insouciance and The Prodigal Son*. Currency (QTC, 3 November)

—— *Sin* 1982 (1978) In *The Overcoat, Sin: Two pieces of Music Theatre*. Currency (Victorian State Opera, Union Theatre, Melbourne, 1 September)

—— *Slam Dunk* 1996 (1995) Currency (La Mama, Napier Street Theatre, Melbourne, 22 June)

—— *This Great Gap of Time* 1984 (1967) In *Squibs: A Collection of Short Plays*. Phoenix Publications, Brisbane (La Mama, 22 October)

—— *Three Old Friends* 1984 (1967) In *Squibs: A Collection of Short Plays*. Phoenix Publications, Brisbane (La Mama, 29 July)

—— *White With Wire Wheels* 2000 (1967) In *Selected Plays*. Currency (University of Melbourne, September)

—— *Who?* 1970 (1968) In *Four Australian Plays*. Penguin, Ringwood (Architecture Theatre, University of Melbourne, April 17)

Hibberd, Jack and John Romeril *Marvellous Melbourne* 1977 (1970) *Theatre Australia*, 2,4:35–44; 2,5:29–39. (APG, 11 December)

Hibberd, Jack and John Timlin *Goodbye Ted* 1983 (1975) Yackandandah (Chevron Hotel, Melbourne, 9 April)

Hilton, Margot *Potiphar's Wife* 1987 (1979) In *Short Plays for the Australian Stage Volume I*, edited by Leonard Radic. Yackandandah, 1987 (Nimrod Theatre, Sydney)

Hodda, Noel *The Secret House* 1989 (1987) Currency (Griffin Theatre Company, Stables Theatre, Sydney, 6 September)

Holman, David *Beauty and the Beast* 1989 (1988) In *No Worries: Three Plays for Children*. Currency (Magpie Theatre, Odeon Theatre, Adelaide, 5 March)

—— *No Worries* 1989 (1984) In *No Worries: Three Plays for Children*. Currency (Magpie Theatre, Theatre 62, Adelaide, 6 March)

—— *The Small Poppies* 1989 (1986) In *No Worries: Three Plays for Children*. Currency (Magpie Theatre, Theatre 62, Adelaide, 1 March)

Holt, Edgar *Anzac Reunion* 1937 In *Best Australian One-Act Plays*, edited by William Moore and T. Inglis Moore. A&R

Hopgood, Alan *And Here Comes... Bucknuckle* 1980 Heinemann Educational, South Yarra, Victoria

—— *And The Big Men Fly* 1969 (1963) Heinemann Educational, South Yarra, Victoria (Union Theatre Repertory Company, Melbourne, June)

—— *The Carer* 2004 (1999) Currency (Bay Street Productions at Chapel off Chapel, Melbourne, 28 October)

BELONGING

———— *The Golden Legion of Cleaning Women* 1979 (1967) Heinemann Educational, South Yarra, Victoria (Melbourne)
———— *Private Yuk Objects* 1999 (1966) In *Plays of the 60s Volume 2*, edited by Katharine Brisbane. Currency (Union Theatre Repertory Company, Melbourne, 6 September)
Hopkins, F. R. C. *Reaping the Whirlwind* 1909 Websdale, Shoosmith Ltd, Sydney
Hopkinson, Simon *Buffaloes Can't Fly* 1984 (1981) Yackandandah (Darwin Theatre Group, The Little Theatre, Adelaide, April)
———— *The Crazy World of Advertising* 1975 (1971) Heinemann Educational, Richmond, Victoria (MTC, November)
Howarde, Kate *Possum Paddock* 1919 In Barbara Garlick, "Australian Travelling Theatre 1890–1935: A Study in Popular Entertainment and National Ideology". Ph.D Dissertation, University of Queensland, 1994 [Appendix C]
Humphries, Barry *A Nice Night's Entertainment* 1981 Currency
———— *The Life and Death of Sandy Stone* 1990 Macmillan, Sydney
Hutchinson, Garrie *Fifteen Rounds with Gorgeous George* 1987 (1985) In *Short Plays for the Australian Stage Volume I*, edited by Leonard Radic. Yackandandah (Melbourne Writers' Theatre, 3 October)
Hutchinson, George *Henry and Peter and Henry and Me* 1985 (1985) Currency (Island Theatre Company, Prince of Wales Theatre, Hobart, Tasmania. 11 October)
———— *No Room For Dreamers* 1981 (1980) Currency (Ensemble-at-the-Stables, 1 January)
Ingleton, Sue *The Passion ... and its Deep Connection with Lemon Delicious Pudding* 1995 (1995) Currency (Playbox, 16 May)
Ireland, David *Image in the Clay* 2004 (1960) In *Plays of the 50s*, edited by Katharine Brisbane. Currency (Pocket Playhouse, 12 May)
James, Andrea *Yanagai! Yanagai!* 2003 (2003) Currency (Playbox, 10 December)
Janaczewska, Noëlle *Blood Orange* 1993 (1993) *Australasian Drama Studies*, 22:81–108 (Death Defying Theatre, Pact Youth Theatre, Sydney, 5 March)
———— *Historia* 1997 (1996) In *Australian Women's Drama: Texts and Feminisms*, edited by Peta Tait and Elizabeth Schafer. Currency (STC's Australian People's Theatre, Wharf 2, 21 February)
———— *The History of Water* 1995 (1992) Currency (STC (New Stages) and Anna Konda Productions, 3 June)
Janson, Julie *Black Mary* 1996 (1996) In *Black Mary and Gunjies*. Aboriginal Studies Press, Canberra (Sydney Street Theatre Space, Sydney, May)
———— *Gunjies* 1996 (1993) In *Black Mary and Gunjies*. Aboriginal Studies Press, Canberra (Belvoir St Theatre, Sydney)
John, Rosemary *Luck of the Draw* 1986 (1985) Currency (Murray River Performing Group, Albury/Wodonga, NSW, 3 July)
Johnson, Eva *Murras* 1997 (1988) In *Australian Women's Drama: Texts and Feminisms*, edited by Peta Tait and Elizabeth Schafer. Currency (Fringe Festival Centre, Adelaide Festival, March)

PLAY LIST

——— *What Do They Call Me?* 1996 (1990) In *Australian Gay and Lesbian Plays*, edited by Bruce Parr. Currency (National Lesbian Festival, Melbourne, January)

Johnson, Patricia *Gladbags* 1984 (1981) Yackandandah (Ensemble Productions, Phillip Street Theatre, Sydney)

Jones, Doris Egerton and Emelie Polini *The Flaw* 1923 (1923) Campbell Howard Collection, University of New England, Armidale, NSW (Criterion Theatre, Sydney, 27 January)

Jones, Graham and Jepke Goudsmit *Undiscovered Land: Voyage 2* 1999 (1997) In *Performing the Unnameable: an anthology of Australian performance texts*, edited by Richard James Allen and Karen Pearlman. Currency (Kinetic Energy Theatre Company, The Edge Theatre, Sydney, 15 October)

Jones, Lyndal *Spitfire 1 2 3...From the Darwin Translations* 1999 (1996) In *Performing the Unnameable: an anthology of Australian performance texts*, edited by Richard James Allen and Karen Pearlman. Currency (Power Station, Melbourne)

Jury, C. R. *The Administrator* 1961 In *The Sun in Servitude and other plays*. F.W. Cheshire, Melbourne

——— *The Battle in the West* 1961 In *The Sun in Servitude and other plays*. F.W. Cheshire, Melbourne

——— *Love and the Virgins* 1958 In *Love and the Virgins and Poems*. The Wakefield Press, Adelaide

——— *The Sun in Servitude* 1961 In *The Sun in Servitude and other plays*. F.W. Cheshire, Melbourne

Katsoulis, Dimitris *The Dowry* 1988 In *Greek Voices in Australia: A Tradition of Poetry, Prose and Drama*, edited by George Kanarakis. ANU Press, Canberra, 1988

Keene, Daniel *All Souls* 1995 (1993) Currency (The Red Shed Company, Adelaide, 20 May)

——— *Cho Cho San* 1987 (1984) Currency (The Universal Theatre, Melbourne, October)

——— *dog* 2003 (1999) In *Terminus and other plays*. Salt Publishing (The Keene/Taylor Theatre Project (Season Nine), The Trades Hall, Melbourne, December)

——— *the eyes* 2003 In *Terminus and other plays*. Salt Publishing, London

——— *the falling man* 2003 In *Terminus and other plays*. Salt Publishing, London

——— *the fire testament* 2003 In *Terminus and other plays*. Salt Publishing, London

——— *The first train* http://www.danielkeene.com/works

——— *Half and Half* 2002 (2002) Currency (The Keene/Taylor Theatre Project in association with Playbox, 3 July)

——— *river* 2003 (1999) In *Terminus and other plays*. Salt Publishing, London (The Keene/Taylor Theatre Project (Season Nine), The Trades Hall, Melbourne, December)

——— *The Serpent's Teeth* 2008 (2008) Currency (STC, 19 April)

BELONGING

―― *scissors, paper, rock* 2003 (1998) In *Terminus and other plays*. Salt Publishing, London (The Keene/Taylor Theatre Project (Season Four), The Trades Hall, Melbourne, September)
―― *the telling* 2003 In *Terminus and other plays*. Salt Publishing, London
―― *terminus* 2003 (1996) In *Terminus and other plays*. Salt Publishing, London (The Red Shed Theatre, Adelaide, September)
―― *To Whom It May Concern and Other Plays* 2000 (1997–8) Black Pepper, Melbourne [*to whom it may concern; a glass of twilight; neither lost nor found; untitled monologue; night, a wall, two men; kaddish; the violin and the rain*] (Keene/Taylor Theatre Project, Melbourne)
Keller, Bruce *Puppy Love* 1985 (1985) Australian Nouveau Theatre Publications, Melbourne (Anthill Theatre, 13 May)
Kemp, Jenny *The Black Sequin Dress* 1996 (1996) Currency (Playbox Theatre, Adelaide Festival, 5 March)
―― *Call of the Wild* 1999 (1989) In *Performing the Unnameable: an anthology of Australian performance texts*, edited by Richard James Allen and Karen Pearlman. Currency (The Church Theatre, Melbourne, Spoleto Festival)
―― *Remember* 1997 (1993) In *Australian Women's Drama: Texts and Feminisms*, edited by Peta Tait and Elizabeth Schafer. Currency, (Gasworks, Melbourne, 27 March)
―― *Still Angela* 2002 (2002) Currency (Playbox, 10 April)
Keneally, Thomas *Bullie's House* 1981 (1980) STC, Sydney (Nimrod Theatre, Sydney, 6 February)
―― *Childermas* 1970 (1968) University of New England Department of University Extension, Armidale, NSW (Old Tote Theatre, Sydney, February 3)
―― *Gossip From the Forest* 1983 (1983) STC, Sydney (STC, Drama Theatre, Sydney Opera House, 5 May)
―― *Halloran's Little Boat* 1975 (1966) Penguin, Ringwood (Old Tote Theatre Company, Jane Street Theatre, Sydney, 15 November)
Kenna, Len *The Putting-down of Ned Kelly* 1995 (1995) Jika Publishing, Bundoora, Victoria (Felix Australia Benalla Easter Arts Festival, Benalla, Victoria, April)
Kenna, Peter *A Hard God* 1999 (1973) In *Plays of the 70s Volume 2*, edited by Katharine Brisbane. Currency (Nimrod Street Theatre, Sydney, 17 August)
―― *An Eager Hope* (1978) (Scott Theatre, Adelaide, 13 March)
―― *Furtive Love* 1980 (1978) Currency (Scott Theatre, Adelaide, 13 March)
―― *Listen Closely* 1977 (1972) In *Three Plays*. Currency (Independent Theatre, North Sydney, 10 May)
―― *Mates* 1996 (1975) In *Australian Gay and Lesbian Plays*, edited by Bruce Parr. Currency (Nimrod Theatre, Sydney, 1 August)
―― *The Slaughter of St Teresa's Day* 2004 (1959) In *Plays of the 50s Volume 2*, edited by Katharine Brisbane. Currency (Elizabethan Theatre, Sydney, 11 March)
―― *Talk to the Moon* 1977 (1963) In *Three Plays*. Currency (Hampstead Theatre Club, London, 16 October)

PLAY LIST

────── *Trespassers Will Be Prosecuted* 1977 (1965) In *Three Plays*. Currency (Independent Theatre, Sydney, 2 May [rehearsed reading])

Kilmurry, Mark *Mercy Thieves* 2003 (2002) Currency (The Studio Company, Darlinghurst Theatre, Sydney, 14 February)

Kirby, Foveaux *Kelver Hartley (a life in progress)* 2004 Boombana Publications, Mt Nebo

Kirby, Margaret *My Body, My Blood* 1996 (1993) Currency (Griffin Theatre Company, Sydney,)

Kittson, Jean *Escape* 1994 (1994) In *Passion: Six New Short Plays by Australian Women*, edited by Ros Horin. Currency (Griffin Theatre Company, Sydney, 29 September)

Koca, Bogdan *Annette and Annette* 1998 (1997) In *My Name is Such and Such, and other plays*. Currency (Pilgrim Theatre, Sydney, 3 January)

────── *Cafe Inferno* 1992 (1992) Bogdan Koca, Sydney (Lookout Theatre Club, Woollahra, Sydney, 13 May)

────── *Gunter's Wife* 1998 (1997) In *My Name is Such and Such, and other plays*. Currency (Pilgrim Theatre, Sydney, 18 March)

────── *My Name is Such and Such* 1998 (1993) In *My Name is Such and Such, and other plays*. Currency (Stables Theatre, Sydney. 4 March)

────── *Sparring Partner* 1998 (1996) In *My Name is Such and Such, and other plays*. Currency (Pilgrim Theatre, Sydney, 7 August)

Krausmann, Rudi *Everyman* 1989 (1978) In *Three Plays*. Hale and Iremonger, Sydney (Nimrod Downstairs)

────── *The Perfection* 1989 In *Three Plays*. Hale and Iremonger, Sydney

────── *The Word* 1989 (1982) In *Three Plays*. Hale and Iremonger, Sydney (School of Drama, University of NSW)

Krauth, Nigel *Muse of Fire* 1985 (1985) Currency (State Theatre Company of South Australia, Playhouse, Festival Centre, Adelaide, 3 August)

Ladds, Dulcie Dunlop *We Have Our Dreams* 1987 (1957) In *Such Stuff as Dreams*, by L. Tarnawski. Boolarong Publications, Brisbane, 1987 (London)

Lapaine, Daniel *Art, Life and the Other Thing* 1985 (1985) In *Interplay '85: Eleven Plays by Young People*. Currency (Seymour Theatre Centre, Sydney, 21 August)

Laughton, Verity *The Mourning After* 1996 (1996) Currency (Playbox, 25 October)

Lawler, Ray *Hal's Belles* 1945 (1945) Manuscript Collection, La Trobe Library, State Library of Victoria, Melbourne (Middle Park Repertory Theatre, Melbourne,)

────── *Kid Stakes* 1978 (1975) In *The Doll Trilogy*. Currency (MTC, 2 December)

────── *Other Times* 1978 (1976) In *The Doll Trilogy*. Currency (MTC, 14 December)

────── *The Piccadilly Bushman* 1998 (1959) Currency [revised edition] (JC Williamson, Comedy Theatre, Melbourne, 12 September)

────── *Summer of the Seventeenth Doll* 1978 (1955) In *The Doll Trilogy*. Currency (Union Theatre Repertory Company, Melbourne, 28 November)

Le Quy, Duong *A Graveyard for the Living* 2002 In *The First Play Collection*. Currency

BELONGING

────── *Market of Lives* 2002 (1998) In *The First Play Collection*. Currency (University of Wollongong, Theatre South)
────── *Meat Party* 2002 (2000) In *The First Play Collection*. Currency (Playbox, 11 October)
Learner, Tobsha *The Glass Mermaid* 1994 (1994) Currency (Playbox, 22 November)
────── *The Gun in History* 1994 (1994) In *Passion: Six New Short Plays by Australian Women*, edited by Ros Horin. Currency (Griffin Theatre Company, Stables, Sydney, 29 September)
────── *Miracles* 1998 (1992) Currency (Vitalstatistix, Waterside Hall, Port Adelaide, 1 August)
────── *Witchplay* 1995 (1987) In *One Small Step and Witchplay*. Currency (Belvoir St Downstairs, Sydney, 6 August)
────── *Wolf* 1992 (1992) Currency (Playbox,)
Lette, Kathy *Grommitts* 1988 (1987) Currency (ATYP, Sailors' Home Theatre, The Rocks, Sydney, January)
Leversha, Pam *Violet Inc* 2000 (2000) In *Inside 2000*. Currency (Playbox Theatre and The Branch, Melbourne, 26 April)
Levkowicz, Valentina *Svetlana in Slingbacks* 2002 (2000) In *Svetlana in Slingbacks and Post Felicity*. Currency (Vitalstatistix, Theatre 62, Adelaide, 27 May)
Lillford, Daniel *Dark Heart* 1997 (1993) In *The La Mama Collection: Six Plays for the 1990s*, edited by Liz Jones. Currency (La Mama, 27 October)
Lindstrom, Tom *Heroic Measures* 1991 (1991) Playbox (Playbox, 28 October)
Lord, Robert *Balance of Payments* 1978 (1972) In *Can't You Hear Me Talking to You?: Eight Short Plays about Lovers and Others*, edited by Alrene Sykes. UQP (Unity Theatre, Wellington, 18 October)
Lumsden, Glenn *Hester Costello Returns From Overseas* 1985 (1985) In *Interplay '85: Eleven Plays by Young People*. Currency (Interplay '85, Seymour Theatre Centre, Sydney, 26 August)
Lurie, Morris *A Visit to the Uncle!* 1979 In *Waterman: Three Plays*. Outback Press, Melbourne
────── *Jangle, Jangle* 1979 In *Waterman: Three Plays*. Outback Press, Melbourne
────── *Waterman* 1979 In *Waterman: Three Plays*. Outback Press, Melbourne
Lyssa, Alison *The Boiling Frog* 1984 (1982) Currency (Nimrod Theatre, Sydney, 12 May)
────── *Pinball* 1996 (1981) In *Australian Gay and Lesbian Plays*, edited by Bruce Parr. Currency (Nimrod Theatre Company, Downstairs Theatre, 9 September)
Lyssiotis, Tes *A White Sports Coat* 1996 (1988) In *A White Sports Coat and Other Plays*. Currency (La Mama, 23 November)
────── *Blood Moon* 1996 (1993) In *A White Sports Coat and Other Plays*. Currency (Theatreworks, Melbourne, 6 March)
────── *The Forty Lounge Cafe* 1997 (1990) In *Australian Women's Drama: Texts and Feminisms*, edited by Peta Tait and Elizabeth Schafer. Currency (Playbox, 16 March)
Macdonald, Donald *Caravan* 1984 (1983) Currency (Ensemble Productions, Playhouse, Sydney Opera House, 13 August)

PLAY LIST

Macdonald, Gabrielle *Like a Metaphor* (2000) (2000) In *Inside 2000*. Currency (Playbox, 12 April)

MacIntyre, Ernest *Let's Give Them Curry* 1985 (1981) Heinemann Educational, Richmond, Victoria (Arts Theatre, UNE, Armidale, NSW,12 September)

Macky, Stewart *The Trap* 1937 In *Best Australian One-Act Plays*, edited by William Moore and T. Inglis Moore. A&R

Maclean, Alanna *Verandahs* 1984 (1980) In *Flags, Verandahs and Other Wombats: Two Australian Plays*. Heinemann Educational, Richmond, Victoria (Leeds University Workshop Theatre, May)

Macleod, Doug *My Son the Lawyer is Drowning* 1987 (1987) Currency (Playbox Theatre, Studio Theatre, VAC, Melbourne, 9 November)

Maher, David *The Wisdom Boys* 1985 (1985) In *Interplay '85: Eleven Plays by Young People*. Currency (Interplay '85, Seymour Theatre Centre, Sydney, 22 August)

Mahjoeddin, Indija Noesbar *The Butterfly Seer* 2000 (1999) In *Three Plays by Asian Australians*, edited by Don Batchelor. Playlab (Playlab, June Writers' Weekend [rehearsed reading])

Mainwaring, Karin *The Rain Dancers* 1998 (1992) In *Sydney Theatre Company: Plays 1*, edited by John Senczuk. Five Islands Press, Wollongong (STC, Wharf 1, 11 March)

Malouf, David *Baa Baa Black Sheep* 1993 Chatto & Windus, London

—— *Blood Relations* 1988 (1987) Currency (STC, Drama Theatre, Sydney Opera House, 24 June)

Mann, Phillip Grenville *Eights Days a Week* 1972 Heinemann Educational, South Yarra, Victoria

—— *How Sleep the Brave* 1981 (1979) Playlab (Ensemble-at-the-Stables Theatre, Sydney, 2 January)

Manning, Ned *Close to the Bone* 1994 (1991) Currency (EORA Centre, Redfern, Sydney, 24 September)

—— *Luck of the Draw* 2000 (1999) Currency (Darwin Theatre Company, Browns Mart Theatre, 6 May)

—— *Milo* 1996 (1994) In *Kingaroy and Milo*. Currency (Wharf 2, Sydney, 27 October)

—— *Us or Them* 1984 (1977) Currency (Childers Street Hall, Canberra, 1 November)

Marshall-Stoneking, Billy *Sixteen Words for Water* 1991 (1991) A&R (STC, Wharf Theatre, Sydney, 13 August)

Masters, Olga *A Working Man's Castle* 1988 (1988) Currency (Theatre South, Wollongong, NSW, 9 July)

Mathew, Ray *A Spring Song* 1985 (1957) Currency; 1985 (Australian Elizabethan Theatre Trust Hamlet company [reading])

—— *The Bones of My Toe* 1964 In *Next Act!*, edited by Richard Beynon and H.G. Fowler. Angus & Robertson, Adelaide 1964

—— *The Life of the Party* 2004 (1960) In *Plays of the 50s Volume 2*, edited by Katharine Brisbane. Currency (Lyric Opera House, Hammersmith, London, 22 November)

BELONGING

———— *We Find the Bunyip* 1968 (1955) In *Khaki, Bush and Bigotry: Three Australian Plays*, edited by Eunice Hanger. University of Queensland Press, St. Lucia (Independent Theatre, Sydney 29 August)
Mathiesen, Ailsa *Swallowing Is A Very Private Thing* 1983 (1979) In *Seven One-Act Plays*, edited by Rodney Fisher. Currency (Darwin Theatre Group, Brown's Mart Theatre, Darwin, 12 September)
Matthews, Harley *We Are The People* 1940 (1940) The Viking Press, Sydney (Bryant's Plahouse, Sydney, March)
Maver, Christopher *The Girl in the Lime Green Bikini* 2003 (2002) Playlab (Judith Wright Centre for Contemporary Art, Brisbane, 2 July)
May, Adam *Rising Fish Prayer* 1998 (1998) Currency (Playbox, 16 September)
Maza, Bob *The Keepers* 1989 (1988) In *Plays From Black Australia*. Currency (Mainstreet Theatre Company, Town Hall, Naracoorte, South Australia, 25 February)
McCart, Greg *A Bed of Ruses* 1993 Yackandandah
McCrae, Hugh *The Ship of Heaven* 1951 (1933) A&R (Independent Theatre Company, Savoy Theatre, Sydney, 7 October)
McKenzie, Sally *Scattered Lives* 2002 (2001) Coalface Communications, The Gap, Queensland (La Boite, 30 April)
McKimmie, Jacqueline *The Kiss* 1978 (1978) In *3 Queensland One-Act Plays for Festivals*. Playlab (Playlab, Brisbane Arts Theatre, 7 May)
McKinney, Jack *Next Door* 1962 In *Australian One-Act Plays: Book 1*, edited by Eunice Hanger. Rigby, Adelaide
———— *The Well* 1968 In *Khaki, Bush and Bigotry: Three Australian Plays*, edited by Eunice Hanger. UQP
McLeod, Marjorie *A Shillingsworth* 1958 (1931) In *Four Period Plays*. Hedges and Bell, Maryborough, Victoria (Garrick Theatre, Melbourne)
———— *Horizons* 1958 (1952) In *Four Period Plays*. Hedges and Bell, Maryborough, Victoria (National Theatre, Melbourne, July)
———— *Mine a Sad One* 1958 (1956) In *Four Period Plays*. Hedges and Bell, Maryborough, Victoria (Town Hall, Swan Hill, 13 March)
———— *Moonshine* 1948 In *Five Plays by Australians*. Dramatists' Club of Australia, Melbourne
———— *Travail* 1934 (1933) In *Eight Plays by Australians*. The Dramatists' Club, Melbourne (Australian Literature Society, Dramatists' Club, Nicholas Building Little Theatre, Melbourne, 4 October)
———— *Within These Walls* 1958 (1936) In *Four Period Plays*. Hedges and Bell, Maryborough, Victoria (Princess Theatre, Melbourne, November)
McNamara, Tony *The Cafe Latte Kid* 1998 (1994) In *Sydney Theatre Company: Plays 1*, edited by John Senczuk. Five Islands Press, Wollongong (STC New Stages, Wharf 2, 27 August)
———— *The Great* 2008 (2008) Currency (STC, 31 May)
———— *The John Wayne Principle* 1996 (1996) Currency (STC, New Stages, Wharf 2, 15 May 1996)
McNeil, Jim *The Chocolate Frog* 1987 (1971) In *Collected Plays*. Currency (Q Theatre Group, AMP Theatre, Sydney 13 July 1971)

PLAY LIST

───── *How Does Your Garden Grow* 1999 (1974) In *Plays of the 70s Volume 2*, edited by Katharine Brisbane. Currency (New Nimrod Theatre, Sydney, 15 October)

───── *Jack* 1987 (1977) In *Collected Plays*. Currency (Nimrod Theatre, Sydney, 17 September)

───── *The Old Familiar Juice* 1987 (1972) In *Collected Plays*. Currency (MTC, Russell Street Theatre, 7 August)

Meredith, Gwen *Ask No Questions* 1940 (1940) Campbell Howard Collection, University of New England, Armidale, NSW (Independent Theatre, North Sydney, August 1940)

───── *Cornerstones* 1956 (1956) Campbell Howard Collection, University of New England, Armidale, NSW (Independent Theatre, North Sydney, April)

───── *Wives Have Their Uses* 1944 (1938) Mulga Publications, Sydney (Theatre Group, Chelsea Club, St James Hall, Sydney, 23 November)

Merritt, Robert J. *The Cake Man* 1999 (1975) In *Plays of the 70s Volume 2*, edited by Katharine Brisbane. Currency (Black Theatre Arts and Culture Centre, Sydney, 12 January)

Messner, G. Florian *Queen of the Night's Revenge* 2000 INBI Group Productions, Sydney; 2000

Metcalfe, Edgar *Garden Party* 1980 (1980) Artlook Publications, Perth (Hole in the Wall Theatre, Perth)

Middlebrook, Douglas *Charlotte* 1979 The Chamber Theatre of Adelaide, Adelaide

Milgate, Rodney *A Refined Look at Existence* 1998 (1966) In *Plays of the 60s Volume 3*, edited by Katharine Brisbane. Currency (Jane Street Theatre, Sydney, 11 November 1966)

Milroy, David *Windmill Baby* 2007 (2005) In *Contemporary Indigenous Plays*. Currency (Yirra Yaakin Theatre Company, Perth, 23 February)

Milroy, David and Geoffrey Narkle *King Hit* 2007 (1997) In *Contemporary Indigenous Plays*. Currency (Yirra Yaakin Theatre Company, Perth, 23 October)

Milroy, Jadah *Crow Fire* 2002 (2002) In *Blak Inside: 6 Indigenous Plays from Victoria*. Currency (Ilbijerri Aboriginal and Torres Strait Islander Theatre Co-operative and Playbox, 19 February)

Misto, John *The Shoe-Horn Sonata* 1996 (1995) Currency (Ensemble Theatre, Sydney, 3 August)

Mooney, Ray *A Blue Freckle* 1984 (1975) Yackandandah (The Players Anonymous Theatre Group, Pentridge Prison, July)

───── *Angel of the Graveyard* 1980 Theatre for Australian Playwrights, Melbourne

───── *Black Rabbit* 1988 (1988) Currency (Playbox Theatre, Studio Theatre, VAC, Melbourne. 8 March)

───── *Everynight, Everynight* 1985 (1978) Yackandandah (Governor's Pleasure Theatre Group, St Martin's Theatre, Melbourne, April)

Moore, William *The Tea-Room Girl* 1910 (1910) T.C. Lothian, Melbourne (William Moore Drama Nights, Turn Verein Hall, 5 October)

BELONGING

Moran, V. J. *Find Me at the Federal* 1962 In *Australian One-Act Plays: Book 1*, edited by Eunice Hanger. Rigby, Adelaide

Morgillo, Antonietta *The Olive Tree* 1990 (1990) *Australasian Drama Studies*, 17:117–55. (Doppio Teatro, Adelaide Festival)

Morphett, Tony *I've Come About the Assassination* 1970 (1966) In *6 One-Act Plays*, edited by Eunice Hanger. UQP (Old Tote Theatre Company, Jane St Theatre, Sydney, 1 October)

Morris, Jill *Almost a Dinosaur* 1988 Currency

Morris, Mary *Two Weeks With the Queen* 1993 (1992) Currency (Toe Truck Theatre, Parramatta Riverside Theatres, Sydney, 14 January)

Moss, Merilee *Empty Suitcase* 2004 (1993) In *At the Crossroads and Empty Suitcases*. Ginninderra Press, Canberra (Women on a Shoestring, Courtyard Studio, Canberra, 31 July)

Motherwell, Phil *Dreamers of the Absolute* 1985 (1978) Yackandandah (APG, November 1978)

────── *Steal Away Home* 1988 (1988) In *Steal Away Home and The Serpent's Fall*. Currency (Playbox, 9 February)

────── *The Surgeon's Arms* 1983 (1980) In *Seven One-Act Plays*, edited by Rodney Fisher. Currency (APG, January)

Mrowinski, Stefan *The White Door* 1982 (1982) Australian Nouveau Theatre Publications, Melbourne (Australian Nouveau Theatre, Anthill Theatre, Melbourne, July)

Mudrooroo *The Aboriginal Protesters Confront the Declaration of the Australian Republic on 26 January 2001 with a Production of* The Commission *by Heiner Müller* 1993 (1996) In *The Mudrooroo/Müller Project: A Theatrical Casebook*, edited by Gerhard Fischer. New South Wales University Press, Sydney (The Sydney Festival, The Performance Space, Sydney, 10 January)

Mueller, Ross *Colosseum* 2003 (2001) Currency (St Martins Youth Theatre, St Martins Youth Arts Centre, Melbourne, 11 October 2001)

────── *No Man's Island* 1997 (1997) In *The La Mama Collection: Six Plays for the 1990s*, edited by Jones Liz. Currency (La Mama, 30 January)

Mulligan, John *The Sex Life of Snails* 1985 (1970) In *Popular Short Plays for the Australian Stage Volume II*, edited by Ron Blair. Currency (Wayside Chapel, Kings Cross, Sydney, November)

Mulvany, Kate *The Danger Age* 2008 (2008) Playlab (La Boite, 28 February)

────── *The Seed* 2008 (2007) Currency (B Sharp, Belvoir St Theatre, Sydney, 19 July)

Murphet, Richard *Quick Death* 1999 (1981) In *Performing the Unnameable: an anthology of Australian performance texts*, edited by Richard James Allen and Karen Pearlman. Currency (La Mama, as part of the *Artaud and Cruelty* season under the title *Quick Death to Infinity*)

Murphy, Tommy *Holding the Man* (Adapted from the book by Timothy Conigrave) 2006 (2006) In *Strangers in Between/Holding the Man*, Currency (Griffin Theatre Company, Sydney, 9 November)

────── *Strangers in Between* 2006 (2005) In *Strangers in Between/Holding the Man*, Currency (Griffin Theatre Company, 11 February)

Murray, Peta *Salt* 2001 (2001) Currency (Playbox, 21 March 2001)

PLAY LIST

―― *Spitting Chips* 1995 (1989) Currency (Toe Truck Theatre, Rocks Theatre, October)
―― *Wallflowering* 1992 (1989) Currency (Canberra Theatre Company)
Murray, Sue *Big Dramas: A Collection of 10 Plays* 2000 Macmillan Education, Melbourne
Murray-Smith, Joanna *Atlanta* 1990 (1990) Currency (Playbox, 3 August 1990)
―― *Bombshells* 2002 (2002) Currency (MTC, 21 December)
―― *The Female of the Species* 2008 (2006) Currency (MTC, 26 August)
―― *Flame* 1994 (1994) In *Passion: Six New Short Plays by Australian Women*, edited by Ros Horin. Currency (Griffin Theatre Company, Stables, Sydney, 27 October)
―― *Honour* 1995 (1995) Currency (Playbox, 14 November)
―― *Love Child* 1998 (1993) Currency (Playbox, 22 June 1993)
―― *Miracles* 1988 (1992) Currency (Vitalstatistix, Waterside Hall, Port Adelaide, 1 August)
―― *Nightfall* 1999 (1999) Currency (Playbox, 16 November)
―― *Rapture* 2002 (2002) Currency (Playbox, 13 November)
―― *Redemption* 1997 (1997) Currency (Playbox, 19 August)
Musaphia, Joseph *The Guerilla* 1976 (1971) In *The Guerilla/Bananas and The Fourth Wall*. Currency Methuen, Sydney (Ensemble Theatre, Sydney, 1 December)
Naish, John *Deuteronomy 24-1* 1957 (1957) Tasmanian Adult Education Board, Hobart (Parish Hall, Suva, Fiji, 30 June)
Nash, Ian *A Boy for Me, A Girl for You* 1983 (1980) In *Show of Strength/A Boy for Me, A Girl For You*. Neptune Press, Newtown, Victoria (MTC, Athenaeum 2, 7 July)
―― *Send-Off* 1986 (1984) Yackandandah (La Mama, 27 June)
―― *Show of Strength* 1983 (1982) In *Show of Strength/A Boy for Me, A Girl For You*. Neptune Press, Newtown, Victoria (La Mama, 26 August)
―― *Two-Up* 1994 (1986) Ian Nash, Melbourne (La Mama)
Nash, Maxine *Programme Completed* 1976 *BIALA*, 1:48–70
Neilsen, Ted *Country Heat* 1990 (1990) The Ballarat City Education Centre, Ballarat, Victoria (Ballarat University College Studio Theatre, 28 March)
―― *The Family Room* 1987 (1985) Yackandandah (Royal QTC, Lyric Theatre, Brisbane, 8 October)
―― *Let Me In* 1983 (1978) In *Seven One-Act Plays*, edited by Rodney Fisher. Currency (Hoopla at the Playbox Theatre, Melbourne, 19 May)
―― *Oh. Quadraphenia* 1984 (1978) Yackandandah (Hoopla Theatre Foundation Ltd, Playbox Theatre, Melbourne, 19 May)
Newcastle, Anthony and Mike Dickinson *Yarnin' Up* 2002 (2002) In *Only Gammon: Three Plays from Kooemba Jdarra*. Playlab (Kooemba Jdarra, Adelaide Festival, 23 February)
Nguyen, Huong, Phi Hai, Pat Rix, and Geoff Crowhurst *Wild Rice* 2002 (1997) Currency (Theatre 62, Hilton, Adelaide, 29 May)
Nimmo, Heather *One Small Step* 1995 (1992) In *One Small Step and Witchplay*. Currency (State Theatre Company of Western Australia, Perth, 20 November 1992)

BELONGING

—— *The Hope* 1987 (1987) Currency (Playbox Theatre, The Studio, VAC, Melbourne, April)

Norton, Danielle and Joanne Morgan *Little Red Riding Hood* 1985 (1985) In *Troupe's Young Playwrights Season: seven plays written by young South Australians*. Currency (Troupe, The Old Unley Town Hall, Unley, South Australia. 11 May)

Nowra, Louis *Albert Names Edward* 1983 (1975) In *Nightmares of the Old Obscenity Master, and other plays: Five Plays for Radio*. edited by Alrene Sykes. Currency Methuen, Sydney (ABC Radio, 15 June; as a stage play: La Mama, 1976)

—— *Byzantine Flowers* (1989) (STC, Wharf Theatre, 30 December 1989. Dir. Kingston Anderson)

—— *Capricornia* 1988 (1988) Currency (Company B, Belvoir St Theatre, Sydney, 23 April 1988)

—— *Così* 1994 (1992) [revised edition] Currency (Company B, Belvoir St Theatre, Sydney, 21 April)

—— *Crow* 1994 (1994) Currency (State Theatre Company of South Australia, The Playhouse, Adelaide Festival Centre, 14 May)

—— *The Golden Age* 1989 (1985) [revised edition] Currency (Playbox Theatre, Studio, VAC, Melbourne 8 February)

—— *The Incorruptible* 1995 (1995) Currency (Playbox, 11 July 1995)

—— *Inner Voices* 2001 (1977) In *Plays of the 70s Volume 3*, edited by Katharine Brisbane. Currency (Nimrod Theatre Downstairs, Sydney, 25 February 1977)

—— *Inside the Island* 1981 (1980) In *Inside the Island/The Precious Woman*. Currency (Nimrod Theatre, Sydney, 13 August)

—— *The Jungle* 1998 (1995) In *Sydney Theatre Company: Plays 1*, edited by John Senczuk. Five Islands Press, Wollongong (STC, Wharf 2, 25 October)

—— *The Language of the Gods* 1999 (1999) Currency (Playbox, 8 September)

—— *The Marvellous Boy* (2005) (Griffin Theatre Company, Sydney, 13 October)

—— *Miss Bosnia* (1995) (La Boite Theatre, Teatar di Migma, Brisbane, 22 July)

—— *The Precious Woman* 1981 (1980) In *Inside the Island/The Precious Woman*. Currency (STC, Drama Theatre, Sydney Opera House, 11 November)

—— *Radiance* 1993 (1993) Currency (Belvoir St Theatre, Sydney 21 September)

—— *Royal Show* (1982) Sydney (Lighthouse Theatre Company, Playhouse, Adelaide Festival Centre, 19 October 1982)

—— *The Song Room* 1983 (1980) In *Seven One-Act Plays*, edited by Rodney Fisher. Currency (ABC Radio, 18 November)

—— *Spellbound* (1982) (Lighthouse Theatre Company, Playhouse, Adelaide Festival Centre, 22 May 1982)

—— *Summer of the Aliens* 1992 (1992) Currency (MTC, Russell Street Theatre, 17 March)

—— *Sunrise* 1983 (1983) Currency (Lighthouse Theatre Company, Adelaide, 19 November)

PLAY LIST

—— *The Temple* 1993 (1993) Currency (Playbox, 27 July)
—— *The Watchtower* (1990) (NIDA, Parade Theatre 31 May)
—— *The Woman with Dog's Eyes* (2004) (Griffin Theatre Company, Stables Theatre, Sydney, 5 October)
—— *Visions* 1979 (1978) Currency (Paris Theatre, Sydney, 17 August)
Nowra, Louis and Brian Howard *Whitsunday* 1988 (1988) Australian Opera, Sydney (Australian Opera, 2 September)
O'Brien, Eris M. *The Hostage* 1928 A&R; 1928
O'Callaghan, Jill *Some Mother's Son* 1998 (1997) Currency (La Mama, September)
O'Connell, Terence and Siobhan McHugh *Minefields and Miniskirts* 2004 (2004) Currency (Playbox, 14 July)
O'Donoghue, John *Abbie and Lou, Norman and Rose* 1993 (1993) Currency (Hunter Valley Theatre Company, The Playhouse, Newcastle, NSW, 9 June)
—— *A Happy and Holy Occasion* 2001 (1976) In *Plays of the 70s Volume 3*, edited by Katharine Brisbane, Currency (Hunter Valley Theatre Company, 1 October)
—— *Essington Lewis: I Am Work* 1987 (1981) Currency (Hunter Valley Theatre Company, The Playhouse, Newcastle, 5 September)
O'Flynn, Mark *Paterson's Curse* 1988 (1988) Currency (Riverina Theatre Company, Wagga Wagga, 12 August)
O'Grady, Desmond *Marriage Gamblers* 1991 Yackandandah
O'Neill, Errol *Faces in the Street* 1993 (1983) Playlab (La Boite, 16 September)
—— *It's MAD* 1995 (1981) In *Challenging the Centre: Two Decades of Political Theatre*, edited by Steve Capelin. Playlab (Popular Theatre Troupe)
—— *The Mayne Inheritance* 2004 (2004) Playlab (La Boite, 13 May)
—— *On the Whipping Side* 1991 (1991) Playlab (Royal QTC, Pilbeam Theatre, Rockhampton, Queensland, 16 August)
—— *Popular Front* 1988 (1986) Playlab (La Boite, 2 April)
O'Neill, Tee *The Dogs Play, and A Few Roos Loose in the Top Paddock* 1999 (1999) Currency (Playbox, 26 May)
O'Toole, John *The Beekeeper's Boy* 1986 (1983) Playlab (Schonell Theatre Downstairs, University of Queensland, May 1983)
Oakes, Russell J. *Enduring as the Camphor Tree* 1967 (1946) Melbourne University Press (Little Theatre, Melbourne, 12 October)
Oakley, Barry *A Lesson in English* 1976 (1969) In *A Lesson in English and The Christian Brothers*. Currency Methuen, Sydney (La Mama, 6 July)
—— *Bedfellows* 1975 (1975) Currency Methuen, Sydney (APG, 3 January 1975)
—— *Beware of Imitations* 1985 (1973) Yackandandah (APG, 24 January)
—— *Buck Privates* 1980 In *The Great God Mogadon and Other Plays*. UQP
—— *Eugene Flockhart's Desk* 1980 (1967) In *The Great God Mogadon and Other Plays*. UQP (Emerald Hill Theatre, Melbourne)
—— *The Feet of Daniel Mannix* 1975 (1971) A&R (APG)
—— *The Great God Mogadon* 1980 In *The Great God Mogadon and Other Plays*. UQP

BELONGING

—— *The Hollow Tombola* 1980 In *The Great God Mogadon and Other Plays*. UQP
—— *Marsupials* 1981 (1979) In *Marsupials and Politics: Two Comedies*. UQP (MTC, September 1979)
—— *Politics* 1981 In *Marsupials and Politics: Two Comedies*. UQP,
—— *Scanlan* 1980 (1980) In *The Great God Mogadon and Other Plays*. UQP (Hoopla, Playbox, Melbourne)
—— *The Ship's Whistle* 1979 (1978) Edward Arnold, Melbourne (APG, 10 November 1978)
—— *Witzenhausen, Where Are You?* 1980 (1967) In *The Great God Mogadon and Other Plays*. UQP (Leeton Dramatic Society, 22 August)
Oliver, Jean *McLarty's Sale* 1964 In *Next Act!*, edited by Richard Beynon and H. G. Fowler. A&R
—— *Pay Cisca Manetti* 1967 In *Australian One-Act Plays: Book 3*, edited by Musgrove Horne. Rigby, Adelaide
—— *Two Jolly Swagmen* 1966 In *First Act*, edited by Richard Beynon and H. G. Fowler. A&R
Oliver, Murray *The Buck Stops Here* 1984 (1984) Currency (Playhouse Theatre, Perth, 6 November)
—— *Confessions From the Male* 1984 (1981) In *Confessions From the Male/Couples*. Currency (Bent Pin Productions, John Forest Senior High School, Morley, Western Australia. 19 June)
Oliver, Murray and Mandy Brown *Couples* 1984 (1982) In *Confessions From the Male/Couples*. Currency (Bent Pin Productions, Rockingham Senior High School, Western Australia. 19 June)
Open City *Sum of the Sudden* 1999 (1993) In *Performing the Unnameable: an anthology of Australian performance texts*, cditoed by Richard James Allen and Karen Pearlman. Currency (Open City, The Performance Space, Sydney)
Order By Numbers *A Few Short Wicks in Paradise* 1995 In *Challenging the Centre: Two Decades of Political Theatre*, edited by Steve Capelin. Playlab (Order By Numbers)
Oswald, Debra *Dags* 1987 (1985) Currency (Canberra Youth Theatre, Seymour Centre, Sydney, 9 May)
—— *Gary's House* 2000 (1996) Currency (Playbox Theatre, Melbourne and Q Theatre, Penrith, NSW, 1 March)
—— *Mr Bailey's Minder* 2004 (2004) Currency (Griffin Theatre Company, Stables Theatre, Sydney, 29 July)
—— *Skate* 2004 (2003) Currency (Australian Theatre for Young People, The Wharf, Sydney, 12 April)
—— *Stories in the Dark* 2008 (2007) Currency (ATYP, 30 April)
—— *Sweet Road* 2000 (2000) Currency (Playbox, 2 August)
Oxenburgh, Dickon and Andrew Ross *The Merry-Go-Round in the Sea* 2006 (1997) Currency (Black Swan Theatre Company, Perth, 15 February)
Palmer, Vance *A Happy Family* 1915 (1921) Campbell Howard Collection, University of New England, Armidale, NSW (Pioneer Players)
—— *Ancestors* 1937 In *Best Australian One-Act Plays*, edited by William Moore and T. Inglis Moore. A&R

PLAY LIST

────── *The Black Horse* 1924 In *The Black Horse and other Plays*. Sydney J Endacott, Melbourne

────── *Christine* 1930 (1930) Campbell Howard Collection, University of New England, Armidale, NSW (Brisbane Repertory Society, 20 November)

────── *The Fledgling* n.d. Campbell Howard Collection, University of New England, Armidale, NSW

────── *Hail Tomorrow* 1947 A&R

────── *Meadowsweet* 1945 Campbell Howard Collection, University of New England, Armidale, NSW

────── *The Prisoner* 1924 In *The Black Horse and other Plays*. Sydney J Endacott, Melbourne

────── *Prisoner's Country* 1959 (1960) Campbell Howard Collection, University of New England, Armidale, NSW (Union Theatre Repertory Company, Melbourne, 18 January)

────── *Telling Mrs Baker* 1924 In *The Black Horse and other Plays*. Sydney J Endacott, Melbourne

────── *Travellers* 1924 In *The Black Horse and other Plays*. Sydney J Endacott, Melbourne

Park, Ruth and Leslie Rees *The Harp in the South* 1987 (1949) Yackandandah (Independent Theatre, North Sydney, 3 March)

Parsons, Nicholas *Dead Heart* 1994 (1993) Currency (NIDA Company, NIDA Theatre, Sydney, 12 May 1993)

Paschalides, Lambis *She Was Spanish* 1988 (1955) In *Greek Voices in Australia: A Tradition of Poetry, Prose and Drama*, edited by George Kanarakis, ANU Press, Canberra, 1988

Patrikareas, Theodore *The Divided Heart* 2000 In *Antipodean Trilogy: Three Greek Australian Plays*, edited by Con Castan. RMIT University Greek Archive Publications, Melbourne

────── *The Promised Woman* 2000 (1963) In *Plays of the 60s Volume 1* edited by Katharine Brisbane. Currency (Sidetrack Theatre, Marrickville, 21 March)

────── *The Uncle From Australia* 2000 (1964) In *Antipodean Trilogy: Three Greek Australian Plays*, edited by Con Castan. RMIT University Greek Archive Publications, Melbourne (The Greek Artists Group, Elizabethan Theatre, Sydney)

Perkins, Elizabeth *A Squeaking of Rats* 1970 (1966) In *6 One-Act Plays*, edited by Eunice Hanger. UQP, 1970 (Twelfth Night Theatre, Brisbane 21 September)

Perrin, Mil *The Flaw* 1983 (1977) In *Seven One-Act Plays*, edited by Rodney Fisher. Currency (Nimrod Theatre, Sydney 7 May)

────── *Is This Where We Came In?* 1985 (1981) In *Popular Short Plays for the Australian Stage Volume II*, edited by Ron Blair. Currency (STC, Stables Theatre, Sydney, 14 November)

Peterson, Ralph *Night of the Ding Dong* 2007 (1954) In *Plays of the 50s Volume 1*, edited by Katharine Brisbane. Currency (London. First performed in Australia: New Theatre, Sydney, 17 October 1959)

────── *The Third Secretary* 1972 Currency

BELONGING

Petsinis, Tom *The Drought* 1994 (1994) Currency (La Mama at the Napier Street Theatre, Melbourne, 24 August)

Phillips, Robert *Technocraton* 1976 (1973) Heinemann Educational, Richmond, Victoria (Q Theatre, Adelaide)

Pinne, Peter N. and Don Battye *Caroline* 1981 (1971) Playlab (St Martin's Theatre, Melbourne, 24 February)

────── *Red, White and Boogie* 1989 (1973) Yackandandah (Le Chat Noir Theatre Restaurant, Melbourne, 27 November 1973)

Pitts, Graham *Emma* 1996 (1991) Currency (Deckchair Theatre, Old Customs House, Freemantle, WA, 15 June)

Pogos, Abe *Strangers in the Night* 1996 (1996) Currency (Playbox, 6 August)

────── *Toby* 2004 (2004) Currency (La Mama, 13 July)

Porter, Charles *Nellie Lacey and the Bushranger* 1944 (1943) In *Six Australian One Act Plays*. Mulga Publications, Sydney (British Drama League Festival of Community Drama, History House, Sydney, 7 September)

────── *Variations on a Printing Press* 1937 In *Best Australian One-Act Plays*, edited by William Moore and T. Inglis Moore. A&R

Porter, Hal *The Professor* 1966 (1965) Faber and Faber, London (Royal Court Theatre, London. 25 August)

────── *The Tower* 1963 In *Three Australian Plays*, edited by HG Kippax. Penguin, 1963

Pree, Barry *A Fox in the Night* 1960 (1958) *Theatregoer* 1,2 (Adelaide Theatre Group, Willard Hall, Adelaide, 28 May)

Price, Norman *Barking Dogs* 2002 (1998) Playlab (Metro Arts Theatre, Brisbane, 16 September)

Prichard, Katharine Susannah *Bid Me To Love* 1974 (1924) In *Brumby Innes and Bid Me To Love*. Currency

────── *Brumby Innes* 1974 (1971) In *Brumby Innes and Bid Me To Love*. Currency [Triad Drama Competition winner, 1927] (APG and Nindethana Theatre, 1 November)

────── *Pioneers* 1937 (1923) In *Best Australian One-Act Plays*, edited by Moore William and T. Inglis Moore. A&R (Pioneer Players 3 December)

Pulvers, Roger *Bertolt Brecht Leaves Los Angeles* 1982 (1979) Yackandandah (Playbox Theatre, Melbourne, 1 June)

────── *News Unlimited!* 1987 (1981) In *Short Plays for the Australian Stage Volume II*, edited by Leonard Radic. Yackandandah, 1987 (La Mama, 5 August)

────── *Yamashita* 1981 (1977) Currency (Hoopla Theatre Foundation, La Mama, 1 December)

Radic, Leonard *A Clean Sweep and Ground Rules* 1984 (1979) Yackandandah (La Mama, 18 October)

────── *Cody versus Cody* 1980 (1975) Playlab (Australian Theatre, Newtown, Sydney, 22 August 1975)

────── *The General* 1987 (1965) In *Short Plays for the Australian Stage Volume II*, edited by Leonard Radic. Yackandandah (Canberra Repertory Society, Riverside Theatre, 8 April)

────── *Sideshow* 1987 (1971) Yackandandah (Newman-St.Mary's Drama Group, Union Theatre, University of Melbourne, 16 June)

PLAY LIST

Radic, Thérèse *A Whip Round for Percy Grainger* 1984 (1982) Yackandandah (Playbox Theatre, Melbourne, 5 May)
—— *The Emperor Regrets* 1992 (1992) Currency (Playbox, 3 October)
—— *Madame Mao* 1986 (1986) Currency (Playbox Theatre, in association with Circus Oz, Studio Theatre, VAC, Melbourne, 23 June 1986)
—— *Peach Melba* 1990 (1990) Currency (Playbox, 8 June 1990)
Radic, Thérèse and Leonard Radic *Some of My Best Friends Are Women* 1983 (1976) Yackandandah (MTC, St. Martin's Theatre)
Rankin, Jennifer *Bees* 1976 (1974) *Theatre Australia*, 1,1:24–28; 1,2:24–28. (MTC, 11 May 1974 [workshop])
Rankin, Scott and Leah Purcell *Box the Pony* 1999 (1997) Hodder Headline, Sydney (Festival of the Dreaming, Sydney 2000 Cultural Olympiad, Playhouse Theatre, Sydney Opera House, 16 September)
Rayson, Hannie *Competitive Tenderness* 1996 (1996) Currency (Playbox, 20 November)
—— *Falling From Grace* 1994 (1994) Currency (Playbox, 9 August)
—— *Hotel Sorrento* 1990 (1990) Currency (Playbox, 27 July)
—— *Inheritance* 2003 (2003) Currency (MTC, Playhouse, VAC, 5 March)
—— *Life After George* 2000 (2000) Currency (MTC, Fairfax, VAC, 1 January)
—— *Mary* 1985 (1982) Yackandandah (Theatre Works Eastern Suburbs Theatre Company at the Playbox Theatre, Melbourne, December)
—— *Room to Move* 1985 (1985) Yackandandah (Playbox Theatre Company, St Martin's Theatre II, Melbourne, February)
—— *Two Brothers* 2005 (2005) Currency (STC and MTC, The Playhouse, Melbourne, 13 April)
Reade, Harry *Bucks' Night at Susy's Place* 1982 Yackandandah
—— *The Naked Gun* 1982 Yackandandah
—— *You'll Die Laughing* 1988 Yackandandah
Reed, Bill *Burke's Company* 1998 (1968) In *Plays of the 60s Volume 3*, edited by Katharine Brisbane. Currency (MTC, 7 May)
—— *Cass Butcher Bunting* 1977 (1976) Edward Arnold, Melbourne (Alexander Theatre Company, Melbourne, 16 June)
—— *Mr Siggie Morrison with his Comb and Paper* 1972 (1972) Heinemann Educational, South Yarra, Victoria (Scotch College Open Air Amphitheatre, Adelaide Festival, 29 February)
—— *Truganinni* 1977 (1970) Heinemann Educational, Richmond, Victoria (The Union Theatre, University of Melbourne, April)
Rees, Leslie *Mother's Day* 1944 (1940) In *Six Australian One Act Plays*. Mulga Publications, Sydney (Bryant's Playhouse, Sydney, 30 March)
—— *Sub-Editor's Room* 1937 In *Best Australian One-Act Plays*, edited by William Moore and T. Inglis Moore. A&R
Reeves, Melissa *The Spook* 2005 (2004) Currency (Company B, Belvoir St Theatre, Sydney, 3 November)
Reid, John Ormiston *Talk of the Devil* 1936 In *Five Plays by Australians*. Dramatists' Club of Australia, Melbourne

BELONGING

―――― *Van Diemen's Land* 1934 (1932) In *Eight Plays by Australians*. The Dramatists' Club, Melbourne (Little Theatre, Fawkner Park, South Yarra, 2 June)

Reynolds, Vicki *Daily Grind* 1995 (1992) *Australasian Drama Studies*, 26:101–40 (Melbourne Workers' Theatre, Theatreworks, 5 May 1992)

Richards, Max *Love Play* 1987 (1972) In *Short Plays for the Australian Stage Volume II*, edited by Leonard Radic. Yackandandah (La Mama, May)

―――― *Sadie and Neco* 1978 (1968) In *Can't You Hear Me Talking to You?: Eight Short Plays about Lovers and Others*, edited by Alrene Sykes. UQP (Canterbury University Drama Society, Christchurch, NZ, July)

Richardson, Wendy *...That Christmas of '75* 1997 (1995) In *Three Illawarra Plays*. Five Islands Press, Wollongong (Theatre South, Bridge Theatre, Wollongong. November 23)

―――― *The Last Voyage of Gracie Anne* 1997 (1993) In *Three Illawarra Plays*. Five Islands Press, Wollongong (Theatre South, Bridge Theatre, Wollongong, 2 September)

―――― *Lights Out Nellie Martin* 1997 (1990) In *Three Illawarra Plays*. Five Islands Press, Wollongong (Theatre South, Bridge Theatre, Wollongong, 16 August)

―――― *Windy Gully* 1989 (1987) Currency (Theatre South, Wollongong, NSW, 4 June)

Rigney, Tracey *Belonging* 2002 (2002) In *Blak Inside: 6 Indigenous Plays from Victoria*. Currency (Ilbijerri Aboriginal and Torres Strait Islander Theatre Cooperative and Playbox, 12 February)

Robertson, Tim *Mary Shelley and the Monsters* 1983 (1975) Yackandandah (APG, 25 March)

―――― *Tristram Shandy – Gent* 1983 (1982) Yackandandah (Nimrod Theatre, Sydney, August)

Robertson, Tim and John Romeril *Waltzing Matilda* 1984 (1973) Yackandandah (APG, November)

Robinson, Bec *Dark, Out There* 1967 In *Australian One-Act Plays: Book 3*, edited by Musgrove Horner. Rigby, Adelaide

Robinson, Keith, William Shakespeare, and Tony Taylor *The Popular Mechanicals* 1992 (1987) Currency (Company B, Belvoir St Theatre, Sydney, 19 November)

Rogers, Susan and Chris Drummond (adapted from Robert Dessaix) *Night Letters* 2004 (2004) Currency (Queen's Theatre, Adelaide, 24 February)

Rogers, Jennifer *Jigsaws* 1988 (1988) Currency (The Hole in the Wall Theatre Company, Perth, 5 Fenruary 1988)

Roland, Betty *Feet of Clay* 1995 (1928) In *Playing the Past: Three Plays by Australian Women*, edited by Kerry Kilner and Sue Tweg. Currency; National Centre for Australian Studies at Monash University, Melbourne

―――― *Granite Peak* 1988 In *The Touch of Silk and Granite Peak*, edited by Philip Parsons. Currency

―――― *Morning* 1937 In *Best Australian One-Act Plays*, edited by William Moore and T. Inglis Moore. A&R

―――― *The Touch of Silk* 1974 (1928) Currency (Melbourne Repertory Theatre, Playhouse, 3 November 1928)

PLAY LIST

—— *The Touch of Silk* [1955 revised version] 1988 In *The Touch of Silk and Granite Peak*, edited by Philip Parsons. Currency
—— *War on the Waterfront* 1986 *Australasian Drama Studies*, 8:74–79
Romeril, John *The Accidental Poke* 1985 (1975) In *Popular Short Plays for the Australian Stage Volume 1*, edited by Ron Blair. Currency (APG, 4 June [Part of *The Hills Family Show*])
—— *Bastardy* 1982 (1972) Yackandandah (APG, 23 August)
—— *Brudder Humphrey* 1971 Monash University, Clayton, Victoria
—— *Chicago, Chicago* 1998 (1970) In *Plays of the 60s Volume 3*, edited by Katharine Brisbane. Currency (Australian Performing Group, Perth Festival, 9 February)
—— *The Floating World* 1982 (1974) Currency [revised edition] (APG, 6 August 1974)
—— *I Don't Know Who To Feel Sorry For* 1973 (1969) Currency Methuen, Sydney; 1973 (La Mama, 18 October)
—— *The Kelly Dance* 1986 (1984) Yackandandah (Bushdance Theatre Company, Troupe Theatre, Unley, Adelaide, 24 May)
—— *Kitchen Table* 1971 Monash University, Clayton, Victoria
—— *Lost Weekend* (1989) (State Theatre Company of South Australia, Adelaide, 12 August)
—— *Love Suicides* 1997 (1997) Currency (Playbox Theatre and Company Skylark, Melbourne, September)
—— *Mickey's Moomba* 1978 *Meanjin*, 37, 3:284–99
—— *Miss Tanaka* 2001 (2001) Currency (Handspan Visual Theatre and Playbox, 21 February)
—— *Mrs Thally F* 1998 (1971) In *Plays of the 70s Volume 1*, edited by Katharine Brisbane. Currency (APG, 16 July)
—— *Top End* (1989) (MTC, Russell Street Theatre, 30 September)
Romeril, John, Jennifer Hill and Chris Anastassiades *Legends* 1986 (1985) Yackandandah (VAC, August 20)
Ross, Kenneth *Don't Piddle Against The Wind, Mate* 1978 (1977) *Theatre Australia*, 2,10; 2,11:33–40 (NIDA, Jane Street Theatre, Sydney, 20 July)
Ross, Lloyd *On the Edge of the Future* 1934 (1933) In *Eight Plays by Australians*. The Dramatists' Club, Melbourne (WEA Little Theatre, Sydney, 2 December)
—— *The Rustling of Voices* 1937 In *Best Australian One-Act Plays*, edited by William Moore and T. Inglis Moore. A&R
Rothfield, Tom *Jam Tomorrow* 1982 (1939) Yackandandah (Torch Theatre, Knightsbridge, London, 16 May)
Rudd, Steele *In Australia: or, The Old Selection* 1987 UQP
Rundle, Guy *Your Dreaming* 2002 (2001) Pluto Press, Sydney (VAC, 1 May)
Rutherford, Mervyn *Departmental* 1979 (1978) Currency (MTC, Russell Street Theatre, 23 May)
Ryall, Philip *The Centenarian* 1985 (1978) In *Popular Short Plays for the Australian Stage Volume 1*, edited by Ron Blair. Currency (Fortune Theatre Company, Canberra, 11 September)

BELONGING

Sam, Maryanne *Casting Doubts* 2002 (2002) In *Blak Inside: 6 Indigenous Plays from Victoria*. Currency (Ilbijerri Aboriginal and Torres Strait Islander Theatre Cooperative and Playbox, 19 February)
Searle, James *The Lucky Streak* 1999 (1966) In *Plays of the 60s Volume 2*, edited by Katharine Brisbane. Currency (Jane Street Theatre, Sydney, 18 October)
Sejavka, Sam *The Hive* 1997 (1990) In *The La Mama Collection: Six Plays for the 1990s*, edited by Liz Jones. Currency (La Mama Theatre, 30 May)
Sewell, Stephen *The Blind Giant Is Dancing* 1997 (1983) Currency (State Theatre Company of South Australia, 15 October)
—— *Dreams in an Empty City* 1986 (1986) Currency (State Theatre Company of South Australia, The Playhouse, Adelaide Festival Centre, 1 March)
—— *Dust* 1997 (1994) Currency (Centre for the Performing Arts, Vision Warehouse, Hindmarsh, South Australia, 24 November)
—— *The Father We Loved on a Beach by the Sea* 1983 (1978) Currency (La Boite, 21 July)
—— *The Garden of Earthly Delights* (1994) (Centre for Performing Arts. Vision Warehouse, Adelaide, 23 November)
—— *The Garden of Granddaughters* 1993 (1993) Currency (Playbox, 20 April)
—— *Hate* 1988 (1988) Currency (Playbox Theatre Company and Belvoir St Theatre, at Belvoir St Theatre, Sydney, 19 November 1988)
—— *It Just Stopped* 2007 (2006) In *It Just Stopped, Myth Propaganda and Disaster in Nazi Germany and Contemporary America Two Plays by Stephen Sewell* Currency (Malthouse Theatre and Company B Bevoir at the CUB Malthouse, Melbourne, 5 April)
—— *King Golgrutha* (1991) (State Theatre Company of South Australia, 26 July)
—— *Miranda* (1989) (La Boite, 8 February)
—— *Myth, Propaganda and Disaster in Nazi Germany and Contemporary America* 2007 (2003) In *It Just Stopped, Myth Propaganda and Disaster in Nazi Germany and Contemporary America Two Plays by Stephen Sewell* Currency (Playbox, 4 June)
—— *The Secret Death of Salvador Dali* (2004) (Griffin Theatre Company, Stables Theatre, Sydney, March 24)
—— *The Sick Room* 1999 Currency (Playbox, 10 March 1999)
—— *Sisters* 1991 (1991) Currency (Playbox, 2 March)
—— *Three Furies* (2005) (Ensemble at The Playhouse, Sydney Opera House, 19 January)
—— *Traitors* 1983 (1979) APCOL/Nimrod, Sydney (APG, 26 April)
—— *Welcome the Bright World* 1983 (1982) APCOL/Nimrod, Sydney (Nimrod Theatre, Sydney, 27 January)
Seymour, Alan *Swamp Creatures* 1955 (1957) Campbell Howard Collection, University of New England, Armidale, NSW (Canberra Repertory Society, November
—— *The One Day of the Year* 1985 (1960) In *Three Australian Plays*. Penguin, Ringwood [revised edition] (Adelaide Theatre Group, Willard Hall, 20 July)

PLAY LIST

Shave, Lionel *A Sirius Cove* 1948 (1935) In *Five Proven One-Act Plays*. The Australian Publishing Company Ltd, Sydney (Bryant's Playhouse, 11 September)
—— *Red and Gold* 1948 In *Five Proven One-Act Plays*. The Australian Publishing Company Ltd, Sydney
—— *That's Murder!* 1948 (1935) In *Five Proven One-Act Plays*. The Australian Publishing Company Ltd, Sydney (Sydney Players' Club, St James Hall. 5 March)
—— *The Resignation of Mr Bagsworth* 1948 (1948) In *Five Proven One-Act Plays*. The Australian Publishing Company Ltd, Sydney (Adelaide Repertory Theatre, 16 July)
—— *Twelve Moons Cold* 1948 (1940) In *Five Proven One-Act Plays*. The Australian Publishing Company Ltd, Sydney (New Theatre Sydney, 23 May)
Shearer, Jill *The Boat* 1978 (1977) In *Can't You Hear Me Talking to You?: Eight Short Plays about Lovers and Others*, edited by Alrene Sykes. UQP (Brisbane Repertory Theatre, 30 March)
—— *Catherine* 1977 Edward Arnold, Melbourne
—— *Echoes* 1980 (1980) In *Echoes and other plays*. Playlab (La Boite. 25 May 1980)
—— *The Family* 1995 (1994) Currency (QTC, Cremorne Theatre, 9 June)
—— *The Foreman* 1977 (1976) In *The New Life/The Foreman*. Currency (Student Theatre, Kelvin Grove CAE, Brisbane, 29 April)
—— *Georgia* 2000 (1999) Currency (La Boite, 15 July)
—— *The Kite* 1980 (1977) In *Echoes and other plays*. Playlab (Brisbane Repertory Theatre, 30 March)
—— *Nocturne* 1980 (1977) In *Echoes and other plays*. Playlab (Brisbane Repertory Theatre, 30 March)
—— *Shimada* 1989 (1987) Currency (MTC, Russell Street Theatre. 25 April)
—— *Stephen* 1980 (1980) In *Echoes and other plays*. Playlab (La Boite, 25 May 1980)
Sheil, Graham *Bali: Adat* 1991 (1987) Currency (La Boite, 22 April)
Shepherd, Catherine *Daybreak* 1942 (1938) Melbourne University Press (Hobart Repertory Theatre Society, Theatre Royal, 30 July)
—— *Delphiniums* 1995 (1943) In *Playing the Past*. Currency (Hobart Repertory Theatre Society, Playhouse, 11 September)
—— *Jane, My Love* 1951 (1951) Campbell Howard Collection, University of New England, Armidale, NSW (Theatre Royal, Hobart, Tasmania, 22 September)
Sherborne, Craig *Look at Everything Twice, For Me* 1999 (1999) Currency (La Mama at the Carlton Courthouse, 3 August)
Shotlander, Sandra *Angels of Power* 1991 In *'Angels of Power' and Other Reproductive Creations*, edited by Susan Hawthorne and Renate Klein, Spinifex Press, Melbourne
—— *Blind Salome* 1985 (1985) Yackandandah (Universal Theatre, Melbourne, 22 May)
—— *Framework* 1984 (1983) Yackandandah; 1984 (Universal Theatre, Melbourne, 22 April)

BELONGING

——— *Is That You Nancy?* 1996 (1991) In *Australian Gay and Lesbian Plays*, edited by Bruce Parr. Currency (Sydney Gay and Lesbian Mardi Gras, Belvoir St Theatre, 2 February)

Sidetrack Performance Group *Citizen X* 2003 (2002) *Australasian Drama Studies*, 42:30–5 (Sidetrack Performance Group, 24 September)

Sidetrack Theatre *Kin* 1988 (1987) Government Publishing Service, Canberra (Sidetrack Theatre)

——— *Out From Under* (1983) *Australasian Drama Studies*, 12/13:35–57 (Sidetrack Theatre)

Simper, Doug *In Search of the Great Australian National Anthem* 1983 (1977) In *Flags, Verandahs and other Wombats*. Heinemann Educational, Richmond, Victoria (Seacombe High School. December)

Simpson, Helen de Guerry *A Man of His Time* 1923 (1923) A&R (Gregan McMahon)

Simpson, Morris Hay *Sending Grannie Off* 1937 In *Best Australian One-Act Plays*, edited by William Moore and T. Inglis Moore. A&R

Somebody's Daughter Theatre and Maud Clark *"Tell Her That I Love Her..."* 1993 (1993) Somebody's Daughter Theatre, Melbourne (Somebody's Daughter Theatre, CUB Malthouse, Melbourne)

Spears, Steve J. *Africa: A Savage Musical* 1978 (1974) In *Early Works*. Outback Press, Melbourne (APG, January)

——— *The Elocution of Benjamin Franklin* 1989 (1976) In *The Elocution of Benjamin Franklin/When They Send Me Three and Fourpence*. Currency (Nimrod Theatre, Sydney, 28 August)

——— *Froggie* 1988 (1985) Yackandandah (Actors' Company, Cleveland, Ohio, USA, June 1985)

——— *Glory* 1988 (1988) Yackandandah (La Mama, 2 November)

——— *King Richard* 1980 (1978) In *Three Political Plays*, edited by Alrene Sykes. UQP (La Boite, 22 September)

——— *Mad Jean: They Reckon She's Crazy Like a Snake* 1978 (1978) In *Early Works*. Outback Press, Melbourne (New South Wales Youth Theatre, Balmain Bijou, Sydney, 21 January)

——— *People Keep Giving Me Things* 1978 In *Early Works*. Outback Press, Melbourne

——— *When They Send Me Three and Fourpence* 1989 (1983) In *The Elocution of Benjamin Franklin/When They Send Me Three and Fourpence*. Currency (Griffin Theatre Company, Stables Theatre, Sydney, 10 July)

——— *Young Mo* 1977 (1976) *Theatre Australia* 1,7:24–32; 1,8:24–33 (Circle Theatre, Adelaide, 15 January)

Spriggins, Florence *The Silver Stars of Freedom* 1936 In *Five Plays by Australians*. Dramatists' Club of Australia, Melbourne

Spunner, Suzanne *Dragged Screaming to Paradise* 1994 (1988) Little Gem Publications, Casuarina, Northern Territory (Paradise Productions, Brown's Mart, Darwin, December)

——— *Running up a Dress* 1997 (1986) In *Australian Women's Drama: Texts and Feminisms*, edited by Peta Tait and Elizabeth Schafer. Currency (Home Cooking Theatre Company, Athenauem 2, Melbourne, 17 September)

PLAY LIST

Stellmach, Barbara *Dark Heritage* 1973 (1964) In *4 Australian Plays*. UQP (Villanova Players, Brisbane)
—— *Dust Is The Heart* 1973 (1961) In *4 Australian Plays*. UQP (Villanova Players, Brisbane, September)
—— *From the Fourteenth Floor You Can See the Harbour Bridge* 1980 (1979) Playlab (Villanova Players, Brisbane)
—— *Hang Your Clothes On Yonder Bush* 1973 (1969) In *4 Australian Plays*. UQP (Cronulla Arts Theatre, Sydney, August)
—— *Legend of the Losers* 1973 (1971) In *4 Australian Plays*. UQP (Mews Playhouse, Randwick, October [rehearsed reading])
Stephen, Adrian *Anchored* 1918 In *Four Plays*. W.C. Penfold, Sydney
—— *Echoes* 1918 (1914) In *Four Plays*. W.C. Penfold, Sydney (Sydney Stage Society
—— *Futurity* 1918 In *Four Plays*. W.C. Penfold, Sydney
—— *The Victor* 1918 In *Four Plays*. W.C. Penfold, Sydney
Stephensen, P. R. *Blasting The Reds* 1983 *Australasian Drama Studies*, 1,2:138–54
Stewart, Douglas *The Fire of the Snow* 1958 In *Four Plays*. A&R
—— *Fisher's Ghost* 1964 In *Next Act!*, edited by Richard Beynon and H. G. Fowler. A&R
—— *The Golden Lover* 1958 In *Four Plays*. A&R
—— *Ned Kelly* 1943 (1942) A&R (Sydney University Dramatic Society, 14 October)
—— *Shipwreck* 2007 (1949) In *Plays of the 50s Volume 1*, edited by Katharine Brisbane. Currency (Metropolitan Theatre, September)
Strachan, Tony *Eyes of the Whites* 1983 (1981) APCOL/Nimrod, Sydney (Nimrod Theatre, Sydney, November 4)
—— *The Harlequin Shuffle* 1985 (1985) Currency (The Stage Company, Space Theatre, Adelaide Festival Centre, 30 May)
—— *State of Shock* 2000 (1986) Currency [revised edition] (Belvoir St Theatre, Sydney, 27 August)
Summons, John *The Coroner's Report* 1985 (1977) In *Popular Short Plays for the Australian Stage Volume II*, edited by Ron Blair. Currency (Nimrod Theatre, Downstairs, 6 May)
—— *Lamb of God* 1979 (1978) Currency (Ensemble Theatre, Sydney, 10 August)
Summy, Irene M. *The Man on the Mountain* 1970 (1967) In *6 One-Act Plays*, edited by Eunice Hanger. UQP (Twelfth Night Theatre, Brisbane)
Sumner, Phil and Jan McDonald *Riff-Raff* 1980 (1979) Heinemann Educational, Richmond, Victoria (WEST Community Theatre, Essendon Civic Theatre, 31 July)
Swenson, Sven *Road to the She-Devil's Salon* 2003 (2003) In *Vertigo and the Virginia and The Road to the She-Devil's Salon: Two plays from the Sundial Series*. Currency (QTC, 7 April)
—— *Vertigo and the Virginia* 2003 (1999) In *Vertigo and the Virginia and The Road to the She-Devil's Salon: Two plays from the Sundial Series*. Currency (QTC, 5 July)

BELONGING

Szeps, Henri *I'm not a Dentist* 2003 (1995) In *One Life, Two Journeys* Currency (Hakoah Club, Bondi, Sydney, 15 October)
—— *Why Kids* 2003 (2001) In *One Life, Two Journeys* Currency (Hakoah Club, Bondi, Sydney, 6 September)
Ta, Binh Duy *The Monkey Mother* 2000 (1998) In *Three Plays by Asian Australians*, edited by Don Batchelor. Playlab (Citymoon, PACT Theatre, Sydney, February)
Taylor, Ariette and Luke Devenish *Disturbing the Dust* 1994 (1994) Currency (Playbox, 15 March)
Taylor, Steve and Kevin Densley *Last Chance Gas* 2003 (1994) Currency (La Mama, 28 April)
Tennant, Carrie *Outback* 1941 In *Three Plays for Little Theatres*. Skewed and Bowman, Sydney
—— *Reprieve* 1941 In *Three Plays for Little Theatres*. Skewed and Bowman, Sydney
—— *Secrecy* 1941 In *Three Plays for Little Theatres*. Skewed and Bowman, Sydney
Tennant, Kylie *Tether a Dragon* 1952 Associated General Publications, Sydney
The Sydney Front *First and Last Warning* 1999 (1992) In *Performing the Unnameable: an anthology of Australian performance texts*, edited by Richard James Allen and Karen Pearlman. Currency (The Sydney Front, The Performance Space, Sydney, 19 November)
Thomas, Michael *The Pier* 1970 (1966) In *6 One-Act Plays*, edited by Eunice Hanger. UQP (Old Tote Theatre Company, Jane Street Theatre, Sydney, 1 October)
Thomson, Katherine *Barmaids* 1992 (1991) Currency (Deckchair Theatre, Old Customs House, Fremantle, Western Australia, 9 November)
—— *Diving for Pearls* 1992 (1991) Currency (MTC, Russell Street Theatre, 30 March)
—— *Harbour* 2004 (2004) Currency (STC, Sydney Theatre, Walsh Bay, January 10)
—— *Navigating* 1997 (1997) Currency (QTC, 16 October)
—— *Wonderlands* 2004 (2003) Currency (Hothouse Theatre, Butter Factory Theatre, Albury Wodonga, June 13)
Thomson, Katherine, Angela Chaplin, and Kavisha Mazzella *Mavis Goes to Timor* 2003 (2002) Currency (Deckchair Theatre, Freemantle Arts Centre, Perth, 7 February)
Throssell, Ric *The Day Before Tomorrow* 2007 (1956) Currency (Canberra Repertory Society, 6 April)
—— *Devil Wear Black* 1955 (1954) Australasian Book Society, Melbourne (Canberra Repertory Society)
—— *For Valour* 1976 (1960) Currency Methuen, Sydney (Canberra Repertory Theatre, August)
—— *Surburban Requiem* 1962 In *Australian One-Act Plays: Book 1*, edited by Eunice Hanger. Rigby, Adelaide
—— *Valley of the Shadows* 1948 (1948) Drama League of Australia, Sydney (Canberra, October)
Thurgood, Nevil *Two Magnificent Melodramas* 1984 Playlab

PLAY LIST

Tighe, Harry *Open Spaces; or, Bush Fire* 1927 (1927) Campbell Howard Collection, University of New England, Armidale, NSW (Queen's Theatre, London, January 1927)
Tomholt, Sydney *Anoli: The Blind* 1936 In *Bleak Dawn and other plays*. A&R
―――― *Bleak Dawn* 1936 In *Bleak Dawn and other plays*. A&R
―――― *The Coming* 1936 In *Bleak Dawn and other plays*. A&R
―――― *The Crucified* 1936 In *Bleak Dawn and other plays*. A&R
―――― *Dimmed Lights* 1936 In *Bleak Dawn and other plays*. A&R
―――― *The Last Post* 1936 In *Bleak Dawn and other plays*. A&R
―――― *Leading Lady* 1936 In *Bleak Dawn and other plays*. A&R
―――― *Life and the Idiot* 1936 In *Bleak Dawn and other plays*. A&R
―――― *Searchlights* 1937 In *Best Australian One-Act Plays*, edited by William Moore and T. Inglis Moore. A&R
―――― *The Woman Mary* 1936 In *Bleak Dawn and other plays*. A&R
―――― *The Women Wait* 1936 In *Bleak Dawn and other plays*. A&R
Tulloch, Richard *Face to Face* 1987 Cambridge University Press, Cambridge
―――― *Hating Alison Ashley* 1988 (1987) Penguin, Ringwood (Toe Truck Theatre, Everest Theatre, The Seymour Centre, Sydney, 3 June)
―――― *Space Demons* 1993 (1989) Currency (Adelaide Festival Centre Trust and Patch Theatre, The Playhouse, 1 April)
Turner, Alexander *All Stations* 1937 In *Hester Siding and other Plays and Verse*. Patersons Printing Press, Perth
―――― *Australian Stages* 1944 Mulga Publications, Sydney
―――― *Centurion* 1937 (1935) In *Hester Siding and other Plays and Verse*. Patersons Printing Press, Perth (Repertory Club, Perth, 5 July)
―――― *Coat-of-Arms* 1937 In *Hester Siding and other Plays and Verse*. Patersons Printing Press, Perth
―――― *Hester Siding* 1937 In *Hester Siding and other Plays and Verse*. Patersons Printing Press, Perth
―――― *Not the Six Hundred* 1937 (1933) In *Hester Siding and other Plays and Verse*. Patersons Printing Press, Perth (Phoenix Club, Meekatharra Hall, 17 October)
―――― *The Old Allegiance* 1937 (1936) In *Hester Siding and other Plays and Verse*. Patersons Printing Press, Perth (Repertory Club, Perth, 20 October)
―――― *One Hundred Guineas* 1937 (1935) In *Hester Siding and other Plays and Verse*. Patersons Printing Press, Perth (Bruce Rock Repertory Club, 17 October)
―――― *Strong Archer* 1937 In *Hester Siding and other Plays and Verse*. Patersons Printing Press, Perth
Tweedie, Phyllis Dorrington *The Queen's Marie* 1934 (1934) In *Eight Plays by Australians*. The Dramatists' Club, Melbourne (Dramatists' Club, Nicholas Building Little Theatre, Melbourne, 20 March)
Upton, John *Machiavelli; Machiavelli* 1986 (1984) Yackandandah (Marion Street Theatre, Sydney, August)
―――― *The Warhorse* 1987 (1980) Yackandandah (The King O'Malley Theatre Company, The Stables Theatre, Sydney, 9 October)
Valentine, Alana *Love Potions* 2006 (2006) In *Savage Grace and Love Potions*. Snowy Owl Press, Sydney (New Theatre, Sydney, 4 February)

BELONGING

—— *Parramatta Girls* 2007 (2007) Currency (Company B, Belvoir Street Theatre, Sydney, 17 March)
—— *Run Rabbit Run* 2004 (2004) Currency (Company B, Belvoir St Theatre, Sydney, 7 January)
—— *Savage Grace* 2006 (2000) In *Savage Grace and Love Potions*. Snowy Owl Press, Sydney (Company gf, Space Theatre, Adelaide Festival Centre, 25 October)
—— *Swimming the Globe* 1999 (1996) Currency (Freewheels Theatre Company, Mission Theatre, Newcastle, 21 August)
Vallack, A. S. *One Year* 1924 Radcliffe Press, Sydney
van Amstell, Pamela *Late Arrivals* 1985 (1980) In *Popular Short Plays for the Australian Stage Volume II*, edited by Ron Blair. Currency (Rocks Players, Rocks Players' Theatre, Leichhardt, Sydney 8 August 1980)
Van Der Werf, Patrick *Moon Babies* 2003 (2002) In *Moon Babies and Dirty Laundry: Two Plays*. Currency (La Mama, February)
Vernon, Barbara *The Multi-Coloured Umbrella* 2004 (1957) In *Plays of the 50s Volume 2*, edited by Katharine Brisbane. Currency (Melbourne Little Theatre, then JC Williamson, Theatre Royal, Sydney, 9 November)
—— *The Passionate Pianist* 1958 (1957) Tasmanian Adult Education Board, Hobart (Inverell Town Hall 22 November)
Vernon, Barbara and Bruce Beaver *King Tide Running* 1967 In *Australian One-Act Plays: Book 3*, edited by Musgrove Horner. Rigby, Adelaide
Version 1.0 *CMI (A Certain Maritime Incident)* 2004 (2004) *Australasian Drama Studies* 32:143–176 (Version 1.0, Performance Space, Sydney, March 26)
Vidler, Edward A. *The Rose of Ravenna* n.d. George Robertson and Company, Melbourne
Vitalstatistix Theatre Company *A Touchy Subject* 1989 (1987) In *A Touchy Subject and Weighing It Up*. Tantrum Press, Adelaide (Vitalstatistix Theatre Company)
—— *Weighing It Up* 1989b (1985) In A Touchy Subject *and* Weighing It Up. Tantrum Press, Adelaide (Vitalstatistix Theatre Company)
Wadds, Gillian M. *Who Cares?* 1988 (1986) Currency (Royal QTC, Cremorne Theatre, 10 July)
Waite, Robyn *The Search* 1985 (1985) In *Interplay '85: Eleven Plays by Young People*. Currency, 1985 (Troupe Theatre, Adelaide, 6 June 1985)
Walley, Richard *Coordah* 1989 (1987) In *Plays From Black Australia*. Currency (Western Australian Theatre Company, Hayman Theatre, Curtin University, Perth, 24 September 1987)
Walshe, Vivienne *God's Last Acre* 2003 (2003) Currency (Playbox, 12 March)
Walton, George Duke *Love Song* 1934 (1934) In *Eight Plays by Australians*. The Dramatists' Club, Melbourne (Dramatists' Club, Nicholas Building Little Theatre, Melbourne, March 20)
Watson, Hugh *A Few Short Wicks in Paradise* 1995 (1985) In *Challenging the Centre: Two Decades of Political Theatre*, edited by Steve Capelin. Playlab (Order By Numbers, La Boite)
—— *Raise the Roof* 1995 (1990) In *Challenging the Centre: Two Decades of Political Theatre*, edited by Steve Capelin. Playlab (Street Arts Community Theatre Company)

PLAY LIST

Watson, Louise *Inside* 1985 (1985) In *Troupe's Young Playwrights Season: seven plays written by young South Australians.* Currency (Troupe, The Old Unley Town Hall, Unley, South Australia, 11 May)
Webb, Peter *Public Dancing* 2001 (2001) In *Inside 01*. Currency (Playbox, 6 June)
Wheeler, John *Garden Fantasia* 1966 In *First Act*, edited by Richard Beynon and H. G. Fowler. A&R [first published 1937]
White, Patrick *A Cheery Soul* 1993 (1963) In *Collected Plays Volume 1*. Currency (Union Theatre Repertory Company, Melbourne, 19 November)
—— *Big Toys* 1994 (1977) In *Collected Plays Volume 2*. Currency (Old Tote Theatre Company, Parade Theatre, Sydney, 27 July)
—— *The Ham Funeral* 1993 (1961) In *Collected Plays Volume 1*. Currency (Adelaide University Theatre Guild, 15 Noveember)
—— *Netherwood* 1994 (1983) In *Collected Plays Volume 2*. Currency (Lighthouse, State Theatre Company of South Australia, Playhouse, Adelaide, 11 June)
—— *Night on Bald Mountain* 1993 (1964) In *Collected Plays Volume 1*. Currency (Adelaide University Theatre Guild, 9 March)
—— *The Season at Sarsaparilla* 1993 (1962) In *Collected Plays Volume 1*. Currency (Adelaide University Theatre Guild, 14 September)
—— *Shepherd on the Rocks* 1987 (1987) In *Collected Plays Volume 2*. Currency (State Theatre Company of South Australia, Playhouse, Adelaide, 9 May)
—— *Signal Driver* 1994 (1982) In *Collected Plays Volume 2*. Currency (Lighthouse Company, Playhouse, Adelaide, 5 March)
Wilcox, Dora *The Fourposter* 1937 In *Best Australian One-Act Plays*, edited by William Moore and T. Inglis Moore. A&R, 1937 (Community Playhouse)
Wilding, Ian *Torrez* 2004 (2004) Currency (Griffin Theatre Company and Black Swan Theatre Company in collaboration with Playbox Theatre, Stables Theatre, Sydney, 29 April)
Wilkinson, Linden *Nice Girls* 1989 (1989) Currency (Playbox Theatre Company, Anthill Theatre, Melbourne, 29 June)
—— *The Night of the Missing Bridegroom* 1994 (1994) In *Passion: Six New Short Plays by Australian Women*, edited by Ros Horin. Currency (Griffin Theatre Company, Stables, Sydney, 29 September)
Wilkinson, Mary E. *The Lighthouse Keeper's Wife* 1995 In *Playing the Past: Three Plays by Australian Women*, editors by Kerry Kilner and Sue Tweg. Currency; National Centre for Australian Studies at Monash University, Melbourne, 1995 [first published in 1922]
Williamson, David *A Conversation* 2002 (2001) In *The Jack Manning Trilogy*. Currency (Ensemble Theatre, Sydney, 5 September)
—— *A Handful of Friends* 1993 (1976) In *Collected Plays Volume 2*. Currency (South Australian Theatre Company, The Playhouse, 20 May 1976)
—— *After the Ball* 1997 (1997) Currency (QTC, Suncorp Theatre, 3 July)
—— *Amigos* 2004 (2004) Currency (STC, Drama Theatre, Sydney Opera House, 8 April)
—— *Birthrights* 2003 (2003) In *Birthrights Soulmates: Two Plays*. Currency (MTC, the Playhouse, VAC, 16 April)

BELONGING

—— *Brilliant Lies* 1993 (1993) Currency (Royal QTC, Suncorp Theatre, 29 April 1993)
—— *Celluloid Heroes* (1980) (Nimrod Theatre Company, Sydney, 2 December)
—— *Charitable Intent* 2002 (2001) In *The Jack Manning Trilogy*. Currency (La Mama, November)
—— *The Club* 1993 (1977) In *Collected Plays Volume 2*. Currency (MTC, Russell Street Theatre, 24 May)
—— *The Coming of Stork* 1986 (1970) In *Collected Plays Volume 1*. Currency (La Mama, 25 September)
—— *Corporate Vibes* 2001 (1999) In *Two Plays: Up For Grabs and Corporate Vibes*. Currency (STC and QTC, Drama Theatre, Sydney Opera House, 30 January)
—— *Dead White Males* 1995 (1995) Currency (STC, Drama Theatre, Sydney Opera House, 9 March)
—— *The Department* 1993 (1974) In *Collected Plays Volume 2*. Currency (South Australian Theatre Company, The Playhouse, Adelaide, 15 November)
—— *Don's Party* 1986 (1971) In *Collected Plays Volume 1*. Currency (APG, 11 August)
—— *Emerald City* 1987 (1987) Currency (STC, Drama Theatre, Sydney Opera House, 1 January)
—— *Face to Face* 2002 (1999) In *The Jack Manning Trilogy*. Currency (Ensemble Theatre, Sydney, 20 March)
—— *Flatfoot* 2004 (2004) Currency (Ensemble Theatre, Sydney, 10 June)
—— *The Great Man* 2000 (2000) In *Two Plays: The Great Man and Sanctuary*. Currency (STC, Drama Theatre, Sydney Opera House, 9 March)
—— *Heretic* 1996 (1966) Penguin and Currency (STC, Drama Theatre, Sydney Opera House, 28 March)
—— *Influence* 2005 (2005) In *Influence/Operator: Two Plays* Currency (STC, Drama Theatre, Sydney Opera House, 18 March)
—— *Jugglers Three* 1986 (1972) In *Collected Plays Volume 1*. Currency (MTC, Russell Street Theatre, 17 July)
—— *King Lear* (1978) (Alexander Theatre Company, Melbourne [adaptation])
—— *Money and Friends* 1992 (1991) Currency (Royal QTC, Suncorp Theatre, 28 November)
—— *Operator* 2005 (2005) In *Influence/Operator: Two Plays* Currency (Ensemble Theatre, Sydney. January 14)
—— *The Perfectionist* 1983 (1982) Currency (STC, Drama Theatre, Sydney Opera House, 20 July)
—— *Sanctuary* 2000 (1994) In *Two Plays: The Great Man and Sanctuary*. Currency (Playbox, 4 May)
—— *Siren* 1990 (1990) Currency (STC, 22 March)
—— *Sons of Cain* 1985 (1985) Currency (MTC, Playhouse, VAC, 26 March)
—— *Soulmates* 2003 (2002) In *Birthrights/Soulmates: Two Plays*. Currency (STC, the Drama Theatre, Sydney Opera House, 13 April)
—— *The Removalists* 1998 (1971) In *Plays of the 70s Volume 1*, edited by Katharine Brisbane. Currency (La Mama, 22 July)

PLAY LIST

——— *Third World Blues* 1997 (1997) Currency (STC, Drama Theatre, Sydney Opera House, 13 March [revised version of *Jugglers Three*])
——— *Top Silk* 1989 (1989) Currency (Festival of Sydney, Kinsela Productions, Greg Hocking and Tim Woods, Gary Penny Productions, at the York Theatre, Seymour Centre, 11 January)
——— *Travelling North* 1993 (1979) In *Collected Plays Volume 2*. Currency (Nimrod Theatre, Sydney, 22 August)
——— *Up for Grabs* [Australian version] 2001 (2001) In *Two Plays: Up For Grabs and Corporate Vibes*. Currency (STC, Drama Theatre, Sydney Opera House, 1 March)
——— *Up For Grabs* [English version] 2002 (2002) Faber and Faber, London (Sonia Friedman Productions and Theatre Royal, Bath at Wyndham's Theatre, London. 13 May)
——— *What If You Died Tomorrow* 1986 (1973) In *Collected Plays Volume 1*. Currency (Old Tote Theatre Company, Drama Theatre, Sydney Opera House, 9 October)
Wilson, Josephine and Erin Hefferon *The Geography of Haunted Places* 1999 (1994) In *Performing the Unnameable: an anthology of Australian performance texts*, edited by Richard James Allen and Karen Pearlman. Currency (Perth Institute of Contemporary Arts)
Winmar, Dallas *Aliwa!* 2002 (2000) Currency (Yirra Yaakin Noongar Theatre, Subiaco Theatre, Perth, 26 July)
Wood, John *On Yer Marx* 1987 (1972) Yackandandah (Nimrod Street Theatre, 7 July 1972)
——— *Ravages* 1992 (1977) Yackandandah (*Dropping In* and *Heels over Head*, La Mama, March 1977; *The Enid Simmons Interview* written for St Martin's Theatre, Melbourne, show called *Ladies Only*. n.d.)
Wright, Tom *Babes in the Wood* 2003 (2003) Currency (Playbox, 26 November)
Yen, Anna *Chinese Take Away* 2000 (1997) In *Three Plays by Asian Australians*, edited by Don Batchelor. Playlab (Gum Yi Productions and the Queensland Performing Arts Trust, Brisbane, 26 August)

WORKS CITED

Aboriginal and Torres Strait Islander Social Justice Commission, *Indigenous Deaths in Custody 1989–1996*, Aboriginal and Torres Strait Islander Commision, Canberra,1996.
Adams, Arthur H., *The Knight of the Motor Launch*, NSW Bookstall Company, Sydney, 1913.
Afford, Thelma, *Dreamers and Visionaries: Adelaide's Little Theatres From the 1920s to the Early 1940s*, Currency Press, Sydney, 2004.
Akerholt, May-Brit, *Patrick White*, Rodopi, Amsterdam, 1988.
Allen, Richard James and Karen Pearlman (eds), *Performing the Unnameable: An anthology of Australian performance texts*, Currency Press, Sydney, 1999.
Alomes, Stephen, 'The Search for a National Theatre', *Voices*, Spring 1993, Vol 3, No. 3, pp. 21–37.
Anderson, Hugh (ed.), *Ballades of Old Bohemia*, Red Rooster Press, Melbourne, 1980.
Andrews, John, 'Melbourne Theatre, 1929–1945: Recession and Response', unpublished manuscript, State Library of Victoria, Latrobe Library, MS 10884, 1979.
Armfield, Neil, 'About *Signal Driver*', performance program, Queensland Theatre Company, Brisbane, 1983.
Arrow, Michelle, *Upstaged: Australian Women Dramatists in the Limelight at Last*, Currency Press, Sydney, 2002.
Ashbolt, Allan, 'Courage, Contradiction and Compromise: Gregan McMahon, 1874–1941', *Meanjin*, no. 37, 1978, p. 332.
Batchelor, Donald, 'Political manoeuvring behind the scenes: the development of the national theatre idea in Australia during the 1940s', *Australasian Drama Studies*, issue 40, 2002, pp. 58–73.
Bedson, Jack and Julian Croft (eds), *The Campbell Howard Annotated Index of Australian Plays 1920–1955*, University of New England, Armidale, 1993.

BELONGING

Binns, Vivienne, *Community and the Arts*, Pluto Press, Sydney, 1991.
Black Chicks Talking, (documentary film), 2002 Film Australia, directed by Leah Purcell, Producer by Bain Stewart.
Bosi, Pino, 'Making a Distinction between "Ethnic" and "Multicultural"', *Writing in Multicultural Australia 1984: An Overview*, Australia Council, Sydney, 1985, pp. 136–8.
Brecht, Bertolt, 'The Popular and the Realistic', in *Brecht on Theatre*, ed. John Willett, Eyre Methuen, London, 1973, pp. 109,112.
Brissenden, R. F., 'The Plays of Patrick White', in *Contemporary Australian Drama* (rev. ed.), ed. Peter Holloway, Currency Press, Sydney, 1987, pp. 290–303.
Burrows, J. F., 'The Four Plays of Patrick White', *Australian Literary Studies*, v. 2, no. 3, 1966.
Burvill, Tom, 'Sidetrack's *Kin*: intervening in multiculturalism', *Australasian Drama Studies*, no. 12/13, 1988, pp. 59–71.
Butler, Judith, *Gender Trouble*, Routledge, New York, 1990.
Buzo, Alex, 'The day of the playwright', *Theatre Quarterly*, no. 26, 1977, pp. 71–3.
——— *The Young Person's Guide to the Theatre and Almost Everything Else*, Penguin, Melbourne, 1988.
Cameron, Neil, *Fire on the Water*, Currency Press, Sydney, 1993.
Campbell, Deborah, '*A Doll's House*: The Colonial Response', in *Nellie Melba, Ginger Meggs and Friends: Essays in Australian Cultural History* ed. Susan Dermody, Drusilla Modjeska and John Docker, Kibble Books, Malmsbury, 1982, pp 192ff.
Capelin, Steve, *Challenging the Centre: Two Decades of Political Theatre*, Playlab Press, Brisbane, 1995.
Carroll, Dennis, *Australian Contemporary Drama* (rev. ed.), Currency Press, Sydney, 1995.
Casey, Maryrose, *Creating Frames: Contemporary Indigenous Theatre*, University of Queensland Press, St. Lucia Qld, 2004.
Castan, Con, 'Greek-Australian Plays', *Australasian Drama Studies*, no. 12/13, 1988, pp. 17–33.
Cherry, Wal, 'Summer of the Seventeenth Doll', in *Contemporary Australian Drama* (rev. ed.), ed. Peter Holloway, Currency Press, Sydney, 1987, pp. 184–8.
Ciccotosto, Emma and Michael Bedworth, *Emma: A Recipe for Life*, Fremantle Arts Centre Press, Fremantle, 1995.
Clarke, John, *A Dagg at My Table: Selected Writings*, Text Publishing, Melbourne, 1998.
Covell, Roger, 'Patrick White's Plays', *Quadrant*, vol. 8, no.1, 1964, pp 7-12.
Cullen, Sue, 'Australian theatre during World War One', *Australasian Drama Studies*, no. 17, 1989, pp. 157–81.
Davidson, Jim, 'Interview [with John Romeril]', in *Contemporary Australian Drama*, ed. Peter Holloway, Currency Press, Sydney, 1981, p. 376.
Davison, Graeme, 'Sydney and the Bush: An Urban Context for the Australian Legend', *Historical Studies*, vol. 17, no. 71, 1978, pp. 191–209.
Davison, P. H., 'Three Australian Plays: National Myths Under Criticism', in *Contemporary Australian Drama* (rev. ed.), ed. Peter Holloway, Currency Press, Sydney, 1987, pp. 203–22.

WORKS CITED

Davison, Remy, 'Outside looking in: an interview with Ray Mooney', *Australasian Drama Studies*, no. 28, 1996, p. 57.

de Groen, Frances, 'Dymphna Cusack's *Comets Soon Pass*: The genius and the potato wife', in *Wallflowers and Witches: Women and Culture in Australia 1910–1945*, ed. Maryanne Dever, University of Queensland Press, St. Lucia Qld, 1994, pp. 91–104.

Dermody, Susan, Drusilla Modjeska and John Docker (eds), *Nellie Melba, Ginger Meggs and Friends: Essays in Australian Cultural History*, Kibble Books, Malmsbury, 1982.

Dever, Maryanne (ed.), *Wallflowers and Witches: Women and Culture in Australia 1910–1945*, University of Queensland Press, St. Lucia Qld, 1994.

Douglas, Dennis and Morgan M. Morgan, 'Gregan McMahon and the Australian Theatre', *Komos*, no. 2, 1969, p. 59 and no. 3, 1969, p. 130.

Dunne, Stephen, 'As Many Pearls As Possible: Gay Theatre in Sydney', unpublished BA (Hons) dissertation, University of Technology, Sydney, 1991.

Dyce, J. R., *Patrick White as Playwright*, University of Queensland Press, St. Lucia Qld, 1974.

Ellis, Bob, 'Go out and write an Australian play (It's not hard)', *Bulletin*, vol. 92, no. 4724, October 1970, pp. 43–4.

Enoch, Wesley, performance program, *Black Medea*, Company B Belvoir, Sydney, 2005.

Fensham, Rachel and Denise Varney, *The Dolls' Revolution: Australian theatre and cultural imagination*, Australian Scholarly Publishing, Melbourne, 2005.

Ferres, Kay (ed.), *The Time To Write: Australian Women Writers 1890–1930*, Penguin, Melbourne, 1993.

Filewood, Alan and David Watt, *Workers' Playtime: Theatre and the labour movement since 1970*, Currency Press, Sydney, 2001.

Fischer, Gerhard (ed.), *The Mudrooroo/Muller Project: A Theatrical Casebook*, University of New South Wales Press, Sydney, 1991.

Fitzpatrick, Peter, *After the Doll: Australian Drama since 1955*, Edward Arnold, Melbourne, 1979.

——— 'After the Wave: Australian Drama Since 1975', *New Theatre Quarterly*, no. 5, February 1986, pp. 55–6.

——— *Williamson*, Methuen, Sydney, 1987.

——— *Stephen Sewell: The Playwright as Revolutionary*, Currency Press, Sydney, 1991.

——— *Pioneer Players: The Lives of Louis and Hilda Esson*, Cambridge University Press, Melbourne, 1995.

Fletcher, Nadia, 'Reg Livermore: a laugh in the wilderness', *Australasian Drama Studies*, no. 26, 1995, pp. 4–21.

Fotheringham, Richard, *Community Theatre in Australia*, Currency Press, Sydney, 1992.

——— *In Search of Steele Rudd*, University of Queensland Press, St. Lucia Qld, 1995.

Fourmile, Henrietta, 'Aboriginal arts in relation to multiculturalism', in *Culture, Difference and the Arts*, ed. Sneja Gunew and Fazal Rizvi, Allen & Unwin, Sydney, 1994, pp. 69–85.

Gilbert, Helen, 'Monumental moments: Michael Gow's *1841*, Stephen Sewell's

BELONGING

Hate, Louis Nowra's *Capricornia* and Australia's Bicentenary', *Australasian Drama Studies*, no. 24, 1994, pp. 29–45.
—— *Sightlines: Race, Gender, and Nation in Contemporary Australian Theatre*, University of Michigan Press, Ann Arbor MI, 1998.
Ginters, Laura, 'Violating the Past: Beatrix Christian', in *The Dolls' Revolution: Australian theatre and cultural imagination*, ed. Rachel Fensham and Denise Varney, Australian Scholarly Publishing, Melbourne, 2005, pp. 238–84.
Glow, Hilary, *Power Plays: Australian Theatre and the Public Agenda*, Currency Press, Sydney, 2008.
Goldsworthy, Kerryn, 'Is It a Boy or a Girl? Gendering the Seventeenth Doll', *Southerly*, vol. 55, no. 1, 1995, pp. 89–105.
Goodall, Jane, 'Some rooms in outer space', *Australasian Drama Studies*, no. 19, October 1991.
Greenaway, Jai, *Political Acts: Lesbian Theatre in Sydney*, Amazon Desktop Publishing, Sydney, 1990.
Grene, Nicholas and Christopher Morash (eds), *The Irish Theatre on Tour*, Carysfort Press, Dublin, 2005.
Griffiths, Gareth (ed.), *John Romeril*, Rodopi, Amsterdam, 1993.
Gunew, Sneja and Fazal Rizvi (eds), *Culture, Difference and the Arts*, Allen & Unwin, Sydney, 1994.
Gurr, Michael, *Days Like These*, Melbourne University Press, Melbourne, 2006.
Hainsworth, J. D., *Hibberd*, Methuen, Sydney, 1987.
Harris, Max, *Ockers: Essays on the Bad Old New Australia*, Maximus Books, Adelaide, 1974.
Hasluck, Sir Paul, *Mucking About: An Autobiography*, Melbourne University Press, Melbourne, 1977.
Heckenberg, Pamela and Philip Parsons, 'The Struggle for an Australian Theatre 1901–1950: Summary of Theatrical Events', in *The Australian Stage*, ed. Harold Love, University of New South Wales Press, Sydney, 1984, p. 127.
Herring, T., 'Maenads and Goat-Song: The Plays of Patrick White' in *Ten Essays on Patrick White: Selected from Southerly 1964–67*, ed. G. A. Wilkes, Angus & Robertson, Sydney, 1970, pp. 147–62.
Hewett, Dorothy, 'Creating Heroines in Australian plays', *Hecate*, no. 2, p. 74, 1976.
Hibberd, Jack, 'How Marvellous Melbourne Came To Life', *Theatre Australia*, vol. 2, no. 4, August 1977, pp. 36–7.
Hibberd, Jack, 'Proscenium-arch blues', in *Contemporary Australian Drama* (rev. ed.), ed. Peter Holloway, Currency Press, Sydney, 1987, p. 126.
Holloway, Peter (ed.), *Contemporary Australian Drama* (rev. ed.), Currency Press, Sydney, 1987.
Hooton, Joy, 'Lawler's Demythologising of the *Doll: Kid Stakes* and *Other Times*', in *Contemporary Australian Drama* (rev. ed.), ed. Peter Holloway, Currency Press, Sydney, 1987, pp. 245–61.
Hope, A. D., 'Standards in Australian Literature', *Current Affairs Bulletin*, no. 19, 26 November 1956, p. 40.
Human Rights and Equal Opportunities Commission, *Bringing Them Home: Report of the National Inquiry into the Separation of Aboriginal and Torres Strait Islander Children from Their Families*, Australian Government Publishing Service, Canberra, 1997.

WORKS CITED

Humphries, Barry, *A Nice Night's Entertainment*, Currency Press, Sydney, 1981.
—— *The Life and Death of Sandy Stone*, Macmillan, Sydney, 1990.
Hunt, Hugh, *The Making of Australian Theatre*, F. W. Cheshire, Melbourne, 1960.
Hunter, Mary Ann, interview with Stephen Sewell, *Australasian Drama Studies*, no. 14, April 1989, pp. 35–9.
J. C. Williamson Papers, Box 2071, State Library of Victoria, Latrobe Library, MS 10052.
Jacobson, Lisa, 'The ocker in Australian drama', *Meanjin*, vol. 49, no. 1, 1990, pp. 137–47.
Jones, Elizabeth, Betty Burstall & Helen Garner, *La Mama: The Story of a Theatre*, McPhee Gribble/Penguin, Melbourne, 1988.
Kelly, Veronica (ed.), *Nowra*, Rodopi, Amsterdam, 1987.
—— (ed.), *Our Australian Theatre in the 90s*, Rodopi, Amsterdam, 1998.
—— *The Theatre of Louis Nowra*, Currency Press, Sydney, 1998.
Kiernan, Brian, *David Williamson: A Writer's Career* (rev. ed.), Currency Press, Sydney, 1996.
Kiernander, Adrian, 'John Bell and a post-colonial Australian Shakespeare, 1963–2000', in *O Brave New World: Two Centuries of Shakespeare on the Australian Stage*, ed. John Golder and Richard Madelaine, Currency Press, Sydney, 2001, pp. 236–55.
Kippax, H. G., 'Australian Drama Since *Summer of the Seventeenth Doll*', in *Contemporary Australian Drama* (rev. ed.), ed. Peter Holloway, Currency Press, Sydney, 1987, pp. 223–39.
—— 'Razzle-Dazzle Over Dog Pack', in *Contemporary Australian Drama* (rev. ed.), ed. Peter Holloway, Currency Press, Sydney, 1987, pp. 283–9.
Kirby-Smith, Virginia, 'The Development of Australian Theatre and Drama, 1788–1964', unpublished PhD dissertation, Duke University, 1969.
Kramer, Leonie (ed.), *The Oxford History of Australian Literature*, Oxford University Press, Melbourne, 1981, p. 209.
Kuch, Peter, 'The Abbey Irish Players in Australia, 1922', in *The Irish Theatre on Tour*, ed. Nicholas Grene and Christopher Morash, Carysfort Press, Dublin, 2005, pp. 69–88.
Lloyd, Vic, 'Dymphna Cusack's *Morning Sacrifice*', *Australasian Drama Studies*, no. 10, 1987, pp. 71–2.
Livermore, Reg, *Chapters and Chances*, Hardie Grant Books, Melbourne, 2003.
Love, Harold (ed.), *The Australian Stage: A documentary history*, University of New South Wales Press, Sydney, 1984.
—— 'Chinese Theatre on the Victorian Goldfields, 1858–1870', *Australasian Drama Studies*, vol. 3, no. 2, 1985, pp. 45–86.
Makeham, Paul, 'Framing the landscape: Prichard's *Pioneers* and Esson's *The Drovers*', *Australasian Drama Studies*, no. 23, April 1993, pp 121–34.
Marr, David, *Patrick White: A Life*, Random House, Sydney, 1991.
—— 'Theatre Under Howard', 9th Philip Parsons Memorial Lecture on the Performing Arts, delivered at the Seymour Centre, Sydney, 9 October 2005. Available online at http://currencyhouse.org.au/documents/ch_d_parsons2005_david_marr.pdf (accessed 10 December 2008).
McCallum, John, 'The *Doll* and the Legend', *Australasian Drama Studies*, vol. 3, no. 2, 1985, pp. 33–44.

BELONGING

—— *Buzo*, Methuen Australia, Sydney, 1987.
—— 'Something With a Cow In It: Louis Esson's Imported Nationalism', *Overland*, no. 108, September 1987, pp. 6–13
—— 'The World Outside: cosmopolitanism in the plays of Nowra and Sewell', in *Contemporary Australian Drama* (rev. ed.), ed. Peter Holloway, Currency Press, Sydney, 1987, pp. 567–80.
—— 'Irish Memories and Australian Hopes: William Butler Yeats and Louis Esson', *Westerly*, no. 2, June 1989, pp. 33–40.
McGillick, Paul, *Hibberd*, Rodopi, Amsterdam, 1988.
Meyrick, Julian, *See How It Runs: Nimrod and the new wave*, Currency Press, Sydney, 2002.
—— *Trapped by the Past: Why Our Theatre is Facing Paralysis*, Platform Papers No. 3, Currency House, Sydney, 2005.
Milne, Geoffrey, *Theatre Australia (Un)limited: Australian Theatre since the 1950s*, Rodopi, Amsterdam, 2004.
Mitchell, Tony, 'Italo-Australian theatre: multiculturalism and neo-colonialism' *Australasian Drama Studies*, no. 10, 1987, pp. 31–48
—— '"Going to the Source": Tes Lyssiotis talks to Tony Mitchell', *Australasian Drama Studies*, no. 12/13, 1988, p. 12.
Moore, T. Inglis, *Social Patterns in Australian Literature*, Angus & Robertson, Sydney, 1971.
Moorhouse, Frank (ed.), *Days of Wine and Rage*, Penguin, Melbourne, 1980.
Morley, Michael, 'Trotsky Cassidy & dancing giants', *The National Times*, 7–13 October 1983, p. 31.
Morley, Sheridan, 'Drama in history', *Sydney Morning Herald*, 11 October 1980.
Nowra, Louis, *Shooting the Moon: A Memoir*, Picador, Sydney, 2004.
Palmer, Jennifer, *Contemporary Australian Playwrights*, Adelaide University Union Press, Adelaide, 1979.
Palmer, Vance, *Louis Esson and the Australian Theatre*, Georgian House, Melbourne, 1948.
Parr, Bruce (ed.), *Australian Gay and Lesbian Plays*, Currency Press, Sydney, 1996.
Parsons, Philip with Victoria Chance (eds), *Companion to Theatre in Australia*, Currency Press, Sydney, 1995.
Pender, Anne and Susan Lever (eds), *Nick Enright: An Actor's Playwright*, Rodopi, Amsterdam, 2008.
Perkins, Elizabeth, *The Plays of Alma De Groen*, Rodopi, Amsterdam, 1994.
Pfisterer, Susan and Carolyn Pickett, *Playing with Ideas: Australian Women Playwrights from the Suffragettes to the Sixties*, Currency Press, Sydney, 1999.
Pram Factory (documentary film), 1994 Film Australia, directed by Anna Grieve and James Manché.
Purcell, Leah, *Black Chicks Talking*, Hodder, Sydney, 2002.
Radic, Leonard, *The State of Play: The Revolution in the Australian Theatre since the 1960s*, Penguin, Melbourne, 1991.
—— *Contemporary Australian Drama*, Brandl & Schlesinger, Blackheath, 2006.
Rees, Leslie, *The Making of Australian Drama: A Historical and Critical Survey from the 1830s to the 1970s*, Angus & Robertson, London and Sydney, 1973.

WORKS CITED

———— *A History of Australian Drama: The Making of Australian Drama from the 1830s to the late 1960s*, (rev. ed.) Angus & Robertson, London and Sydney, 1978.

———— *Hold Fast to Dreams: Fifty Years in Theatre, Radio, Television and Books*, Alternative Publishing Cooperative, Sydney, 1982.

Ridgeman, Jeremy, 'Interview: Louis Nowra, Stephen Sewell and Neil Armfield talk to Jeremy Ridgeman', *Australasian Drama Studies*, no. 2, 1983, pp. 105–23.

Robertson, Tim, *The Pram Factory: The Australian Performing Group Recollected*, Melbourne University Press, Melbourne, 2001.

Roland, Betty, *The Eye of the Beholder*, Hale & Iremonger, Sydney, 1984.

———— *An Improbable Life*, Collins Australia, Sydney, 1989.

Rundle, Guy, *Your Dreaming*, Pluto Press, Sydney, 2002.

Schaefer, Kerrie, 'Staging Seduction: The Sydney Front and the postmodern geography of theatre's bodies and spaces', in *Body Show/s*, ed. Peta Tait, Rodopi, Amsterdam, 2000.

———— *Women and the Bush: Forces of Desire in the Australian Cultural Tradition*, Cambridge University Press, Melbourne and Cambridge, 1988.

Sheridan, Susan, *Along the Faultlines: Sex, Race and Nation in Australian Women's Writing*, Allen & Unwin, Sydney, 1995.

Shoemaker, Adam, *Black Words, White Page: Aboriginal Literature, 1929–1988*, University of Queensland Press, St. Lucia Qld, 1989.

Sierz, Aleks, *In-Yer-Face Theatre: British Drama Today*, Faber and Faber, London, 2001.

Smith, Vivian (ed.), *Letters of Vance and Nettie Palmer 1915–1963*, National Library of Australia, Canberra, 1977.

Stanwell, John and Anne Jones, *'The Logan City Story'*, in *Community Theatre in Australia*, ed. Richard Fotheringham, Currency Press, Sydney, 1992, pp. 79–88.

Stargazer (pseud.), 'The Australian Play', *Lone Hand*, no. 1, May 1907, p. 104.

Sturm, Terry, 'Drama', in *The Oxford History of Australian Literature*, ed. L. Kramer, Oxford University Press, Melbourne, 1981, p. 209.

Summers, Anne, *Damned Whores and God's Police: The Colonisation of Women in Australia*, Penguin, London, 1975.

Sumner, John, *Recollections at Play: A Life in the Australian Theatre*, Melbourne University Press, Melbourne, 1993.

Sykes, Alrene (ed.), *Australian Drama Productions, 1950–1969*, University of Queensland Library, St. Lucia Qld, 1984.

Tait, Peta, *Converging Realities: Feminism in Australian Theatre*, Currency Press and Artmoves, Sydney, 1994.

———— *Original Women's Theatre: The Melbourne Women's Theatre Group 1974–77*, Artmoves, Melbourne, 1993, pp. 45–6.

———— (ed.), *Body Show/s: Australian viewings of live performance*, Rodopi, Amsterdam, 2000.

Tait, Peta and Elizabeth Schafer, *Australian Women's Drama: Texts and Feminisms*, Currency Press, Sydney, 1997.

Tait, Viola, *A Family of Brothers: The Taits and J.C. Williamson: A Theatre History*, Heinemann, Melbourne, 1971.

BELONGING

Thomson, Helen, 'Gardening in the Never-Never: Women Writers and the Bush', in *The Time To Write: Australian Women Writers 1890–1930*, ed. Kay Ferres, Penguin, Melbourne, 1993, pp. 19-37.
Walker, David, *Dream and Disillusion: A Search for Australian Cultural Identity*, Australian National University Press, Canberra, 1976.
Waterhouse, Richard, *From Minstrel Show to Vaudeville: The Australian Popular Stage, 1788–1914*, University of New South Wales Press, Sydney, 1990.
—— *Private Pleasures, Public Leisure: A History of Australian Popular Culture since 1788*, Longmans, Melbourne, 1995.
Watson, Hugh, '"All 4114 All": Writing For Street Arts in Logan City', in *Challenging the Centre: Two Decades of Political Theatre*, ed. Steve Capelin, Playlab Press, Brisbane, 1995, pp. 159-69.
Watt, David, 'The Popular Theatre Troupe and Street Arts: Two Paradigms of Political Activism', in *Challenging the Centre: Two Decades of Political Theatre*, ed. Steve Capelin, Playlab Press, Brisbane, 1995, pp. 13-33.
Watt, David and Graham Pitts, 'Community Theatre as Political Activism: Some Thoughts and Practices in the Australian Context', in *Community and the Arts*, ed. Vivienne Binns, Pluto Press, Sydney, 1991, pp. 199-133.
Wilde, William H., Joy Hooton and Barry Andrews, *The Oxford Companion to Australian Literature*, Oxford University Press, Melbourne, 1985.
Wilkes, G. A. (ed.), *Ten Essays on Patrick White: Selected from Southerly 1964–67*, Angus & Robertson, Sydney, 1970.
Willet, John (ed. and trans.), *Brecht on Theatre*, Eyre Methuen, London, 1973.
Williams, Margaret, *Drama*, Oxford University Press, Melbourne, 1977.
—— *Australia on the Popular Stage, 1829–1929*, Oxford University Press, Melbourne, 1983.
—— 'Mask and Cage: Stereotype in Recent Drama', in *Contemporary Australian Drama* (rev. ed.), ed. Peter Holloway, Currency Press, Sydney, 1987, pp. 327-33.
—— *Dorothy Hewett: the Feminine as Subversion*, Currency Press, Sydney, 1992.
Wolf, Gabrielle, *Make It Australian: The Australian Performing Group, the Pram Factory and New Wave Theatre*, Currency Press, Sydney, 2008.
Woolacott, L. L. *Playwriting: An unconventional textbook*, Currawong Publishing, Sydney, 1942.
Zuber-Skerritt, Ortrun (ed.), *David Williamson*, Rodopi, Amsterdam, 1988.

INDEX

Note: Page numbers in bold type (e.g. **301–3**) indicate the most detailed discussion of the topic. Page numbers in italics (e.g. *106–7*) indicate illustrations.

7:84 company (UK), 266, 277

A

Ab Intra Theatre (Adelaide), 17
Abbey Theatre (Dublin), 5, 22, 32, 142
 see also Irish drama
Aboriginal characters
 19th century, vii, 1, 302
 early 20th century, 24, 29–30, 38, 42, 44–8, 56, 61, 66–8, 70, 72, 302
 ethnic theatre, 283, 290
 Hewett, 122
 New Wave, 156
 since 1990s, 343, 349
 Williamson, 156, 183
Aboriginal playwrights, 301, 313, 315, 345
Aboriginal theatre, **301–25**
 in 1960s and 1970s, 44, 68, **301–3**
 in 1980s and 1990s, ix, 267, 272, 300, **304–21**
 white writers, **321–5**; early 20th century, 67–8, 70, 302; in 1970s, 148; in 1980s, 205, 223, 229–31; since 1990s, 360, 362, 377
absurdist drama, 74–5, 93, 132, 134, 142, 149, 156, 187, 189–90
 1980s, 353
 De Groen, 194
 Sewell, 211
 since 1990s, 376
Achurch, Janet, 13
Acropolis Now (TV series), 283
Adams, Arthur H., 17, **19–22,** 94, 373
 plays: *Galahad Jones*, 20; *Gallipoli Bill*, 19; *Mrs Pretty and the Premier*, 20, 21; *Tapu*, 4, 19; *The Forty Thieves*, 19; *The Wasters*, 20
 The Knight of the Motor Launch, 21
Adelaide Festival, 87, 89, 92, 94
Adelaide Repertory Theatre, 4, 15
Adelaide University Theatre Guild, 92, 94, 101
Afford, Max, 46
 plays: *Lady in Danger*, 14; *Mischief in the Air*, 14
AIDS plays, 274, 275, 378
Akerholt, May-Brit, 112
Akhmatova, Anna, 197, 200
Albee, Edward: *Who's Afraid of Virginia Woolf?*, 14
Allen, David, 145
Allen, Peter, 248

461

BELONGING

Allen, Richard James: *Performing the Unnameable* (with Karen Pearlman), 330
Anders, Doug, 137
Anderson, Tammy: *I Don't Wanna Play House*, **316,** 319
Andrews, Benedict, 92, 98, 378
Angus & Robertson (publisher), 75
animals, 1, **6,** 17
Anzac tradition, 63, 85, 86, 87–8
APG. *see* Australian Performing Group
Aristophanes, 130, 149
Aristotle, 366
Armfield, Neil, 92, 95, 96, 100, 102, 103, 105, 108, 143, 319
Armstrong, Millicent, 52
    plays: *As The Moon Sets*, 52; *At Dusk*, 52; *Drought*, 25–6; *Fire*, 52; *Goblin Gold*, 52
Arrabal, Fernando, 149
Art-in-Working-Life movement, 276
art theatre. *see* repertory & amateur theatres
Artaud, Antonin, 137
Ash, Kathryn, 377
    Flutter, 328, 377
Ashbolt, Allan, 13, 15, 18
The Aunty Jack Show (Grahame Bond and Rory O'Donoghue), 164
Australia: You're Standing In It (ABC TV), 269
Australian Broadcasting Commission (later, Corporation; ABC), 60, 269
Australian Drama Nights (Melbourne), 17
Australian Elizabethan Theatre Trust, 15, 53, 78
Australian Labor Party, 172, 189, 355, 357
    see also Whitlam, Gough
Australian National Playwrights Conference, 170, 210
Australian Performing Group (APG, Melbourne), 44, 135, 141, **143–5,** 188, 234, 267
    playwrights: Hibberd, 3, 143, 144, 148, 151, 170; Oakley, 146, 164–5; Romeril, 3, 143, 144, 155, 156, 157, 161, 165; Sewell, 213; Williamson, 167, 170
    Stasis Group, 137, 142, 143

vaudeville history plays, 3, 143, **163–6,** 240
'Australianness'
    before 1970s, ix, 5, **6–14,** 21, 24, 34, 78, 80, 84, 87
    Bicentennial plays, 219
    New Wave, 140, 154, 156, 160, 188–9, 206–7, 209–10, 327
    post-New Wave, 265, 267, 281, 327
    see also nationalist drama
authenticity, **10,** 21, 24, 35, 38, 68, 284
Ayres, Tony, 275
    The Fat Boy, 275–6

B

Babare, Dalmazio, 364
Bailey, Bert, 5, 7, 8, 9, 12, 19, 20, 373
    plays: *On Our Selection*, viii–ix, 5, **7–9,** 17, 24, 30, 33, 78, 148, 240, 373; *The Squatter's Daughter* ('Albert Edmunds,' i.e. Edmund Duggan and Bert Bailey), 6
Baker, George Pierce: *Dramatic Technique*, 11
Bakes, John, 155, 278
Bakhtin, Mikhail, 128
Balodis, Janis, 287, **288–94,** 362
    plays: *Ghosts* trilogy *[Too Young for Ghosts, No Going Back, My Father's Father]*, 288–90; *My Father's Father*, 288, 289, **290**; *No Going Back*, 288, 289, **290**; *Too Young For Ghosts*, 288, **290**; *Wet and Dry*, **290–1,** 292–3
Barclay, Edmund, 46
Barry McKenzie Holds His Own (film), 128
Baruch, Kester, 17
Bates, Sandra, 170
Baudelaire, Charles, 149
Beckett, Samuel, 94, 131, 132, 365, 366
    Waiting for Godot, 150, 235, 366–7
Beeby, George S.: *The Banner*, 59
Bell, Hilary, 271
    plays: *Fortune*, 328; *Wolf Lullaby*, 328
Bell, John, 144, 146, 224–5
Bell Shakespeare Company, 144
Bellbird (TV series), 60

INDEX

belonging, x, 24, 49, 228, 374, 379
Belvoir Street Theatre (Sydney), 82, 105, 143, 225, 230
Bennett, Arnold, 13
Bennett, Roger
    plays: *Funerals and Circuses*, 314–15; *Up the Ladder*, 315–16
Benyon, Lissa: *Come in Spinner* (with Nick Enright), 249
Beresford, Bruce, 129
Betty Can Jump (APG), 267
Betzien, Angela, 377
    Children of the Black Skirt, 377
Beynon, Richard
    plays: *Simpson J.202*, 85; *Summer Shadows*, 85–6; *The Shifting Heart*, **85–6,** 114, 286
Bicentennial (1988), 68, 219, 230, 259
Bidenko, Kristina, 254–5
Big Brother (TV series), 98
The Big Chill (film), 340
Big hART, 155, 278, 316
Biggles (Michael Boddy, Marcus Cooney and Ron Blair), 149, 164
Blair, Ron, 144, **146–7**
    plays: *Biggles* (with Michael Boddy and Marcus Cooney), 149, 164; *Flash Jim Vaux*, 146, 164; *Hamlet on Ice* (with Michael Boddy and Marcus Cooney), 146, 160; *Last Day In Woolloomooloo*, 147, 375; *Mad, Bad and Dangerous to Know*, 146; *Marx*, 146; *President Wilson in Paris*, 146; *The Christian Brothers*, 146, **147**
Blak Inside (festival), 319–21
Blewett, Dorothy, 46
    plays: *Quiet Night*, 60; *The First Joanna*, 54, **55–6**
Blue Hills (radio series), 60
Blundell, Graeme, 143, 145, 170
Boddy, Michael, 146
    plays: *Biggles* (with Ron Blair and Marcus Cooney), 149, 164; *Hamlet on Ice* (with Ron Blair and Marcus Cooney), 146, 160; *The Legend of King O'Malley* (with Bob Ellis), 136–7, 143, 146, **163–4,** 166, 240

Bond, Grahame
    Boy's Own McBeth (with Jim Burnett), 164
    TV shows: *The Aunty Jack Show* (with Rory O'Donoghue), 164; *Wollongong the Brave* (with Rory O'Donoghue), 164
Borghesi, Anna, 102
Bosi, Pino, 282
Bostock, Gerald L., 302
    Here Comes the Nigger, 302
Bovell, Andrew, 147, 182, 329, 347, **360–3**
    Lantana (film), 360–2
    plays: *After Dinner*, 360; *Confidentially Yours* (monologues), 362; *Holy Day*, 205, 259, 360, **362–3,** 377; *Like Whiskey on the Breath of a Drunk You Love*, 360; *Scenes From a Separation* (with Hannie Rayson), 335; *Speaking in Tongues*, 360–2; *The Ballad of Lois Ryan*, 360; *The Ship of Fools*, 360; *Who's Afraid of the Working Class?* (with Patricia Cornelius, Melissa Reeves, Christos Tsiolkas, and Irine Vela), 362, 375
Boyd, Martin, 284
The Boys in the Band, 14
Brainrot (Melbourne University), 142, 149, 154
Bran Nue Dae (Jimmy Chi and Kuckles), 163, **313–14,** 316, 318, 323
Brandenstein, Carl von, 45
Brand, Mona, 18, 61, **70–3,** 88, 126, 212, 213, 279
    New Theatre revues: *I'd Rather Be Left*, 70; *On Stage Vietnam*, 70
    plays: *Flood Tide*, 26; *Here Under Heaven*, 71; *No Strings Attached*, 72–3; *Pavement Oasis*, 286; *Strangers in the Land*, 72
Bread and Puppet Theatre (USA), 266, 278
Brecht, Bertolt
    community & political theatre and, 266, 287, 300

463

BELONGING

nationalists and, 88
playwrights and: Hewett, 114;
  Hibberd, 154; Keneally, 136;
  Nowra, 227, 234; Rayson, 338;
  Reed, 147; Romeril, 161, 162;
  Sewell, 211, 212; White, 100, 114
Bren, Frank, 142
Bridges, Mike, 105
Briggs, Tony: *The Sapphires*, 318
Brisbane, Katharine, 44, 70, 93, 167
Brisbane Repertory Theatre, 66
Brodney, Spencer (Leon Brodzky), 43
  Rebel Smith, 43
Brodzky, Leon. *see* Brodney, Spencer
Brook, Peter, 141–2
  The Empty Space, 141
Brooks, Mel: *The Producers*, 207
Brooksbank, Anne, 182
Brown, Frank, 42, **43**
  plays: *Andeganora* (with Louis Esson), 30, 33; *Mates* (with Louis Esson), 43
Brown, Tom, 134
Brown, Paul, 279
  Aftershocks, 279
Bryant's Playhouse (Sydney), 94
Buchanan, Alfred Johnson, 1
The Bulletin (journal), 75
Burnett, Jim: *Boy's Own Macbeth* (with Grahame Bond), 164
Burstall, Betty, 142
bush comedy & drama
  Doll school, 78–81, 83–7, 89
  early 20th century, 7–9, **23–49,** 51–4, 57–8, 69, 74, 76, 349
  gothic, 31, 101, 328, 374
  New Wave, 133, 161
  opposition to city, x, 21, **23–49**
  since 1980s, 226, 287, 337–9, 349, 351–2
  see also country town comedies & dramas; family sagas; station dramas
bush legend, 6–7, 10, 21, **23–38**
  women in, x, **47–9**
Butler, Judith: *Gender Trouble*, 271
Buzacott, Martin: *Kingaroy*, 322–3
Buzo, Alex, 57, 91, 127, 139–40, 144, **187–93**
  plays: *Big River*, 188, **192**; *Coralie Lansdowne Says No*, 188, **190–1,** 192, 193, 258; *Macquarie*, 188; *Makassar Reef*, 188, **191–2**; *Martello Towers*, 188, **191,** 192, 193; *Norm and Ahmed*, 75, 127–8, 135, 136, 156, 187, 188, **189**; *Normie and Tuan*, 189; *Pacific Union*, 188; *Rooted*, 136, 140, 187, 188, **189–90**; *Shellcove Road*, 188; *Stingray*, 188; *The Front Room Boys*, 136, 140, 143, 187–8, **190,** 335; *The Marginal Farm*, 188, **192–3**; *The Roy Murphy Show*, 190; *Tom*, 188, **190,** 335
Bynder, Wayne, 308–9
Byrne, Gerald, 42

C

Caine, Peggy: *Who'll Come A-Waltzing*, 14
Cameron, Neil, 278
Capsis, Paul, 207
  Boulevard Delirium, 207
  The Lost Echo, 207
Carleton, Stephen, 377
  Constance Drinkwater and the Final Days of Somerset, 377
Carroll, Peter, 147
Casson, Lewis, 3
Castan, Con, 284, 285
celebratory plays, 122, 151–2, 172, 240, 242, 298
censorship, 135, 136, 156, 187, 189
Charged Up (Street Arts), 227
Charrington, Charles, 13
Chater, Gordon, 9, 239–40
Cheetham, Deborah: *White Baptist Abba Fan*, 315
Chekhov, Anton, 144, 168
  The Cherry Orchard, 115–16
Cherry, Wal, 145
Chi, Jimmy: *Bran Nue Dae* (with Kuckles), 163, **313–14,** 316, 318, 323
Chikamatsu, 161–2
  Sonezaki Shinju (The Love Suicides at Sonezaki), 162
Chobocky, Barbara: *The Raid* (film), 299
Christian, Beatrix, 271, **328**

464

INDEX

Jindabyne (film), 328
   plays: *Blue Murder*, 328; *Fred*,
      328; *Old Masters*, 328; *The
      Governor's Family*, 328
Ciccotosto, Emma: *Emma: A Translated
   Life*, 295
Circus Oz, 145
cities. *see* bush comedy & drama; urban
   plays
Claire, Jennifer, 269
   The Butterflies of Kalimantan, 269
Clarendon Hotel (Katoomba), 207
Clark, John, 122, 134, 136, 170
Clark, Manning: *Manning Clark's
   History of Australia* (John Romeril,
   Tim Robertson and Don Watson),
   230
Clark, Maud: *"Tell Her That I Love
   Her..."* (with Somebody's Daughter
   Theatre), 205–6
Clarke, Doreen, 145, **270–1**
   plays: *Bleedin' Butterflies*, 270;
      Farewell Brisbane Ladies, 270–1;
      Roses in Due Season, 270
Clarke, John (Fred Dagg), 71, 77, 79
Clarke, Terence
   musical plays: *Summer Rain* (with
      Nick Enright), 247, **248–9**;
      The Venetian Twins (with Nick
      Enright), 247, **248–9**
class
   early 20th century, 41, 67, 76
   in 1960s, 61, 87–8
   late 20th century, 161, 250, 257,
      279–80, 281, 345
   see also middle-class drama;
      underclass drama; working-class
      drama
Clayton, Syd, 137
Clifton, Marshall, 117
Coburn, Anthony: *The Bastard Country*
   (aka *Fire on the Wind*), **53–4**, 84,
   286, 328
Cold War, 65, 70, 377
Collie, Therese, 279
   Out of the Blue (A Jailbird's Story),
      205
commercial theatres
   early 20th century, 2–8, 10, **11–14**,
      17–22, 24, 28, 63, 373

   in 1950s and 1960s, 53, 78, 126,
      141
communism, 44, 64, 87, 113–14, 118,
   125, 175, 210, 214, 276, 279
   see also socialism
Community Playhouse (Sydney), 16
community theatre
   Enright, 247, 249, 252
   Hewett, 122
   identity and, 265–7, **276–9**, 300,
      327
   immigrants & ethnicity, 34, 281–4,
      298, 300
   New Wave, 140, 155, 166, 171
Company B (Sydney), 68, 143, 230,
   279, 321, 324
Compton, Jennifer, 268–9
   plays: *Barefoot*, 268; *Crossfire* (aka
      No Man's Land), 268; *The Big
      Picture*, 269
Conabere, Sydney, 36–7
Confidentially Yours (monologues), 362
Conigrave, Timothy, 274, 275
   Holding the Man, 275, 276
   plays: *Like Stars in My Hands*, 275;
      Thieving Boy, 275
Conley, Boris, 364
Cook, Adam, 252
Cook, Patrick, 71
Cooney, Marcus, 146
   plays: *Biggles* (with Ron Blair and
      Michael Boddy), 149, 164;
      Hamlet on Ice (with Ron Blair
      and Michael Boddy), 146, 160
Coppin, Tyler, 96
Cornall, Jan: *At the Crossroads*, 271
Cornelius, Patricia, 279
   Who's Afraid of the Working Class?
      (with Andrew Bovell, Melissa
      Reeves, Christos Tsiolkas, and
      Irine Vela), 362, 375
Cortese, Raimondo, 85, 147, 375–6
   plays: *Features of Blown Youth*,
      375–6; *Roulette*, 376; *St Kilda
      Tales*, 376
cosmopolitanism. *see* new
   internationalists
Costello, Peter and Tim, 339
Costi, Angela: *Panayiota*, 294
country town comedies & dramas

BELONGING

early 20th century, **57–61,** 70, 73–4
since 1960s, 89, 121–2, 123, 134, 148, 348, 374, 377
Coustas, Mary, 283
Cowell, Brendan, 374, 376
  Morph, 374
Cramphorn, Rex, 137, 142, 145
Cranney, P.P. (Pat), 279
  The Logan City Story, 277
Cribb, Reg, 376
Crocodile Dundee (film), 132
Crowhurst, Geoff: *Wild Rice* (with Huong Nguyen, Phi Hai, and Pat Rix), 297
Crystal Palace movie parlour (Perth), 119
Cullen, Max, 102
Cummins, Peter, 152, 153, *158–9*
Currency Press, 127, 188
Curtis, Stephen, 105
Cusack, Dymphna, 46, 61, **62–6**
  Come in Spinner, 249
  Jungfrau, 66
  plays: *Anniversary,* 63; *Comets Soon Pass,* 64; *Morning Sacrifice,* 63–4; *Pacific Paradise,* 65, 77; *Red Sky at Morning,* 26, **62–3;** *Second Rhapsody,* 63; *Shallow Cups,* 63; *Shoulder the Sky,* 64–5; *The Golden Girls,* **65–6,** 69

D

Dadaism, 130
Dagg, Fred (John Clarke), 71, 77, 79
Daily Mirror (Sydney), 92
Dampier, Alfred: *Marvellous Melbourne,* 3, 163
Dann, George Landen, 46, 61, **66–70,** 88, 213, 230, 302, 321, 349
  plays: *Caroline Chisholm* (aka *A Second Moses*), 66; *Fountains Beyond,* 66, 67; *How Far Returning,* 54, 66, 68; *In Beauty It Is Finished,* 66–7, 69; *No Incense Rising,* 68, **69;** *Ring Out Wild Bells!,* 70
Darrell, George, 6
  plays: *The Double Game,* 6; *The Sunny South,* 6
Davidson, E. Coulson: *The Forerunners,* 44

Davis, Arthur Hoey. *see* Rudd, Steele
Davis, Essie, 102
Davis, Jack, ix, 302–3, **304–11,** *308–9,* 313, 318, 319, 322
  plays: *Barungin: Smell the Wind,* 230, 302, 305, **310;** *Honey Spot,* 304–5; *In Our Town,* **305,** 306; *Kullark,* 304, **305–6,** 307, 311, 320; *Moorli and the Leprechaun,* 304; *No Sugar,* 305, 307, 310, 311, 314; *The Dreamers,* 230, 305, **306–7,** *308–9,* 310–11
Davison, P.H., 85
Dawn, Gloria, 124
De Groen, Alma, 187, **193–201,** 267, 342
  plays: *Chidley,* 195; *Going Home,* 193, **195,** 200; *Perfectly All Right,* 194; *The After-Life of Arthur Cravan,* 137, **194;** *The Girl Who Saw Everything,* 200; *The Joss Adams Show,* 194; *The Rivers of China,* 193, **196–7,** *198–9,* 200; *The Sweatproof Boy,* 194; *The Woman in the Window,* 193, 196, **197,** 200; *Vocations,* 193, **195–6;** *Wicked Sisters,* 182, 193, **200–1,** 337
Death Defying Theatre (Sydney), 278, 298
Deckchair Theatre, Fremantle, WA, 295
Delacroix, Eugène: *Liberty Leading the People,* 260
Delval, Marcel, 363–4
Depression (1930s), 2, 14, 68, 124, 248, 270
Dessaix, Robert: *Night Letters,* 378–9
Devanny, Jean, 279
  Paradise Flow, 87, 286
Devine, George, 94
Dickens, Charles, 65, 243
  A Christmas Carol, 242
Dickins, Barry, 239, **241–5**
  plays: *A Dickins' Christmas,* 242; *Beautland,* 244; *Lennie Lower,* 242, **243–4;** *Mag and Bag* (aka *The Horror of Nature Strips*), 244; *One Woman Shoe,* 243; *Remember Ronald Ryan,* 244–5; *Royboys,* 244; *The Banana*

INDEX

Bender, 244; *The Bridal Suite*, 243; *The Death of Minnie*, 243; *The Fools' Shoe Hotel*, 242, 375–6; *The Golden Goldenbergs*, 242
The Dismissal (TV series), 171
Dobell, William: *The Dead Landlord*, 94
documentary drama, 328
Doll school, **84–90,** 91, 114, 123
Doll trilogy. *see* Lawler, Ray
Doyle, John and Greig Pickhaver (Roy Slaven and H.G. Nelson), 128, 190
Drake, Elizabeth, 331
Drake-Brockman, Henrietta, 46
  plays: *Men Without Wives*, 26, 27, **47–9,** 101; *The Man From the Bush*, 27
Drummond, Chris, 379
Duggan, Edmund
  plays: *My Mate: A Bush Love Story*, 6; *On Our Selection*, viii–ix, 5, **7–9,** 17, 24, 30, 33, 78, 148, 240, 373; *The Squatter's Daughter* ('Albert Edmunds,' i.e.Edmund Duggan and Bert Bailey), 6
Duigan, John, 151
Duncan, Catherine: *Sons of the Morning*, 54
Dunstan, Graham: *Project Ghostfisher*, 278
Dürrenmatt, Friedrich: *The Visit*, 360
Dutton, Geoffrey, 94
Dwyer, Kerry, *158–9*

E

Earley, Eric: *The Custodians*, 322
Eastwood, Larry, 147
eclecticism, 124, 209, 223, 300
Edgerton, Joel, *254–5*
'Edmunds, Albert' (Edmund Duggan and Bert Bailey)
  plays: *On Our Selection*, viii–ix, 5, **7–9,** 17, 24, 30, 33, 78, 148, 240, 373; *The Squatter's Daughter*, 6
Edwards, Gale, 170
El Teatro Campesino, 266, 278
Elisha, Ron, 239, **246–7**
  plays: *Choice*, 246; *Einstein*, 246; *Esterhaz*, 246; *In Duty Bound*, 246; *Pax Americana*, 246; *Safe House*, 246; *The Levine Comedy*, **246,** 247; *Two*, 247
Elizabethan Theatre Trust. *see* Australian Elizabethan Theatre Trust
Elliott, Sumner Locke
  Rusty Bugles, **74–5,** 78
Ellis, Ben, 376
  plays: *Falling Petals*, 376; *Post Felicity*, 376; *These People*, 376
Ellis, Bob, 181–2, 210
  plays: *The Duke of Edinburgh Assassinated* (with Dick Hall), 164; *The Legend of King O'Malley* (with Michael Boddy), 136–7, 143, 146, **163–4,** 166, 240
Emerald Hill Theatre (Melbourne), 145
Enoch, Wesley, 66, 68, 230, 316, 318, 321
  plays: *Black Medea*, 318; *The 7 Stages of Grieving* (with Deborah Mailman), 315, **316–18,** 319; *The Sunshine Club*, 65, 318
Enright, Nick, 147, 239, **247–56,** 263, 272, 362
  Lorenzo's Oil (film) (with George Miller), 249
  plays: *A Property of the Clan*, 247, **252–3,** 279; *Blackrock*, 253, **254–5,** 256; *Cloudstreet* (with Justin Monjo and Tim Winton), 249; *Come in Spinner* (with Lissa Benyon), 249; *Country Music*, **248,** 249; *Daylight Saving*, 248; *Good Works*, 251–2; *Mary Bryant* (with David King), 247, 248, **249;** *Miracle City* (with Max Lambert), 247, 248, **249;** *Mongrels*, 249–50; *On the Wallaby*, 248; *Spurboard*, 247; *St James Infirmary*, 250–1; *Summer Rain* (with Terence Clarke), 247, 248–9, **248–9;** *The Boy From Oz*, 247, 248; *The Venetian Twins* (with Terence Clarke), 247, 248; *Variations*, 247
Ervine, St John, 23, 29
Esson, Hilda, 22, 35, 38, 39

Esson, Louis, x, 3, 17, **28–39,** 40, 163, 364
   melodrama, 10, 11, 22, 31–2
   nationalist drama, 4, 19–22, **28–39,** 43, 57, 75, 78, 141–2, 373
   naturalism, 2, 4, 41, 62, 785
   Palmer, Vance: *Louis Esson and the Australian Theatre*, 39
   plays: *Andeganora* (with Frank Brown), 30, 33; *Australia Felix*, 34; *Ballades of Old Bohemia*, 34–5; *Dead Timber*, **29–30,** 33; *Mates* (with Frank Brown), 43; *Mother and Son*, **30–1,** 33, 34; *Shipwreck*, 22, 34, **38–9,** 45, 108, 328; *Terra Australis*, 34; *The Battler*, 5, **31–2,** 33, 57, 73; *The Bride of Gospel Place*, 35, 85; *The Drovers*, **28–9,** 30, 33, 43, 48, 83, 187; *The Quest*, 34; *The Sacred Place*, 33, 35, 87, 286; *The Southern Cross*, 33, 34; *The Time Is Not Yet Ripe*, 21–2, 33, 34, **36–7,** 373, 374; *The Woman Tamer*, 33, 35; *Vagabond Camp*, 30, 33, 43
   realism, 10, 20, 22, 30–1, 35, 38, 43
   underclass drama, 33
ethnicity, 34, 266, 281–3, **284–300**
Euripides
   plays: *Medea*, 318; *The Bacchae*, 135, 329; *Women of Troy*, 259, 377–8
Everage, Edna. *see* Humphries, Barry
expressionism
   Dickins, 242, 244
   Hewett, 114, 115, 118
   Hibberd, 150
   migrant theatre, 300
   Romeril, 157, 160
   Sewell, 212, 216
   White, 93, 99, 114

F

Facey, A.B.: *A Fortunate Life*, 245
Fairlea Women's Prison, 206
family sagas
   Aboriginal, 313
   early 20th century, 54–6
   in 1950s, 54–6, 59, 65
   in 1980s, 85–6, 192, 214, 227–31, 233
   Kenna, 123–5
   migrant theatre, 286, 288, 294
   since 1990s, 220, 236, 251, 337, 374
   White's *Signal Driver*, 94, 104–5
Farwell, George, 46
feminist theatre
   Aboriginal, 313
   early 20th century, 62, 66, 268
   in 1970s, 81, 118, **267–8,** 270
   in 1980s and 1990s, 33, **268–71,** 272–3, 279–80, 281, 342
   New Wave, 180, 191, 196, 200
Fensham, Rachel, 271, 328
Ferguson, Dale, 100
Festival of the Dreaming (1997), 315
FILEF: *Nuovo Paese*, 278
Filiki Players, 287
'The Firm.' *see* Williamson's, J.C.
Fischer, Margaret, 272
   The Gay Divorcee, 273
Fisher, Rodney, 170
Fitton, Doris, 16, 94
Fitzpatrick, Kate, 102
Fletcher, Nadia, 208
Flood, Les, 113, 114
Forde, Margery and Michael Forde: *Way Out West: Legends and Larrikins*, 3
Foster, Lynn: *There is No Armour*, 54, 55
Fotheringham, Richard, 276, 279
   plays: *Fallout and Follow Me*, 276; *The White Man's Mission* (with Albert Hunt), 166, 276
Frankland, Richard J.: *Conversations with the Dead*, 320–1
Freewheels Theatre (Newcastle, NSW), 252
Freudian psychology, 101, 273, 328
Friedman, Betty, 333
Fuller, Michael, *308–9*
Futcher, Michael, 291
   plays: *A Beautiful Life* (with Helen Howard), 291, **299–300;** *The Drowning Bride* (with Helen Howard), 291, 294

INDEX

G

Gage, Mary: *The New Life*, 284
Gallacher, Frank, *198–9*
Gallipoli. *see* Anzac tradition; World War I
Gallipoli (film), 171
Galsworthy, John, 13, 22
Gantner, Carrillo, 145
Garland, Nicholas, 127
gay and lesbian drama
    1960s and 1970s, 124–6, 202–4, 245, 272, 274
    since 1980s, 251–2, 256, 266–7, **272–6,** 279–80, 281, 283
Gay Theatre Company (Sydney), 274
Geoghegan, Edward: *The Currency Lass*, 135
Gerald, Jim, 3
ghetto theatre, **281–4**
Giannopoulos, Nick, 283
Gilbert, Kevin, 301–2
    The Cherry Pickers, **301,** 302
Gilbert and Sullivan, 2, 12, 249
Gillies, Max, 71, 153, 165, 166
Glow, Hilary: *Power Plays*, 344
Gogol, N.V., 149
    The Overcoat, 154
Goldoni, Carlo: *The Venetian Twins*, 248
Gooding, Tim: *The Last Resort* (with Louis Nowra), 238
Gore, Sandy, *36–7*
Gorky, Maxim, 375
    The Lower Depths, 73, 285
Gorman, Clem, 239, **245**
    plays: *A Fortunate Life*, 245; *A Manual of Trench Warfare*, 245; *A Night in the Arms of Raeleen*, 245; *The Harding Women*, 245; *The Last Night Club*, 245
Gow, Michael, 239, **256–63,** 272
    plays: *1841*, 219, 230, **259–60,** 262; *Away*, **256–8,** 259, 262; *Europe*, 259; *Furious*, **260–1,** 262; *On Top of the World*, **258–9,** 262; *Sweet Phoebe*, 259, **261–2**; *The Fortunes of Richard Mahony*, **262,** 284; *The Kid*, **256,** 261; *Toy Symphony*, 262–3
GP (TV series), 60
Granville Barker, Harley, 15

Gray, Oriel, 88
    Bellbird (TV series), 60
    plays: *Burst of Summer*, 61, 67; *Sky Without Birds*, 87, 286; *The Torrents*, 59, 60, 77
Green, Kristin (Williamson), 182
Greer, Germaine, 342
Gregan McMahon Players, 16
Griffin Theatre Company (Sydney), 63, 238, 256, 258, 268–9, 276
Grotowski, Jerzy, 137
Guattari, Félix, 271
Gunew, Sneja, 283
Gurdjieff, Georgei, 196
Gurr, Michael, 160, 242, 329, 347, **352–60,** 362
    plays: *A Pair of Claws*, 353–4; *Crazy Brave*, 353, **357–8**; *Imitation Real*, 353; *Jerusalem*, 353, **356–7**; *Julia 3*, 333, 355, **358–60**; *Magnetic North*, 353; *Sex Diary of an Infidel*, 353, **354–5**; *The Simple Truth*, 353, **358**; *Underwear, Perfume and Crash Helmet*, 353, **355–6**; *What You Wanted*, 353
Gurr, T. Stuart: *Collits' Inn* (with Varney Monk), 63

H

Hage, Ghassan, 345
Hai, Phi: *Wild Rice* (with Huong Nguyen, Pat Rix, and Geoff Crowhurst), 297
Hair, 14, 207
Hall, Dick: *The Duke of Edinburgh Assassinated* (with Bob Ellis), 164
Hall, Ken G., 9
    The Silence of Dean Maitland (film), 75
Hall, Rodney: *A Return to the Brink*, 323
Hanger, Eunice, 83, 85, 86
    plays: *2D*, 60; *Flood*, 60, 64, 77, 87, 89, 286
Hanson, Pauline, 337–8
Harding, Alex, 274
    plays: *Blood and Honour*, 274; *Only Heaven Knows*, 274–5
Harding, John
    plays: *Enuff*, 320; *Up the Road*, **319,** 320

BELONGING

Hardy, Frank: *Faces in the Street*, 230
Hardy, Jonathan: *Jungfrau*, 66
Harkness, Alan, 17
Harris, Max, 140
Harrison, Wayne, 170
Harrison, Jane: *Stolen*, 318
Hasluck, Paul, 15
Haylen, Leslie, 46
Healey, Tom, 256
Heckenberg, Pamela, 11
Hefferon, Erin: *The Geography of Haunted Places* (with Josephine Wilson), 330, 374
Hemensley, Kris, 142
Hepworth, John
  The Beast in View, 85
  The End of the Rainbow, 85
Herbert, Xavier, 162
  Capricornia, 68, 229, 230–1
Hewett, Dorothy, 57, **113–22**, 181, 242, 267–8
  Bobbin' Up, 113
  plays: *Bon-Bons and Roses for Dolly*, 116, **119**, 120, 137; *Catspaw*, 116; *Golden Valley*, 120; *Jarrabin*, 122; *Joan*, 116, 117, **119**; *Mrs Porter and the Angel*, 115, 120; *Nowhere*, 122; *Pandora's Cross*, 120; *Song of the Seals*, 120; *Susannah's Dreaming*, 120; *The Beautiful Mrs Portland*, 116, 117; *The Chapel Perilous*, 116, **117–19**, 121; *The Fields of Heaven*, 122; *The Golden Oldies*, 116, 117, **120**; *The Man From Mukinupin*, **121–2**, 314; *The Tatty Hollow Story*, 116, 119, **120**; *This Old Man Comes Rolling Home*, 89, 114, 136
Hibberd, Jack, 127, 139–40, 144, **148–54**, 163, 165, 167, 209, 242
  plays: *A Stretch of the Imagination*, 117, 148, 149, **152–4**; *A Toast to Melba*, 165; *Captain Midnight VC*, 165; *Death Warmed Up*, 154; *Dimboola*, 148, **151**, 152, 166, 170; *Glycerine Tears*, 150; *Goodbye Ted* (with John Timlin), 151–2; *Just Before the Honeymoon*, 149; *Liquid Amber*, 152; *Marvellous Melbourne* (with John Romeril), 3, 143, 163, 240; *Mothballs*, 149; *No Time Like the Present*, 149; *O*, 149; *Odyssey of a Prostitute*, 154; *One of Nature's Gentlemen*, 142, 149; *Peggy Sue*, 150–1; *Squibs*, 154; *The Les Darcy Show*, 165; *The Prodigal Son*, 154; *This Great Gap of Time*, 149; *Three Old Friends*, 142, 149; *White With Wire Wheels*, 128, 140, 142–3, **150**, 171, 188; *Who?*, 142, 149
The Hills Family Show (APG), 166
historical dramas, 51, 53, 126, 135, 182, 213, 259, 374
  see also vaudeville history plays
Hitchcock, Alfred, 52
Hogan, Paul, 132
Hole-in-the-Wall Theatre (Perth), 145
Hollywood, 84, 85
Holt, Bland, 6
Home Cooking Theatre Company (Melbourne), 269–70
homosexuality. *see* gay and lesbian drama
Hoopla Productions (Melbourne), 145
Hope, A.D., 51
Hopgood, Alan, **133–4**, 136
  plays: *And Here Comes... Bucknuckle*, 134; *And The Big Men Fly*, **133**, 134, 152; *Private Yuk Objects*, 134, 136; *The Golden Legion of Cleaning Women*, 133–4
Horler, Ken, 144
Horniman, Mrs, 22
Howard, Brian: *Whitsunday* (with Louis Nowra), 238
Howard, Helen
  plays: *A Beautiful Life* (with Michael Futcher), 291, **299–300**; *The Drowning Bride* (with Michael Futcher), 291, 294
Howarde, Kate, 7, 12, 20
  Possum Paddock, 7, 24
Hullabaloo Theatre Company (Sydney), 274
Human Body, 137

470

INDEX

Humphries, Barry (Edna Everage), 91, 98, 126, **127–32**, 136, 160, 180, 208, 210, 376
   Barry McKenzie Holds His Own (film), 128
   performances: *A Nice Night's Entertainment*, 127; *An Audience with Dame Edna*, 132; *Back with a Vengeance*, 131, 132; *Days of the Week*, 127; *Excuse I*, 128; *The Dame Edna Experience*, 128; *Wild Life in Suburbia*, 128
Hunt, Albert, 276
   The White Man's Mission (with Richard Fotheringham), 166, 276
Hunt, Hugh, 15, 53, 83, 88, 94
Hunter Valley Theatre Company, 279
Hutchinson, Garrie, 145
Hutchinson, George
   plays: *No Room For Dreamers*, 195; *The Ballad of Billy Lane*, 279

I

Ibsen, Henrik, 32
   A Doll's House, 13
I'd Rather Be Left (New Theatre revue), 70
identity-based drama, **265–80**, 282, 301, 327
Ilbijerri Aboriginal and Torres Strait Islander Theatre Co-operative, 318, 319
immigrants & refugees, vii–ix
   early 20th century, 35, 52–3, 86–7, 284, 286
   in 1950s to 1970s, 53, 60, 82, 85, 115, 284–6
   since 1980s, 233, **281–300**, 345, 376
   see also ethnicity; multiculturalism
Independent Theatre (Sydney), 16, 74
Indigenous theatre. *see* Aboriginal theatre
Ingleton, Sue, 166, 269
   The Passion...and its Deep Connection with Lemon Delicious Pudding, 269
internationalism, 5, 378
   see also new internationalists

Ireland, David: *Image in the Clay*, 230
Irish drama, 22, 32, 43, 364, 375
   see also Abbey Theatre (Dublin)
Irwin, Steve, 132

J

Jaffer, Melissa, 106–7
James, Andrea: *Yanagai! Yanagai!*, 319
James, Clive, 131
Janaczewska, Noëlle, 279, **297–9**
   plays: *Blood Orange*, 298–9; *The History of Water*, 297–8
Jane Street theatre (Sydney), **134–7**, 145, 167, 170
Janson, Julie: *Black Mary*, 316
'JCWs.' *see* Williamson's, J.C.
Jeffrey, Tom, 172
Jesus Christ Superstar, 207
Jindabyne (film), 328
Joffe, Mark, 232
John, Alan, 103
Johnson, Eva, 272, **313**
   plays: *Murras*, 272, **313**; *What Do They Call Me?*, 272, **313**
Jones, Doris Egerton: *The Flaw* (with Emelie Polini), 14
Jones, Gillian, 103
Jones, Henry Arthur, 13
Joyce, James: *Portrait of the Artist as a Young Man*, 111
Junction Theatre (Adelaide), 278
Jungian psychology, 101, 273

K

Kane, Sarah, 375
   Blasted, 227
Kantor, Michael, 92, 329, 378
Keene, Daniel, x, 147, 182, 329, 347, 362, **363–71**, 375, 378
   plays: *a glass of twilight*, 366; *All Souls*, **364–5**, 370; *Cho Cho San*, 363, **364**; *Half and Half*, 368–9, **371**; *kaddish*, 367; *neither lost nor found*, 366; *night, a wall, two men*, 366–7; *river*, 371; *terminus*, 370; *Terminus and other plays*, 364; *the eyes*, 370–1; *the fire testament*, 371; *the first train*, 367; *the rain*, 367, 369; *the violin*, 367; *to whom it may*

471

concern, **365–7,** 371; *To Whom It May Concern and Other Plays [to whom it may concern; a glass of twilight; neither lost nor found; untitled monologue; night, a wall, two men; kaddish; the violin and the rain],* 364, 365; *untitled monologue,* 366

Keene/Taylor Theatre Project (KTTP), 363–4, 371

Kelly, Veronica, 223

Kemp, Jenny, 271, **330–3**
plays: *Call of the Wild,* 331; *Remember,* 331; *Still Angela,* 332–3; *The Black Sequin Dress,* 331–2

Keneally, Thomas
plays: *Bullie's House,* 230, 321; *Childermas,* 135, 136; *Halloran's Little Boat,* 135, 136

Kenna, Peter, **123–5,** 147, 249–50, 272
plays: *A Hard God,* 89, 123, **124–5,** 348; *An Eager Hope,* **125,** 286; *Furtive Love,* 125; *Listen Closely,* 123; *Mates,* 124; *Talk to the Moon,* 123; *The Cassidy Album [A Hard God, Furtive Love, An Eager Hope],* 124–5; *The Slaughter of St Teresa's Day,* 85, 123, 124; *Trespassers Will Be Prosecuted,* 123, 148

Kennedy, Patricia, 367

Kickett, Denise, 283

King, David: *Mary Bryant* (with Nick Enright), 247, 248, **249**

Kingsley, Henry, 284

Kippax, H.G., 27–8, 80, 88, 94
Three Australian Plays (ed.), 89–90, 126

Kirby-Smith, Virginia, 15

Koehne, Graeme, 232

Kooemba Jdarra (Brisbane), 315

Kosky, Barrie, 329, 364, 377–8
The Lost Echo, 329, 377

Krape, Evelyn, 166

KTTP. *see* Keene/Taylor Theatre Project

Kuckles. *see* Chi, Jimmy

L

La Boite Theatre (Brisbane), 213

La Mama (Melbourne), 135–7, **142–5**
Hibberd, 142–3, 148, 151, 167
Keene, 363
Oakley, 145–6
Romeril, 142–3, 156–7, *158–9,* 167, 376
Williamson, 167, 170

Lacan, Jacques, 47

Ladds, Dulcie Dunlop: *We Have Our Dreams,* 53

Ladies Night in a Turkish Bath, 13

Lambert, Max
Miracle City (with Nick Enright), 247, 248, **249**

Lane, William, 41, 279

Lantana (film), 360–2

larrikin drama
character type, viii
New Wave precursors, 71, 126, 133, 135
New Wave proponents & successors, 139, 163, 216, 240, 259, 265; Dickins, 242, 244; Hibberd, 151, 163, 209; Oakley, 146; Romeril, 156, 163, 230; Spears, 240; Williamson, 171, 175, 182
see also vaudeville history plays

The Last Bastion (film), 171

Lawford, Ningali: *Ningali,* 315

Lawler, Ray, 40, 83, 242
Kid Stakes, 82–3
Other Times, 82–3
Summer of the Seventeenth Doll, 40, 58–9, 64, **77–84,** 87; opening success, 14, 17, 28, 53, 73, **76–8,** 133, 168; 'school' of, **84–90,** 91, 114, 123; trilogy [with *Kid Stakes* and *Other Times*], **81–3,** 289
The Piccadilly Bushman, 14, 83–4

The Lawsons (radio series), 60

Le, Hung, 283

le Brun, Bobby, 3

Le Quy, Duong, 296
plays: *A Graveyard for Living,* 296; *Market of Lives,* 296; *Meat Party,* 296

Learner, Tobsha, 271, 327, **342–4**
plays: *Miracles* (aka *Miracle*),

INDEX

343; *The Glass Mermaid*, 337, **344**; *The Gun in History*, 343; *Witchplay*, 344; *Wolf*, 342–3
Leeton Dramatic Society, 145
The Legend of King O'Malley (Michael Boddy and Bob Ellis), 136–7, 143, 146, **163–4**, 166, 240
Leichhardt, Ludwig, 289–90
lesbian theatre. *see* gay and lesbian drama
Levkowicz, Valentina: *Svetlana in Slingbacks*, 296
Lighthouse Company (Adelaide), 103, 106–7
Lipscombe, W.P.: *Pommy* (with Victor Weston), 14
Little Theatres. *see* repertory & amateur theatres
Littlewood, Joan, 277
Livermore, Reg, 187, **206–8**, 284
  performances: *Betty Blokk Buster Follies*, 206, 207; *Firing Squad*, 207; *Home Sweet Home (Leonard's Last Hurrah)*, 207; *Mother Goose*, 207; *Red Riding Hood, the Speed Hump and the Wolf*, 207; *Sacred Cow*, 207; *Santa on the Planet of the Apes*, 207; *Son of Betty*, 207; *The Good Ship Walter Raleigh*, 133; *Wish You Were Here*, 207; *Wonderwoman*, 207
Llewellyn-Jones, Tony, 36–7
Lloyd Webber, Andrew, 249
Locke Elliott, Sumner: *Rusty Bugles*, **74–5**, 78
Lone Hand (journal), 12, 15, 18, 19
Longford, Raymond, 5, 8–9
Lorenzo's Oil (film) (Nick Enright and George Miller), 249
Lothian, T.C., 17
Lowe, Barry: *Writer's Cramp*, 274
Lyndon, Simon, *254–5*
Lyssa, Alison, 272
  plays: *Pinball*, 272, **273**; *The Boiling Frog*, 273–4
Lyssiotis, Tes, 282, **287–8**
  plays: *A White Sports Coat*, 287; *Blood Moon*, 287, **288**; *The Forty Lounge Café*, 287–8; *The Journey*, 287

M

McDonagh, Martin, 375
McDonald, Garry, 9, 240
McDougall, Duncan, 16
McGrath, John, 266, 277
McGuiness, Lee, *292–3*
McKern, Leo, 9, 76
Macky, Stewart, 42
  The Trap, 42
McLeod, Marjorie
  plays: *Horizons*, **52–3**, 87, 286; *Mine a Sad One*, 53; *Within These Walls*, 53, 54, 55
McMahon, Gregan, 4–5, 15, 16, 18, 21, 22, 44
McNamara, Tony, 374
  plays: *The Give and Take*, 374; *The John Wayne Principle*, 374; *The Unlikely Prospect of Happiness*, 374; *The Virgin Mim*, 374
McNeil, Jim, 187, **201–4**, 205, 249–50, 275, 302
  plays: *How Does Your Garden Grow*, 202–3; *Jack*, 203–4; *The Chocolate Frog*, 202; *The Old Familiar Juice*, 202
Magois, Séverine, 363–4
Mailman, Deborah, 319
  The 7 Stages of Grieving (with Wesley Enoch), 315, **316–18**, 319
Malouf, David, 24
  Blood Relations, 230, **321–2**
Malthouse (Melbourne), 329, 378
Mamouney, Don, 155
Manning, Ned
  plays: *Close to the Bone*, 230, 322; *Luck of the Draw*, 230, 322
Manning Clark's History of Australia (John Romeril, Tim Robertson and Don Watson), 230
Mansfield, Katherine, 196–7
Marber, Patrick, 375
Mardi Gras (Sydney), 272, 274
Marr, David, 112, 167
Martin, David N., 3
Masefield, John, 13
Mathew, Ray
  plays: *A Spring Song*, 74; *The Bones of My Toe*, 74; *The Life of the*

473

BELONGING

Party, 74; *We Find the Bunyip*, 73–4, 77, 78
Matrix Theatre, Brisbane, 291
Maugham, Somerset, 13
Maupassant, Guy de, 149, 154
Maurice, Furnley, 42
Maver, Christopher: *The Girl in the Lime Green Bikini*, 275
The Mavis Bramston Show (TV series), 71, 126
May, Adam: *Rising Fish Prayer*, 324
Maza, Bob: *The Keepers*, 312–13
Mc. *see* Mac
Melbourne Festival of the Arts, 207
Melbourne Repertory Theatre, 16, 21
Melbourne Theatre Company, 36–7, 133, 141–2, 188, *198–9*
Melbourne Women's Theatre Group, 143, 267, 280
Melbourne Workers' Theatre, 360, 362, 375
    Who's Afraid of the Working Class (*see* Bovell, Andrew)
    Who's Afraid of the Working Class? (Andrew Bovell, Patricia Cornelius, Melissa Reeves, Christos Tsiolkas, and Irine Vela), 362, 375
Melbourne Writers' Theatre, 204
Mellor, Aubrey, 122, 144, 145, 170
melodrama
    19th century, 1–2, 6, 89, 373
    early 20th century, 2, 6, 8, **10**, 17, 24, 54, 62, 86; Esson, 10–11, 22, 31–2; Roland, 11, 28, 54, 58
    Doll school, 84
    Hewett, 117
    New Wave, 3, 163, 204
    since 1990s, 339, 377
    White, 94, 101
Menzies, Robert, 368–9
Meredith, Gwen, 71, 94, 377
    plays: *Ask No Questions*, 60; *Wives Have Their Uses*, 60
    radio series: *Blue Hills*, 60; *The Lawsons*, 60
Merritt, Robert J., 302–3
    The Cake Man, ix, **302–3**
Mews Theatre (Sydney), 301
Meyerhold, V.E., 92, 154, 211

Meyrick, Julian: *See How It Runs*, 141, 144
Michelakakis, George, 282
Michell, Keith, 94
middle-class drama
    Aboriginal theatre, 304, 313, 325
    Adams, 20
    Cusack, 62
    early 20th century, 4
    Gow, 259
    J.C. Williamson's, 2–3
    Lawler, 80, 82–3
    New Wave, 9, 93, 139, 189, 193, 195
    Phillip Street revues, 70
    repertory theatres, 15–16
    White, 93, 98, 102, 110
    Williamson, 139–40, 168, 172–3, 176–9, 182, 184–5
    women playwrights, 267, 327, 333–4, 339–40, 342, 352
migrants. *see* ethnicity; immigrants & refugees; multiculturalism
Milgate, Rodney
    plays: *A Refined Look at Existence*, 135–6; *At Least You Get Something Out of That*, 136
Miller, George: *Lorenzo's Oil* (film) (with Nick Enright), 249
Milller, Harry M., 14
Mills, Richard: *Batavia* (opera), 76
Milne, Geoffrey, x, 242
Milroy, Jadah: *Crow Fire*, 320
Milson, John, 145
Mo (Roy Rene), 3, 207, 240
modernism, 93, 132, 140
Molière: *Don Juan*, 248
Monash University, 167
Monjo, Justin: *Cloudstreet* (with Nick Enright and Tim Winton), 249
Monk, Varney: *Collits' Inn* (with T. Stuart Gurr), 63
Mooney, Ray, 204–5
    plays: *A Blue Freckle*, 204; *Black Rabbit*, **205**, 230, 259; *Everynight, Everynight*, 204–5
Moore, George, 32
Moore, William, 17
    The Tea-Room Girl, 17
Morgillo, Antonietta: *The Olive Tree*, 294

INDEX

Morphett, Tony
   plays: *I've Come About the Assassination*, 134–5; *The Rise and Fall of Boronia Avenue*, 136
Morse, Helen, 367
Moss, Merilee: *Empty Suitcase*, 271
Mozart, W.A.: *Così Fan Tutte*, 234
Mueller, Ross, 376
Mulgan, Alan, 42
multiculturalism, 87, 180, 266–8, 272, 281–3, **284–300**, 313, 333, 345
Mulvany, Kate: *The Seed*, 377
Mundey, Jack, 103
Murphy, Tommy
   plays: *Holding the Man* [adapted from the book by Timothy Conigrave], 276; *Strangers in Between*, 276
Murray-Smith, Joanna, 271, 327, **339–42**, 362
   plays: *Atlanta*, 340; *Bombshells*, 342; *Flame*, 340; *Honour*, 340; *Love Child*, 340–1; *Nightfall*, 341–2; *Rapture*, 342; *Redemption*, 341; *The Female of the Species*, 342
Musgrove, George, 2
Music Hall Theatre Restaurant (Sydney), 3
musical theatre, 2–3, 13, 65, 117, 230, 247–9, 313–14
My Darling Patricia, 374
The Mystery of the Hansom Cab, 133

N

National Institute for Dramatic Art (NIDA), 122, 134, 248
National Theatre for the Deaf, 278
National Theatre (Perth), 121
nationalist drama
   early 20th century, viii, 4, 7, 9, 11–12, 15, 17, **18–22**, 24, 78; Esson & Pioneer Players, 4, 19–22, **28–39**, 43, 57, 78, 141–2, 373
   Doll school, 76, 78, 87–8, 132, 168
   new internationalists and, 209–12, 238
   New Wave, 3, 5, 76, 126–7, 139–41, 188–9, 259
   since 1990s, ix, 327, 333, 345, 375, 378
   see also 'Australianness'
naturalism
   early 20th century, 10, 35, 41–2, 62, 78
   new internationalists, 209–10, 212
   New Wave, 88, 156–7, 373, 376
   since 1990s, 333, 376, 379
   White, 93–4
   Williamson, 127, 168–9
   see also realism
Nelson, H. G. (Greig Pickhaver), 128, 190
Nevin, Robyn, 100, 170
New Australians. *see* immigrants
New Fortune theatre (Perth), 117
new internationalists, **209–38**, 263
New Theatre movement, 18, 70–1, 126, 135
New Wave, 3, 9, 40, 88, **139–66**, 327, 373
   J.C. Williamson's and, 14
   late period, 239–41, 245, 248, 257, 259, 263
   new internationalists and, 140, 147, 157, 160, 187, 209–10, 216, 233, 238
   playwrights: Blair, 144, **146–7**, 164; Buzo, 139–40, 143–4, 187–9, 192; De Groen, 187, 193–5; Hewett, 117; Hibberd, 139–40, 142–4, **148–54**, 156, 163, 165–6; Humphries, 126, 127, 128, 132, 160; Kenna, 123, 124, 147–8; Livermore, 187, 206; McNeil, 187, 201, 204; Oakley, **145–6**, 155, 164–5; precursors, **133–4**, 276, 301; Reed, 147–8; Romeril, 139, 142–4, 148, **155–63**, 165–6, 376; White, 91, 93, 103, 117, 126, 160; Williamson, 139–0, 144, 151–2, 155, 167–8, 170–5, 187–8, 195, 373–4
   precursors, 18, 64, 71, 89, 135
   successors, 265–7, 300, 343, 353
New Women, 54, 58, 59
Newcastle (NSW), 252
Newcastle Workers' Cultural Access Committee, 279
Ngapartji, Ngapartji (Big hART), 278
Nguyen, Huong: *Wild Rice* (with Phi

475

BELONGING

Hai, Pat Rix, and Geoff Crowhurst), 297
NIDA. *see* National Institute for Dramatic Art
Nightshift (Melbourne), 142
Nimrod Theatre (Sydney), 123–4, 141, **143–5,** 146–7, 164, 167, 190, 224–5, 240, 268
  Women and Theatre Project, 272
Nindethana Theatre, 44
Norman, Leslie: *Season of Passion*, 84
Nowra, Louis, 57, 103, 117, 140, 147, 160, 182, 210, **223–38,** 239, 263
  anthology: *The Cheated*, 237
  autobiographies: *Shooting the Moon*, 238; *The Twelfth of Never*, 238
  films: *Black and White*, 238; *Heaven's Burning*, 238; *K-19*, 238; *Map of the Human Heart*, 238
  libretti: *Love Burns*, 232; *Whitsunday* (with Brian Howard), 238
  novels: *Abaza: A Modern Encyclopedia*, 237; *Palu*, 237; *Red Nights*, 237; *The Misery of Beauty*, 237
  plays: *Albert Names Edward*, 224; *Byzantine Flowers*, 229, 230; *Capricornia*, 68, 219, **229–31;** *Così*, 232, **233–4,** 238; *Crow*, 228, **229,** 230, 232; *Ice*, 237; *Inner Voices*, **224–5,** 226, 230, 236; *Inside the Island*, **226–7,** 228, 230; *Miss Bosnia*, 232, 235; *Radiance*, 230, 232, 238; *Spellbound*, 226; *Summer of the Aliens*, 232, **233,** 296; *Sunrise*, 226, **227–8,** 230, 235, 238; *The Boyce Trilogy [The Woman with Dog's Eyes, The Marvellous Boy, The Emperor of Sydney]*, 178, 219, 238; *The Emperor of Sydney*, 238; *The Golden Age*, ix, 226, **228–9,** 230; *The Incorruptible*, 232, 234, **235;** *The Jungle*, 232, 234, **235–6;** *The Language of the Gods*, 236–7; *The Marvellous Boy*, 238; *The Precious Woman*, 226, **227,** 228;

The Song Room, 224; *The Temple*, 232, **234–5;** *The Watchtower*, 226, 228; *The Woman with Dog's Eyes*, 238; *Visions*, 226
  telemovies: *Displaced Persons*, 238; *Hunger*, 238; *The Lizard King*, 238
  TV series: *The Last Resort* (with Tim Gooding), 238
Nuovo Paese (FILEF), 278

O

Oakley, Barry, **145–6,** 155, 164–5
  plays: *A Lesson in English*, 145–6; *Bedfellows*, 146; *Beware of Imitations*, 164–5; *Eugene Flockhart's Desk*, 145; *Marsupials*, 146; *Scanlan*, 146; *The Feet of Daniel Mannix*, 146; *The Great God Mogadon*, 146; *The Ship's Whistle*, 165; *Witzenhausen, Where Are You?*, 145
Observer (London) competition, 86
O'Casey, Sean, 17
ocker style, 160, 269
  'sons of Ocker' (New Wave), 140, 165, 188–9, 265, 301
O'Connor, Caroline, 186, 342
O'Donoghue, John: *A Happy and Holy Occasion*, 89
O'Donoghue, Rory
  The Aunty Jack Show (with Grahame Bond), 164
  Wollongong the Brave (with Grahame Bond), 164
O'Ferrall, Ernest, 42
Old Tote Theatre (Sydney), 75, 134, 135, 142, 281
Oliver, Jean: *Pay Cisca Manetti*, 286
Olivier, Laurence, 12
Olympic Games
  Melbourne (1956), 76
  Sydney (2000), 315
On Our Selection, viii–ix, 5, **7–9,** 17, 24, 30, 33, 78, 148, 240, 373
  see also Rudd, Steele (Arthur Hoey Davis)
On Stage Vietnam (New Theatre revue), 70

INDEX

O'Neill, Errol, 279
  plays: *Faces in the Street*, 279; *On the Whipping Side*, 279; *Popular Front*, 279
O'Neill, Eugene, 17, 34, 88, 375
  The Iceman Cometh, 73, 285
opera & operetta, 2–3, 5
  see also Gilbert and Sullivan
Opera Australia, 76
Orton, Joe, 353
Oswald, Debra, 60, 89, 271, 327, 339, 347, **350–2,** 362
  plays: *Dags*, 350–1; *Gary's House*, 350; *Mr Bailey's Minder*, 352; *Skate*, 351; *Sweet Road*, 351–2
Otto, Barry, 234
Outback Press, 241
Ovid, 329
  Metamorphoses, 207, 377

P

Packer, Frank, 243
PACT (Sydney), 137
Palmer, Nettie, 40
Palmer, Vance, 5, 22, 23, **40–2,** 43, 62, 68, 78, 302, 321, 329
  Louis Esson and the Australian Theatre, 39
  plays: *A Happy Family*, 40, 60; *Ancestors*, 41; *Christine*, 41, 60; *Hail Tomorrow*, 41, 279; *Meadowsweet*, 41; *Prisoner's Country*, 42, 71; *The Black Horse*, 41; *The Fledgling*, 41; *The Prisoner*, 41; *Travellers*, 41
Palomares, Simon, 283
Papua New Guinea, 324
Parade Theatre (Sydney), 102, 248
Parfitt, Trevor, *308–9*
Parsons, Philip, 11, 175
Parsons, Nicholas: *Dead Heart*, 230, **324–5**
Parups, Elise, 291
Patrikareas, Theodore, 284–7
  plays: *Antipodean Trilogy [The Promised Woman, The Uncle from Australia, The Divided Heart]*, 285–7; *The Divided Heart*, 285, **286,** 287; *The Promised Woman* (aka *Throw Away Your Harmonica, Pepino*), **285–6,** 287; *The Uncle From Australia*, 285, **286,** 287
Pearlman, Karen: *Performing the Unnameable* (with Richard James Allen), 330
Penguin Books, 143
Performance Syndicate (Sydney), 137, 142, 145
Perkins, Elizabeth, 194
Perkins, Rachel, 232
Perth Festival, 136, 142–3, 157, 188, 307
Perth Repertory Club, 15
Petsinis, Tom: *The Drought*, 294
Phillip Street revues (Sydney), 70, 126
Pickhaver, Greig (H.G. Nelson), 128, 190
Pinero, Arthur Wing, 13, 14
Pinter, Harold, 132, 135, 149, 156
Pioneer Players (Melbourne), 5, 12, 16, 21, 22, 32, **40–3,** 142
pioneering plays, **51–76,** 147, 259
  see also bush legend; station dramas
Pirandello, Luigi: *Henry IV,* 146
Pitts, Graham, 155, 279, **295**
  Emma, 279, **295**
Plautus, 286
Play Society, 16
Playbox Art Theatre (Sydney), 16–17
Playbox Theatre (Melbourne), 122, 145, 154, 235, 318–19, 329, 363, *368–9*, 378
Playwrights Advisory Board prize, 59, 77
Playwrights Conference. *see* Australian National Playwrights Conference
Police Rescue (TV series), 60
Polini, Emelie, 14
  The Flaw (with Doris Egerton Jones), 14
Politely Savage, 374
political drama
  1940s to 1960s, 70–3, 113–14, 126
  Aboriginal theatre, 320
  Dickins, 245
  Elisha, 246
  Gow, 259
  Hewett, 113–14, 118–19, 122
  identity & community theatre, 265, 267, 276

migrant theatre, 282, 286, 298, 310
new internationalists, 210–14, 216–17, 219–23, 234–5
New Wave, 71, 139–41, 143, 145–6, 164, 166, 188–9
since 1990s, 327, 329, 333–4, 337–9, 344, 352–8, 374, 377
Spears, 241
White, 102–3, 108, 111
Williamson, 168, 176–80, 182
see also socialism
Popular Theatre Troupe (Brisbane), 145, 166, 276, 277–8
Porter, Hal, 126
The Professor, 126
The Tower, 126
Possum Paddock, 7, 24
postmodernism, 128, 140
Pram Factory (Melbourne), 143, 148, 151, 152, 167
Prichard, Katharine Susannah, 17, 42, **43–6,** 62, 68, 88, 113, 212, 230, 276, 279, 302, 321
plays: *Bid Me To Love*, 44; *Brumby Innes*, 33, **44–6,** 48, 53; *Forward One*, 44; *Intimate Strangers*, 44; *Pioneers*, 25, 43; *Solidarity*, 44; *The Great Man*, 43; *The Great Strike*, 44; *The Women of Spain*, 44
prison playwrights, viii, **201–6,** 250
Private Eye (magazine), 127
professional class. *see* middle-class drama
professional theatre, 15–16, 61, 73, 78, 84, 89, 141, 170, 247
propaganda, 70–1
Proust, Marcel, 153
Puccini, Giacomo: *La Bohème*, 35
Pullan, Ru: *Curly on the Rack*, 85
Purcell, Leah: *Box the Pony* (with Scott Rankin), 315, **316**

Q
Q Theatre, 252
Queens Theatre (Adelaide), 379
Queensland Theatre Company, 66, 145, 258, 262
Quentin, Robert, 134, 142

R
Racine, Jean: *Phèdre*, 259
The Raid (film), 299
Rankin, Scott, 155, 278
Box the Pony (with Leah Purcell), 315, **316**
Ravenhill, Mark, 375
Rayson, Hannie, 57, 89, 271, 294, 327, **333–9,** 342, 374
plays: *Competitive Tenderness*, 335–6; *Falling From Grace*, 334–5; *Hotel Sorrento*, 333–4; *Inheritance*, 57, 333, **337–9**; *Life After George*, 182, 333, **336–7**; *Mary*, **294–5,** 333; *Room to Move*, 333; *Scenes From a Separation* (with Andrew Bovell), 335; *Two Brothers*, 178, **339**
realism
early 20th century, 6, **10,** 11, 23–8, 57, 62; Esson & Pioneer Players, 10, 20, 22, 30–1, 35, 38, 43
Gow, 258
Hewett, 114, 115, 117, 120
migrant theatre, 300
new internationalists, 209, 377
New Wave, 124, 147, 258, 373
since 1990s, 374, 376
social, 279, 327, 331
socialist, 71
urban ('backyard'), 53, 80, 83, 86, 88–9, 132
White, 91, 93–5, 99, 105, 108, 114
see also naturalism
Red Ladder (UK), 266
Reed, Bill, 147–8
plays: *Burke's Company*, 147; *Cass Butcher Bunting*, 148; *Mr Siggie Morrison with his Comb and Paper*, 148; *Truganinni*, 148, 230, 231
Rees, Leslie, 11–12, 62, 77, 327
Reeves, Melissa
plays: *The Spook*, 377; *Who's Afraid of the Working Class?* (with Andrew Bovell, Patricia Cornelius, Christos Tsiolkas, and Irine Vela), 362, 375
Rene, Roy (Mo), 3, 207, 240

INDEX

repertory & amateur theatres (Little Theatres)
    early 20th century, 4–5, 11–13, **14–17**, 18–19, 21–2, 24, 53–5, 63
    Hewett, 117
    in 1950s and 1960s, 18, 61, 71, 84, 89
    White, 93, 94, 101, 108
Repertory Theatre (Melbourne), 16, 21
Return Fare (UTRC revue), 127
Returned Services League, 87
Richardson, Henry Handel: *The Fortunes of Richard Mahony*, 262, 284
Rigney, Tracey: *Belonging*, 320
Riverina Theatre Company, 324
Rix, Pat: *Wild Rice* (with Huong Nguyen, Phi Hai, and Geoff Crowhurst), 297
Roberts, Rhoda, 315
Robertson, Tim, 151, **165**
    plays: *Manning Clark's History of Australia* (with John Romeril and Don Watson), 230; *Mary Shelley and the Monsters*, 165; *Tristram Shandy – Gent*, 165; *Waltzing Matilda (*with John Romeril), 165
Robinson, Bec: *Dark, Out There*, 286
The Rocky Horror Show, 207
Rogers, Susan, 379
Roland, Betty, 46, 62, 279
    plays: *Granite Peak*, 56; *Morning*, 56–7; *The Touch of Silk* (1928), 10–11, 25, 54, 55, 57–8; *The Touch of Silk* (1955 revised version), 11, 28, 58, 77
Romeril, John, 57, 139, 142, 144, 148, **155–63**, 167, 211, 212, 223, 279, 295, 376
    plays: *Bastardy*, 156, 375; *Black Cargo*, 155; *Brudder Humphrey*, 156; *Chicago, Chicago* (aka *The Man from Chicago*), 143, 156, **157**; *Dr Karl's Cure*, 156; *I Don't Know Who To Feel Sorry For*, 156–7, *158–9*, 375; *Kitchen Table*, 156; *Lost Weekend*, 155, **161**; *Love Suicides*, 155, **161–2**; *Manning Clark's History of Australia* (with Tim Robertson and Don Watson), 230; *Marvellous Melbourne* (with Jack Hibberd), 3, 143, 163, 240; *Miss Tanaka*, 155, 161, **162–3**; *Mr Big the Big Big Pig*, 156; *The American Independence Hour*, 156; *The Floating World*, 156, 157, **160–1**; *The Kelly Dance*, 165–6; *Top End*, 155, **161**; *Waltzing Matilda (*with Tim Robertson), 165; *Whatever Happened to Realism*, 156, 187
Rosnan, Alice Grant, 15
Rothfield, Tom: *Jam Tomorrow*, 284
Rubinstein, Deirdre, 362
Rudd, Steele (Arthur Hoey Davis)
    Dad and Dave Come to Town, 9
    Dad Rudd, M.P., 9
    On Our Selection (*see On Our Selection*)
    Our New Selection, 9
    The Rudd Family, 8
Rundle, Guy
    The Big Con, 165
    Your Dreaming, 165
Rush, Geoffrey, 103
Russell Street Temperance Hall (Melbourne), 40

S

Sam, Maryanne: *Casting Doubts*, 319–20
San Francisco Mime Troupe, 266
Schaupp, Karin, 186
Schumann, Peter, 278
Scott, Ian, *198–9*
Scribe, Eugene, 11
*Scripsi (*journal), 154
SeaChange (TV series), 60
Searle, James: *The Lucky Streak*, 135
See How They Run, 13
Senczuk, John, 43
sentimentality, 62–4, 181, 183, 233, 244, 245, 286
set clichés, 24–6, 55, 192
settlers. *see* pioneering plays
Sewell, Stephen, 57, 117, 140, 147, 157, 160, 182, 210, **211–23**, 238–9, 263, 339, 353
    plays: *Dreams in an Empty City*, 214, **217–18**, 219, 221, 234;

Dust, 221–2; *Hate*, **219**, 220, 227, 230; *It Just Stopped*, 211, 223; *King Golgrutha*, 221; *Myth, Propaganda and Disaster in Nazi Germany and Contemporary America*, 211, 216, 218, **222–3**; *Sisters*, 219–20; *The Blind Giant Is Dancing*, 176–7, 214, **216–17**, 222; *The Father We Loved on a Beach by the Sea*, 213; *The Garden of Earthly Delights*, 221, **222**; *The Gates of Egypt*, 211, 223; *The Golgrutha Trilogy [King Golgrutha, Dust, The Garden of Earthly Delights]*, 211, **221–2**; *The Secret Death of Salvador Dali*, 211, 223; *The Sick Room*, **220–1**, 227; *The United States of Nothing*, 211, 223; *Three Furies*, 211, 223; *Traitors*, 213; *Welcome the Bright World*, **214–16**, 222

Seymour, Alan
  plays: *Swamp Creatures*, 77, 328; *The One Day of the Year*, 85, 86, **87–8**, 89, 94, 126

Shakespeare, William, 120, 121, 144, 162, 229, 240, 256, 378
  plays: *A Midsummer Night's Dream*, 257; *King Lear*, 257–8; *Romeo and Juliet*, 40; *The Tempest*, 321; *Titus Andronicus*, 259; *Twelfth Night*, 127

Sharman, Jim, 92, 100, 102, 103, 105, 135, 142

Sharp, Martin, 240

Shaw, George Bernard, 13, 14, 22, 353
  Heartbreak House, 108, 109

Shirley, Arthur: *The Breaking of the Drought*, 6

Shotlander, Sandra, 272–3
  plays: *Blind Salome*, 272–3; *Framework*, 272; *Is That You Nancy?*, 273

Sidetrack Performance Group (Sydney), 278, 285

Sidetrack Theatre (Sydney), 155, 278
  plays: *Down Under the Thumb*, 283; *Kin*, 283; *Out From Under*, 283

The Silence of Dean Maitland (film), 75

Slaven, Roy (John Doyle), 128, 190

Smith, Martin: *Love Has Many Faces*, 274

Smith's Weekly, 66

socialism, 18, 40, 43, 52, 64, 71, 130, 177, 279
  see also communism; political drama

Somebody's Daughter Theatre, 205–6
  "*Tell Her That I Love Her...*" (with Maud Clark), 205–6

Sontag, Susan, 235

Sorlie's (tent-show), 3

Spears, Steve J., 239–41
  plays: *Africa: A Savage Musical*, 241; *Early Works*, 241; *King Richard*, 241; *Mad Jean: They Reckon She's Crazy Like a Snake*, 241; *People Keep Giving Me Things*, 241; *The Elocution of Benjamin Franklin*, **239–40**, 241; *When They Send Me Three and Fourpence*, 241; *Young Mo*, **240**, 241

Spence, Bruce, 153, 170

Spielman, Dan, 368–9

Spunner, Suzanne, 269–70
  plays: *Dragged Screaming to Paradise*, 270; *Running up a Dress*, **269–70**, 295

The Squatter's Daughter ('Albert Edmunds,' i.e.Edmund Duggan and Bert Bailey), 6

Stables Theatre (Sydney), 143

'Stargazer,' 12, 18

Stasis Group (Melbourne), 137, 142, 143

State Theatre Company of South Australia, 63, 103, 221, 378

state-subsidised companies, 17, 78, 133, 247

station dramas, **51–4**, 71, 74, 192, 226, 337, 377

STC. *see* Sydney Theatre Company

Stewart, Douglas, 75–6
  plays: *Ned Kelly*, 76, 126; *Shipwreck*, 75–6; *The Fire on the Snow*, 75, 136; *The Golden Lover*, 75

Stoppard, Tom, 144

Strachan, Tony
  plays: *Eyes of the Whites*, 324; *State of Shock*, 323–4

INDEX

Street Arts Community Theatre Company (Brisbane), 277–8
Strindberg, August, 93, 331
subsidised state companies, 17, 78, 133, 247
suburban drama, x
    early 20th century, 62
    Gow, 259
    Hewett, 115, 120
    Humphries, 130, 132
    Kenna, 124
    New Wave, 93, 126, 156, 160, 207
    Nowra, 233
    since 1990s, 332–3, 351, 376
    White, 93, 98–9, 102, 126
Summers, Anne, 81
Sumner, John, 17, 92, 133, 141–2, 242
surrealism, 93, 157
Sutherland, Joan, 9
Swan River Stage Company, *308–9*
Sweeney Todd, 133
Swenson, Sven: *Vertigo and the Virginia*, 377
The Sydney Front, 137, 330
    plays: *Don Juan*, 330; *First and Last Warning*, 330, 374; *The Pornography of Performance*, 330
Sydney Opera House, 174
Sydney Theatre Company (STC)
    Kosky, 329, 377
    playwrights: Cusack, 63; Enright, 254–5, 279; Gow, 258, 259; Kenna, 124; White, 92, 95; Williamson, 167; Wright, 377–8
    Wharf Revue, 71
Sydney Theatre (Walsh Bay), 349
Synge, J.M., 5, 20, 22, 32, 80
    plays: *Riders to the Sea*, 33; *The Playboy of the Western World*, 32, 33; *The Shadow of the Glen*, 5; *The Tinker's Wedding*, 33

T

Ta, Binh Duy: *The Monkey Mother*, 297
Tait brothers, 2, 4, 12–14, 18
    see also Williamson's, J.C. ('JCWs,' 'The Firm')
Tarantino, Quentin, 234
Tasker, John, 92, 94
Taylor, Ariette, 363

Taylor, Tony, 166
Tennant, Carrie, 16
tent-shows, 3, 7, 249
Terror Australis (Jane Street revue), 135, 142
terrorism, 299, 358, 359
The Aunty Jack Show (Grahame Bond and Rory O'Donoghue), 164
The Big Chill (film), 340
The Boys in the Band, 14
The Bulletin (journal), 75
The Dismissal (TV series), 171
'The Firm.' *see* Williamson's, J.C.
The Hills Family Show (APG), 166
The Last Bastion (film), 171
The Lawsons (radio series), 60
The Legend of King O'Malley (Michael Boddy and Bob Ellis), 136–7, 143, 146, **163–4**, 166, 240
The Mavis Bramston Show (TV series), 71, 126
The Mystery of the Hansom Cab, 133
The Raid (film), 299
The Rocky Horror Show, 207
The Silence of Dean Maitland (film), 75
The Squatter's Daughter ('Albert Edmunds,' i.e. Edmund Duggan and Bert Bailey), 6
The Sydney Front, 137, 330
    plays: *Don Juan*, 330; *First and Last Warning*, 330, 374; *The Pornography of Performance*, 330
The Theatre (journal), 19
The Wog Boy (film), 282, 283
The Year of Living Dangerously (film), 171
The Theatre (journal), 19
theatre restaurants, 3, 151
Theatre West (Melbourne), 278
Theatre Workshop (UK), 277
theatres, writers without, **40–6**
Thomas, Michael: *The Pier*, 135
Thomson, Brian, 100, 103
Thomson, Katherine, 57, 60, 89, 271, 327, 339, **347–50**
    plays: *Barmaids*, 347; *Diving for Pearls*, **348**, 349, 350; *Harbour*, 349–50; *Navigating*, 348–9; *Wonderlands*, 57, **349**
Thorndike, Sybil, 3

thrillers, 2, 14, 52, 146, 212, 214–18, 222, 339, 354
Thring, Frank W., 63
Tide Theatre Company, 363
Tighe, Harry: *Open Spaces; or, Bush Fire*, 25, 27
Timlin, John: *Goodbye Ted* (with Jack Hibberd), 151–2
Tivoli circuit, 3, 275
Toe Truck Theatre, 324
Tomholt, Sydney, 40
  plays: *Anoli The Blind*, 86, 286; *The Women Wait*, 33
Treharne's company (Adelaide), 15–16, 19, 22
Triad (journal), 18
  playwriting competition, 33, 44
Tribe, 137
Troupe Theatre (Adelaide), 145, 165
Trust Players, 53
Tsiolkas, Christos: *Who's Afraid of the Working Class?* (with Andrew Bovell, Patricia Cornelius, Melissa Reeves, and Irine Vela), 362, 375
Turn Verein Hall (Melbourne), 17
Turner, Alexander, 46

U

underclass drama
  Bovell, 182, 329
  Cortese, 376
  Dickins, 241
  Esson, 33
  Gow, 256
  Keene, 182, 329, 363, 375
  women's theatre, 269–70, 339, 347, 350–2
Union Theatre Repertory Company (Melbourne), 17, 78, 92, 127, 133, 242
University of New South Wales, 135
  Drama Foundation, 134
  School of Drama, 134
  see also National Institute for Dramatic Art (NIDA); Old Tote Theatre; Parade Theatre
urban plays
  early 20th century, 19, 21, 33–4, 58, 373
  in 1950s and 1960s, 28, 53, 76, **77–90**
  in 1990s, 269, 328–9
  New Wave, 147, 149, 156
  White & Hewett, 94, 120
  see also bush comedy & drama; suburban drama
Urban Theatre Projects (Sydney), 278

V

Valdez, Luis, 277–8
Valentine, Alana
  plays: *Parramatta Girls*, 328; *Run Rabbit Run*, 328
Varney, Denise, 271, 328
vaudeville, 3, 93, 104, 114, 206–7, 242
vaudeville history plays, 18, 146, 147, **163–6**
  see also larrikin drama
Vela, Irine: *Who's Afraid of the Working Class?* (with Andrew Bovell, Patricia Cornelius, Melissa Reeves, and Christos Tsiolkas), 362, 375
verbatim theatre, 328
Vernon, Barbara: *The Multi-Coloured Umbrella*, 14, 84
Vietnam War, 122, 129, 134, 136, 139, 164, 173, 250, 257, 276, 318, 323, 377
Vitalstatistix Theatre Company (Adelaide), 273

W

Wagner, Richard, 256
Wales, Robert: *The Grotto*, 85
Walker, Kerry, 103
Wallace, George, 3
Walley, Richard, 311
  Coordah, 311–12
Watson, Don: *Manning Clark's History of Australia* (with John Romeril and Tim Robertson), 230
Watson, Hugh, 277, 279
  plays: *A Few Short Wicks in Paradise*, 277; *Raise the Roof*, 277
Watt, David, 265, 266, 278
Webster, John, 20
Wedekind, Frank, 17
Welfare State (UK), 266
Weston, Victor: *Pommy* (with W.P. Lipscombe), 14

INDEX

Whaley, George, 9
Wharf Revue, 71
Wherrett, Richard, 144, 147, 191, 239
White, Patrick, 27, 89–90, **91–112**, 113, 114, 117, 120, 160, 187, 275, 333, 376
    award to artists, 194
    novels: *Riders in the Chariot*, 97; *The Burnt Ones*, 97
    plays: *A Cheery Soul*, 92, 93, 98, **99–100,** 104, 111, 116, 120, 126; *Big Toys*, 93, **102–3**; *Bread and Butter Women*, 94; *Netherwood*, 94, 103, **108–9,** 112; *Night on Bald Mountain*, 92, 94, **101–2**, 108, 113, 115; *Return to Abyssinia*, 94; *School for Friends*, 94; *Shepherd on the Rocks*, 91, 92, 94, 103, 108, **109–12**; *Signal Driver*, 92, 94, 102, **104–8,** *106–7*, 343; *The Ham Funeral*, 3, 89, 91, 92, **94–6,** 97, 104, 108, 111, 333; *The Season at Sarsaparilla*, 92, 93, **97–8,** 102, 111, 126
Whiteley, Brett, 175, 185
Whitlam, Gough, 128, 129, 130, 172–3, 175, 182
Who's Afraid of the Working Class? (Andrew Bovell, Patricia Cornelius, Melissa Reeves, Christos Tsiolkas, and Irine Vela), 362, 375
Wilde, Oscar, 34, 194
    The Soul of Man Under Socialism, 34
Wilding, Ian, 376
Williams, Lynne, *198–9*
Williams, Margaret, 10, 29, 148, 153–4
Williams, Tennessee, 80
Williamson, David, **167–86**
    Adams as precursor, 20
    autobiographical element, 117
    films: *Gallipoli*, 171; *Phar Lap*, 171; *The Last Bastion*, 171; *The Year of Living Dangerously*, 171
    naturalism, 127, 168–9
    new internationalists and, 210, 223
    New Wave and, 139–40, 144, 151–2, 155, 167–8, 170–5, 187–8, 195, 373–4
    plays: *A Conversation*, 171, **184**; *A Handful of Friends*, 174, **181–2,** 185; *After the Ball*, 175, **180–1,** 182; *Amigos*, 186; *Birthrights*, 186; *Brilliant Lies*, **179–80,** 183; *Charitable Intent*, 171, **184–5;** *Corporate Vibes*, 183; *Dead White Males*, 169, **180,** 181; *Don's Party*, 136, 167, 170, **172–3,** 175, 181, 182; *Emerald City*, 168, 170, 176, **177,** 185; *Face to Face*, 170, 171, **184**; *Heretic*, 169, **180,** 181; *Influence*, 186; *Jugglers Three*, 173–4; *Lotte's Gift*, 186; *Money and Friends*, 170, 176, **178–9;** *Operator*, 177, **186;** *Sanctuary*, 180; *Scarlett O'Hara at the Crimson Parrott*, 186; *Siren*, 177, **178**; *Sons of Cain*, 176–7; *Soulmates*, 179, 182, **185**; *The Club*, 133, 152, **174;** *The Coming of Stork*, 128, 140, 167, 169, **171,** 180, 188; *The Department*, 170, **174**; *The Great Man*, 179, **182–3,** 337; *The Jack Manning Trilogy [Face to Face, A Conversation, Charitable Intent]*, 168, 170–1, 182, 183, **184–5;** *The Perfectionist*, 170, **175–6,** 177, 181; *The Removalists*, 167, 168, 170, **171–2,** 173; *Third World Blues* [revised version of *Jugglers Three*], 174; *Top Silk*, 176, **177–8;** *Travelling North*, **175,** 180, 181, 337; *Up for Grabs*, 171, 177, 179, 182, **185**; *Up For Grabs* [English version], 185; *What If You Died Tomorrow*, 168, **174,** 175, 181, 185
    TV series: *The Dismissal*, 171
    women playwrights and, 333, 342
Williamson, Kristin (Green), 182
Williamson's, J.C. ('JCWs,' 'The Firm'), 2–5, 12–14, 16, 18–19, 44, 84, 122
Wilson, Josephine: *The Geography of Haunted Places* (with Erin Hefferon), 330

BELONGING

Wimmin's Business (solo performances), 315
Winmar, Dallas: *Aliwa!*, 318–19
Winton, Tim: *Cloudstreet* (with Nick Enright and Justin Monjo), 249
The Wog Boy (film), 282, 283
Wogarama (revue), 283
Wogs Out of Work (revue), 283
Wollongong the Brave (Grahame Bond and Rory O'Donoghue), 164
women, 1, 58, 63–4, 66
    Aboriginal theatre, 313, 318
    in bush legend, x, **47–9**
    migrant theatre, 295
    New Wave, 193
    red witches, 113, 268, 349, 373
    Williamson, 176, 182
    see also feminist theatre; New Women
Women On A Shoestring Theatre Company (Canberra), 271
women playwrights, 46, 60, 137, 268, 270–1, 313, 327–8
women's theatre, **266–71**, 328, 331–3, 335, 340–5
    see also feminist theatre
Women's Theatre Group (Melbourne), 143, 267, 280
Wood, John, 103, *106–7*
Woolacott, L.L., 18, 44
working-class drama
    1970s, 89, 124, 147, 213
    1980s, 85, 223, 229, 244, 267, 270, 279–80
    1990s, 252, 279, 327, **348–50**, 362
World War I, 57, 63, 121, 194, 226–7, 245
World War II, 9, 53–4, 63, 64–5, 71, 74, 118, 228–9, 274–5, 377
Worm's Eye View, 13
Wright, Tom, 377–8
    plays: *The War of the Roses*, 378; *Women of Troy*, 377–8

Y

Yang, William. *see* Young, Willy
The Year of Living Dangerously (film), 171
Yeats, W.B., 5, 22, 32–3, 35

Young, Willy (William Yang)
    plays: *Childhead's Doll*, 137; *Cooper and Borges*, 137; *Interplay*, 137